T5-CWL-531

E U R O P E

White Sea

FINLAND

N. Dvina

Gulf of Bothnia

Lake Onega

Lake Ladoga

Svir

Helsinki ★

Gulf of Finland

★ Tallinn

ESTONIA

Baltic Sea

Riga ★ LATVIA

Volga

★ Moscow

LITHUANIA

Dvina

Vilnius ★

RUSSIA

RUSSIA

URAL MTS.

★ Minsk

BELARUS

See Asia map for eastern Russia.

POLAND

Vistula

★ Warsaw

Kiev ★

Don

Volga

UKRAINE

Dnieper

SLOVAKIA

CARPATHIANS

KAZAKHSTAN

★ Bratislava

MOL.

★ Budapest

Chişinău ★

HUNGARY

Sea of Azov

greb

ROMANIA

Belgrade ★

Bucharest ★

BOSNIA & HERZ.

Danube

CAUCASUS

Sarajevo ★

SERBIA

Black Sea

Caspian Sea

Prishtina

MONT.

★ Sofia

GEORGIA

Podgorica

KOS.

★ Skopje

BULGARIA

Tbilisi ★

Tirana ★

MAC.

ARM.

AZERBAIJAN

ALB.

Ankara ★

Yerevan ★

Baku ★

TURKMENISTAN

GREECE

Aegean Sea

TURKEY

Athens ★

Ionian Sea

Rhodes

ELBURZ MTS.

Euphrates

★ Tehran

Crete

CYPRUS

SYRIA

Tigris

Mediterranean Sea

Beruit ★

Damascus ★

Baghdad ★

LEBANON

IRAN

ISRAEL

IRAQ

THE GREENWOOD
ENCYCLOPEDIA OF
WORLD
POPULAR CULTURE

The Greenwood Encyclopedia of
World Popular Culture

General Editor

GARY HOPPENSTAND

Volume Editors

MICHAEL K. SCHOENECKE, North America

JOHN F. BRATZEL, Latin America

GERD BAYER, Europe

LYNN BARTHOLOME, North Africa and the Middle East

DENNIS HICKEY, Sub-Saharan Africa

GARY XU and VINAY DHARWADKER, Asia and Pacific Oceania

THE GREENWOOD
ENCYCLOPEDIA OF
WORLD
POPULAR CULTURE

EUROPE

Gary Hoppenstand
General Editor

Gerd Bayer
Volume Editor

GREENWOOD PRESS
Westport, Connecticut • London

Library of Congress Cataloging-in-Publication Data

The Greenwood encyclopedia of world popular culture / Gary Hoppenstand, general editor ; volume editors, John F. Bratzel ... [et al.].
    p. cm.
  Includes bibliographical references and index.
  ISBN-13: 978-0-313-33255-5 (set : alk. paper)
  ISBN-13: 978-0-313-33316-3 (North America : alk. paper)
  ISBN-13: 978-0-313-33256-2 (Latin America : alk. paper)
  ISBN-13: 978-0-313-33509-9 (Europe : alk. paper)
  ISBN-13: 978-0-313-33274-6 (North Africa and the Middle East : alk. paper)
  ISBN-13: 978-0-313-33505-1 (Sub-Saharan Africa : alk. paper)
  ISBN-13: 978-0-313-33956-1 (Asia and Pacific Oceania : alk. paper)
  1. Popular culture—Encyclopedias. 2. Civilization, Modern—Encyclopedias. 3. Culture—Encyclopedias. I. Hoppenstand, Gary. II. Bratzel, John F. III. Title: Encyclopedia of world popular culture. IV. Title: World popular culture.
HM621.G74   2007
306.03—dc22   2007010684

British Library Cataloguing in Publication Data is available.

Library of Congress Catalog Card Number: 2007010684
ISBN-13: 978-0-313-33255-5 (Set)
ISBN-10: 0-313-33255-X

ISBN-13: 978-0-313-33316-3 (North America)
ISBN-10: 0-313-33316-5

ISBN-13: 978-0-313-33256-2 (Latin America)
ISBN-10: 0-313-33256-8

ISBN-13: 978-0-313-33509-9 (Europe)
ISBN-10: 0-313-33509-5

ISBN-13: 978-0-313-33274-6 (North Africa and the Middle East)
ISBN-10: 0-313-33274-6

ISBN-13: 978-0-313-33505-1 (Sub-Saharan Africa)
ISBN-10: 0-313-33505-2

ISBN-13: 978-0-313-33956-1 (Asia and Pacific Oceania)
ISBN-10: 0-313-33956-2

First published in 2007

Greenwood Press, 88 Post Road West, Westport, CT 06881
An imprint of Greenwood Publishing Group, Inc.
www.greenwood.com

Printed in the United States of America

The paper used in this book complies with the Permanent Paper Standard issued by the National Information Standards Organization (Z39.48–1984).

10 9 8 7 6 5 4 3 2 1

To Ines

CONTENTS

Contents

FOREWORD

Popular culture is easy to recognize, but often difficult to define. We can say with authority that the current hit television show *House* is popular culture, but can we say that how medical personnel work in hospitals is popular culture as well? We can readily admit that the recent blockbuster movie *Pirates of the Caribbean* is popular culture, but can we also admit that what the real-life historical Caribbean pirates ate and what clothes they wore are components of popular culture? We can easily recognize that a best-selling romance novel by Danielle Steel is popular culture, but can we also recognize that human love, as ritualistic behavior, is popular culture? Can popular culture include architecture, or furniture, or automobiles, or many of the other things that we make, as well as the behaviors that we engage in, and the general attitudes that we hold in our day-to-day lives? Does popular culture exist outside of our own immediate society? There can be so much to study about popular culture that it can seem overwhelming, and ultimately inaccessible.

Because popular culture is so pervasive—not only in the United States, but in all cultures around the world—it can be difficult to study. Basically, however, there are two main approaches to defining popular culture. The first advocates the notion that popular culture is tied to that period in Western societies known as the Industrial Revolution. It is subsequently linked to such concepts as "mass-produced culture" and "mass-consumed culture." In other words, there must be present a set of conditions related to industrial capitalism before popular culture can exist. Included among these conditions are the need for large urban centers, or cities, which can sustain financially the distribution and consumption of popular culture, and the related requirement that there be an educated working-class or middle-class population that has both the leisure time and the expendable income to support the production of popular culture. Certainly, this approach can encompass that which is most commonly regarded as popular culture: motion pictures, television, popular fiction, computers and video games, even contemporary fast foods and popular fashion. In addition, this approach can generate discussions about the relationship between popular culture and political ideology. Can popular culture be political in nature, or politically subversive?

Can it intentionally or unintentionally support the status quo? Can it be oppressive or express harmful ideas? Needless to say, such definitions limit the critical examination of popular culture by both geography and time, insisting that popular culture existed (or only exists) historically in industrial and postindustrial societies (primarily in Western Europe and North America) over the past 200 years. However, many students and critics of popular culture insist that industrial production and Western cultural influences are not essential in either defining or understanding popular culture.

Indeed, a second approach sees popular culture as existing since the beginning of human civilization. It is not circumscribed by certain historic periods, or by national or regional boundaries. This approach sees popular culture as extending well beyond the realm of industrial production, in terms of both its creation and its existence. Popular culture, these critics claim, can be seen in ancient China, or in medieval Japan, or in pre-colonial Africa, as well as in modern-day Western Europe and North America (or in all contemporary global cultures and nations for that matter). It need not be limited to mass-produced objects or electronic media, though it certainly does include these, but it can include the many facets of people's lifestyles, the way people think and behave, and the way people define themselves as individuals and as societies.

This six-volume *Encyclopedia of World Popular Culture*, then, encompasses something of both approaches. In each of the global regions of the world covered—North America, South America, Europe, the Middle East, Sub-Saharan Africa, and Asia—the major industrial and postindustrial expressions of popular culture are covered, including, in most cases, film; games, toys, and pastimes; literature (popular fiction and nonfiction); music; periodicals; and radio/ television. Also examined are the lifestyle dimensions of popular culture, including architecture; dance; fashion and appearance; food and foodways; love, sex, and marriage; sports; theater and performance; and transportation and travel. What is revealed in each chapter of each volume of *The Greenwood Encyclopedia of World Popular Culture* is the rich complexity and diversity of the human experience within the framework of a popular culture context.

Yet rooted within this framework of rich complexity and diversity is a central idea that holds the construct of world popular culture together, an idea that sees in popular culture both the means and the methods of widespread, everyday, human expression. Simply put, the commonality of national, transnational, and global popular cultures is the notion that, through their popular culture, people construct narratives, or stories, about themselves and their communities. The many and varied processes involved in creating popular culture (and subsequently living with it) are concerned, at the deepest and most fundamental levels, with the need for people to express their lifestyle in ways that significantly define their relationships to others.

The food we eat, the movies we see, the games we play, the way we construct our buildings, and the means of our travel all tell stories about what we think and what we like at a consciously intended level, as well as at an unintended subliminal level. These narratives tell others about our interests and desires, as well as our fundamental beliefs about life itself. Thus, though the types of popular dance might be quite different in the various regions of the world, the recognition that dance fulfills a basic and powerful need for human communication is amazingly similar. The fact that different forms of popular sports are played and watched in different countries does not deny the related fact that sports globally define the kindred beliefs in the benefits of hard work, determination, and the overarching desire for the achievement of success.

These are all life stories, and popular culture involves the relating of life's most common forms of expression. This *Encyclopedia of World Popular Culture* offers many narratives about many people and their popular culture, stories that not only inform us about others and how they live, but that also inform us, by comparison, about how we live.

INTRODUCTION

POPULAR CULTURE IN EUROPE

GERD BAYER

Even though Europe has seen more than its share of interior division, including two major wars in the past century and decades of Cold War tension, it often is summarized as one homogenous entity when looked at from the outside. Yet, the interior differences are great and lasting. Decades after the fall of the Berlin Wall in 1989, the unofficial end of the Cold War, the formerly divided Eastern and Western Europe remain largely separate. While the Western states continue to have higher prosperity, some of the Eastern states, and especially the rural hinterlands, have not yet managed to recover from the end of socialist planning.

For the purpose of this volume, Europe is defined by oceanic geographic borders in the north, west, and south (the North Sea, the Atlantic, and the Mediterranean, respectively) and by the Bosporus in the southeast, making at least a section of Turkey part of Europe. Those states of the former Soviet Union that border on traditional Eastern European nations such as Poland or Romania are also considered a part of Europe. Thus, Ukraine and Belarus are covered, along with the Baltic states. However, due to the difficulty in coming across hard data about many of the eastern countries, some of the chapters can only give cursory information about the eastern parts of Europe.

Given the centuries of recorded history in many European states, it comes as no surprise that national traditions have developed that differentiate many nations within Europe. Although some differences might be more perceived than actually existing, the fact remains that the lifestyles range widely between, say, Sweden and Spain or between Belgium and Bulgaria. At the same time, and in particular with regard to popular culture, the tendencies in many European countries lean towards global fashions. Thus, much of the music, clothing, and dancing and many of the films, books, and foods that Europeans enjoy as part of their everyday life have become international in perspective and flavor. However, this should not necessarily be understood as foreign domination. On the contrary, Europe has exported such global trends as the pizza, originally "invented" in Italy.

European popular culture thus presents itself as both homogenous and diverse: as simultaneously rooted in century-old traditions (as visible in ethnic dances, for example) and belonging to the global village of info- and entertainment. In several of the chapters, the authors emphasize the importance of the Internet for shaping patterns of media consumption or styles of fashion. Indeed, popular culture is changing rapidly, with neomania often dictating a quick turnover rate, often in the service of large international corporations and their financial interests. At the same time, though, popular culture has always enabled its practitioners to speak out against the dominant or hegemonic power and thus serves as a necessary counterbalance to the larger cultural sphere.

THE CHAPTERS IN THIS BOOK

Eckard Wolf, a practicing architect, describes Europe's diverse **Architecture** as being determined by popular demand, by the visionary power of architects and also by the needs of urban development. In fact, Wolf's chapter shows how the process of building has both private and civic functions: providing comfortable housing for individuals as well as creating a sense of public space. The different climates and associated lifestyles of the various regions of Europe have also brought about a range of different building styles. The differing economic situations across the continent have supported a luxurious interest in design and aesthetics in some parts of Europe, while other parts struggle with the difficult task of providing adequate housing to the countless people who continue to migrate from the countryside into the cities, but also from the colder regions in the North to the sunny beaches of the Mediterranean.

Art historian Joy Sperling outlines how **Art** has been a central part of European national identity for a long time. Her chapter not only shows that the field of art covers a wide array of aesthetic practices, ranging from photography, textiles, and ceramics to sculpture and painting; it also brings out the national traditions and situates them in the historical development of the various regions of Europe. Sperling also emphasizes the importance of popular art in the creation of national identities. The ever-changing borders of Europe have had a substantial influence on the role that popular art plays for creating a sense of identity and continuation. Like other chapters in the book, the art section stresses the relationship of the market to popular art, showing how "the artifacts of popular culture are produced with the expectation that they will be purchased on the open market."

Heike Grundmann, in the chapter on **Dance**, provides a comprehensive overview over the various traditional and modern dance styles that have evolved in Europe. Taking a comprehensive look at popular dance forms, Grundmann shows that "Western dance has always embraced a variety of ritualistic folk dances, social dances enjoyed by many different levels of society, and skilled theatrical dances often in conjunction with opera." Her chapter, accordingly, covers polka and wedding dances alongside developments in competitive ballroom dancing and ballet. While the latter emphasizes the global importance of European patterns of dancing, the survival—and in some cases even the revival—of ethnic dances seem to indicate that many Europeans also long for belonging to a cultural unit smaller than the official European Union.

Malin Lidström Brock shows in her chapter on **Fashion and Appearance** how patterns of dressing changed in Europe in response to both social changes that led to more prosperity and technological developments that made various articles of clothing machine-producible and thus more affordable. In the twentieth century, the difference between tailor-made fashion and factory-produced garments has increasingly disappeared. In the globalized world of the twenty-first century, many Europeans shop at stores belonging to the same multinational corporations, making it difficult to speak of national fashion trends. Ethnic or folkloristic dress is increasingly falling out of fashion. The internationalization of the fashion industry has, however, also led to the development of new fashion centers beyond France and Italy. In addition, fashion has become a normal topic of discourse: "Fashion is acknowledged, debated, and criticized on television and in newspapers, popular magazines, and academic journals." The changing body shape of Europeans (mostly toward higher obesity rates) puts additional pressure on appearance and logos, creating an ever-growing consumer base for the latest fashion trends (and follies).

Written by film scholar Robert von Dassanowsky, the chapter on **Film** provides a detailed overview over both the history of European cinema and the wide range of national traditions as they developed over the past one hundred years. Without doubt, the cinema must belong to the most popular leisure activities of countless people. Dassanowsky's article shows how cinema exists and develops under different national and cultural environments, being influenced by the environment, both financial and political, within which filmmakers have to work. The power of the visual image has repeatedly led to censorship and the banning of films, emphasizing the force that cinema can unleash. While much of Europe seems enthralled by Hollywood productions of greater or lesser quality, art cinema is very much alive and well in many European countries. Many of the smaller films from Europe may never see global circulation, but they certainly contribute to a national sense of popular culture. With film depending also on the spoken word, the costly problem of translating or dubbing films may contribute to more regional or national developments within this art form.

Enno Lohmeyer's chapter on **Food and Foodways** may prove difficult to readers whose blood sugar level is low while sitting down with the text. His comprehensive analysis of both the production and the consumption side of food culture describes a wealth of different dishes and food traditions that is both highly informative and extremely appetite inducing. Lohmeyer links the food traditions of the various countries to their larger cultural and geographic situations, showing how food production shapes national economies, and how historical legacies survive in the flavors and names of various dishes. The chapter also provides the readers with countless examples of popular national food and drink traditions, many of which may be available in metropolitan restaurants or supermarkets around the world.

In her chapter on **Games, Toys, and Pastimes**, Maja Mikula presents contemporary gaming in the historical context of individual countries' traditions and developments. Having outlined the history of toy making in Europe in the context of the technological developments, Mikula goes on to show that toys, like many other objects of pop culture, have by now become a commercial commodity that is driven by market parameters and financial concerns. She also shows the toy market in a stage of transition as a result of the impact of the virtual revolution: with a generation of youngsters growing up computer literate (if not necessarily alphabetically literate), computer games and game consoles often replace traditional toys and games in the eyes of both teenagers and young adults.

Luca Prono's chapter on **Literature** serves as a wonderful example how difficult it can be to differentiate between popular and "high" art. Although professional literary critics may often belittle crime fiction or autobiographies, both types of literature find readers in their millions in many European countries. At the same time, veritable high-art authors such as Günter Grass or Umberto Eco clearly also find favor with the mass reader, turning their books into objects of popular art. The popularity of such authors also contributes to the financial successes of their books, an important aspect in the publishing world of the twenty-first century. Prono argues convincingly that literature also has to be seen as a system of production, turning the book and thus literature into an object shaped by the market economy. Prono's chapter also includes information about literature for children, cookbooks, and nonfiction titles, thus taking a rather comprehensive look at the system of popular literature.

In the chapter on **Love, Sex, and Marriage**, Annette Olsen-Fazi presents European ways of living at "the vanguard of what might be a new social order." While patterns of sexual contact are becoming ever more permissive and the age for first coitus is rapidly decreasing, marriage and parenthood are becoming less popular or moved to later stages of life, if they are desired at all. While romantic love appears in polls as a desired goal, the reality of many people's love life seems marked by short and even casual contact with sexual partners. Olsen-Fazi's chapter also addresses such problematic aspects as sexually transmitted diseases, human trafficking, and prostitution. Most European countries provide some sort of sexual education, with contraception available to most who seek it, two tendencies that surely contribute to the thinking on the issue. Beyond addressing all these complex issues, the chapter also provides a detailed account of the various courting and marriage traditions as they have evolved in the different European countries.

In the chapter on **Music**, musicologist Andreas Jacob shows how in most European countries national traditions and formats coexist with international, mostly Anglo-American products. While many national markets currently experience similar tendencies, with shrinking sales in the CD market and high levels of piracy, local traditions still survive. As with other popular art forms that rely to some extent on language, as in the lyrics of pop songs, popular music retains elements of local flavor. In addition, countries do have individual forms, as the Schlager in the German-speaking regions, or the Fado in Portugal. A further finding of the chapter is that not all European countries share the same relative interest in the various genres of popular music. Indeed, as Jacob points out in his introduction, what counts as popular music is independent from generic differences, at least if one takes widespread success as indication for the popularity of a musical form. So, while pop songs or rock music appear in most countries, many societies also consume classical music or jazz as popular art forms.

Christina Svendsen's chapter on **Periodicals** provides detailed analyses of the numerous national reading (and skimming) traditions as they relate to newspapers and tabloids, cooking and sports magazines. Like the chapter on literature, Svendsen's work makes obvious how many different languages coexist in Europe, making for numerous small linguistic markets. With readers of newspapers also looking for local or at best national information, the market for many popular periodicals is as diverse as few other popular objects described in this volume. The differences in reading patterns as described for the various countries provide further insights in national characteristics. However, the growing importance of transnational publishing houses, often producing different language editions of the same publication, also leads to a decrease in the importance of national traditions within the reading patters for newspapers and magazines.

Holger Briel presents the state of European **Radio and Television** in a way that both introduces the most important technological developments in the radio and television markets and portrays the unique broadcasting situations in the various European countries as they evolved during the twentieth century. Many countries still go through phases of increasing privatization, making life for public broadcasting a difficult mission. In many countries, a pattern evolves wherein public networks compete with quality information and news against private broadcasters who lure their audiences with sex and crime. The often transnational organization of private media empires provides them with resources that especially smaller countries and their public media can hardly compete with. The growing importance of the Internet as a source of information and entertainment also changes the media landscape in many European countries.

Written by sport historians Stephan Wassong and Thomas Zawadzki, the chapter on **Sports and Recreation** provides not only a comprehensive historical survey of the development of sports from a leisurely pastime to both competitive sports and mass phenomenon. Taking England as the homeland of modern sports as a case study, the two authors situate the development of popular sports in the context of the rise of urban culture and as a consequence of the Industrial Revolution. They also point out the importance of political and ideological developments for the growth of sports and for the inclusion of working-class and female athletes. In their individual country sections they describe European countries in terms of their favorite sports, also offering specific information about such data as amount of money spent on supporting popular sports and the average number of hours different age groups spend engaging in sports.

In the chapter on **Theater and Performance**, Kevin Brown argues that not only is the line between high art and popular art a difficult one to draw; it is also important to realize that many forms of popular culture already exist in a state of dependence on government funding. The situation of state theaters makes it clear that popular culture can also be part of the hegemonic system, making it twice difficult to distinguish popular from elite art forms. As the historical sections of the chapter show, many forms of "elite" theater started out as strictly popular art forms, only later acquiring the reputation of high art. The focus on performance alongside theater enables Brown to take a wider look at popular theatrical art forms.

The chapter on **Transportation and Travel**, co-authored by geographer Martin Sachs and Gerd Bayer, shows Europe to be a highly networked and densely linked continent. Many of the means of transportation, such as the railroad or the automobile, were in fact first developed in Europe. It is hardly a surprise, then, to find that when Europeans travel, they can pick from a wide range of transportation choices. At the same time, Europe is both the place of departure and highly popular destination for many tourist travelers. While in general the direction of travel is from the cooler north to the warmer Mediterranean, making Italy, Spain, and France popular destinations, travel patterns also feature other seashores and the spectacular mountain areas of the Alps. Since many travel options are rather costly, like the plane, the overall wealth of most European countries favors the development of such a dense network of trains, highways, and airports.

ARCHITECTURE

ECKARD WOLF

The European cultural space contains a broad variety of regional features. The man-made environment consists of architecture, infrastructure, artificial landscapes, and urban structures and is also shaped by the characteristics of other cultural domains. For centuries there were extensive cultural exchanges among almost all regions, which led to a kind of linear development in the history of European cities and architecture. However, the rich variety of regional specifics and the influence of the general development created specific identities depending on local situations. More often than not multiple factors, such as scenic characteristics or cultural traditions, combine to create local features. In addition to the history and development of the cultural identity, one should not underestimate other factors, such as technological advances, availability of materials and energy, climatic characteristics, constraints or possibilities of landscape and nature, and, last not least, the social and political framework.

STEPS IN ARCHITECTURE HISTORY

To understand the architectural and urban situation in today's Europe it is necessary to look briefly at a number of steps in the history of architecture over the last hundred years that form the basis to nearly all professional and intellectual discussions in the architectural and urban fields. The development that at last led to the architecture and urbanism of the twenty-first century started at the end of the nineteenth century with historicism, a building design that imitates historic styles. Historicist buildings are spread all over Europe: the neo-Baroque Opéra in Paris, the neo-Classical Palace of Justice in Brussels, or the buildings of the Ringstrasse in Vienna. Historicism ruled when Gottfried Semper (1803–1879) defined the aesthetic appearance of architecture as a system of symbols—the language of architecture. Semper went on to build the famous Opera and Zwinger in Dresden. But because this language was connected to imperial systems, the Jugendstil movement in Vienna and the Arts and Crafts movement in Great Britain tried, around 1900, to come up with more independent artistic expressions. This was the origin of

1

JUGENDSTIL

Jugendstil (also called art noveau, modern style, stile liberty, and modernismo) was a European art style that sought to end the traditional style of historicism and replace it with new forms and ornaments, often derived from organic patterns. It also resisted the institutionalized teaching of art and, in fact, seceded from the academies. One of the origins of the stylistic ornaments was the drawings of William Morris and the Arts and Crafts movement. Some of the most important architects of this movement were Victor Horta (1861–1947) in Brussels, Hector Guimard (1867–1942) in Paris, Antoni Gaudi (1852–1926) in Barcelona, and Charles Rennie Mackintosh (1868–1928) in Glasgow.

something like an "objective" aesthetics, based on real life and new hierarchies in the wake of the rising modern times.

The beginning of modernism as an architectural style around 1920 came at a time of disintegrating traditional ideas of design, construction, and material. At the same time, a lively discussion was under way about what the meaning of architecture should be. What is known as Modern or International Style has been very influential for all kinds of building aspects, such as design, construction, and urban development. As an example of the idea of connecting professional design to the aesthetic of everyday life in the architecture of the early twentieth century there is the accidental style of Josef Frank (1895–1967), who had been criticized by his modern colleagues because of his inconsistent interior design in his contribution to the Weissenhofsiedlung near Stuttgart (1927), which itself was a key moment for introducing Modern ideas from the German Bauhaus and other design schools to a larger audience. Frank was one of the founders of the Austrian Werkbund and leader of the Werkbundsiedlung in Vienna. In his architectural contribution to the Weissenhofsiedlung, a semidetached house, he showed an interior design that was defined by an accidental assemblage of different things, not presented as a unique style. Later, the buildings of the Belgian architect Lucien Kroll (born 1927) formed a contemporary equivalent. Kroll integrates the creativity of the clients in his architecture and leaves it "unready," to be completed by them. His most famous work is the student dormitory in Louvain, Belgium.

The wish to express a regional or national style dates back to the seventeenth century and has not died out even today, for instance in Hungary, where Imre Markovecz (born 1935) initiated a Hungarian school of architecture. Markovecz started his career within the socialist administration. He developed his own organic style based on traditional elements of the Hungarian culture as a symbol against the official doctrine of industrialized architecture. He has been influenced by Frank Lloyd Wright, Antoni Gaudi, and Rudolf Steiner. A typical example of his architecture was the Hungarian pavilion at the World's Fair in Seville in 1992.

Beside the frequent accusation that it produced boring results, Modern architecture did not fit well into the grown urban fabric and could not integrate the general needs for narrative, symbolic, expressive, and communicative issues in architectural forms. The program of Modern architecture has therefore been declared a failure by such critics as Peter Blake. In the late 1970s new ideas, expressed in buildings and urban design as well as in theoretical considerations, dealt with the void between the elaborate architecture and popular flavor, between anonymous architecture and local traditions. These new ideas are known as Postmodernism. Its feature can be considered to be an overcoming of the totalitarian requirements of modernism and a farewell to the idea of objective solutions for problems that are situated in very different contexts.

DYNAMICS INFLUENCING THE ARCHITECTURAL DEVELOPMENT

Industrial and political developments changed the framework of lives all across Europe. A number of new phenomena arose. First, a dramatic development of housing standards followed from the increased need for living space from about 1900 onward until the middle of the twentieth century. Later, with the oil shock and ensuing energy shortage in the 1970s, an ecological discussion began that changed the material, technical, and constructive aspects of building. The demographic growth in the late nineteenth and the early twentieth century first caused plentiful building activity and created a market for industrial prefabricated dwelling structures; later, the demographic decrease toward the end of the century led to the need for new strategies to preserve the existing level of infrastructure. The ongoing process of urbanization is a reason for large and growing agglomerations, no more to be called cities, such as the Ruhrgebiet in Germany or the Glattal or Simmattal in Switzerland. An increasing economic orientation on consumption created new types of buildings, such as shopping malls and supermarkets. All these are developments throughout the western part of Europe. During the Cold War the Eastern countries followed a different development. Today, the economic success of the European Union influences the development in the countries around it, and the prestigious products and lifestyle of Western culture and economy cause strange phenomena at times, such as the revival of a "postmodern" style in the Russian architecture of the rich.

POSTMODERNISM

In response to new tendencies in the architecture design of the 1960s and 1970s, Charles Jencks first called this development Postmodernism. In his book *The Language of Postmodern Architecture*, he described the connection between modern architectural techniques and mostly traditional architectural aspects as a replacement of modernity. The architecture simultaneously communicated with the public and with the engaged architects. Unlike this double code the former director of the Frankfurt Architecture Museum, Heinrich Klotz, saw in this development a position of function and fiction. After late modernism no longer applied denotation, the new architecture once again had narrative, symbolic, and fictional elements. The architectural symposia of the International Design Center in Berlin in the early 1970s, where the problematic modern urban design was designed, were important for the European scene. Postmodernism is a pluralistic style that cannot be defined consistently, as the wide range of buildings shows: the expressionistic buildings of Gottfried Böhm, the rationalistic architecture of Aldo Rossi and Matthias Ungers, the classicistic designs of Mario Botta, the art and architecture of Haus Rucker & Co., the poetic style of Hans Hollein, or the new urbanism of Rob Krier. But it is worth noting that postmodernity is a return to local, regional, and traditional features with new intentions.

WHAT IS POPULAR ARCHITECTURE?

To refer specifically to popular architecture, some aspects must be noted. There was a period in the 1960s in which Pop is found as a deliberate style in architecture. It existed mainly in drawings, technical utopias, and environmental fantasies and will not be further described here. For the present purpose, the term *popular architecture* refers to the main part of the man-made environment throughout the whole history of human buildings. Traditional

THE DEVELOPMENT OF HOUSING STANDARDS: A CASE STUDY

As an example for the progress of architecture and housing standards in Europe, the French development is typical for the change which occurred during the first five or six decades of the twentieth century.[1] Middle-class citizens already had large apartments with individual bedrooms. The situation for workers and rural families was different. Around 1900, three or four beds commonly stood in one room of the rural population. To raise the standard they built new rooms, but often the living space was very poor. Even in the cities, many people lived in one-room apartments: in Nantes about 19 percent, in Lille, Lyon, and others about 16 percent. A census from 1906 shows that in cities with more than five thousand inhabitants, 26 percent were living with more than two persons in one room, 36 percent lived one or two people to a room, only 17 percent had their own room, and about 21 percent had more than one room to live in. This was the situation until about 1950. There was a lack of social housing, because of missing capital and no profit-oriented construction because of low rent fixing. In 1954 a population census showed an undeveloped general standard. From the 13.4 million apartments surveyed, less than 60 percent had running water, only about a quarter had lavatories in the apartment, and a little more than 10 percent had showers, bathrooms, and central heating.

From the 1950s on, the situation changed dramatically. In 1953 there were 100,000 new apartments built, in 1959 about 300,000, in 1965 about 400,000, and from 1972 until 1975 about 500,000 apartments each year. The change not only increased the number of people who owned their own apartments; the size and quality of living spaces also developed. It had become normal to provide each apartment with a kitchen, a living room, and a master bed room as well as at least one additional bedroom. Every room had to be at least 9 square meters (about 100 square feet) in area. Every apartment had to have a lavatory, a bathroom, and individually controllable central heating.

So only twenty years after the disastrous 1954 census, the general situation showed apartments of 3.5 rooms with an average space of about 20 square meters (about 220 square feet) each. All people living in one household had an average living space of about 24 square meters (about 260 square feet). The housing service standard rose to about 97 percent of apartments having running water, 70 percent with lavatories within the apartment, 65 percent having showers or bathroom, and about 50 percent of the apartments having central heating. This quantitative development changed the quality of family life.

architecture history and theory has generally underestimated this aspect of the unknown builders and buildings. The Vienna architect Bernard Rudofsky was one of the first to bring anonymous architecture to the attention of the public with his exhibition, titled "Architecture Without Architects," held at the Museum of Modern Art in 1964. Until the end of the nineteenth century, architecture was clearly separated into, on the one hand, the mass of anonymous buildings erected by craftsmen and, on the other, the architecture of high culture, described in architecture history.

The historic distinction between high culture and anonymous design has transformed into both an elaborate professional perception of form and figure and what is liked by the masses. In recent years, there exists a professional interest in "vernacular" design, as seen in Port Grimaud. Even Le Corbusier, the French-Swiss architect who at one point planned massive housing projects, had a hand in this with his houses in Jaoul in Neuilly in 1953. Breaking with his white Cubist ideology, Corbusier combined vernacular elements of Paris with Mediterranean elements, designing an exotic ensemble wthithin the urban structure. At least on an industrial level, this kind of design plays a major role.

THE ROLE OF THE ARCHITECT

The role of the architect has changed fundamentally over the twentieth century. From the position of artistic creators of ambitious artworks, they developed into experts in all built elements of the man-made environment: buildings and urban structures. Today there is no country in Europe without its detailed building code. The international activities of the UNESCO world heritage, for example, show the current tendencies to have complete control over all aspects of building and urban development everywhere. Popular architecture today is still made by freelance architects, but it seems to be that the industrialized architects contribute a greater number of buildings.

THE ALPINE REGION

This area is located in different countries: southern Germany, Austria, northern Italy, and Switzerland. The similar architectural situations in the connecting upper Bavarian and Black Forest areas in Germany are included here as well.

In earlier days, the region was a difficult place to live because of the harsh agricultural and economic conditions. Today it is a prosperous space because of tourism and because of its position as a transit spot between southern and northern Europe.

In general the area is not very densely populated: 100 inhabitants per square kilometer in Austria and about 180 inhabitants per square kilometer in Switzerland. On a microlevel, however, it becomes obvious that the valleys and plains are densely populated, sometimes with cities growing along the valleys. Tourism has for a long time supported the survival of folkloristic culture. Therefore the architecture of this area is to be seen as a model poised against the dominant traditions of popular architecture elsewhere. In the contemporary public debate, there are two differing positions. On one hand there is a very modern and well-designed contemporary architecture scene that is very well accepted in the whole professional world. On the other hand there is a populist, even nostalgic demand to go back to traditional structures and forms. This, however, does not refer to a longing for a return to the real and original kinds of buildings, because they are mostly primitive constructions made out of local materials: stone, wood, and earth. What the nostalgic designers wish for is an architecture that serves as a symbol of tradition but contains the new qualities of living as well as catering to mass tourism.

The Swiss Chalet and Other Ideal Types of Houses

The Swiss chalet was the house of the free farmers in the country who first got rid of absolutistic power. Since then this house, offering a scenic view of alpine panoramas, has become a symbol for freedom. The architectural design of broad and humble massive stony house, covered by huge overlapping pitched roofs, has metamorphosed into a symbol for the values of homeland and freedom in different countries. Something similar is the Black Forest house as a very characteristic construction, with deep hipped roofs, outside and inside walls constructed in wood, and wooden weatherboards on the roof. A third type of building that works as model for contemporary buildings comprises the Bavarian and the Tyrol types of farmhouses. They are built of stone or wooden two-story constructions with balconies running around the house beneath far overlapping roofs.

The contemporary types of domestic buildings try to copy such types. The symbols found in this architectural language express the desire for a beautiful life. Extremely overdrawn are the tourist hotels in the skiing areas of the Alps in Bavaria and Tyrol. The roof covers multistory houses with a number of balconies. Behind them are many little holiday apartments and hotel rooms. The size is about five times as large as the traditional, but they have the same ornaments cut into the wooden balustrades and gable boards.

In the early 1980s the public became interested in architectural design in rural areas, supported by television series that taught details about rural architecture, traditional proportions, window size and sash bars, fences, and rural gardening. The series *Bauen und Bewahren auf dem Lande* [Building and Restoring in the Country] was very popular.[2] In imitation of it, people created a regional style that transcended local features.

Spreading Cities and Supermarkets

As in other regions of Europe, the processes of industrialization, of urbanization, and of demographic growth and increasing infrastructure areas such as airports, wide streets, and business parks generated new townscapes and new types of architecture. In Switzerland, the spreading settlements in suburban and outskirts areas received names as if they were new cities, such as Glattalstadt or Limmattal around Zurich.[3] In Innsbruck, the economically successful city has grown into the surrounding valleys. The settlements contain several types of buildings: multistory, semidetached, terraced single-family houses in various styles, sizes, and qualities as elsewhere in Europe. As in other such agglomerations, a new type of suburban settlement has emerged that is called *Zwischenstadt* (in-between city).

A contemporary and popular contribution to this kind of cultural development is the unique supermarket buildings in the area of Tyrol. The "M-Preis" markets are architecturally designed supermarkets that show a characteristic design of high quality. This successful family enterprise speaks in an architectural language that is direct and contemporary. It tries to represent the quality of the food and nonfood offerings. Beyond the architectural staging of transparency, liberality, and freshness, the architecture generates a positive shopping event.

Vienna and Its Housing Programs

One could say that Vienna is the easternmost point of the Alps. At the same time, Vienna is an important place for European architecture. Many architectural innovations originated in Vienna, such as the Frankfurter Küche, designed by the Vienna architect Margarete Schütte-Lihotzky, which is today the industrialized model for nearly all kitchens in Europe. One could also say that the idea of social housing had its first relevant expression in the housing program of the 1920s in Vienna.

Similarly to the French development the lack of private living space led to an extensive culture of public institutions such as pubs and cafes. This is the origin of the typical

Vienna coffee house. But in contrast to France, the attraction of the coffee houses did not vanish with the rise in social housing projects, because of the small size of the apartments. From 1923 to 1934, under a program instigated by the social-democratic authority, about 65,000 apartments were built in constructions such as the famous Karl-Marx-Hof.[4] This was about 10 percent of all apartments. The Nazis tried to compete with their own programs but, in the long run, caused the destruction of about 180,000 apartments in Austria, which was about 28 percent of those in Vienna, about 33 percent of those in Linz or Graz, and 88 percent in Wiener Neustadt. After the war about 150,000 communal apartments were rebuilt.

As of the first decade in the twenty-first century, Vienna was again trying to be innovative in housing culture. The programs in the early 1990s, however, were located in the suburbs. Different kinds of terraced housing settlements were designed by famous architects, even including some kinds of environment-friendly houses. But the architectural ambition was made obsolete by the contemporary need of living space in consequence of a new urbanization boom.

THE BALKAN STATES

If diversity is typical of Europe, the Balkan area can count as the most European part of it. For centuries there were multiethnic, multiconfessional, and multilingual influences oscillating among different ethnic populations. Within this territory, which covers about 285,000 square kilometers and has a population of about 26.6 million, the most successful example for the process of transforming into the Western model is Slovenia; other follow-up states, however, still are among the poorest areas within the former socialist realm.

Socialist idea and policy did not generate the same results in Slovenia or Bosnia as in the other socialist countries, even in such other Balkan countries as Bulgaria and Romania. Already the nonaligned policy of President Tito created the basis for this development. Apart from the multiethnic configuration of the region, the religious configuration is an important and, in Europe, unique criterion of the cultural development. The Balkans for a long time were part of the Ottoman Empire and thus influenced by the traditions of Islam.

Normality in the North

Although cities in Yugoslavia were neither many nor large, the industrialization process changed the economic situation of the people from the agricultural sector to the industrial or the service sector during the socialistic and postsocialistic times.[5] This was the general process, but there were large regional differences between north and south. In Slovenia about 45 percent of the territory has Alpine or sub-Alpine topography, and the population changed from being over 50 percent agrarian in 1991 to as little as 7 percent. Today 70 to 80 percent of the population lives in urban agglomerations, where about four-fifths of workplaces are located.

The socialist municipal authorities in Slovenia tolerated illegal, self-provided housing construction. In the 1970s detached, privately owned houses made up about half of the annual housing production. Before 1991, privately owned real estate made up about 67 percent of all domestic buildings. This increased to 88 percent after 1991. As a result of the housing and land policy of the past, housing manifests itself in two distinct forms: tall, multistory buildings of nonprofit or public housing with a high concentration of inhabitants (33 percent), and often unplanned single-family housing with low density (63 percent),

COLD WAR BUILDING POLICIES

During the Cold War, all socialist countries blocked private activities. The programs for maintaining old buildings were given up in favor of building new industrialized structures, mostly large scale housing estates. There are exceptions, such as in hilly environments or in Hungary, where fortunate circumstances led to the maintenance of regional traditions. This is found in the Western countries too, but in quite different implementations. The residential market in the West required a broader variety of housing types. There were also differences in public buildings. In the Eastern countries these were cultural centers where the workers' everyday life was supposed to get transformed. In the West, on the other hand, there are buildings of consumption, which serve as facilities for the rapid turnover of industrial products on the market. Since the great changes after the end of the Cold War, the Eastern countries have tried to turn around and catch up to the Western standard, which is seen as a higher state of development.

characterized by insufficient traffic and services. The lack of efficient planning control today continues with irregular growth. Maribor, the second largest city in Slovenia, contains about 11 percent city area, 66 percent suburban area, and 23 percent other types. The development created a large amount of traffic. Accordingly, the average travel time within the Ljubljana agglomeration grew from about 22 minutes in 1993 to about 45 minutes in 1999. As a result there are two problems: high pressure on the land and building market, and a lack of affordable living space.

War Coverage in the South

Development in the southern part of what had been Yugoslavia was extremely handicapped by the war. Today there are many activities to manage the basic needs for living space. Tents and wooden barracks have to be counted as popular living spaces too. In some areas the NATO Kosovo Force (KFOR) found about two-thirds of the buildings damaged, about 25 percent totally destroyed. The regular forms of living space are still poor. To look at Kosovo, for example, about 10 percent of the households live in one room, one-third have two, and about one-fifth have more than three rooms. More than 90 percent of the people heat with wood stoves. In rural areas 44 percent of the people have to get their water out of fountains, whereas in the cities about 94 percent of the apartments have running water. However, 99 percent of the houses are privately owned.

Bosnia and Herzegovina are areas with a strong Muslim influence, and this is to be seen in the housing culture as well. The structure of Sarajevo,[6] the greatest and most interesting town in the area, shows the historical phases of architecture and urban development as the multiethnic culture of the city, which is supported by the citizens. They understood the conflict not as ethnic but as a conflict between rural and urban culture. The Ottoman city, as one of the oldest parts, is built like an amphitheater with the dense living quarters, called *mahalas*, on the surrounding hills and infrastructure such as the university, the market, shops and workshops, spas and restaurants in the downhill center. The *mahalas* contain five important institutions necessary for Islamic society: a local mosque, a funeral place, a fountain, a bakery, and a school. The houses are surrounded by gardens and located so as not to block sunlight from the others. It is an old custom to ask one's neighbors when one wants to build, but the people of today often forget to ask the municipality.

To rebuild the city, art activities and architectural and urban reconstruction are important features of the urban culture of this area. A symbol of the multiethnic past and future is the Stari Most bridge in Mostar, originally built in 1566. After demolition it was rebuilt before 2004, literally connecting the Eastern and Western cultures.

EASTERN EUROPE

Before World War II, Eastern Europe showed quite diverse cultural characteristics. In architecture and urban development there were many regional features similar to the European development. The traditional structures still existed and were complemented by new additions. One could find beautiful buildings and urban ensembles of all stylistic periods up to the time when modern development took place. Examples are, on the one hand, Prague,[7] a city in its old plan mainly undistorted, and, on the other hand, Bucharest,[8] known as "the Paris of the Balkans," huge parts of whose inner quarters were demolished to make room for the dictator Ceausescu's colossal and pretentious palace and his idea of a socialist metropolis. Where wars did not leave their marks old buildings have survived, as in the city cores of Kiev or Lviv in Ukraine,[9] Krakow in Poland,[10] and Riga or Tallinn in the Baltic states.[11] But because of the housing policy of the socialist governments, they are badly degenerated, often uninhabitable, and threatened by present-day building development.

Together with Russia, Eastern Europe makes up about two-thirds of Europe. It consists of Poland, the Czech Republic, Slovakia, and Hungary to the west; the Baltic States to the north; and Romania and Bulgaria to the south. This is an area of about 6.0 million square kilometers and houses a population of about 270 million. In broad terms, the socialistic policies turned the area, specifically in architecture and urban terms, into a space of homogeneous development for about fifty years, between 1945 and the end of the twentieth century. From 25 to 35 percent of all apartments in these countries are prefabricated multistory houses in large-scale projects in the cities or on their fringes, which adds up to 35 to 40 million apartments with 100 to 120 million inhabitants. In the 1980s two-thirds of the people in Russia lived in cities. The contrast is starkly shown in Germany, where in the socialist Eastern part such apartments made up about 18 percent, but in the Western part only 2 percent, of all apartments.[12]

The postsocialistic development is marked by a search for cultural roots and the attempt to reach Western European standards. This is true for every country. The non-Russian countries, which understand themselves as having been occupied countries, try to distance themselves within their new development from the socialist period and reach back to the architectural design of the times before the war. There are several lines of development to observe. First is the renovation activity such as the preservation of the Art Noveau district in Riga, the wooden central-city houses of Tallinn, the maintenance of the pearls of sanatoriums in the Czech Republic[13] or the feudal or historic urban fabric of St. Petersburg or Budapest. But the situation varies widely according to the region.

Individually important are symbols of status, expressed in such architectural elements as bay windows or little towers, ornaments, and expensive materials such as natural stone. Banks and office buildings were built of steel and glass. But the architectural style of individual dwellings, especially, falls back to an approved architectural language of representation, associated with power and wealth. In some cases the role models are earlier styles such as the so-called Cossack style in Kiev; in other cases a semi-postmodern or modern style is the model. Western architecture is a model, but with an important difference. The connection is to prewar times in style and expression. Even the Stalinist historical style is again in vogue, as in the Triumf Palas in Moscow, the tallest residential building in Europe, which was built in 2006.[14] Especially in the Russian areas, building has to be as pretentious as possible.

The Socialistic Housing Policy

This development in housing started in the 1920s as a result of the Russian revolution. The idea of the new socialistic city disregarded the dense fabric of the old European towns and preferred instead a light- and air-flooded, green, loose settlement. Social hygiene was to develop through urban space and architectural equality. The early model appointed more or less all steps of development until the great political change. There were large dwelling houses, parallel or rectangularly situated, with flat and wide space in between for green space or a large axis to represent socialistic life in parades. This concept of a linear industrial city was an assembly of modular elements of the same size and character containing a number of dwelling houses and infrastructural buildings such as shopping or cultural institutions. In the beginning there were five-floor houses. In a dynamic development phase after World War II there were about 11 million apartments built within three years, and the amount of prefabricated building parts in the late 1950s increased from 25 to 70 percent.[15] Later the houses got higher, up to twelve floors.

This development was only interrupted by a stylistic phase, which is today called Stalinist romantic houses, concentrating on traditional technical skills and historic ornaments. We find examples in every former socialist capital from East Berlin to Moscow. When renovated, they are attractive living spaces because of their size and configuration.

By contrast, the apartments of the functionalistic phases were very small, of low quality, and with bland design. The economic benefit of the building industry was of the greatest importance, not architectural design or construction quality. But every apartment had its own kitchen, bathroom, running water, and district heating (heat supplied to multiple buildings from a central plant). The people coming from simple, rural wooden houses appreciated the new comfort, even if they had to give up their privately owned house and piece of land. The location of the inhabitants in the city districts or at the city fringes depended on their status within society. Military functionaries, politicians, and intellectuals moved into the attractive parts. The common people had to live elsewhere.

In the settlements, urban life was very austere because of the lack of public institutions. Eating out in a restaurant was difficult. Simple cafes and lunchrooms served simple and quick food options. The public and service buildings were located in the open areas between the housing blocks. Artfully designed and heavily decorated, these buildings aspired to show architecture as an idealistic and heroic thing to form a feeling of historical optimism in the society. With such names as Palace of the Young Pioneers, Palace of the Soviets, or Palace of Culture, these public buildings, such as cinemas, music or sports halls, could not deny the absence of meaning and identification.

The Russian Dacha: An Old and New Tradition

Originally *dacha* meant any kind of housing with a piece of land used for recreation in the suburban areas.[16] All well-situated town people had datchas. In the 1920s the dachas of companies were socialized and transformed into governmental privileges for executives and functionaries. After 1950 the increasing number of dachas served as symbols for individual living, private property, and self-produced agricultural products. About 38 to 50 million Russian households today have a piece of land to grow their own agricultural products. In the times of change, Russian society overcame the economic problems of the political change with their own food production even though it was uneconomical. Food on the market would have been cheaper than the work for self-production, but it was not available or affordable because of high unemployment. This food maintenance of the Russian population had a retarding effect on urbanization.

Under the current process of growing prosperity, the dacha as a substitute food source will lose its relevance. It will remain as a recreation place for those with the necessary income. Therefore the houses and the character of the whole thing depend on what the owner invests. The building variety ranges from simple and traditional to representative and pretentious, from old wooden houses to massive villas.

Markovecz the Hungarian: A Regional Feature

In the socialist era, architecture was made by institutions, not by persons. There were no individual architects who decided about design, material, and construction. Sometimes, however, regional particularities brought up discrepancies from the socialist mainstream based on individual preferences. In Lithuania, Poland, the Czech Republic, and other countries, architects tried to work out a regional style before the war. Now there are attempts to connect back to these traditional elements. One of the most famous examples of a regional feature based on traditional forms, symbols, and culture is the work of the Hungarian architect Imre Markovecz. His career started within a governmental planning institution. But as an autonomous intellectual he could develop his own style, which is known as organic architecture. Mainly in churches and cultural buildings, he realized his idea of traditional symbols and forms that continue the old folklore culture. He started a movement of architectural inspiration of younger architects that for some years dominated the scene.

FRANCE AND THE BENELUX COUNTRIES

In terms of territory, France is the largest country in Europe, covering about 544,000 square kilometers. France is marked by a high level of centralization, with a few cities and the capital Paris. In general, though, it is a very low-density country, with only about 110 inhabitants per square kilometer. World War II did not leave as much damage to the architectural structures in France as in other countries; therefore settlement development took another direction than, for example, in Germany, which is otherwise comparable in standards and technique. The French way of housing development is more concentrated on contemporary solutions than on preservation of old structures. But preserving the old while building the new is also a typical way of thinking.

Changes in Living Following Architectural and Urban Development

The old cities contained social structures of neighborhoods, of social interaction and control. The communication structure, for example, was preserved—women's contact places in shops and men's assembling places in taverns and cafes. This institutionalized social behavior along architectural types in the urban fabric changed in the wake of the arising housing development. Around 1920 there were about 500,000 taverns in France, which means more than 1 tavern for 100 inhabitants. As a consequence of urbanization and developments in housing construction, public behavior and the places to communicate in the neighborhood often vanished. Supermarkets became common, and the rents were too expensive for little cafes. The typical cafes or restaurants of today are only a remnant of the old tradition.

New Towns as New Villages

The fast growth of the housing market in the latter half of the twentieth century is not a matter of a single housing policy. To manage the increase of urban population and the lack of sufficient living space, there have been numerous housing programs with predominantly public housing in the often poor suburbs (*banlieues*) of Paris and other French cities. The old city cores became attractive but expensive locations once they were renovated. In the late 1960s and early 1970s, a structured program of new developments in Paris existed. But, parallel with this, the abolition of restrictions to residential development in the outskirts led to an uncontrolled suburban development.

The new towns show a new kind of living quality as is to be seen in the films of Eric Rohmer. These settlements are composed like middle-sized towns with central functions such as supermarkets, colleges, administrative services, and offices, as in Cergy-Pontoise, located northeast of Paris and home to about 200,000 inhabitants. The most famous of these new towns, because of its architect, Ricardo Bofill, was built in Noisy le Grand, Marne-la-Vallée. Bofill arranged the architectural design of the multistory houses with huge classical ornaments to interpret the houses as oversized villas. This is the background of Rohmer's film *L'Ami de Mon Amie*, which portrays a new kind of small-town life, where the people accidentally meet outside stores, as they did in villages about 50 years ago.

The Character of Individual Housing

The suburban, rural, and provincial situation is totally different. The big cities produce their suburban structures similar to the new towns. People migrate first to new settlements and later move on to the surrounding country. The desire to live in one's own house and garden is still alive, especially in the minds of young families and middle-class people. So there are existing settlements of detached and terraced houses in the suburban or rural regions.

The individual living space is gradually connected to the public sphere. All houses have a representative front facing the public, like a little piece of front garden with a low fence. Usually, it is possible to look from the living room to the public space, so the children may play supervised nearby. The back area of house and garden is reserved for private activities protected by higher fences and oriented to the inner rooms.

The architectural design depends on regional traditions, such as the Mediterranean terracotta-colored buildings or the white heavy-looking constructions of Brittany. Most private houses in France are built with pitched or hipped roofs, one or two floors high.

The Low Countries: Netherlands and Belgium

The most densely populated states in Europe are the Netherlands, with about 475 inhabitants per square kilometer, and Belgium, with about 350 inhabitants per square kilometer. Together they have about 53 million inhabitants, about half in each country. At the same time, both countries are home to the greatest amount of sprawl in Europe outside the large agglomerations such as the Ruhrgebiet in Germany or the megalopolis agglomerations such as Paris or London. The industrialized agriculture of the Netherlands has to be viewed in connection with the limited amount of land, which has to feed the population. For that reason, the Netherlands has frequently created new land by filling up parts of the ocean, initially to be used as agricultural land. Together with Great Britain the two countries have the largest number of single-family houses of all European countries, more than 70 percent of all units.[17]

Randstad

With twenty-four municipalities of over 20,000 inhabitants in 1900, the urbanization process got off to a late start in the Netherlands compared to other areas.[18] Around 1910, the settlement development was greatly influenced by the British Garden City concept with its concentric circles; this concept was soon displaced by free-standing housing blocks, terrace houses, and high-rise apartment houses. As of 2006, housing production is dominated by professional developers. About 10 percent of the units in the Netherlands are self-provided houses.[19] The general process is based on planned and standardized dwelling structures.

Because of the differences between the old land, situated in the southwest, where the historical grown settlements and old cities were situated, and the area in the northeast where new land created empty spaces, the country has been divided in two parts. Urban planners therefore coined the term *Randstad* for the southwestern region including the urbanized areas between Amsterdam and Rotterdam. This may be the very origin of generating development ideas on a supraregional level, which has been a famous element of the Dutch architects.

Following postwar reconstruction there were small scale housing projects built, seldom more than two stories high. Their rectangular layout consisted of row after row of houses, a model still seen in countless districts such as Pendrecht in Rotterdam. In the late 1960s, megastructures came into vogue. From that time stems the large type of project called the *bijlmermeer*, consisting of large multistory housing blocks for about 100,000 inhabitants on a hexagonal plan, as in the new town developments southeast of Amsterdam. The physical separation of different traffic was a major theme then on different levels or, in the case of the Bijlmermeer, to create an undisturbed green space for everybody. Between the 1980s and the end of the twentieth century, the development returned to small scale projects, sociability, new subdivisions and street patterns, new types of dwellings, and finally to a revival of the concentrated urban structures.

Today there are two movements to be seen in architectural development. The famous Dutch architects understand the problem of urban sprawl, and the young, especially, make unusual comments: at the EXPO 2000 exposition,[20] there was a building made of stacked pieces of landscapes by the architects MVRDV.[21] The most extreme idea was published by Rem Kohlhas, who suggested a division of the country into one densely settled area in the southwestern part as a unique urban space, leaving the open space in the northeastern part without settlements.

As in other regions, a conservative idea of architecture and urban space came up from the 1980s onward as well as the impact of postmodernity. Business buildings and ambitious settlements were designed in classical and historical styles. A definition stated by Rob Krier, who is one of the most important representatives of what is often called New Urbanism, is that traditional architecture is a pure invention of the mind. For architects like him, traditional architecture is just as modern as so-called modern architecture, which claimed only an unjustified monopoly on the concept of modernity.[22]

Peri-Urbanization

Although the Netherlands has some of the most restrictive building regulations, the Dutch people have gotten used to sitting in traffic jams and seeing open space only between urban structures. This is common also to the situation in Belgium, where the process of urbanization has continued because of property interests. But in contrast to the Dutch, the 79 percent of single-family house units in Belgium are mainly (60 percent) self-provided buildings. What the Belgians long for is the single-family house surrounded by a garden and a garage for the inevitable car. The peri-urban phenomenon belongs to a systematic context in which driving a car plays a key role that is hardly limited by politics. Therefore, outside of the big cities, Belgium is to be seen as a vast suburban area full of single-family houses situated in green gardens.[23]

GERMANY

Located in the middle of Europe, Germany has the largest population (82.5 million), a medium-size population density, but a dense network of cities, which as of 2006 was home to more than 80 percent of the population.[24] Its development has been influenced by history in a unique way.

The results of World War II and the period of the Cold War until 1989, when Germany was divided into two states, created a specific situation in all economic sectors, in social and cultural features, and, naturally, in urban development and architecture. The two parts of Germany together provide a model for the two political systems that dominated Europe for about fifty years. But even beyond that, living spaces, public or individual, have changed dramatically from the beginning of the twentieth century. Starting from a predominantly rural culture with sporadic islands of concentrated industrialized locations, with mainly traditional housing produced slowly over centuries, the German landscape changed rapidly to become an urbanized and industrialized consumer society. At the beginning of the twentieth century, most houses and apartments did not have running water, private bathrooms, or central heating. In the countryside, there was no sewer service for the most part, but people enjoyed living in what they considered to be a well-ordered architectural environment. A dramatic change of this man-made environment started with the housing projects in the 1920s and 1930s.

The Urban and Architectural Situation in the West

After the widespread destruction of buildings during World War II and what were considered, at the time, necessary demolition projects to accommodate the growing car traffic, urban development and the fast rebuilding of the cities created numerous new buildings in the 1950s and 1960s. The architecture of the urban multistory houses of that time is marked by cheap materials and construction, simple utilities such as oil stoves, and bathrooms with no windows. The cities in the center of Germany, especially, such as Kassel, Bielefeld, or Braunschweig, sometimes look faceless and devoid of historical contexts. They do, however, have wide streets and generous traffic arteries. The economic miracle of the 1950s put an end to the postwar depression and caused a housing shortage. With the onset of general prosperity, people realized that the architectural and urban environment was rarely pleasant or inviting, as Alexander Mitscherlich commented in a famous book *Die Unwirtlichkeit unserer Städte* [The Inhospitability of Our Cities]. This realization led to a changed perception of the urban environment and finally introduced broad activities in building renovation, preservation in historic buildings, and what has since been called "repairing the cities."

During the increasing urbanization of the late twentieth century, all cities grew into the surrounding areas and suburbs, creating a new kind of urban living space called *Zwischenstadt* (in-between city).[25] This growth is a result of migration from the rural areas and from the city cores and relies on increased individual car ownership. Now the western cities are surrounded by areas that are economically powerful because of prospering industries, middle-class people living in areas of detached or denser settlements of terraced houses using the infrastructure of the cities.

The Single-Family Detached or Semidetached House

The most popular kind of house has a gabled roof, red tiles, white facade, wooden or plastic windows with sash bars, and an attached garage and garden. The inner arrangement of the rooms is mainly separated into two stories, the second often under the roof. A living room is located on the ground floor, together with the dining room and kitchen. Many people prefer open-floor plans, influenced by the American way of life. Sometimes the master bedroom is also located on the ground floor, but in most houses it is on the upper floor along with other bedrooms. Sometimes each bedroom has its own bathroom. Often there is a guest lavatory near the front door. Every house has to be connected to the public sewer service, the public water and electric power system, and a public road. Even though each family wants to have their own style, variety is often limited to a choice of bathroom tiles and kitchen furniture.

Living in the City

The attraction of living in the city has changed historically. For a long time, young families and everybody who could afford it preferred to move into their own homes, which led to the growth of suburbs. On the other hand, rented apartments are still a popular and affordable living space for many Germans. Many people with limited incomes live in multistory apartment complexes. During the social housing programs in the 1950s and 1960s, there were new settlements built in the inner cities. During the 1970s, there were large projects at the edges of the old town plan, such as Märkisches Viertel in Berlin (about 17,000 units built in the 1960s for about 40,000 inhabitants) or Neuperlach in Munich (started in 1968, there were about 38,000 inhabitants by 1976). Based on the ideas of modernist architecture and urban design, the buildings of six to, sometimes, twenty stories and more pretended to preserve a modern level of living quality: small kitchens with all appliances, living rooms with integrated dining corners and balconies, full bathrooms, and a number of bedrooms. The size of the rooms was limited, for example children's bedrooms with 10 to 12 square meters. All apartments had central heating, and the buildings had elevators. The settlements were complemented by shopping centers, schools, and some cultural facilities to maintain a kind of local identity.

Until the 1980s the older buildings in the inner cities remained unattractive. The rediscovery of the quality of the architectural space was a result of student and alternative living at the end of the 1970s, first institutionalized on a commercial level in 1989, through the International Building Exposition in Berlin. Before that, rebuilding a city often meant razing it and rebuilding according to the contemporary technical and architectural state of the art. Especially in Berlin, whole city blocks were demolished to build new structures. The process came to be called *Kahlschlagsanierung* (clear cutting reconstruction). The conflict about the demolition of the buildings of Kettenhofweg in Frankfurt in the early 1970s also became famous. Around the turn of the millennium, the old quarters with renovated building structures in the inner cities had become an attractive living space for the young urban people.

The City Core

Migration out of the city, the unattractive living space in the old, unrenovated architecture, and the lack of parking space led at first to empty cities. But the dissatisfaction with modern urban planning, together with the growing offer of consumer goods and increasing consumption in the last twenty or thirty years began to change the function of the architectural scenery in the city cores. Especially in the urban ensembles that showed something like an old town, tourism became an important economic factor. In the 1970s the building of car-free pedestrian zones changed the adjacent buildings into expensive locations for retail trade and department stores. Today the city centers are a consumer's and tourist's paradise: a setting of intact urban environments and cultural identities, home to a wide range of stores; but the shops and warehouses have a new competitor.

Shopping Centers, Outlet Stores, and Building Centers

Today, shopping, outlet, garden, and building centers are popping up in the outskirts and, recently, at important traffic junctures in the municipal area. They compete with the traditional places of shops and warehouses in the inner cities and thereby also challenge the traditional way of life. In particular, the shopping centers constitute a new kind of urban space and a new kind of urban activity. Some such places have restaurants, cafes, fast food and an array of shops, sometimes even cinemas and galleries.

The Urban and Architectural Situation in the East

The single-family house areas and the rise of shopping centers in the outskirts, as well as the change of the historical city core, are phenomena that also started in eastern Germany after reunification in 1989, spurred by a backlog of demand. Prior to that date, the urban development had followed a different path for years and produced some specific details in popular living and space. First, the city fabrics were changed by a building industry that provided a very limited number of architectural solutions. This consisted of residential buildings of the type WB 70. These buildings were made with precast concrete slabs and had very little variety across East Germany. They were simple rectangular concrete boxes, six to ten stories high, with flat roofs. All apartments had the same floor plan, small rooms, windowless bathrooms, and no elevators. The surrounding green space was rarely landscaped; instead there were parking lots in between. If one entered these projects the impression was just a variety of tail fins or headlights of mostly identical cars that came in a handful of colors. Looking up to the narrow balconies, one could sometimes find an attempt at individualism in the coloring of the back walls of the balconies. Frequently, the old buildings were neglected, and they often degenerated. In some cases, for example in Berlin, the housing policy led to the demolition of large areas of inner-city buildings, to be replaced with the socialistic urban fabric.

THE MEDITERRANEAN AND SOUTHERN EUROPE

This area, from West to East, covers the Iberian peninsula, Italy, Greece, Turkey, and the Mediterranean islands. Along with the widespread phenomena of demographic growth, urbanization, and the continued change from an agricultural to an industrial economy the

Mediterranean area shows some additional features. Because of the frequent lack of laws, public regulations, and public housing, urban growth in these areas often leads to chaotic consequences. Improvised and self-made structures have generated a model for mass architecture.

Older structures also exist. As a result of the area's importance as a tourist destination there are, on the one hand, huge metropolises that can compete with any European city and, on the other hand, quaint (and sometimes artificial) fishing villages. Barcelona can claim one of Europe's most impressive outdoor shopping and leisure malls, the Ramblas, which is not only a commercialized postcard theme but a lively artery of urban life. Naples, for example, claims one of the largest historic city cores. It survived both World Wars and the development schemes of recent decades for the most part unharmed.

Uncontrolled Settlements

One of the most dynamic and fast-growing agglomerations is Istanbul, whose characteristics are rather modern and rarely show signs of an Islamic tradition. In fact the massive process of migration, the growing need for living space, and continued economic growth have all drastically changed the fabric of the city. In 1950, 85 percent of the population lived in an agricultural environment.[26] In 1990, 60 percent of the population lived in cities, but 50 percent of them depended financially on agricultural activities. The population of Istanbul grew tenfold over the next fifty years. In spite of several censuses, the precise population of Istanbul is unknown; it is put at approximately 10 to 15 million. Migration of the poor rural population generated nine-tenths of the urban settlement. Other Turkish cities, such as Ankara, Adana, or Antalya, grew because of tourism, and Diyarbakir because of Kurdish migration. Today, two-thirds of the Turkish people live in agglomerations.

In the late 1950s, Istanbul's municipal authority destroyed a great number of the traditional wooden houses, driving broad traffic arteries through the body of the city. Until then, Istanbul was a pedestrian city. Between 1959 and 1963 illegal settlements started. These settlements grew from 25,000 to 100,000 people, living at distances of 15 to 45 kilometers from the city. Today 60 percent of the city territory consists of illegal or uncontrolled settlements, and the migration still goes on at a rate of about 1000 houses a day.

The illegal individual settlement process starts with the so-called *Gecekondu*, which means "what is built in one night." These are small barracks or one-room houses built quickly, using cheap materials. Later the district will take on suburban characteristics by rebuilding the sites with multistory concrete frameworks, broadening the streets, and connecting all locations to the urban infrastructure.

The almost Mafia-like housing industry builds multistory houses, always using the same plan. The houses are separated narrowly, seldom plastered, but expandable on the top. If the maximum height is reached, the buildings get an individually designed roof to give them a characteristic outfit. There are about 50,000 households in Istanbul that can afford something different. For them, investors create so-called garden cities within the municipal area, which provide a permanent holiday feeling with private security.

The urbanization process everywhere in the southern European countries produced similarly unorganized settlements. Madrid was surrounded by a belt of substandard housing settlements until some public housing projects were started there.[27] In Rome, the *borgate* settlements began in the 1940s and lasted until the 1960s, with self-erected barracks. They were later reengineered by a legalizing post-urbanization process, which often dislodged the original settlers, as Pasolini showed in his film *Accatone*.

In Lisbon the illegal settlers are called *clandestinos* and at first live in "barracks." In 1984 the clandestine apartments made up about 25 to 40 percent of the apartment market. But the uncontrolled settlements created multifunctional districts. People bought the sites with savings by the whole family and, gradually, built houses as best as they could afford. Sometimes they sold the second half of the site at a profit. Many settlements remain unfinished for years, but the people go on building with great pleasure and a sense for detail and color, so that at the end picturesque ensembles emerge.

A Touristic Metropolis and Its Opposite

An urban feature often seen at tourist places around the Mediterranean coastlines, and especially on the islands such as Malta or Mallorca, are projects of big hotels and multistory apartment houses with countless balconies looking out at the sea, surrounding a little village core. In wintertime these are ghost towns with very few inhabitants, but during the summer they are full of life. An extraordinarily successful and unique example is Benidorm, which has about 50,000 permanent residents, but in August contains nearly 400,000 people.[28] At the beginning of the Benidorm development there were no height limitations but a minimum distance of 14 meters between the buildings. As a result, more and more high-rise apartment buildings, facing the south and the sea, were erected. Because of the discontinuity of the facades, it became difficult for the street to become the most important urban element. Benidorm is set off from other tourist destinations by its tall buildings. In fact, out of a total of 200 skyscrapers in Spain, 132 are in Benidorm, only 43 in Madrid. Benidorm ranks third in Europe with regard to the number of skyscrapers after London and Milan. Since 1973 Benidorm has been the most visited tourist destination in Europe. The number of tourists per year is above 5 million. There is capacity for more than 220,000 tourists. Benidorm has more hotel beds than any other city in Europe other than London, Paris, and Madrid.

Not far away, on the southern coast of France about 5 kilometers from St. Tropez, a more traditional project fulfills the idea of living in paradise. Port Grimaud is an artificial village designed by the architect Francois Spoerry in the late 1960s. The whole village was erected continuously in one construction process. Although the buildings were planned by one hand and partly constructed with prefabricated components, the completed village boasts a picturesque design because of variations in the outer elements, such as windows, doors, and balconies. The model was the traditional rural Provencal style with its typical roof tiles, a palette of ocher and terra cotta colors, a maximum height of three stories, pitched or pent roofs, and a varying disposition of the facade elements. The marine settlement was planned for about 35,000 inhabitants; 7 kilometers of canals and fourteen bridges make sure that every house is connected to a pedestrian way and a waterway. Cars are banned from the village, but a boat of no more than 3 meters draft can reach every corner of the village.[29]

In Grimaud as well as in the hills along the Mediterranean coast it is fashionable to build houses in the old style. Massive constructions with shutters, which are closed during the day against the heat, and a flat pitched roof with monk-and-nun roof tiles in terra cotta colors are varied in different houses with balconies and terraces, swimming pools, and gardens.

SCANDINAVIA

Scandinavia is located on the northern edge of Europe, connected through Denmark to central Europe. Some important cities such as Copenhagen, Stockholm, and Helsinki are located around the Baltic Sea, opening a new economic and cultural conurbation with the Baltic countries in the future. For much of the hinterland up north, the area is very sparsely populated, mostly below 25 inhabitants per square kilometer. The total population of the Nordic countries is about 85 million, about the same as that of Germany.

Even though these are relatively small countries, they have developed ways of construction, living culture, and design that have become influential worldwide. The traditional wood construction practices, which are elaborated, for example, in the Norwegian stave churches, go back to a long tradition in using the materials. The method of construction with vertical boards driven into the ground is developed within the history of wooden constructions in Norway on to an elaborated construction style. The design of bent cams and rafters to support the roof construction was adopted from shipbuilding; the roof was understood as an inverted ship with its bent ribs. These wooden constructions are unique examples of the Northern wood construction art, comparable only with Russian religious architecture.

Wooden constructions can produce simple and functionally designed but warm and comfortable rooms in an inhospitable climate where winter lasts for almost half the year. Wooden constructions can be built in all places, all times, and all temperatures. The application of traditional knowledge to the conditions of modern developments such as urbanization and industrialization, which also had an impact on architectural and urban Scandinavia in the twentieth century, brought a new culture of living into the world.

A New Culture of Living

The starting point of what is known as the Scandinavian furniture design can be set at the publication of *Beauty for Everybody* by Ellen Key and the watercolors of Carl Larrsons, published in his book *House in the Sun*.[30] In his art, Larrsons exhibited the rooms and the way of life in his house in Sundborn, which is shown today as the origin of the modern Nordic way of living. At the low point of the standard of living in Sweden at the beginning of the twentieth century, there began a movement to change architectural and cultural features that was connected to international discussions. So the reduced classicism of Heinrich Tessenow fitted in with the traditional design and construction of the Nordic sphere. The living space and its furnishing was a central topic of the work of architects until the 1960s and has become so again in the twenty-first century.

Furnishings and equipment of apartments were systematically developed in architectural and functional aspects. The designers tried to integrate new functions into the traditional architecture, such as bachelor studios with a separate entrance in times when the houses were overcrowded, or multipurpose rooms with kitchen appliances in a living space to change the use of a room according to need. In test kitchens, architects experimented with design and functional configuration of furniture, fixtures, and appliances.

Out of a cultural background of prefabrication and functional approach, the Nordic countries generated the production of cheap, modern-designed furniture sold as a kit and assembled at home. In the mid 1960s, there were various Swedish firms producing cheap models of stools, tables, shelves, and wardrobes. Since then, IKEA has brought this style to the far corners of the world. The company opened its first store in 1965, in competition to "Domus-Interior-Decoration-Store," a cooperative society. The connection of architecture and living standard, expressed in the unity of construction and the functional design, lives on in the vacation homes of the Swedish people. About 50 percent of the population owns them.

Development of Swedish Housing

The idea of prefabrication was derived from the traditional kind of wooden constructions in rhythmic structures. The Swedish development started with a growing need for additional living space. For example, in 1945 about 29 percent of the population lived in a room with more than one person.[31] About 44 percent of the units were one-room apartments or houses. Through innovative developments in furnishing, designers found solutions connected to tradition and oriented to modern standards. Already in the 1920s, Nordic governments started producing prefabricated and standardized building programs for detached, terraced, and multistory houses. In Sweden, areas are counted as urbanized in settlements of 200 inhabitants or more with a distance between houses of 200 meters or less. Although there was an attitude of experimentation, the ultimate solutions integrated the needs of the people and of the general program and did not break the connection to traditional culture. Not revolutionary but rather new, architects sometimes found very specific solutions, such as the Y-shaped multistorey house with three wings jutting out from a central staircase, all surrounded by green spaces. From the beginning the diversification of materials and colors, individual details in the facades, participation of the inhabitants in planning, and sometimes self-organized construction were basic standards. The Swedish prefabs are successful in other European countries as a model of architecture, and not only because of the homely colors of the one- or two-story pitched-roof wooden houses.

The neighboring countries, Norway and Finland, do not differ much. The architects of these regions, such as Erskine from Sweden, Alvar Aalto from Finland, Sverre Fehn from Norway, or Arne Jacobson, are mostly famous for their architectural work, which is embedded in the general Nordic culture, and for their furniture design as a functional design usable every day.

THE UNITED KINGDOM

Great Britain was the very first country to engage in a process of capitalist industrialization. The growth of railroads, shipping, and heavy industries led to a massive urban development as a consequence of the migration of workers to the industrialized areas concentrated in or near cities. But just as the development reached its climax, when about 48 percent of employment was in industrial jobs, the dynamic turned. From 1955 to 1983 the industrial numbers fell to 34 percent of all jobs. Afterward, the shrinking process accelerated. These developments also feature in the urban dynamic. In Manchester or in Liverpool, both industrial centers, the number of inhabitants decreased between 1930 and 2002 by about 49 percent and 45 percent, respectively.[32] The rise and fall of cities influenced architectural features for the people.

Britain, with a population of about 26.5 million, spearheaded several important European issues. The industrial inventions repressed the agricultural structures and forced urban growth across the continent. The Arts and Crafts Movement aimed to supersede the predominant imperial symbolic language in arts and architecture and opened, along with the Jugendstil movement in Vienna, the cultural scenery to modern times. In the phase of industrial development at the end of the nineteenth century, the idea of the garden cities started with Ebenezer Howard's book *Tomorrow: A Peaceful Path to Social Reform*, first published in 1898 and later renamed *Garden Cities of To-Morrow* for its second edition of 1902. Following the ideas, two garden cities were built during Howard's lifetime (1850–1927): Letchwork in 1903 and Welwyn Garden City, finished in 1928. To organize the unregulated and dynamic growth of the urban agglomerations, it would be channeled into new cities of about 30,000 people each, out in rural surroundings. The design of the new settlements consisted of concentric structures that separated functions with green spaces in between. The garden city concept was the model for many urban concepts in foreign situations such as new or satellite towns as an idea. The most effective result of this early twentieth-century idea in Great Britain was its transformation into the greenbelt concept, evolved in the 1980s to restrain urban sprawl. But the attempt to manage urban containment and protect the rural surrounding did not notice the overspill when it really came. The result is to be seen in the outskirts of London or even Belfast, where settlements come up far outside beyond the greenbelt, such as Basildon or Crawley, expanding new towns in a distance of about 30 kilometers.

The English Cottage and Urban Development

Since life in cities and urban agglomerations displaced rural vernacular architecture, the typical English terraced houses emerged as a consequence of extensive and economically defined building processes. Two-story brick houses with small front yards and little gardens with about 80 square meters in the back were built everywhere in Great Britain throughout the twentieth century. A well-designed front face and the sewage pipes outside on the back facade are some characteristics of this type.

As of 2006 the production of housing has been driven by risk-averse, least-cost strategies. Speculative house-building attracts negative and often hostile comments in relation to quality and design. The architecture is not necessarily sensitized to user needs. The standardized layouts and limited house-types have a low range of variation and minimal sense to good design. So typically there are a kitchen, a little cloakroom, and a dining and sitting area on about 50 square meters on the ground floor and some sleeping rooms and a bathroom above.

The situation in the urban regions changed dramatically in the last 25 years. In particular, the industrial centers such as Manchester or Liverpool had to manage fundamental social and economic change. Today there are extensive areas with terraced or twin houses from the nineteenth and twentieth centuries that exceed the need for living space. Between 1956 and 1976, about 43 percent of residential structures in Manchester were built outside of the municipality. In 2001, about 500 hectares within the city area were filled with empty houses or brown land. During the 1980s about 12,000 people a year left Liverpool. As there was no more need for housing, the value of terrace-houses in the Manchester and Liverpool area declined in 2000 to about a sixth of the general value in Great Britain. About a third of the municipal area remains undeveloped.[33] In conjunction with a new urban policy to encourage the inner cities, there was a dramatic rise in apartment production in the early twenty-first century. In 2002 more apartments than houses were constructed.[34] But since companies traditionally had the house market in their grip, they control apartment production too.

The Change of the City Cores

The industrial change left constructions and space without further disposition in attractive positions within the city plan. Also in the industrial subcenters in Northern England, new projects started in city districts formerly used by industry. "Concert Square" is an old industrial construction started in Liverpool that imitates an architectural system of the European continent, mixing up living, leisure, and business space. An old warehouse was reconstructed as a first project in 1995 with eighteen apartments and 2,800 square meters of business and leisure space. Another, the former Bryant and Match Factory, was converted into 2,500 square meters of business space in 2001, using an old water tank as an architectural sign of identification. In Manchester in 2000, 25 apartments were built in Britannia Mills, a former warehouse.[35]

A world famous inner-city redevelopment area and the biggest of its type—about 22 square kilometers—is the Docklands area in London. Starting in the mid-1970s it contains today a new landmark as an emblem for London, the Canary Wharf Tower. Between 1981 and 1998 the workplaces increased from 10,000 to 70,000, and the population grew from 30,000 to about 80,000. Many buildings were erected with interesting architecture, which even won a number of awards.[36]

RESOURCE GUIDE

PRINTED SOURCES

Architektur im 20. Jahrhundert. Frankfurt am Main: German Architecture Museum, 1995–96. 9 catalogues to exhibitions about different countries.

Ariés, Philippe, and Georges Duby, eds. *A History of Private Life*. 5 vols. Cambridge, MA: Belknap Press of Harvard University Press, 1987–1991.

Asensio Cerver, Francisco. *European Architecture*. Barcelona: Atrium International, 2000.

Blake, Peter. *No Place like Utopia: Modern Architecture and the Company We Kept*. New York: W. W. Norton, 1996.

Campi, Mario, Franz Bucher, and Mirko Zardini. *Annähernd perfekte Peripherie: Glattalstadt/Greater Zurich Area*. Basel/Boston/Berlin: Birkhäuser, 2001.

Certeau, Michel de. *The Practice of Everyday Life*. Minneapolis: University of Minnesota Press, 1998.

Creese, Walter L. *The Search for Environment: The Garden City—Before and After*. Baltimore: Johns Hopkins University Press, 1992.

Droste, Magadelena. *Bauhaus, 1919–1933*. Köln: Taschen, 2002.

Dubois-Taine, Geneviève, ed. *European Cities: From Helsinki to Nikosia—Insights on Outskirts*. Brussels: ESF COST, 2004.

Dyroff, Hans-Dieter, ed. *Art Nouveau/Jugendstil Architecture in Europe*. Bonn: German Commission for UNESCO, 1988.

Engel, Barbara. *Öffentliche Räume in den Blauen Städten Russlands* [Public Spaces in the Blue Cities of Russia]. Tübingen, Germany: Wasmuth, 2004.

Fainstein, Susan S., and Scott Campbell, eds. *Readings in Urban Theory*. Oxford: Blackwell, 2002.

Franzén, Mats, and Jean-Marie Halleux, eds. *Dynamics*. Brussels: METL/PUCA, 2004.

Gold, John R., and Margaret M. Gold. *Cities of Culture: Staging International Festivals and the Urban Agenda, 1851–2000*. Aldershot, UK: Ashgate, 2005.

Goldhoorn, Bart, and Philipp Meuser. *Capitalist Realism: New Architecture in Russia*. Berlin: DOM, 2006.

Goodman, David, ed. *The European Cities and Technology Reader: Industrial to Post-Industrial City*. London/New York: Routledge, in association with the Open University, 1999.

Gottdiener, Mark. *Postmodern Semiotics: Material Culture and the Forms of Postmodern Life*. Oxford: Blackwell, 1995.

Hitchcock, Henry Russell, and Philip Johnson. *The International Style*. New York: W. W. Norton, 1996.

Howard, Ebenezer. *Garden Cities of To-Morrow*. F.J. Osborn, ed. Cambridge, MA: MIT Press, 1965.

Ikonnikov, Andrei. *Russian Architecture of the Soviet Period*. Moscow: Raduga, 1988.

Jencks, Charles. *Modern Movements in Architecture*. Harmondsworth, UK: Penguin, 1985.

Katz, Peter. *The New Urbanism: Toward an Architecture of Community*. New York: McGraw-Hill, 1994.

Klotz, Heinrich. *20th-Century Architecture: Drawings, Models, Furniture from the Exhibition of the Deutschen Architekturmuseums, Frankfurt am Main*. London: Academy Editions, 1989.

Krier, Leo. *Architecture: Choice or Fate*. Windsor, UK: Andreas Papadakis, 1998.

Kunstler, James Howard. *The City in Mind: Notes on the Urban Condition*. New York: The Free Press, 2001.

Le Galès, Patrick. *European Cities: Social Conflicts and Governance*. New York: Oxford University Press, 2002.

Mitscherlich, Alexander. *Die Unwirtlichkeit unserer Städte*. Frankfurt: Suhrkamp, 1965.

Oswalt, Philipp. *Atlas of Shrinking Cities*. Ostfildern, Germany: Cantz, 2006.

Oswalt, Philipp. ed. *Schrumpfende Städte*. Ostfildern, Germany: Cantz, 2004.

Parker, Simon. *Urban Theory and the Urban Experience: Encountering the City*. London/New York: Routledge, 2004.

Pevsner, Nikolaus. *An Outline of European Architecture*. Harmondsworth, UK: Penguin, 1958.

Rudofsky, Bernard. *Architecture without Architects*. New York: Museum of Modern Art, 1964.

Shamiyeh, Michael, ed. *What People Want: New Populist Tendencies in Architecture*. Basel/Boston/Berlin: Birkhäuser, 2005.

Shiel, Mark, and Tony Fitzmaurice, eds. *Screening the City*. London: Verso, 2003.

Talen, Emily. *New Urbanism and American Planning: The Conflict of Cultures*. New York: Routledge, 2005.

Wieland, Dieter. *Bauen und Bewahren auf dem Lande*. Bonn: Deutsches Nationalkomitee für Denkmalschutz, 2003.

Zhuravlev, Anatolii Mikhailovich, A.V. Ikonnikov, and A.G. Rochegov. *Arkhitektura Sovetskoi Rossii* [Architecture of Soviet Russia]. Moscow: Stroiizdat, 1987.

FILMS

Accattone (Italy, 1961). Directed by Pier Paolo Pasolini. Realistic film about street life in 1960s Rome.

L'ami de mon amie [My Girlfriend's Boyfriend] (France, 1987). Directed by Eric Rohmer. Filmed in the New Town Marne-le-Vallée.

L'arbre, le maire et la médiàtheque [The Tree, the Mayor, and the Mediatheque] (France, 1993). Directed by Eric Rohmer. About the building of a multimedia house in small-town France.

Berlin Alexanderplatz (Germany, 1931). Directed by Piel Jutzi. Film version of one of the most famous city novels.

Berlin: Symphonie einer Großstadt [Berlin: The Symphony of a Great City] (Germany, 1927). Directed by Walter Ruttmann. Homage to urban life in early twentieth-century Germany.

El bola [The Pellet] (Spain, 2000). Directed by Achero Mañas. Teenagers growing up in suburban Madrid.

Carne trémula [Live Flesh] (Spain, 1997). Directed by Pedro Almodóvar. Set in post-Franco Spain.

Caro diario [Dear Diary] (Italy, 1994). Directed by Nanni Moretti. Wonderful motor scooter ride through Rome.

Chelovek s kino-apparatom [The Man with the Movie Camera]. (USSR, 1929). Directed by Dziga Vertov. Lyrical portrait of city life.

A Clockwork Orange (UK, 1971). Directed by Stanley Kubrick. Partly set in dystopian townscapes of International Style architecture.

Dekalog (Poland, 1989). Directed by Krzysztof Kieślowski. About anonymous life in socialist housing estates.

Der Himmel über Berlin [Wings of Desire] (Germany, 1987). Directed by Wim Wenders. On an angel learning about human life in Berlin.

Lisbon Story (Germany, 1994). Directed by Wim Wenders. Urban life and culture in Lisbon.

Lola rennt [Run, Lola, Run] (Germany, 1998). Directed by Tom Tykwer. Fast-paced film set in Berlin.

Naked (UK, 1993). Directed by Mike Leigh. Gloomy film on drifters in London.

Les quatre cents coups [The 400 Blows] (France, 1959). Directed by François Truffaut. Sad life of a young urban boy.

Raï (France, 1995). Directed by Thomas Gilou. About multicultural gang-life in suburban Paris.

The Way We Live (UK, 1946). Directed by Jill Craigie. Postwar film about town-planning ideology.

MUSEUMS

Design Museum, Shad Thames, London SE1 2YD, UK. http://www.designmuseum.org/. Major design
   museum that also covers architecture.
Deutsches Architekturmuseum, Schaumainkai 43, 60596 Frankfurt am Main, Frankfurt, Germany.
   http://dam.inm.de/. History and current state of architecture; with changing exhibitions.
Fondation Le Corbusier, 8–10, square du Docteur Blanche, 75016 Paris, France. http://www.fondation
   lecorbusier.asso.fr/. Includes material on Le Corbusier's urban planning projects.
Pinakothek der Moderne, Kunstareal München, Barer Strasse 40, D-80333 Munich, Germany.
   http://www.pinakothek.de/pinakothek-der-moderne/. Museum on modern and contemporary
   art with section on architecture.

GALLERIES

Az W (Architekturzentrum Wien), Museumsplatz 1, im MQ, A-1070 Vienna, Austria.
Galerie Aedes, Christinenstr. 18–19, 10119 Berlin, Germany. http://www.aedes-galerie.de/.
La Galerie d'Architecture, Paris, 11, rue des Blancs Manteaux, 75004 Paris, France.
   http://www.galerie-architecture.fr/flash/index.html.

NOTES

1. Case study data gathered from Ariés and Duby 1987 (in Resource Guide), vol. 5.
2. See Wieland 2003 (in Resource Guide) and http://www.br-online.de/land-und-leute/himmel/.
3. Campi et al. 2001 (in Resource Guide); Maresa Schumacher et al., "The Zurich Limmattal," in
   Dubois-Taine 2004 (in Resource Guide).
4. *Architektur im 20. Jahrhundert, Österreich* (in Resource Guide); *Stadtbauwelt* 86.24 (1995. June 10).
5. Data of this article taken from Metka Sitar, "The Dynamics of Urbanization Processes in Slovenian
   Towns and Settlements," in Franzén and Halleux 2004 (in Resource Guide).
6. For Sarajewo see *Bauwelt* 46/2000 (2000, December 8).
7. On Prague see *Bauwelt* 83.39/40 (1992, October 23).
8. See Lionel Duroy, "Das Massaker von Bukarest" [The massacre of Bucharest], *Stadtbauwelt* 80.24
   (1989, June 23); *StadtBauwelt* 87.36 (1996, September 27).
9. On Russian cities see *Stadtbauwelt* 83.48 (1992, December 28); *Stadtbauwelt* 90.12 (1999, March
   12) (Moscow); *Stadtbauwelt* 86.48 (1995, December 29) (Magnitogorsk).
10. On Krakow see *Bauwelt* 84.4 (1993, January 22).
11. On Tallinn see *Bauwelt* 85.43 (1994, November 11).
12. Heike Liebmann, "Genese, Stand und Perspektiven der Großsiedlungen in Osteuropa" [Genesis,
   status, and perspectives of the large-scale estates in Eastern Europe], *Stadtumbau in Großsiedlungen* 2
   (April 4.2006), Information zur Raumentwicklung. Bonn: Bundesamt für Bauwesen und
   Raumordnung, 2006.
13. On the Czech Spas see *Bauwelt* 83.33 (1992, August 28).
14. Philipp Meuser, "Jenseits von Kommunismus und Kapitalismus" [Beyond Communism and Cap-
   italism] *Deutsches Architektenblatt* 38.8 (2006).
15. See Engel 2004 (in Resource Guide).
16. Irina Chekovskich, "Datschenkultur" [Culture of Dachas], in Oswalt 2004 (in Resource Guide).
17. See Jean-Marie Halleux, "Outskirts Dynamics and New Residential Developments in Belgium," in
   Franzén and Halleux 2004 (in Resource Guide).
18. Hans Ibelings, *20th Century Urban Design in the Netherlands*, (Rotterdam: Netherlands Architecture Institute Publishers, 1999).
19. See Franzén and Halleux 2004 (in Resource Guide).

20. Marijke Kuper, ed., *Nine+One – Ten.Young.Dutch.Architectural.Offices* (Amsterdam: Netherlands Architecture Institute Publishers, 1997).
21. "MVRDV, Winy Maas, Jacob van Rijs and Nathalie de Vries, Niederländischer Pavillon," *Arch+* 149/150 *Medienarchitektur* (April 2000).
22. Hans Ibelings, *Unmodern Architecture: Contemporary Traditionalism in the Netherlands* (Rotterdam: Netherlands Architecture Institute Publishers, 2004).
23. Data taken from Franzén and Halleux 2004 (in Resource Guide).
24. Data of population, density, areas etc. are taken from http://www.europa-waechst-zusammen.de and *Raumordnungsbericht 2000*, vol. 7 (Bonn: Bundesamt für Bauwesen und Raumordnung, 2000) and *Raumordnungsbericht 2005*, vol. 21 (Bonn: Bundesamt für Bauwesen und Raumordnung, 2005).
25. See Thomas Sieverts, "Zwischenstadt—zwischen Ort und Welt, Raum und Zeit, Stadt und Land" [In-between City—between Location and World, Space and Time, City and Landscape], *Bauwelt Fundamente* 118 (1997).
26. Data on Istanbul taken from *Bauwelt* 89.36 (1998, September 25).
27. See Andres Walliser and Carlos Bruquetas Callejo, "Urban Outskirts in Madrid," in Dubois-Taine 2004 (in Resource Guide).
28. José Miduel Iribas, "Benidorm: The Reasons for Success," in *What People Want: Populism in Architecture and Design*, edited by Michael Shamiyeh (Basel: Birkhauser 2005).
29. See http://www.cote.azur.fr/annuaire/site-guides-port-grimaud-infos_3450.htm or http://www.grimaud-provence.com.
30. Data taken from Claes Caldenby, ed., *Architektur im 20. Jahrhundert—Schweden* (Munich: Prestel, 1998).
31. Ibid.
32. Alan Kidd, "Rise and Fall of Manchester," in Oswalt 2004 (in Resource Guide).
33. Ibid.
34. Bob Imrie, *Accessible Housing: Quality, Disability and Design* (New York: Routledge, 2006).
35. Deborah Mulhearn, "Urban Splash: New Entrepreneurs of Reurbanization," in Oswalt 2004 (in Resource Guide).
36. See http://www.geographie.uni-erlangen.de/london/docklands/revital.htm and Peter Davey, "Die Docklands in London: eine gründlich missverstandene Herausforderung," *Stadtbauwelt* 79.48 (1988, December 23).

JOY SPERLING

European countries do not have what can be described as an autonomous popular culture such as that found in the United States, although the United Kingdom and Ireland are possible exceptions to this rule. In continental Europe and Scandinavia, European popular culture is inevitably a derivation of high culture that has filtered down into society as an acquired taste or as the conscious retrieval of folk traditions and art as a mechanism for coping with the dislocations brought about by rapid economic and political changes or for consolidating a national identity. The variations within Europe are quite significant and are divided into six regions along cultural and artistic fault lines: Central Europe, Eastern Europe, the Iberian Peninsula, Scandinavia, Southeastern Europe, and Western Europe. These geographic divisions do not imply that Europe does not share significant cultural and artistic commonalities, but that there are significant differences in addition to those commonalities that have emerged over time.

Central Europe is dominated by the cultural and artistic trends that have emerged within a group of countries that are German-speaking or have a long historical entanglement with either Germany or Austria: these include Poland, Hungary, Switzerland, Czechoslovakia, and Slovenia. Eastern Europe now consists of the Russian Federation and those republics of the former Soviet Union that have a European rather than a Eurasian cultural heritage, including the three Baltic States (Estonia, Latvia, and Lithuania), Belarus, and Ukraine. Spain and Portugal constitute Iberia. These two countries possess a distinctly Roman Catholic culture, closely related languages, and a political history dominated by a series of authoritarian governments. They have been historically separated from the rest of Europe by the geographic barrier formed by the Pyrenees. The four Scandinavian countries (Sweden, Norway, Finland, and Denmark) have developed a common Nordic identity and have forged a well-marketed and immediately recognizable Scandinavian design aesthetic. Southeastern Europe contains the most disaggregated group of countries, but those countries are tied together by a common history, particularly defined by the regional competition between the Austro-Hungarian and Ottoman empires. In addition to that political competition, the region was riven by the civilizational competition between Christianity and Islam. For the countries of southeastern Europe, art and popular culture emerged as an assertion of national and civilizational identity. Finally, Western Europe is the most diverse and includes Belgium, the Netherlands, the United Kingdom, and Ireland, as well as France and Italy.

While the political and geographic boundaries provide a clear structure for this chapter, its content—popular art—is less easy to define. Some continue to argue that popular culture is indistinguishable from folk culture. The contrast between the development and omnipresence of popular culture in the Anglo-Saxon countries, particularly in the United States and Great Britain, and its relative absence in the countries of continental Europe strongly suggests that these two categories of culture are distinct and separable. There is a general agreement that folk and popular culture can be easily differentiated from high culture, but once again, significant differences arise between the continental Europeans and the Anglo-Saxons. Popular culture and high culture have become interpenetrated in Britain and the United States while retaining their essential character, but on the European continent high culture remains relatively insulated from popular and folk culture (other than as a source of appropriation). The common ground shared by popular and high culture is found in the existence of a sophisticated and highly developed market for the goods produced in each sphere. Yet, popular culture, unlike high culture, requires a capitalist market economy animated by a hyperconsumerism that reaches into everyday life. The absence of popular culture in much of Central, southeastern, and Eastern Europe may be directly attributed to the cultural and economic pall that Communism cast over those nations for almost forty-five years; it is no accident that a popular culture emerged in West Germany but was absent in East Germany. Both high culture and folk culture are, respectively, elite preoccupations with a fairly narrow clientele and an organic expression of national or regional culture unmediated by the market. Moreover, the artifacts of popular culture are produced with the expectation that they will be purchased on the open market in competition with other goods; folk culture is thus produced by individuals to meet their own needs. The following discussion amply demonstrates that popular culture is underdeveloped or absent in much of Europe and is dependent upon the appropriation of high or folk culture. Moreover, it is also clear that American popular culture not only validates European popular cultures but largely determines their form and content.

CENTRAL EUROPE: GERMANY, AUSTRIA, CZECHOSLOVAKIA, HUNGARY, POLAND, SLOVENIA, AND SWITZERLAND

Germany

By 1871 Otto von Bismarck had consolidated the German Empire after a series of successful wars with Austria and Denmark. Berlin was the capital between 1871 and 1945. After World War II, Germany was truncated and divided into the Federal Republic of Germany (FRG) and the German Democratic Republic (GDR), allied with the United States and the Soviet Union respectively. The two German states were united in 1990 after the Berlin Wall fell in 1989. Berlin has since been restored as Germany's capital city.

Photography

By 1900 Berlin and Dresden had the largest camera-manufacturing centers in Europe, boasting the firms of Zeiss, Voigtländer, and Agfa, which produced lenses, cameras, chemicals, film, albums, and even postcards for all of Europe. Between 1880 and 1918, photography spread to the German lower middle classes in the form of snapshot cameras and photographically illustrated magazines, in which Germany also led the world. Between 1914 and 1918, many soldiers took cameras to war. In 1925 Leitz's Leica camera swept the world, replacing glass with hand-held film cameras; in 1926 Zeiss-Ikon became one of Europe's largest photographic companies; and in 1936, Agfa and Kodak (Germany) introduced color film.

In 1928 the Dephot photo agency was founded in Berlin to assist press photographers, but its tenure was short. In 1933 the Illustrated Press Department was established by the Propaganda Ministry, and all press photographers and photo agencies came under ministerial control (with the exception of the American Associated Press until 1941). After 1945 Berlin lost its prewar role in German photojournalism, although new German magazines were established elsewhere, such as the *Revue* (Munich) and the *Neue Illustrierte* (Cologne).

Sculpture

Between 1895 and 1901, perhaps the largest German sculptural display was created on Berlin's Siegesallee in front of the Reichstag. It comprised monuments narrating almost 800 years of German leadership. This vast collection was dismantled after 1945. Between the wars, but especially after 1933, Nazi sculpture in Germany tended to be characterized by over-life-size figures of German youth. Much of this sculpture has not survived. It is somewhat ironic that the most popular sculpture of recent years in Germany was the 1995 *Wrapped Reichstag* by Christo and Jeanne Claude, a piece that celebrated German democracy but followed the tradition of megalomaniacal power, nationalism, and gigantism evident in so much of earlier German sculpture.

Interiors

Around 1900 German interior design was heavily influenced by the English Arts and Crafts style. By 1918, however, English style was no longer acceptable, and the clean, stripped, flexible spaces and forms of German Functionalism dominated home design of the interwar period until 1933. The 1927 *Weissenhofsiedlung* model housing complex of flats in Stuttgart, designed by the *Deutscher Werkbund*, was based on each apartment having a single large, flexible, functional room to be used as a combination living area/bedroom/workroom/study. The apartments included neutral furniture that occupied minimum space and standardized woven or brightly colored patchwork rugs. The tubular steel and leather furniture of such designers as Walter Gropius, Marcel Breuer, Ludwig Mies van der Rohe, and Hans Poelzig was the ideal, but it was so expensive that only the wealthy could afford it. After 1945 the desperate need to shelter the homeless and dispossessed created a demand for simple housing with small spaces and inexpensive, functional furniture that could fulfill several needs, for example, being able to be converted from a bed to a table to a desk to a chair.

Ceramics

German porcelain has always been a source of national pride. All kinds of decorative ceramics are mass-produced for the domestic, export, and tourist markets. Fine porcelain was first produced at Meissen in 1740. The factory made vases, coffee and tea services, and its speciality, small figure groups. In 1913 Paul Scheurich Rocoso further enhanced Meissen's reputation by reviving the famous porcelain figurine groups, although with exaggerated gestures. These revivals are the mainstay of the company today.

In 1905 the Rosenthal-Porzellan Manufaktur in Selb (Bavaria) produced Donatello, a completely undecorated service. The company enjoyed success in the postwar period as a niche producer of high-quality and well-designed coffee and tea services, as well as tabletop objects.

The M. I. Hummel Company began in 1935 in the northern Bavarian region of Germany through the partnership of Sister Maria Innocentia Hummel (born Berta Hummel), who loved to draw children, and Franz Goebel, the head of a porcelain-making company. The company continues to make popular figurines of children, in various poses and costumes, that are avidly collected worldwide.

Jewelry

Around 1900 Pforzheim became the center of enamel manufacture and painting in Germany, with a number of artists producing a range of products, from hair ornaments and large brooches to silver cigarette cases. Of particular note were complex copies of Swiss mechanical singing-bird boxes and other automata that were made until the 1920s with enamel produced in Pforzheim. By 1940 many of the Pforzheim factories had introduced mass-produced and inexpensive jewelry. Today Pforzheim maintains an international reputation for the production of both expensive and cheap jewelry. Idar-Oberstein is still one of world's largest gem and hard-stone centers.

Austria

In 1904 Carl Otto Czeschka signaled the popular revival of Austrian folklore with his publication of the illustrated *Märchen-Kalender für das Jahr 1905* [Fairy-Tale Calendar for the Year 1905] and his widely known *Die Nibelungen* (1909). In 1923 Felix Salten wrote *Bambi*, the story of a fawn in the Austrian forest, which achieved global fame and was ultimately translated into numerous illustrated books and made into a Walt Disney animated film (1942). Other notable Austrian illustrators include Angelika Kaufmann and Susi Weigel.

Photography

In 1864 Vienna hosted Central Europe's first international photography exhibition, with roughly 400 cameras and over 1,100 photographs. In 1879 the invention of the photogravure process precipitated a boom in the photographic publishing of illustrations in books and magazines, and as posters and postcards. Much of this trade was connected to the popular side of the Austrian revival or to tourism: the photographs portrayed landscape and city views or urban and rural genre images. The genre photographs of "Old Vienna," for instance, represented completely mythic Vienna types (*Wiener Typen*) such as washerwomen, musicians, cabbies, or street urchins, many of which were actually actors posed in photographic studios. Between 1918 and 1938, economic failures and a diminished commercial market caused many Austrian photo studios to close. The

Manassé Studio did thrive, however, producing glamor and nude photographs for an upper-class clientele.

Porcelain

In 1718 the Wiener Porzellanmanufaktur was established in Vienna as the second factory in Europe after Meissen. It rivaled Meissen's production from the outset with a range of chocolate beakers, coffee cups, pipes, walking-stick handles, cutlery-handles, terrines, candelabra, holy-water stoups, clock cases, and mirror frames. The Wiener Porzellanfabrik Augarten was established in 1922 to reproduce traditional Viennese porcelain wares, including floral dinner services, animal figures, and rococo figurines.

Czechoslovakia

The Czechs and the Slovaks underwent an amiable divorce after the end of the Cold War; however, their tangled historical relationship and long-term identification (at least externally) as Czechoslovakians argues for joint treatment rather than individual treatment of the current Czech Republic and Slovakia. In the late nineteenth century, Czech visual artists drew on national identity, history, folklore, and legend in their work. In 1948, however, Communism imposed the norms of Socialist Realism on Czech visual imagery.

Illustration

Czech book illustration has a distinguished history. Josef Lada, the Czech writer and illustrator of traditional folktales, was best known for his illustration of Jaroslav Hasek's *The Good Soldier Svejk* (1924) and of his own *In-and-Outside Tales* (1939) and *Naughty Tales* (1946), in which he parodied famous Czech folktales. His illustrations come out of the tradition of caricature. Prior to the imposition of Socialist Realism in the 1950s, Slovakia had a relatively well-developed graphic tradition that had begun around 1900, represented by the work of Eugen Krón (1882–1974) and Koloman Sokol (1902–2003).

Photography

A truly independent photographic tradition in Czechoslovakia emerged in 1918 with Czechoslovak independence. The New Czech Photography exhibition in 1930 captured this development, presenting an impressive array of modernist, documentary, scientific, technical, architectural, and published periodical photography. Two major exhibitions took place in the 1930s: the Czech Surrealist Art exhibition (1935) and the 100 Years of Czech Photography exhibition (1939). In 1942 photographic freedoms were quashed under the Nazi Protectorate and then under the Soviet occupation after 1948.

Karel Klietsch invented the photogravure and rotogravure processes (1877–1890), which provided fast and cheap photographic reproduction. His invention was used for several important Czech photographic books, including Tyrsky and Jindrich Heisler's *Na Jehlách Techto dni* [On the Needles of These Days] (1945) and Josef Sudek's *Fotografie* (1956). Karel Plicka, whose *Praha ve Fotografii* (1940) was published in gravure, has remained in print for over fifty years. Although limited artistic freedom was briefly restored in 1968 with the Prague Spring, Koudelka, who documented that period with photographs, was later forced into exile.

Hungary

Photography

In the 1920s many of Hungary's best-known photographers left when confronted with Admiral Miklos Horthy's right-wing government. They included Kertész, Moholy-Nagy, Brassaï (Gyula Halasz), Robert Capa (Endre Erno Friedman), Cornell Capa, Martin Munkácsi, Nicholas Muray, György Kepes (the inventor of holography), and Rudolf Balogh, who worked for the progressive *Est* newspaper. Some photographers, such as Klára Langer and Kata Sugár, stayed. In 1945 Socialist Realism photographic norms were imposed. Ata Kandó documented the Hungarian uprising in 1956, but the photographs were only published in the West. In 1990 the Museum of Hungarian Photography (HMP) was opened in Kecskemét to house the 75,000 items that had been collected since 1958.

Interiors

Between the 1870s and 1900, thirteen bentwood furniture factories were established to meet domestic demand; Endre Thék was the largest of them. At the Paris Exposition Universelle of 1900, Ödön Faragó and Pál Horti exhibited prize-winning furniture and carpet designs. In the 1930s factories mass-produced an inexpensive and wide range of furniture and carpet styles, including historical revival styles.

Poland

Between 1819 and 1939, Poland enjoyed what must have seemed like a moment of independence sandwiched between almost two centuries of German and then Russian domination that only ended in June 1989. The events of the 1848 revolution and the beauty of the landscape around Kraków were especially well-covered themes in art. The Kapist group focused on folklore. Many Polish homes were decorated with explicitly patriotic prints and paintings referring to the partition(s) of Poland. After 1949 artists working within the constraints of Socialist Realism included Helena Krajewska, Juliusz Krajewski, and Tadeusz Trepkowski.

Decorative Arts

Nineteenth-century Polish interiors were characterized by an interest in Polish revival styles, such as bentwood furniture or Zakopane-style pieces based on furniture from the Tatra Mountains. In 1926 an artists' cooperative was founded in Warsaw to design relatively inexpensive, functional furniture with folk art decorations, often in wickerwork. In 1949 the Cepelia Folk Art Trade Cooperative began producing a range of modern, revival, and folk furniture, and its designers specialized in wickerwork. Mass-produced furniture was produced in state-owned factories

Slovenia

In the mid-nineteenth century, the growing middle-class art-buying public commissioned solidly bourgeois portraits by artists such as Mihael Stroj and collected romantic

Slovenian landscapes by artists such as Anton Karinger and Marko Pernhart or by printmakers such as Johann Nolli. Around 1900 the artistic group Vesna (Spring), which included Gvidon Birolla, Maksim Gaspari, and Hinko Smrekar, among others, actively sought to revive the imagery and forms of Slovenian folk art.

Decorative Arts

The Ljubljana region was the center of ceramics, specifically creamware production, in the nineteenth century. The Dvor cast iron foundry, founded in 1796 and claiming to be the largest of its time, served the entire region. By the nineteenth century, the Samassa bell foundry (founded 1729) in Ljubljana had taken over much of the cast iron trade, producing products for churches and homes. Around 1900 bentwood furniture was produced by the factories of Naglas and Mathian, both in Ljubljana.

Switzerland

Swiss theater and advertising posters, as well as book and magazine illustrations, have been of a consistently high quality for a long time because of the complex demands of meeting the needs of four national languages in one tiny market. The search for a Swiss identity was illustrated in Johanna Spyri's alpine novel, *Heidi* (1881), and much later in Selina Chönz and Alois Carigiet's Romansh-language *Schellen-Ursli* [Ursli and the Bells] (1945), about the search for the largest cowbell. Jörg Steiner and Jörg Müller wrote the politically motivated *Der Bär, der ein Bär bleiben wollte* [The Bear Who Wanted to Be a Bear] (1976). In 1994 Müller's illustrations won a Hans Christian Andersen Medal for distinguished contributions to children's literature. Hans Fischer had a long career as an illustrator and caricaturist for the magazine *Nebelspalter*. His first illustrated book, *Die Bremer Stadtmusikanten* (1944), was still in print in the 1990s.

Photography

In 1852 Carl Durheim took some of the first police photographs in Bern, followed in 1900 by Rodolphe Archibald Reiss in Lausanne. Photographs of the Swiss landscape produced for the tourist industry proved more lucrative, however. The competition for alpine views was fierce between Charnaux frères (since 1870) and Jullien frères (since 1880) in Geneva, although Fred Boissonnas (since 1900) transformed Swiss tourist photography from a local trade to an international business by expanding his business into Greece and Egypt in the 1920s. In the illustrated press, Arnold Kübler transformed the *Zürcher Illustrierte* into a photographic journal by 1929 and included the work of staff photographers Hans Staub, Ernst Mettler, Paul Senn, Gotthard Schuh, and Jakob Tuggener.

Glass

The most popular Swiss glass is Flühliglas, an engraved glass cut with Swiss heraldic designs; animals such as bears, stags, or lions; romantic scenes, such as couples toasting one another; farmers or workers; romantic symbols such as flowers, birds, or burning hearts; and drinking slogans. The last Flühli glassworks closed in 1869, but production was transferred to Hergiswil.

Clocks and Watches

Although Switzerland boasts of the most venerated names in watchmaking—Vacheron Constantin, Patek Philippe, Breguet, Jaeger LeCoultre, and Girard Perregaux—Swatch is the firm responsible for designing watches that have defined popular taste for watches worn as fashion accessories.

Textiles

Switzerland remains one of the world's leading producers of lace and embroidery. By the 1880s competition with Nottingham in England made the Swiss embroidery industry fight for its life; in the 1920s the industry declined because fashion and trade policies had changed. In the 1930s Appenzeller embroidery was revived and popularized by the nationalistic *Heimatstil*. Black silk or horsehair lace caps that are part of the traditional Swiss costume were also produced in Bern, Jura, Greyerzerland, and Lauterbrunnental. Novelty laces, including straw and horsehair laces produced in Steckborn on Lake Constance, are now made mostly for tourists.

EASTERN EUROPE: RUSSIA, UKRAINE, BELARUS, AND THE BALTIC STATES

Russia

As the Russian empire expanded into Eurasia in the nineteenth century, Russians still looked to Western Europe for their cultural cues. However, as the increasingly vast and diverse nation also looked inward to examine its own histories, cultures, and folklores, the popular art of the time also became increasingly diverse and local. Regional artists investigated their national origins through the production of cheap popular prints (*lubok*), which some artists, such as Kuz'ma Petrov-Vodkin, related to the icon-painting tradition. The avant-garde artists Mikhail Larionov and Natal'ya Goncharova drew directly from the flat, decorative qualities of folk art. After 1917 Russian graphic art became increasingly decorative as a wave of nostalgia for the prerevolutionary period swept through the Russian art world, exemplified by the work of Alexandre Benois, Anna Ostroumova-Lebedeva, Yevgeny Lansere, and Sergey Chekhonin.

During World War II, many posters and agitational forms of art (referred to as "agitprop") were produced in the Soviet Union. After 1945 numerous very large war memorials honoring the fallen were erected throughout the Soviet Union by sculptors such as Yevgeny Vuchetich. After 1945, almost in reaction to the horrors of war, landscape painting became very popular among artists such as Sergey Gerasimov, Georgy Nissky, and Nikolay Romadin, while rural life was portrayed by Arkady Plastov, V. F. Stozharov, and Sergey and Aleksey Tkachov.

Illustration

Fairy tales and folktales, often written for children but produced by mainstream illustrators, predominated nineteenth-century Russian book and magazine illustration. In 1934 these illustrated books were banned under Soviet cultural policy. In the provinces, illustrators and writers were asked to Russify their work by writing in Russian and creating distinctly

Russian images. Since 1991 the development of private-sector publishing firms has been slow, and the best Russian illustrators, including Gennady Spirin, Alexander Koshkin, and Boris Diodorov, have signed contracts with higher-paying Western publishers.

Photography

The business of C. E. de Hahn and Bulla opened as one of Russia's first picture agencies; between 1914 and 1918, Karl Bulla and his sons, Alexander and Viktor, documented both World War I and the Russian Revolution. Lenin recognized and used the power of the photographic image as an instrument of propaganda. He used photographic posters and films in cities, on agitprop trains, and on steamers throughout Russia's rural regions, as well as printed photographs in press journals such as *Pravda*, *Izvestia*, *Rabochaya Gazeta*, and *Ogonyok*. Millions came to know Lenin's face through Pyotr Otsup's portrait photograph of him. Later Soviet propaganda, such as the "USSR in Construction" campaign, targeted foreign audiences rather than Soviet residents, and the Unionbild agency distributed the images.

THE FIGHT FOR DOMINANCE IN SOVIET ART AND CULTURE

In the early twentieth century, the Russian vision refocused inwardly and eastwardly after almost two centuries of Western influence, a development accompanying the Soviet government's 1918 decision to move the capital from St. Petersburg to Moscow. The Soviet Union sought to create a functional, national, and rational visual culture, but this vision was contested throughout the 1920s. Two major rival groups vied for dominance. The Constructivist avant-garde group of abstract artists and designers such as El Lissitzky, Aleksandr Rodchenko, and Malevich created the infamous Black Square for the theater, took photographs, and designed furniture and posters. The AKhRR (Association of Artists of Revolutionary Russia) on the other hand, embraced nineteenth-century Russian realism, drained of its regional and local emphasis, and explored Soviet themes and principles.

Between 1941 and 1945, Soviet photographers such as Alpert, Baltermants, Khaldei, Boris Kudoyarov (the siege of Leningrad), Petrussov, and Shaikhet produced some of the war's most powerful photographs for the newspaper *Frontovaya Illustratiya* and the TASS agency. After World War II, thousands of photographers returned to socialist realist photography, including Baltermants, who documented the announcement of Stalin's death in 1953. Boris Mikhailov has become the most famous and celebrated Russian photographer since 1991.

Interiors

After 1917 a severe furniture shortage in Russia produced a government decree soliciting the design of interior furnishings for the working classes. While El Lissitzky designed built-in furniture in 1922 that formed a single whole with the house, Aleksandr Rodchenko designed furniture for a Workers' Club in 1925 that included fold-away equipment for meetings, a wall-mounted newspaper rack, a slide projector stand, and a fold-away chess table. The 1920s represented the great age of Soviet furniture design, but it came to an end with the abolition, expropriation, and redistribution of private property, including furniture. After 1946 interiors for apartments and institutions became increasingly institutionalized. The furniture was made more cheaply with wood finishes using chipboard, textured paper, and hot-molding processes. This trend continued into the 1970s with synthetic materials and collapsible sectional components. In the 1980s Russian designers again revived traditional folk motifs; an example is Andrey Vasnetsov's Russian Restaurant (1980) at the International Trade Centre in Moscow.

Ceramics

The major Russian porcelain factory in the nineteenth century was the Auerbach Factory in Tver', which produced ceramics with grapevine and leafy designs that were hand painted at first but later prepared using transfer printing. While many factories closed after 1917, the factory at Tver' continued to produce mugs decorated with educational and sports images and slogans into the 1930s. More recently, 300 patterns have been discontinued and 800 new patterns have been introduced. The single- and limited-edition pieces are highly prized today, but the mass-produced items are of poor quality. Since 1945 Gzhel has reemerged as an important center for ceramics.

Until the 1930s the Soviet Union used porcelain objects for propaganda purposes, both at home and abroad, or displayed them at European and American trade fairs to earn hard currency. Yet, in the 1920s and 1930s, decorative porcelain accounted for a small amount of the ceramic industry's output: its valuable production lines were needed to refit the nation, its infrastructure, and even its people. Consequently, it produced electrical fittings, scientific instruments, false teeth, and glass eyes. In the 1970s traditional Russian styles were reproduced at many factories, but since 1991 the transition to the market economy has been difficult.

Glass

In 1900 Russia was one of Europe's largest glass manufacturers, producing major diplomatic gifts and presentation pieces. In 1918 the industry was nationalized and severely constrained by acute shortages of labor, fuel, and raw materials. In the 1940s Russian glass design showed enormous energy and creativity, but the industry was curtailed first by redirection of energy to the war effort and then by the destruction caused by the war itself. After 1945 many glass factories were rebuilt, but since glassmakers were reassigned to research laboratories, new decorative designs emerged only slowly. By 1957, however, 100 new designs had been created. Some folk designs were also revived. Since the 1960s, 70 percent of Russian glass production has been decorative crystal and pressed glass in a wide range of colors.

Gold

Nineteenth-century Russian gold work was known throughout Europe. Carl Fabergé, located in St. Petersburg and jeweler to the Russian Imperial Household, had 500 employees in 1914. Fabergé objects, reflecting the European tastes dominating the St. Petersburg market, combined European elegance with Russian opulence and exquisite technical quality. Fabergé perfected a range of colors for translucent enamels that he applied over a guilloche ground and decorated with gold work. In 1918 the company closed and Fabergé left the country.

In the 1940s and 1950s, the Leningrad Jewelry Factory produced commissions for gold and silver objects. In the 1960s and 1970s, traditional Russian jewelry was revived with the production of headdress pendants, silver necklace sets, amethyst necklaces, earrings, and rings that valued craft over precious stones. Since the 1980s, gold and silver brooches, pendants, bracelets, and earrings have been mass-produced at the Ural'skiye Samotsvety Works (Urals Gem Works), but quality remains problematic owing to a shortage of well-trained, professional staff.

Ukraine

A traditional practice in almost every Ukrainian home is the creation of hand-painted designs on walls, furniture, toys, paper, and particularly on Easter eggs. The geometric and stylized decorations on blown eggs, often with white linear patterns over a single color, are now produced mostly for the tourist trade and for export, and are popular all over the world.

Belarus

Belarus borders Russia to the east, Ukraine to the south, and Poland to the west. It was annexed in 1922 as the Belorussian Soviet Socialist Republic and regained its independence in 1991. In the nineteenth century, Jan Chrucki was a very successful portrait, landscape, genre, and still-life painter. Yehuda Pen painted landscape paintings and scenes of local Jewish life. In 1917 Marc Chagall became commissar for the arts in Vitebsk, and other teachers in the province included Kazimir Malevich and El Lissitzky. In 1919 Vera Yermolayeva was sent to Vitebsk to direct the art school. After the breach between Malevich and Chagall, art in Belarus faded into the representation of local themes and styles once again.

THE BALTIC STATES

Estonia

In the 1860s national identity, local customs, and folklore became major themes in Estonian painting and popular printmaking. In the mid-1890s, a number of illustrated periodicals were established. Estonia was one of the more industrialized regions of the Russian empire; during the brief time the country enjoyed independence prior to World War II, Estonian culture developed until it was suppressed again in 1939 after the Soviet annexation. Beginning after independence in 1991, an Estonian visual culture has slowly emerged.

Latvia

In 1921 the Latvian Academy of Art opened in Riga. Popular realism was encouraged at the expense of other styles. After 1945 Latvian art was forced to adopt official Soviet themes and styles.

Lithuania

In 1907 Vilnius hosted its first art exhibition, featuring works by Lithuanian painters, sculptors, architects, and folk artists; established the Lithuanian Art Society; and organized eight more exhibitions before 1914. In 1918 Lithuania claimed independence, and in 1920 the Lithuanian Art Society was reopened in Kaunas (Vilnius was occupied by Poland at this time), in conjunction with the existing Society of Artists for theater, music, literature, and fine arts. A new archaeological commission was charged with collecting the nation's fine and folk art, while the art group ARS was charged with encouraging a national artistic regeneration based on folk-art traditions.

In the aftermath of World War II, many Lithuanian artists were still active but were forced to work from refugee camps. By 1949 exhibitions of Lithuanian art in diaspora communities had moved from refugee camps to German galleries and museums; Lithuanian illustrated books were also published and widely distributed. Beginning in about 1950, many artists began moving to Australia, Canada, France, and the United States. A few remained in Lithuania and produced art through the 1960s and 1970s, notably the painters Augustinas Savickas and Vincas Kisarauskas, and the sculptor Teodoras Kazimieras Valaitis; their work featured Lithuania's historical and cultural heritage.

IBERIAN PENINSULA: SPAIN AND PORTUGAL
Spain

A national revival style between 1874 and 1900 characterized Spanish popular art as modernism (the Catalan version of art nouveau) became popular. In the late nineteenth century, Mariano Fortuny y Marsal painted small genre pictures; Darío de Regoyos painted landscapes in Basque country and made Casas, posters for tobacco and alcohol companies; and Joaquín Sorolla y Bastida painted very popular scenes of women and children on the beaches of Valencia, all of which were collected by Spain's middle class as well as by its industrial and financial magnates. Between 1923 and 1975, political instability, civil war, and the Franco dictatorship alienated artists and cut Spain off from the rest of Europe. Those cultural ties were only reestablished after the death of Franco in 1975 and then were deepened after Spain joined the European Community in 1986.

Photography

In 1863 Jean Laurent's studio in Madrid compiled the first photographic catalog, including several hundred photographs of art works in Spain, which was distributed throughout Europe. Tourist photographs of Spain's major architectural sites, especially the Alhambra at Granada, were always popular. The Spanish Civil War was covered to an unprecedented level by the international press, but very little attention was or is paid to Spanish photographers. After 1945 the Spanish economy could not support a full-fledged commercial photographic economy or a photographic press corps. The major Spanish photographer until the economic recovery in the 1950s was José Ortiz-Echagüe.

Interiors

At the turn of the twentieth century, the courtly and the industrial middle classes clashed in a battle between old and new, between revivalism in Andalusia and cosmopolitanism in Catalonia. Thus, there was the revival of the *cortijo* (farmhouse) style in Andalusia and the *casona* (country-house) style in Cantabria. Three Madrid palaces—Marquesa de Bermejillo, Conde de Casal, and the Conde de las Almenas—are now museums decorated with velvet curtains, damasks, *sillónes fraileros* (friars chairs), and carved cupboards with Mudéjar patterns. On the other hand, in Barcelona, Gaudí's modernism is evident in the Casa Calvet (1898–1904), the Casa Battló (1904–06), and the benches in the Park Güell (1900–14). Gaudí's furniture was organic and asymmetrical, designed to serve multiple purposes. In the early decades of the twentieth century, modernism waned as a radical movement, but it was still popular with the Catalan public. Outside Catalonia, however, many Spanish homes were still gloomy and filled with heavy, ornate furniture. In 1929 Ludwig Mies van der Rohe introduced the Barcelona chair at the German Pavilion of the Exposició Internacional. It struck such a chord in Spain that the designer contracted with MAC (Muebles de Acero Curvado), which started to manufacture his designs.

Ceramics

Until 1900 Catalonian ceramics were dominated by tiles that initially depicted the lives of saints, romantic scenes, and mythology, and later displayed a blue cherry pattern and a polychrome *Bañolas* with figures and flowers. Around 1900 several modernist (art nouveau) designers used ceramic tiles with floral designs on the walls of halls, staircases, and kitchens; Gaudi pioneered their use on monumental structures.

Embroidery

A small but highly specialized couture trade of hand embroidery survived in Barcelona until 1939. Spanish folk embroidery, with its exquisite bands of openwork on handwoven linen sheets and covers with fringes or bobbin-lace edging, had identifiable regional styles. In the nineteenth century, hand knitting flourished and lace knitting was particularly popular; machine-knit textiles were still produced in the Barcelona area throughout the twentieth century. Macramé, a Moorish-decorated knotted fringe, was revived in the nineteenth century and enjoyed a global revival beginning in the 1960s. Heavy Spanish lace, in both black and white silk with large floral patterns and made by hand or by machine, has always been extremely popular in Spain.

Portugal

Rafael Bordalo Pinheiro launched several popular illustrated journals in the nineteenth century. In *Columbano Bordalo*, Pinheiro portrayed everyday Portuguese life, and José Malhoa painted sentimental images of rural life that were very popular with the middle classes. Carlos Botelho created Lisbon landscapes but also worked as an illustrator and cartoonist.

Illustration

Around 1900, with growing numbers of Portuguese books and newspapers being published, the quantity and range of work for illustrators increased. Several artists collaborated fruitfully with children's book authors, a particularly important aspect of publishing since at the time three-quarters of Portuguese children were illiterate. In 1945, at the height of President António de Oliveira Salazar's power as head of state, these books emphasized traditionalism, patriotism, and nationalism. Later, more humor and irony appeared.

Photography

Portugal industrialized slowly and thus had a small and relatively weak middle class for most of the nineteenth century. Consequently, photography was slow to establish a commercial base in the country. In 1875 José Júlio Rodrigues founded the photography section of the Portuguese Directorate-General of Geographical Works, which organized a national photographic exhibition. In 1932 Salazar restricted the use of cameras in public; official photography, such as the images of Domingos Alvão, became increasingly pictorialistic, representing traditional ways of life.

Scandinavia: Sweden, Denmark, Norway, and Finland

The Nordic countries of Sweden, Denmark, Norway, and Finland share a common history and culture, but there are also significant differences among them. Swedish, Danish, and Norwegian are related languages, for example, but Finnish is not a Scandinavian language. Still, there is an identifiable Scandinavian cultural identity.

Sweden

Sweden was culturally cosmopolitan in the nineteenth century, although a Swedish national phase developed at midcentury. At this time, artists increasingly represented the ancient sagas of Swedish gods and heroes, and popular art focused on nationalistic themes. Although portraiture continued to dominate the market, moody northern landscapes with Scandinavian versions of elves and fairies by artists such as Nils Jakob Blommér or Johan August Malmström were popular, as were dramatic shipwreck scenes by Marcus Larson and peasant genre works by Kilian Zoll, Johan August Malmström, or Bengt Nordenberg. By the 1920s several artists, including Hilding Linnqvist and Axel Nilsson, began painting Swedish imagery that became very popular.

Printmaking and Illustration

Nordic publishers faced small markets segmented by language. Consequently, many books and magazines have relied on high-quality illustrations as a major means of communication. By 1900 both Sweden and Denmark regularly published cheap illustrated books and magazines, international classics in translation, and Scandinavian originals, which were distributed inexpensively through schools. Elsa Beskow wrote and illustrated over forty picture books about the magical transformations of people and landscapes in a small Swedish town between the 1890s and the 1920s. In 1906 Selma Lagerlöf, who won a Nobel Prize for literature, wrote *The Wonderful Adventures of Nils*, originally an illustrated geography book. In the twentieth century, Arne Ungermann illustrated Jørgen's *Wheel* and then, with Jens Sigsgaard, published *Paul Alone in the World* (1942), the most popular Danish picture book of all time. The Swedish illustrator Gustaf Tenggren produced almost fifty illustrated children's books, selling fifteen million copies, including *A Dog of Flanders* (1924) and *The Poky Little Puppy* (1942). More recently, illustrators of Swedish children's books have included the Norwegian Alf Prøysen (*Old Mrs. Pepperpot* and *Fam Ekman*); the Danes Dorte Karrebæk, Lilian Brøgger, Egon Mathiesen, Arne Ungermann, Otto S. Svend, and Ib Spand Olsen; and the Swede Sven Nordqvist (*Festus and Mercury*).

Interiors

Bent birch-wood and laminated plywood furniture by Bruno Mathsson in the 1920s; functionalist furniture by Gunnar Asplund, Sven Markelius, Uno Åhrén, and Hakon Ahlberg in the 1940s; and interiors with large windows, undecorated walls, and simple interior wood finishes on teak, gabon, and imported woods in the 1950s made Swedish design synonymous with simplicity and elegance. After 1950 modular furniture, mass-produced from laminates and chipboard that was inexpensive and required only do-it-yourself assembly became popular. In the 1980s, this furniture style began to be marketed through the IKEA and Domus shops and catalog, along with a plethora of sofas and armchairs in leather (or imitations) designed for easy television viewing, cheap beds and desks, and all kinds of gadgets designed to attract the impulse buyer. Inexpensive but well-designed furniture from Scandinavia continues to be popular around the world, especially in Western cultures.

Denmark

Nineteenth-century popular Danish art tended toward nostalgic or romantic rural genre scenes and national landscapes such as those painted by Christen Dalsgaard, Frederik Vermehren, and Johan Julius Exner. The Skagen painters, including Anna and Michael Ancher, specialized in local seascapes and the lives of fishermen.

Illustration

There has been a lively Danish vernacular printmaking tradition in woodcut, lithograph, and wood engraving since the eighteenth century. Artists working in this tradition produced penny prints, a full range of popular prints, and chest letters (*kistebrev*) that illustrated themes ranging from military, aristocratic, and royal portraits to moral and biblical scenes to contemporary current events. Hans Christian Andersen, the novelist and playwright, is best remembered for four collections of fairy tales published between 1835 and 1872 that were illustrated and translated worldwide. The best known are the *Little Mermaid*, the *Little Match Girl*, and the *Ugly Duckling*, all of which have been adapted for opera, theater, film, books, magazines, and all kinds of merchandise.

Interiors

In the 1920s several major Danish cabinetmakers abandoned the traditional Danish decorating aesthetic of tapestry-covered walls, gilt-leather-carved wooden panels, stucco, and tiles in favor of mass-produced furniture. In 1928 Mogens Koch developed a shelving system and a folding chair (1933) that are still used widely in Danish homes and offices. In 1942 Morgensen used Danish pine for a range of simple, inexpensive furniture styles designed for small apartments, while Arne Jacobsen designed a number of innovative chairs—called the Egg, the Swan, and the Ant—using organically formed laminated wood with steel legs, in addition to floral curtains and wallpapers. Wegner also made widely disseminated shell chairs in wood. In the 1950s the Danish *Snedkermestrenes Møbeludstilling* [Cabinetmakers' Furniture Exhibition] became the European forum for new furniture design. It was revived in 1983 as the *Snedkernes Efterårsudstilling* [Cabinetmakers' Autumn Exhibition].

Ceramics

In 1843 the Royal Court Terracotta Factory in Copenhagen was established as the factory creating high-quality decorative wares, copies of antique Greek vases, and small Parian reproductions of famous sculptures, all at a superior technical standard and qualitatively competitive internationally. In 1863 the Aluminia Fajancefabrik in Copenhagen was established to produce inexpensive transfer-printed daily ware to compete in foreign markets. In the twentieth century, Bjørn Wiinblad created decorative works based on Nordic folklore for the Nymølle Fajancefabrik in Kongens Lyngby. Grethe Meyer designed for the Kongelige Porcelainsfabrik. In 1987 the Kongelige Porcelainsfabrik and Bing & Grøndhal merged to form Royal Copenhagen. Among its offerings are collectible porcelain figurines and annual Christmas plates.

Norway

In the nineteenth century, many artists in Norway were self-taught; many traveled from town-to-town in the mountains of Telemark and Hallingdal and the settlements on the west coast with illustrated magazines, patterns books, an entire range of prints, and even photographs in addition to their painting supplies. These artists were called 'rose painters' and the 'Telemark rose' is the identifying mark of west Telemark painting.

Sculpture

Gustav Vigeland became internationally known in Norway for nearly two hundred sculptures in Vigelandspark, Oslo (1924), including free-standing pieces, fountains, and relief sculptures. In 1953 Knud Steen created a huge fountain sculpture in Sandefjord called the *Whale Hunter*, in which six whale hunters in an open boat are lifted by a whale.

Interiors

In 1929 Herman Munthe-Kaas designed a cantilevered, tubular steel chair, but functionalist design was not as strong in Norway as in the other Nordic countries. The exception was the way laminated wood was used by Ingmar Relling in his Siesta chair (1965) and by Ingvar Dyste in his Laminette stackable chair (1966). Norwegian designers were also interested in ergonomics: Petter Opsvik designed the Trip-trap chair for children (1973) and, with Svein Gusrud and Hans Christian Mengshoel, developed the radical and hugely popular Balans chair, which supports the knees but has no back (1979).

Finland

In the nineteenth century, the Finnish language and culture became a symbol of national identity and defiance against Russia. Like Norwegians, Finnish artists trained in Düsseldorf and Paris but returned to Finland to paint national landscapes, genre scenes, and images. Magnus and Ferdinand von Wright studied in Dresden and returned to paint idyllic Finnish landscapes, while landscape and genre painter Albert Edelfelt studied in Paris. Around 1900 Juho Rissanen painted gently humorous genre scenes, while Hugo and Simberg painted fairy tales.

Interiors

In the 1930s Finnish Functionalism was restricted to public buildings and tended to be site specific, but it achieved more popularity after 1945 as the country urbanized. In 1927 the first Finnish furniture exhibition was held in Helsinki. In 1929 Alvar Aalto designed curved plywood armchairs for the Paimio tuberculosis sanatorium. In 1932 the Asko factory began to produce functionalist furniture, and by the mid-1930s, Alvar Aalto's Artek company designs made Finnish furniture design identifiable on the international stage.

The Russo-Finnish War and its aftermath devastated Finland: after 1945, refugees from Karelia, representing one-fifth of the total population, had to be housed. Thus, basic housing design was central to Finnish postwar design. In the 1950s and 1960s, Finnish housing design was simple and clean, based on an open plan with large windows that embraced nature and included natural wood and stone. In the 1970s smaller urban apartments left little room for individuality; furniture was often prefabricated and constructed at home, while rooms focused on the television and sofa.

SOUTHEASTERN EUROPE: BULGARIA, ROMANIA, SERBIA, BOSNIA-HERZEGOVINA, CROATIA, ALBANIA, AND GREECE

In the nineteenth century, the emergence of national and cultural identities, the establishment and formalization of separate written languages, and an interest in local history and folklore led to the preservation of some widely diverse tales throughout the Balkan states that have sometime been connected to their independence movements. Early collections of folklore and folktales in the region were frequently published with illustrations for adults as well as for children. Similarities and differences in stories depended on geographical, historical, political, and cultural contexts. For instance, while Ukrainian folktales have much in common with Russian and Polish tales, the folktales of Serbia, Croatia, Slovenia, Bosnia-Herzegovina, and Macedonia are usually related to ancient Greek lore or mix Christian and Islamic traditions. Bulgarian folktales often included liberation narratives owing in part to 500 years of Turkish occupation. Croatian tales draw attention to Croatian landscapes, an idealized peasant life, and a mythologized childhood.

Bulgaria

In 1878 Bulgaria gained independence from Ottoman rule, and for the next twenty years, the country's visual culture was dominated by images of battle scenes, military victories, and national heroes. Illustrations of historic events in the form of lithographs were particularly popular; around the turn of the twentieth century, this emphasis gave way to images of national identity based on folktales and legends. In the 1920s the work of Vladimir Dimitrov-Maistora was particularly popular. At the same time, more than 400 public sculptures and monuments focusing on the theme of national freedom were produced in stone, concrete, and metal; for example, *Monument of Freedom* (1925) at Shipka Peak by Aleksandr Andreev. In the 1980s, a new sculptural program was initiated to celebrate 1,300 years of the Bulgarian state.

Interiors

Industrialization had little impact on Bulgarian interiors until 1900. Until that time, most furniture and some ceilings were still traditionally carved or decorated with folk patterns of twigs, buds, leaves, and fruit. The most significant piece of furniture was a large colored dowry chest (*rakla*), but other objects included low tables, stools, and most importantly, an icon (or icon copy) in one corner with an icon stand and lamp. The wood-carvers at Tryavna, represented by the Vitanov family (particularly Koyu Vitanov) produced everything from carved doors to cutlery, all made from pine or beech wood. After industrialization, however, traditional low beds and three-legged stools disappeared, although the *rakla* was and is still used to store valuables.

Romania

Romanian art was dominated by the Byzantine icon tradition until the mid-nineteenth century, when Western engravings and illustrated books became available. In the early twentieth century, Constantin Stahi produced portraits and still lifes of Romanian subjects, but his satirical drawings and caricatures were especially in demand. Between 1900 and 1939, the illustrated press employed and distributed the work of artist/illustrators such as Camil Ressu and Iosif Iser. Between 1960 and 1989, posters and book illustration dominated Romanian visual culture. Since 1989, there has been an attempt to reestablish normal artistic activity.

Traditional Romanian homes had usually been decorated with ceramic stoves, wooden floors, and silk wall hangings. Around 1900, industrialization brought about increasingly eclectic interior styles, and at about the same time, the first popular ceramics were produced in Romania. At the 1939 World's Fair in New York, Nora Steriadi exhibited several enormous ceramic and glass mosaic pieces illustrating Romanian history and folktales, but many others have been lost. Large quantities of nineteenth- and twentieth-century silver survive, as do quantities of the very popular decorated copper.

LITERATURE IN THE COLLAPSED AUSTRO-HUNGARIAN EMPIRE: THE SEARCH FOR CULTURAL IDENTITY

After 1918 the collapse of the Austro-Hungarian Empire produced a large number of independent or quasi-independent states. Between 1946 and 1989, however, national identities in this region were molded to fit the collective identity central to the ideology of the governing Communist regimes. As a consequence, many writers and artists had to homogenize or at least Russify their work—a requirement imposed with particular rigor in Albania and Romania. Ironically, one remarkably unrestricted creative area was children's literature, particularly if the theme appeared nonsensical. This arena was exploited by subversive writers and illustrators, such as Bulgaria's Assen Bosev and Croatia's Grigor Vitez and Luko Paljetak. Since 1989 many of the same nations have attempted to reestablish their national and cultural legacies, although the highly developed Western European and American publishing industries for fairy tales and fantasy have proven to be difficult competitors for them. Also, since each country wants to emphasize its ethnic, religious, and linguistic identity, a charged political situation in the region prevents collaboration in illustration and publishing among these countries.

Serbia

By 1900 Serbian popular art was replete with images of Serbia's historic and contemporary figures in popular print and photographic forms. In the 1890s many of these images were disseminated even more widely using the fast and cheap reproductive technique of oleography. Serbian photographers created much of the important documentary photography of the Balkan Wars (1912–13) and some of the most powerful photographs from the front lines in World War I—the Serbian army had issued every officer a Kodak camera and film. In the twentieth century, the Serbian tradition of popular prints flourished through illustrated books, poster design, and commercial art.

Decoration

Houses were often furnished simply, with a central hearth, a large copper or iron kettle for water, a large earthenware dish (*crepulija*) for baking bread, low tables, and three-legged stools. Either handwoven rag rugs or fine reversible rugs (*kilims*) covered floors. Pirot, in eastern Serbia, was the center of kilim production. By the late-nineteenth century, kilims were woven on vertical looms using both traditional Slavic designs and newer Eastern patterns. The Tree of Life was one of the more popular patterns; it included geometrical representations of human figures, animals, plants, and flowers.

A variety of textiles and embroidery styles typical of the Serbian national costume were revived in the late nineteenth century. Byzantine and Islamic influences were marked by the velvet, silk, and fur added to more traditional linen and wool garments, while patterned and embroidered woolen socks worn beneath shoes with upturned toes remained distinctive characteristics of Serbian costume. Most embroidery designs continue to be deeply symbolic; the peony image, for instance, stands for the blood shed in the 1389 Battle of Kosovo.

Serbian ceramics for everyday use were produced from local clays; decorated with paint or a black soot, flour, and powdered tree bark combination pigment; and incised with simple patterns of parallel lines in straight, wavy, or cross-hatched designs. Thinner-walled pots, dipped in slip and painted with red patterns that were sometimes partly tin or lead glazed, were used to hold water and wine.

Bosnia

Painting, popular printmaking, and photography in Bosnia were naturalistic as well as illustrative of Bosnian history and culture over the last two centuries. Little has survived. The more permanent, formal, and monumental character of sculpture has made that art form a more durable marker of the Bosnian visual culture. The Partisan cemetery in Mostar (1965) and the Memorial to the Revolution (1970–72) on Mount Kozara are important examples.

The Bosnian visual culture is a rich admixture of two rural traditions: European and Ottoman. Ottoman Turkish culture is especially visible in Bosnian urban interiors, textiles, and ceramics, owing to the long residence of wealthy Turkish families in major Bosnian towns and cities. The central focus of many nineteenth-century Bosnian homes was a brass samovar used for both heat and cooking. Metal dishes and ceramics, the most prized of which were souvenirs from Mecca or blue-and-white Chinese-ware flasks were stored on high shelves in Bosnia homes, while the large cupboard (*musandera*) and carved chests with mirrors and painted floral decoration stored more precious possessions.

Highly decorated textiles continued to be handwoven and hand decorated well into the twentieth century. Jewelry was mostly the preserve of urban Bosnians and was heavily influenced by Ottoman Turkish jewelry fashions. The changes to Bosnian visual culture after World War II were both dramatic and abrupt as a result of the imposition of the orthodox Communist aesthetic. The changes in the 1990s were just as abrupt, but these were initiated by the disintegration of Yugoslavia and the attending civil conflicts.

Croatia

Croatia had very little visual culture until the 1850s when Bishop Josip Juraj Strossmayer founded several drawing schools in larger towns. Within a generation, a modest group of illustrators, lithographers, and some painters had established a body of images that spoke of Croatian history, landscape, and urban and rural culture to a fairly wide audience. The Graphic Croatia lithography workshop was established in Zagreb in 1850. Likewise, there was little public sculpture of public appeal before 1850. From 1945 until 1957, the popular arts in Croatia were dominated by socialist realism; since then, the economic domination of the West has made it difficult for a distinctly Croatian popular visual culture to emerge.

Albania

Albanian popular visual culture in the nineteenth century was a composite of European baroque and Islamic imagery. Indeed, the same artists were often commissioned to decorate both churches and mosques. The interiors and facades of both Christian and Moslem Albanian homes in towns and cities were likewise decorated by the same artisans. Albanian landscapes and prints representing its people and folk traditions permeated Albanian visual culture until 1900. After 1945 socialist realism dominated the Albanian art and visual culture. Painters working from the 1960 to the 1980s produced realistic prints and some monumental wall paintings, such as Sali Shijaku and Myrteza Fushekati's 1981 *Partisan Attack*.

Decoration

In the nineteenth century, potters in Mat manufactured ceramics, while potters working in Gojan (near Pukë), Farkë (near Tiranë), Bradvicë, and Kavajë produced thrown ceramic objects. The various terracotta pipes, candleholders, cups, plates, and cult objects were often decorated with carved surfaces and multicolored glazes. After 1945 the state potteries in Kavajë (1948) produced functional ceramics; Tiranë (1950) produced dinnerware, decorated plates, vases, flower pots, and decorated tiles with multicolored glazes, such as those used for the restaurant interior of the Youth Park in Tiranë. In Vlorë and Korçë, traditional terracotta vases were decorated with images from folklore or animals created using multicolored glazes. Multicolored glass panes for dormer windows and partitions, decorated with plant forms, geometric patterns, and arabesques, have been used in Albanian ecclesiastical and domestic architecture since the sixteenth century. The state glassworks established after 1945—the Tiranë Glass Factory, the Kavajë Glassworks, and the Korçë Glass and Ceramics Factory—continue to mass-produce glass partitions, often decorated with folk motifs.

Embroidery

Differences in the embroidered Albanian folk costume were frequently used to identify the region of the wearer. In the nineteenth century, the 140 embroidered types cataloged were produced in local workshops or in homes. Very finely embroidered blouses were decorated with silk and cotton, and outer clothing (*zhupja* or *cibun*) was elaborately embroidered in red with multicolored braids. Southern Albanian carpets, rugs, and blankets were also highly prized. After 1945 state combines were created in Tiranë, Berat, Korçë, and Shkodër to produce carpets, knitwear, and fabrics.

Greece

From 1453 to 1821 Greece was under Turkish rule, and the only truly Greek visual culture before 1821 was found on the Ionian Islands. Although there was little recent visual culture from which to draw on after independence, many Greek artists and illustrators used national subjects, such as the War of Independence, while others drew on ancient Greek and philhellenic subjects. Important artists included Theodoros Vryzakes, Nikiforos Lytras, Nikolaos Gysis, and Theophilos. In the twentieth century, modern Greek identity was explored by artists such as Yannis Tsarouhis.

Photography

In 1891 Greece could boast of only twenty-seven professional photographers. Since then, historical sites and classical sculpture have been the mainstays of the commercial photography that supplies the tourist market. There has also been an enormous increase in amateur photography. The Greek, illustrated press gained acclaim during the Balkan Wars in the early twentieth century. During the 1950s several Greek photographers emerged as dance and portrait photography specialists, including Spiros Meletzis, Dimitris Harissiadis, and Kostas Balafas.

WESTERN EUROPE: FRANCE, BELGIUM, THE NETHERLANDS, ITALY, THE UNITED KINGDOM, AND IRELAND

France

As one of the largest European nations and one of those with the most clearly defined national cultural identity, French visual culture tended to dominate continental Europe in the nineteenth century. At the end of World War I, the conservative avant-garde art of Renoir and the more colorful Cubist paintings were appropriated purely for their visual decorative attractiveness. Cubist forms were integrated into art deco imagery and used in murals on the walls of luxury stores, ocean liners, and movie theaters. After World War II, Paris declined as a major art center; the artists who had fled in 1939 did not return. Since then, French popular art has focused on mythologizing and merchandizing its nineteenth-century past.

Illustration

French lithographic production and distribution was widespread in the nineteenth century. In the 1890s Henri Toulouse-Lautrec made posters for the Moulin Rouge, and Alphonse Mucha provided the same for the actress Sarah Bernhardt. He also designed her costumes and the decor for her productions. In 1931 Jean de Brunhoff published the illustrated *Histoire de Babar, le petit éléphant* [The Story of Babar, the Little Elephant], which melded together popular visual culture, colonial vision, and French cultural identity. In 1943 Antoine de Saint-Exupéry produced a similar cultural statement in *Le Petit Prince*. In 1961 René Goscinny and Albert Uderzo revived interest in France's ancient Gallic past and

THE POPULARITY OF DAGUERREOTYPE PHOTOGRAPHY

The Daguerreotype, the earliest phase of true photography, was distinct in several ways. First, it was a direct positive form of photography and not reproducible. Second, its inventor, Louis-Jacques-Mandé Daguerre (1787–1851), had commercial motives when he experimented with the process: he was searching for a way to gain a commercial advantage in France and in Europe more generally. The incredible detail and veracity of daguerreotype photography created a worldwide sensation within weeks. One year after Daguerre's announcement, there were thousands of photographers all over the world, and Paris had dozens of operators. Daguerreotype portraits dominated by 1849, but Talbot's calotype emerged as the preferred process for architectural photography, precisely because of its reproducibility. The state-funded Mission Héliographique (1851) recorded the historic monuments of France in calotype form. Other travel books using calotypes included Maxime Du Camp's photographs of Egypt (1849–51), Eugène Piot's of Italy (1851), and Auguste Salzmann's of Jerusalem (1854).

mythology with the still famous *Astérix le Gaulois*.

Photography

In 1927 the mass-marketed, photographically illustrated magazine *Vu* was established in Paris. In the 1930s French photojournalists increasingly moved to hand-held cameras such as the Leica, Rolleiflex, and Contax to produce pictures for these magazines; independent picture agencies were founded in tandem, including Alliance-Photo (established by Pierre Boucher) and Rapho (established by Charles Rado) to distribute photographs to the international press and publishing industries. In the 1940s many photographers either left Paris, abandoned photography, or had their work censored by the Vichy government. Later, French photojournalism in Vietnam, for example, and commercial photography in portraiture, advertising, and fashion set new benchmarks for excellence. French fashion magazines such as *Vogue, Jardin de la mode, Elle*, and *Marie-Claire* and photographers such as Sieff, Helmut Newton, Frank Horvat, and Guy Bourdin continue to set continental European standards.

Interiors

The 1889 Paris Exposition Universelle sought to reestablish French preeminence in the decorative arts. In 1895 S. Bing established La Maison de l'Art Nouveau. Bing's art nouveau was a critical success that swept Europe, but the style was not popular at home. German designs proved more popular with the French public before 1914. After 1945 functionalist school designs seemed more appropriate for the rapid and inexpensive rebuilding of France's war-torn cities. In the 1980s President François Mitterrand broke with conservative design tradition and commissioned modernist Philippe Starck to redecorate his refurbished private apartments in the Elysée Palace.

Metal

Around 1900 Héctor Guimard designed decorative Art Nouveau ironwork for Parisian architecture. At the same time, a number of ceramicists and glassmakers also used decorative wrought iron frames for goblets, lamps, vases, and chandeliers. In the late 1920s, art deco designers used decorative wrought iron for staircases, tables, and lamps.

Jewelry

In 1925 the jewelry companies of Boucheron (1858) and Cartier (1897) developed simple designs, but at the same time used fabulously brilliant and hugely expensive gems. Cartier, in particular, became known for a new stone setting that eliminated cloisins between stones, allowing light to refract through the gem without hitting the metal bands, thus enhancing the brilliance—and expense—of the gem.

Belgium

The nineteenth-century Belgian and French visual culture were inextricably linked. However, evidence of an interest in specifically Belgian folk culture and history emerged by 1850, notably in the historical genre paintings of Henry Leys. His artistic output was based on early Flemish art, such as that found in the Council Chamber of Antwerp Town Hall, or on the rural genre paintings of Ferdinand De Braekeleer and Jean-Baptiste Madou. In 1860 Charles De Groux painted a version of the *Last Supper* that he set in a Walloon (Belgian Francophone) peasant home.

Interiors

By 1900 French art nouveau and English Arts and Crafts influences were synthesized in Belgium in the work of Victor Horta, who designed elaborate interiors for nouveau riche clients in Brussels. Henry Van de Velde collaborated with Liège, a manufacturer, and the Brussels furnishing company Céline Dangotte to produce more affordable versions.

Glass

The Walloon glass factory tradition, *bousillage*, was established in the nineteenth century and involved glassworkers making objects for personal use or for gifts during their breaks. These blown, drawn, and multicolored decorated glass objects (*bousillés*) were sometimes shaped as horses, merry-go-rounds, baskets, trumpets, or paperweights, and they have become highly sought after as collectors' items.

Textiles

Flanders is one of the most important centers for lace in the Western world. The well-known, cobweb-fine eighteenth-century Flemish bobbin laces are not only manufactured in towns for which they are named, but in fact Valenciennes lace is also made in Ghent, Enghien, and elsewhere; Mechelen lace is also made in Brussels and Valenciennes; and Brussels lace is also made in Binche and Liège. With the collapse of the Second Empire in 1871, the Belgian lace industry lost much of its market. The major factories limped along on a reduced scale until around 1900, but even then were unable to compete with machine-produced lace. By 1914 the industry was in ruins. A small but slow recovery has occurred since 1945, owing mostly to the tourist trade.

The Netherlands

Sluijters, a fashionable Amsterdam portrait painter, was generally agreed to be the greatest Dutch artist of the pre-1945 era, despite the avant-garde reputations of the De Stijl artists Piet Mondrian and Theo van Doesburg. It was not until several years later that Mondrian's primary-colored, grid-like paintings were appropriated for their decorative qualities and achieved a popular appeal in the Netherlands.

After 1945, The Hague school took two very different directions in popular art: one was inspired by outsider art, as in Willem Witsen's woodcut townscapes or Jessurum de Mesquita's animal prints; the other was inspired by the almost obsessive naturalism found in the work of Dirk van Gelder and Jan Mankes, and in the prints of Jeanne Bieruma Oosting and M. C. Escher. The Netherlands produced a vast array of illustrated books, magazines, and photographs throughout the nineteenth and twentieth centuries. The best-known illustrator, however, was Leo Lionni, who wrote and illustrated over thirty picture books between 1959 and 1994, including *Inch by Inch* (1960) and *Alexander and the Wind-up Mouse* (1969). In the 1980s the crossover writers and illustrators Joke van Leeuwen and Wim Hofman have also achieved international fame.

Between 1870 and 1900, Dutch photography was dominated by portraiture and scientific photography. After World War II, the Netherlands became an advertising center for photography in Europe, characterized by radical design. Nonetheless, Dutch photo history is still largely neglected in many mainstream photo histories, even though it is well documented at home.

Interiors

At the turn of the twentieth century, the growing Dutch middle class wanted houses that were dark, crowded, and cluttered. Furniture was heavy, dark, and upholstered; windows were hung with heavy curtains; and the interior was richly decorated. The new century swept in with the Arts and Crafts philosophy of simple, honest housing, the women's movement, and socialism. In the Netherlands, Willem Penaat's interest in low-cost design for the working classes resulted in simplified designs and basic furniture production. He used local or imported batik printing for upholstery, tablecloths, and wall fabrics.

The journal of the avant-garde movement De Stijl (1917–31) advocated a very different design aesthetic based on gray tones or primary colors, inexpensive materials, and flexible divisions of space. Very few De Stijl interiors were ever realized, the most famous being Gerrit Reitveld's Schröder House in Utrecht, but the style exerted considerable influence. In the 1920s functionalism in the Netherlands became more aggressively standardized, abstract, and functional. By 1935 this bare, underfurnished aesthetic gave way to the revival of more traditional Dutch wooden furniture and fabrics with large floral prints. Metz and Company in Amsterdam and The Hague even became direct agents for the Arts and Crafts products of Liberty and Company of London.

Italy

In 1900 Italy was poor and politically unstable. The Venice Biennale was the only regular national art exhibition. Several radical artists turned to futurism before World War I, but many more avoided it. The Florentine painter and printmaker Ottone Rosai, for instance, one of Italy's most popular artists in the early twentieth century, portrayed the ancient streets and hills in and around Florence in a folk art style. In 1930 Mussolini's personality cult of Roman imperialism mandated an official style, but it was not widely implemented.

Photography

Italian photography developed slowly, but once it took hold, it dominated Europe. To meet the needs of the growing numbers of middle-class tourists who flocked to Italy in the nineteenth century, printed travel books and tourist guides were first published with daguerreotypes and calotypes and then with wet-plate drop-in photographs. By 1920 Alinari photographs of Italian art and architecture, landscapes, and genre scenes of peasant girls, traveling musicians (*pifferari*), fisher folk, glass makers, and gondoliers were distributed all over the world. Between 1922 and 1943, Fascist-era photography was used for propaganda. In 1932, for instance, an exhibition in Rome featuring thousands of photographs marked the tenth anniversary of the March on Rome. Photojournalism was officially subject to censorship, but in practice it was largely unaffected. In the 1940s and 1950s, photoromance (*fotoromanzo*), a form of serialized novel with photographs, was very popular.

Metal

An entire industry produced copies of small works of art in copper, bronze, and base metals throughout Italy in the nineteenth century. Around 1900, increasing numbers of small domestic decorative objects were also produced in bronze and copper, particularly in the Stile Liberty (Art Nouveau) that included trays, statuettes, inkwells, and ashtrays. Many were also produced in even less costly materials such as brass, pewter, and cast iron. In the twentieth century, particularly after World War II, Italian design was epitomized by the family-owned firm Alessi, which produced a wide range of high-quality stainless steel products for the kitchen.

The United Kingdom

In the nineteenth century, the United Kingdom emerged as a political and economic power with global reach. Expanding British wealth created the domestic demand for luxury- and middle-class goods. From the 1860s to 1900, a staple of British painting was a hazily painted, romanticized, and usually somewhat eroticized languid female figure, sometimes in contemporary costume but sometimes in classical or "other" dress, draped over some piece of furniture. The popularity of painting declined in tandem with the downturn in the British economy after 1900. In 1946 the Arts Council of Great Britain attempted to revive a flagging visual culture, but it was only in the 1960s that British art and popular culture finally caught the attention of the rest of the world. Unfortunately, the economic and artistic optimism of the 1960s was very short lived; British art and culture did not reemerge on the world stage until the late-1990s when the new racial and ethnic mix in the country created some exciting new directions in British art.

Sculpture

Early nineteenth-century English town squares and parks were decorated with sculptures of national heroes such as Lord Nelson. By midcentury, however, public interest in sculpture was generated by several widely publicized commissions, and competitions for monuments, which included sculptures of Lord Nelson (the largest monument being in Trafalgar Square, London), Sir Robert Peel (d. 1850), the Duke of Wellington (d. 1852), Prince Albert (d. 1861), and Queen Victoria herself (d. 1901). The most controversial English sculpture of the nineteenth century, ironically, was a classical subject—Alfred Gilbert's nude *Eros*—for Piccadilly Circus, London. Sculptors Henry Moore and Barbara Hepworth later established significant international critical reputations.

Prints

In 1901 Beatrix Potter self-published her first book, *Peter Rabbit*, using a small format. Potter integrated her text-and-image layout and produced a series of exquisitely rendered watercolors of small, local animals such as rabbits, mice, and frogs, which were placed throughout her, sometimes, subversively ironic and humorous tales. J. M. Barrie was a popular playwright in London when he met a family of boys in Kensington Gardens (1897) who inspired him to write the play and later the book *Peter Pan*. Barrie completed the play, titled *Peter Pan, or The Boy Who Wouldn't Grow Up*, for the 1904 Christmas season in London. Barrie followed the show's stunning success in London and New York with the serialization of the story and its illustration by Arthur Rackham. A. A. Milne published *Winnie the Pooh*, the first of four books about his son, Christopher Robin, and his stuffed animals, in 1920. All four of the books, illustrated by E. H. Shephard, became bestsellers and have remained in print ever since.

Photography

In 1904 the *Daily Mirror* was the first daily newspaper to be completely illustrated using photography, and it was the first newspaper to hire photographers on a freelance basis. In doing so, the *Daily Mirror* created the business of modern photojournalism, in which a team of photographers work in fierce competition with one another in relentless pursuit of the best, closest, and, if possible, most scandalous image of the hottest new subject. More genteel publications such as the *Picture Post* and *Queen*, and newspapers such as the *Observer*, did not demand such scandal-driven photographs. In the 1960s several major daily newspapers began publication of Sunday color supplements, made possible by relatively inexpensive color printing, which became a source of visual information about England's new popular culture role as a music and fashion center for young people. The concept of the "swinging sixties" in London was promoted through the work of a number of young models (such as Twiggy) and fashion designers (such as Mary Quant) in some carefully designed photographic advertising, television imagery, and a sweep of feature stories in the Sunday supplements. Since the 1960s, English popular photography has not been able to separate its identity from that of American photography except in the area of illustrated books, for which the Dorling Kindersley Press has reinvigorated a distinctly British vision.

Interiors

In 1862 William Morris and the English Arts and Crafts Movement reacted against both the mass-produced and the revival style designs to establish an English country cottage style. The Orchard at Chorleywood (1900), by C. F. A. Voysey, was designed with lighter and simpler interiors, whitewashed walls, and seating fitted into window bays and inglenooks around fireplaces. The design spread to the middle and suburban classes from 1905 to the 1920s through a series of housing developments soon after the building of the 1918 Metroland railway and the underground extensions.

Ceramics

After 1925 Clarice Cliff revived the English ceramics industry with the Newport Pottery's popular range of Bizarre and Fantasque designs—distinctive, brightly colored geometric wares with conical or triangular handles. In 1933 Keith Murray at Wedgwood created the Bournvita design for mugs, and over one million were sold in fourteen months. The Utility Scheme, which was a government rationing program started during World War II, limited production to white and ivory wares until 1952, but new designs subsequently emerged using primary colors, maroons, and grays. In the mid-1960s several factories introduced English versions of oven-to-table ware in brown and speckled glazes to try to compete with American-made Pyrex glassware. Wedgwood china, along with many other brands, remains very popular in the United Kingdom, the United States, and throughout Europe.

Glass

Around 1900 Stourbridge and Birmingham emerged as centers for handmade ornamental glass, while work in pressed glass remained located in Manchester and the northeast. During World War I, many factories retooled to make industrial and medical glass, but after the war, England was flooded with cheap glass imports from Belgium, Germany, and Czechoslovakia. It was only with the imposition of tariffs in 1931 that the pressed-glass industry began to revive by imitating fine crystal glass and by producing vases, figures, and trinket sets in a range of green, blue, pink, and amber colors. Jobling created a line called Opalique in imitation of Lalique's opalescent glass. By 1960 colored glass produced in Stourbridge had virtually disappeared.

Scotland

In 1826 the Royal Scottish Academy for Art was established in Edinburgh, and by 1850 a large, vigorous artistic community was active in the city. The somewhat obsessively detailed narrative genre paintings of Thomas Faed and Noel Paton were particularly popular. Later, the more sentimental, nationalistic art of William McTaggart and George Paul Chalmers resonated more with the public. In the 1880s the so-called Glasgow boys—James Guthrie, W. Y. MacGregor, E. A. Walton, James Paterson, and others—created similar images.

Interiors

After 1850 Glasgow took the lead from Edinburgh in design. The work of Charles Rennie Mackintosh was published widely throughout Europe. Hill House in Helensburgh, Strathclyde, built for Walter Blackie (1904), and his own home (1906) were Mackintosh's best known domestic interiors. Around 1900 Glasgow became a center for international furniture design. Morrison and Company sold high-quality furniture worldwide, including fittings for luxurious railway carriages. The Scottish Cooperative Wholesale Society in Beith produced lower-end furniture. In the 1920s Whytock and Reid sold jazzier furniture with exotic veneers. After 1945 Scottish manufacturers made resin-bonded wood laminate, developed for the aircraft industry; Herbert Morris and Company marketed the Allegro and Cloud ranges of tables made of this kind of laminated plywood (1948–49).

Textiles

Tartan is associated traditionally with Scotland. The chief characteristic of any tartan is a brightly checked wool twill fabric based on a simple two-color check arrangement of colored threads, which run the same in the warp and the weft. The tartan is part of the Highland dress for men, and the kilt was originally also worn as a shawl. The original tartan was simply a wool twill fabric. It could be plain or colored, and it was used for blankets as well as clothing. Today, there are a vast number of patterns, and each pattern is imbued with great mystical meaning. The patterns are nineteenth-century inventions and were only linked to clans at that time.

Wales

Most of the popular art of Wales in the past century has included painted landscapes and portraits of the mining communities—a trend that reached its height with the 1950s Rhondda Group, named after a valley in South Wales, and in the art of Ernest Zobole.

Sculpture

John Goscombe served as adviser for the Welsh Pantheon of National Heroes, created for the Marble Hall in City Hall, Cardiff. The project involved eleven sculptures, was completed in 1916, and included Henry Pegram's *Llywelyn ap Gruffydd* (1914–16), one of the most celebrated images of Welsh culture. After 1900 John Goscombe created a number of medals as part of the Eisteddfod movement as well as an Eisteddfod chair elaborately carved with national imagery. Several other significant Celtic revival chairs were carved between 1910 and 1930, along with some important Welsh revival wrought ironwork. There are many popular Celtic designs, plus the iconic Welsh dragon, crafted in gold, silver, other metals, and wood, sold throughout the world.

The Republic of Ireland (Eire)

After 1922 many Irish artists painted romantic realist images of the new Irish Free State. Paul Henry and Maurice MacGonigal painted the landscapes of the west of Ireland; Rose Barton, Mildred Anne Butler, and John Keating painted romantic national images; and James Humbert Craig and Harry Kernoff painted urban subjects of Dublin. Elizabeth Corbet Yeats established the Dun Emer Press in 1902 and the Cuala Press in 1908 to revive Irish publishing and illustration. Cuala published the poems of William Butler Yeats, with illustrations by Jack B. Yeats, as well as illustrations of poems and fairy tales by stained glass artist Harry Clarke. The Irish Arts Council was established in 1951.

Ceramics

The Dubliner David McBirney established the Belleek Porcelain Factory in 1857 in Belleek, County Fermanagh. McBirney, who also owned shares in the Sligo and Bundoran

Railway, had a railway line built directly to the factory to help with distribution. Belleek produced three kinds of wares: utilitarian earthenware decorated with transfer printing; stoneware that included vases but also telegraphic insulators; and its most famous, very thin, nacreous-luster glazed porcelain that was formed into delicate openwork baskets, centerpieces, vases, and assorted wares. Around 1870 the factory concentrated production on porcelain for sale to export markets in Britain, Europe, Canada, America, Australia, and South Africa. The Belleek company was sold in 1884, and then again in 1918 and 1984. It now reissues older designs, relies mostly on the tourist market, and remains the predominant ceramics factory in Ireland.

Glass

In the eighteenth century, Irish glassworkers followed the glass markets of London because Irish glass could only be exported through England. In 1771 Benjamin Edwards moved from Bristol to Tyrone, and in 1776 he established a glass factory in Belfast that produced clear and colored glass, plain and cut-glass wine glasses and decanters, and chemical and enameled wares. In 1777 England imposed punishing taxes on all English glass, causing a mass migration of skilled glassworkers from Bristol and Stourbridge to Ireland. In 1779 Ireland was granted permission to export lead glass tax free to America, the British colonies, France, Spain, and Portugal. Thus, Irish glass factories began to produce large quantities of superbly crafted, deeply cut, thick-walled glass that became the envy of the world. In the nineteenth century, at the height of Irish glass production, the deeply cut designs in large flat diamond patterns on glasses, decanters, mirrors, and half-chandeliers placed in front of mirrors deliberately used the facets and short, sharp, carefully arranged prismatic cuts of the diamond shapes to make candlelight or gaslight dance and glitter brilliantly in reflection and refraction. As of 1825, there were eleven lead glass factories in Belfast, Dublin, Waterford, and Cork. The Glass Excise Act (1825), however, introduced a tax on Irish glass by metal weight, sending the Irish industry into decline. Glassworks survived in Cork until 1841, in Waterford until 1851, in Belfast until 1868, and in Dublin until 1893. Waterford Glass Limited was founded in 1947 to produce copies of the eighteenth-century glass that had made the name famous. The company and many others like it continue to thrive today, but they largely execute nineteenth-century designs.

Textiles

Irish lace was also popular far beyond the small country itself. In 1808 John Heathcoat invented a machine to make cotton net. Embroidered net laces were produced at Carrickmacross, County Monaghan; appliqué cambric on net in Limerick; tambour (chain stitch) and run (darn) on net in Kells, County Meath; and both styles and a variety of laces were made at country estates and convent schools. Crochet, which was taught during the famine at many convent and Church of Ireland centers, used linen thread rather than woolen yarn. It remained a cottage industry into twentieth century, especially in the west of Ireland. Several varieties of embroidery were similarly produced: sprigging (white cotton thread on white linen, sometimes using floral designs); Mountmellick (white knitted cotton on white satin using wild-flower designs); Marlfield (colored wool on wool with art nouveau designs); and Kells (wool on wool with Celtic revival designs). The Irish cottage industry still produces knitted Aran sweaters, which were originally made for fishermen, with family designs knitted into each one; today many Aran sweaters are machine-knitted. Around 1893 a loom that was small enough to fit into a cottage home and cheap enough to be purchased by a farmer-weaver helped to create the cottage industry in the production of Donegal tweeds, which remain in commercial demand today.

RESOURCE GUIDE

PRINT SOURCES

Armstrong, Walter. *Scottish Painters: A Critical Study*. London: Seeley, 1888.

Auty, Robert, and Dimitri Obolensky, eds. *An Introduction to Russian Art and Architecture*. Cambridge: Cambridge University Press, 1980.

Bell, Sam Hanna, Nesca A. Robb, and John Hewitt, eds. *The Arts in Ulster*. London: Harrap, 1951.

Bird, Alan. *The History of Russian Painting*. Boston: Hall, 1987.

Boase, T. S. R., ed. *The Oxford History of English Art*. 9 vols. Oxford: Clarendon, 1952–78.

Clark, Timothy J. *The Painting of Modern Life: Paris in the Art of Manet and His Followers*. New York: Knopf, 1985.

Crookshank, Anne, and the Knight of Glin. *The Painters of Ireland, ca. 1660–1920*. London: Barrie & Jenkins, 1979.

Deuchler, Florens, ed. *Ars Helvetica: Die visuelle Kultur der Schweiz/Arts et Culture Visuels en Suisse*. 13 vols. Disentis: Pro Helvetia, 1987–93.

Dobrowolski, Tadeusz, and Helena Blumówna, eds. *Historia sztuki polskiej* [History of Polish Art]. 3 vols. Krakow: Wydawnictwo Literackie, 1965.

Fallon, Brian. *Irish Art, 1830–1990*. Belfast: Appletree, 1994.

Ford, Boris, ed. *The Cambridge Guide to the Arts in Britain*. 9 vols. Cambridge: Cambridge University Press, 1988–90.

Gijsen, Marnix. *Modern Sculpture in Belgium*. Brussels: Ministry of Foreign Affairs, 1952.

Glassie, Henry H. *Turkish Traditional Art Today*. Bloomington: Indiana University Press, 1993.

Granath, Olle. *Another Light: Swedish Art since 1945*. Malmö: Swedish Institute, 1978.

Hewitt, J., and M. A. Catto. *Art in Ulster*. 2 vols. Belfast: Blackstaff Press, 1977.

Historia de l'art català. 8 vols. Barcelona: Edicions 62, 1983–87.

Historia del arte hispánico. 6 vols. Madrid: Editorial Alhambra, 1978–80.

Horat, Heinz, ed. *1000 Years of Swiss Art*. New York: Hudson Hills, 1992.

Hulten, Pontus, and Germano Celant. *Italian Art, 1900–1945*. New York: Rizzoli, 1989.

Hütt, Wolfgang. *Deutsche Malerei und Graphik, 1750–1945*. Berlin: Henschelverlag Kunst und Gesellschaft, 1986.

Introducción al arte español. 9 vols. Madrid: Sílex, 1989–94.

Irwin, David G., and Francina Irwin. *Scottish Painters at Home and Abroad*. London: Faber, 1975.

Kent, Neil. *The Triumph of Light and Nature: Nordic Art, 1740–1940*. London: Thames & Hudson, 1987.

Kubler, George, and Martin Soria. *Art and Architecture in Spain and Portugal and Their American Dominions*. Harmondsworth, UK: Penguin, 1959.

Lindgren, Mereth. *A History of Swedish Art*. Stockholm: Signum, 1987.

Lord, Peter. *The Visual Culture of Wales: Imaging the Nation*. Cardiff: University of Wales Press, 2000.

Macmillan, Duncan. *Scottish Art, 1460–2000*. Edinburgh: Mainstream, 2000.

Marien, Mary Warner. *Photography: A Cultural History*. Upper Saddle River, NJ: Prentice Hall, 2006.

Renda, Günsel, et al. *A History of Turkish Painting*. Geneva: Palasar, 1988.

Sarabianov, Dmitrii Vladimirovich. *Russian Art, from Neoclassicism to the Avant-Garde: Painting—Sculpture—Architecture*. New York: Abrams, 1990.

Strickland, Walter G. *A Dictionary of Irish Artists*. 2 vols. Dublin: Maunsel, 1913.

Thomson, Richard. *Monet to Matisse: Landscape Painting in France, 1874–1914*. Edinburgh: National Gallery of Scotland, 1994.

MUSEUMS

Bauhaus Museum, Berlin, Germany. http://www.bauhaus.de/. Covers all aspects of Bauhaus design including art, architecture, ceramics, design, and photography.

Centre Pompidou, Paris, France. http://www.centrepompidou.fr/. The *Centre national d'art et de culture Georges Pompidou* offers a vast collection of modern and contemporary European art.

Guggenheim Bilbao, Bilbao, Spain. http://www.guggenheim-bilbao.es. Strong permanent collection with modern and contemporary art and changing exhibitions.

Kunsthalle Wien, Vienna, Austria. http://www.kunsthallewien.at/. Exhibitions of contemporary art, video installations, and new media.

Pinakothek der Moderne, Munich, Germany. http://www.pinakothek.de/pinakothek-der-moderne/. Collection of twentieth- and twenty-first-century art, graphics, architecture, and design.

Tate Modern, London, England. http://www.tate.org.uk/. Extensive collection of post-1900 modern art.

Victoria and Albert Museum, London, England. http://www.vam.ac.uk. Vast range of collections, including photography, fashion, metalwork, ceramics, photography, furniture, and sculpture.

HEIKE GRUNDMANN

The history of Western dance is characterized by great diversity and rapid change as Western dancers showed a constant eagerness to find or create new fashions. Western dance has always embraced a variety of ritualistic folk dances, social dances enjoyed by many different levels of society, and skilled theatrical dances often in conjunction with opera. The renewal of European dance coincided with the turn from the nineteenth to the twentieth century. The years before World War I saw an almost frantic search for new forms, a radical questioning of values previously taken for granted, a craze for individual expression, and a more dynamic way of life. Two trends were evident in the rapid development of dance: the renewal of established forms of dance, especially the ballet, and the revival of old forms of social dance and folk dance.

Ethnic dance has found its way into contemporary theater and ballet and the cross-fertilization in the field of popular and social dances has created a widely various scene in Europe that remains strongly influenced by North American forms of popular music and dance.

BALLROOM DANCE

Ballroom dance is a style of partner dance that originated in Europe and is now enjoyed both socially and competitively around the globe. The definition of "ballroom dance" depends on the era. Formerly, balls (from Latin *ballare* = to dance) featured Minuet, Quadrille, Polonaise, Pas de Gras, Mazurka, and other popular dances of the day, which are now placed into the category of historical dances. In times past, ballroom dancing was "social dancing" of privileged classes, leaving "folk dancing" for the lower classes. Today ballroom dancing is much more democratic, and the boundaries between once-polarized ballroom and folk dances become blurred. Most competitive ballroom dances were social or folk dances before being formalized as ballroom dances. Dance historians usually mark the appearance of the Twist in the mid 1960s as the end of social partner dancing, and they credit what was then called the Latin Hustle for bringing it back in the late 1970s. The ballroom dances were thoroughly revolutionized through infusions of new vitality from South American, Creole, and black sources.

BALLET PROMOTION

It was not a choreographer or even a dancer who spread the Russian ballet through Europe and the Americas but an impresario, or promoter-manager: Sergej Diaghilev.

"Strictly ballroom"—that is, competitive ballroom dancing—relies on extensively studied and formalized techniques. The following divisions of contemporary ballroom dance are recognized: International Standard/Ballroom (Waltz, Tango, Viennese Waltz, Foxtrot, Quickstep) and International Latin (Cha-Cha-Cha, Samba, Rumba, Paso Doble, Jive). In addition, American Smooth (Waltz, Foxtrot, Tango, Viennese Waltz) and American Rhythm (Cha-cha-cha, Mambo, Rumba, Bolero, East Coast Swing) are widely popular in the United States.

All the dances mentioned above can be and are danced socially in numerous dance clubs, schools, and studios. In addition, the less standardized Nightclub dance category is recognized, which includes dances such as Lindy Hop, West Coast Swing, and Hustle. Another category recently formalized in Europe is the Latin Swing class: Tango Argentino, Mambo, Lindy Hop, Swing Boogie (sometimes also known as Nostalgic Boogie), and Disco Fox. There is also a Rock 'n' Roll dance variant accepted as a social dance.

BALLET

In the 1890s, the centre of ballet shifted from France to Russia. There, the renowned French-born choreographer Marius Petipa collaborated with composer Pyotr Ilyich Tchaikovsky on lavish story ballet spectacles that brought Romantic ballet to a pinnacle of technical virtuosity.

Diaghilev's interest in dance began while he was a member of a small circle of intellectuals in St. Petersburg who fought to bring Russia's arts onto the wider European scene. His *Ballets Russes*, formed in 1909, appeared worldwide under various names for thirty years.

George Balanchine (1904–1983) was trained at the Imperial school in St. Petersburg. He later joined Diaghilev's company in Monte Carlo and went on to the United States, where he founded the School of American Ballet. With Balanchine, the music came first: he is remembered for saying that he wanted the audience to "see" the music and to "hear" the dance. His ballets are exotic, abstract, and mostly plotless, although the structure of a piece frequently has an emotional subtext that gives it a meaning beyond the mere dancing.

The United States, Great Britain, and the former Soviet Union have the best-known companies and the largest audiences. However, there are important ballet companies throughout the world that continue to recreate the classics and enrich the contemporary repertoire, for example, the Royal Danish Ballet, the Royal Swedish Ballet, Germany's Stuttgart Ballet, the Dutch National Ballet, and a number of French ballet companies. Ballet is also performed by national companies in Prague, Budapest, and other European cities. The last two decades have brought important innovations in genre as contemporary narrative ballet, folklore, abstract ballet, which is danced to all kinds of music, and experimental ballet combine the high art of ballet with popular art forms.

MODERN DANCE, FREE DANCE, AND *AUSDRUCKSTANZ*

Although sometimes applied to a category of twentieth-century ballroom dances, "modern dance" as a term usually refers to twentieth-century concert dance. Shedding classical ballet technique, costume, and shoes, a few dancers started to rebel against the rigid constraints of Classical Ballet and practiced "free dance." From the 1890s onwards, Loïe Fuller, Isadora Duncan, and Ruth St. Denis developed their own styles of barefoot free dance and laid the foundations of American modern dance. In Europe, Rudolf von Laban, Émile Jaques-Dalcroze, and François Delsarte developed theories of human movement and methods of instruction that led to the development of European modern and Expressionist dance (*Ausdruckstanz*). Other modern-dance pioneers are Ruth St. Denis and Ted Shawn, who specialized in highly theatrical and exotic tableaux, or stage pictures. Like the opera-ballets of the eighteenth century, their pieces satisfied an audience's hunger for a glimpse of foreign people and places. Influenced by the actress Sarah Bernhardt and the Japanese dancer Sado Yacco, Ruth St. Denis developed her own translations of Indian culture and mythology.

In Germany, Mary Wigman and Rudolf von Laban established modern dance vocabularies based on natural body shapes and movement. In "abstract dances," dancers dressed in elaborate, disguising costumes and were choreographed to create the effect of colors and geometric forms moving in space, rather than to portray individuals or relationships. The dancer obeyed the laws of the body and of the room; the human became an intermediary between technology and theatrical act. In 1931 Hanya Holm went to America as an assistant of Mary Wigman, which led to a crossing between German *Ausdruckstanz* and the American modern dance. Holm founded the New York Wigman School of Dance in 1931.

Both Postmodern dance and Contemporary dance build upon the foundations laid by Modern dance and form part of the greater category of twentieth-century concert dance. Postmodern dance hailed the use of everyday movement as valid performance art and advocated novel methods of dance composition. Claiming that any movement was dance, and any person a dancer (with or without training), early postmodern dance was closely aligned with the ideology of modernism.

SOCIAL DANCE

Popular and social dances were created by and for the upper classes in the past, yet have gained a mass influence and wide distribution in the twentieth century. Social dance today is international and reflects the democratization of dance more clearly than any other contemporary dance form. Whereas the term "popular dance" is often used for dances of the twentieth century only, "social dance" usually signifies the dances of the more urban or affluent members of society who attend upper-class social meetings such as the Viennese Opera Ball. It also sometimes refers to recreational folk dances in opposition to ceremonial or ritual folk dances.

By the end of the nineteenth century, social dance steps had become exhausted and no longer reflected the character of the emerging contemporary world. In addition, around 1900 the centre for the development of popular dance shifted from Europe to America. Instead of America importing English or French steps, dances spread from America to Europe. In 1889, American bandmaster John Philip Sousa's "Washington Post March" gave birth to the two-step, followed by the cakewalk of 1893. It was with the cakewalk in the 1890s that the first indigenous African-American dance became a national dance fashion and then spread to Europe. Ragtime, with its lively, syncopated rhythms, also had roots in black American music and emerged in the late 1890s. It gave rise (around 1910) to a popular craze for dances imitating animals, such as the Grizzly Bear, the Bunny Hug, and the Turkey Trot, in which syncopated arm gestures simulated wing movements and the feet moved with one step to each beat.

Social dance from then on was and is largely dominated by global influences. The dances of the 1910s and 1920s with their kicks, swinging arms, mobile torsos, and blaring rhythms, reflected a euphoric sense of prosperity and freedom. The black influence in jazz dominated in the 1920s with the Shimmy and the Charleston, a form of the Jitterbug. By 1924, the Charleston had become the rage first in Paris and then in the rest of Europe, as audiences were beguiled by the elegant Josephine Baker. In 1928 another American classic, the Lindy Hop, burst on the scene. The Jazz Age of the 1920s came to an end with the stock-market crash in 1929.

In the 1930s big band swing emerged as the new musical sound. Wanting respite from the Great Depression, people eagerly watched motion-pictures with the dancers Fred Astaire and Ginger Rogers. The Fox Trot, a fast dance from about 1913, returned in the 1930s in a slower, smoother version. At the 1939 World's Fair, a Samba orchestra played at the Brazilian pavilion. Soon, popular culture was swept with a rage for South American dances such as the Rumba, Mambo, Samba, and Conga Line. The Latin forms and sensual hip movements became popular at a time when women were gaining increased freedom, working in factories and managing homes and businesses while men were away at war during the 1940s. World War II interrupted dance evolution in the 1940s, but the 1950s brought the Merengue and Cha-Cha-Cha.

In the 1950s the sensuous movements of the Latin dances became the provocative hip rolls of rock star Elvis Presley. Rock and roll became a national phenomenon when the song "Rock Around the Clock" by Bill Haley and the Comets was featured in the film *The Blackboard Jungle* (1955), and the television show *American Bandstand* began its telecasts of dancing teenagers.

By the early 1960s, the Lindy was becoming outdated, rock 'n' roll became rock, and the Twist enjoyed brief popularity. During the civil rights era, in dances such as the Watusi, Monkey, Frug, Jerk, Hitchhike, and Pony, males and females danced face to face as solo improvisers, expressing freedom and individualism. An infusion of American interpretations of African dance forms was apparent not only in the dances' names but in movements of rippling spines, hip rotations, and hand-jive gestures. The 1950s closed with people jitterbugging to rock music. With the 1960s came the Bossa Nova and disco dancing, the latter producing dozens of individualized, free-moving dances, such as the Twist.

Several contradictory trends appeared in the 1970s and 1980s. Couple dancing, shunned by the individuality of the 1960s, returned in the 1970s with the Hustle (the Lindy Hop cut down to half-time) and other elaborately choreographed dances performed to disco music, a simple form of rock with strong dance rhythms. Alongside the disco movement, which dominated the 1970s and 1980s, the more outrageous punk rock movement brought in its wake slam dancing, which involved leaping, jumping, and sometimes physical attack. At the same time, in an impulse to nostalgia, the big-band sound was revived with Fox Trots, Waltzes, and Jitterbugs.

With the rise of rap music in the 1980s came break dancing, a street dance that combined acrobatic and martial-arts movements. This acrobatic solo dancing began among urban blacks and incorporated various spins on the back, head, and arms, as well as quick footwork, handstands, and other moves. Hip Hop and its panoply of musical (rap), graphic (graffiti), and dance expressions erupted in the 1980s. A number of trends, including the hip-gyrating Lambada and the Macarena, emerged in the 1980s and 1990s.

In general, since the 1960s, popular dance in the West has moved away from any prescribed sequence of movements and physical contact between participants, the dancers performing as individuals with no distinction between the male and the female role. In the 1990s, there are few named dances. The prevailing free style combines many different styles and is described by musical types of funk, reggae, house, club, and rap. Older ballroom and regional dance forms are kept alive at dance studios and by special dance clubs, and at weddings, formal charity balls, and government functions. European couple dances such as the Waltz and Fox Trot continue to be performed. Like contemporary American popular music, popular dancing tends to be percussive. Dancers do not sweep across the floor in large group patterns, but remain stationary, the feet stomping, sliding, hopping, while the arms punch the air or swing in counterpoint. The dance floors are crowded, bodies are close, yet the dancers move as individuals, despite "bump and grind" fashions with plenty of bodily contact. Dancing in America as well as in Europe tends to be age-specific, with fourteen- to twenty-five-year-olds engaging in the most dance activity. The role of composers of popular dance music in this development cannot be overestimated, nor can the many other elements that popularized American social dance throughout the world during the first half of the twentieth century. Major influences were vaudeville, musical comedy, films, and the popularity of such dancing stars as Fred Astaire and Gene Kelly. Further reinforcement came from the accompanying technology, such as the mass impact of dance music on radio, record, and tape, and, more recently, the dance images on television (MTV) or DVD.

The twentieth century, perhaps more so than any other age, was characterized by border crossing and international movements of dance. Although many dances can be traced back to folkloristic roots, they have developed into global movements. Popular dance can be regarded as a specifically Western phenomenon, influenced by the tradition of the theater and music of individual countries and only rarely spreading to areas other than the North American and European spheres.

AUSTRIA

Austria's most famous dance was and is the Waltz, a dance in 3/4 time, done primarily in closed position, the commonest basic figure of which is a full turn in two measures using three steps per measure. It first became fashionable in Vienna in the 1780s, was disapproved at first on account of its assumed lasciviousness, then spread to many other countries within the next few years. The Waltz is sometimes assumed to be a descendant of the Lavolta; others suggest the Ländler evolved into the Waltz. The Viennese Waltz became outdated in the 1920s but, since the 1930s, had its comeback in Germany and Austria. The most important social event where the Waltz is danced is the Vienna Opera Ball (Wiener Opernball), first held in 1936.

In Austria, folk dances in general are known as *Folkloretänze* (folklore dances), whereas the Austrian type of folk dance is known as *Volkstanz* (literally "people's dance"). In folk dancing, the Waltz and the Polka are slightly different from their counterparts in standard ballroom dancing. The famous Schuhplattler dance goes back to early courtship displays (*Balztanz*) of men who wanted to impress young ladies, and an older form of the dance can be traced back to the eleventh century. Initially the style was free without rules. Usually in 3/4 time, one carries out a series of jumps and hip movements to the time of the music. Characteristically the dancers rhythmically strike their thighs, knees and soles of the feet, and stamp with the feet. Nowadays the dance is usually performed out of tradition, maintaining the older customs, and as part of the activities of *Trachtenvereine* (that is, societies which maintain traditional dress, songs and culture of earlier days). Other Austrian folk dances are Boarischer Eiswalzer, Hiatamadl, Jägermarsch, Krebspolka, Kreuzpolka, Kuckuckspolka, Lunzer Boarischer, Mazurka, Neudeutscher, Polka, Poschater Zwoaschritt, Rediwa, Rheinländer, Siebenschritt, Studentenpolka, Zwiefacher. Some well-known folk

THE "SILENT DANCE"

In Bosnia-Herzegovina and Croatia, the "silent dance" tradition arguably resulted from the Turkish prohibition of native song and dance, where the only musical accompaniment to the dance is the sound of the dancers' feet and jingling costume ornaments.

dance festivals in Vienna are that of the *Alpenverein*, the Autumn Dance at Schloss Belvedere, the Ländler dances, the Kathreintanz, and the summer dances.

Austria is also a country with a very lively ballet scene. Ballet companies are attached to the opera houses of several Austrian cities (Baden bei Wien, Graz, Innsbruck, Klagenfurt, Linz, Salzburg, and St. Pölten), though until recently their prime function has been performing in operas. Historically, the main center of dance activity has been Vienna, and ballet performances there also take place at the Theater an der Wien and the Volksoper. There is a small but growing number of independent dance companies such as Eva-Maria Lerchenberg-Thony's Tanztheater Company in Innsbruck as well as new moves to encourage the pofile of dance, such as the biannual dance festival in Vienna and the Austria Dance festival in Graz.

THE BALKANS: SLOVENIA, CROATIA, SERBIA AND MONTENEGRO, BOSNIA-HERZEGOVINA, MACEDONIA, AND ALBANIA

Dance has always been a significant means of cultural identity and community involvement for ethnic Balkans. The main historical themes of their dances are resistance and heroism in an area fraught with a past of cultural, religious, and ethnic tensions. The area includes Bosnian Muslims, Orthodox Christian Serbs, Roman Catholic Croats, Jews, and Roma (Gypsies). Contemporary political boundaries are relatively new and do not reflect the lines of dance migrations. Religious influences, be they Catholic, Orthodox, or Islamic, also have shaped the themes and occasions for Balkan dance. As a result of the wars, religious identification and adherence to religious rules have increased among Bosnians, Croats, and Serbs.

In Slovenia and Croatia, dances show the effect of Catholicism and the long influence of the Austro-Hungarians: Western hand-clapping, stamping, arm-swinging, and partner dances with symphonized sound, such as Waltzes and Polkas, soon became part of the repertoire. Certain traditional dances are performed on religious holidays such as Christmas and Easter, yet they often have pre-Christian ritual embellishments and Eastern symbolism. Dances also display a defiant, warrior-like posture and a sense of collective power in the Slavic Kolo, a dance in which the dancers form a circle which moves like a snake. The Padushka Kolo, called the "cripple dance" because of its limping step, is also found in Bulgaria. Between World War I and World War II, the Kolo became something of a national dance in Serbia, traditionally beginning any ball. Innovations such as the Komitsko dance of Macedonia reveal the region's history of resistance, depicting mountain warriors challenging their historical Turkish occupiers. The Aramiska, a male warrior dance, remembers outlaw bands that fought nineteenth-century Turkish governors.

Spectacular dances such as magical sword dances, the dance-drama *Moresca*, and ritual "shaking" dances are particularly memorable forms of Croatian dance. The Lindjo is a Dalmatian folk dance common at weddings in the city-state of Dubrovnik, with string accompaniment on the lijerica and the direction of the lead dancer/caller.

The fusion of Byzantine, Ottoman, Western European, Russian, Slavic, and Roma influences has created hybrid art forms. Serbia has absorbed the Csárdás, a Hungarian couple dance adopted and changed by the Slovaks and Croats under the Austro-Hungarian Empire. Slavic music now accompanies the dance, and Croatian or Slovakian Csárdás feature faster, freer steps than the Hungarian version. Wherever the Austro-Hungarians held political influence, couple dances such as Polkas and Waltzes have been popular since the 1800s. Turkish influence can be seen in large-scale town dances in the province of Kosovo, and Austrian influence is clear in the couple dances popular in Vojvodina. Kolos and Lesnos are the most common formations in Macedonia, and Macedonia's characteristic asymmetrical rhythms give the region a most rich and varied folk tradition. Lesno, meaning "easy dance," is a walking dance (Polonaise) with many regional and musical variations. Men's and women's-only dances continue to be popular, such as the bride's dance for weddings. Greek dances such as the Sta Tría and Syrtós are also common. Drmes is the famous "jiggling dance" from the region of Posavina (Bosnia and Croatia), a traveling circle dance. The Greek Baidoúska, an often asymmetrical rhythm dance with quick-slow beat, is performed with a step on the quick beat.

Most Balkan dances involve the form of the circle, considered since pre-medieval times to be a magic shape and impenetrable by evil forces. Women generally display a greater degree of restraint and modesty in their movements, avoiding the sometimes flamboyant and higher steps of the men. In Albania, because of Islamic influences, women and men often do not dance together in public. Another consistent characteristic is that the beats of Balkan music and the step timing of Balkan dance do not always match exactly; instead, a dancer's individual bodily rhythm unifies the dance.

Slovenia has two subsidised opera and ballet houses, the SNG (Slovene National Theater) Ljubljana Opera and Ballet and the SNG Maribor. In 1918 the first Slovene professional ballet ensemble and ballet school were established, and in 1946 the second ensemble began work in Maribor. Modern dance in Slovenia goes back to the end of the nineteenth century, and in 1929 a school for modern dance was opened by Meta Vidmar, a student of Mary Wigman. Other choreographers and dancers before World War II included Pia and Pino Mlakar (who led the ballet theater for 15 years), Katja Delak, Marija Gradnik, and Marta Paulin, who trained two influential Slovene dancers, Lojzka Žerdin and Živa Kraigher. In the 1990s, fifteen independent organizations were established by Slovene dancers and choreographers, with the Ljubljana Dance Theater as their only performance premises. One of the internationally acclaimed dance companies is EnKnap, established by Iztok Kovač, which has engaged around seventy dancers and musicians from several countries in its international coproductions and has also produced several dance films.

In Croatia, ballet has a tradition of 130 years. The most important ensemble, the Ballet Troupe Croatia, is a professional classical ballet touring company consisting of dancers of the Croatian National Ballet in Zagreb. It was formed in 1994 under the artistic leadership of Svebor Sečak, the principal dancer of the Croatian National Ballet in Zagreb, and has since given more than 250 guest performances all throughout Croatia and other European countries with its programs.

Albania has an Opera with ballet and folk music and dance ensembles that operate under the control of the national state TV and Radio; Serbia has its Ballet of the National Theater in Belgrade, yet the arts in most Balkan countries still suffer from the effects of Communist rule and war.

BALTIC STATES (LATVIA, LITHUANIA, ESTONIA)

The Baltic states have traditionally been a bridge between the West and the East, torn between the dominance of Western states such as Germany and Sweden on the one hand and Russia on the other. In all three Baltic states—Estonia, Latvia, and Lithuania—song and dance festivals have been an integral part of national culture for more than a century. There is a Song and Dance Festival in Latvia every four to five years, with the number of amateur singers and dancers usually being around 20,000. Folkdance and song are two important traditions in Latvian culture, and the company Daile, founded in 1968, is heading the folk dance scene. Latvian dances are rooted in pairs of dancers, solo dances are a rarity. The International Folk Dance Festival "Sudmaliņas" is the only stage folk dance festival in the Baltic States, which has been organized every three years since 1992. The festival has attracted dancers from Latvia and countries all over the world. An important role in the cultural life of Riga, the capital of Latvia, is assigned to amateur groups and artists. As of 2005 there were 303 amateur performing and arts groups, 84 choirs, and 43 folk dance groups.

The first full-length ballet produced in Latvia, *La Fille mal gardée*, was performed at the National Opera House in Riga in 1921. In 1932, a ballet school was founded in Riga, and Alexandra Fedorova strongly influenced teaching and choreography, staging ballets from the Russian repertoire in the 1920s and 30s. After the war, Elena Tangieyeva-Birzniece created the first Latvian-Soviet ballet, *Laima*. The most internationally known contemporary dance company of Latvia (founded in 1996) is Olga Zitlukhina Modern Dance Company.

Lithuania had a lively ballet scene since the sixteenth century till it was suppressed by Slavonic influences, especially since the occupation of Lithuania by czarist Russia in 1795. Lithuania became independent of Russia after the Revolution of 1918, and reflecting this momentous political change, culture in Lithuania became more sensitive to its specifically national identity. The National Lithuanian Theatre opened in 1920 with a production of *La Traviata* that included ballet scenes. During World War II Lithuania experienced invasions by both Nazi and Soviet armies. After the war the company was re-formed, but the repertoire still focused mainly on Russian classical ballet. In 1990 Lithuania regained its independence, foreign choreographers were invited to create works, and there were new opportunities for dancers.

In addition to reinterpreting traditional ballet with new choreography, there is a lively interest in modern dance. The annual international contemporary dance festival, Naujasis Baltijos Sokis (New Baltic Dance), takes place every spring, an event indicating the growing trend towards an international dance style. Rasa (founded in 1967) is the oldest folk dance ensemble in Lithuania, where singing and dancing usually go together.

Ballet in Estonia is based at the two opera houses, Estonia Theater in Tallinn and Vanemuine in Tartu, and professional dance dates back to the beginning of the twentieth century. As a result of lack of funding, many dancers have left the country, including Thomas Edur and Agnes Oaks, who went to England. Modern dance emerged in the 1990s with the Dance Theater Nordstar, founded by Saima Kranig in 1991, and Fine 5, founded in 1993 by the choreographer René Nömmik.

Estonia underwent a period of national awakening in the 1860s, with the first Song Festival organised in 1869. The first Estonian Games, Dance, and Gymnastics festival, held in 1934, was a precursor to the present Dance Festival. Dance Festivals since the 1950s have been held at the Kalev Central Stadium in Tallinn, with growing numbers of participants each year, usually together with the Song Festival. The greatest Dance Festival of all times (the ninth) took place in 1970 with over 10,000 performers.

The Dance Festival is a performance with a certain theme, where the dancers in their bright national costumes form several colorful patterns on the dance field. At the beginning of the 1960s, the number of youth choirs, orchestras, folk-dance groups and participants had increased to such a level that there arose a need for a separate festival, and the Youth Song and Dance Festivals was organized. The first was held in 1962, and the festivals now take place every five years. In July 2004 about 100,000 people participated in the twenty-fourth Song Celebration and the seventeenth Dance Celebration, either as performers or spectators.

BELGIUM

Ballet dance was a rather late development in Belgium and was restricted for the most part to Brussels and Ghent. In 1816, a permanent corps de ballet was established at the Théâtre de la Monnaie opera house in Brussels. In 1841, the Royal Opera was founded in Ghent, a dance academy followed seven years later. After World War I, a resident ballet company was established at the Monnaie, and ballet productions began to proliferate. Efforts by Elsa Darciel, Lea Daan, and Isa Voos helped to develop expressionst modern dance in the 1930s. In 1947, the first independent ballet company in Belgium, Ballet Belge, was formed, and in 1960 Maurice Béjart (born in 1927) founded the Ballet of the Twentieth Century in Brussels. Béjart established himself as one of the most important choreographers on the international ballet scene. The Rosas company and Ultima Vez are the major Belgian proponents of contemporary dance at the moment. The Amperdans festival in Antwerp is one of the major venues for dance companies in Belgium.

Folk dance traditions in Belgium are closely related to religious festivals, archery celebrations, or harvesting, and many folkloric customs originate from old Germanic paganism. In May, the planting of the maypole is celebrated, and a ribbon dance and popular dances are alternated with May songs. A remainder of the morris dance can also be found in Flanders. The Flemish Sword Dance, performed two weeks before Easter, is related to British forms of Sword Dance. Folk art traditions are no longer automatically passed on from generation to generation but stay alive only through the efforts of over 130 folk dance groups in Flanders. Historical dances (e.g., Walloon dances) of the Renaissance are performed with minute attention to detail regarding the costumes and the authenticity of the dance steps. Flemish dances are suites based on the Polka, the Waltz, Scottish dancing, and the Mazurka and demand an exceptionally high level of technique and cohesion on the part of the dancers. These dances vary from easy community dances to real choreographies that, as regards to the steps and figures, build on the tradition.

BULGARIA

Bulgarian culture has been influenced successively by Byzantine, Islamic, and Greek traditions. Orthodox Christian religion and culture and Islamic influence have survived Communist rule.

As in Macedonian dance, asymmetrical rhythms are fundamental to Bulgarian dance. The focus of the dancers is on their footwork and line cohesion. Sexually segregated line dances are most popular. Balkan dance has a common appeal because of its use of the circle, a shape embodying community, harmony and unity. Horo, a chain circle dance, is a popular form led by the first and last dancers marked with handkerchiefs, who signal dancers to spiral in and out from the ends of the line. The lively Bulgarian couple dance Rachenitsia Horo has spread to Romania and Yugoslavia as a popular wedding dance for both genders. In Romania, the dance is called a Hora, or skylark dance, because its speeding tempo and grapevine step imitate a bird's path.

Bulgarian folk dances are intimately related to the music of Bulgaria. A distinctive feature of Balkan (and Bulgarian) folk music are the asymmetrical meters, built up around various combinations of "quick" and "slow" beats. The metrical accents are based on varying musical notations (e.g., quarter, eighth, or sixteenth notes), which are, however, often simplified in performance. Common Bulgarian folk dances are the Paidushko Horo, a men's dance, the Chetvorno Horo, the Pravo Horo, the Sandansko Horo, the Daichovo Horo (a circle dance where a leader calls what the circle should do next), the Petrunino Horo, and the Elenino Horo. Line dances include the Trite Puti, which is quick-quick-slow, the Eleno Mome, the Gankino or Kopanitsa, the Acano Mlada Nevesto, and the Buchimish. A men's dance such as the Chope dance is often accompanied by bagpipes and drums. Many of the men's dances are formed by each man holding the belt or sash of the man on either side. Bulgarian folk music is unusual, displaying complex harmonies and rhythms. The chief folk musical instruments are the gaida (bagpipe) and the kaval (wooden shepherd's flute).

Bulgaria's National Opera and Ballet is situated in the capital Sofia and focuses strongly on the classics with the National Academy of Music responsible for the education of new dancers.

THE CZECH REPUBLIC

Ballet activity is concentrated in the capital, Prague, with the Prague Ballet, founded in 1964, and the Prague National Theatre Ballet, founded in 1883. The repertoire consists largely of contemporary Czech choreography, especially ballets by Ogoun and Smok. After 1970, the Prague Ballet was reformed as Prague Chamber Ballet.

Popular Bohemian folk dances from the 1830s are the Zwiefacher and the Polka (meaning "field" or "half" or "Polish girl"). Polka is not only a 2/4 beat dance but also a genre of dance music, common both in Europe and America. In the nineteenth century polkas were composed by the leading composers of ballroom music (including both Johann Strausses), and examples occur in art music by Bedrich Smetana, Antonin Dvorak, and others. In the early days of the Polka's worldwide success story it was accompanied by related Bohemian dances (Trasak, Skocna, Rejdovak), and local dancing masters introduced their own variants. Typical instruments are the accordion, tuba, and piano. In America, various styles of Polka have been developed (especially among the Polish population of North America), such as Chicago Honky, Chicago Push, or Cleveland styles.

FRANCE

France has traditionally been the country with the most lively ballet scene. Paris remained the ballet capital of the world until the 1890s, when the center of ballet moved to Russia. After 1945 many small, adventurous companies emerged both within and outside Paris. During the 1970s, the ballet scene began to look to a younger audience by bringing in work by modern choreographers, and between 1983 and 1989 a new, controversial period started at the Paris Opera Ballet under the direction of Rudolf Nureyev.

Much contemporary popular music and dance in France is of international origin, combining sounds from West, Central, and North Africa, the Caribbean, and Latin America, though the old chanson tradition is undergoing something of a revival, and rap has taken strides. Meanwhile jazz and classical music continues to thrive. There are several excellent regional companies and festivals of innovative dance that bring in the best international talent. The French regional contemporary dance companies include Régine Chopinot's troupe from La Rochelle, Jean-Claude Gallotta's from Grenoble, Mathilde Monnier's from

Montpellier, Karine Saporta's from Caen, and Joëlle Bouvier and Régis. As of 2003, France had 11,300 actors and dancers, 16,200 musicians and singers, 250 music, opera, and dance festivals, and 8700 Variété artists.

France is composed of very different regions, each keeping its traditions and its local language; therefore French traditional dancing encompasses a huge range of geographically and culturally separate groups that can be roughly divided as follows.: Central French dances are the Bourrées in 2 and 3-time, Mazurkas, Waltzes, Branles, and Schottisches found in various forms; they form the core of the central French dance repertoire. The origin of most of these dances is rather unclear, but most of France's folk dances are descendants of early circle dances or Branles, and they were originally accompanied only by song with no instruments. The dances gradually increased in complexity, and the form of the dances developed from a circle, to sets of couples in a circle, to broken chains and couple dances. Brittany can be further split into Eastern, French- and Gallo-speaking Haute Bretagne (where the dances include An Dro, Hanter Dro, Laridé, and Rond de St. Vincent) and the Western, Breton-speaking Basse Bretagne (where the dances include the Gavotte, Plinn, and Kost ar C'Hoat). The Fest Noz (night dance) is widespread in summertime. People gather in their hundreds to dance to the traditional An Dro, Suite Gavotte, Suite Plinn, and Suite Fisel. At such an event one can hear two symbolic local instruments: the bombarde, a loud and high-pitched relative of the oboe, and the biniou, a kind of small bagpipe, although nowadays folk-rock bands have added guitars and a rhythm section to this traditional duet. Béarn, in the southwest, is the home of the Branle d'Ossau, Sauts, and Rondeaux in chains and in couples. The Basque country, straddling the Spanish border, features more Sauts and Fandangos. The Alps are home to the lively Rigodons, with their links to English country dancing. Alsace, on the German border, features 5- and 8-time Waltzes, Zwiefachers from Germany, and contredanses.

GERMANY

Although often considered an American phenomenon, the evolution of modern dance can also be traced to Germany. Regular ballet performances started in Berlin after World War I at the State Opera (Staatsoper). The leading figures in German modern dance after the war were Rudolf von Laban, who had set up his school in Munich in 1910, and his student Mary Wigman, who also ran an influential school of expressionist dance. Only in 1928, when Laban's *Schrifttanz* was published under the title *Kinetography*, did dance become describable by a general system of notation. Laban described not only the movements on the ground, but those of the entire body.

Laban's pupils Mary Wigman and Kurt Jooss became the great examples who turned his ideas into reality. Kurt Jooss intended to give the *ballet d'action* the face of the twentieth century. He argued in 1928 that classical ballet had to find a common base with modern dance. Dance was for him a dramatic story, with a minimum of decorations, and he regarded pirouettes and entrechats as anachronisms. After studying with Laban, Wigman performed in Germany and opened her own school in Dresden (1920). She became the most influential German exponent of expressive movement (*Ausdruckstanz*). Wigman choreographed and danced in Talhoff's *Das Totenmahl* 1930 in Munich, a monumental show against war and death, in which each movement was to have the power of conjuration, without paying heed to beauty. Although Wigman's school was closed by the Nazis, she reopened it in Berlin in 1948. In contrast to her expressionist dance were the harmless and beloved Wiesenthal sisters, Bertha, Else, Martha and especially Grete Wiesenthal.

Another movement was the Abstract Dance (*Abstrakter Tanz*), a term used by Oskar Schlemmer to describe the dance aesthetic he developed at the Bauhaus, Weimar, during the mid 1920s. Dancers were turned into mechanical figures, dressed in elaborate, disguising costumes and were choreographed to create the effect of colors and geometric forms in space, rather than to portray individuals or relationships. After World War II the company continued in what was then East Berlin. Berlin's second opera house, the Charlottenburg, which opened in 1912, is today home to the Berlin Opera Ballet. In the field of modern dance, Pina Bausch became a leading dancer, choreographer, and company director and one of the most influential avant-garde artists on the European dance scene. An heir to the German expressionist dance tradition of *Ausdruckstanz*, she stresses in her productions ideas such as feelings of alienation, anguish, frustration, and cruelty rather than the elaboration of pure movement.

Among German ballet companies today the Stuttgart Ballet and the Frankfurt Ballet are the most internationally recognized. The Leipzig Ballet symbolizes the rebirth of dance in the former East Germany.

Germany is also the place of lively folk dance traditions. The Schuhplattler and Zwiefacher are danced all over Bavaria. The main distribution area of the Zwiefacher is Lower Bavaria, Hallertau, and Upper Palatinate; it is also known in the Black Forest, Austria, Alsace, the Czech Republic, and Sudetenland. The main feature of this dance is the alternation between even and odd time signatures (e.g., from three to two beats per bar). An increase in the popularity of this dance type is directly credited to Michael Eberwein, who collected more than 100 Zwiefacher songs/dances during his lifetime. The Schottische was a German folk dance that consisted of a series of chassés and hops done to 2/4 and 4/4 music. There were also combination dances such as the Polka-Redowa and Polka-Mazurka. The Schuhplattler is a traditional dance of courtship display from Bavaria and Austria in which the men perform complicated jumps, slapping their thighs in time with the music, while the ladies twirl, showing off their traditional dress. Some of these dances may tell a story, such as a dating couple, or depict a trade, such as a miller or woodcutter. Nowadays the dance is usually performed out of tradition, maintaining the older customs, and as part of the activities of Trachtenvereine (societies that maintain traditional dress, songs and culture), especially at the Oktoberfest in Munich or the *Musikantenstadl*, a well-known TV show.

GREECE

Greece is one of the few places in the world where folk dance is still kept alive. In ancient times, dance, song, and music were all integral parts of the theater: in fact, the Greek word *choros* referred to both dance and song. Dance has its place in some ceremonial customs that are still preserved in the Greek villages, such as "dancing the bride" during a wedding. Dance occasions and styles are well correlated with Greek Orthodox Church rituals, holidays, and the pre-Lenten carnival.

Most dances move counterclockwise, with an open circle being the most common formation. Leaders often improvise and embellish the basic step pattern, while other dancers stay closer to the original pattern. Four of the most popular pan-Hellenic dance forms include the Sta Tría, a very ancient dance form copied throughout the dance world; Tsámikos, a free-style dance in a slow-quick count with a leader directing the general group direction; Hassaposervikos, a mainland dance with ever-increasing speed and a rapid step; and Syrtós (Kalamatianós), one of the most common dances in Greece and danced all over the world in Greek communities. A famous Greek dance is the Pentozali.

The Pentozali was done by armed warriors during ancient times. The rhythm is provided by a *lyra* (a kind of fiddle, not the ancient Greek lyre), and the dancers, holding hands, start dancing slowly in a circle. As the music quickens, so do the steps and the dance reaches a frenzied speed, ending suddenly when the lyra stops. Traditional Greek dances such as the Hasapiko, the Tsámikos, and the Kalamatianós continue to be performed at weddings and other celebrations. Another group of dances originated in Asia Minor, which was a part of Greece for centuries: Hassaposervikos, Karsilamas, Zeibekikos. The rediscovery of the old rebetika songs, and the effort of contemporary Greek musicians to return to the roots of Greek music, popularized these traditional but forgotten rhythms and the corresponding dances. Today, Hasapiko, Hassaposervikos, and Zeibekiko are included in the program of the Greek tavernas along with Syrtós and Karagouna. Syrtaki was created for the movie *Zorba the Greek* to music written by Theodorakis. It starts with a slow tempo that is danced in the steps of Hasapiko and eventually becomes faster and danced in the steps of Hassaposervikos. Tsifteteli is an example of a transplanted dance. It originated in the Oriental belly dance and then developed into a free dance. In each region local dances are preserved because of people's love for dancing, regional customs, and the efforts of local cultural organizations. Other private efforts include the Dora Stratou Dance Theater and the Peloponnesian Folklore Museum.

HUNGARY

Hungary is a country with both a lively ballet and a folk dance scene. The State Opera House in Budapest, opened in 1884, comprises the national ballet ensemble, which still dominates dance activity in Hungary, despite many other companies. In Szeged, the first professional provincial company was established in 1946. The Szeged Contemporary Dance Company was established in 1987, under the name of Szeged Ballet, after the return of Zoltán Imre. Other companies are the Ballet Sopianae at the National Theater at Pécs, founded in 1960 by Imre Eck, who created a repertory of youth-oriented political ballets in a modern style. This company, now known as Pécs ballet, is still very popular and has toured widely in Europe and America. The Györ Ballet, founded in 1979 by Iván Marcó, is Hungary's only classical company to be financially independent of a theater.

Despite lack of funds, a considerable independent modern dance scene has developed, and the Hungarian Contemporary Dance Festival, founded in 1992, is proof to that. Among the best-known modern groups to emerge are Artus, which was founded by Gábor Goda in 1985 and performs mixed-media works fusing poetry, dance, and acrobatics; TazDanz, founded by Péter Gerzson-Kovács in 1991, which combines jazz, folk dance, and text; the Sabo Company, founded in 1990, which is strongly influenced by Anne Teresa de Keersmaeker, an important proponent of postmodern dance; and the Bozsik company, led by Yvette Bozsik, whose works, such as *The Miraculous Mandarin* (1995), draw on folk dance and the styles of Wigman and Bausch. Based in Paris and Budapest, the Compagnie Pál Frenák is committed to developing and presenting the dance-language of choreographer Pál Frenák, which is based on the sign language system of the deaf and mute.

Although Hungarian folk music is no longer a key characteristic of rural life, recent years have seen the growth of an urban-centered folk revival movement known as the *tánchaz* (dance house). The format usually consists of about an hour of dance-step instruction followed by several hours of dancing accompanied by a live band, which might include some of Hungary's best folk musicians. Hungary has famous ensembles promoting native folk dance, such as the Hungarian Stage Folk Ensemble, founded in 1949. The Budapest Dance Ensemble is one of the oldest, yet freshest folk dance groups from Central Europe. Established in 1958, it became part of the Hungarian State Folk Ensemble in 1998.

In the nineteenth century Hungarian folk dance (*népi tánc*) was still a traditional part of the folklore, chiefly in the life of the peasantry. Hungary's national couple dance, the Csárdás (from *csárda*, a tavern, beer house), sometimes called the "Tango of the East," had developed from a folk dance into a dance of the upper classes. Csárdás is of Magyar and Roma origin, and it is characterized by a variation in tempo: it starts out slowly (*lassú*) and ends in a very fast tempo (*friss*). Women wear wide (often red) skirts, and partners hold and embrace each other in close proximity. The recruiting dance Verbunkos (derived from the German word *werben*, which means "to enrol in the army") is an eighteenth-century solo men's dance and music genre of the Hussars.

Karikázó is a circle dance (*karika*, ring), performed mostly by women without music and accompanied by the singing of folksongs. The chain and circle forms were popular all over Europe during the Middle Ages, and they are the most archaic forms of folk dance found in Hungary. Ugrós, or jumping dances, are solo or couple dances that are accompanied by old-style music with accent on the second measure. The jumping dances originate from the same medieval source as the weapon dances (Haiduk), but in this dance family no implement was used, and because of this, more dancelike footwork developed. Ciganytánc and the first half of Szenyeri Paros belong to this dance family.

ITALY

Italy is regarded as the birthplace of ballet, and many Italian ballet masters served in France and other countries at court entertainments during past centuries. When ballet became an art of the theater, Milan become the main center with the opening of the Scala Theater in 1778. The Imperial Academy of Dancing was established in 1813 and produced famous ballerinas. In Rome, the ballet school of the Teatro dell'Opera was founded in 1928 and staged several productions of the classics. Italy has major international festivals, such as Nervi-Genoa, Verona, Spoleto, and Castiglioncello, which have strongly promoted dance. Some small, independent companies have succeeded in challenging the opera house companies, notably Aterballetto, directed by Mauro Bigonzetti, which is resident at both the Balletto di Toscana and Milan Ballet (founded in 1997). In general, modern dance has not gained an influence such as in other European countries.

Italian folk dances are performed at festivals, weddings, and celebrations to reflect and remind the Italians of their past. Italian folk dance has an ancient history: preserved under volcanic ash in the ruins of Pompeii were friezes of dancers, which inspired movements used to create Italian folk dances. The most famous Italian folk dance, the Tarantella (Tarentule, Tarentella, Tarantel) is a circle dance, performed clockwise in 6/8 time and characterized by the rapid whirling of couples.

Men and women perform the same step for the Tarantella, which requires that the dancers constantly switch feet. Danced to a mandolin and tambourines played by the dancers, the Tarantella is a lively, improvised aerobic dance for men and women alike. A staple of Italian weddings, it is also the theme song of some Italian restaurants and has appeared in films such as *The Godfather*.

Other Italian folk dances are the Ballo Sardo from Sardinia. The Saltarello dance is also popular throughout the region of Central Italy. La Raspa is now known as the Mexican Hat Dance, but it was first danced in Europe and southern Italy with a pointed instead of flexed foot. CountroDanso, from the northern part of Italy, has a French influence.

Costuming is very simple because the dancers were peasants, not members of the royal court. Women wear a long, brightly colored full skirt of cotton or a heavier fabric in a solid or a printed pattern.

NETHERLANDS

Amsterdam has traditionally been the center for ballet in the Netherlands, with the first performances dating back to the seventeenth century. After the success of Romantic ballet in the nineteenth century, ballet was reduced to operatic functions in the 1890s, despite visits by Loïe Fuller, Isadora Duncan, and Anna Pavlova. Today the most important companies in the country are the Scapino Ballet, the Dutch National Ballet, and the Netherlands Dance Theatre. The Netherlands' oldest ballet company, the Scapino Ballet, was founded in 1945 in Amsterdam by Hans (Johanna) Snoek to provide performances for children, but the company now also performs a wide-ranging adult repertoire. The Dutch National Ballet (Het Nationale Ballet), based in Amsterdam, was formed in 1961. The troupe originally covered a huge repertoire of classic and new works, and the dancers were also expected to perform in Opera productions. The Netherlands Dance Theater (NDT), which was founded in 1959 and is based in The Hague, is one of the most successful dance companies in the world. Eschewing the classics and the hierarchy of classical ballet, the company built up a repertoire of experimental Dutch work with a modern dance slant. The company became the first in Europe to give its members classes in modern dance technique. American modern dance choreographers such as John Butler, Anna Sokolow, and Glen Tetley worked with the NDT and heavily influenced its style. In 1975 the company was artistically revived by the Czech choreographer Jiri Kylián, who also created two smaller offshoot companies, NDT2 for junior dancers and NDT3 for dancers of retirement age.

Traditional Dutch dances are often called *Folkloristisch* and sometimes *Boerendansen* (farmer dancing). The main Dutch contribution to world dance is the Klompen dance, the dance in wooden shoes (clogs, Dutch *klompen*) that created rhythms based on the sounds of the feet, yet without spectacular movements. Well-known Dutch dances are Baanopstekker (Achtehoek), Boerenplof, Polka Janny Lint (Friesland), Riepe Riepe Garste, Slaapmuts, Skotse Fjouwer, Langdans, Horlepiep, IJswals, Hakke-Toone, and Klapdans. Many of these dances are traditional in certain regions of the Netherlands only and are performed in the costumes of that region. Festival occasions for Dutch folk dance are the Meiboom (maypole) celebrations and the Tulip Time Festival, which has been celebrated since the late 1920s and has grown by now into a major tourist event.

POLAND

Ballet in Poland goes back to the sixteenth century Polish courts. Indeed, Warsaw, under Russian occupation after 1794, became a center of ballet. Modern dance became influential in Poland between the two World Wars and was taught at private schools. In 1937 the Polish Ballet was founded and financed by the government to promote Polish ballet abroad. After World War II, companies in smaller cities emerged. In 1973 the independent Polish Dance Theater was founded; it is still the major company in Poland. After the end of Communist

> ## TARANTELLA: AN EARLY CURE
> Tarantella (meaning "small tarantula") is thought to have been an early remedy for a tarantula bite: you dance until you sweat the poison out of your body.

rule in 1989, Polish dance culture underwent substantial restructuring. The Silesian Dance Theatre was established in 1991 in the city of Bytom.

The Polonaise and the Mazurka are the most famous Polish dances. The Polonaise is a stately processional dance, performed by couples who walk around the dance hall; the music is executed in 3/4 time and moderate tempo. Dancing the Polonaise requires a straight, upright posture with no movement of hips, smooth and elegant hand gestures, and the head held high. The greatest composer of polonaises in classical music was Fryderyk Chopin, whose works for piano made this dance the musical symbol of Poland and Polishness.

The Mazurka is a general term for a series of Polish folk dances in triple meter that originated in the plains of Mazovia around Warsaw. The dances comprise the Mazur or Mazurek, the Obertas or Oberek, and the Kujawiak from the neighboring district of Kujawy. The Mazurka was originally performed exclusively as a classic dance and consisted of numerous figures and steps. In the Mazurka, all the couples follow a leader. Sometimes the woman will kneel down while her partner executes a chasse around her, then they reverse the manoeuver. The Polacco is a sister dance to the Mazurka, also written in 3/4 time. It can be graceful and melancholic and other times lively.

The Krakowiak is one of Poland's national dances, and it recounts the story of the invasion of the Tartars—complete with their dancing horse, the Lajkonik. The Nowo Sadecki is an exuberant village dance from the town of Nowy Sacz. The Rzeszowski from Poland's southeast features beautiful costumes combined with eye-catching spins. The Goralski from high in the Carpathian Mountains is completely unlike any other dance in Poland, because it features very athletic and acrobatic performances by the men including their characteristic axe leaping. The Lubelski from the city of Lublin is another brisk and lively folk dance comprising several segments including a Polka, an Oberek, and a gypsy dance. The Kujawiak-Oberek from the Kujawy area of Poland combines the very energetic Oberek with the stately Kujawiak. The most balletic of Poland's national dances, it employs much classical technique and features a number of energetic lifts.

ROMANIA

Romania has been controlled for much of its history by foreign powers, including the Ottoman Empire and Austria-Hungary. The population includes ethnic Romanians, Hungarians, and Roma populations. Although Romania has been influenced by divergent Western trends, it also has a well-developed indigenous folk culture.

While typical mixed-gender Balkan circle and line dances are sometimes performed in Romania, the most common forms are improvised men's dances, women's circle dances, and couple dances. Dances are generally grouped under their region, despite myriad village variations, such as the Kalotaszeg, Mezoseg, and Szekely regional dances. Improvisation is a key component of dance and music, especially in the couple dances. As in Croatia and Hungary, flamboyant male dances are popular, especially among youth. Men often leap onto large drums and dance, perform fancy footwork around glass bottles, or dance with sticks and knives.

Wallachia is home to the taraf bands, which are perhaps the best-known proponents of Romanian folk culture. Dances associated with tarafs include Brâu, Geamparale, Sârba, and Hora. The fiddle leads the music, with the cimbalom (hammered dulcimer) and double bass accompanying it. Lyrics are often about heroes such as the Haidouks, legendary Robin Hood–like heroes of Romanian folklore. Many traditional Romanian tunes are based on music of the Roma people, thousands of whom once wandered through the countryside.

Folk themes and music by the Roma (lăutari) have inspired vibrant pop and rock traditions in modern Romania.

Romania's capital, Bucharest, had a corps de ballet established in 1898, which presented stagings of the Ballets Russes and early Soviet repertories before World War II. After the war, many new state-subsidized schools were established, producing such major dancers as Ileian Illiescu, Elena Dacian, and Alexa Mezincescu. Since 1993, the Romanian Opera of Bucharest Ballet Company has been run by Illiescu and Mihai Babuska. Smaller modern dance groups such as the Contemp, Orion Ballet, or Marginalii Dance Group, and Studio DCM have engaged in experimental work.

SPAIN AND PORTUGAL

Traditional music and dance in Spain have been preserved almost completely till the late twentieth century, as it was not until then that Spanish music and dance began to be influenced more intensely by other cultures through media and travel. Spanish dance can be categorized in six groups: flamenco, classical Spanish dance (called *estilización*), folklore, eighteenth-century dances, ballet (classical dance), and castanets. The roots of Spanish folk dance reach back to the court entertainments of the Moorish caliphs; the theatrical dance dating from the reign of Ferdinand and Isabella; sixteenth-century courtly dances such as the Zarabanda, Chacona, Pasacalle, and Folía; and the liturgical dances (*los seises*) that are still performed in the cathedral at Toledo.

Spain is divided into seventeen diverse regions, and each takes pride in its unique traditions and the way they contribute to the whole of Spanish culture. Bagpipes can be heard in some of Galicia's music, and the sword dance (*la danza de espadas*) and Muñeira are widely known there. Dances in Valencia include Fandango, a lively couple's dance in triple meter with guitar and castanets accompanying, and Jota, a quick folk dance in triple meter accompanied by the use of bamboo castanets. Catalonia's most important circle dance is the Sardana. Andalusia is the home of flamenco music that is highly ornamented and very improvisational. Flamenco is a song (*cante*), guitar music (*guitarra*), and dance (*baile*) style that is strongly influenced by the Roma (called *gitanos* in Spanish), but it has its deeper roots in Moorish musical traditions. Flamenco dance is performed with castanets to fast, vigorous rhythms and is considered by many to be a Spanish heritage treasure. Nuevo Flamenco, or New Flamenco, is a recent variant of flamenco which has been influenced by modern musical genres such as rumba, salsa, pop, rock, and jazz. Sevillanas are another variation on the theme, from Seville. During the second half of the nineteenth century, flamenco began to change from an intimate social dance to a professional art form.

Neoclassical Spanish dance is the rebirth of classical Spanish dance during the late nineteenth century. Drawing on flamenco, folk, and school dance roots, Neoclassical Spanish dance developed through the genius of the Argentine-born Spanish dancer La Argentina (Antonia Mercé y Luque), who was the first to dance to music of leading Spanish composers, such as Isaac Albéniz. She founded her own company in 1928. Spanish ballet traditions also tended to adhere to their Spanish roots. The Teatro del Licea in Barcelona and the Teatro Real in Madrid had ballet companies, and the latter also a ballet school. The Ballet de Madrid, founded in 1927 by La Argentinita (Encarnación López Julvez), incorporated Spanish themes, music, and dance into choreographies and made Spanish dance a worldwide phenomenon. The government sponsored the National Dance Company of Spain (now National Ballet of Spain). Classical ballet never got real hold of Spain; even the Ballet Clásico, founded in 1979, focuses on contemporary works.

Portugal is closely allied to Spain by its geographical position and by their common origin, yet each of its provinces has to some extent dances and dance-music peculiar to itself. Many remains of old Moorish civilization persist, and the traces of Saracen culture are greater in Portugal than even in southern Spain. The principal dance of a Romaria, a festival held in honor of a saint, is named the Fofa, a kind of national dance performed by couples that includes elements attributed to African or Brazilian influence. These dances are not especially graceful, but slow in movement and similar to Oriental dances. The dances are generally innocent and decorous; they resemble Quadrilles, with hops and skips but without much spirit, and the faces of the performers maintain a solemn gravity. Portugal is famous for its Ballets ambulatories, which are religious processions with dances, in imitation of the Tuscan pomp.

Fado is the traditional song of Portugal, just as flamenco is in Spain. The fado, originally known as the Brazilian fado, was a mixture of dance and song from Brazil in the late 1700s, namely the Spanish Fandango, Lundu (Baia), and the Fofa. When this new music reached Portugal, these dances and song came to a head with the black sailors and formed the Fado.

SWITZERLAND

The dances of eastern Switzerland are similar to those of Alpine Germany and Austria, the dances in the Western cantons are similar to those of France, and those in the South to Italy. Most Swiss dances are couple or group dances using the steps of popular ballroom dances of the nineteenth century: Mazurka, Waltz, Schottische, and Gallop. Perhaps because of the austerity of the Calvinist religion, not many traditional dances have survived, and many of the folk dances performed today are reconstructions based on traditional dance figures that were collected and set to either traditional tunes or especially composed ones. Very few ritual dances have remained, and those are usually danced at "driving out the winter" ceremonies, carnival, spring, and harvest celebrations. Swiss dances are more sedate and earthbound than their German counterparts. The Swiss folk dance movement has traditionally been closely allied with the Swiss Costume Association, which fosters every aspect of folk art.

Switzerland has no national ballet, but companies are attached to opera houses in Zurich, Bern, Basel, St. Gall, Lucerne, and Geneva. Modern dance came into the country with Rudolf von Laban setting up his Dance Farm near Locarno and later his school in Zurich. Dancer Charlotte Bara built herself the Teatro San Martino at Ascona and staged modern dance performances there. Independent modern dance companies have emerged, such as Compagnie Philippe Saire and the Compagnie DRIFT, one of the most interesting European ensembles.

RUSSIA, UKRAINE, AND BELARUS

Just before the turn of the century, in the 1890s, the center of ballet moved from France to Russia. There the renowned French-born choreographer Marius Petipa collaborated with composer Pyotr Ilyich Tchaikovsky on lavish story ballet spectacles that brought ballet to a pinnacle of technical virtuosity. These ballets included *Swan Lake*, *The Sleeping Beauty*, and *The Nutcracker*. Petipa also created works that continued to challenge dancers with their technical and artistic demands, including *La Bayadère Act II*, *Paquita*, and *Don Quixote*. In 1909, the Russian impresario Sergej Diaghilev brought together some of Russia's most talented dancers, choreographers, composers, singers, artists, and designers in his company, the

Ballets Russes. The troupe took Paris by storm as it introduced whole new aspects of classical ballet to the world. During its 20-year existence, Ballets Russes offered new scores by composers such as Igor Stravinsky, Sergei Prokofiev, Maurice Ravel, and Claude Debussy; décor and costumes by Leon Bakst, Aleksandr Benois, Pablo Picasso, Andre Derain, Georges Braque, Henri Matisse, Georges Rouault, and other major artists; choreography by Mikhail Fokine, Vaslav Nijinsky, Bronislava Nijinska, Leonide Massine, and George Balanchine; and dancers such as Nijinsky, Tamara Karsavina, and Anna Pavlova. The ballets included Fokine's *Scheherazade, The Firebird, Petrouchka,* and *Les Sylphides*; Nijinsky's *The Rite of Spring* and *L'Apres-Midi d'un Faune*; Bronislava Nijinska's *Les Noces* and *Les Biches*; and George Balanchine's *Apollo* and *Prodigal Son*.

In Russia herself, the conservatism of the directorate stifled new creativity. Great talents had to leave the country to develop their potential. After the Russian Revolution in 1917, Tsarist patronage was replaced by the State authority and avant-garde principles were developed, but by 1932 Socialist Realism demanded realistic stagings and politically correct themes. Opera houses were established in major towns and cities, but Moscow and Leningrad remained the centers of dance. In the late 1950s, Soviet ballet began to enjoy international prestige as the Bolshoi troupe and the Kirov troupe went on tours abroad. In the 1990s, under the new democracy, economic and political reforms have led to a radical decline in state funding for the arts, and many companies have to tour most of the time to sustain themselves.

Russia has also a long and lively folk dance tradition. Troika (meaning three-horse team or gear) is a widespread Russian folk dance, where a man dances with two women. The dancers imitate the prancing of horses pulling a sled or a carriage. Similar folk dances are known among other Slavic peoples, such as the Polish Trojak. Barynya is a fast Russian folk dance and music. The dancing was without special choreography and consisted mainly of fancy stomping and traditional Russian squatwork. There are a number of scenic, more refined versions of the dance. Traditional dances such as the Drobushki, Kamarinskaya, Kazachok, Khorovod, Trepak, and Yablochko are also widespread. Kamarinskaya is a Russian traditional dance that is mostly known today from the Russian composer Glinka's opus. Khorovod is an art form of the Eastern Slavs, a combination of a circle dance and chorus singing that goes back to ancient Greece.

SCANDINAVIA

Scandinavia is the common name for Denmark, Norway, and Sweden, with Iceland and Finland often included. Scandinavian turning dances usually consist of a turning figure and a resting figure. The oldest documented Scandinavian dances are called Bygdedans, meaning regional, country or village dances. There are several categories of Scandinavian dances. Gammaldans (old time dance), which includes the Hambo, Waltz, Schottische, Mazurka, and occasionally Tango, are dances known over most of the Scandinavian countries.

The Swedes separate dance into three main categories: Song dances (including song games and long dances); village dances, which include the Bygdedans and Gammaldans; folk dances (figure dances). Bygdedans are primarily danced to violin or Hardanger fiddle. Polska is a category of traditional Swedish dance form with three beats per measure and a wide variety of forms. Hambo is a form of Polska. Another form of Scandinavian dancing is group dancing, often done in a quadrille or square formation. In Sweden dance festivals in summer include Ranseter, Varmland in June, Musik vid Siljan, Falun, and Rattviksdansen Folklore Festival in July.

The Norwegians divide dance into four main categories: Bygdedans, Gammaldans or Runddans, Turdans, and Songdans. There are Springar, Gangar, Springleik, Springdans, Rudl/Rull, Pols, and Halling. Gammaldans or Runddans (old dance or round dance) are what we might call the ballroom dances of Scandinavia. Runddans describes the action of the dances. Dance couples usually turn clockwise while dancing and progressing counterclockwise around the dance space. European dances have become assimilated to Scandinavian culture and have taken on a character of their own.

People practicing folk dance are a small part of the population, mostly in clubs and courses or at local community centres. Historically the local Bygdedans would be found at events within a region, at May Day, midsummer, Jonsok, and Olsok, or St. Olaf's day or New Year. In Norway there is a community of people who travel to the various dance music *kappleik*(s) (meaning competitions and festivals). Some dance music festivals are part of an historical market week, such as Kongsbergmarken and Rorosmartnan in February.

The Royal Danish Ballet in Copenhagen has dominated Danish dance since the eighteenth century. The company was revived under Harald Lander's direction (1932–51) and gained a worldwide reputation. There are a couple of small modern dance companies despite lack of official support, such as the New Danish Dance Theatre and Uppercut Danseteater. Norway's only ballet company is the Norwegian National Ballet in Oslo, founded in 1945. Sweden has a long ballet tradition that goes back to the seventeenth century. The Gothenburg Opera Ballet, the company of Birgit Cullberg, and the Scandinavian Ballet are important companies.

TURKEY

Before World War II, theatrical dance in Turkey was present only in the form of touring foreign dance companies. In 1948, a national ballet school was set up in Istanbul. In 1968, the first work by a Turkish choreographer, Sait Sökmen, was performed, called Cark (The Wheel). In 1970 the Istanbul State Ballet was founded, and contemporary dance is represented by Modern Dance Turkey, founded in 1993 in Ankara.

Turkish folk dances have different characteristics based on region and location and are generally danced at weddings, journeys to the mountains in the summer, when sending sons off to military service, and during religious and national holidays. Many of the dagger, sword, and knife dances are expressions of male valour and courage. The best-known folk dances are the Bar, Halay, Horon, Kasik Oyunu, Kilic Kalkan, and Zeybek. Bars are dances performed by groups in the open, side-by-side, hand, shoulder, and arm-in-arm in 5/8 and 9/8 measures. They are spread, in general, over the eastern part of Anatolia. Halay is performed to a large extent in eastern, southeastern, and central Anatolia, and it is one of the most striking dances. It has a rich figure structure and varied rhythmic elements. Halays are mostly performed with drum-zurna combination as well as with kaval (shepherd's pipe), sipsi (reed), cigirtma (fife), or baglama (an instrument with three double strings played with a plectrum), or performed when folk songs are sung. Horon, or the round dance, is a typical folk dance of the Black Sea coastal area and its interior parts. Horons appear very different from the folk dances in other parts of the country with their formation of tempo, rhythm, and measure. Horon is performed by men only, dressed in black with silver trimmings.

Kilic Kalkan, the Sword and Shield Dance of Bursa, represents the Ottoman conquest of the city. It is performed by men dressed in early Ottoman battle dress who dance to the sound of clashing swords and shields without music. Zeybek is an Aegean dance of colorfully dressed male dancers, called "Efe," that symbolizes courage and heroism, The Zeybek dances, with their swashbuckling mood of adventure appropriate to the bandits who performed them. Zeybek dances are formed, in general, of 9/8 measures and have a variety of tempos such as very slow, slow, fast, and very fast. It is necessary to regard Turkish folk music and folk dances as two complementary aspects of one art form.

SPOON DANCE

Kasik Oyunu, the Spoon Dance, is performed from Konya to Silifke and consists of gaily dressed male and female dancers clicking out the dance rhythm with a pair of wooden spoons in each hand.

UNITED KINGDOM AND IRELAND

Great Britain and Ireland both have a longstanding tradition of ballet and modern dance, with theatrical dance dating back to the eighteenth century. In the nineteenth century, two London theaters, the Alhambra and the Empire, were leading in the development of dance. Other companies are the English National Ballet (founded in 1950), the Scottish Ballet (1969), and the Northern Ballet Theatre in Leeds. Modern Dance goes back to the influence of Martha Graham, who had visited London in the 1950s. Dance Umbrella, founded in 1978 by Van Bourne, is the country's most important company for new choreography.

Ninette de Valois was responsible for development of dance in Ireland through her eight years of collaboration with the Abbey Theatre (1926–34) in Dublin, where she staged some plays by W. B. Yeats. In 1945 the Cork Ballet Company was founded by Joan Denise Moriarty, who also founded the professional Irish Ballet Company in 1974, which later became the Irish National Ballet. Several groups teach and perform modern dance, the most well-known being John Scott's Irish Modern Dance Theatre.

England boasts a rich tradition of folk dances that are still widely practiced today. Morris dancing goes back to fertility rituals in pagan times. By beating sticks, waving handkerchiefs and jingling bells, evil spirits were to be chased away and the stamping of feet was supposed to stamp fertility out of the ground. Today, there are three predominant styles of Morris Dancing, and different traditions within each style named after their village of origin. The Cotswold Morris is a dance from the English Cotswolds, normally danced with handkerchiefs or sticks to embellish the hand movements. It consists of a dance group of six people, a musician, and a "fool," accompanied by a violin, a concertina, or a melodeon. The North West Morris is more military in style and often processional, while the dance style has characteristics of reel and country dances. The dancers' costumes are, in comparison to others, very colorful. The Border Morris from the English-Welsh border represents a simpler, looser, more vigorous style, normally danced with blackened faces in keeping with the mysterious winter festivities. The dances have often become complex, involving many invented and evolved steps, figures, and choruses.

Sometimes considered a type of Morris is the sword dance, which includes both Rapper Sword and Long Sword traditions. The Rapper Sword dance from Northumbria is performed with short swords—flexible spring steel "rappers" with two hilts—by five dancers. The Long Sword dance is a hilt-and-point sword dance from Yorkshire performed on Boxing Day or Plough Monday. Unlike many traditional dances in England, which are mainly performed by revival teams, Long Sword dances are often still performed by their own village teams.

There is also Hoodening, which comes from East Kent, and the Abbots Bromley Horn Dance, dating back to the eleventh century. Six of the twelve dancers in it carry the horns (reindeer antlers); they are accompanied by the musician playing an accordion or violin,

Maid Marian (a man in a dress), the Hobby-horse, the Fool (or Jester), a youngster with a bow and arrow, and another youngster with a triangle.

Maypole dancing is also still practiced widely. Dancers dance in a circle, each holding a colored ribbon attached to a central pole. By the movements of the dancers the ribbons are intertwined and plaited either on to the pole itself or into a web around the pole. The dancers may then retrace their steps exactly in order to unravel the ribbons. English Country Dance (ECD) is another form of folk dance, revived by Cecil Sharp. It is a social dance form that dates from the late sixteenth century. ECD continues today as a social dancing form, in Britain, the United States, and around the world. There are also descendants of ECD, such as Scottish country dance, contra dance, and perhaps square dance.

Céilí (cèilidh, céilidh) is a traditional Gaelic social dance gathering in Ireland and Scotland. Formerly, there were céilís in most town and village halls on Friday or Saturday nights and even now they are not uncommon in rural parts, especially the Gaelic-speaking regions. The general format of céilí dancing is the set. A set consists of four couples, with each pair facing another in a square or rectangular formation. Each couple exchanges position with the facing couple, and also facing couples exchange partners. About half of the dances in the modern Scots ceilidh are couple dances performed in a ring. The céilí has become a favourite at wedding parties all over the United Kingdom, together with jigs, reels, polkas and hornpipes as accompaniment. As a form of entertainment that gets everybody involved on the floor, the céilí is increasingly chosen as the culmination of wedding celebrations.

Irish step dancing (sometimes referred to as "Irish dance") is a type of recreational and competitive folk dance, often performed at céilís, that has been recently popularized by the world-famous *Riverdance* and *Lord of the Dance*. Whereas set dancing involves all present, whatever their skill, step dancing is usually reserved for show, being performed only by the most talented of dancers. An organized step dance competition is referred to as a *feis*. Tap dance was also influenced by Irish step dancing. Unlike soft-shoe dancing, hard-shoe dancing involves rhythmic and very fast striking of the floor with the tips of the shoes.

Scottish country dancing (SCD) is a form of social dance involving groups of mixed couples of dancers tracing progressive patterns according to a predetermined choreography. SCD is often considered a type of folk dancing, although it derives from the courtly dances of the Renaissance and, as a form of ballroom dancing, predates the more modern styles of the Quadrille as well as couple dances like the Waltz. It nearly died out and had to be revived in the 1920s. Scottish country dances are categorized as reels (including hornpipes), jigs, and strathspeys according to the type of music to which they are danced. The first two types (also called quick-time dances) feature fast tempos and quick, lively movements. The third type (strathspey) has a much slower tempo and a more formal, stately feel. The Strathspey is unique to Scottish country dancing. At Scottish weddings there is nearly always a dancing following the meal. Usually this takes the form of a ceilidh to live traditional music. The first dance is led by the bride and groom, followed by the rest of the bridal party, and finally the guests.

Highland dancing is one of two basic types of Scottish dancing that can be seen at nearly every modern-day Highland Games event. Highland dancing has much in common with ballet, with which it shares common roots in the classical dances of earlier times. In many ways, Highland dancing evolved from solo step dancing, but while some forms of step dancing are purely percussive in nature, Highland dancing involves not only a combination of steps but also some integral upper body, arm, and hand movements. Highland dancing should not be confused with Scottish country dancing, which is both a social dance like ballroom dancing and a formation dance like square dancing.

RESOURCE GUIDE

PRINTED SOURCES

Adshead-Lansdale, Janet, and June Layson. eds. *Dance History: An Introduction*. London: Routledge, 1994.

Allenby Jaffé, Nigel. *Folk Dance of Europe*. Kirby Malham, UK: Folk Dance Enterprises, 1990.

Anderson, Jack. *Ballet and Modern Dance: A Concise History*. Princeton, NJ: Princeton Book Company, 1992.

Au, Susan. *Ballet and Modern Dance (World of Art)*. London: Thames and Hudson, 2002.

Banes, Sally. *Writing Dancing in the Age of Postmodernism*. Hanover, NH: Wesleyan University Press, 1994.

Beliajus, Vyts. *The Dance of Lithuania*. Chicago: F. Summy, 1951.

Benbow-Pfalzgraf, Taryn, ed. *International Dictionary of Modern Dance*. Detroit.: St. James Press, 1998.

Billman, Larry. *Film Choreographers and Dance Directors: An Illustrated Biographical Encyclopedia with a History and Filmographies, 1893 through 1995*. Jefferson, NC: McFarland, 1997.

Carter, Alexandra. *The Routledge Dance Studies Reader*. London: Routledge, 1998.

Carter, Alexandra, ed. *Rethinking Dance History: A Reader*. London: Routledge, 2004.

Cohen, Selma Jeanne, and Katy Matheson, eds. *Dance as a Theatre Art: Source Readings in Dance History from 1581 to the Present*. Princeton, NJ: Princeton Book Company, 1991.

Cohen, Selma Jeanne, ed.. *International Encyclopedia of Dance*. Oxford: Oxford University Press, 1998.

Craine, Debra, and Judith Mackrell. *The Oxford Dictionary of Dance*. Oxford: Oxford University Press, 2000.

Dodds, Sherril. *Dance on Screen: Genres and Media from Hollywood to Experimental Art*. Basingstoke, UK: Palgrave, 2001.

Driver, Ian. *Tanzfieber: Von Walzer bis HipHop. Ein Jahrhundert in Bildern*. Berlin: Henschel, 2001.

Dunin, Elsie Ivancich. *Dance Occasions and Festive Dress in Yugoslavia*. Los Angeles: University of California Los Angeles, 1984.

Dziewanowska, Ada. *Polish Folk Dances & Songs: A Step by Step Guide*. New York: Hippocrene Books, 1999.

Felföldi, László. *Essays on Folk Music and Folk Dance of Central and Eastern Europe*. Budapest: Akad. K., 1994.

Flett, Joan, and Thomas M. Flett. *Traditional Dancing in Scotland*. London: Routledge and Kegan Paul, 1985.

Franks, A. H.. *Social Dance: A Short History*. London: Routledge and Kegan Paul, 1963.

Gurzau, Elba Farabegoli. *Folk Dances, Costumes and Customs of Italy*. Newark, NJ: Folkraft Publishing Company, 1969.

Hunt, Yvonne. *Traditional Dance in Greek Culture*. Athens: Centre for Asia Minor Studies, 1996.

Jaffé, Nigel Allenby. *Folk Dance of Europe*. Skipton: Folk Dance Enterprises, 1990.

Jankovic, Ljubica, and Danica Jankovic. *Dances of Yugoslavia*. London: Max Parrish & Co., 1952.

Koegler, Horst. *The Concise Oxford Dictionary of Ballet*, 2nd edition. London: Oxford University Press, 1982.

Lawson, Joan. *European Folk Dance*. London: Sir Isaac Pitman & Sons, 1962.

Reynolds, Nancy and Malcolm McCormick. *No Fixed Points: Dance in the Twentieth Century*. New Haven, CT: Yale University Press, 2003.

Rust, Frances. *Dance in Society*. London: Routledge and Kegan Paul, 1969.

Raffé, W.F. *Dictionary of the Dance*. revised edition. London: Barnes and Company, 1975.

Rinaldi, Robin. *European Dance: Ireland, Poland, and Spain*. Philadelphia:Chelsea House, 2004.

Sorrell, Walter. *The Dance Through the Ages*. New York: Grosset and Dunlap, 1967.

Sorrell, Walter. *Dance in Its Time*. New York: Columbia University Press, 1986.

White, Joan W., ed.. *Twentieth-Century Dance in Britain: A History of Major Dance Companies in Britain*. London: Dance Books, 1985.

Wingrave, Helen, and Robert Harrold. *Aspects of Folk Dance in Europe*. London: Dance Books, 1984.

WEBSITES

BalletTanz: Europe's Leading Dance Magazine. November 2006. Friedrich Berlin Verlagsgesellschaft mbH. Accessed November 2, 2006. http://www.ballet-tanz.de/. The companion site to the European dance magazine, *BalletTanz,* featuring articles dealing with the past, present, and future of dance and dancers.

Conrad, Jenni. *Introduction to Balkan Dance, Music and Costumes.* Accessed December 2, 2005. http://www.arts.wa.gov/progFA/balkandance/fabalkandance1.html. This site offers information covering a brief history of the Balkans and their dance traditions.

Critical Dance Forum and Ballet Dance Magazine. Updated October 2006. CriticalDance. Accessed November 2, 2006. http://www.ballet-dance.com/. A site focusing on ballet and other forms of expressive dance.

Culture Kiosque – The European Guide to Arts and Culture Worldwide. Updated November 2, 2006. Euromedia Group, Ltd. Accessed November 2, 2006. http://www.culturekiosque.com/dance/. A site with articles covering different performing and fine arts, including a section dedicated to dance.

Dance Magazine. Updated 2006. Dance Magazine, Inc. Accessed November 2, 2006. http://www.dancemagazine.com/index.php. Website for popular magazine dedicated to dance and the dancer's lifestyle.

Dancilla. Updated September 9, 2006. Accessed November 2, 2006.http://www.dancilla.com. Information about folk dances, videos, instructions, music, and costumes.

Estonian Song and Dance Festivals. Updated July 9, 2004. Accessed December 2, 2005. http://www.vm.ee/estonia/kat_174/pea_174/4645.html. A look at the history of Estonia's Song and Dance Festivals until 2004.

German Folkdancing. Updated November 11, 2003. Accessed December 2, 2005. http://www.germandance.org. General information on German folk dance in the United States.

Kyriacou, Charlie. *Greek Folk Dance Resource Manual.* Updated December 2004. Accessed December 2, 2005. http://www.filetron.com/grkmanual/. Documents different sources of information regarding Greek folk dancing.

List of Folk Dance Links Sorted by Origin. Updated 2005. Farlex, Inc. Accessed December 2, 2005. http://encyclopedia.thefreedictionary.com/List%20of%20folk%20dances%20sorted%20by%20origin.

Patsidou, Lena. *History and Evolution of Greek Dance.* Updated 2004. Accessed December 2, 2005. http://www.annaswebart.com/culture/dancehistory/introduction.html. A site with information about the origins of Greek dance.

Reusch, Amy. *Contemporary Modern Dance Companies.* Updated May 25, 2005. Accessed December 2, 2005. http://www.dancer.com/dance-links/modern.htm. Links of contemporary and modern dance companies.

Richoux, Donna. *Folk Dancing in the Netherlands.* Updated October 8, 2006. Accessed November 2, 2006. http://www.euronet.nl/~trio/. Provides links, information and recommendations for those looking to participate in a dance troupe, company, or class in the Netherlands.

Shapiro, Robert B. *Folk Dance Information.* Updated October 22, 2002. Accessed December 2, 2005. http://www.recfd.com/resources.htm. Links to different Internet sources that focus on the different genres of folk dance.

Square Dance and Round Dance in the Slovak Republic and in the Czech Republic. Updated April 15, 2002. Accessed December 2, 2005. http://www.square-dance.sk/.

Terleckaite, Jurate. *Short History of 20th Century Dance in Lithuania.* Updated August 2003. CriticalDance. Accessed December 2, 2005. http://www.criticaldance.com/features/2003/Lithuania_20030800.htm. An article giving a brief description of the role ballet played in twentieth-century Lithuania.

Volkstanz.at. Updated September 3, 2005. Accessed December 2, 2005. http://www.volkstanz.at/. A site dedicated to Austrian folk dance.

VIDEO/DVD

Billy Elliot: I Will Dance (2000). Directed by Stephen Daldry.

Burn the Floor (1999). Directed by David Mallet and Anthony van Laast.

Carmen (1983). Directed by Carlos Saura, starring Antonio Gades, Laura del Sol.

Celtic Tiger (2005). With Michael Flatley.

Dancing on Dangerous Ground (2000). Directed by Jeremy Sturt.

Explosive Dance (1998). Directed by Ross MacGibbon.

Feet of Flames (1997). With Michael Flatley.

Lord of the Dance (1997). With Michael Flatley.

Salsa & Amor (1999). Directed by Joyce Bunuel.

Zorba the Greek (1964). Directed by Michael Cacoyannis, starring Anthony Quinn and Alan Bates.

FASHION AND APPEARANCE

MALIN LIDSTRÖM BROCK

Since the Middle Ages, Paris has been the dominant fashion capital of the world, competing successfully with cities such as London, Milan, and lately, New York. The *Oxford English Dictionary* traces the word fashion in connection to dress back to 1576, but until the 1800s, fashion in Europe was largely synonymous with *haute couture*, which is French for skilled sewing or stitching. Before the introduction of mass-produced clothing, so-called *couturiers*, or master dressmakers, could be found in every larger European capital, working for the courts and the aristocracy. Ordinary men and women were dependent on tailors, seamstresses, or their own sewing skills for new clothes.

By the mid-1800s, the invention of the sewing machine and the popularity of women's fashion magazines meant that ordinary people could aspire to become fashionable faster. New fashion was depicted in magazines on so-called fashion plates, and suppliers like Vogue, Butterick, and Weldon provided diagrams and dress patterns to be used by seamstresses and at home. The European middle classes were growing wealthier, and it became important for them to show off their new status and prosperity through their physical appearance. The emergence of department stores also facilitated and influenced consumer habits. The first department store in Paris, the Bon Marché, opened as a small shop in 1838 and later evolved into a proper department store with a range of shops and wares under one roof. In stores like this one, members of the middle class could find everything they needed and catch up with the latest trends. Shopping for clothes and displaying one's fashion sense became part of many people's leisure pursuits.

At the end of the nineteenth century, clothes were mass-produced in garment factories, but *haute couture* still dominated European fashion trends. This continued into the first half of the twentieth century, when two world wars left their mark on how people dressed. The 1920s saw a new freedom in dress for women, as the bra gradually took the place of the corset and dress lines became straighter and more fluid. Hairstyles were shorter, and cosmetics were no longer hidden under the counter but sold openly in department stores. Sports also influenced fashion, and suntans became popular. In the 1940s, clothes were rationed and statutory rules regulated prices and limited the use of fabrics. In the United Kingdom, the so-called "utility mark" guaranteed that clothes had been produced according to wartime restrictions. In Germany, France, and Italy, women's fashion was interpreted and negotiated in the context of Nazi and fascist ideals of the female.

After World War II, French designer Christian Dior launched the "new look," a style that consciously refuted the rationing of fabrics. The 1950s also saw young Europeans inspired by American youth culture, particularly its music and dress. French couture's domination was finally broken in the 1960s when London suddenly set the fashion rules for the young. "Swinging London" became the catchphrase for a whole generation of designers and their customers. *Prêt-à-porter*, or ready-made designer clothes, were sold in smaller boutiques and designed by young British art school graduates who wanted to distance themselves from the fashion produced by the couturiers. Designs were youthful, informal, and included items like kaftans, miniskirts, and wide-brimmed hats. Second-hand clothing also became very popular. Youth culture eventually changed what everyone wore, and casual wear came to dominate popular dress. From the 1960s onward, the lifestyles of many young people could be categorized into various sub- and countercultures in which members shared the same interests, politics, ethnicity, or sociogeographical background. In many cases, participants dressed to differentiate themselves from the rest of society or from other groups.

In postwar Eastern and Central Europe, socialist governments struggled to dominate a consumer culture that, like the rest of Europe, took its cues from Paris and London. Western fashion was desired for its exclusivity and was frowned upon by authorities because of its capitalist connotations. The breakdown of the Soviet Union and a growing capitalist market in the 1980s led to a new freedom expressed in clothing and the development of a commercial fashion merchandising industry. The 1980s was also the decade when fitness training in gyms in the form of aerobics or weight lifting, became popular in Europe. In the 1990s, minimalism, a style characterized by discreet clothes and a noticeable lack of accessories, was the most prominent trend on the catwalks and in the streets.

In the early twenty-first century, high fashion is dominated by the *prêt-à-porter* industry while European cities such as Paris, London, and Milan are attracting both new and established talents. Italy has taken a step forward as an important force in fashion, and several talented designers have emerged from Belgium. American and Japanese designers are also making important contributions to the European fashion scene. The majority of fashion houses have been bought up by luxury goods conglomerates, and the houses' image and sales have been heightened by the appointment of new designers and the branding of perfumes and cosmetics. In some cases, the centralized ownership has led to friction with designers who say their creativity has been stifled by corporate directives. Despite this friction, the designs created in the couture houses are often considered more avant-garde than those of the *prêt-à-porter*. It is the *prêt-à-porter* that often inspires mass-produced fashion aimed at the so-called "high street," that is, neighborhoods that have a high concentration of fashion stores, such as the Champs-Elysées in Paris or Oxford Street in London. The globalization of popular culture means that new fashion spreads quickly among geographical and social groups, and it is becoming increasingly difficult to make national distinctions based on how people dress. Immigration, traveling, and newly introduced religions have also led to a cross-fertilization of styles and cultures that are largely independent of fashion marketing. Fashion is acknowledged, debated, and criticized on television and in newspapers, popular magazines, and academic journals. Museums regularly present fashion exhibitions that attract large crowds and much media attention. Advertising in women's magazines, and increasingly in magazines for men, is still the most effective way to reach fashion customers.

Some fashion magazines with small editions but an influential readership, such as Britain's *Face* and *i-D* and the continental magazines *Dutch* and *Purple*, have proven particularly important for the creation and dissemination of cutting-edge fashion. The combined efforts of their editors, photographers, and stylists have resulted in new and often controversial styles, such as the heroin chic look in the mid- and late 1990s. Celebrities also influence popular fashion. Contemporary fashion icons in Europe include British model Kate Moss, European royal princesses Mary of Denmark and Letizia of Spain, and the fictive characters in the American sitcom *Sex and the City*.

Home shopping, especially mail-order shopping, is popular in Northern Europe, and buying on the World Wide Web is on the increase. Local stores and boutiques compete with retailers who manufacture their own clothes at competitive prices. All large Western European retailers outsource their production. Poland and Bulgaria are some of the biggest clothing suppliers; however, China, Turkey, and Hong Kong top the list. Currently Europe is the largest market in the world for textile and clothing products. Europe is also the world's leading exporter of textiles and the third largest exporter of clothing. The large-scale production of clothes has grown to an enormous business, involving predictions, marketing, distribution, stores, and mail order. It has also led to the development of

THE BEAUTY IDEAL IN EUROPE

A very slender beauty ideal is typical for all Western industrialized countries. In the European Union, anorexia nervosa affects approximately 1 percent of girls and women between the ages of 12 and 25, but the disorder also occurs in men and older people.[1] Slimming products are sold throughout Europe for €95,500 million annually.[2] In 2002, almost 231 million Europeans attempted a diet, but only four million managed to keep their thinner figures for longer than a year.[3]

Obesity has become a new health problem. Greece and the United Kingdom have some of the highest rates of obesity in Europe with nearly a quarter of their populations affected. When the number of overweight people is also taken into account, several countries report that well over 50 percent of the population is affected.[4] And the problem is getting worse, especially in Eastern Europe.

academic programs focusing on fashion design, marketing, and merchandise development. Fashion studies can be separated into two further categories: historical and cultural studies of fashion. There is a seemingly endless stream of new fashion books, published mostly by university presses. Supplementing these books are popular books on fashion and appearance that cater to the general reader. European best sellers include *French Women Don't Get Fat* (2005) by French author Mireille Guiliano (which became an American best seller as well), *What Not To Wear* (2002) by British authors Trinny Woodall and Susannah Constantine (which is also a popular British television show, with a U.S. television version also on the air), and *Guide to Elegance: A Complete Guide for the Woman Who Wants to Be Well And Properly Dressed for Every Occasion* (2003), first published in the 1960s by French author Genevieve Dariaux.

AUSTRIA

Austria is a wealthy nation by EU standards, but retail sales are lower than in many other European countries and prices are comparatively high. In 2005, the total sales value for clothing was €7 billion, while the total sales value for cosmetics was over €1.2 billion.[5] Outdoor activities such as skiing, mountaineering, swimming, and hiking are popular leisure pursuits and play a large part in Austrians' physical fitness and general appearance. Nevertheless, about 14 percent of the women and 10 percent of the men are obese, and more than 50 percent of 15-year-old girls are, or feel that they should be, on a diet.[6]

In general, Austrians care a great deal about their appearance. Popular fashion is classic in style but includes elegant sportswear. Children do not wear uniforms in school and dress much like children and young people elsewhere in Europe, favoring designer brands like Nike and Levi's. Contemporary Austrian fashion owes many of its characteristics to traditional folk costumes, the so-called *Trachten*. For women, the *Tracht* consists of a close-fitting bodice with an apron in a different color, worn over a blouse of cotton and lace. Men wear *Lederhosen*, knee-length trousers made from leather, and jackets and hats made in a heavy wool fabric. They sometimes wear a *Steireranzug*, a man's garment made of gray or brown wool. Once worn by everyone in the country on weekends and for parties, these types of clothes are now worn mostly at weddings, balls, and for other formal occasions. They are generally mass-produced and come in many different fabrics and price ranges. The mass-produced woman's costume is referred to as a *Dirndl*. Tostmann is a well-known contemporary Austrian *Dirndl* maker. The revival of interest in traditional crafts and dress has led the *Steireranzug* to become a semi-official national costume for men. The *Tracht* has also inspired modern Austrian fashion to include some of its traditional elements, such as colorful embroidery and the use of *Loden*, a heavy and water-resistant wool fabric.

Contemporary Austrian fashion manufacturers that use *Tracht* elements in their collections include Sportalm and Geiger, whose knitted sweaters, updated Tyrolean jackets, and *Loden* coats are very popular both in Austria and abroad. Austria's most successful and well-known fashion designer is Helmut Lang. His minimalist and understated take on classic suits, jackets, trousers, and T-shirts is a good example of how far Austrian fashion has traveled from its *Tracht* origins. Other popular Austrian designers are Schella Kann, Michel Mayer, Hermine Span, and Wendy & Jim.

Austrian retailing is largely underdeveloped, and the country relies on foreign retailers and franchises. Popular European fashion retailers that cater to women, men, and children are Sweden's H&M, the United Kingdom's Marks & Spencer, and Holland's C&A. Austrian clothing and textile retailers include Don Gil (for men), Huber Holding and Palmers (underwear), and Mary Kindermoden (for women and children). Other successful Austrian exports are products by Wolford, one of the world's largest manufacturers of stockings. The company was founded in 1950 and was the first producer of hipster tights (1970), fashionable support tights (1977), and the lightest pantyhose in the world (1992). Austria exports clothing worth almost €2 billion annually.[7] The largest foreign markets for Austrian fashion and clothing are Germany, France, the United Kingdom, and Switzerland. Partly because of subcontracting overseas, China is the main supplier of clothes to Austria, accounting for 15.5 percent of all imports, followed by Hong Kong, Indonesia, and Bangladesh.[8]

The Austrian cosmetics supply is almost entirely dependent on foreign imports. Beiersdorf (Germany), L'Oréal (France), Schwarzkopf & Henkel (Germany), and Procter & Gamble (United States) are the most dominant cosmetics and toiletries companies. Cosmetics are often bought in grocery chain stores that are increasingly selling their own brands. Austrians are following the general European trend of buying "new" kinds of beauty products, such as sun protection and special skin-care products.

THE BALKANS: SLOVENIA, CROATIA, SERBIA AND MONTENEGRO, BOSNIA-HERZEGOVINA, MACEDONIA, AND ALBANIA

The Balkan countries are slowly recuperating from life under Communist rule and the after-effects of the war that broke up the former Yugoslavia into several autonomous states. There is very little information available on consumer habits and trade in the region, but there are significant differences among the six countries. Croatia and Slovenia have come relatively far in developing a market economy, whereas Serbia and Montenegro is the most recent and last country to begin the transition process. Large parts of the population in the Balkan region live below the poverty line. Money is spent on basic necessities, such as water, electricity, and rent, which leaves little to spend on clothes. In Croatia, 11 percent of the population is obese, and 46 percent is overweight.[9] The situation is similar in the other five countries, but participation in sports and other active leisure pursuits are becoming more popular. Cars are said to be one reason that many people are overweight. The number of cars since the war has increased by 400 percent.[10]

As the markets in the six countries grow, the demand for fashionable clothes is intensifying. Albanian sales of clothing and footwear increased by 27 percent between 2004 and 2005.[11] The attempt to satisfy the desire for fashion has taken a similar form in all the Balkan countries. Low-cost items from Asia and Turkey are offered to the majority of the population whereas a small group of wealthy people buys imported luxury brands from Europe. Popular foreign retailers in the region include the British Marks & Spencer and Miss Selfridges, as well as the Spanish Zara. This competition is a new experience for many domestic retailers who are not used to adjusting their production to consumer wishes.

In many Muslim communities in the Balkans, dress is still traditional and gender-specific. Women typically wear long skirts, cover their hair with a scarf, and, in some more conservative households, hide their face behind a veil. Nevertheless, the majority of people in the Balkans are influenced by trends from Western Europe, and it is not unusual to see young women wearing miniskirts or bikinis on the beach. The difference in dress is most pronounced between people in the countryside and those in large cities. International travel, the emergence of the Internet, and, in some areas, a local rave party culture have been particularly influential in the spreading of new trends.

Work dress codes are fairly conservative, depending on the company and the position. Men typically wear suits or sports jackets, and women wear skirts or trousers. Domestic fashion designers are trying their luck on the very competitive international market but suffer from a lack of sponsorship. The clothing and textile industries in the region export mostly to Europe but are facing strong competition from China. In 2004 Croatia exported clothes to the European Union valued at €495 million, which amounted to a quarter of the country's total exports to Europe.[12] The cosmetics and toiletries market in the Balkans is dominated by multinational companies such as Unilever (Netherlands/United Kingdom), Procter & Gamble (United States), and Beiersdorf (Germany). Dental care and bath products are the current best sellers.

BELGIUM

The Belgian population is divided into the Dutch-speaking Flemish in the north, the French-speaking Walloons in the south, and a large group of German speakers in the east. Despite this ethnic diversity, Belgian dress codes are discreet and neutral. The Belgian clothing market is strong. The annual sales value for clothing in 2005 was €9.6 billion, whereas the sales value for cosmetics reached almost €1.600 billion.[13] Despite a high awareness of weight-related health problems, 63 percent of Belgian men and 41 percent of Belgian women are overweight; 14 percent of men and women are classified as obese.[14] Belgian fashion is typically pan-European, and people generally dress well in public. In large cities such as Brussels and Antwerp, corporate culture dominates, and most people wear business-type suits to work. There is an emphasis on cleanliness and tidiness, and hair and general appearance is conservative in style. In less formal work settings, a more relaxed style is often seen, although extremely casual wear is saved for days at home.

Women in their forties and older are dressing in a more youthful fashion, and fashion for mature women has become more casual. Most young Belgians follow the latest trends in fashion. One of the most vivid Belgian subcultures in the late 1980s and 1890s emerged around rave dance parties. Raves inspired new fashions, including hooded sweaters, wide trousers, and high-tech fabrics. Belgium also has a small but active rap music scene; participants wear clothes similar to their American counterparts.

In contrast to but also complementing the conservative and neutral fashion of Brussels, Antwerp has seen the emergence of several fashion designers who have reached international stature. Usually referred to as the "Antwerp six," the designers include Dirk Bikkembergs, Ann Demeulemeester, Walter van Beirendonck, Dreis van Noten, and Martin Margiela. Their designs are typically simple but sophisticated clothes in high-tech fabrics. In 1990 Margiela presented clothes with the seams on the outside, causing a stir in the international fashion press. The design was quickly copied onto mass-produced fashion. Antwerp has developed into Belgium's fashion capital, mainly because of the fashion program at Antwerp Royal Academy of Fine Arts. Recent graduates of the Academy include a new generation of successful Belgian designers, such as Veronique Branquinho, Raf Simons, Anke Loh, and the duo A. F. Vandevorst. The number of fashion shops in Antwerp continues to grow, and in 1998 an international fashion center was founded in the city by the Flanders Fashion Institute.

Belgium has a well-developed clothing and textile industry. In 2002 the country exported clothing valued at €10.3 billion. In comparison, imports were valued at €6.7 billion.[15] Belgium also has a number of strong domestic clothes retailers, such as Olivier Strelli (for men and women), Chamail (knitted fashion), Archie Pell (for men and women), Cortina (shoes), and Van de Velde (underwear). They are in competition mainly with German, French, and Dutch companies. Not surprisingly, Belgian women favor a natural but wholesome look, both in clothes and makeup. Increasingly, they are buying cosmetics and skin-care products in supermarkets, where selections have been expanded to include more high-profile brands and products. L'Oréal (France) remains the leading company, followed by Beiersdorf (Germany) and Unilever (United Kingdom/Netherlands).

BULGARIA AND ROMANIA

Bulgaria and Romania are two of the poorest countries in Europe. Social inequality is widespread and is not expected to diminish in the near future. Attitudes about fashion are very similar in both countries. The demand for consumer goods such as clothes and cosmetics is low and concentrated in the larger cities where people have a relatively high disposable income. In 2005 the annual sales of clothes in Bulgaria was valued at €300 million with €178 million spent on cosmetics.[16] In Romania, sales of clothes and cosmetics amounted to €638 million and €367 million, respectively.[17]

About 11 percent of men and 16 percent of women in Bulgaria are obese, and more than half of the adult population is classified as overweight.[18] In Romania the situation is even worse. One-fourth of Romanian women are categorized as obese, and more than 60 percent of the population is overweight.[19] Lack of exercise, consuming the traditional fat-laden fare, the emergence of fast food, and an increase in television watching are said to be the culprits.

Until the twentieth century, everyday peasant dress in Bulgaria and Romania was a plainer version of their traditional folk costumes. The most common Bulgarian folk costume for women is still the *soukman* dress, which includes a richly embroidered pinafore, a chemise, an apron, and a belt. Men's clothes are typically white or black and consist of a tuniclike chemise and trousers. Romanian folk costumes are based around a unisex shirt, worn by both men and women. The men's version is usually knee-length, belted, and worn over trousers and leggings. Women wear a shorter version of the shirt tucked into a wide skirt protected by two aprons. Romania's early upper class did not find fashion inspiration in folk culture, but in the dress worn in the Ottoman Empire (Romania was a suzerainty). In the 1800s European dresses were accessorized with turbans and cashmere shawls before wearers adapted completely to Western dress. Bulgaria's proximity to the Ottomans and life under German rule had a similar influence on the dress of wealthy people.

Today folk costumes are a rare sight, except in societies specializing in the study of traditional dance and art. Under the rule of socialist president Ceausescu, Romanian clothes were seen as strictly functional, and emphasis was placed on conformity and anti-individualism. Violations of the official dress code, which dictated dress, hairstyle, and general appearance, were viewed as ideologically incorrect behavior. In Bulgaria the Communist government discriminated against ethnic minorities such as Turks and Tartars by banning their traditional dress. These days, dress codes in both countries are westernized and informal, especially among the younger generation, although older people tend to stick to the simplicity and functionality of earlier times.

The demand for fashionable clothes is high among young people and urban professionals, but a brand-new coat costs the average buyer about 80 percent of his or her monthly disposable income.[20] After the fall of Communism, shops and markets filled up with old-fashioned clothes, brought in by foreign importers who saw the high demand for Western clothing as an opportunity to get rid of old stock. Second-hand clothing, frequently imported from the West, has become popular among people who are looking for affordable ways to add a sense of fashion and style to their wardrobes. Some groups have stuck to their own fashion. More than one million Roma, or Gypsies, live in Romania and Bulgaria. Roma women typically wear wide pantaloonlike underwear with wide chintz skirts, colorful blouses, and head scarves. Younger women and girls sometimes wear modern clothing but keep their long hair.

Domestic fashion designers in Romania and Bulgaria cater to a very small segment of the market and suffer from a general lack of sponsorship. Once fashion was sold in small, privately owned, local shops or large Soviet-inspired supermarkets. More recently, the market has become vitalized by the arrival of foreign retailers. In Bulgaria Stambouli from Cyprus has set up several mini-department stores under the name Bonjour. There are no mail-order businesses or shopping malls in either country. Temporary "malls" are created through recurring bazaars and markets. Nevertheless, the number of shopping streets, arcades, and smaller stores is growing. The Bulgarian clothing sector employs around 40,000 people and consists of more than 3,200 companies.[21] This growth is largely the result of outsourcing by American and Western European fashion retailers. Consequently Bulgaria exports much of its production, mainly sweaters, blouses, and T-shirts, to the European Union. In Romania the garment and textile industries make up more than 25 percent of the country's total exports.[22] Italy, Germany, France, and the United Kingdom are the major export destinations.

Women in both countries increasingly buy cosmetics and skin-care products directly from salespeople visiting their homes, a market led by the American company Avon. Aroma Cosmetics is the largest domestic cosmetics company in Bulgaria; in that country, buyers are slowly shifting from economy brands to mid-price brands such as Estée Lauder (United States) and Hugo Boss (Germany). Popular products include anti-aging products and anti-cellulite creams. In Romania, basic toiletries such as toothpaste, shampoo, and bath products still account for almost half of all cosmetics sales.

THE CZECH REPUBLIC

The transition from life under the Soviet Union to membership in the European Union has been economically and politically turbulent, but the Czech Republic has fared better than many of its Central and Eastern European neighbors. The standard of living for most Czechs has increased significantly, and people are spending more money on clothes and beauty products. In 2005 annual sales reached €8.4 billion for clothing and €960 million for cosmetics and toiletries.[23] Clothes are still expensive, and wages are comparatively low. On average, a woman must spend almost half her disposable monthly income for a winter coat.[24] Like most Europeans, Czechs favor a slim and healthy physique, and Czech women are known throughout Europe for their beauty. The former model Paulina Porizkova, a beauty icon of the 1980s, and supermodel Karolina Kurkova are both Czech. Unfortunately more than 26 percent of Czech women are obese, and more than 60 percent of adults are overweight.[25] In the Czech Republic, 15-year-old girls are very concerned about their weight; 67 percent have been on a diet or believe that they should be.[26]

The Czechs have a long history of interest in fashion. In the second half of the nineteenth century, women's clothes were influenced by romantic feelings of patriotism. When department stores sprang up in Prague, Czechoslovakia's first fashion magazine, *Lada*, tried to reconcile new fashions with traditional Czech folk costumes but soon gave up in favor of complete conformity to European fashion. Men's clothes were the first to be mass-produced. By the end of the nineteenth century, women's so-called "top clothes," that is, jackets and raincoats, were also machine-made on an industrial scale. Under Soviet rule, attempts were made to "re-educate" Czech women, and new fashion magazines were published under strict ideological control. Plain and functional were the two watchwords. Women reacted by making their own clothes, and Western patterns from Burda and Vogue became very popular. Today Czech fashion is completely westernized, although a certain simplicity can be discerned among the older generation who grew up under Communist rule. Czechs usually dress informally at work and at home and rarely wear suits. Men prefer sports jackets or, depending on the work, blue overalls. Exceptions are employees of big or international organizations; their dress codes lean toward a more general corporate style.

Popular international retailers include the British Marks & Spencer, the Dutch C&A, and the French Kookaï. Bata, a well-known and popular Czech shoe retailer, can also be found in other countries. In the Czech Republic, it is customary to remove one's shoes in the hallway of homes and slip into a pair of house shoes or *bačkory*. Czechs are very brand conscious, and department stores in larger cities sell upscale fashions, including Gucci, Dolce & Gabbana, and Calvin Klein. In the 1980s, exclusive fashion boutiques kept their doors locked even when they were open for business, admitting only Western tourists and wealthy Czech customers. Contemporary domestic fashion designers include Tatiana Kovarikova and Monika Drapalova. The country's clothing exports still exceed its imports, but increased labor costs mean that the industry has met with competition from China and other Eastern European countries where labor is cheaper. Czech women prefer foreign brands of cosmetics and toiletries, but the domestic companies Astri Praha and Setuza are also popular. A growing preoccupation with keeping up a youthful appearance means that Czechs are buying more anti-aging products, firming creams, and makeup products.

ESTONIA, LATVIA, AND LITHUANIA

Estonia, Latvia, and Lithuania are commonly referred to as the Baltics. The three countries were annexed by the Soviet Union after World War II, and the domestic clothing industries ended up under strict Soviet ideological control. Since independence in the early 1990s, people in the Baltic states have become more interested in fashion. No trade statistics exist on the sales value of clothes and cosmetics in any of the Baltic countries, but it is safe to assume that both have increased dramatically in the last two decades. Despite low wages, young people like to keep up with Western European and American fashion trends. Generally people dress more formally than in the neighboring Scandinavian countries, and clothes in the workplace confirm traditional gender roles. Women frequently wear skirts and high heels, even in winter; men prefer suits or sports jackets. Status is important, but the wearing of luxury brands is still reserved for the few. Of the three nationalities, Estonians dress most like Scandinavians, and the Lithuanians dress most conservatively. Traditional folk costumes are more frequently worn in Lithuania than in the other two countries. As with most European folk costumes, Lithuanian dress differs from region to region. The women's dress typically consists of a skirt, blouse, an apron decorated with embroidery, and amber jewelry. Men wear trousers, a shirt, and a vest.

More than 50 percent of men and 55 percent of women in Estonia are overweight, and in Latvia 10 percent of men and 17 percent of women are obese.[27] The prevalence of obesity is higher in Lithuania than in the other two countries. From 65 to 75 percent of Lithuanians are overweight or obese, but these numbers are thought to have declined in recent years.[28]

Foreign retailers such as Germany's Hugo Boss, Spain's Mango and Zara, and Italy's Benetton have entered the Baltic market. Department stores are very popular, especially in the capitals. Finland's Stockmann has recently opened a large store in Riga, Latvia. Domestic fashion designers are becoming more numerous, but they still struggle to establish themselves outside their respective countries. Juozas Statkevièius is one of Lithuania's most famous designers. The garment industry in the Baltic countries caters mainly to foreign retailers, such as Zara (Spain), H&M (Sweden), Kappahl (Sweden), and KarstadtQuelle (Germany). The industry employs about 120,000 workers, and half of these come from Lithuania.[29] In Estonia and Latvia, about 16 percent of all employed persons work in the fashion industry, compared to 19 percent in Lithuania.[30] More than 80 percent of the clothes made there are exported to the European Union.[31] The cosmetics and toiletries market in the region is dominated by L'Oréal (France), Procter & Gamble (United States), and Beiersdorf (Germany). Hair-care products are especially popular among Baltic women.

FRANCE

For many, France is synonymous with impeccable style and high-quality fashion. This reputation is also reflected in its sales. In 2005, the country's total sales value for clothing was €39.9 billion and €10.5 billion for cosmetics.[32] True to stereotype, French women buy more accessories and perfume than other Europeans. Perfume is also a big export product. The total sales value for fragrances was €1.9 billion in 2005.[33] The French population as a whole is getting older, and more people live in single-person households. This group consists of socially active people with relatively high wages who spend a lot of their money on clothes and cosmetics. Although many French people are buying expensive quality items, the same people are also buying cheaper goods, such as supermarket cosmetics and clothing.

The beauty ideal includes a very slim physique, but overweight people in France constitute about 35 percent of the adult population.[34] When the entire population is considered, 11 percent are obese.[35] In 2002 the French spent €13.8 billion on diet products.[36] French people typically pay much attention to their own and others' appearances. Clothes are seen as a reflection of the wearer's social status. Popular fashion for women is feminine and classic, whereas French men in corporate jobs dress much like their Belgian neighbors. Suits are typically dark, even in summer. Men shop for comfort and luxury, and British-inspired styles are very popular. Sportswear for everyday use is worn mostly by children. French urban street fashion is inventive and individual. The *culture métissée*, or "hybrid culture," of young French men and women from various ethnic backgrounds has resulted in new styles. In the early 1980s, so-called *sapeurs*, groups of young male Congolese immigrants, turned fashion into an obsession by wearing only the latest Parisian couture or convincing knockoffs. The brand Xuly Bët by designer Lamine Kouyate mixes African dress and Parisian thrift-shop finds. Recent freestyle sports like *le parkour*, or free-run, have popularized high-tech sportswear. In March 2005 the French government banned religious clothing from public schools, including girls' head scarves, causing protests from both Muslim and Sikh communities.

The French industry's influence over international fashion trends goes back to medieval times. France's early monarchy and strong government encouraged the establishment of professional guilds in Paris. During the reign of Louis XIV, a luxury goods market was developed that helped secure France's reputation as a producer of quality items. Although the guilds were officially dissolved by the 1800s, to this day Paris remains a center for excellent taste, workmanship, and style. In 1945 the magazine *Elle* was launched, and it is still the most popular fashion magazine in France. In 1947 Christian Dior introduced his so-called "new look," a style defined by a dress with a widely flared skirt and a wasplike waist. It was quickly copied by mass manufacturers and became very popular. French fashion icons of the 1960s included actress Brigitte Bardot as well as singers Jane Birkin and Françoise Hardy. Popular French fashion producers are Chanel, Dior, Yves Saint Laurent, Louis Vuitton, and Hermès. Yves Saint Laurent's feminine take on the male suit has become a fashion classic. Vuitton bags and Hermès silk scarves and leather goods are best-selling status symbols among wealthy French women. Louis Vuitton belongs to France's leading clothing company, Louis Vuitton Moët Hennessy (LVMH), which employs 56,000 people worldwide and had gross sales of €12,600 million in 2004.[37] LVMH is a luxury goods conglomerate that also sells perfumes, watches, and wine. Popular clothing retailers include domestic low-price companies Monoprix, Prisunic, and Etam as well as Spain's Zara, Sweden's H&M, and Italy's Benetton. Many French women also buy their clothes from small boutiques or department stores. La Redoute is France's largest mail-order company for clothes; it regularly hires well-known French designers such as Jean-Paul Gaultier and Sonia Rykiel to design small collections for its catalogs. Clothes are increasingly being manufactured in countries like Tunisia and Morocco where wages are low. French women use color cosmetics more than other European women. As the population grows older, the French also spend more money on skin care, especially anti-aging creams. Recent best sellers also include sun protection products. The heat wave in 2003 meant that the French also spent more money on bath products and deodorants. Men's products show particular growth. French cosmetics company L'Oréal is the world's largest cosmetics firm and the most popular one in France. It manufactures mainly skin-care products, perfumes, and toiletries, and includes popular brands such as Biotherm, CCB, Cacharel, Garnier, Helena Rubinstein, Kérastase, Lancôme, and Shu Uemura.

GERMANY

In 2005 Germany's total sales value for clothing was €58.8 billion, which puts it in the lead of the European market.[38] The fashion market is diverse, and Germans have access to a wide variety of clothes in different price ranges. Typically a German woman spends around

20 percent of her monthly disposable income on a coat in a mid-price range.[39] The average age of Germans is rising, and German clothes manufacturers are increasingly taking into account the tastes and preferences of older customers. Atelier Goldner Schnitt and Afibel are two brands that cater exclusively to the elderly.

Obesity rates in Germany are high. More than 22 percent of men and women are clinically obese, and over 75 percent of men and 59 percent of women overweight, which makes the country's weight problem one of the most serious in Europe.[40] In 2002 Germans spent €9.55 billion on diet products.[41] Despite this, Germans favor a healthy physique, and a sporty, natural look is often preferred to a more visibly "made-up" face.

Work dress codes are casual, with the exception of people in corporate finance and similar careers. Suits are rarely worn even in so-called white-collar professions. Mainstream German tastes lean toward simplicity and discretion and often include sportswear elements. When Germans dress up, they tend do so with the intention of not sticking out too much. Young Germans dress very casually. Children are brand conscious and some sports labels have achieved an almost cultlike status among older children and youth. Popular names are Adidas, Puma, Nike, and Levi's. Another trend in Germany is the fashion worn by young political activists. The typical clothes worn by these groups are baggy jeans, hooded sweaters, and long scarves. Dreadlocks and body piercing are other common trademarks. In 2005 so-called "terrorist chic" fashion was debated in the German press. The style includes military parkas and T-shirts covered in revolutionary symbols. Critics objected to the fashion in reviews of an art exhibition, "Regarding Terror: The RAF Exhibition," and argued that both phenomena glorified terrorists by turning them into popular icons. Fashion in Germany has been politicized before. In the 1930s the Nazi government began a boycott of Jewish-owned department stores in Berlin and Vienna. The boycott was the first step in the so-called "Aryanization" of the German and Austrian clothing industries, and it ended with the government's confiscation of Jewish property and deportation of its owners. This caused an abrupt end to the prominence of Berlin and Vienna as fashion capitals.

After the war, the clothing industry in East Germany was regularized by the state. In 1952 the Institut für Kleiderindustrie (Institute for Clothing Industry) was founded in an attempt by the East German government to gain complete control over production and design. Clothes were made with simplicity and practicality in mind. In West Berlin, independent designers were free to establish their own houses and brands. The 1970s saw the development of gay and lesbian subcultures that found fashion inspiration in the punk music scene, leather fetishism, and the cabarets of the 1930s. Today Berlin still represents anti-establishment fashion with an edge. More conventional but internationally known German fashion brands include Escada, Strenesse, Joop, and Hugo Boss. Jill Sander is Germany's best-known designer, with the exception of Karl Lagerfeld, who is stationed in Paris and also designs for Chanel. Labels in the mid-price range include Etienne Aigner (clothes and accessories for women), Adidas-Salomon (sportswear), and Peter Kaiser (shoes).

Germany has the largest home shopping market in Europe; it accounts for more than 5 percent of all retail sales in the country.[42] The main e-shop retailers are KarstadtQuelle and Otto, which dominate almost 50 percent of the e-market.[43] These days more people are shopping to suit their exact preferences by mixing high-end products and cheaper goods. The German shopping center Centr O is the biggest in Europe, and factory outlets are becoming very popular. Germany subcontracts most of its clothing manufacturing abroad and imports nearly half of all the clothes produced in Eastern Europe. The country's other main garment supplier is China. German women also prefer a fresh and clean feeling when it comes to cosmetics and toiletries. Germany has two of the three largest producers of

THE POPULARITY OF H&M

Swedish clothing company H&M (Hennes & Mauritz) is one of Europe's most popular chain stores. It designs cheap but trendy clothes, mainly for men and women between eighteen and forty-five. It also produces children's clothing and its own brand of cosmetics. The company operates over 1200 stores in more than thirty countries and continues to expand. Germany is H&M's biggest market and accounts for nearly 30 percent of its sales.[44] More than half of its clothing is made in Asia; the rest is manufactured primarily in Europe. Founder Erling Persson opened the first women's clothing store in 1947, naming it Hennes (Swedish for "hers"). He later bought the hunting and men's clothing store Mauritz Widforss. In 2000, the company opened its first U.S. store on Fifth Avenue in New York, and there were long lines on opening day. Design collaborations have taken place between H&M and well-known *prêt-à-porter* designers Karl Lagerfeld (2004) and Stella McCartney (2005).

cosmetics and toiletries in the world: Beiersdorf, which produces Nivea (hand and body care) and Schwarzkopf (hair products). Products that promote wellness and health are particularly popular.

GREECE

Greece is a Mediterranean country that includes many small islands, where a large part of the population lives. In 2005 the sales value was €8.374 billion for fashion and €1.09 billion for cosmetics.[45] Sales figures suggest that Greeks are buying more clothes than they used to. The tourists that come to the islands every summer give the impression that Greeks wear mostly shorts and T-shirts, but domestic dress codes are semiformal, and the older generation dresses very traditionally and in accordance with the teachings of the Greek Orthodox church. Widows typically wear head scarves and dress in black. Older men on the islands wear traditional fishermen's garb that includes shirts and knitted sweaters. The intense heat in summer means that daytime clothes are less formal than evening wear. Most young women prefer body-hugging feminine clothes, whereas many men wear trousers and short-sleeved shirts. Greek people like to dress up, and weddings are typically lavish affairs. The groom generally wears a dark suit, and the most common bride's gown is wide-skirted and covered in white lace. School uniforms are mandatory, and children often dress up in Greek folk costumes at national celebrations.

The most popular leisure pursuit is walking, or just taking a stroll, which also includes meeting up with friends and going out for dinner. Greece and Cyprus have the highest obesity rates in Europe. Studies suggest that as many as 36 percent of the women are obese and more than 75 percent of the total population is overweight.[46]

The retail company Sprider, a subsidiary of Hatziioannou Holdings, sells casual wear for the whole family and operates several outlets. Sprider sells its own products, but it also sells brands such as Adidas (Germany) and Fruit of the Loom (United States). Sex Form is a popular domestic lingerie manufacturer that also caters to Petit Elephant (luxury children's underwear) and Aline (underwear). Popular foreign clothes retailers include Zara (Spain), Gant (United States), and French Connection UK (United Kingdom). Contemporary Greek fashion designers are adding such classic Greek elements to their designs as clothes that are draped around the body. Deux Hommes, Angelos Fretzos, and Sofia Kokosalaki are recurring names in the international fashion press. The Greek clothing and textiles industry is export-oriented. In the last few years, many of the industry's jobs have been lost to countries where labor costs are lower. Greek women stick to basics when buying cosmetics and toiletries. Shampoo, bath products, and dental hygiene products are among the most popular items, but there is also a growing demand for more exclusive skin-care and sun protection products. L'Oréal (France) dominates the sector, followed by Unilever (United Kingdom/Netherlands) and Procter & Gamble (United States).

HUNGARY

Since the fall of Communism, the standard of living in Hungary has improved, and the market for clothes and cosmetics has increased dramatically. Yet social inequality is on the rise, and Hungarian clothing consumption is only about 40 percent of the European average.[47] In 2005 the total sales value was €858 million for clothing and €650 million for cosmetics and toiletries.[48] Like so many people in Central Europe, a lot of Hungarians are overweight, and more than 20 percent of men and women are obese.[49] Dress codes depend on the workplace, but Hungarians tend to dress semiformally or even casually at work. In summertime, many women prefer body-hugging, revealing clothes. Children do not wear school uniforms. Young people dress fashionably and are very brand conscious. A lively music culture has resulted in alternative fashion similar to that found in large cities such as Berlin, Paris, and London. The desire for fashionable clothes can also be explained by restrictions on clothing once imposed by the Communist government. Despite these restrictions, Hungarians have always found ways to protest silently through dress. In the sixteenth century, the country's domination by the Austrian Habsburgs resulted in a nationalistic revival that was frequently expressed through the wearing of Hungarian folk costumes. In an attempt to support the emerging domestic textile industry, the Hungarian aristocracy of the 1840s wore dresses made from domestic textiles. After World War I, Hungarians in Romania wore clothes and fabrics in the Hungarian national colors to protest against Romania's incorporation of the once Hungarian regions in which they lived. The Communist government became extra sensitive to any kind of opposition through clothing after the 1956 Hungarian uprising. A revolutionary pin on a coat lapel could cost a student his or her place at university.

The everyday use of traditional folk costumes disappeared in the early twentieth century when factory-produced items took the place of homemade garments. These changes were pragmatic as increasing numbers of men and women left the countryside to look for work in the cities, work that required other types of dress. Men typically wore overalls, loden coats, and cloth cap berets, except in the 1950s, when small groups of men dared to wear the so-called "teddy boy" look made popular by British and American young men. Today Hungarians are free to dress as they please. The imminent arrival of international retailers such as H&M (Sweden), C&A (Holland), and Zara (Spain) will expand their choices further. Two-thirds of the Hungarian population live in cities, and that is where most new shops are opening up, in traditional locations like Budapest's Váci Utca. Factory-outlet malls are found in the outskirts of towns and larger cities. Between 1998 and 2002, the market for cosmetics and toiletries increased by 42 percent.[50] Half of all cosmetics are imported. The main suppliers are Unilever (United Kingdom/Netherlands), Procter & Gamble (United States), and Beiersdorf (Germany). Color cosmetics and skin care are popular women's products, whereas Hungarian men are increasingly buying deodorants, mostly as a result of intense advertising on billboards and television. Specialist cosmetics stores such as Yves Rocher (France) and Lush (United Kingdom) are also gaining more customers, but Hungarians still buy most of their beauty products in the supermarket.

ITALY

Italians are famous throughout Europe for their fashion sense and high-quality products. The country is the world's biggest exporter of high-fashion clothing and one of Europe's main exporters of general clothing and textiles. In 2002 the total sales value for clothes was €41.586 billion and €8210 billion for cosmetics and toiletries.[51] Great weight is put on *fare la bella figura*, loosely translated as making a favorable impression, which extends to the clothes a person wears. Italians tend to make social judgments based on people's sense of style and the quality of their clothes. This is important in all social situations. Work suits are generally dark in neutral muted colors. Women wear makeup daily, take great care with their hair, and tend to sacrifice comfort for fashionability. Prominent display of jewelry is popular and still considered a sign of prosperity. Neutral colors, such as black, brown, navy, cream, and white, are popular for all age groups. Young Italians are very fashionable and quick to jump on new trends. Italy is predominantly Catholic, and religion still influences what people wear, especially for worship and in mourning. In northern Italy, fashion is more businesslike than in the poorer—but less conservatively dressed—southern parts.

Obesity rates are fairly low, less than 10 percent of the population.[52] In 2002 Italians spent €14.1 billion on diet products.[53] Beauty standards are conventional but rigid; a suntan, well-kept hair, and a shapely figure are considered beautiful on both women and men. The contemporary Italian fashion industry owes much of its present success to American investors and the work of a single man, Marchese Giovanni Battista Giorgini. In 1951 Giorgini brought all the leading Italian designers of the day together in Milan, where their creations were presented to international buyers and the world fashion press. Today Italian fashion houses such as Versace, Dolce & Gabbana, Giorgio Armani, Pucci, Salvatore Ferragamo, and Gucci are well-known luxury-goods producers. Marni is a privately owned fashion house whose original and wearable creations have become very popular among young Hollywood actresses and other wealthy women. Other popular Italian fashion houses are Krizia, Cerruti, Trussardi, Missoni, and Romeo Gigli.

As would be expected, Italian companies dominate the clothing industry in Italy, whereas foreign companies dominate the cosmetics and toiletries counters. The majority of clothes are still made in Italy, but much of the production is outsourced to countries with lower labor costs. Benetton (for men, women, and children) is a very large fashion retailer of clothing in the mid- to low-price range. Other domestic mid-price companies are Moschino (for women), Agnona (for women), and Loro Piana (for men and women). Fashion outlets are very popular and are situated in close proximity to large cities or production sites. Perfumes and colognes are best-selling products among both men and women. Despite a slowing economy, Italians still spend money on expensive beauty and hygiene products. These purchases are made mostly in pharmacies and drugstores. L'Oréal (France) is the dominant cosmetics company in Italy; it produces some of its products near Turin, employing 20,000 people.[54] Other large cosmetics and toiletries companies are Procter & Gamble (United States) and Lever Fabergé (United Kingdom/Netherlands).

THE NETHERLANDS

The Netherlands is one of the most ethnically diverse countries in Europe. The traditional folk costume, typically worn by the commercially created Dutch "cheese girl," is used at festive events by a quickly diminishing segment of the population and is predicted to be entirely extinct in about twenty years. At present, the largest group of regular costume wearers, around 1000 people, live in the conservative eastern Dutch village of Staphorst. In 2002 the annual sales value for clothes was €6.4 billion, with €1.48 billion for cosmetics.[55] Business dress in the Netherlands is semiformal but depends on the workplace and the position of the employee. Generally the higher people are in the social hierarchy, the more informal and individual is their dress. Like the Belgians, the Dutch prefer a clean and tidy-looking appearance, and like the Germans, they do not like to draw too much attention to themselves. A strong sense of egalitarianism also contributes to discretion in dress. Wealth and privilege are not usually displayed through clothes.

Sports and leisurewear is increasingly worn for all occasions, including work, and a growing number of sportswear consumers are over thirty-five years old. Practicality and high quality are favored over quick fashion fads. Dutch children are becoming more brand conscious, and designer collections made especially for children by Versace, DKNY, and Dolce & Gabbana can now be bought in several large cities. The Dutch lifestyle is very healthy, and obesity rates are at a low 10 percent of the population.[56] Beauty ideals are based on looking natural and healthy, but the market for cosmetics and toiletries has grown by 29 percent in the last five years.[57]

The clothing market is highly fragmented, and the Dutch have a large selection of fashion retailers from which to choose. An increase in the number of one-person households has also increased sales in fashion and cosmetics. The majority of retailers are foreign, and popular stores include H&M (Sweden). Dutch C&A is one of the largest fashion retailers in Europe. Imports account for about 80 percent of available products, but many imports are the products of Dutch companies that have outsourced their production to countries with low labor costs.[58] Other domestic fashion retailers include sportswear companies Bemontex, Campri Leisure Dynamic, Fros International, Sport Service Benelux, and Texton Fashion.

Dutch designers of the 1960s were conservative in style and designed mostly classic clothes for older women. Today the most famous designers in the Netherlands are the design duo Victor & Rolf, whose clothes are inspired by the arts, the theater, and deconstructive fashion of the 1990s. Dutch women are experimenting more with hair color, which has increased sales of colorants and special shampoos. Color cosmetics are also popular products. Dutch men are concerned with their image and are buying more skin-care and body products than before. Most Dutch people buy foreign-brand cosmetics and toiletries in drugstores, such as the Dutch drugstore chain Kruidvat.

POLAND

A third of the Polish population is under eighteen, and young people are the country's main fashion customers. On average, Polish buyers of fashion have a disposable income that is only 40 percent of their Western European counterparts.[59] A mid-price winter coat will cost a woman around 60 percent of her disposable monthly income.[60] In 2005 the sales value for clothes was €4.2 billion with €1.9 billion for cosmetics and toiletries.[61]

The elderly population in Poland dresses conservatively and discreetly. The Polish favor a formal dress code at work and prefer traditional suits to sports jackets. Women often wear skirts or dresses. Obvious displays of wealth are generally frowned upon. The beauty ideal in Poland is feminine and requires high maintenance. The most recent study (1996) of obesity in Poland reported that around 10 percent of the population is obese.[62] Probably that figure is much higher. Poland lacks a tradition of regular exercise, and the consumption of alcohol and fatty foods is high.

Although Poland has often been under the control of foreign governments, the country developed its own folk costumes quite early. In the 1600s a national costume, inspired by

Slavic dress, came into existence. The *jerkin*, a caftan that can also be found in Finnish and Iranian folk costumes, is still an integral part of the male regional dress. Folk costumes are still worn for special occasions, such as church processions, village feasts, and weddings. The female costume consists of an embroidered blouse under a velvet corset and a plain or flower-patterned skirt covered by a linen or tulle apron. Men's costumes include a jerkin and wide white trousers adorned with blue or red stripes and held up by a broad leather belt. The outer dress is a coat decorated with trimmings and fringes. The *rogatywka*, a cap adorned with a peacock's feather, and the *magierka*, another type of hat, are sometimes part of the outfit.

After World War II, Communism largely determined fashion trends. Nearly half the Polish work force consisted of women whose clothes were designed with functionality and durability in mind. Perhaps as a result, Polish women now take great pride in their looks and like to emphasize their femininity. Most lingerie sold in Poland is produced domestically and sells in the mid- to low-price ranges. Popular and fashionable lingerie brands are International Wieslaw Jonczyk, Lemax Lingerie, Corin, Gorsenia, and PIK. Popular foreign brands include Chantelle, Maidenform, Calvin Klein, and Passionata. About fifty foreign fashion retailers have established shops in Poland. Some of the most popular are British women's wear brands Part Two, River Island, and Wallis, and Sweden's H&M. Other popular brands are Italy's Esprit and Spain's Zara. Second-hand clothing is also very much sought after.

A recent slump in the Polish economy has meant that cheaper cosmetics and toiletries are currently among the best-selling products. This might explain why Poles are buying fewer deodorants and men's grooming products. Direct sales are becoming more popular, with the American company Avon in the lead. Avon's best-selling products in Poland are color cosmetics and nail- and skin-care merchandise. Procter & Gamble (United States) still sells the most products overall, mainly in hair care and oral hygiene. Polish women buy the majority of their cosmetics and toiletries in supermarkets and no longer buy such items from drugstores or outdoor markets. As the Polish become more prosperous, sales of so-called "new products," such as sun-care products and depilatories, are expected to rise.

RUSSIA, UKRAINE, AND BELARUS

The European part of the former Soviet Union is a growing market for fashionable clothes. In 2005 the total sales value for clothes in Russia was €15.34 billion, whereas cosmetics sold for €6.78 billion.[63] The same year, the total sales value for clothing in Ukraine amounted to around €1.56 billion.[64] Belarus lacks statistical information on its clothing and cosmetics sales. The three countries are undergoing a phase of dramatic social upheaval. Social inequality is widespread, and many people can only afford to spend money on absolute essentials. Because of illegal trade and incomplete statistical information, it is difficult to know just how the wealth in the three countries is distributed and to how much of it there is.

Popular fashion ranges from luxury goods to inexpensive basics. As in many former Eastern European countries, Russia, Ukraine, and Belarus have developed a clothing market that is dominated by counterfeit products and unfashionable goods, and many people still have not caught up with current European trends. A small but profitable part of the market provides luxury clothing to the new upper classes. For most groups, elegance and formality are the favored watchwords. Many people wear suits to work, but work dress can also be a blue overall. Generally colors are muted and discreet. An exception was the bright orange worn to support Ukrainian president Yushchenko during the country's general elections in 2004. Schools often have a uniform requirement. Young people covet American sports brands, but older people in large cities prefer more classic styles. In many parts of the area, winters are cold and long. As a consequence, knitted sweaters and durable outerwear are both popular and necessary, but it is not unusual to see women also wearing high heels in wintertime.

Russian tennis stars Maria Sharapova and Anna Kournikova are examples of the new sporty beauty ideal, but obesity is a serious problem in all three countries. In Russia more than 54 percent of the population is overweight, whereas 66 percent of the population in Belarus weighs too much.[65] The countries provide no national statistics on obesity, but reports indicate that the situation is the most acute in the countryside. In Ukraine 7 percent of the men and 20 percent of the women are obese.[66]

Half of all sales in Ukraine take place in open-air markets and bazaars. Department stores, drugstores, and permanent outlets account for all other sales. More than 90 percent of Ukrainian clothing factories produce their goods in the framework of outsourcing schemes designed by Western European and American manufacturers.[67] Belarus is also dependent on its clothing and textile industry. The middle classes in Ukraine are increasing in numbers, and Western mid-price brands are gaining in popularity. A well-known Ukrainian fashion designer is Oleksiy Zalevsky. In Russia economic setbacks have resulted in a diminishing middle class, but the luxury goods market is still flourishing. Russian designers are focusing mostly on creating exclusive *haute couture* for a handful of wealthy customers. One well-known *prêt-à-porter* designer who has broken that trend is Max Chernitsov. Exclusive clothes and accessories are imported from Italy, Germany, and France. China is the major country of origin for more affordable shoes and clothing. Kalina is the leading domestic cosmetics company in Russia, but foreign companies like Avon (United States), Oriflame (Sweden), Procter & Gamble (United States), and Schwarzkopf (Germany) dominate the market, which is expected to become one of the leading cosmetics and toiletries markets in Europe. Counterfeit products are a major problem; such products are said to constitute about 40 percent of all sales.[68]

Despite low incomes, most Ukrainians prioritize health and attractive looks. Accordingly skin and body hygiene products are very popular. Sun-care products and perfume are other best sellers. Avon (United States) competes with Oriflame (Sweden) for home-based sales, and Sephora, a chain owned by LVMH (France), is establishing itself in the country.

SCANDINAVIA

Scandinavia encompasses Denmark, Norway, and Sweden. Iceland and Finland are also often included in this region. Sweden dominates both the fashion industry and retailing in Scandinavia. In 2005 the total sales value for clothes in Sweden was €7.03 billion and €1.14 billion for cosmetics.[69] Sales figures in Norway and Denmark were somewhat lower. In Finland the total sales value for clothing in 2005 was €2.25 billion and €670 million for cosmetics.[70] Iceland has a very small population, which explains the modest sales value for clothes in 2004 of only €126 million.[71] The population in all five countries is aging, but all age groups are highly fashion conscious and quick to adapt to changing trends.

Working women without families are Scandinavia's main consumers of clothing, shoes, and cosmetics. Because of the cold winters, clothes tend to be practical and functional rather than decorative. Materials are predominantly natural fibers. Clothes are often cut close to the body, and light colors for both men and women are popular in summertime. Otherwise muted colors in neutral tones are preferred. Norwegians are the wealthiest people in Scandinavia, and they spend the most on clothing, particularly fashionable sportswear and shoes. Egalitarianism is the dominant social value in all five countries, and actual social inequality is the lowest in Europe. As a consequence, there are few outward signs of

101

hierarchy and status in the workplace. Work dress codes vary between casual and semiformal and are not necessarily dependent on a person's social position. Scandinavian men usually wear separates, such as a sports jacket with a pair of khakis or jeans to work. Unlike most Europeans, they also wear light suits, often in linen, in the summertime. Children's clothes are casual and inspired by sportswear. School uniforms are not required. The northern parts of Scandinavia have a population of around 80,000 Sami, whose main livelihood is reindeer breeding. Traditional Sami costumes vary, but they are often dark blue and decorated with pewter embroidery and colorful borders. Today the costume is worn mostly at weddings and when the Sami wish to emphasize their culture and origins.

Hiking, skiing, or just spending a lot of time outdoors are popular leisure pursuits in Scandinavia, and the common beauty ideal is sporty and natural. Makeup is generally understated. Obesity rates in Denmark, Norway, Iceland, and Sweden are very similar. Around 11 percent of both men and women are obese.[72] In Finland the rates are higher: 19 percent of men and women suffer from obesity.[73]

Scandinavians are proud of their long tradition of functional design and tend to patronize domestic fashion brands. Popular Swedish fashion designers and brands are Anna Holtblad and J. Lindeberg. Mid-price-range brands like Filippa K and Tiger Of Sweden are also very popular. Best-selling quality sportswear retailers include Fjallraven and Peak Performance. Diesel (Italy) and Polo Ralph Lauren, Gant, and Marlboro Classics (all of the United States) are foreign brands that sell well in Sweden. The most common fashion retailers in Scandinavia are all Swedish: H&M, KappAhl, and AB Lindex. Denmark also has a long tradition of clothes production. The majority of clothing is nevertheless imported, mostly from China, Germany, and Turkey. Dressman and Cubus are two popular Norwegian retailers. Icelanders are considered the most fashionable and trend conscious of all Scandinavians, whereas Finnish fashion is sophisticated and understated. A popular Finnish brand, Marimekko, produces both clothes and home design and is well-known worldwide for its bold design and bright fabrics. Rukka and Lutha are two Finnish sportswear brands that work with telecom company Nokia to produce skiwear that also incorporates wireless technology.

Sweden has a fairly well-developed cosmetics and toiletries industry. Brands such as Invima and Oriflame are sold predominantly in people's homes. Lilleborg is the largest domestic cosmetics company in Norway. After the Swiss, Norwegians buy the most cosmetics and toiletries in Europe. L'Oréal (France) dominates the Finnish market but competes with the domestic company Lumene. Popular products in all five countries include items for sun and skin care. Products and brands specifically aimed at men are also selling very well. Unilever (United Kingdom/Netherlands), L'Oréal (France), Beiersdorf (Germany), and Procter & Gamble (United States) are the largest international retailers on the market.

SPAIN AND PORTUGAL

Spain and Portugal have large clothing industries. Spain's economy is both larger and more stable than Portugal's, although its spending power is still below the EU average. In 2005 the sales value for clothes in Spain was €18.75 billion, and almost €6 billion were spent for cosmetics and toiletries.[74] For Portugal, the sales value was €4 billion for clothes and €1.14 billion for cosmetics and toiletries.[75] Both the Spanish and Portuguese are very conscious of style, and the work dress code in both countries is conservative. Spanish men prefer suits in dark colors, and women favor classic and feminine styles, preferring skirts and dresses to trousers. Natural materials and comfort are other determining criteria when the Spanish and Portuguese go shopping. In Portugal work dress codes are more relaxed than in

Spain, but the quality of clothes remains important. Both nationalities also add great importance to immaculate clothes and hair. Catholicism is the predominant religion, and clothes worn to church and on other religious occasions reflect the need for modesty and propriety. Older generations still wear simple and functional clothes, whereas young people are more fashionable and conscious of style. Quality sportswear is popular, both for its comfort and the status it brings. School uniforms are not compulsory in either country.

In Spain 11 percent of men and 15 percent of women are obese, and more than half of the population is reportedly overweight.[76] In Portugal 13 percent of men and 26 percent of women are obese.[77] Spanish princess Letizia, with her tiny physique and immaculate choice of clothes, is a good example of the typical Latin beauty ideal that reigns in the two countries.

Both Spanish and Portuguese women are becoming more brand conscious, although only the more affluent parts of the population can afford domestic designs. Popular Spanish designers include Adolfo Dominguez, Sybilla, and Agatha Ruiz de la Prada. Contemporary Portuguese designers include Fátima Lopes, Ana Salazar, and Jose Antonio Tenente. The roots of Spanish fashion can be traced back to early Iberian culture. The most famous type of dress, the flamenco dress, originated in the work dresses of nineteenth-century Andalusian women who accompanied livestock traders to Prado de San Sebastián. Gradually the meetings turned into festivals, and the dresses came to be associated with the festivities and flamenco. Adornments include lacing and ruffles, and the dresses are often accessorized with Manila shawls, flowers, and silk fans. Contemporary flamenco dresses come in many colors and styles, but the basic figure-hugging body and layers of ruffles are always present.

The Spanish textile and clothing industry accounts for 10 percent of Spain's industrial employment.[78] About 70 percent of the domestic production is exported to the European Union, mainly to France, Portugal, Italy, the United Kingdom, and Germany.[79] Popular domestic mid- and low-price fashion retailers include Zara (for men and women), Massimo Dutti (for men), Springfield (for men), and Mango (for women). Popular Spanish shoe labels are Camper, Lotusse, and Pura López. In Portugal, the textile industry has a long tradition. It employs about one-quarter of the country's work force and is responsible for 22 percent of total Portuguese exports.[80] Like Spain, Portugal also relies on fashion retailers from other countries. Zara (Spain), H&M (Sweden), Marks & Spencer (United Kingdom), and Gap (United States) are some of the most popular companies. Most people buy their clothes in large shopping centers or department stores. Puig Beauty and Fashion is the largest Spanish manufacturer of cosmetics and toiletries. The Portuguese market is dominated by L'Oréal (France), Unilever (United Kingdom/Netherlands), and Beiersdorf (Germany). Hair-care products sell very well in Portugal; Spanish men are buying more products aimed specifically at them. In Portugal, direct sales in people's homes is also a popular distribution method. The home-selling market is dominated by Avon (United States) and Oriflame (Sweden).

SWITZERLAND

The Swiss clothing market is small, but the population as a whole is one of Europe's most affluent. On average women spend only 11 percent of their disposable monthly income on a winter coat in the mid-price range.[81] The Swiss also buy more shoes than other Europeans and are the continent's biggest buyers of cosmetics. Most Swiss consumers are willing to spend substantial sums on clothing and shoes; sales of both high-cost brands and cheaper goods have increased. In 2005 the country's total sales value for clothing was €4.25 billion, and 1.42 billion were spent for cosmetics.[82]

Dress codes at work are semiformal. Men typically wear dark suits, and women wear skirts or dresses in classic styles and neutral colors. Some professionals dress more casually, and jeans at work are not an unusual sight. As would be expected, good shoes are an important aspect of the Swiss dress code. A well-known Swiss shoe retailer is Bally. Although many Swiss dress casually, they generally look neat and clean. Children prefer sports brands such as Nike and Adidas, and jeans and sneakers are worn daily. Sports such as snowboarding and skateboarding also influence young people's dress. High-tech sportswear is also increasingly worn off the slopes. The Swiss geography and climate allow for an active lifestyle, and obesity rates are at only 10 percent, but they are rising.[83] Only 42 percent of Swiss fifteen-year-old girls have ever dieted or thought about doing so.[84] Switzerland relies heavily on other countries to supply it with clothes. In 2003 Germany and Italy were the main producers of imported clothing. The domestic clothing industry consists of less than 200 companies.[85] Some of the more popular designer brands are Akris, Ida Gut, Christa de Carouge, and Trudie Götz's Trois Pommes. Strellson and Ritex are popular menswear brands. Italian luxury brands such as Versace, Armani, and Krizia are sold in department stores or in exclusive boutiques in larger cities. Low-price retailers such as H&M (Sweden), Mango (Spain), and Zara (Spain) are also very popular. All major cosmetics companies do very well in Switzerland. Two domestic cosmetics and toiletries companies are Gaba and Sprig. The most popular products are color cosmetics and skin-care products. Perfume also sells well. Deodorants and sun protection are other best sellers. The Swiss prefer to buy their cosmetics and toiletries in upscale department stores or in large supermarkets.

TURKEY

With a population of 72 million and 65 percent of its total population under age thirty-five, Turkey has the potential for becoming the second largest market in Europe.[86] In 2005 the total sales value for clothing was €9.53 billion with €1.513 billion spent for cosmetics and toiletries.[87] Social inequality in Turkey is higher than in most other European countries. On average a Turkish woman must spend three times her monthly disposable income for a winter coat.[88] Nevertheless, income levels are rising, mostly in urban areas, where 75 percent of the population lives.[89]

More than 25 percent of Turkish men and women are overweight; 24 percent of women and 15 percent of men are obese.[90] Despite its being a predominantly Muslim country, Turkey has legislated against religious dress in public offices and universities, where women are not allowed to wear head scarves and men cannot sport a beard. In the early 1900s, leader Mustafa Kemal Atatürk initiated a reform to "westernize" Turkey by abolishing traditional Turkish dress in favor of Western-style clothing. His so-called "hat law," enacted in 1925, prohibited Turkish men from wearing the traditional fez but encouraged Western headgear such as the bowler hat. The first legislation regarding clothing in the area was initiated in the 1700s during the reign of Süleyman the Magnificent. He created special rules regarding the clothing of Muslims, Christians, Jews, clergy, tradesmen, and state and military officials. Today traditional Turkish dress is worn only for special occasions and varies according to region. The traditional costume for women usually consists of a shirt and trousers worn under an *üçetek*, an outer garment, which is covered by an apron. Men typically wear a shirt, trousers held up by a girdle, and a *cepken*, a short embroidered jacket. Often the costumes are made of a silk and cotton striped fabric, manufactured in the city Gaziantep.

Contemporary dress codes are conservative. Until 2003 women in government jobs were not permitted to wear trousers to work. Men typically wear a suit and tie, whereas women dress in a skirt suit or a skirt and a blouse. In the rural parts of the country, women sometimes wear long or ankle-length skirts and long-sleeved blouses. Many observant Muslim women wear a head scarf and a light cover-all topcoat when they go out in public, and some also prefer to wear a black veil. In the urbanized parts of Turkey, children and young people are heavily influenced by Western fashion, and jeans are frequently worn by both men and women under thirty. Miniskirts, bikinis, and shorts can also be seen on the beach and in the streets.

In large cities such as Ankara and Istanbul, exclusive department stores sell foreign brands like Donna Karan and Prada. Contemporary Turkish-born fashion designers include Rifat Ozbek, Hussein Chalayan, and Atil Kutoglu. Gonul Paksoy's knitted sweaters are very popular both in Turkey and abroad. Popular domestic fashion retailers for both men and women include Vakko, Beymen, and Mudo. Domestic retailers such as Janine Tekstil also design for and export to customers in the Middle East. The oldest department store in Istanbul is Yeni Karamürsel, or YKM, which opened in the mid-twentieth century. The Turkish buy most of their clothes in boutiques and bazaars, usually situated in the city centers. British retailer Marks & Spencer has also opened several stores in Istanbul.

The Turkish clothing and textile industry is one of the largest in the world and plays a significant role in the country's economy. In 2004 total clothing and textile exports reached €3.215 billion.[91] The main markets include Russia, the United States, and members of the European Union, accounting for 64 percent of the country's total clothing exports, but the country is facing increased competition from low-wage Asian countries such as China.[92] An interest in Western lifestyles and successful advertising campaigns contributed to increased sales of foreign toiletries and cosmetics in 2000. Since the economic crisis of 2001–02, the Turkish are buying cheaper domestic cosmetics and toiletries. Popular domestic brands include Gulcicek Kimya, Haci Sakir, Canan Kozmetik, and Banyo Malzemeleri. The home-selling market is dominated by Oriflame (Sweden). Sales of color cosmetics, fragrances, and skin-care products remain very low. The most popular products are shampoo and other hair-care items. Most Turkish people buy their toiletries and cosmetics in retail outlets and supermarkets.

UNITED KINGDOM AND IRELAND

The United Kingdom (UK) is the second largest economy in the European Union. The fashion industry is highly segmented and offers British people a lot of choice when buying clothes. In 2005 the total sales value for clothing was €49.85 billion, and €8.9 billion were spent for cosmetics and toiletries.[93] In Ireland, the sales value for clothes was €2.3 billion with €550 million spent on cosmetics.[94] Irish household incomes are higher than the EU average, and the market for fashion has grown rapidly in the last five years.

In both countries, suits are worn at work, but many offices have implemented a policy of "dress-down Fridays" when it is acceptable to dress more casually. Casual clothes have come to dominate many areas of everyday life, and country casual is a popular look for people living in rural areas. This style typically includes waxed cotton jackets, tweed suits, and corduroy trousers. Sportswear is also very popular. Obesity rates are high; more than 21 percent of men and 23 percent of women in the United Kingdom are obese, and the number of overweight people is increasing faster in the United Kingdom than anywhere else in Europe.[95] A survey conducted in 1990 suggests that 55 percent of men and 35 percent of women in Ireland are overweight, and obesity affects over 15 percent of the population.[96] Several popular fashion retailers such as H&M (Sweden), Marks & Spencer (United Kingdom), and New Look (United Kingdom) have introduced plus-size collections. The United Kingdom has a long tradition of fashion design and high-quality tailoring. In the 1960s, young British fashion became popular worldwide. Successful designers included Mary Quant and Barbara Hulanicki, founder of the inexpensive brand Biba. Their clothes combined youthful design with reasonable prices. British style icons of the 1960s were models Twiggy and Jean "the Shrimp" Shrimpton, as well as singer Marianne Faithfull.

Today the clothing market is more specialized than ever and caters to a wide variety of people. Large chain stores such as Next and River Island (United Kingdom), Zara (Spain), H&M (Sweden), and Gap (United States) account for more than three-fourths of all sales. Strict retail laws that limited the size of shops and price of goods have been abolished in Ireland. The result has been an influx of popular retailers such as Zara (Spain) and H&M (Sweden). Two British department store operators, House of Fraser and Harvey Nichols, are also expected to open Irish outlets. Well-known Irish fashion designers are Paul Costelloe, Louise Kennedy, and John Rocha. Milliner Philip Treacy is also Irish. Influential British fashion designers include Paul Smith, Stella McCartney, Alexander McQueen, and John Galliano. Vivienne Westwood entered the fashion arena with the emergence of punk music and culture. Anti-authoritarian and anarchistic, punk has continued to influence both high and mass-produced fashion long after the movement's demise. Earlier subcultures did not reject the typically British style but transformed it. The 1950s "teddy boys" exaggerated and changed the typical Edwardian suit, whereas the "mods" of the 1960s preferred tight-fitting, immaculately tailored suits. West Indian immigrants brought with them the fashions of the Caribbean and mixed them with typical British clothing items such as the reefer coat. In the 1980s, Doc Marten's boots became popular after being worn by so-called "skinheads."

In the early twenty-first century, rap music and rave parties have helped popularize high-tech sportswear and American sports brands. Football (soccer) is another style inspiration. Football player David Beckham is a contemporary British male fashion icon. School uniforms are compulsory in both countries. The majority of British and Irish exports go to the European Union, especially to France and Germany. The United Kingdom also exports shoes to the United States, the Republic of Ireland, Germany, and Japan. Imported clothes in the United Kingdom come mainly from Germany, Italy, and Hong Kong, whereas imports to Ireland are mostly from the United Kingdom, and Germany. The British buy most of their clothes in department stores, followed by chain stores, boutiques, and sports shops. Until recently Irish people preferred local, smaller shops to large retailers. Color cosmetics, skin-care, and bath and shower products sell well in the United Kingdom, but sun-care and baby products are current best sellers. Men's skin-care products are also becoming more popular. No cosmetics company controls more than 10 percent of the market, but Procter & Gamble (United States), L'Oréal (France), and Lever Fabergé (United Kingdom/Netherlands) are all active in the British market.[97] The same multinational companies dominate Irish sales. Like the British, the Irish buy most of their cosmetics and toiletries in department stores and supermarkets.

RESOURCE GUIDE

PRINT SOURCES

Bond, C. *New Fashion in Sweden*. Stockholm: The Swedish Institute, 2003.
Breward, C. *Fashioning London: Clothing and the Modern Metropolis*. Oxford: Berg, 2004.
Constantine, S., and T. Woodall. *What Not to Wear*. London: Weidenfeld Nicolson Illustrated, 2002.
Cumming, V. *Understanding Fashion History*. London: Costume & Fashion Press, 2004.
Cunningham, P. A., and S. V. Lab, eds. *Dress and Popular Culture*. Bowling Green: Popular Culture Press, 1991.

Dariaux, G. *A Guide to Elegance: For Every Woman Who Wants to Be Well and Properly Dressed on All Occasions.* New York: William Morrow, 2004.

Derycke, L., and S. van de Veire. *Belgian Fashion Design.* Gent–Amsterdam: Luidon Editions, 2000.

Farkas, E. "Political Resistance in Hungarian Dress." *Voices* 30 (Spring–Summer 2004): 42–46.

Guenther, I. *Nazi Chic? Fashioning Women in The Third Reich.* Oxford: Berg, 2004.

Guiliano, M. *French Women Don't Get Fat: The Secret of Eating for Pleasure.* New York: Knopf, 2005.

Hewitt, P., and M. Baxter. *The Fashion of Football: Soccer from Best to Beckham, From Mod to Label Slave.* Edingurgh:Mainstream Publishing, 2004.

Lobenthal, J. *Radical Rags: Fashions of the Sixties.* New York: Abbeville Press, 1990.

Mugglestone, D., and R. Weinzierl, eds. *The Post-Subcultures Reader.* Oxford: Berg, 2004.

Navaro-Yashin, Y. "The Veil as a Commodity." Pp. 82–85 in *Faces of the State: Secularism and Public Life in Turkey.* Princeton: Princeton University Press, 2002.

Paulicelli, E. *Fashion under Fascism: Beyond the Black Shirt.* Oxford: Berg, 2004.

Ruane, C. "Clothes Make the Comrade: A History of the Russian Fashion Industry." *Russian History* 23:1–4 (1994). 311–44.

Steele, V. *Paris Fashion: A Cultural History.* Oxford: Berg, 1998.

Stitziel, J. *Fashioning Socialism: Clothing, Politics and Consumer Culture in East Germany.* Oxford: Berg, 2005.

Tulloch, C., ed. *Black Style.* London: V&A, 2005.

Turnau, I. *History of Dress in Central and Eastern Europe from the Sixteenth to the Eighteenth Century.* Translated by I. Szymanski. Warsaw: Institute of the History of Material Culture, 1991.

Uchalová, E., and M. Zeminova. *Fashion in Bohemia*: *From the Waltz to the Tango 1870–1914.* 2 vols. Prague: Museum of Decorative Arts, 1994.

Waddell, G. *How Fashion Works: Couture, Ready-to-Wear and Mass Production.* Oxford: Blackwell Publishing, 2004.

White, N. *Reconstructing Italian Fashion: America and the Development of the Italian Fashion Industry.* Oxford: Berg, 2000.

Wood, M. *We Wore What We'd Got: Women's Clothes in World War II.* Exeter: Warwickshire Books, 1989.

Young, A. *Women Who Become Men: Albanian Sworn Virgins.* New York: Berg, 2000.

POPULAR FASHION MAGAZINES

Amelia. Stockholm: Amelia Publishing Group, since 1995.

Brigitte. Hamburg: Gruner & Jahr, since 1965.

Cosmopolitan. London: Hearst, since 1886.

Elle. Paris: Hachette, since 1945.

Esquire. London: National Magazine, since 1991.

FHM. London: Emap Metro, since 1992.

Freundin. Munich: Scherz Verlag GmbH.

Glamour. Greenwich, CT: Condé Nast, since 1941.

Good Housekeeping. New York: International Magazine Co., since 1916.

British GQ. London: Condé Nast.

Men's Health, New York: Rodale.

Tatler. London: Condé Nast, since 1901.

Vogue Italia. Edizioni Condé Nast Spa.

WEBSITES

Currie, C., et al., eds. *Health and Health Behaviour of Young People.* World Health Organization. Accessed May 5, 2005. http://www.hbsc.org/downloads/Int_Report_00.pdf. Statistics on dieting among girls.

Economist Intelligence Unit. Updated August 16, 2006. Economist Group. Accessed May 5, 2005. http://www.eiu.com/ Regularly updated consumer statistics and forecasts.

International Obesity Task Force. *EU Platform on Diet, Physical Activity and Health*. Updated March 15, 2005. European Association for the Study of Obesity. Accessed May 5, 2005. http://europa. eu.int/comm/health/ph_determinants/life_style/nutrition/documents/iotf_en. pdf. Obesity statistics.

Euromonitor International. Updated 2006. Euromonitor International. May 6, 2005. http://www. euromonitor.com/c osmeticsandtoiletries. Regularly updated cosmetics and toiletries forecasts.

Eurostat. UpdatedAugust 16, 2006. Statistical Office of the European Communities. Accessed May 5, 2005. http://epp.eurostat.cec.eu.int/portal/page?_pageid=1090,30070682,1090_33076576&_dad=portal&_schema=PORTAL. Regularly updated European trade and consumer statistics.

INFOMAT: Fashion Industry Business Information. Updated 2006. InfoMat, Inc. May 10, 2005. http://www.infomat.com/. An online guide to over 350,000 businesses in the fashion industry.

World Health Organization, Regional Office for Europe. Updated August 10, 2006. World Health Organization. Accessed May 6, 2005. http://www.euro.who.int/. Obesity statistics.

VIDEOS/FILMS

Another Country. (United Kingdom, 1984). Directed by Marek Kanievska, starring Rupert Everett. Features classic British men's fashion.

Belle de Jour. (France, 1967). Directed by Luis Bunuel, starring Catherine Deneuve. Features French fashion designed by Yves Saint Laurent.

Cabaret. (United States, 1972). Directed by Bob Fosse, starring Liza Minelli. Features period costumes from 1930s Berlin.

The Cook, the Thief, His Wife and Her Lover. (United Kingdom, 1989). Directed by Peter Greenaway. Features clothes by Jean-Paul Gaultier.

"Dedicated Follower of Fashion" *Routes of Rock* (documentary). (United Kingdom, 1999). Directed by Nigel Simpkiss. Describes how London became the center of fashion in the 1960s.

Tacones Lejanos (High Heels). (Spain, 1991). Directed by Pedro Almodóvar. A Spanish take on the classic Chanel suit.

Le Mépris. [Contempt] (France, 1963). Directed by Jean-Luc Godard, starring Brigitte Bardot. Brigitte Bardot's influential look is introduced.

Prêt-à-Porter. (United States, 1994). Directed by Robert Altman, starring Marcello Mastroianni, Sophia Loren, and Tim Robbins. Portrait of the Paris fashion industry.

Punk and the Pistols (documentary). (United Kingdom, 1995). Directed by Paul Tickell. Punk rock music's influence on fashion.

Quadrophenia. (United Kingdom, 1979). Directed by Franc Roddam, starring Phil Daniels, Leslie Ash, Sting, and Garry Cooper. Period recreation of Mod style.

Uncut—Men Talk (documentary). (United Kingdom, 1992). Directed by Richard Jobs. Interviews with men who became obsessed with their appearance in the 1980s.

ORGANIZATIONS AND MUSEUMS

Camera Nazionale Della Moda Italiana, Via Gerolamo Morone 6. I-20121, Milano, Italy. http://www.cameramoda.it/. Promotes and coordinates the development of Italian fashion.

Deutsches Historisches Museum, Unter den Linden 2, 10117 Berlin, Germany. http://www.dhm.de/. The collection consists of 8000 items from the mid-1700s to the present.

Euratex, 24, Rue Montoyer; Bte. 10, B-1000 Brussels, Belgium. http://www.euratex.org/. Promotes the interests of the European clothing industry.

Fédération Française de la Couture du Prêt-À-Porter des Couturiers et Des Créateurs de Mode, 100-102, Faubourg Saint-Honoré, 75008 Paris, France. http://www.modeparis.com/. Represents the craftsmen and craftswomen in the French fashion professions.

Livrustkammaren, Slottsbacken3 S-111, 30 Stockholm, Sweden. http://www.lsh.se/livrustkammaren/. Small but unique collection of coronation dress and other royal robes from the 1600s.

Musée de la Mode et du Textile, 107, rue de Rivoli, Paris, France. http://www.museums-of-paris.com/musee_fr.php?code=355. A total of 81,000 items from the 1700s to the present day, including 35,000 accessories.

Musée Galliera/Musée de la Mode de la Ville de Paris, 10, avenue Pierre Ier de Serbie, 75116 Paris, France. http://www.paris.fr/musees/musee_galliera/. A collection of 15,000 garments and 40,000 accessories from the 1700s to the present.

Museo del Traje, 2 Avda. Juan de Herrera, Madrid, Spain. http://museodeltraje.mcu.es/. A collection of fashion from the 1700s to the 1900s. Includes Spanish traditional costumes.

Museum of Costumes, Bath, Assembly Rooms, Bennett Street, Bath, UK BA1 2QH. http://www.museumofcostume.co.uk. A collection of 30,000 objects and clothes for men, women, and children from the late 1500s to the present.

Victoria & Albert Museum (V&A), Cromwell Road, London, UK SW7 2RL, http://www.vam.ac.uk/. Items in the collection date from the 1600s to the present. One of the world's largest museums with 63,000 objects.

Wien Museum, Karlsplatz, A-1040 Vienna, Austria. http://www.wienmuseum.at/frameset.asp. The collection is of Europe's largest at 20,000 items. Mainly fashion from the 1800s and 1900s.

NOTES

1. Gunborg Palme, "Characteristics of Anorexia Nervosa," Oct 28, 2003. From *Web4Health*. http://web4health.info/en/answers/ed-dia-anorexia-character.htm.
2. *Datamonitor: Shifting Consumer Attitudes about Weight Loss.* (London: Datamonitor Plc., 2005).
3. Ibid.
4. *EU Platform on Diet, Physical Activity and Health.* Brussels: International Obesity Task Force. EU Platform Briefing Paper, March 15, 2005.
5. *Executive Briefing Austria.*(The Economist Intelligence Unit, 2005). http://www.eiu.com/.
6. C. Currie, K. Hurrelmann, et al. *EU Platform on Diet, Physical Activity and Health, IOTF 2005*, and *Health Behavior among School-Aged Children: A WHO Cross-National Study (HBSC) International Report.* World Health Organization (WHO) Policy Series: Health Policy for Children and Adolescents Issue 1 (Universität Beilefeld, 2000). http://www.hbsc.org/downloads/Int_Report_00.pdf.
7. *Executive Briefing: Austria* (EIU, 2005).
8. Ibid.
9. Maja Baretić and Stjepan Balić, "Overweight and Obesity in Croatia." *Diabetologia Croatica: Journal Of Diabetes, Endocrinology And Metabolic Diseases* 31.2 (2002). http://www.idb.hr/diabetologia/02no2-3.pdf.
10. John Pucher and Ralph Buhler. "Transport Policies in Central and Eastern Europe." Pp. 43–61 in K. J. Button and D. A. Hensher (eds.), *Handbook of Transport Strategy, Policy, and Institutions*, Oxford: Elsevier Press, 2005.
11. *Albania's Foreign Trade Developments during the First Nine Months of 2004.* Albanian Center for International Trade (ACIT), 2004. http://www.acit-al.org/publications/reports/QuartRepIII2004.pdf.
12. *Executive Briefing: Croatia* (EIU, 2005).
13. *Executive Briefing: Belgium* (EIU, 2005).
14. *EU Platform on Diet, Physical Activity and Health* (IOTF, 2005).
15. *Executive Briefing: Belgium* (EIU, 2005).
16. *Executive Briefing: Bulgaria* (EIU, 2005).
17. *Executive Briefing: Romania* (EIU, 2005).
18. *Highlights on Health in Bulgaria.* (World Health Organization: Regional Office for Europe, December 2001). http://www.euro.who.int/Document/E73818.pdf.
19. *Obesity in Europe: The Case for Action* (Copenhagen: IOTF, 2002). http://www.iotf.org/media/euobesity.pdf.
20. *Executive Briefing: Bulgaria* and *Executive Briefing: Romania* (EIU, 2005).
21. *Executive Briefing: Bulgaria* (EIU, 2005).

22. *Executive Briefing: Romania* (EIU, 2005).
23. *Executive Briefing: The Czech Republic* (EIU, 2005).
24. Ibid.
25. *EU Platform on Diet, Physical Activity and Health* (IOTF, 2005).
26. *Health Behavior among School-Aged Children* (World Health Organization, 2000).
27. *Highlights on Health in Estonia* (World Health Organization, Regional Office for Europe, December 2001). http://www.euro.who.int/document/e74339.pdf. Also *European Obesity Rates*, (IOTF, 2005).
28. *Highlights on Health in Lithuania* (World Health Organization: Regional Office for Europe, March 2001). http://www.euro.who.int/document/e72373.pdf.
29. Jozef de Coster. "EU Membership Could Dampen Baltic Clothing Exports." *International Market News*, January 21, 2004 (Hong Kong: Trade Development Council). http://www.tdctrade.com/imn/04012103/clothing120.htm.
30. Ibid.
31. Ibid.
32. *Executive Briefing: France* (EIU, 2005).
33. Ibid.
34. *EU Platform on Diet, Physical Activity and Health* (IOTF, 2005).
35. Ibid.
36. *Datamonitor: Shifting Consumer Attitudes about Weight Loss.* (London: Datamonitor Plc., 2005).
37. http://www.lvmh.com/. Accessed March 20, 2005.
38. *Executive Briefing: Germany* (EIU, 2005).
39. Ibid.
40. *EU Platform on Diet, Physical Activity and Health* (IOTF, 2005).
41. *Datamonitor: Shifting Consumer Attitudes about Weight Loss* (London: Datamonitor Plc., 2005).
42. *Executive Briefing: Germany* (EIU, 2005).
43. Ibid.
44. Beisada, Alex. *H&M*. http://www.hoovers.com/. Accessed March 2006.
45. *Executive Briefing: Greece* (EIU, 2005).
46. *EU Platform on Diet, Physical Activity and Health* (IOTF, 2005).
47. *Executive Briefing: Hungary* (EIU, 2005).
48. Ibid.
49. *EU Platform on Diet, Physical Activity and Health* (IOTF, 2005).
50. *Executive Briefing: Hungary* (EIU, 2005).
51. *Executive Briefing: Italy* (EIU, 2005).
52. *European Obesity Rates* (IOTF, 2005).
53. *Datamonitor: Shifting Consumer Attitudes About Weight Loss* (London: Datamonitor Plc., 2005).
54. *Executive Briefing: Italy* (EIU, 2005).
55. *Executive Briefing: The Netherlands* (EIU, 2005).
56. *EU Platform on Diet, Physical Activity and Health* (IOTF, 2005).
57. *Executive Briefing: The Netherlands* (EIU, 2005).
58. Ibid.
59. *Executive Briefing: Poland* (EIU, 2005).
60. Ibid.
61. Ibid.
62. *EU Platform on Diet, Physical Activity and Health* (IOTF, 2005).
63. *Executive Briefing: Russia* (EIU, 2005).
64. *Executive Briefing: Ukraine* (EIU, 2005).
65. *Highlights on Health in the Russian Federation.* World Health Organization, Regional Office for Europe, December 1999. http://www.euro.who.int/document/e72504.pdf. Also *Highlights on Health in Belarus* (World Health Organization: Regional Office for Europe, December 2000). http://www.euro.who.int/document/e72016.pdf.

66. *International Comparisons: Ukraine* (World Health Organization, Global InfoBase Online, 2002). http://www.who.int/ncd_surveillance/infobase/web/InfoBasePolicyMaker/CountryProfiles/Quick Compare.aspx?UN_Code=804&rptCode=BQC&dm=5.

67. *Executive Briefing: Ukraine* (EIU, 2005).

68. *Executive Briefing: Russia* (EIU, 2005).

69. *Executive Briefing: Sweden* (EIU, 2005).

70. *Executive Briefing: Finland* (EIU, 2005).

71. *Executive Briefing: Iceland* (EIU, 2005).

72. *EU Platform on Diet, Physical Activity and Health* (IOTF, 2005).

73. Ibid.

74. *Executive Briefing: Spain* (EIU, 2005).

75. *Executive Briefing: Portugal* (EIU, 2005).

76. *EU Platform on Diet, Physical Activity and Health* (IOTF, 2005).

77. Ibid.

78. *Executive Briefing: Spain* (EIU, 2005).

79. Ibid.

80. *Executive Briefing: Portugal* (EIU, 2005).

81. *Executive Briefing: Switzerland* (EIU, 2005).

82. Ibid.

83. *Highlights on Health in Switzerland* (World Health Organization: Regional Office for Europe, September 2001). http://www.euro.who.int/document/e73485.pdf.

84. *Health Behavior among School-Aged Children* (World Health Organization, 2000).

85. *Executive Briefing: Switzerland* (EIU, 2005).

86. *Executive Briefing: Turkey* (EIU, 2005).

87. Ibid.

88. Ibid.

89. Ibid.

90. Husrev Hatemi, Volkan Demirhan Yumuk, et al. "Prevalence of Overweight and Obesity in Turkey." *Metabolic Syndrome and Related Disorders* 1.4 (2003), pp. 285–290.

91. *Executive Briefing: Turkey* (EIU, 2005).

92. Ibid.

93. *Executive Briefing: United Kingdom* (EIU, 2005).

94. *Executive Briefing: Ireland* (EIU, 2005).

95. *Health Survey for England 1994–2003.* Office for National Statistics. January 2006. http://www.statistics.gov.uk/.

96. *Highlights on Health in Ireland* (World Health Organization: Regional Office for Europe, September 1998). http://www.euro.who.int/document/E62012.pdf.

97. *Executive Briefing: United Kingdom* (EIU, 2005).

FILM

ROBERT VON DASSANOWSKY

France is commonly recognized as the nation that popularly introduced European film art. The first screening of a motion picture to a paying audience took place in Paris in 1895, with the showing of short films by photographer Louis Lumière. The premiere of his work met mixed response in European capitals between 1895 and 1897: with adulation in Vienna and Berlin (people in the latter city had already seen films by the Skladanowsky brothers two months prior); with curiosity in Madrid and Rome (the Italians patented the Albertini Kinetograph in 1895); as a novelty in London music halls; and with outright hostility in Athens, where some members of the audience reportedly fainted while others threw stones at the screen.

The showing of imported films (usually French or American) predated the start of many national film industries. Some cinemas were an aspect of a larger imperial development (for example, Czech/Slovakian, Hungarian, and some Balkan cinemas were part of Austria's art and industry until 1918; Polish and Baltic films were suppressed by Czarist Russia). The first films made in Europe were recordings of appearances by monarchs and political leaders, daily life, erotic scenes, theatrical productions, and sporting events (the first significant Greek film was a newsreel of the 1906 interim Olympic Games). Film was used as propaganda (newsreels and fiction films) during World War I, and the new political/military use strengthened some cinemas (Austria and Germany), while the loss of cast, crew, and financing to the war effort weakened others (France, Great Britain). The subsequent alteration of Europe's map in 1918 brought with it emerging national cinemas in the newly established or reestablished states of Central and Eastern Europe (Hungary, Poland, Czechoslovakia, Yugoslavia, Lithuania, Latvia, and Estonia). The American film industry flooded the European market following World War I, taking advantage of the economic disaster of the postwar years that reduced European production power and distribution and turned audiences to Hollywood film. Nevertheless, by the mid-1920s, most national cinemas had established a traditional studio structure and a star system. Strongly defined national styles and directions were evident: monumental biblical epics and socially critical melodrama in Austria; theatrical translations in Great Britain; *Film d'art*, impressionism and surrealism in France; expressionism in Germany; monumental Roman and early

Christian period epics in Italy; historical themes and formalist experimentation in the early Soviet Union; and folkloric melodramas and *zarzuelas* in Spain.

Sound was a difficult hurdle for some European cinemas, given the costly process of refitting studios during a period of general economic depression, but following Hollywood's first sound "talkie" film in 1927, Germany led Europe with *Der blaue Engel* [The Blue Angel] (1930). Although it was not the first German or European sound film, it added fresh impetus to Berlin's industry rivalry with Hollywood and made a star of Marlene Dietrich. Many nations continued to produce and show silent films into the mid-1930s. New cinema palaces were created throughout Europe, and publications ranging from fan magazines to theoretical texts emerged as cinema became the popular mass entertainment source for most Europeans.

The rise of fascism and Soviet Stalinism altered the direction of many national cinemas and their relationships with the international market. Beginning in 1922, Fascist Italy encouraged artistic modernism and film industry development; however, the industry focused on the production of period epics and melodramas to support its cultural ideology and to provide escapism. From 1933 on, Nazi Germany ejected Jews and other unwanted racial and social elements from its "Aryanized" industry, centralizing its production of opulent entertainment and historically/culturally celebratory films, as well as racist and geopolitical propaganda, at the nationalized UFA studio outside Berlin. Ardent Catholicism and censorship inhibited Spanish film. To a lesser extent, Austria also wrestled with creating a moral cinema. Until annexation, it simultaneously satisfied German import demands with a racially exclusive industry and also differentiated the nation from Germany with its secondary Hungarian and Czechoslovakian co-produced films, not for distribution in Germany, which featured German émigré and independent Austrian talent . After 1938 the Czech film industry was Germanized, but Switzerland banned Nazi German films. During World War II, French film retreated into entertainment genres and symbolism couched in period fantasies. Polish film was banned, and the industry was eventually obliterated by German occupation. Soviet film was forced to abandon experimentation for strong censorship and political control under Stalin.

The postwar era meant a revision of much of the European film industry resulting from the massive wartime destruction, the banning of fascist-associated film talent, the introduction of Soviet Communism into Eastern Europe, the economic and sociopolitical reconstruction in Western Europe, and the glut of Hollywood films that often attracted audiences away from national product.

AUSTRIA

Given the nature of the Austro-Hungarian Empire, Austrian film was multicultural from its inception and tended to remain so throughout its history, mirroring American cinema, to which it contributed many talents, styles, and genres over the twentieth century. Vienna's film industry employed such Austrian filmmakers as Robert Wiene, Carl Mayer, Fritz Lang, and G. W. Pabst before opportunity prompted their move to Berlin and brought them international reputations. Other émigré Austrians such as Erich von Stroheim, Josef von Sternberg, and Billy Wilder actually began their film careers in Berlin or in Hollywood. Sound brought the creation of a genre that has become synonymous with the interwar Austrian cinema: the "Viennese Film." Developed by screenwriter Walter Reisch and director Willi Forst (the latter also became its most famous actor), these elegantly stylized and heavily atmospheric melodramas, complete with rich musical scores, dealt with historical or fictional musical artists who sacrifice love for their art. The first, *Leise flehen meine Lieder* (1933, remade in English as *Unfinished Symphony*, 1934), became an international sensation, and its follow-up, *Maskerade* [Masquerade] (1934), made a star of ingénue Paula Wessely, who reigned as Austria's dramatic film diva through the 1950s and as the doyenne of German language theater. With the *Anschluss*, the annexation of Austria by Germany in 1938, Vienna was given a specific role in the film production structure of the Third Reich as the center of lavish operetta, period comedy, and entertainment films.

The four-power division of Austria, beginning in 1945 and lasting until the long-delayed return of full sovereignty in 1955, hurt the return of Austrian film to the world market. The central studio, Rosenhügel, was placed under Soviet administration, while supplementary sites and facilities were damaged or controlled by the other Allies. Nevertheless, film production resumed on a limited basis in 1946. The first new studio to produce independently was Belvedere-Film, and it discovered several major talents in its short run, including actress Nadja Tiller and comedian Günther Philipp. Nazism and the war were for the most part avoided, although director Karl Hartl offered a family epic that dealt with recent Austrian history, *Der Engel mit der Posaune* [The Angel with a Trumpet] (1948), which brought actor Oskar Werner to fame. Films on Mozart, Schubert, Empress Maria Theresa, and Beethoven helped reconstruct a cinematic national "identity" couched in the imperial past. A state-funded, all-star sci-fi fantasy/comedy/historical pageant about a futuristic Austria still under Allied control, *1. April 2000* [April 1, 2000] (1952) failed as an internationally aimed "event film" and a plea for national sovereignty, but it has since become a cult film. The most important genre to emerge from the 1950s, which marked a "boom" in Austrian film production, was the Imperial Epic, created by veteran Ernst Marischka and his rival, newcomer Franz Antel, who specialized in audience-pleasing comedies (featuring the "dream comedy team" of veteran stars Paul Hörbiger and Hans Moser) and who would remain Austria's most prolific commercial directors into the next century. These lavish, color historical romances of nineteenth-century aristocratic Vienna brought Austria back into the world market. Its best representative is Marischka's *Sissi* trilogy (1955–57) about the young lives of Emperor Franz Joseph and Empress Elisabeth (Sissi), which launched actress Romy Schneider.

While Willi Forst reinvented his style and ultimately retired from filmmaking in the late 1950s, and the Imperial Epics devolved into musical comedies by the early 1960s, it was the *Heimatfilm*, or provincial film, that attracted the largest German-speaking audiences. These romance dramas, present in Austrian and German film since the 1920s, used the beauty of alpine settings and the "purity" of the rural world to enforce a moralistic ideology. Subgenres of the *Heimatfilm* also developed rapidly, until the formula faded in the 1960s or was transformed by sex comedies.

With the emergence of television and the artistic powerhouse of Austria's national network, ORF, the demise of many of the stars and filmmakers of the 1930s and 1940s, the dilution of film style and content in large multinational co-productions, and the lack of national subsidies, Austria's commercial industry disappeared in the 1960s. While there was no mainstreamed new wave movement to take its place, isolated, highly experimental film based in Actionist performance art evolved from such artists as Peter Kubelka, Ferry Radax, Kurt Kren, Günther Brus, and Peter Weibel. Audiences were alienated by these examples of shock art, which attacked traditional forms and bourgeois complacency, and turned to television.

The late 1970s marked the measured return of narrative films, although these were small, local productions rarely screened in the remaining cinemas or exported. A few attempts at large commercial co-productions failed, but Valie Export emerged as one of the leaders of international feminist filmmaking, and her work found a limited mainstream audience

MICHAEL HANEKE AND THE NEW AUSTRIAN FILM

It is clear that the new era in Austrian film has been in the making for some time, emerging from the impecunious experiments of the 1970s to current global interest, and developing through artistic and theoretical concerns rather than for commercial interests. Much of this journey has been based on the development of the Austrian nation during the past several decades as its society continues to wrestle with its identity and geopolitical role. Michael Haneke's work has stimulated international cinema discourse on a level not seen since the French New Wave or New German Cinema. His breakthrough as a filmmaker came with his very first feature, *Der siebente Kontinent* in 1989; that film joins two later films, *Benny's Video* (1992) and *71 Fragmente einer Chronologie des Zufalls* (1994), to form a trilogy on the social alienation and narcissism nurtured by the age of video and computers. *Caché* (2005), however, has opened debate on the American reception of contemporary European filmmaking. Haneke's study of a Parisian couple unhinging in the paranoia caused by surveillance videos anonymously deposited at their front door was made in France with French actors, but the film, with its Austrian director/writer and crew, is regarded even by the French as an "Austrian" film. A critical and popular success across the continent, *Caché* found gold at Cannes and garnered awards for Best European Film and Best European Director at the 2005 European Academy Awards; it was rejected as Austria's official entry for the Best Foreign Language Oscar of 2005 because it was shot in French.

throughout Europe. With ORF becoming a major film financing source, and a national subsidy program finally announced in 1980, more narrative films found limited commercial or television screenings. These were revisions of traditional Austrian genres, such as the *Heimatfilm*, which became neorealistic, exploring political corruption in Christian Berger's *Raffl* (1984) and the Nazi past in Wolfram Paulus's *Heidenlöcher* (1985). Socially critical film focused on racism, xenophobia, sexual repression, and psychological abuse, usually presented through dramas about family dysfunction or the outsider: Peter Patzak's *Kassbach* (1979); Michael Haneke's *Der siebente Kontinent* [The Seventh Continent] (1989) and *Benny's Video* (1992). Veteran director Franz Antel returned with a popular tragicomic generational saga dealing with Austria's place in Central Europe beginning with the *Anschluss*, as seen through the eyes of a Viennese butcher and his family, in *Der Bockerer* [The Stubborn Mule] (1981) starring Karl Merkatz. The film proved that the Nazi period in Austria was now a topic for commercial film. Axel Corti and Nikki List also gained international attention for their work in historical drama and comedy, respectively.

The films of the 1990s to the present, funded by a network of systems and European co-productions, have found international attention at film festivals and have become known as New Austrian Film. Haneke's *Funny Games* (1997) became the first Austrian film to compete at Cannes since the 1950s, and Barbara Albert's award-winning *Nordrand* [City Skirts] (1999) led the strong female presence in Austrian film in the twenty-first century (Barbara Gäftner, Ruth Mader, Ruth Beckerman). Haneke's *Die Klavierspielerin* [The Piano Teacher] (2001), based on 2004 Nobel Prize–winning Austrian author Elfriede Jelinek's metaphor on self-abusive repression in the high-culture and economically prosperous atmosphere of Austria, has found international audiences and acclaim. So, too, has Ulrich Seidl's *Hundstage* [Dog Days] (2001), a similar examination of the dark side of Vienna's pristine suburbs.

Austrian filmmakers are moving toward becoming a more unified force with political influence, as well as working to increase subsidies and control of national festivals and film promotion. Cinema theaters have returned in the form of luxurious multiplex houses that attract sizable numbers, and art house screenings of classic or rediscovered films have also become popular draws through the restoration and marketing efforts of the Film Archive Austria (FAA). The Viennale and Diagonale Film Festivals are considered major national and international venues. While American blockbusters and some German comedies still hold the box office, Austrian films once again attract a respectable domestic interest.

The population of Austria is 8 million. Cinema admissions for 2004 totaled 19,316,023 at 562 screens.

BALKAN CINEMA: SERBIA/MONTENEGRO/YUGOSLAVIA, SLOVENIA, CROATIA, BOSNIA-HERZEGOVINA, MACEDONIA, ALBANIA

Serbian film traditionally dominated Balkan cinema in its development phase in the early twentieth century and during the existence of the Yugoslavian state that was created following World War I. With the establishment of a Communist regime in 1945, state control, limitation of foreign imports (mostly from Soviet bloc nations), and expansion of the industry for propaganda purposes allowed for the first continuous production of all genres of film in Yugoslavia's history. As Tito's dictatorial regime distanced itself from strict Soviet influence, Yugoslavian film, when compared with that of other Eastern bloc countries, managed to be the most Western European in terms of quality, style, and production structures. Artistic and production competition emancipated the cinema from Soviet socialist realism and increased both local and international recognition of Yugoslavian film. Important directors of the period include Rados Novakovic, Vojislav Nanovic, and Vladimir Pogacic, who received the first major film festival award (first prize at Czechoslovakia's Karlovy Vary) for a Yugoslavian film. The most popular theme of the 1950s and 1960s was Yugoslavia's role in World War II, but Zivorad Mitrovic shifted the genre and audience taste to adventure film. Co-productions with Western European countries (Austria, Norway, Germany, Great Britain) also boosted local production and the use of studio sites in the 1960s and 1970s. A new generation of Serbian filmmakers including Goran Paskaljevic, Srdjan Karanovic, Goran Markovic, Dejan Karaklajic, and Darko Bajic (educated in Belgrade, but also in Prague and in other European film centers), attracted national and foreign critical interest in the following two decades.

Yugoslavia's dissolution in the 1990s resulted in over 250 films about the various conflicts, and it also freed the national cinemas of Slovenia, Croatia, Bosnia, and Macedonia, which had had only minor representation in Yugoslavian cinema. These newly established states suffered from the lack of even the minor state support found in post-Communist Eastern Europe, and it took about five years for new production structures to emerge after war and independence. Nevertheless, a passion for the development of recognized national cinema cultures is evident in all the post-Yugoslavian states.

Slovenia, which had avoided war during the breakup of Yugoslavia, launched a Film Fund in 1993. The low level of financial support and the continuing box office dominance of foreign features made filmmakers turn to "small," low-budget contemporary films that attracted a relatively impressive portion of the overall audience. These films deal with social criticism, reflections on Slovenian nationhood, and the alienation of postmodern urban life, similar to recent New Austrian Film. Igor Sterk's *Ljubljana* (2001), which portrays the young generation of the nation's capital, is a standout among these films. Notable directors include Damjan Kozole, Janez Lapjane, and Andej Kosak.

In contrast, Croatia has seen the shuttering of most of its cinema theaters. Those that remain open screen Hollywood films, but even these have low attendance levels. Although audiences prefer to stay home and watch Croatian and international films on television, national directors find interest in their work at film festivals. Directors such as Viko Ruic, Mladan Juran, and Dalibor Matanic focus on contemporary themes of cultural intolerance, urban alienation, or Croatia's recent history.

Bosnia, which has had an independent cinema for half a century, has had little established studio support. Nevertheless, Bosnian filmmakers have earned a higher level of importance as representatives of the national culture than have the country's writers or even its leaders. Double Cannes Film Festival winner Emir Kusturica (*Bila jednom jedna zemlja* [Underground], 1995), Oscar winner Danis Tanović (*Nikogarsnja zemlja* [No Man's Land], 2001) and European Academy Award winner Ahmed Imanmovic (*10 Minuta* [10 Minutes], 2002) are more famous than any other figures in public life. Lack of national funding (which is often promised but undelivered) is the main reason that only one or two feature films are produced every two to three years, but when they appear, they do not fail to attract large audiences. Bosnian films tend to deal with the aftermath of the Balkan War, refugee dramas, and tragicomedies on contemporary life. The Sarajevo Film Festival was launched in 2002, and CineLink, a platform to showcase scripts from Bosnia-Herzegovina, Croatia, Serbia, and Montenegro for potential producers, promises a growth in cinematic cooperation beween the nations of the former Yugoslavia.

The Skopje Film Festival was founded in 1998 to help boost the cultural promotion of Macedonia's capital. Albania had some co-productions with the Soviet Union during the 1950s (although Communist, the country professed its alliance with China rather than with the USSR), but its post-Communist cinema is nearly nonexistent. Its few theaters show imports. Serbia and Montenegro (the new name for the former post-union Yugoslavia) shows a distinct preference for the escapism of comedy and romantic dramas in response to current economic hardships. Despite the fact that cinema ticket prices have risen 75 percent in the last few years, audiences are loyal to the national product, and half of the top ten box office hits between 2001 and 2003 were Serbian films.

The population of Serbia and Montenegro is 8.5 million. Cinema admissions for 2004 totaled 4.68 million at 195 screens. The population of Slovenia is 1.98 million, and cinema admissions for 2004 totaled 3 million at 100 screens. The population of Croatia is 4,381,352. Cinema admissions for 2004 totaled 2,656,543 at 55 screens. The population of Bosnia-Herzegovina is 3 million. There are no available admission figures for the country's 25 screens. There are no current figures regarding admissions or screens in Macedonia and Albania.

BALTIC CINEMA: LITHUANIA, LATVIA, ESTONIA

Although the nations of Lithuania, Latvia, and Estonia all have their distinct linguistic, historical, and cultural traditions, they have been strongly linked by the geopolitics of the nineteenth and twentieth centuries. Following the fall of Czarist Russia, these nations found brief independence in the interwar period but were once again swallowed up by the Soviet Union. Much of their national culture was forbidden or destroyed. Reestablished after the dissolution of the Soviet Communism, the three independent Baltic states have continued their regionalism through shared history and through membership in the European Union.

The Lithuanian Newsreel Studio was founded following the Soviet annexation of the Baltic states in World War II. Approximately three feature films, forty documentaries, and forty newsreel journals were produced during this period and into the postwar era. The films were heavily censored and of a propagandist nature, but the technical quality was on par with Soviet film. This production firm was expanded into the Lithuanian Film Studios in 1956. In order to demonstrate Soviet cultural control, all Baltic films were produced in association with Russian facilities or even made in Russia, including the Lithuanian feature *Maryte* (1947), which was produced at the Mosfilm Studio with Lithuanian actors. *Zydrasis horizontas* [The Blue Horizon] (1957) directed by Vytautas Mikalauskas, was the first Baltic film to be made independently. Lithuanian film drew both Soviet and international attention at film festivals from the 1960s into the 1980s. Important films include Raimondas Vabalas's *Zingsniai nakti* [The Footsteps at Night] (1962); Vytautas Zalakevicius's *Vienos dienos kronika* [The Chronicle of a Day] (1963); and Algimantas Puipa's *Amzinoji sviesa* [The Eternal Light] (1987).

In 1987, director Sarunas Bartas established Kinema, the first independent Lithuanian studio. Following independence, national funding was problematic, and Lithuanian cinema was completely overshadowed by foreign imports. Nevertheless, several new film companies were founded, and approximately two feature films and ten documentaries have been made each year since the beginning of the 1990s. Given the small production numbers, Lithuania has had an inordinate presence at international film festivals and has won an impressive number of awards. Current filmmakers of note include Vytautas Zalakevicius, Diana and Kornelijus Matuzevicius, Andrius Stonys, Janina Lapinskaite, and Valdas Navasaitis. Lithuania has solved some of its financial support problems by developing co-productions with Germany. Its most recent films have focused on the nation's fight for independence, in such films as Jonas Vaitkus's historical drama, *Vienui vieni* [Utterly Alone] (2004), about a legendary partisan and his heroic exploits against the Soviets. The 2003 Vilnius Spring Festival screened around sixty foreign films as well as Lithuanian work.

The early Soviet film industry benefited greatly from the revolutionary work of Latvia's Sergei M. Eisenstein, who today is considered one of the great directors in international cinema history. The first Latvian color film, a propaganda documentary entitled *Soviet Latvia*, was awarded the Special Jury Prize at Cannes in 1951. Latvia established the European Documentary Film Symposium in 1977 and the International film forum "Arsenals" in 1986. Juris Podnieks, one of Latvia's most critically acclaimed filmmakers, chronicled the collapse of the Soviet Union in his *Hello, Do You Hear Us?* (1989). In 1989, the same year as the breakup of the Warsaw Pact, Ivars Seleckis became the first Latvian filmmaker to be awarded the European Academy Award for his documentary *Crossroad Street*. At about the same time, Latvia established the Academy of Culture, which also offers film production training. The nation has one of the lowest state film subsidies in Europe, but this has not stopped production and audience interest. Women are strongly represented among the new generation of filmmakers. In addition to Anna Viduleja, whose film *Pitons* [The Python] (2003) provides a metaphor on the totalitarian state, there is filmmaker Mika Kaurismäki as well as screenwriter Margarita Pervenecka.

Estonia constructed its large Riga Film Studio in 1963. The Estonians have proven to be no less a cinema-audience nation than Latvia and Lithuania and are particularly proud of their national products. In 2002 the film *Nimed marmortahvlil* [Names in Marble] by Elmo Nüganen, about a student who joins in the fight for Estonian independence in 1918, sold 136,000 tickets, beating the all-time record set by the American film *Titanic*. Estonian animators are now considered among the best in Europe, and television has begun to screen Estonian-made documentaries. There is a current effort to educate the nation about its film history, which was suppressed under the Soviet Union; cinema pioneers are celebrated, and their films are being restored and screened. In 1994 the Estonian director Jaan Kolberg directed the second film about the national hero Jüri Rumm. This romantic historical epic about a horse thief in Czarist Estonia included most of the nation's best-known film actors.

The population of Lithuania is 3,698,500; there are no admission figures available for the 83 screens. The population of Latvia is 2.4 million. Cinema admissions for 2004 totaled 1,908,390 at 35 screens. The population of Estonia is 1.36 million. Cinema admissions for 2004 totaled 1.56 million at 81 screens.

Lithuania, Latvia, and Estonia are represented by an umbrella organization, Baltic Films, which promotes their films at global festivals and seeks to distribute their films on the world market.

BENELUX CINEMA: BELGIUM, NETHERLANDS, LUXEMBOURG

Dutch film began early, but foreign imports dominated the market. Unlike other cinematic "regions" in Europe (the Baltic states, Switzerland's relationship with German and Austrian cinema) or artificially linked cinemas (Czechoslovakia, Yugoslavia), there has been a movement toward and interest in collaboration among the Netherlands, Belgium, and Luxembourg, which have formed a multilingual cinema in addition to the development of individual national cinemas.

In the Netherlands, Joris Ivens emerged as a world-class filmmaker in early sound and continued mostly in documentary films until his death in 1989. Fons Rademakers was the leading director of the 1950s and 1960s, as was the award-winning documentarian Bert Haanstra (who briefly worked with French director Jacques Tati). The increasing use of English following World War II has also encouraged Dutch filmmakers to move to the United States or to Great Britain. An example of newer Benelux successes emigrating abroad is Paul Verhoeven, whose intense but entertaining films on sexual relationships and the Dutch past (*Turkish Delight*, 1973; *Soldier of Orange*, 1977; *Spetters*, 1980) brought international focus to Dutch cinema. Other examples are cinematographer Jan de Bont and the Dardenne brothers, Jean-Pierre and Luc. Several internationally known actors began their careers in Verhoeven films, including Rutger Hauer and Jeroen Krabbé. Dutch film is currently supported by both government subsidies and private investment generated by a tax incentive law, which has an uncertain future. Children's films create a healthy box office, while features by directors Ben Sombogaart, Pieter Kuipers, Maria Peter, and Theo van Gogh have earned critical praise. Dutch co-production supports the works of Danish director Lars von Trier and Britain's Peter Greenaway. Infrequently, a Dutch film manages to break into the roster of Hollywood-dominated, top ten box office hits, as was the case with Pim van Hoeve's romantic teen comedy, *Volle maan* [Full Moon] (2002).

Belgium, a bilingual country (French and Flemish), had a stronger relationship with France than with the Netherlands in its early film, and its industry came to be dominated by France's Pathé company. The first Belgian studio was built by Alfred Machin outside Brussels, and producer Hippolyte De Kempeneer led the displacement of the French by Belgian talent in nationally produced film. The 1930s were dominated by Charles Dekeukeleire and Henri Storck as well as by documentary filmmakers André Cauvin and Gérard De Boe, whose experimental style gained European fame. The "Belgian School" of documentary filmmaking also influenced narrative filmmakers Gaston Schoukens and Jan Vanderheyden, who concentrated on bringing Belgian literature to the screen. Following World War II, Belgian animation was notable, but film production suffered from the lack of a government subsidy (finally begun in 1964) and from American, French, and Dutch imports. André Delvaux, (*Un soir, un train* [One Night, a Train], 1968) and Roland Verhavert (*De Loteling* [The Conscript], 1974) emerged as major filmmakers, and co-production between the Benelux countries became common. In the 1980s and 1990s, Marc Didden,

Robbe de Hert, Chantal Akerman, Benoît Poelvoorde, Marleen Gorris, and Oliver Gourmet returned the cinema to film festivals and international art houses, earning one Oscar and several top awards at Cannes. Belgium has a relatively large set of festivals for a small country: the Mons Romantic Film Festival, the Brussels Fantasy Film Festival, the Ghent Film Festival, and the Namur Film Festival.

Luxembourg's size, its cinematically dominant neighbors, and its three official languages (German, French, and Letzebuergesch), have made it a natural for film import rather than for production. Director René Leclère dominated Luxembourg's film industry in the 1930s and 1940s. Bady Minck, who makes her films in Luxembourg and Austria, and Laurent Brandenbourger have recently received attention at European film festivals. It was the amateur film scene, however, that was responsible for creating a true Letzebuergesch-language cinema in the early 1980s, and one Letzebuergesch film is now released every two years. In 1989 the National Center of the Audiovisual was created, and the National Fund of Support for Audiovisual Production was founded in 1990. Use of this fund has allowed Luxembourg to attract international producers, and co-productions have significantly raised the nation's film production: approximately 110 films were made in Luxembourg between 1899 and 1990, whereas 120 films were produced between 1990 and 1999.

The population of Belgium is 10.31 million. Cinema admissions for 2004 totaled 24.5 million at 514 screens. The population of the Netherlands is 16.1 million. Cinema admissions for 2004 totaled 24.1 million at 596 screens. The population of Luxembourg is 441,300. Cinema admissions for 2004 totaled 1.4 million at 25 screens.

BULGARIA

Bulgarian audiences have traditionally embraced foreign films. The over 200 cinema theaters of the 1930s and 1940s screened mostly imports. With the onset of the Communist era following World War II, the state made considerable funding available for the expansion and promotion of the national cinema to serve state propaganda aims. The number of theaters increased twenty-fold between the onset (1945) and the fall of the Marxist regime (1989). Film production also grew substantially during these years. Ironically, although Communist ideology preferred a deconstruction of national culture, this support developed audience desire for a national cinema and turned them away from a traditional interest in imports (these were now Soviet and other Eastern bloc films). A national film festival, the Golden Rose in the city of Varna, was founded in 1977.

Censorship, ideological restrictions, and state funding were all extinguished with the end of the Communist regime. The drop in local film production was met by audience return to foreign films and by a general drop in cinema attendance. With the return of some national funding, and despite poor film distribution and continuing popular disinterest, critics and cineastes hailed the 2002 Golden Rose Festival as the beginning of a revival of the national cinema. Ljudmil Todorov, who has become one of Bulgaria's best-known directors since the fall of Communism, took the top prize at the festival for *Emigrants* (2002), a tragicomedy about socioeconomic conditions in contemporary Bulgaria. Other popular filmmakers are Krassimir Krumov, Konstantin Bonev, and Ivanka Gravcheva. The Sofia Film Festival, Bulgaria's premier cinematic showcase, has helped bring filmmakers to Bulgaria and has stimulated international interest in Bulgarian productions since the mid-1990s. The election of ex-king Simeon II as Prime Minister in 2001 brought with it a new government attitude toward the national cinema, as Simeon's party pledged to increase and secure development. Bulgaria's EU membership may also bring changes in this sector. The Black Sea Star Film

Festival, held simultaneously in three cities, was launched in 2002 to further national interest in local production.

The population of Bulgaria is 7.85 million. Cinema admissions for 2004 totaled 24.5 million at 202 screens.

CZECHOSLOVAKIA/CZECH REPUBLIC AND SLOVAKIA

Czechoslovakia was truncated by Nazi Germany in 1938, which turned the Czech portion of the nation into the "Protectorate of Bohemia and Moravia" and attempted a Germanization of its culture. Prague's Barrandov Studios became the third site of Nazi Propaganda Minister Goebbels's film program, after Berlin and Vienna. Its role was to serve as a secondary production site and as a source of films made for southeastern European Axis states and occupied territories. Following World War II and the Sovietization of the reestablished Czechoslovakia, Czechoslovak film fell into a period of decline, offering the same type of propaganda dramas and documentaries found across Eastern Europe during the late 1940s and the 1950s.

With the attempts to liberalize its Stalinist socialism in the 1960s, and the influence of the French New Wave, the film industry was revitalized by the critical and artistic visions of such directors as Jan Kadar, Milos Forman, Jiri Menzel, Elmar Klos, Vojtech Jasny, Jan Nemec, Ivan Passer, and Vera Chytilova. Many of this new generation of filmmakers were graduates of FAMU, Prague's Film and Television School at the Academy of Performing Arts. Audiences returned to the cinema after having rejected the hard-line Czechoslovak and other Eastern European and Soviet films that had dominated cinemas and television. This first true new wave of film in the Eastern bloc garnered swift international attention and acclaim: both Kadar and Klos's Slovak film, *Obchod na korze* [The Shop on Main Street] (1965), and Menzel's Czech film, *Ostre sledovane vlaky* [Closely Watched Trains] (1966), won several European film festival awards and Oscars for Best Foreign Language Film. Slovakian filmmakers rose to greater national and international notability, particularly Jaromil Jireš and Juraj Herz. The Prague Spring of 1968, which sought to create "socialism with a human face" to the point of independence from Soviet dictates, was crushed by the Soviet invasion in August of that year. It brought an end to the new wave movement, and it reestablished strong censorship and a propaganda-aimed film industry. Many filmmakers were forbidden to work or departed the country for international production (Passer, Nemec, Forman). Somewhat distant from the concentrated site of Soviet repression, Slovak filmmakers in Bratislava were able to sidestep some of the censorship and create more experimental and socially critical films.

With the fall of Communism in 1989, Barrandov Studios was privatized, and filmmakers were no longer guaranteed funds from the new government. Financial support for the industry came with foreign productions that employed the Prague studio as an economically and technically advantageous alternative to other production sites in Europe. Prague, Bratislava, and other cities have often been used to represent pre-World War II Europe in films since their historical architecture is similar to what had existed in Vienna, Budapest, Berlin, and even in Paris, and has not been damaged or greatly altered. Films of the 1990s took on the past with honesty and criticism, reconnecting with the style of the Czech and the lesser-known Slovak New Wave and managing to bring national audiences back to the theaters. This period brought a new roster of notable filmmakers, including David Ondricek, Jan Sverak, Jan Hrebejk, Sasa Gedeon, and Petr Zelenka. The tradition of Czech puppet animation of the 1970s and 1980s found new life in the visions of internationally acclaimed master of grotesque animation Jan Švankmajer, who influenced a new generation of experimental animators such as Jiri Barta. Milos Forman moved into the first rank of international directors with the Oscar-winning Hollywood-based films *One Flew over the Cuckoo's Nest* (1975) and *Amadeus* (1983).

The Czech Film Center was created in 2003 to promote films at festivals, and Barrandov remains popular with foreign productions. The Czech Karlovy Vary Film Festival is considered one of the major competitive venues for European and international film, and a few Czech films break into the nation's top ten box office hits, which are dominated by American and British film. Slovakian feature film production is still scant, but documentaries are filling the gap with such works as Matej Minac's award-winning *Nicholas Winton—Sila l'udskosti* [Nicholas Winton—The Power of Good] (2002), about the British man who rescued over 600 Czechoslovakian Jewish children in 1939 by bringing them across Nazi Germany to Britain. The nation's entry into the European Union brings some promise of European co-production and funding. American films are Slovakia's only box office hits.

The population of the Czech Republic is 10.27 million. Cinema admissions for 2004 totaled 10.92 million at 754 screens. The population of Slovakia is 5.4 million. Cinema admissions for 2004 totaled 3.01 million at 312 screens.

THE CZECH FILM INDUSTRY

The relationship between Slovak and Czech filmmaking did not end with the establishment of the separate states in 1992; Slovak filmmakers such as Jurai Jakubisko and cinematographer Marin Strba continue to work in the Czech Republic. But film was not promoted in Slovakia during the post-breakup government of Vladmir Meciar, and production came to a near standstill by the mid-1990s. In the Czech Republic, a difficult transition to capitalism was echoed in films that either romanticized or satirized the Communist past or unflinchingly critiqued urban life. By 2000 Czech television co-financed most productions, as film does not receive direct support from the Prague government. Nevertheless, the Czech audiences are staunchly supportive of their film industry, which managed to produce twenty features in 2002. Although these new films have difficulty in being distributed beyond the nation's borders, they have made their mark in recent international film festivals.

FRANCE

The Allied liberation of France immediately destroyed the careers of Nazi collaborators, and the unprotected domestic film market was dealt a blow by the creation of the CNC (National Center of Cinema), the strongest film finance program in postwar Europe. The period between 1945 and 1959 has been unfairly disparaged as "papa's cinema," an era of unremarkable conservatism in French film, for it experienced box office and critical successes in the postwar films of interwar giant Marcel Carné, in Robert Bresson's Catholic spirituality, and through Henri-Georges Clouzot's suspense dramas, which brought Yves Montand to the screen. Clouzot's Hitchcock-like *Les Diaboliques* [Diabolique] (1955) also made an international star of Simone Signoret. Comedies by Jacques Tati took on the absurd aspects of France's industrialization and modernization during the Fourth Republic, while Jean Cocteau represented the avant-garde, and Jean-Pierre Melville moved between experimental and mainstream film influenced by American action cinema. Hollywood turned to Parisian subject matter during this decade, with musicals and romances starring French actors Charles Boyer, Maurice Chevalier, Leslie Caron, and Louis Jordan, but French audiences and critics dismissed these as American cultural colonialism and cliché-ridden fantasies.

STYLES IN FRENCH CINEMA

No less than five different French film style movements marked the final decades of the twentieth century. Heritage cinema, led by Truffaut's detailed occupation period drama, *Le Dernier metro* [The Last Metro] (1980), moved toward literary adaptations and period works. "The Look" was introduced by Jean-Jacques Beineix's *Diva* (1981) and included Luc Besson and Léos Carax as its creators. The style focused on youth themes and drew audiences that appreciated innovative art direction and the stylish, postmodern pastiche. Bertrand Tavernier emerged with films on marginalized social groups and issues in a gritty realism hat became known as *le jeune cinema*. The Women's Film, led by Coline Serreau, Diane Kurys, Claire Denis, and Josiane Balasko, is broader in theme definition and ranges from popular genres with a distinct female focus to autobiographical stories and feminist deconstructions/adaptations of Heritage film genres.

Along with the earlier Italian neorealism, the French New Wave is considered the most powerful shift in cinematic aesthetics during the mid-twentieth century. It brought international acclaim to its artists and its style, influenced other arts and national cinemas during the 1960s, and has continued to be an inspiration in filmmaking. The directors associated with the movement had met during the 1950s at the Paris Cinematheque (founded in 1936; now among the most impressive film archives in the world) and were all influenced by the theoretical publication *Cahiers du cinema* and critic André Bazin, who advocated sociopolitical criticism, realism, and a personal, literary-like style. Although the French New Wave paid homage to Hollywood's melodramas and low-budget features, it moved against the dominant cinema of the time with on-location filming, improvisational dialogue, hand-held camera work, radical editing experiments (the jump-cut), and socially critical stories that also used the urban settings as "character." Among the most notable creations are Jean-Luc Godard's *A bout de souffle* [Breathless] (1959) with Jean-Paul Belmondo; François Truffaut's *Les 400 Coups* [The 400 Blows] (1959); Alain Resnais's *Hiroshima mon amour* [Hiroshima My Love] (1959) and his fragmented memory puzzle *L'Année dernière a Marienbad* [Last Year at Marienbad] (1961); Truffaut's love triangle starring Jeanne Moreau, *Jules et Jim* [Jules and Jim] (1962); Godard's *Le Mepris* [Contempt] (1963), which gave 1950s sex-symbol Brigitte Bardot a significant dramatic role; Agnes Varda's *Cléo de 5 à 7* [Cleo from 5 to 7] (1962); and Jacques Demy's all-sung romantic drama, *Les Parapluies de Cherbourg* [The Umbrellas of Cherbourg] (1964), which introduced Catherine Deneuve to lasting stardom.

The growing student protests leading to a general strike that threatened to bring down the French establishment in 1968 radicalized the remnants of the French New Wave. Godard took on a far-leftist stance with a shock/black comedic attack on the Parisian bourgeoisie, Western capitalism, and trendy pop/rock-youth culture in *Week-end* (1967) and, working with Maoists, created propagandist collages. He soon disowned this work and returned, as did most of the former New Wavers, to more traditional and commercial structures in the 1970s and 1980s. Realism continued to hold sway in examinations of recent history and contemporary society, which brought actors Isabelle Huppert and Gerard Depardieu to fame. But the fall of censorship during the 1960s and the decline of cinema audiences, resulting from increased television viewing and a general fatigue following the cinema-saturated 1960s, also generated a long series of soft-porn features, lead by Just Jaeckin's *Emmanuelle* (1974), and light comedies starring veteran clown Bourvil.

By the turn of the current century, most of the French actors recognizable globally were female: Isabelle Adjani, Emmanuelle Béart, Sophie Marceau, Juliette Binoche, Julie Delpy, and Audrey Tautou; the latter starred in Jean-Pierre Jeunet's stylish but sentimental comedy

Amelie (2001), a major international hit. Despite a recent move toward sex and violence in the work of art house filmmakers, Jeunet's film suggests the commercial route for French film success in the early twenty-first century. The French remain among Europe's most engaged film audiences, with cinema attendance reaching a record 186 million in 2002, thanks to multiplex systems and a modernization of art houses. France is America's smallest film market in Europe, not only because of the national pride in its leadership of the art form—the annual Cannes Festival is arguably the most important competitive film festival and market in the world—but because many recent French films have also rivaled Hollywood productions for pure entertainment value. As auteur/art films have become increasingly less popular, mainstream films find large audiences in France and abroad: Francois Ozon's *8 Femmes* [8 Women] (2001) a kitschy, socially critical, comedic whodunit, was a broad European hit, and Christophe Gans's *Le Pacte des Loups* [Brotherhood of the Wolf] (2001) mixed French history, trendy gothic horror, and computer-generated effects for successful global escapism.

The population of France is 58.5 million. Cinema admissions for 2004 totaled 184.5 million at 5280 screens.

GERMANY

Germany's pioneering production site, UFA, which had been nationalized to produce lavish entertainment and propaganda films under the Nazi regime, fell under the control of the Soviets in 1945, who assisted in the creation of DEFA, the state-controlled film company for the German Democratic Republic (GDR, Communist East Germany). The company was the first in postwar Germany to create a film dealing with the immediate past, *Die Mörder sind unter uns* [The Murderers Are Amongst Us] (1946) that moved in a neorealist direction and connected with the proletarian films of the Weimar Republic. Although also following the Soviet socialist realist dictates until the 1970s, East German film tended toward a more subtle and artistic use of Marxist ideology in its early "rubble films" and later traditional genres. The Federal Republic of Germany (FRG, West Germany) moved its film industry to Hamburg, then Munich. While the West German film industry also began with works that dealt with the conditions of the postwar nation, it rapidly moved toward solid escapist entertainment, reinventing the lavish styles of the 1940s in musicals, costume dramas, and comedies. Many were remakes of earlier films; others followed the style of the strong Hollywood presence in its cinemas. By the 1950s, the royal melodrama and the *Heimatfilm*, or provincial drama, both influenced by these genres' boom in Austria, became among the most popular genres in West German cinema, rivaled only by emerging pop musicals, which launched singers and comedians who crossed over into recording and television. A new generation of stars appeared, often shared with Austrian film: among them, O. W. Fischer, Ruth Leuwerick, Curd Jürgens, Hildegard Knef, and Maria Schell. As Hollywood film and German television sapped the audience, production moved to cheaply produced sensationalism, sex comedies, and adult-themed docudramas.

Rejecting what they saw as the "bankruptcy" of commercial film, a group of young filmmakers created the Oberhausen Manifesto in 1962, which demanded a break with the past and the creation of socially critical and artistic filmmaking. While these films, which were often derivative of styles from France, Italy, and Sweden, garnered some critical acclaim, they soon faded because of a lack of financial support and popular disinterest. By the 1970s a second generation of auteur filmmakers had arrived, whose productions were supported by the publicity efforts of Alexander Kluge. He encouraged the government to act as a patron to film, which would represent a progressive and artistically important Germany to the world in what became known as New German Cinema. Films made by Werner Herzog (*Aguirre,*

125

NEW GERMAN CINEMA

New German Cinema used the production values of commercial film genres for its critical political, social, and sexual explorations; it was known for the distinctive personal style of its filmmakers, for its technical excellence, and for the way it commented on German popular film of the past, which it in many ways parodied and deconstructed. With the conservative government of Helmut Kohl and the shift in the film financing policy during the 1980s, New German Cinema fell into decline, its talents moving to television, independent co-production, or working abroad. The reunification of the two German states in 1990 brought with it a new generation of filmmakers and subject matter. Having put the Nazi period "into history," post-reunification cinema looks at the absurdity of sociopolitical norms and toward a fresh melding of popular and critical/artistic style in comedies and dramas.

der Zorn Gottes [Aguirre, Wrath of God], 1972), Margaretha von Trotta (Die verlorene Ehre der Katherina Blum [The Lost Honor of Katherina Blum], 1975), Rainer Werner Fassbinder (Die Ehe der Maria Braun [The Marriage of Maria Braun], 1978), Volker Schlöndorff (Die Blechtrommel [The Tin Drum], 1979), Helma Sanders-Brahms (Deutschland bleiche Mutter [Germany Pale Mother], 1980), and Wim Wenders (Paris, Texas, 1984) rapidly gained international attention and acclaim, as did many of their new actors (Hanna Schygulla, Barbara Sukowa, Bruno Ganz).

In 1992 director Volker Schlöndorff revitalized the UFA/DEFA studio as a cutting-edge production site and museum. By the turn of the twenty-first century, German cinema had regained international interest at the competitive Berlinale Festival and other regional events through auteur/commercial films that are informed by postmodern edginess, such as Tom Tykwer's Lola rennt [Run Lola Run] (1998) and Wolfgang Becker's Good Bye Lenin! (2003), and through a presence in Hollywood film (Wolfgang Petersen, Michael Ballhaus, and Roland Emmerich).

The population of Germany is 82,474, 729. Cinema admissions for 2004 totaled 163.9 million at 4,868 screens.

GREECE

Although Greece began filmmaking during roughly the same period as other European nations, its cinema did not seriously emerge until World War II. The founding of the Hollywood-style Finos film company in 1943 and its genre features marked the first accomplished attempt at entertaining the Greek audiences with a national film culture. A star system developed, which gave Greece its classic film diva, Aliki Vouyouklaki. Directors of the 1950s include Niko Tsiforos, Dimis Dadiras, Yiorgos Tzavellas, and Alekos Sakellarios. The latter two were among the most successful and helped develop a national audience loyal to Greek film. Tzavellas's work could break box office records beyond any import, and Sakellarios directed over fifty films, which are today considered classics.

The melodramas and comedies of the 1950s were rejected by Grigoris Grigoriou, who was influenced by Italian neorealism and who introduced a Greek version of the style with Bitter Bread (1951). The three most influential figures in 1960s Greek cinema began in this movement: Cypriot director Michael Cacoyannis, director Nikos Koundouros, and actress Melina Mercouri. Cacoyannis's best-known film abroad is Zorba the Greek (1964), but his cinematic adaptations of Euripidean tragedies earn greater respect by the nation's cineastes. The French New Wave influenced a New Greek Cinema movement of auteur filmmaking, which distanced itself from commercial film and attempted to reach the world market. It was, however, far more than a translation of experimental style. Politically, it defied and rejected the dictatorship that existed from 1967 to 1974; artistically, it attempted to question concepts of Greek culture and society in a period in which the arts became dominated by American influences. Theo Angelopoulos's *Reconstruction* (1970) and Alexis Damianos's *Evdokia* (1971), both of which deal with social constrictions and the notion of freedom, are standouts in this period.

In the 1980s and 1990s, Angelopoulos led a return to more commercial film, winning the top prize at Cannes for his work *Eternity and a Day* (1998). Greek audiences strongly supported the national cinema until the emergence of a new youth market around 2000, which seemed to prefer American films. While exhibition and attendance are currently at an all time high through the creation of regional multiplex cinemas, Greek cinema (including Greek entertainment genre films) has now been reduced to limited appearances at art houses. Nevertheless, new Greek productions, which now feature the first group of female filmmakers in the nation's cinema history, have been embraced by the critics as fresh and important. Narrative films tend to focus on the contemporary working class, youth culture, and the urban milieu, but the recent past also surfaces in Robert Manthoulis's cinematic tapestry *Lilly's Story* (2002), which explores the history of Greek repression.

The population of Greece is 10.9 million. Cinema admissions for 2004 totaled 14.8 million at 440 screens.

HUNGARY

Alexander Korda and Mihaly Kertesz (Hollywood's Michael Curtiz) created significant films during the silent era in Budapest and Vienna before earning fame in London and Hollywood, respectively. Interwar Hungarian actors also moved easily among Budapest, Vienna, and Berlin. Communist control following World War II expanded the cinema to serve state purposes; however, the failed 1956 revolution did not result in the type of heavy censorship and ideological emphasis Czechoslovakian film would experience after 1968, and filmmakers Miklos Jansco, Zoltan Fabri, and Marta Meszaros attempted to lift the style above the proscribed Socialist Realism. By the 1980s two directors had emerged who, in opposite ways, marked the development of the national cinema beyond Communist dictates: Bela Tarr, whose noncommercial, experimental style attracted a cult following, and Istvan Szabo, whose films *Mephisto* (1981), *Colonel Redl* (1984), and *Sunshine* (1999) focused on the Central European (Hungarian/Austrian/German) experience in the twentieth century. Szabo has become Hungary's best-known artistic/commercial filmmaker and has led Hungarian co-productions with a variety of European nations.

Unlike other nations emerging from Communism, Hungary quickly developed a booming film industry based on an impressive national funding policy, private investment, new production companies, and several state-of-the art facilities. Even today, while theaters are still filled mostly with American, French, and German productions, Hungarian films do respectable business, and the favorable funding attracts international co-productions. Gabor Herendi's comedy about a Hungarian American who returns to Hungary and pretends he is a Hollywood film mogul, *Valami Amerika* [A Kind of America] (2003), which targeted youth audiences, has been the greatest success in the post-Communist era. Herendi is now considered the "Hungarian Steven Spielberg," and national audiences await his films with anticipation.

The population of Hungary is 10.5 million. Cinema admissions for 2004 totaled 15,228,000 at 585 screens.

IRELAND

Irish film has had the most culturally contentious history in European cinema, given that the country has suffered no wartime destruction or totalitarian experiences. Throughout the early history of the art, the Catholic Church criticized filmmakers for being a detrimental influence on Irish society. Leftists have considered the industry to be a force promoting capitalist exploitation and class repression, while Republican movements have called for a cinema that would enforce a unified nation, or else have condemned the Irish cinema as a propaganda source for continued British imperialism. Vast emigration from Ireland in the nineteenth and twentieth centuries created a shadow cinema industry in Britain and Hollywood, which reduced the Irish nation and its people to stereotypes that were too often accepted by the interwar national cinema. Irish and British filmmakers and actors have regularly participated in each other's cinemas, and the founding of Ireland's Ardmore Studios brought in many British and American film projects. The mainstay of Irish cinema has been national literature. Sean O'Casey's plays continue to figure importantly among these films, and there have long been whimsical, neorealistic, or epic versions of period rural tales.

The Irish cinema attained world-market status in the 1980s when it began to respond to the clichéd representations of the nation and its people that have been staples of American and British film. Among the filmmakers who have led this new era are director Stephen Frears (*Prick Up Your Ears*, 1987; *The Grifters*, 1990; *Mary Reilly*, 1994); screenwriter Shane Connaughton (*My Left Foot*, 1989; *The Playboys*, 1992; *Run of the Country*, 1995); director Jim Sheridan (*In the Name of the Father*, 1993; *In America*, 2002); director Pat O'Connor (*A Month in the Country*, 1987; *Circle of Friends*, 1994); director Neil Jordan (*The Company of Wolves*, 1985; *Mona Lisa*, 1986; *The Crying Game*, 1992; *Interview with the Vampire*, 1994). Male actors from Ireland have attained global fame in both national and international film in recent decades: Peter O'Toole, Richard Harris, Liam Neeson, Pierce Brosnan, Stephen Rea, Colin Farrell, Patrick Bergin, Milo O'Shea, and Gabriel Byrne (also a producer and director); female actors other than Hollywood's Golden Age stars (Maureen O'Sullivan and Maureen O'Hara) are less well-known. Films like *Michael Collins* (1996) and *The General* (1998) have also brought a corrective view that contrasts with the reductivity of Irish history and culture found in American popular culture. The "troubles" of Ireland's past and present— the division of the country produced by political and religious loyalties, periods of economic misery, and the violence of the IRA—dominate contemporary Irish film and co-productions (*The Butcher Boy*, 1998; *Patriot Games*, 1993; *Angela's Ashes*, 2000).

The national cinema tends to move between low-budget and medium-size works, which ensures the filmmaker control of the work. There has, however, been a sensitivity to Irish culture and politics even in foreign-dominated co-production, as in *The Magdalene Sisters* (2002), which had an Irish cast but was shot in Scotland by Scottish director Peter Mullan, or in Joel Schumacher's *Veronica Guerin* (2002), which was only partially supported by an Irish cast and technical crew. An exhibition boom has led to all-time-high box office figures, with admissions exceeding 18 million, but the top-ten money-making films from 2001 through 2003 were all American.

The population of the Republic of Ireland (not including Northern Ireland) is 3.91 million. Cinema admissions for 2004 totaled 17.3 million at 326 screens.

ITALY

Roberto Rossellini's *Roma citta aperta* [Rome Open City] (1945) is considered the first postwar neorealist film. It was begun during the German occupation of the country and examined the unusual Catholic/Communist underground alliance against fascism, making a star of Anna Magnani, whose role as an impoverished and unwed pregnant widow raising a child broke cinematic ground. The movement, which not only severed Italian film from fascist and Hollywood dominant styles, had a permanent influence in international film art. Shot on location in black and white, the style is known for its documentary photographic quality as well as for a content that examines the experiences of the working classes, first in a war-torn environment and later in the urban dystopia of the Italian Republic.

Emulated by nearly every European postwar cinema, the Italian cinema seemingly owned this revolutionary direction, based on the landmark creations of Rosselini's "rubble films" *Paisan* (1946) and *Germania anno zero* [Germany Year Zero] (1947); Vittorio De Sica's sad portraits of reconstruction and poverty such as *Shoeshine* (1946), *Ladri di biciclette* [The Bicycle Thief] (1948), and *Umberto D.* (1951); and Luchino Visconti's look at the pessimism of peasant society in *La terra trema* [The Earth Trembles] (1948). As social and economic reform took place and deprivation was no longer seen as a major topic, neorealist films concentrated on the loneliness and alienation of the individual in the industrial/urban world and in hierarchical social constructions. A second phase of the style moved in a more commercial, hybrid direction and brought such masterworks as Giuseppe De Santis's *Riso amaro* [Bitter Rice] (1949), which added a sex symbol (Silvana Mangano) who is obsessed with American pop culture to its proletarian setting. As the Italian audience began to demand melodrama and comedy, the style became less socially critical and more "entertaining" by the 1950s. Hollywood genres returned (musicals, crime films), and new directors such as Dino Risi moved between artistic and entertainment modes with accomplishment. The neorealists transformed themselves between the late 1950s and the early 1960s: Rossellini (whose scandalous affair with Ingrid Bergman shifted his work to emotional and psychological themes) and De Sica (who moved into mainstream filmmaking) abandoned purely realist aesthetics, and Visconti developed an operatic historical imagery that would dominate his later work.

The Hollywood connection was firmly established through the co-production genre of the "Spaghetti Westerns," led by Sergio Leone. These films brought fame to film composer Ennio Morricone as well as to stars who had emerged mostly from mainstream entertainment cinema between the 1950s and the 1970s, and who had moved into international film: Sophia Loren, Marcello Mastroianni, Gina Lollobrigida, Virna Lisi, Monica Vitti, Dominique Sanda, and Giancarlo Giannini. Although realist-tinged and politically critical films were made in the 1960s, such as Ermanno Olmi's *Il posto* [The Sound of Trumpets] (1961) and Gillo Pontecorvo's *The Battle of Algiers* (1966), Michelangelo Antonioni and Federico Fellini broke with neorealism entirely and shaped Italian film in the 1960s. Antonioni explored perception and psychology in *L'avventura* [The Adventure] (1959), swinging London in *Blow-up* (1967), and the burnout of America's hippies in *Zabriskie Point* (1969). But it was Fellini's influential, surrealistically tinged examinations of the human experience in *La Dolce Vita* (1959) and *8 1/2* (1963) that generated the greatest international acclaim.

The 1970s were marked by the neodecadent movement, which attempted to analyze the sexual roots of Fascism through lavishly melodramatic film style: Visconti's *La caduta degli dei* [The Damned] (1969), Bernardo Bertolucci's *The Conformist* (1970), and Liliana Cavani's *Il portiere di notte* [The Night Porter] (1974) were all outdone by Pier Paolo Pasolini's highly controversial transference of the depravity of De Sade's *120 Days of Sodom* to the final days of Mussolini's Republic of *Salò* (1975). Fellini looked at a youth's experiences under Fascism in the autobiographical *Amarcord* (1974), and Tinto Brass exploited the style with the soft-porn *Salon Kitty* (1976), followed by the part-all star/part-hardcore historical epic *Caligula* (1977) before the trend expired.

The Fascist past received a more neorealist and ironic treatment in Ettore Scola's *Una giornata particolare* [A Special Day] (1977) and two decades later, in the Oscar-winning hit *La vita è bella* [Life Is Beautiful] (1998), a Chaplinesque tragicomedy set in a concentration camp, directed by and starring actor Roberto Benigni. The brothers Vittorio and Paolo Taviani and Emmanno Olmi returned mainstream Italian cinema to a gentle realism in the 1980s and 1990s, although audiences also liked the Hollywood exploitation-style horror films of Dario Argento, the topical comedies of Mario Monicelli, and the polyglot work of Italian international directors such as Franco Zeffirelli (*Tea with Mussolini*, 1999) and Michael Radford (*Il Postino* [The Postman], 1994). There is an auteur and neo-neorealist school among new directors, but these filmmakers refuse to cater to mainstream tastes, although several films have had breakthroughs with national and international audiences, such as Giuseppe Tornatore's *Cinema Paradiso* (1988). The kitschy, box office megasuccess from Benigni, *Pinocchio* (2002), suggests what is now truly popular, but artistic films such as Nanni Moretti's *The Son's Room* (2001) continue to win awards and cult appreciation.

Cinema attendance has dropped significantly since 2001, and although releases average about 100 each year, few manage to make it into the critical or box office top thirty. The Berlusconi government's severe cuts in film funding and open disregard for Italy's film industry have led to antigovernment demonstrations. The Venice Film Festival is one of the major international cinema venues, although Italy has numerous other specialized and regional festivals.

The population of Italy is 57.8 million. Cinema admissions for 2004 totaled 49.7 million at 3,700 screens.

NORDIC CINEMA: DENMARK, NORWAY, FINLAND, ICELAND

Although of different languages and cultures, the Nordic or Scandinavian cinemas have traditionally been dominated by Swedish imports. Nonetheless, each of the Nordic countries has developed its own national cinema. One of the first countries to begin film production was Denmark, whose early silent film was as popular as that of the United States or Germany in the international market. Legendary Danish pioneer Carl Dreyer made only a few films in his career (mostly during the 1920s and 1930s), but his style continues to be studied by historians and artists internationally. Much of Denmark's film talent emigrated to work in Berlin or Hollywood prior to World War II. Danish films following the war were either unremarkable or paralleled Swedish films by having a reputation for adult themes during the 1960s and 1970s. By the 1980s a new generation of filmmakers, including Billie August (*Pelle the Conqueror*, 1988), Lars von Trier (*Zentropa*, 1991; *Dancer in the Dark*, 2000), and French-born Gabriel Axel (*Babette's Feast*, 1987), had attracted domestic and world audiences and had won awards.

Government funding in Denmark has increased in recent years, and an upward trend in production is evident. Approximately three to four of the top-ten domestic box office successes are Danish films.

Norway did not begin actual national production until the 1920s since its audiences preferred to watch Swedish and Danish film. Rasmus Breistein is considered the nation's most important early filmmaker. Edith Carlmar, the first female director in Norway and a specialist in film noir, and Aren Skouen, a neorealist, helped raise cinema attendance to its peak in the 1950s. In the 1980s and 1990s, Norwegian film had managed to reach beyond its domestic audience, and the directors Nils Gaup, Ola Solum, and Pal Sletaune were attracting international attention at festivals. While production has increased since 2000, with contemporary society and relationship films by Brent Harmer, Jens Lien, and Unni

Straume, few Norwegian films crack the top ten box office hits, which are dominated by Hollywood imports.

Finland has also had a national cinema since the silent era, but it was not well-known internationally or even among the Nordic audiences. Edvin Laine and Jorn Donner were the dominant directors of the 1950s and 1960s. By the 1980s, Finnish film seemed to be dominated by the Kaurismäki brothers, Mika and Aki, who worked independently of each other but shared actors and technical crew. Although foreign films dominate the Finnish box office, Aki Kaurismäki has continued to impress the critics and draws a cult following in art house theaters. Renny Harlin, who became a Hollywood director during the late 1980s, is Finland's major film talent export.

Iceland has created a strong governmental support for film archiving and promotion in recent years and averages about five feature film productions per year. These are usually set in a rural milieu, with Baltasar Kormakur's

DOGME 95

Lars Von Trier created the "Dogme 95" movement, which revisited neorealism and the French New Wave in rejecting genre films and insisting on hand-held camera work, rough visual and sound editing, and a departure from art direction. The manifesto has strongly influenced independent filmmakers around the world. The style has been variously praised and attacked because it can serve to "liberate" the camera as well as excuse a lack of filmmaking craft. Nevertheless, Dogme filmmaking has appeared in most European cinema since the late 1990s. Von Trier has more recently moved to a more radical experimentalism with minimalist sets (chalk lines rather than scenery) that obliterate any illusion of reality (*Dogville*, 2003).

Hafið [The Sea] (2002), a family drama set in a fishing village, representative of the style and quality. In addition to being very popular domestically, this film has received several national and international awards. Documentaries dominate film production, and these often deal with controversial subjects. Small-budget digital video features earn both critical and audience respect, but the few attempts at international market genre films have usually failed at the box office and with critics. Films on Icelandic literature and films from debut filmmakers are the current popular wave with audiences.

The population of Denmark is 5.4 million. Cinema admissions for 2004 totaled 12.9 million at 358 screens. The population of Norway is 4.5 million. Cinema admissions for 2004 totaled 12 million at 401 screens. The population of Finland is 5.2 million. Cinema admissions for 2004 totaled 7.7 million at 354 screens. There are no current figures regarding cinema admissions or screens in Iceland.

POLAND

The reestablishment of the Polish state following World War II was controlled by the Soviet Union. The film industry was nationalized and fell under the same Stalinist propaganda precepts as those of other Eastern bloc states. Alexander Ford, who had been making films since the early 1930s, continued to be an influence in postwar Polish film with works such as *The Young Chopin* (1951) that avoided Socialist Realism by using historical and biographical themes. Andrzej Munk followed Ford's style and historical escapism with notable skill, but it was Andrzej Wajda who emerged as the leading director of the postwar era. With his debut film *Pokolenie* [A Generation] (1954), Wajda set the tone for Polish neorealist style and examination of Nazi occupation. Its ambiguity toward Marxism and its vivid characters helped it become an instant sensation for an audience that had tired of Polish and Soviet propaganda

POLISH PROGRESSIVE FILM

By the 1960s, Poland had produced some of the most progressive cinema in the Eastern bloc, and films by a new generation of directors—Wojciech Has, Jerzy Kawalerowicz, and Roman Polanski—filled theaters. The French New Wave particularly influenced Polanski, who began his career as an actor and screenwriter. His *Nóz w wodzie* [Knife in the Water] (1962) allowed him to move his explorations of the dark side of human existence into French, British, and American vernacular with award-winning style and influence. Krystof Zanussi and Krystof Kieslowski emerged in the 1970s to move Polish cinema into a phase of social criticism that transcended neorealism or influences from the French New Wave. Poland's Solidarity movement was captured by Wajda in *Człowiek zżeleza* [Man of Iron] (1981), which featured Solidarity leader and future president Lech Walesa. It was hailed by critics and audiences alike and went on to win at Cannes, but it was banned four months after its release by General Jaruzelski, who declared martial law in order to crush the Solidarity movement and forestall a Soviet invasion. Also forbidden was Ryszard Bugajski's critical look at Communist repression, *The Interrogation* (1982), which was not seen until its Cannes Festival screening in 1990.

film. Wajda's follow-up was the tragic look at the Polish underground in *Kanal* [Canal] (1957). But *Popiół i diament* [Ashes and Diamonds] (1958) has become his most famous film. It made a star and nonconformist sex symbol of young actor Zbigniew Cibulski and overtly dealt with anti-Soviet sentiments at the end of the war. Wajda's 1968 *Wszystko na sprzedaż* [Everything for Sale], influenced by the French New Wave and British satire, took on Polish filmmaking and introduced Daniel Olbrychski, who has remained one of Poland's best-known actors.

Wajda spent much of the 1980s working abroad, and his French production of *Danton* (1983), set in the aftermath of the French Revolution, allegorized the imposition of martial law in Poland. In the post-Communist 1990s, Wajda began to treat Polish history with *Pan Tadeusz* (1999), adapted from the famous poem by Adam Mickiewicz. The film was a major box office success, as Poles sought heroic aspects of their long-suppressed history. Krystof Zanussi's *Barwy ochronne* [Camouflage] (1977) led a movement known as the "cinema of moral concern," which strove to undertake a moralist examination of Polish life and recent history. *Dekalog* [The Decalogue] (1988), *Krótki film o miłości* [A Short Film about Love] (1988), and *Krótki film o zabijaniu* [A Short Film about Killing] (1988) brought an Oscar and world fame to Krystof Kieslowski. His more metaphysical works of the 1990s, particularly what has become known as the three colors trilogy (*Blue*, 1993; *White*, 1994; *Red*, 1994) have influenced French and other European postmodern cinema.

Zanussi's former assistant and screenwriter Agnieszka Holland attained acclaim for *To Kill a Priest* (1988) and for her Oscar-nominated look at a Jewish boy caught between Communism and Nazism in *Europa, Europa* (1991). Like cinematographers Jerzy Zielinski, Hubert Taczanowski, two-time Oscar winner Janusz Kaminski (*Schindler's List*, 1993; *Saving Private Ryan*, 1998), and other film artisans of her generation, Holland has moved in an international direction and often works abroad.

Obviously influenced by the popularity of Wajda's historical epics and in an effort to capture world audiences, Polish film has moved toward larger-scale projects in the 1990s. National reception has been positive, and Polish films share the top-ten box office hits with American, British, and German films. Notable among these recent epics are Jerzy Hoffman's trilogy on Polish life in the seventeenth century; Jerzy Kawalerowicz's *Quo Vadis* (2001), Poland's most expensive film to date; and Jadwiga Baranska's *Chopin, Pragnienie Miłości* [Chopin, Desire for Love] (2002). Roman Polanski returned to his homeland and to his own past as a child of the Holocaust to direct the Oscar-winning *The Pianist* in 2002. But economic questions facing the country as a new member of the European Union, a significant reduction in state funding for film, political scandal, and lack of popular trust in the current government has given rise to more small-budget, independent film productions and a new phase of socially critical filmmaking.

The population of Poland is 40 million. Cinema admissions for 2004 totaled 25.9 million. There are no current figures regarding the number of screens in the country.

PORTUGAL

The giant of Portuguese cinema is Manoel de Oliveira, who began filmmaking with the silent era and remains active into his nineties with one film per year. He is the top award-winning director in the nation, and his work has been given several retrospectives in the United States. João César Monteiro founded the small New Portuguese Cinema movement in the 1960s as an experimental and socially critical attempt to break from entertainment and genre films. By the 1970s, he had become recognized as a major force in the national cinema, and he continued to make provocative films to his death in 2003 with films such as *A Comédia de Deus* [God's Comedy] (1995), which was awarded the Jury's Special Prize at the 1995 Venice Film Festival. Teresa Villaverde, who began her career in acting, now represents the style and success of the next generation of Portuguese filmmakers. Her themes deal with youth conflict, and her work has brought award-winning Portuguese actress Maria de Medeiros to international attention.

Portuguese national cinema has for most of its history avoided the Hollywood studio production model and has been director controlled. It survives today as a result of heavy state funding and co-production with television studios. The exhibition venues are very limited (around 550 screens), and since Portuguese films rarely break into the global market beyond importation to Brazil, only about ten features are made a year; success is measured by modest audience numbers (150,000). Yet the highbrow quality of Portuguese films, which usually deal with isolation, solitude, and a desire for transcendence, are frequently praised at international film festivals for their poetic style. A new crop of films has also explored Portugal's colonial links to Africa and Brazil. Portugal's most expensive film in its cinema history, *A selva* [The Jungle] (2002) by Leonel Viera, an adaptation of a novel by Ferreira de Castro that examines the life of a young monarchist forced into Brazilian exile in 1812, became the biggest hit of the year among national films. The new generation of filmmakers is less meditative than its predecessors and is looking more critically at urban life and familial dysfunction (Antonio Ferreira, Joaquim Sapinho). There are no current figures regarding admissions or screens in Portugal.

ROMANIA

The small Romanian film industry was nationalized and placed under the dictates of Stalinist Socialist Realism following World War II. The financial support received from the state, which owned the film production and distribution companies, led to the first active program to export Romanian films across Eastern Europe. Like Czechoslovakian cinema of the period, most Romanian films were based on literature. Sergiu Nicolaescu is the best-known director of the era, whose work in different genres attracted a wide national audience. The first film to gain critical attention beyond the borders of the country was Victor Iliu's *Moara cu noroc* [The Lucky Mill] (1957). The expansion of the industry under

Communism resulted in the opening of the Buftea Studios in 1959. Romania captured the Cannes Film Festival prize for best direction with Liviu Ciulei's *Padurea spanzuratilor* [The Forest of the Hanged] (1965), ushering in a minor new wave period. Romania has also excelled in animation, led by Ion Popescu-Gopo (the founder of the country's animation film school), whose *Scurta istorie* [Short History] (1957), a Cannes Festival winner, is typical of the national style. Directors active in the 1960s through the 1980s include Iulian Mihu, Manole Marcus, Malvina Ursianu, Gheorghe Vitanidis, and Serban Marinescu. Censorship was strengthened after the Prague Spring in 1968, and although dictator Nicholae Ceausescu was first greeted as a progressive leader, his brutal oppression became infamous and ultimately curtailed the film industry.

Censorship and ideological restrictions were lifted immediately after the collapse of Communism, but the new freedom did not boost film production since state support vanished with the economic crisis of democratic restructuring. Despite the glut of foreign films that regularly win at the box office, Romanian film has slowly regained popular interest during the last decade through works by Lucian Pintilie, Mircea Daneliuc, Radu Gabra, and Dan Pita. Despite the political pressures and changes, the number of Romanian cinema theaters increased steadily between 1938 (338) and the late 1970s (6,275). Romanian films, such as Pita's *Hotel de luxe* (1992), which was awarded the Silver Lion at the Venice Festival, manage to find both national and international critical acclaim. The desire by filmmakers to locate wider national audiences was given a boost in 2002, when two productions—a lowbrow television spin-off comedy, *Garcea si oltenil* [Garcea and the Oltenians] by Sam Irvin, and the more sophisticated fantasy by Nae Caranfil, *Filantropia*—joined a top-ten box office success list made up of American imports. National production is still weak, but Romanian filmmakers are taking on controversial subjects, criticizing post-Communist society, and encouraging a new generation of artists.

The population of Romania is 21.68 million. Cinema admissions for 2004 totaled 5.32 million at 247 screens.

RUSSIA, UKRAINE, BELARUS

Following a period of theory creation and influential experimentation (stylistic and technical innovations, nondogmatic social criticism) under Lenin by directors Eisenstein and Pudovkin, Stalin's oppressive regime constrained subject and form, instituting a propagandistic conservatism in the arts known as Socialist Realism. Russia's most popular form of mass entertainment was reduced to a doctrinaire celebration of leader, system, and worker. World War II allowed for some freedom of expression so that film could serve as anti-German propaganda and as a showcase of Soviet political, social, and cultural superiority, but even this was lost with the extreme repression of the postwar era and Soviet imperialist consolidation. Belarusian productions were integral to Soviet cinema from its onset, with Victor Turov emerging as a major director in the 1950s and 1960s. The Belarusfilm studio outside of Minsk was the center for ideological documentaries throughout the 1940s and has become a site of international co-production since the 1990s. The cinema of Ukraine, a nation subject to Stalinist genocidal policies in the 1930s, was suppressed, but its most important director, Alexander Dovzhenko, had created classics in the late 1920s and was able to produce documentaries at Moscow's Mosfilm Studio. Since 1957, the Ukranian Kyiv production site bears his name.

Filmmakers became more daring and critical in the 1970s and 1980s, but production became increasingly mass-oriented and formulaic as propaganda waned. Only a few films were considered progressive or artistic and could find foreign interest (Tarkovsky's *Solyaris* [Solaris], 1972), but these were ignored or given very limited distribution at home. During the *Glasnost* of Gorbachev, imports finally appeared from beyond Eastern Europe, and filmmakers dared to approach Russian life as it really was (Sergei Solovyov's *Assa*, 1988). With the collapse of the Soviet Union and state funding, control and censorship evaporated—films now deal with topics that include sexuality, crime, urban squalor, gulags, the Chechen War, and Stalin—but production is expensive and limited to independent projects (about twenty-five major films a year) funded with venture capital or developed through European co-production. National stars or Hollywood hits secure box office success. Nevertheless, Russian film is showcased at, and international filmmakers are attracted by, the St. Petersburg Film Festival. Belarus celebrated the eightieth anniversary of its film industry in 2004, and Belarusfilm and the annual Minsk International Film Festival

POST-TOTALITARIAN CINEMA

"The Thaw," as it is known, came with Khrushchev's rejection of Stalin's overt totalitarianism and ultimately resulted in a gentle form of youth culture in film during the early to mid-1960s. Led by Andrei Tarkovsky and Marlen Khutsiyev, this semi–new wave style questioned urban life and social norms, but it had no influence beyond the mild and tolerated protest of the moment. Lavish megabudget historical and literary-based epics were attempted (Sergei Bondarchuk's six-hour *Voyna I mir* [War and Peace], 1968), and director Andrei Konchalovsky moved from these films to eventually direct in Hollywood. With the smashing of the Prague Spring, the period of liberalism in Soviet cinema was ended and replaced by a period of stagnation.

exemplify a positive outlook for the small industry and its co-productions with Russia. The faltering Ukrainian film industry (dropping from forty features a year in 1991 to ten in 2002) was given a boost in 2002 with new state-funded film development legislation. The three studios at Dovzhenko, Odessa, and Yalta hope to attract both increased domestic production as well as joint ventures with Russia and Europe since funding is aimed at independent producers not studios.

The population of Russia is 150 million. Cinema admissions for 2004 totaled 45 million at 18,200 screens. The population of Belarus is 10.5 million. Cinema admissions for 2004 totaled approximately 10.5 million at 152 screens. There are no current figures regarding cinema admissions or screens for Ukraine.

SPAIN

Spain lost its influential filmmaker, surrealist Luis Buñuel, early in its cinema history when he settled in France. The dictatorship of Francisco Franco, following the Spanish Civil War and lasting until 1975, significantly hampered the film industry in artistic growth. Genre films were dominant, and these were influenced by censorship and ideological propaganda. Still, Luis Berlanga and Juan-Antonio Bardem created notable work in the 1950s and 1960s (Bardem was jailed in the 1970s as a leftist). During this time, Spain was seen as an attractive venue for foreign films, particularly as a location for European westerns and American epic films. Between 1959 and 1964, American producer Samuel Bronston created several U.S./Spanish films with international stars in a grandiose Hollywood style (*King of Kings, El Cid, The Fall of the Roman Empire*). Censorship became less strict in the 1960s, and some formerly banned foreign films were allowed release, including early Buñuel. Despite the limited number of imports and narrow distribution, Spanish film continued to draw major audiences. Carlos Saura, Mario Camus, and Manuel Summers emerged with gentle experimentation, social criticism, and more adult topics. Saura, particularly, gained the attention of Spanish cineastes and the international audiences with his veiled and symbolic criticisms of Franco's Spain in the 1970s. Franco's death, the establishment of a constitutional monarchy that supported democracy, and the dropping of censorship unleashed a new cinema from directors Pedro Almodovar, Julio Medem, Bigas Luna, and Fernando Trueba that openly dealt with the Civil War, dictatorship, class conflict, gender roles, sexuality, and the contemporary urban environment. Among many new faces, actors Antonio Banderas and Carmen Maura became internationally recognized stars.

Spanish films have been well marketed and distributed abroad, winning many prizes including the 2004 Best Foreign Film Oscar for Alejandro Amenábar's *Mar adentro* [The Sea Inside] (2004). While the critical edge of Spanish film is being continued by young, often first-time filmmakers, many of the major productions are currently Hollywood-influenced genre films. A few female filmmakers are beginning to emerge, but men still dominate the mainstream industry. The second biggest box office hit in Spanish cinema history came with Javier Fesser's technically accomplished all-star live-action translation of Spain's cartoon spies of the 1960s, *La gran aventura de Mortadelo y Filemón* [The Big Adventure] (2002), which managed to bring three generations of Spaniards to the cinemas. It also demonstrated that Spanish Civil War films, critical social dramas, and experimental works were no longer popular. Most of the top ten box office successes are Hollywood films.

The population of Spain is a little over 40 million. Cinema admissions for 2004 totaled 19.02 million at 4039 screens.

SWEDEN

Swedish post–World War II films often took on the problems arising from Sweden's "neutrality" during German occupation, such as Hampe Faustman's *Främmande hamn* [Foreign Harbor] (1948). Sjöberg's *Fröken Julie* [Miss Julie] (1950), based on the Strindberg play, attacked the Swedish class system, explored gender roles, and introduced a symbolic eroticism that paved the way for greater frankness in Nordic cinema. Ingmar Bergman's subtle commercialization of mystical and psychological themes brought international attention to Swedish cinema during the following two decades. His brilliant ensemble casts moved easily from sophisticated comedy in *Sommarnattes leende* [Smiles of a Summer Night] (1955), to the Cold War allegory set in plague-ridden medieval Sweden, *Det sjunde inseglet* [The Seventh Seal] (1956), to elegiac memory pieces such as *Smultronstället* [Wild Strawberries] (1957). By the 1960s, Bergman's films had moved toward an innovative minimalism and made international stars of actors Bibi Anderson, Max von Sydow, Ingrid Thulin, Liv Ullmann, and cinematographer Sven Nykvist.

Despite Bergman's continued success, Swedish film floundered in the early 1960s as American imports and television attracted the national audience. Bo Widerberg led an anti-Bergman campaign on the basis that his films had no connection with modern society and its problems. Widerberg's films, such as *Barnvagnen* [The Baby Carriage] (1962) and *Kärlek 65* [Love 65] (1965) displayed a new interest in physical love and in taboos that lay beneath Sweden's placid popular image. His greatest international success, however, was an uncharacteristic period romance that ignored sex and violence and relied on Mozart's music: *Elvira Madigan* (1967). Vilgot Sjöman and Jan Troell continued Widerberg's frankness, the former with the controversial *Jag är nyfiken—gul* [I Am Curious—Yellow] (1967), his filmed "experience" of a young woman's quest to find herself socially and sexually, which attracted both public fascination and censorship battles in Sweden and the United States. Sexploitation films masquerading as serious continuations of Sjöman's style followed, stereotyping Sweden as a haven for adult filmmaking and ardent sexuality through the 1960s. In 1968 FilmCentrum was launched as a distributor for films that were ignored by the Swedish Film Institute, and more experimental protest films were able to find an audience. The decade ended with the work of Jonas Cornell and Kjell Grede, both Swedish New Wave outsiders, who moved feature films back into intelligent and coherent narrative style.

With the confrontational experimentation over, the 1970s opened with Jan Troell's *Utvandrana* [The Emigrants] (1971), an example of the neoclassic Swedish cinema, which returned to poetic historical panoramas and mystical flavoring. This film about the hardships of nineteenth-century Swedes in the American Midwest garnered several Oscar nominations, including that of Best Picture. Comedies reemerged in the films of Jan Halldorf, Lasse Hallström, and Hans Iveberg, but these were mostly formulaic and harmless farces about sex or domestic life. Gösta Ekman found popularity as a major comic actor in a series of films that rarely found export but were box office successes at home. The most resilient and exportable series for decades have been films based on the *Pippi Longstocking* children's books by Astrid Lindgren. Ingmar Bergman's films of the 1970s and early 1980s used various topics and styles and were greeted as masterworks by international cineastes: *Viskningar och rop* [Cries and Whispers] (1973), recalled the minimalism of the director's films of the 1960s; *Autumn Sonata* (1977) marked Ingrid Bergman's singular return to Swedish cinema; and the opulent *Fanny and Alexander* (1982) provided a throwback to early period films. Liv Ullmann, Bergman's longtime featured star and partner, has also turned to film direction.

Although there has been less exportation of film during the last two decades, Lasse Hallström's Oscar-nominated *Mitt Liv som Hund* [My Life as a Dog] (1985) returned international attention to Swedish film, but he then departed for Hollywood and international productions. A mix of classic Swedish surrealism and blunt critical realism can be found in the films of the current generation of cinema artists, which includes Lukas Moodysson. Production of films remains high—around twenty-five new films a year since 2001—although current productions are aimed at domestic entertainment rather than at artistic triumph at festivals and foreign distribution. Swedes are ardent filmgoers, and Sweden's annual Göteborg Film Festival is one of Europe's important cinema events. The population of Sweden is 8.9 million. Cinema admissions for 2004 totaled 18.3 million at 1,176 screens.

SWITZERLAND

The distinct language areas of Switzerland allowed for foreign film dominance from the earliest days of cinema. Unlike other nations, Swiss cinema not only had to fight American imports, but also highly popular French, German, Austrian, and Italian films at the box office. The mid-1930s marks the start of the career of the country's most famous director, Leopold Lindtberg, who produced twelve features between 1935 and 1953, all considered national classics. His postwar work garnered him international attention: *Die letzte Chance* [The Last Chance] (1945) was awarded a Hollywood Golden Globe, and the Austrian co-produced *Die Vier im Jeep* [Four in a Jeep] (1951), about the Allied occupation of Vienna, has become one of Switzerland's most famous films. In the 1950s and 1960s, Swiss film was aimed at domestic audiences in both dialect and subject matter, varying between the urban landscape of Zurich in features directed by Kurt Früh and the provincial or historical films of Franz Schnyder. Influenced by the French New Wave, the Francophone directors dominated Swiss film by the mid-1960s, and a New Swiss Film, which broke away from the genres of the 1950s, was founded by Jean-Louis Roy, Claude Champion, and Francis Reusser. The films of Alain Tanner and Michel Soutter broke into the international market, and French New Wave director Jean-Luc Godard settled in Switzerland in the 1970s.

Internationally known Swiss-born or immigrant actors have only seldom worked in the national cinema: Ursula Andress, Marthe Keller, and Austrian-born actor/director Maximilian Schell are examples. The Swiss-German film collaboration offered successful documentaries during the 1970s, and a new generation of more socially and politically critical German language and German-Swiss dialect films was created by directors Kurt Gloor, Rolf Lyssy, Fredi Murer, and Daniel Schmidt. Their films were critically praised at home and managed distribution abroad. Outstanding among these is Markus Imhoof's *Das Boot ist voll* [The Boat is Full] (1981), which took on the national policy toward immigration during World War II, and two Oscar winners: Richard Dembo's *Diagonale du fou* [Dangerous Moves] (1984) and Xavier Koller's *Reise der Hoffnung* [Journey of Hope] (1990). Current filmmakers of note include Silvio Soldini, Jakob Berger, Luke Gasser, and Patricia Plattner, and their themes range from social and political satire to psychological drama.

The Swiss are among the most avid filmgoers in Europe, with recent movie tickets per capita outpacing totals in Germany and Austria, but the Swiss have in recent years somewhat neglected their own product, which has only taken in about 3 percent of the market share. Only one Swiss film, *Ernstfall in Havana* [Crisis in Havana] (2002), directed by Sabine Boss, has managed to break into the top ten box office successes, which are mostly American, German, and French films. The population of Switzerland is 7.26 million. Cinema admissions for 2004 totaled 18.81 million at 511 screens.

TURKEY

Film was introduced to Istanbul in 1895, but the medium was exclusively used for the entertainment of the Ottoman sultan. Public screenings began with the establishment of the first cinemas in 1908. Short films were produced by the government during World War I, but it was upon his return from Germany in 1922 that theater artist Muhsin Ertuğrul ushered in the new era of feature filmmaking with the first privately owned production company, Kemal Film. Bedia Muhavvit and Neyyire, the first Moslem female actors in Turkish film, appeared in *Ateşten Gömlek* [The Ordeal] (1923) and subsequently became the nation's earliest stars. The film received its premiere in April 1923, six months prior to the founding of the Turkish Republic. *Bir Millet Uyanıyor* [A Nation Awakens], a war of independence epic directed by Ertuğrul in 1932, is considered one of the greatest masterworks of the interwar period.

Following World War II, several new studios and production companies were established, and in 1946 the Film Producers' Association was formed, along with other professional film organizations. In 1948 Turkey's first film festival was established in Istanbul. Cinematically, the years between 1950 and 1970 are known as the "Cinema Artists Period" because of the emergence of important directors, who led the development of the national film beyond the entertainment genres of the 1930s and 1940s. Notable filmmakers included Lütfi Akad, Atıf Yılmaz, Metin Erksan, Memduh Ün, Osman Seden, Nejat Saydam, Nevzat Pesen, Orhan Aksoy, and Hulki Saner. Akad's *Kanun Namına* [In the Name of the Law] (1952) introduced realistic concepts to Turkish filmmaking, which had been dominated by stylized studio productions. A period of socially critical films followed, of which Metin Erksan's *Gecelerin Ötesi* [Beyond the

Nights] (1960) is a prime example. The introduction of color followed, but Italian and French styles influenced younger filmmakers, who preferred to work in black and white.

International attention came to Turkish cinema with *Denize İnen Sokak* [A Street Leading to the Sea] (1960) directed by Atilla Tokatlı, when it received an honorable mention at the Locarno Film Festival and was screened at the Venice and the Karlovy Vary Film Festivals in 1961. Erksan's neorealist rural film *Susuz Yaz* [Dry Summer] (1964) amplified the new interest in Turkey when the film received the Golden Bear at the Berlinale Film Festival and was praised at Venice. The decade brought a new set of influential filmmakers to the screen, such as Halit Refiğ, Fevzi Tuna, Duygu Sağıroğlu, Erdoğan Tokatlı, Bilge Olgaç, and Tunç Başaran. National interest in Hollywood and European film had been modest in the postwar years, and desire for Turkish film had grown so strongly since the 1950s that by 1966 saturation had been reached with the production of 240 features that year. This inflation of product led to a glut of poor-quality exploitation films; however, export of the best works found a fascinated European audience, and a "Turkish Films Week" was held in Paris in 1968.

Television did not find wide appeal in Turkey until the 1970s, and with it, cinema attendance and film production declined. Yılmaz Güney's *Umut* [Hope] (1970) opened the decade to a more experimental new wave era. Emigration and the alienation of the Turkish worker abroad became the subject of several films, and popular actress Türkan Şoray, whose directorial debut *Dönüş* [The Return] (1973), was screened at the Moscow Film Festival, became the first female filmmaker to find acclaim. By the 1980s, comedies dominated the remaining cinemas, and dramatic films stressed the search for personal identity, particularly among the female characters. Şerif Gören's *Derman* [Remedy] (1983) went further and depicted the revolt of women against second-class status and male domination in Turkish villages. Audiences returned somewhat to the cinemas in the 1990s in support of the new auteurial filmmaking style, but production remained low (thirty-three films in 1991). Kurdish subject matter was introduced by directors Şahin Gök and Ümit Elçi, who hoped to influence the political atmosphere in the Middle East. Films produced for television dominated production by the mid-1990s, which led to the closure of many cinema theaters. The creation of several private television networks added to this problem, but they also helped reintroduce the nation to its cinema history by broadcasting older films, many for the first time.

Topics during 1990s spanned the widest possibilities of culture, from the conservative and religious to the progressive and alternative. *Minyeli Abdullah* [Abdullah from Minye] (1990) by Yücel Çakmaklı, one of many Islamic-themed films during the decade, set a nationwide box office record. In 1995, a group of directors formed the Turkish Cinema Foundation and produced *On Yönetmen İki Film* [Ten Directors, Two Films] based on ten short-subject film scripts dealing with love and tolerance. An example of the growing co-production with other European countries was the Turkish/Italian/Spanish film *Hamam* [Turkish Bath] (1997) by Ferzan Ozpetek, about an unhappily married Italian man who inherits a Turkish bathhouse in Istanbul and ultimately comes to question his sexuality when he meets the son of the family that manages the bath. It was a successful import in twenty countries, received several festival awards, and became controversial only when the government of Turkey refused to nominate it for a Best Foreign Film Oscar because of its homosexual content. The German co-production of *Lola ve Bilidikid* [Lola and Bilidikid] (1999), directed by Kutluğ Ataman, also approached gay subject matter and scored awards at festivals in Oslo and New York.

Serious government interest in the national cinema has produced low interest rates for loans and easier terms for investment, along with assistance for artists and film companies suffering financial difficulties. The Ministry of Culture has established a Turkish film unit to support distribution abroad and has allocated funds to produce films and to solve infrastructure problems. Incentives for building new cinemas throughout the country have resulted in multiplex theaters and an IMAX theater in Ankara. Film production currently hovers at about fifteen to twenty features per year. Comedies continue to be highly popular, such as the Egyptian co-produced hit, *Mumya firada* [Mummy on the Run] (2002), by first-time director Erdal Murat Aktas. Famed comedy writer/actor Zeki Alasya and television comedian Levent Kirca often appear on the big screen. In contrast to other European cinemas, the documentary is relatively neglected and has only had one recent commercial release, Tolga Örnek's *Hittiler* [The Hittites] (2003). Although large-scale epics find box office success, such as Ziya Öztan's look at the collapse of the Ottoman Empire in *Abdulhamid düserken* [The Fall of the Red Sultan] (2003), small neorealist films such as Ümit Ünal's digitally shot *Nine* (2003), about the investigation of the death of a street girl, and the films of the late Nuri Bilge Ceylan, have received critical praise. Ceylan's *Distant* (2003) received the Grand Jury Prize at Cannes and best actor awards for Muzaffer Özdemir and Mehmet Emin Toprak, whose characters and stories from previous Ceylan films have gained a cult following in Turkey.

Hollywood blockbuster films have gained audiences during the last two decades and have ultimately overtaken Turkish films for a greater share of the top ten box office successes. The Istanbul Film Festival is recognized globally as a specialized competitive event, with an annual attendance that exceeds 100,000, and is considered a prime showcase for international distributors. Additionally, there are a number of smaller or regional film festivals. The population of Turkey is 65 million. Cinema admissions for 2004 totaled 23 million at 980 screens.

THE UNITED KINGDOM (GREAT BRITAIN AND NORTHERN IRELAND)

During the 1930s, major Hollywood companies absorbed the failing British film industry, and the Anglo-American partnership created a classic film period that was more technically and stylistically sophisticated and had a ready market in America. Britain's film history was served by the creation of the National Film Archives and the British Film Institute (BFI), which developed into one of the world's most respected institutes of cinema preservation and study. Production was downscaled during World War II. The Rank Organization became the dominant rival in production and distribution to Austrian-Hungarian émigré producer Alexander Korda's London Films in the postwar years. Big-budget films (*The Red Shoes, Great Expectations, Oliver Twist*) demonstrated that London could keep up with Hollywood, but the financial demands were not sustainable. Instead, small budget-films shaped the British film style of the 1950s. With the onset of television and the emergence of the BBC, British film looked toward attracting national audiences with local topics and culture, which included the popular comedies produced by the Ealing Studios. A new set of British actors, which included Richard Burton, Jack Hawkins, Laurence Harvey, and Peter Finch, attracted international interest. While the BBC produced some of the best artistic fare in the medium, cinema theaters shuttered and film production slumped.

Two factors helped create the British New Wave in the late 1950s and early 1960s: directors such as Joseph Losey, John Houston, and Stanley Kubrick relocated to Britain to escape the McCarthy era in the United States and would eventually bring American financing and co-production to British cinema; and a new youth market was lured into the cinemas with the fading of censorship and the reflection of its popular interests on screen. Filmmakers inspired by new waves in Europe created neorealistic portrayals of contemporary British society and its problems: *Look Back in Anger* (1958), *Saturday Night and Sunday Morning* (1960), and *A Taste of Honey* (1961) represent the breakthrough. With the new youth culture of music and style led by the Beatles, the Rolling Stones, and others, the myth of "Swinging

London" became an international concept that was also promoted in film. Epics by David Lean (*Lawrence of Arabia*, 1962; *Doctor Zhivago*, 1965; *Ryan's Daughter*, 1970); stylish social commentaries such as *The Servant* (1963), *Georgy Girl* (1966), and *Alfie* (1966); and the James Bond series reinvigorated the cinema and introduced Peter O'Toole, Michael Caine, Peter Sellers, Albert Finney, Sean Connery, Rita Tushingham, Alan Bates, Tom Courtney, Richard Harris, Julie Christie, Terrence Stamp, David Hemmings, Donald Pleasance, Paul Scofield, and the Redgraves—Corin, Lynn, and Vanessa—to world audiences.

Along with the crossover between popular music and film in such works as *Help!* (1965), there was also a psychedelic phase of internationally co-produced spy spoofs and satires that, at its burnout, funneled its remains into the surreal television and later film comedy of Monty Python in the 1970s. The end of the decade signaled the end of the "mod" style, and the American funding that had helped buoy production in the 1960s evaporated in the wake of a U.S. recession. Although Richard Attenborough and Ken Russell moved from acting and television, respectively, to film direction with notable success, many more talents moved into television, and studios were closed or hired out for Hollywood production.

Resurgence began with the internationally acclaimed *Chariots of Fire* (1981). Two images of Britain, aimed at the international market, dominated the Thatcher era: a romanticized view of the British Empire embodied in films that were elegantly produced (many by the Merchant-Ivory team) and not as devoid of sociopolitical criticism as has been suggested (*A Passage to India*, 1984; *A Room With a View*, 1986); and the localized small film dealing with regional culture, economic decline, sexuality, immigration, racism, and the working class milieu (*Gregory's Girl*, 1980; *My Beautiful Laundrette*, 1986), often co-financed by the progressive Channel 4 television network. *A Fish Called Wanda* (1988) represented the type of subject matter that lured back American money for material that would play well in both countries. The 1990s also saw independently and regionally (Scotland, Wales) created films that would not compromise on content or style, including controversial work by Peter Greenaway and Derek Jarman as well as Mike Newall's smash comedy *Four Weddings and a Funeral* (1994), which moved Hugh Grant to stardom; Peter Cattaneo's equally popular *The Full Monty* (1997); Mike Leigh's *Secrets and Lies* (1995); and Ken Loach's *Sweet Sixteen* (2002).

Audience attendance has steadily risen since the late 1980s, and by 2002, annual cinema admissions totaled about 170 million. Britain has overtaken Germany to become the biggest film market in Europe, and although ticket prices are the highest in the European Union, British box office produces the largest gross. The population of the United Kingdom is 58.7 million. Cinema admissions for 2004 totaled 175.9 million at 3258 screens.

AUDIENCE POPULARITY AND AWARDS

The most popular films in all European countries based on box office receipts for the last decade have been American blockbusters (expensively produced adventure and science fiction films), followed by American comedies and then national comedies. Video and DVD rental for home viewing is as popular in all Western and Central European countries as in the United States and is growing in availability in Eastern and southeastern European countries. Given the dominance of American films at the cinema theaters, national productions often receive their largest audience through video/DVD rentals or television broadcasts.

The European Film Academy (EFA), founded in 1989 and headquartered in Berlin, reflects the mission of the Academy of Motion Picture Arts and Sciences (the Oscar awards) in the United States with its own pan-European cinema presentations, programs, and

EUROPEAN FILM ACADEMY (EFA) BEST PICTURE AWARDS

1988: *Krótki film o zabijaniu* [A Short Film about Killing] (Poland)

1989: *Topio stin omichli* [Landscape in the Mist] (Greece/France)

1990: *Porte Aperte* [Open Doors] (Italy)

1991: *Riff-Raff* (Great Britain)

1992: *Il Ladro di Bambini* [The Stolen Children] (Italy/France/Switzerland)

1993: *Urga* [Close to Eden] (Russia/France)

1994: *Lamerica* (Italy/France)

1995: *Land and Freedom* (Great Britain/Spain/Germany)

1996: *Amor omnie* [Breaking the Waves] (Denmark/Sweden/France)

1997: *The Full Monty* (Great Britain)

1998: *La Vita è bella* [Life Is Beautiful] (Italy)

1999: *Todo sobre mi madre* [All about My Mother] (Spain)

2000: *Dancer in the Dark* (Denmark/Germany/Netherlands/United States/Great Britain)

2001: *Amélie* (*Le Fabuleaux Destin d'Amélie Poulain*) (France)

2002: *Hable con ella* [Talk to Her] (Spain)

2003: *Good Bye Lenin!* (Germany)

2004: *Gegen die Wand* [Head-On] (Germany/Turkey)

2005: *Caché* [Hidden] (Austria/France)

2006: *Das Leben der Anderen* [The Lives of Others] (Germany)

annual televised awards (formerly called the "Felix" but now known as the EFA Awards), which recognize seventeen categories, including the Jameson People's Choice Awards voted for by cinema audiences across Europe. The BAFTA (British Academy of Film and Television Arts) Award, founded in 1947, concentrates on English language cinema and is often understood as a sister award to the Oscars. Television broadcasts of these award presentations garner large international audiences. A few other countries have similar Oscar-like televised national media awards (usually produced by major media firms or publishers) that include prizes for film, television, music, and audience popularity. Well-known examples are the Bambi Awards in Germany and the Romy Awards in Austria. But the most respected film awards in Europe remain tied to the important film festivals: the Palme d'Or (Golden Palm) of the Cannes Film Festival (France); the Golden Lion of the Venice Biennale (Italy); the Golden Bear of the Berlinale, or Berlin International Film Festival (Germany); the Golden Shell of the San Sebastian Film Festival (Spain); the Crystal Globe of the Karlovy Vary International Film Festival (Czech Republic); the Alexander Award of the Thessaloniki International Film Festival (Greece); the Joseph Plateau Awards of the Flanders International Film Festival (Belgium); the awards for independent and experimental film at the International Film Festival Rotterdam (Netherlands); and the awards of the Stockholm International Film Festival (Sweden), the Edinburgh International Film Festival (Scotland), the Cork Film Festival (Ireland), and the Warsaw International Film Festival (Poland).

RESOURCE GUIDE

PRINT SOURCES

General European Film

Dyer, Richard, and Ginette Vincendeau, eds. *Popular European Cinema*. New York: Routledge, 1992.

Ezra, Elizabeth, ed. *European Cinema*. Oxford: Oxford University Press, 2004.

Forbes, Jill, and Sarah Street, eds. *European Cinema: An Introduction*. London: Palgrave Macmillan, 2001.

"Great Directors Series," *Senses of Cinema* (Australia). http://www.sensesofcinema.com.

Horton, Andrew James, ed. *Kinoeye: New Perspectives on European Film*. http://www.kinoeye.org. Resources on Central, Eastern, Balkan, Baltic, and Post-Soviet cinemas.

Nowell-Smith, Geoffrey. *The Oxford History of World Cinema*. Oxford: Oxford University Press, 1999.

Rosenthal, Daniel, ed. *Variety International Film Guide* (annual). Los Angeles: Silman-James Press, 2004ff. Current release, box office, festival, publication information.

Sklar, Robert. *Film: An International History of the Medium*. New York: Abrams, 2002.

Vincendeau, Ginette, ed. *Encyclopedia of European Cinema*. New York: Facts on File, 1995.

National Cinemas

Barton, Ruth. *Irish National Cinema*. London: Routledge, 2004.

Besas, Peter. *Behind the Spanish Lens: Spanish Cinema under Fascism and Democracy*. Denver: Arden, 1985.

Bondanella, Peter. *Italian Cinema: From Neorealism to the Present*. New York: Continuum, 2003.

Cunningham, John. *Hungarian Cinema: From Coffee House to Multiplex*. London: Wallflower Press, 2004.

Dassanowsky, Robert von. *Austrian Cinema: A History*. Jefferson, NC: McFarland, 2005.

Gillespie, David. *Russian Cinema*. New York: Longman, 2002.

Goulding, Daniel J. *Liberated Cinema: The Yugoslav Experience, 1945–2001*. Bloomington: Indiana University Press, 2002.

Hake, Sabine. *German National Cinema*. London: Routledge, 2001.

Haltof, Marek. *Polish National Cinema*. New York: Berghahn, 2002.

Hames, Peter. *The Czechoslovak New Wave*. Berkeley: University of California Press, 1985.

Hjort, Mette. *Small Nation, Global Cinema: The New Danish Cinema*. Minneapolis: University of Minnesota Press, 2005.

Holloway, Ronald. *The Bulgarian Cinema*. Rutherford: Fairleigh Dickinson University Press, 1986.

Ioradanova, Dina. *Cinema of the Other Europe: The Industry and Artistry of East Central European Film*. London: Wallflower, 2003.

Kosanovic, Dejan. *Serbian Film and Cinematography 1896–1993*. Serbian Unity Congress. http://www.serbianunity.net/culture/history/Hist_Serb_Culture/chw/Cinematography.html.

Lanzoni, Remi. *French Cinema: From Its Beginnings to the Present*. New York: Continuum, 2004.

"The Rise and Rise of Greek Cinema." *Greece Now*. http://www.greece.gr/Culture/VisualArts/GreekFilmOverview.stm.

Soila, Tytti, Astrid Soderbergh Widding, and Gunner Iverson. *Nordic National Cinemas*. London: Routledge, 1998.

Staedeli, Thomas. *The Swiss Film*. http://www.cyranos.ch/sf-e.htm.

Street, Sarah. *British National Cinema*. London: Routledge, 1997.

Taylor, Richard. *The BFI Companion to Eastern European and Russian Cinema*. London: BFI, 2000.

Thys, Marianne. *Belgian Cinema/Le Cinema Belge/De Belgische Film*. Brussels: Royal Belgian Film Archive. Amsterdam: Flammarion, 1999.

Triana-Toribio, Nuria. *Spanish National Cinema*. London: Routledge, 2003.

WEBSITES FOR EUROPEAN FILM RESOURCES

Internet resources below are listed in order by country. They include national film organizations, film festivals, and other resources. Some are in the language of the country, but many are in English.

General

European Film Academy (EFA): http://www.europeanfilmacademy.org/.

Austria

Austrian Film Museum: http://www.filmmuseum.at.
Austrian Film Commission: http://www.afc.at.
Diagonale Film Festival (Austria): http://www.diagonale.at.
Film Archive Austria: http://www.filmarchiv.at.
Viennale International Film Festival (Austria): http://www.viennale.at.

Belgium

Flanders Film Festival (Belgium): http://www.filmfestival.be/.
Royal Film Archive Belgium: http://www.ledoux.be.
Wallonie Bruxelles Image (Belgium): http://www.cfwb.be

Bulgaria

Bulgarian Ministry of Culture: http://www.culture.government.bg/.

Bosnia-Herzogovina

Cinematheque of Bosnia and Herzogovina: http://www.kinotekabih.ba.
Sarajevo Film Festival (Bosnia and Herzogovina): http://www.sff.ba.

Croatia

Croatian Film Clubs Association: http://www.hfs.hr.

Czech Republic

Czech National Film Archive: http://www.nfa.cz.
Karlovy Vary International Film Festival (Czech Republic): http://www.kviff.com.

Denmark

Odense Film Festival (Denmark): http://www.filmfestival.dk.

Estonia

Estonian Film Foundation: http://www.efsa.ee.
Estonian Black Nights Film Festival: http://www.poff.ee.
Estonian National Archive: http://www.filmi.arhiiv.ee.

Finland

Espoo Ciné Film Festival (Finland): http://www.espoocine.org/; www.melies.org/.
Helsinki Film Festival (Finland): http://www.hiff.fi.
Tampere Film Festival (Finland): http://www.tamperefilmfestival.fi.

France

Cannes Film Festival (France): http://www.festival-cannes.org.
Centre National de la Cinématographie (France): http://www.cnc.fr.
Cinémathèque de Toulouse (France): http://www.lacinemathequedetoulouse.com.
Cinémathèque Francaise: http://www.cinemathequefrancaise.com.
Clermont-Ferrand Film Festival (France): http://www.clermont-filmfest.com.
Institute Lumière (France): http://www.institut-lumiere.org.

Germany

Berlinale Film Festival (Germany): http://www.berlinale.de.
Deutsches Filminstitut, DIF (Germany): http://www.deutsches-filminstitut.de/.
Deutsches Filmmuseum Frankfurt am Main (Germany): http://www.deutsches-filmmuseum.de.
Filmfest Hamburg (Germany): http://www.filmfesthamburg.de.
Filmfestival Max Ophüls Prize (Germany): http://www.max-ophuels-preis.de/.
Filmmuseum Berlin-Deutsche Kinematek (Germany): http://www.filmmuseum-berlin.de.
Münchner Filmmuseum (Germany): http://www.stadtmuseum-onlin.de/filmmu.htm.
Oberhausen Film Festival (Germany): http://www.kurzfilmtage.de.

Great Britain

British Academy of Film and Television Arts (BAFTA): http://www.bafta.org.
British Film Institute: http://www.bfi.org.uk/.
Leeds Film Festival (Britain): http://www.leedsfilm.com.
London Film Festival (Britain): http://www.lff.com.

Greece

Thessaloniki International Film Festival (Greece): http://www.filmfestival.gr.

Hungary

Hungarian Motion Picture Foundation: http://www.mma.hu.

Iceland

Icelandic Film Centre: http://www.icelandicfilmcentre.is.
National Film Archive Iceland: http://www.kvikmyndasafn.is.

Ireland

Cork Film Festival (Ireland): http://www.corkfilmfest.org.
Irish Film Board: http://www.filmboard.ie.
Irish Film Institute: http://www.irishfilm.ie.

Italy

Fondazione Cineteca Italiana: http://www.cinetecamilano.it.
Fondazione Federico Fellini (Italy): http://www.federicofellini.it.
Giffoni Film Festival (Italy): http://www.giffoni.it.

MIFED-Milan (Italy): http://www.mifed.com.
Museo Nazionale del Cinema (Italy): http://www.museonazionaldelcinema.org.
Pesaro Film Festival (Italy): http://www.pesarofilmfest.it.
Venice Film Festival (Italy): http://www.labiennale.org.

Lithuania

International Film Festival Film Spring (Lithuania): http://www.kino.lt.
Museum of Theater, Music and Cinema Vilniaus (Lithuania) http://www.teatras.mch.mii.lt.

Luxembourg

Media Desk Luxembourg: http://www.mediadesk.lu.

Netherlands

International Film Festival Rotterdam (Netherlands): http://www.filmfestivalrotterdam.com.
Filmmuseum (Netherlands): http://www.filmmuseum.nl.
Netherlands Film Festival: www.filmfestival.nl.
Utrecht Film Festival (Netherlands): http://www.filmfestival.nl.

Norway

Bergen Film Festival (Norway): http://www.biff.no.
Haugesund International Film Festival (Norway): http://www.filmfestivalen.no/.

Poland

Crakow Film Festival (Poland): http://www.cracowfilmfestival.pl.
Film Polski (Poland): http://www.filmpolski.com.pl.
Polish National Film Library: http://www.fn.org.pl.
Warsaw International Film Festival (Poland): http://www.wff.org.pl.

Portugal

Cinemateca Portuguesa (Portugal): http://www.cinemateca.pt.
Portuguese Institute of Cinema: http://www.icam.pt.

Russia

Moscow International Film Festival (Russia): http://www.miff.ru.
Saint Petersburg Festival of Festivals (Russia): http://www.filmfest.ru.

Scotland

Edinburgh International Film Festival (Scotland): http://www.edfilmfest.org.uk.
Scottish Screen Archive: http://www.scottishscreen.com.

Serbia and Montenegro

Belgrade International Film Festival (Serbia and Montenegro): http://www.fest.org.yu.
Yugoslav Film Archive (Serbia and Montenegro): http://www.kinoteka.org.yu.

Slovakia

Slovak Film Institute: http://www.sfu.sk.

Spain

San Sebastian Film Festival (Spain): http://www.sansebastianfestival.ya.com.
Filmoteca Espanola (Spain): http://www.cultura.mecd.es/cine/film/filmoteca.isp.
Valencia International Film Festival (Spain): http://www.ff.umea.com.
Valladolid Film Festival (Spain): http://www.seminci.com.

Sweden

Göteborg Film Festival (Sweden): http://www.filmfestival.org.
Stockholm Film Festival (Sweden): http://www.filmfestivalen.se.

Switzerland

Cinémathèque Suisse (Switzerland): http://www.cinematheque.ch.
Fribourg Film Festival (Switzerland): http://www.fiff.ch.
Locarno Film Festival (Switzerland): http://www.pardo.ch.
Nyon Film Festival (Switzerland): http://www.visionsdureel.ch.
Swiss Film Center: http://www.swissfilms.ch.

Turkey

Istanbul Film Festival (Turkey): http://www.istfest.org.

Ukraine

Kiev International Film Festival (Ukraine): http://www.molodist.com.

ARCHITECTURE

ARCHITECTURE: Zwinger Palace in Dresden serves as a perfect example of Historicism. Courtesy of the Library of Congress.

ARCHITECTURE: Park Guell in Barcelona, designed by architect Antonio Gaudi. Courtesy of Shutterstock.

ARCHITECTURE: Playa Levante in the late afternoon, Benidorm, Spain. Courtesy of Shutterstock.

ARCHITECTURE: The picturesque villiage of Positano, Italy. Courtesy of Shutterstock.

ART: The delicate Fabergé egg is a beautiful example of French workmanship. Courtesy of Shutterstock.

ART: Kazimir Malevich's *Suprematism*, ca. 1917. © Erich Lessing / Art Resource, NY.

DANCE

DANCE: Mary Wigman performs at the Chanin Theater in New York, 1931. © Bettmann/Corbis.

DANCE: Flamenco Dance has survived without many changes since its folk roots. Courtesy of Shutterstock.

FASHION AND APPEARANCE

FASHION AND APPEARANCE: Exclusive shopping at Milan's Galleria Vittorio Emanuele II, completed in 1878. Courtesy of Shutterstock.

FILM

FILM: Adrien Brody stars in Roman Polanski's 2002 film, *The Pianist.* Courtesy of Photofest.

FILM: Arno Frisch (as Paul), Stefan Clapczynski (as Schorschi) in Michael Haneke's 1997 film, *Funny Games.* This is the first Austrian film to compete at Cannes since the 1950s. Courtesy of Photofest.

FOOD AND FOODWAYS

FOOD AND FOODWAYS: A traditionally decorated Ukrainian restaurant. Courtesy of Shutterstock.

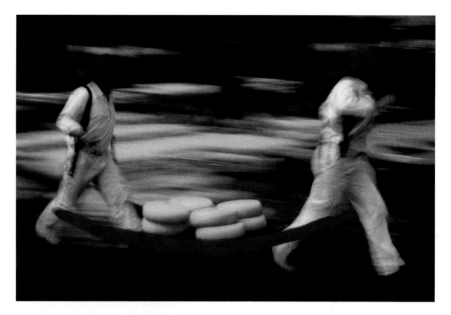

FOOD AND FOODWAYS: Cheese "weighers" in Amsterdam. Courtesy of Corbis.

FOOD AND FOODWAYS: Arrangement of an assortment of petit four cakes on a white dish. Courtesy of Shutterstock.

FOOD AND FOODWAYS: A plate of Adana Kebab (Kebap) with rice and salad. Courtesy of Shutterstock.

FOOD AND FOODWAYS: Sumptuous platter of flat breads served with red pepper hummus dip, crab dip, olives and grilled haloumi cheese. Courtesy of Shutterstock.

FOOD AND FOODWAYS: A well stocked wine shop in Tuscany, 2005. Courtesy of Shutterstock.

FOOD AND FOODWAYS

ENNO LOHMEYER

In the late nineteenth and early twentieth centuries, life in Europe saw some of its most dramatic political, economic, social, and cultural changes, which also influenced agriculture and the way people produced and prepared foods. The Industrial Revolution not only led to a mass exodus from the country to the city; it also improved the working conditions of those who remained on their farms. The use of machines meant that fewer people were needed in the process of production, and traditional farms, in which all members of the family, supported by a group of farmhands, were involved in tending animals and planting and harvesting crops, slowly gave way to more specialized, business-oriented and less labor-intensive enterprises, a development that is still going on in many Eastern European countries. Agricultural research came up with new varieties of economically useful plants that yield better harvests and enabled farmers to produce larger quantities, necessary to feed the constantly growing population. Chemical industries started to supply fertilizers, pesticides, and herbicides, which protected plants against diseases and made the farmland more productive. When it was necessary in former times for fields to lie fallow following a strict cycle, land could now be used constantly without lengthy and costly resting periods. Modern technology, especially the introduction of cooling devices, made it possible to store food for longer periods, which became more and more important because of the migration of people. During the Middle Ages, the population mostly lived in villages and small towns, close to the providers of their food, but that situation changed when industrialization lured people to the cities. There, food was scarce and had to be brought from the country, requiring better transportation and storage techniques.

World War I (1914–1918) meant a major setback in keeping the food flow going and brought starvation back to European households, especially in the cities, where the newly established working class had many difficulties to make ends meet in the first place. The beginning of the twentieth century also saw happier days, however. The so-called Golden Twenties brought glamor, gaiety, and an open mind, at least to the big urban centers in the West. The entertainment business boomed, and those who could afford it frequented bars and restaurants, which became more and more accessible even for members of the lower classes. With the rise of industrialization, eating habits had gradually started to

DINING OUT

Eating out in a restaurant traditionally means sitting down at a table, selecting food from some sort of menu, and being served by waiting staff. There is quite often a special occasion for a trip to a restaurant: a holiday, a birthday, a family reunion, a business meeting. One enjoys a good meal and spends time together with family and friends, or talks business over lunch or dinner, without necessarily paying attention to the clock. At the same time, people have always had a yearning for snacks on the side. English fish and chips, Dutch herrings, French crêpes, German bratwurst, and Turkish kebab have been sold in the streets for centuries. They are cheap, easy to get on the way home or to work; one does not have to dress up, and reservations are not required. This type of food is just simply fun and has been part of folk festivals forever. The modern American idea of fast food, however, reached Europe only after World War II and has slowly spread from the west to the east and the north to the south. Most of the major chains have restaurants at least in the bigger cities, and there is considerable competition from local chains nowadays as well. Because modern working hours leave little room for traditional lunch breaks, a quick, easy, and relatively affordable meal is appealing to many consumers. Nevertheless, unlike in the United States, fast-food restaurants still attract mostly young people in Europe, whose financial means are limited and who enjoy a less formal setting. Especially in rural and more conservative areas, many consumers criticize the quality of the food and resent having to eat with plastic utensils. Indeed, the way fast food is prepared and served is of concern for many environmentally conscious people, and waste regulations are strict.

change in general. Whereas farmers' families in previous centuries were more or less self-sufficient, both blue-collar and white-collar workers were forced to buy their food in shops specializing in local products, but also in those imported from the colonies overseas. Potatoes, from Peru, had already been introduced in the sixteenth century and soon became one of the main staples, especially in Central Europe and on the British Isles, but other vegetables and fruits, such as bananas and even oranges and lemons, considered common nowadays, were still quite rare and exotic in most European countries at the turn of the century. Coffee and tea, even though introduced much earlier, also reached the average consumer only after World War I. Having to work in a factory or an office meant that mealtimes and the social setting of eating had to be moderated as well. Since the working day requires a certain rhythm, it was not possible any more to have the main meal in the middle of the day, as was common mainly in Central and Eastern Europe. The long midday breaks enjoyed in Mediterranean countries could not be maintained, either, which meant that their principal meals in the evening had to be set at an earlier time during the day. These modern work requirements forced families to reserve their meal traditions for the weekend, resulting in the strict division between workdays and Sundays that is so typical of modern European society, in contrast to past centuries, when the demands of farm animals and seasons dictated life of the rural masses.

On the other hand, restaurants of all sorts are more affordable now and are a positive alternative to home cooking, especially on weekends and holidays. Since people travel more, they are familiar with foreign cuisines, which supports a need for and an interest in ethnic restaurants that can be found in basically all major European cities. Eating is not only a means to supply the body with essential nutrition; it has become an art form and a new type of social entertainment. There are endless numbers of magazines and TV shows trying to encourage their audience to be more adventurous or to rediscover the recipes of their ancestors. TV chefs have become as famous as pop stars, and cooking itself has turned into a popular pastime for the rich and famous as well as for average people.

AUSTRIA

The mountainous terrain of the eastern Alps covers 60 percent of modern Austria,[1] and vast areas of the country are covered with forests and woodlands. Tourism is one of the major income sources for the Austrian economy, which also derives its high standard from industrial enterprises, whereas only 0.8 percent of the labor force worked in the sector of agriculture and forestry in 2004.[2] With more than two million inhabitants, the Austrian capital, Vienna, is the biggest city in the whole Alpine region and has dominated cultural, social, and political life for centuries. The Viennese cafés or *Kaffeehäuser* have traditionally been the place for members from all groups of society to meet and to discuss important matters of the day.

Coffee is taken seriously in Austria, and even though modern consumers in other Western countries can now choose from a large variety of different kinds of coffee beverages, Austrians have always enjoyed this privilege. There is *Franziskaner*, for example, dark coffee with a little more milk, which gives it the color of a Franciscan's robe; *Pharisäer*, strong black coffee with whipped cream, served with a small liqueur glass of rum; *Kaisermelange*, a cup of black coffee with raw egg yolk and brandy on the side.

Wine has been cultivated in Austria for more than 2000 years, and even though Austrian wines are not as widely known as those of France and Italy, they are of high quality. *Grüner Veltliner* is a dry white wine of a pale straw color; *Schilcher* is a rosé wine, mostly produced in the region of Styria; and *Zweigelt* is a popular red wine. In August 1784, Emperor Josef II decreed that foods, wine, and juices could be sold by anybody who wished to do so. This tradition has survived up to the present day in the form of the *Heuriger*, a small inn, where the owner is allowed to sell

HEALTH CONSCIOUSNESS AND DIET

Up to the first half of the twentieth century, feeding a family did not so much mean watching out for fat, cholesterol, carbohydrates, and other excesses in their diet, because the economy was bad, money was scarce, and for many Europeans it was still difficult to satisfy their basic nutrition needs. With the end of World War II, though, health and beauty concerns came to play an important role, especially in Western society, where obesity and inappropriate nutrition cause many diseases. When the British model Twiggy (Lesley Hornby) showed off her extremely slender body to the fashion world of the 1960s, women all over Europe tried to follow her example. Even though it is difficult to compete with Twiggy, her beauty ideal, as far as body weight goes, has not changed much up to the present day. Diet programs try to outdo each other, and members of both sexes join fitness clubs to keep in shape. They also pay attention to what they eat, not only for beauty but also for health reasons. Due to advanced medical research, we know what foods to avoid. To be sure, there have always been fitness programs and spas, and pharmacies, drugstores, and certain other specialty shops have always sold health-oriented food, but there is greater awareness and interest in society nowadays. Many consumers are willing to pay extra for organic produce that has not been treated with chemicals and has not been genetically modified. Products low in fats and carbohydrates are on the market, and meat from free-range animals, which have not been injected with hormones, is preferred. The number of vegetarians, who eat neither meat nor fish, and vegans, who refuse any animal products, is on the rise. Long-forgotten herbs and natural remedies have been rediscovered as well, and they compete with traditional medical treatment.

151

his own wine, typically from the previous vintage, to customers who enjoy simple local wines. Modern state regulations, however, require that a *Heuriger* may be open only for a limited period each year. Brandy made from different fruits and herbs, including rowan-berries and the roots of the Alpine gentian, are popular with Austrians as well as with tourists, and so is rum, mostly used for coffee and tea mixed drinks.

The Viennese eat in a restaurant at least once a week, more often than their fellow citizens in other parts of the country. Regardless of where it is prepared, at home or in a restaurant, the *Wiener Schnitzel*—a boneless cut of veal, breaded and fried—is known worldwide. *Tafel-spitz* is made from rump steak boiled in broth. It is then cut in slices and served with horse-radish. *Bosner* is a kind of hot dog, although it is made with bratwurst, curry, and cayenne pepper, and the bread is usually toasted. The city of Salzburg is known for its *Nockerln*; their main ingredients are eggs, sugar, and some flour. The city of Linz gave the world the *Linzer Torte*. Its dough is made with lots of ground hazelnuts and then covered with a layer of *Ribiselgelee* or black currant jelly. A layer of dough on top in lattice shape gives the cake its typical appearance. The *Hotel Sacher* in Vienna created the famous *Sacher-Torte*, a chocolate cake with apricot jam in between the layers.

THE BALKANS: ALBANIA, BOSNIA AND HERZEGOVINA, CROATIA, MACEDONIA, SERBIA AND MONTENEGRO, SLOVENIA

Albania is one of Europe's poorest nations and still largely agricultural, with about 72.2 percent of its workforce engaged in that sector in 2001.[3] During Communist rule, the land was collective property and not well managed. Even though most of it has been privatized since 1992, farmers still have a hard life in Albania and make very little profit. They grow grains, mostly wheat and maize, but also watermelons (about 292,000 tons in 2004) and tomatoes (about 169,000 tons).[4] Food processing companies employ many of the indus-trial workers and turn food into an important business factor for the Albanian economy.

The states sharing the territory within the borders of the former republic of Yugoslavia have both a Communist heritage and a lifestyle influenced by the Mediterranean Sea. It was easier for Yugoslav citizens to leave their country than for those in other Communist states, and Balkan cuisine was part of the early ethnic-cooking wave that swept over Europe in the second half of the twentieth century, long before Communism collapsed.

The Balkan region is generally known for its grilled meats, such as *ražnjići*, which is pork cut into cubes and then grilled on skewers. *Ćevapi*, like the Turkish kebab, is prepared in a similar fashion, only here ground meat, spiced and shaped into little rolls, is used. *Ćevapi*, which is nowadays mostly known in its diminutive form, *ćevapčići*, originates in Serbia, where pork is preferred, whereas the Moslem nations Turkey and Bosnia use lamb or beef. *Pasulj corba* is the famous Serbian bean soup, made with white beans, different cuts of pork, peppers, potatoes, leek, and celery. *Đuveč* is a rice dish with pork, tomatoes, and bell and hot peppers, originally created in Serbia as well. Peppers of all sorts can be found in many Balkan dishes. *Pasticada* is a type of stew, popular along the coast. It is made with marinated beef, cooked in wine with onions. The Dalmatian coast in Croatia is also famous for its dried ham, called *prsut*. It is served as an appetizer with *paski sir*, hard sheep's milk cheese. There is *kastradina*, dried mutton, as well, and *osoljena*, salted fish.

Different kinds of nuts and seeds are not only served as appetizers but used as ingredients for desserts, too. *Prekmurska gibanica* is a strudel-like pastry filled with curds, apples, and poppy seeds. Desserts tend to be rather sweet and are often flavored with honey and rose water. Wine has been cultivated on the Balkan Peninsula for millennia, and, especially, red wines from Kosovo are internationally known. These wines are on the sweet side, too, and have a high alcohol content. Seventy percent of all the plums harvested in the Balkan states usually end up in *šljivovica*, a clear liquor popular as an aperitif or after a rich meal.

THE BALTIC STATES: ESTONIA, LATVIA, AND LITHUANIA

The three Baltic republics have been under Russian influence for centuries, and only in 1990 did they become independent modern republics, albeit still struggling with their Russian heritage. Many of their food traditions are similar to those of their huge neighbor to the east, Russia, and also to those of Poland, which has always had close connections especially to Lithuania. All three countries are situated on the shores of the Baltic Sea, which means that fishing plays an important role for their economies as well as for their eating habits. Even though the Baltic republics are probably the most economically advanced of the former Soviet republics, farming still plays an important role, employing 17.8 percent of the labor force in Lithuania, 15.5 percent in Latvia, and 7 percent in Estonia.[5] The large urban centers such as the capitals Vilnius, Riga, and Tallinn, offer all the amenities of modern cities with supermarkets and restaurants of all sorts, but life in some rural areas, especially along the Russian border, is still very simple, with few opportunities for gastronomic entertainment and rather basic shopping possibilities.

Baltic cuisine has never required the reputation of being particularly fancy; which is one reason why expensive restaurants there hardly serve traditional local dishes. The ingredients used for some of them, such as pig's head and ears, do not necessarily appeal to modern taste buds, but the food is rich and tasty. For breakfast, many people like hearty dishes made with fish, sausages, and cheese. Salads tend to be served with a creamy mayonnaise sauce, and soups are equally rich. In Latvia, sorrel soup made with pork, hard-boiled eggs,

FOOD CUSTOMS UNDER COMMUNIST RULE

The states in Eastern Europe are still young with regard to their post-Communist identity, but they all look back to a long cultural history. Ancient civilizations once settled there, such as the Thracians, who lived in what is now Bulgaria from 3500 BC until the Roman occupation. The Romans brought military dominance to the countries they conquered, but they also spread their way of living, including the art of wine making. After the Romans came the Ottomans with their exotic cuisine and strict Islamic food rules. Most countries in the east adopted Christianity toward the end of the first millennium and fought to keep their food traditions alive. The result was a cuisine with local, Roman, and Turkish elements, even though many of the ancient civilizations left few traces. When Communism gripped the east during the twentieth century, its ideology of uniformity threatened local food traditions again. Factories produced cheap and simple foods, and state-owned farms cultivated those vegetables and fruits their leaders considered most useful for the people. Diversity and old, supposedly bourgeois ideas were not encouraged. In addition to ideological constraints, mismanagement quite often led to poor harvests, which made feeding a family difficult at times. Economic hardships and strict government control could not completely destroy the old way of life, and since the Iron Curtain came down at the end of the 1980s, the new nations have proudly revived their food traditions. Restaurant visits are still unaffordable for many citizens, especially in rural areas, but it is possible to enjoy private parties openly, lavishly displaying the typical eastern hospitality, even if the means are modest. Shopping possibilities in the bigger cities have almost reached Western standards, and most consumers are eager to embrace the offers of capitalism, which had been denied to them for so long.

sour cream, barley, and potatoes is popular. There is green soup in Estonia, which gets its name from a variety of vegetables, cooked with lots of onions and bacon. *Capelinai* are eaten in Lithuania, especially when guests are expected. They are a type of dumplings, made from raw and boiled potatoes, filled with ground beef, curd, or mushrooms. Mushrooms are popular in all three Baltic states, as are other fruits and vegetables that can be found in the wild. Potatoes are also a main staple and can find their way into soups, stews, pies, puddings, pancakes, and other dishes. *Vederai* is a type of sausage, made from potatoes or barley with lots of bacon, cracklings, and pig intestines. *Piragi* are a Latvian yeast pastry filled with bacon and onions. In Estonia, there is *russolje*, pickled herring with turnips, and *täidetud basikarind* is stuffed veal roast. *Bliny* are small pancakes, often filled with sour cream or fish. *Kama* is a mush usually made from a variety of grains and ground beans or peas. In Estonia, people like to eat it as a dessert with milk or whipping cream, but it is also popular for breakfast, when it is mixed with fresh berries, honey, or *kefir*, a dairy product particularly loved in Eastern European countries.

Since there are many beekeepers in rural Baltic areas, honey is used not only for cooking but also for producing sweet liqueurs and wines. Regular wine is usually imported from Russia and is preferred sweet as well, whereas beer is preferred as a light variety. As for their Russian neighbors, vodka is probably still the most popular alcoholic spirit for the vast majority of adult consumers in Estonia, Latvia, and Lithuania, where it is distilled in large quantities. For more than hundred years, the liquor company *AS Liviko* in Tallinn has produced *Vana Tallinn*, a strong liqueur with vanilla and cinnamon extracts, which is a favorite for coffee mixed drinks.

BELGIUM AND LUXEMBURG

Belgium is a highly industrialized country, where only 4.2 percent of the labor force worked in the agricultural sector in 2001;[6] in Luxemburg it was 1.3 percent in 2002.[7] The proximity to France is responsible for the French influence on Belgian cuisine, which also has Flemish roots.

Soupe à l'Ardennaise is a soup from the Ardennes region and features chicory, an herb of which Belgians are especially proud. *Lapin à la Flamande* is a rabbit dish, prepared in a stewpot with prunes and brandy. Because Belgium is situated on the coast of the North Sea, there are also many seafood dishes on the menu. *Moules frites* is probably the most famous of them, mussels cooked with vegetables and then served with French fries—which, in spite of the name, are a Belgian invention. *Pommes frites*, as they are called in French, were probably first created in the seventeenth century, when poor fishermen fried sliced potatoes instead of fish. *Waterzooi de poissons* is a famous fish soup, which traditionally also contains eel. Luxemburgers like old-fashioned, rural dishes, such as *geheck*, a soup made from innards. As a dessert both in Belgium and Luxemburg, waffles or *gauvres* may be served with whipped cream, fresh fruits, or just simply sugar. They are also popular with people of all age groups as a snack.

Chocolate is another delicacy for which Belgium has become famous; brand names such as Godiva and Guylian are known worldwide.

In 2003, Belgians produced about 16 million hectoliters of beer,[8] which has been brewed there for centuries. In 1366 the Den Horen brewery was founded, which changed its name to *Artois* in 1717 and became one of the biggest and most renowned companies. After several mergers, it was integrated into the InBev brewing company in 2004.[9] Within the borders of Belgium, abbey beers with about 70 different brands are very popular. The recipes of these beers are owned by the abbeys that originally brewed them, even though today many of them are produced by different companies under license. Abbey beers should not be confused with Trappist beers, which are still manufactured in the community of the monastery. There are six brands of Trappist beers, most of which have a strong alcoholic content. Unique to Belgium are the lambic beers, fermented with natural yeast, which gives them a distinct taste. These beers can be blended to produce gueuze, or flavored with cherries to make kriek.

BULGARIA

Traditionally, agriculture plays an important role in Bulgaria, but the country has been considerably industrialized since World War II. In 2001, 25.6 percent of the work force were employed by the agricultural sector, which accounts for more than 12 percent of the gross national product.[10] Farmers grow wheat (about 4 million tons in 2004), sunflower seeds (1.1 million tons),[11] tobacco, vegetables and fruits, especially grapes, which are used for producing wine and brandy.

Slivova, a brandy made from plums, is traditionally produced in many rural areas in Bulgaria each fall. The production is executed on a grander scale nowadays, resulting in many liters of *slivova* for export. The mild and sunny Bulgarian climate not only attracts tourists to the country but also creates different kinds of wine for local use and export. Most of all, however, Bulgarian cuisine is known for its large variety of dairy products, especially its famous yogurt. *Sirene* is a cheese made from goat's milk, which is often cut into very thin slices and served with *shopska salata*, a traditional salad made from fresh tomatoes and cucumbers that are available on every country market in Bulgaria.

Bulgaria does not have a long restaurant tradition. In previous centuries, travelers used to stop at monasteries to eat, but nowadays cities such as Sofia and many of the tourist resorts on the Black Sea are filled with excellent restaurants of high standards. Eating in a restaurant can become a cultural experience, when live music is played and dancing takes place in the

THE GROCERY STORE

Grocery shopping in Europe has changed considerably over the past four decades, and the traditional grocery and mom-and-pop shops have mostly become institutions of the past, even though rural areas in the former Communist countries in the east are still behind the trend. Most Europeans buy their food in supermarkets nowadays, which are usually owned by a few national chains. As in the United States, many of these supermarkets require a large amount of space and are moved out of the cities, to which modern consumers can adjust depending on their cars. For certain articles, though, many consumers still prefer to shop at the local baker's, butcher's, fishmonger's, and the bigger the city, the more specialty stores offer their goods to those customers willing to pay a higher price. Open-air markets have not completely disappeared either; at a time when freshness is in demand, they are actually quite popular again. In Western countries, it is not necessarily the local farmers who sell their produce, but rather vendors who specialize in supplying this type of market and in satisfying the somewhat distinguished palate of their customers. Since the role of women has changed as well, not all women spend a large portion of time preparing food for their families, as used to be common in previous centuries. Supermarkets meet this change of traditions very well, since they offer in one store everything necessary for cooking, including ready-to-eat meals, which are not yet, however, as popular as in the United States. Canned and frozen supermarket food has replaced the old custom of preserving and canning fruits and vegetables at home, which is, however, still popular with many housewives, mostly not out of necessity but rather to keep up traditions and to serve their families food out of the ordinary.

background. Traditionally, Bulgarians love to eat, and a festive meal consists of several different courses. *Kyopolu* may be served as an appetizer, a paste made from roasted eggplants and green peppers. *Tarator* is a yogurt soup with cucumbers and walnuts. There are many dishes made with cheese, such as *purzheni chushki s sirene*, small or medium-sized hot peppers filled with *sirene* or *brynsa*, made from sheep's milk. The peppers are then fried and served as appetizers. *Banitsa* is a pastry made from puff pastry dough and filled with *sirene* or *brynsa*. It is baked in the shape of an S and served hot or cold as an appetizer, or with drinks. Religious holidays all have their traditional dishes and rituals, some of which go back to Thracian days.

CZECH REPUBLIC AND SLOVAKIA

Both the Czech Republic and Slovakia are among the most economically advanced countries of Eastern Europe, and in 2002 only 6.2 percent of the labor force were employed by the agricultural sector in Slovakia and 4.4 percent in the Czech Republic. The two countries are highly industrialized, and foods and live animals totaled only 3 percent of Czech exports in 2004.[12] The remaining farmers who still work the land produced about 5 million tons of wheat and 2.3 million tons of barley in the Czech Republic (2004),[13] and 1.6 million tons of sugar beets and about 1.6 million tons of wheat in Slovakia.[14]

Another crop the Czech Republic and Slovakia specialize in is hops. This herb is needed for brewing beer, and the Czech Republic can proudly look back to a long tradition of brewing excellent beer. With about 17.7 million hectoliters of beer brewed in 2001, the Czech Republic is one of the world's leading beer producers.[15] The most popular beer is Budějovický Budvar from the town of Čéské Budějovický, which is named *Budweis* in German, so it is truly a Budweiser, just as Pilsener comes from Plzeň; in the United States, Budějovický Budvar is marketed as "Czechvar."[16] Because of a competitive market, many of the smaller breweries had to close after 1990. Several of the bars across the country produce their own beer in microbreweries, such as U Fleků in Prague, which serves a special dark beer.

Apricots, grown in the warmer climate zones of the two countries, are used to produce fruit schnapps, but also to make a variety of desserts. *Meruňkové knedlíky* are dumplings made from potatoes or curds and filled with apricots. Many different kinds of curds and cottage cheeses are used for cooking and baking. *Halušky* is a Slovak dish made from sheep or goat curds and is also served as a dessert. Dumplings or *knedlíky* are still very popular to accompany meat dishes. Bread dumplings are the most common ones nowadays.

Pork roast or *vepřová pečené* is a very popular dish and is traditionally served with dumplings and sauerkraut. Sirloin or *svíčková*, which is usually marinated before it is cooked, is another typical meat for festive occasions.

FRANCE

Next to Italian, French cuisine has required a reputation worldwide that is hard to beat, and culinary masterpieces created by French chefs are especially praised above others by connoisseurs for their superb quality. There are publications on French cooking in almost any language, and French chefs spread their expertise around the world, where restaurants offering French food tend to be on the pricy side. In France itself, there is a vast variety of restaurants, cafés, brasseries, and bistros—all of which words, internationally used, are borrowed from the French language. Like most national cuisines, French cooking consists of regional components, and traditionally cooks in the south with its Mediterranean influence prepare different dishes than those in Brittany or in Alsace, but they all share the enthusiasm for eating and drinking good food.

Only 4.1 percent of the labor force were employed by the agricultural sector in 2002,[17] but French farmers are still very influential in public life and produced about 39.7 million tons of wheat in 2004 and 5.2 million tons of wine in 2002.[18] France is famous for its red wines form Burgundy and the Bordeaux region, but wine is produced in many areas of France, and Alsace and Languedoc-Roussillon, especially, cultivate excellent white and rosé wines, too. Since 1855, the year of the World Exposition in Paris, there has been a classification of French wines that nowadays consists of four grades, with *appellation d'origine controlée* as the highest category. Estates producing award winning wines include Margaux, Mouton-Rothschild, Lafite, Latour, and Haut-Brion. Champagne is a sparkling wine, and only those wines produced in five *départements* roughly corresponding to the historic region of Champagne are allowed to bear the name. The same restrictions concerning the name are true for *cognac* and *calvados*. True calvados, a brandy made form apple cider, originates in a limited area in Normandy, and the real cognac, a brandy made from white wine, is only distilled in the vicinity of Cognac, mainly in the *département* of Charente.

A stereotypical French breakfast consists of *baguette* (wheat bread in the shape of a stick, known in the United States as "French bread"), butter, jam, and a small cup of coffee. There is also *café au lait*, coffee with milk, and *café crème*, coffee with steamed milk added. *Brioche* is a round pastry with a small elevation, and for *pain au chocolat*, puff pastry is filled with chocolate sauce.

A festive meal in the evening consists of many different courses, and meat and side dishes are usually served separately. As appetizer, there may be *foie gras*, goose or duck liver paste, or *confit*, any kind of meat cooked in fat and then served cold as a spread. Mussels and snails are popular appetizers, and occasionally one may find frog legs on the menu. *Bouillabaisse* from Provence is a rich fish soup, which is called *bourride*, when refined with fresh cream. The south is also home to the famous *salade niçoise* and to *ratatouille*, a vegetable stew with eggplants, tomatoes, peppers, zucchini, and onions. *Bourbaguian*, a specialty from Monaco, is a type of pizza with vegetables, eggs, and rice. Provençal cooking cannot do without garlic and olive oil; both are main ingredients of *aïoli*, a mayonnaise used as a complement for all kinds of dishes. White and black truffles are the rarest and most expensive mushrooms that add a special touch, for which French cuisine is so famous. Frenchmen like their beef rare, but there is also a lot of pork available, and rabbit and horsemeat are specialties in many areas. The number of cakes and pastries served as dessert is endless; *charlotte*, a light sponge-cake with cream or fruits, is one example. *Crêpes*, very thin pancakes with any kind of sweet or salty filling, are available at every street corner, and no proper French dinner would be complete without a selection of cheeses from cow's, sheep's, or goat's milk. Camembert, for example, a soft cheese from cow's milk, is a creation from Normandy.

GERMANY

German food has the reputation of being rich and heavy, but as with most modern cuisines, this is only true for certain traditional dishes, which are not on the menu anymore for many young people. Since the various regions of Germany have historically had certain independence, there are also regional differences in cooking. Most of all, Germany is known for its beer gardens, which can be found all over the country nowadays, but tend to be more common in the south and in the Berlin area. Traditional Bavarian beer gardens permit their customers to bring their own food, as long as they buy a beverage there. Altogether, there are about 1,270 breweries in Germany, which produced more than 106 million hectoliters of beer in 2001.[19] Weihenstephan in Munich, founded in 1040, is the oldest brewery, and Warburger Brauerei is one of the biggest. Since Roman days, wine has also been cultivated along the Rhine and other rivers in the south, and especially German white wines, such as Riesling, have acquired fame around the world. Weizenkorn is a clear liquor made from wheat, and the mountainous regions in the south and east are famous for their herbal and fruit liqueurs.

Agriculture employed 2.3 percent of the labor force in 2004,[20] and farming has changed considerably during the late twentieth century. Most farmers specialize in one or two crops nowadays and run their farms like any other enterprise. In the first decade of the twenty-first century, German farmers produced 25.4 million tons of wheat, 25.3 million tons of sugar beets, and 599,000 tons of cabbage a year;[21] a large amount of the latter ends up as *Sauerkraut*. It is the Romans again who brought the technique of making sauerkraut to Austria and Germany, and sauerkraut and other cabbage preparations have been popular ever since, especially as winter dishes. Traditionally, sauerkraut would be served with *Eisbein*, pig's knuckles, but when leaner meat is asked for, other cuts of pork may be substituted. For a festive meal, many consumers still prefer pork over beef, but poultry is on the rise as well, and there has always been a stuffed goose for Christmas, accompanied by red cabbage and potato dumplings. Potatoes may be served boiled, fried, mashed, baked, as a salad, dumplings or as pancakes; they have always been the main side dish for meat, and only recently have they had competition form rice and pasta.

It seems that every German region is proud of its own local *Bratwurst*, which is usually grilled outdoors at family reunions, as a snack in the city or at folk festivals. Traditionally, it is served with a slice of bread and some mustard only, but a ketchup-curry sauce is popular now as well. People in rural areas are particularly fond of stews with peas, beans, lentils, or prunes and other dried fruits.

Even though many young people like *Müsli* or cereal for their breakfast nowadays, Germans traditionally start their day with different kinds of bread or bread rolls, butter, and selection of jams, honey, cheeses, and cold meat cuts, which are usually called *Wurst*. German bread comes in colors from white to black and is made from wheat or rye, often with whole grains. Multigrain breads, to which occasionally more unusual ingredients such as nuts, raisins, or pumpkin seeds are added, are available as well. For centuries, the city of Nuremberg has been the center of gingerbread production, which is particularly popular at Christmas and at fairs. Because lunch is considered to be the main meal of the day, bread tends to be served for supper or *Abendbrot* as well. Open sandwiches, buttered and covered with cheese or slices of *Wurst*, are typical and may be supplemented with salads and potato dishes. There is an endless variety of different cold cuts of meat, from salamis, hams, and jellied meats to liver and blood sausages.

The correct time to serve cake is four o'clock in the afternoon, when cafes and *Kaffeehäuser* are popular meeting points, especially on weekends. For *Schwarzwälder Kirschtorte*, or Black Forest cake, cocoa is added to the batter. The cake is then cut and layered, with whipped cream and cherries in between. As a regular dessert, different kinds of custard may be served or just simply fruit. Ice-cream parlors, usually of Italian origin, have been popular for decades now, as have other restaurants serving ethnic food.

GREECE

The mild Mediterranean climate allows Greek farmers, 15.8 percent of the labor force in 2002,[22] to grow oranges (about 772,500 tons in 2004), olives (2.1 million tons), cotton (about 359,000 tons), and also soybeans and tobacco.[23]

Because of the summer heat, Greeks traditionally like to have their main meal in the evening, preferably late. Unlike in other countries, even in restaurants Greeks tend to order for the whole table to share, instead of getting individual dishes. Many of the Greek appetizers are popular worldwide, and it is sometimes even forgotten that they are of Greek origin. There is the farmer's salad, for example, *horietiki salata*, made with fresh tomatoes, cucumbers, peppers, onions, olives, and *feta* cheese, made from sheep's milk. *Tzatziki* is made from unsweetened Greek yogurt with olive oil, thinly sliced cucumbers, and lots of garlic. *Taramosalata* is made from fish roe, and *dolmadakia* are grape leaves filled with rice, spices, and onions. As a main course or *kyria piata*, fish may be served or rabbit, lamb, or goat meat, whereas pork and beef were traditionally rarely used for meat dishes. *Mousakas* is a kind of soufflé made with eggplants and ground meat. Other dishes, such as *gyros*, pork or lamb grilled on a spit, and *souvlaki*, lamb skewers, are Greek in origin but have only gained their reputation through Greek restaurants abroad. *Baklava*, created in Turkey, has become a typical eastern Mediterranean dessert. It is made with puff pastry filled with walnuts and almonds or pistachios and soaked in a sweet, spicy syrup.

Retsina is a typical Greek white or rosé wine that gets its distinctive taste from being treated with pine-tree resin. The island of Samos is home to a sweet dessert wine made from muscadine grapes. *Mavrodaphne* is a red wine fortified with brandy, a technique typical for certain Mediterranean wines. *Ouzo* is a liquor made from a combination of pressed grapes, berries, and herbs, including star anise and licorice, which give it its typical flavor. Dissolving anise oils are also responsible for its whitish, clouded color, when mixed with water. Ouzo is considered by some to be Greece's national drink, whereas *Metaxa*, a brandy created by Spyros Metaxa in 1888, is probably its most famous spirit worldwide. The typical Greek coffee is strong and served in small cups with the coffee grounds in it.

HUNGARY

In spite of its Communist history, Hungary is one of Europe's fastest-growing and most open economies with a high standard of living. Half of Hungary consists of good, fertile soil, ideal for producing sunflower seeds (1.2 million tons in 2004), maize (8.3 million tons), and apples (680,000 tons).[24] In 2002, 6.2 percent of the labor force were employed by the agricultural sector, which was responsible for 6 percent of all Hungarian exports.[25] One product exported all over the world is *Tokaji* (Tokay), a sweet dessert wine from the northeast of Hungary, near the town of Tokaj. There are two kinds of *Tokaji*: *Tokaji Szamorodni* and *Tokaji Aszú*. Both of them get their bouquet and flavor from mold with which some of the grapes are infected. *Tokaji Aszú*, however, contains additional, especially selected grapes, which give the wine a superior quality. Red wines from the region of Eger, such as *Egri Bikavér* or Bull's Blood, are famous as well. Altogether, 541,000 tons of wine were produced in 2001.[26] *Unicum* is a bitter liqueur, made for over 150 years from a blend of forty herbs, and it can be enjoyed as an apéritif or after a meal, thus helping digestion.

As in most Eastern European countries, food traditions either go back to rural cooking or to the cuisine of the aristocracy, whereas the middle classes have started only rather lately to contribute to the rich Hungarian cuisine. Of all Hungarian dishes, goulash is probably the most famous one. What Hungarians call *gylás*, however, is a thick beef soup cooked with onions and potatoes, whereas what foreigners usually think of as goulash is *pörkölt*: meat stewed with onions and paprika and often softened with *tejföl* or sour cream—another ingredient Hungarians like to add to a variety of dishes. *Paprikás csirke* is chicken cooked in broth with paprika, and *Debreceni töltött káposzta* is ground meat wrapped in cabbage leaves. This dish has its origin in the city of Debrecen, which is also famous for its sausages. Because the Danube flows through Hungary, and there is also Lake Balaton with its many tourist resorts, fish is a common alternative to meat. *Fogos* or pike-perch is served either breaded and fried or grilled, and then there is *hálaszlé*, a spicy fish soup cooked with tomatoes, green peppers, and paprika.

IBERIAN PENINSULA: SPAIN AND PORTUGAL

The two westernmost European countries, Spain and Portugal, share the Iberian Peninsula and are under Mediterranean influence, which is responsible for long, warm nights and late dinner times. Because both states look back to a long seafaring history, exotic spices and foods were already brought to the peninsula centuries ago and were integrated into local dishes early on. The mild climate allows cultivating citrus fruits; almost 2.7 million tons of oranges were harvested in Spain in 2004.[27] Spanish farmers, 5.9 percent of the labor force in 2002,[28] also produced about 3.8 million tons of tomatoes and almost 5 million tons of olives.[29] Food products totaled 12 percent of all Spanish exports in 2004.[30] In Portugal, 12.3 percent of the labor force were still employed by the agricultural sector in 2002.[31] In many rural areas, it is also still possible to find quaint little villages with traditional grocery stores and small bars.

Soups and stews are traditional dishes all over Spain. Stew, or *cocido*, prepared in Castile should contain chickpeas, beef, bacon, chicken, blood sausage (*morcilla*), vegetables, mostly white cabbage, and *chorizo*, a dry pork sausage made with lots of garlic and paprika, which gives it its typical red color. *Sopas mallorquinas* is a similar stew, served on the island of Mallorca, where *sopas* is this case does not refer to the plural of *sopa* or soup, but to the slice of bread which is put into the bowl the stew is served in. *Caldeirada* is a rich Portugese soup made with fish and other sea foods. Because Portugal has a long coastline, fish has always played an important role; *bacalhão* or stockfish is especially popular. In Spain, there is *paella*, of course, which originates in Valencia and is made with round-grain rice flavored with saffron, olive oil, and garlic, which is then cooked with seafood or meat. *Gazpacho* is a famous vegetable soup, which is usually served cold. *Tapas* are snacks eaten in bars, since restaurants traditionally only serve complete meals.

The list of desserts is endless; one possible choice is *flan*, a type of caramel custard. *Mantecados* are pastries baked with lard, and *polvorones* are made from almonds. As in France, cheese may be offered as dessert as well: *manchego*, for example, sheep's milk cheese from central Spain, or *queso de Burgos*, a curdlike cheese from the city of Burgos. Spain and Portugal are also famous for their wide variety of wines. Spain's wine growers alone produced about 3.6 million tons in 2002,[32] and no other country produces more white wine than Spain. People in the north of Portugal are proud of their *vinho verde*, green wine, where "green" actually means new. *Vinho verde* may refer to red, rosé, or white wine, and it is put on the market while it is still lightly sparkling. Port, which gets its name from the country, is red wine fortified with alcohol. The same is true for sherry, white wine originally from the city of Jerez de la Frontera in Andalucia, which English merchants started to market in the eighteenth century. It has been particularly successful with British consumers ever since.

ITALY

Italian cuisine is famous and loved all over the world, and there is hardly a city in the Western Hemisphere that does not have a restaurant serving some kind of Italian food. Bread, wine, and olives are part of the Italian *dolce vita*. 4.43 million tons of wine were produced in 2002,[33] and much of it was exported. Grapes that make the famous Italian red wines are, for example, Sangiovese, Montepulciano, and Nebbiolo. In 2004, Italian farmers, 5.3 percent of the labor force,[34] also produced 4.5 million tons of olives and 2.1 million tons of oranges.[35]

Italian bread is traditionally made from wheat, such as *focaccia*, a flat bread from the Ligurian coast, which is often baked with herbs and was already known to the Etruscans. *Ciabatta* is another wheat bread; it was originally baked in a big flat shape, but is sold in a variety of different shapes today.

Some people consider focaccia to be the forerunner of pizza. Since the mid 1700s, there has been some kind of pizza in southern Italy, prepared only with olive oil, tomatoes, and basil or oregano. Cheese was added at the end of the nineteenth century, and these four ingredients are still used nowadays for making pizza, even though fresh tomatoes are usually replaced with *salsa pizzaiola* or tomato sauce, and several other components can be added according to taste. In the nineteenth century, Italian emigrants also took pizza to the United States, where it became even more popular than in its home country.

Another food made from wheat is pasta, which can be freshly made at home or bought as a dry staple. Pasta comes in all kinds of shapes, forms, and colors, from *anelli* through *lasagne, ravioli, spaghetti* (Italy's most famous dish), and *tortellini* to *ziti*—the list is endless. Rice was introduced to Italy during the Renaissance and has ever since been grown in the valley of the river Po. Round-grain rice is used to make *risotto*, which may be served with *ossobuco* or veal knuckles.

Mortadella di Bologna is a type of pork sausage, often flavored with pistachios. *Salami* is another dry sausage, which is eaten cold and sliced as an appetizer. It was originally made from donkey or mule meat, but pork or beef is used nowadays, as well as lots of garlic. *Prosciutto di Parma* is air-dried ham from the regions of Piemonte and Emilia-Romagna.

Italy's cheeses are also known worldwide. There is, for example, *parmigiano reggiano* or parmesan, which is used for pasta dishes, whereas mozzarella was originally used as

SUN, SEAFOOD, AND WINE: MEDITERRANEAN CUISINE

Life in the countries in and around the Mediterranean Sea, from Portugal in the west to Turkey in the east, has many things in common. Long, hot, and relatively dry summers dominate and make visitors from the north forget their own, quite often dismal weather conditions. Life seems to be so much easier when the sky is blue and the sun is shining, which did not go unnoticed on members of the British high society, who discovered the French *Côte d'Azur* near Nice and Monaco as a perfect vacation destination in the nineteenth century. Since then, sun-hungry travelers from all social classes and countries have learned to appreciate the Mediterranean charm, and tourism has become one of the most important industries along the coast. It has changed life in once-forgotten fishing villages for better or worse, and new tourist resorts are still being built. For many people, the typical Mediterranean lifestyle means eating outdoors by the sea, seafood perhaps, but definitely bread, olives, and a glass of wine. The Greek island of Crete can be regarded as the European cradle of olive oil and wine; both were first cultivated there millennia ago. Olive oil is essential for Mediterranean cooking and is almost exclusively used when "oil" is asked for—including such nonfood uses as the ceremonial anointing of kings and the sacraments of the Catholic Church (for which it is often mixed with balsam). It comes in different quality groups in shades from green to yellow, and in different price ranges. The olives themselves are used as appetizers and in salads and pastes, and they may be added to a variety of other pasta, meat, or seafood dishes. The early Greeks relied on olive oil to treat injuries, for cosmetics, and as fuel for their lamps.

pizza cheese and, together with tomatoes, basil, and olive oil, makes a lovely salad called *caprese*.

Traditionally, Italians have their main meal in the evening, which consists of several courses, at least as a festive dinner. As *antipasti*, salads or cold meat cuts may be served, *primi piatti* might consist of pasta dishes or *gnocchi di patate*, a type of potato dumplings. *Polenta*, a cornmeal mush, may be used instead of pasta in the northern regions of Italy. Soups, such as *minestrone*, made from a variety of vegetables, would be served as *primi piatti* as well, whereas fish and meat dishes make up *secondi piatti*. There is a vast assortment of *dolci* or desserts as well, such as *zabaglione*, made from eggs and wine. *Tiramisù*, originally created in Venetia, is a layered dessert made with *mascarpone* cheese and cake dough soaked in liquor. A cup of *espresso* or *cappuccino* usually finishes the meal.

NETHERLANDS

The Netherlands are a small, mostly flat, and low country by the North Sea. The land is fertile and very intensively cultivated by, in 2002, about 3.1 percent of the labor force.[36] Tomatoes from the Netherlands are known and sold all over Europe, and Dutch farmers produced 645,000 tons of them in 2004.[37] Although the Netherlands are highly industrialized, food products and live animals amount to 19 percent of all exports.[38] In addition to vegetables, farmers and the food industry produce large amounts of dairy products, especially cheese. In 2002, Dutch cows gave 10.8 million tons of milk.[39] Among the vast array of Dutch cheeses, Edam and Gouda are the most famous ones, both named after the cities where they were produced originally. Edam and Gouda are semi-hard cheeses made from cow's milk, traditionally with a fat content of about 40 percent; there are low-fat varieties available nowadays, however. Both cheeses are usually round with a waxed rind, and Gouda, especially, may be sold young or mature.

The Dutch are a very open-minded and liberal people who love to socialize and to eat out in restaurants offering everything from fast food to high-quality dishes, from traditional Dutch to international cuisine. Due to the former colonial links to Indonesia, southeastern Asian dishes are especially popular with many Dutch consumers. *Saté*, small meat skewers, served with a hot Asian sauce and sweet potatoes or fried bananas, may be available in an Indonesian restaurant. Traditionally though, the Dutch love their fish from the North Sea, most of all herring, which is eaten slightly salted and almost raw as a snack, sold everywhere in the streets, or served as part of an elaborate fish meal. *Hutspot* is a stew made with mashed potatoes and vegetables, a dish which is known as *hochepot* by the Flemish neighbors in Belgium. *Erwtensoep* is a pea soup, traditionally cooked with different cuts of pork, including sausages and pickled pork knuckles.

The Dutch usually eat a light breakfast with bread and sweet spreads, such as *hagelslag* or chocolate streusel, washed down with a *kopje koffie*—a coup of coffee, which may be offered at any time of the day, even though the Dutch are also fond of black tea. The main meal of the day, *avondeten*, traditionally takes place in the evening and may be completed with a dessert, *toetje*. Pancakes are popular and may be turned into a cake, called *flensjes*, when up to seven pancakes are piled up with a layer of apple sauce or jam in between the individual pancakes. *Olie bollen*, a kind of doughnut with raisins and currants, are served on New Year's Eve. Heineken is the biggest brewing company in the Netherlands, and with a production of about 121.8 million hectoliters of beer per year, it ranks fourth in the world. Heineken was founded in 1863, even though the actual brewery is about 300 years older.[40] The Grolsche Bierbrowerij in Enschede was founded in 1615 and produces about 3.2 million hectoliters of beer annually.[41] Although its name comes from the same source as *gin* in English, *jenever* is a stronger, clear liquor, which the Dutch enjoy as an aperitif.

POLAND

Poland is a very traditional country, rooted to the soil, and 50 percent of its farming is still done by small family-owned businesses, even though they are not as self-sufficient as they used to be.

Soil is fertile in Poland, and 29.8 percent of the labor force were employed by the agricultural sector in 2002; less than twice as many people work for the industry. Food and live animals totaled 8 percent of all Polish exports in 2004,[42] including the famous Christmas geese. In 2004, Polish farmers produced almost 14 million tons of potatoes, but also 927,900 tons of carrots, 250,200 tons of cherries, and other fruits and vegetables.[43] Honey is produced in large quantities by beekeepers and exported especially to the countries of the European Union, which Poland joined in 2004.

The consumption of hard liquor has decreased over the past decades, even though vodka is still very popular. Popular brands are Sobieski or Wyborowa, but the most spectacular kind is Wódka Żubrówka, which is produced exclusively in Poland. Each bottle of this vodka contains a blade of grass, which gives the liquor its typical aroma. Poland is also a country of beer lovers; Żywiec, Okocim, and Tyskie are some popular brands. Tea is more common than coffee, which is quite often prepared in the Turkish style: with coffee grounds and lots of sugar.

There are more than seventy kinds of smoked pork sausages or *kiełbasa*, which are not only known in their home country. *Bigos*, another famous Polish dish, has been around for centuries and was very famous with the old aristocracy. Its main ingredients are meat and white cabbage. Nowadays, *bigos* is a typical dish for a festive New Year's Eve party. Polish culture is rich in splendid church ceremonies, and each religious holiday traditionally requires a special meal. As a devout Catholic nation, Poland keeps Christmas Eve as a day of abstinence—that is, there is no meat served, but hosts and guests still enjoy an extensive meal that quite often consists of twelve courses, as a reminder of Jesus' twelve Apostles. It is also tradition to leave one chair empty, in case an additional guest arrives unexpectedly.

ROMANIA AND MOLDOVA

In spite of severe economic problems caused by Communist mismanagement, both Romania and Moldova, Europe's poorest country, are blessed with very fertile regions, suitable for growing a variety of crops. Because industry is still underdeveloped, 51 percent of the labor force were employed by the agricultural sector in Moldova in 2001, and many of its citizens find work abroad. Foods, including wine, totaled 15 percent of Moldovan exports in 2003, and 33 percent of all exported goods went to Russia.[44] When the Russian government announced a ban on all Moldovan wine imports on March 27, 2006, Moldova's economy was hit by yet another crisis.[45]

In Romania, 36.4 percent of the labor force were employed by the agricultural sector in 2002.[46] Most of the farms are still relatively small and produce such crops as maize (14.5 million tons in 2004), cabbage (919,100 tons), and sunflower seeds.[47] One of the few pleasures ordinary people had under the very rigid Communist regime was keeping up the old tradition of food preparation. The Turks, especially, left an important culinary heritage, which can be regarded as one of the fundamental elements of modern Romanian cuisine.

Mamaliga, made from ground corn and similar to Italian *polenta*, is typically served with *pastrama*, meat that is salted, smoked, and then simply grilled. Both words are of Turkish origin, as is *ghiveci* (from *güveç*, an earthen pot used to prepare it), a stewlike dish with meat and a variety of vegetables, including hot peppers and even grapes. *Ghiveci* has the reputation of being Romania's national dish and expresses as such a proud Christian opposition to 500 years of Muslim food rules, because bacon is needed for its preparation, as well as wine. Romania's mild climate along the Danube river is responsible for excellent wines, which are served even before fermentation has been completed in small garden restaurants, called *mustarii*. *Mititei*, small sausages made from ground beef and lots of garlic, grilled on an open fire, are traditionally eaten with this kind of wine and are so popular that they are even served in first-class restaurants in the capital.

RUSSIA, UKRAINE, AND BELARUS

People in the vast areas that once constituted the Soviet Union, including present-day Russia, Ukraine, and Belarus, have created food traditions that go back at least to the ninth century. Over the centuries, a cultural identity has been shaped by various ethnic groups, each of whom contributed some foods to the national table. Threatened by Communist uniformity, these old food traditions have been revived since the 1980s. Before 1990, restaurants were far less common in the Soviet Union than in the West, and visits there were reserved for special occasions. Nowadays, eating out has become more popular, especially in the bigger cities, where fast food can also be found, either in sit-down places or at street kiosks. The Russian fast-food company Russkoe Bistro is a fierce competitor for American burger chains.

Russia, Ukraine, and Belarus are among the world's largest producers of grain and potatoes. In 2004, Russia alone produced 45.4 million tons of wheat, 36 million tons of potatoes, and 21.9 million tons of sugar beets.[48] In 2004, foods and agricultural products made up 18 percent of all Russian imports, whereas food exports are generally low. 13.4 percent of the Russian labor force were employed by the agricultural sector in 2002, 19.8 percent in Ukraine and 11.3 percent in Belarus.[49] Festive meals usually start with cold appetizers, such as pickled herring or caviar, which is made from fish roe. *Borshch*, a native of Ukraine, is one of the world's great soups. For the main course, meat dishes may be served, for example *pel'meni* (Siberian dumplings) or *plov* (rice pilaf), and, of course, potatoes and vegetables. Tea, quite often prepared in a samovar, follows the meal together with an assortment of desserts.

One Russian product known and sold all over the world is vodka. Up to the 1970s, the Soviet Union claimed the rights to market liquors named *vodka*, and even though the legal situation has changed today, vodka is still produced in Russia, Ukraine, and Belarus; Stolichnaya being one of the most prestigious brands. Sparkling wine produced on the Crimean peninsula in Ukraine has also been a popular alcoholic beverage for export since the late nineteenth century.

SCANDINAVIA: DENMARK, FINLAND, ICELAND, NORWAY, SWEDEN

Together with Russia, the four Scandinavian countries and Iceland are Europe's northernmost outpost, with parts of Finland, Norway, and Sweden being north of the Arctic Circle. Farming, therefore, is possible only in the southern parts of these countries. Fishing, hunting, and forestry are conducted in the north, and the native people, the Sami, keep reindeer. Iceland is situated just south of the Arctic Circle in the North Atlantic Ocean, but its interior is mountainous and covered with lava terrain, and the cold northern climate allows agriculture only in the coastal area. The Scandinavian states are among those with the highest living standards in the world, famous for their social system. In Denmark, Sweden, and Norway, less than 4 percent of the labor force were employed by the agricultural sector in 2002,[50] in Finland 5.4 percent,[51] and in Iceland 7.3 percent (but this number refers mainly to fishery). Sixty percent of all Icelandic exports are fish products.[52] In 2004, Swedish farmers produced 1.7 million tons of barley, 925,000 tons of oats, and about 2.4 million tons of wheat.[53] Danish farmers managed to double that amount and also harvested about 3.6 million tons of barley,[54] a large quantity of which is used for the brewing industry. All together, agricultural products amounted to 23.3 percent of all Danish exports in 2003,[55] including their famous cheeses.

Costs of living are high in Scandinavia, and alcohol, especially, is heavily taxed and usually sold only in stores with a special liquor license. Only beverages with very low alcohol content may be sold in regular supermarkets, where most consumers shop nowadays. Because of the relatively short growing season in most areas of Scandinavia, fresh food was traditionally available only during the summer, when meat was dried, smoked, or salted to preserve it for the long winter months. Some vegetables, such as potatoes and turnips, could be stored for longer periods; others were pickled; and fruits were canned or dried as well. Since restaurants are expensive, international and local fast-food chains are popular with many Scandinavians, who traditionally also enjoy buffet-style eating. The Swedish *smörgåsbord* is known all over the world. *Smörgås*, or *smørrebrød* in Danish, are slices of bread with fish, meat, or eggs, but the buffet usually also offers all kinds of salads and other meat and fish dishes. In previous centuries in the very north, regular bread was served only for special occasions, because the grains grown there, mostly barley and oats, are not very suitable for yeast breads. Scandinavia is famous nowadays for its crisp bread, called *knäckebröd* in Swedish and *näkkileipä* in Finnish. The company Wasabröd is the world's largest producer of this type of crisp bread, and even though the company has been owned by the Italian food producer Barilla since 1999, it was founded by the Swede K. E. Lundström in 1919 and still has its headquarters in the Swedish city of Filipstad.

All Scandinavian countries heavily depend on fish for their meals; herring and stockfish are especially popular. *Lutfisk* (in Swedish) or *lutefisk* (in Norwegian) is stockfish first soaked in lye, then in water, and eventually cooked and served with a white sauce, a dish that is part of a traditional Christmas dinner. Herring is prepared in all shapes and forms and may be served at any time of the day. *Surströmming* is a traditional Swedish way of preparing herring, which is first fermented in barrels, after having been slightly salted, and then finishes the fermentation in cans. When the cans start to "move" about six months later, the cans may be opened and the fish eaten. A less smelly dish is smoked salmon, a fish that is still abundant in the many Scandinavian rivers. Meatballs, called *köttbullar* in Swedish and *kjottkaker* in Norwegian, are another popular dish. *Gammel danske kaus* is made from corned beef, herring, potatoes, onions, and red beets; it is traditional in Denmark, but certainly not to everybody's liking. The same is true for *súrsaðir hrútspungar* in Iceland, ram testicles marinated in sour milk. Because sheep are the main farm animals in Iceland, their meat, including unusual cuts and pieces, have been used for Icelandic dishes for centuries. People in Iceland traditionally also ate whale and seal meat. Coffee is a popular beverage in Scandinavia; the Finns and Swedes especially love it. With an average of nine (in Finland) or four (in Sweden) cups a day per person, they head the world list of coffee consumers per capita. Coffee and a special bread with currants as a symbol against hunger and thirst is also presented by the blonde Luzia (St. Lucy), when she arrives with her crown of candles on December 13 every year to bring light into the dark northern nights. Vodka is distilled especially in Finland, and *aquavit*, a clear liquor with anise extracts, is another typical spirit in Europe's north.

SWITZERLAND

Switzerland is a small, wealthy country, situated completely within the Alps with high mountains and superb skiing areas but with little room for farmland, which was cultivated by about 4 percent of the labor force in 2004.[56] In 2002, Swiss farmers produced about 1.4 million tons of sugar beets, 526,700 tons of potatoes, and about 3.9 million tons of milk.[57] Even though Swiss agriculture is very effective and highly modernized, many cattle herds still roam the Alpine pastures high above the villages in summer, a technique that has been practiced for centuries. The Swiss food industry is very successful, especially Nestlé, which is one of the biggest companies in its line in the world. Swizerland's high living standard accounts for high food prices, and eating out in one of the numerous excellent restaurants can become a costly event, especially for tourists.

Because of Switzerland's unique political history, many international organizations have their headquarters or at least major branches there, resulting in the presence of international hotels and cooking schools in such cities as Zurich, Lausanne, Montreux, and Geneva. Also because of its diverse ethnic background, Swiss cuisine contains many regional elements, even though centuries of statehood have created nationwide traditions and dishes. *Birchermüesli*, for example, is one of the first cereals created on European ground. It is traditionally made with oat flakes, milk or yogurt, and different kinds of shredded fruits. Another dish that enjoys international popularity is hash browns, called *Rösti* in Switzerland, where the actual potato pieces are a little bigger than in American fast-food restaurants. *Rösti* may be served to accompany *Zürcher Geschnetzeltes*, thinly sliced veal and mushrooms simmered in a white wine and cream sauce.

The Alpine pastures with all their wild herbs provide ingredients for medicines and cosmetics, but they also make excellent food for cows, whose milk is then used to produce Switzerland's world famous chocolates and cheeses with their typical holes. Emmentaler and Appenzeller are the best-known ones, and Sbrinz is the hardest type, which is grated to flavor soups and pasta dishes. Greyerzer is also available around the world under its French name, Gruyère. All these cheeses are traditionally produced in the shape of a wheel and are exported worldwide. A typically Swiss way of enjoying cheese is by having a *fondue du fromage*, which has been prepared in the French-speaking parts of Switzerland and in Savoy for centuries. *Fondue du fromage* uses a special pot, called a *caquelon*, which is heated over a small flame, called the *rechaud*. Cheese such as Greyerzer is then melted in the pot and mixed with wine, spices, garlic, and some *kirsch*, one of the many kinds of fruit liqueur popular all over the Alpine region. Pieces of bread are then dipped into the cheese mixture with especially long forks. *Fondue* and *raclette* are most fun when they are enjoyed with a group of people, preferably in winter. To prepare *raclette*, a large piece of cheese, such as Ganser or Bagne, was traditionally placed next to a fire. After it had melted, the cheese was transferred to a plate and then eaten with potatoes and pickled vegetables. *Basler Leckerli* is a kind of gingerbread produced in the city of Basel, and a variety of fruitcakes and tarts are popular all over Switzerland. Especially in the southwestern parts of the country, wine has been cultivated since Roman days, but it is rarely ever exported.

TURKEY AND CYPRUS

Only the small westernmost part of Turkey, Thrace, officially belongs to Europe, separated from the rest of the country and the vast Asian continent by the Bosporus strait at the entrance to the Black Sea. Its ancient metropolis, Istanbul, although no longer Turkey's capital, is a bustling city, a mixture of old and new, Orient and Occident. Modern supermarkets are side by side with Oriental bazaars, and among the Western restaurants and fast-food places there are traditional coffee houses, where only men gather to play board games and to sip mocha, strong Turkish coffee, or sweet tea. Tea, served in small glasses at any time of the day, is also a sign of hospitality. Turkey is not yet as industrialized as its neighbors in the West, and 33.2 percent of the labor force were still employed by the agricultural sector in 2002.[58] Turkish farmers produced 21 million tons of wheat in 2004, 1.6 million tons of hazelnuts, and about 202,000 tons of tea.[59] The climate in some areas also allows growing fruits and vegetables, which amounted to 5 percent of all Turkish exports in 2004.[60] The island of Cyprus in the eastern Mediterranean Sea also profits from its southern location and produces tons of fruits every year, including about 25,000 tons of lemons and limes in 2004 and even about 10,500 tons of bananas.[61] The fishing fleet provides the country, which is divided into a Turkish and a Greek part, with plenty of fish and other seafood. Agriculture offered jobs for 8 percent of the Greek and Turkish Cypriot labor force in 2001.[62]

Since Turkey is predominantly an Islamic country, the Koran has determined food traditions for centuries. There are certain foods that are *haram* and may not be eaten, whereas others are *halal* and safe to eat for all religious believers. *Haram* refers in particular to meat and excludes meat from carnivorous animals, including pigs, but there are also regulations on how to butcher acceptable animals. In general, it is traditional for a Turkish family to sit down at the table and to eat together, especially for the main meal in the evening, a custom not always observed any more in the West. A Turkish breakfast usually means wheat bread, cheese from sheep's milk, olives, and tea. Farmers in remote rural areas may still start their day with a bowl of hearty soup. Traditionally, there is only a light lunch, such as sandwiches made with *pide*, a thin flat bread. *Lahmacun* is similar to pizza, usually prepared with ground meat and spices such as cumin and sumac.

Dinner is the time to eat properly and to discuss the events of the day. A festive meal begins with *meze*, a selection of appetizers, and *rakı*, a clear liquor, flavored with anise. *Rakı* has been around since the fifteenth century and is usually mixed with water, which gives it a milky appearance. For *meze*, there may be just simply slices of tomatoes, cucumbers, and sausage, but rather elaborate sauces and salads may be served as well. Hummus is a mush made from chickpeas, tahini is a sesame paste, and baba ghanoush is a similar dish, one of over forty eggplant creations. *Cacık* is made from yogurt with cucumbers and garlic. As in Greece, grape leaves stuffed with rice or ground meat, called *dolma*, are popular as appetizers as well. As main course, lamb and mutton are traditionally the most common meat types, but beef is becoming more and more available as well. Ground lamb or beef, shaped into balls, well seasoned, and then grilled, is called *köfte*. For *türlü*, ground meat, onions, potatoes, string beans, zucchini, eggplants, and tomatoes are layered in a pot and cooked slowly. The internationally most known Turkish dish, however, is kebab *(kebap)*, which has become one of Europe's favorite fast foods over the past decades. Traditionally, *kebap* refers to ground meat, usually lamb, grilled on charcoals. For *döner kebap*, thinly sliced lamb and ground lamb are pressed on a spit, which is positioned vertically on a grill. While the spit is slowly turning around, the cooked outer layer of meat is cut off and served with a yogurt sauce, tomatoes, and peppers on flat bread. To accompany meat dishes, rice may be served or bulgur, a parboiled wheat product similar to North African couscous. For the poorer rural population, bulgur still remains the main food of the day. Although originally from India and Persia, *halvah*, made from sugar, honey, sesame seeds and oil, is a popular dessert, as well as *baklava* and *kadayıf*, puff pastries with nuts, drenched in syrup.

UNITED KINGDOM AND IRELAND

Despite certain reservations from some continental gourmands, the United Kingdom and Ireland have long gastronomic traditions and are famous for their pubs, cozy country inns, and large breakfasts with potatoes, eggs, bacon, sausages, toast, and jam. Because of the Gulf Stream, the weather is rather settled with mild winters and not very hot summers, even though the Irish west coast and the Scottish Highlands especially have rougher weather conditions. The main crops are wheat, 15.5 million tons of which were produced in the United Kingdom in 2004; sugar beets, with about 8.8 million tons; and potatoes, with about 6.4 million tons.[63] Britain was one of the first countries to embrace industrialization in the nineteenth century, and only 1.4 percent of the British labor force were employed by the agricultural sector in 2003, whereas in Ireland 6.4 percent were. As in many other areas of Europe, the conditions for smaller farms are getting more and more difficult, forcing a large number of farmers to give up their trade. Still, food products amounted to 3 percent of all British exports in 2004.[64] Fish is also an important economic factor for the two island states, and fish and chips, quite often flavored with vinegar, is probably the most famous traditional fast food in the United Kingdom. Britain's long history as a colonial power is also the reason for all kinds of exotic influences on local British cooking; Indian cuisine with spices such as curry and *garam masala* is especially popular today.

One of the most traditional British dishes is roast beef and Yorkshire pudding, which is made from flour, eggs, milk, and fat. Black pudding has blood as one of its main ingredients, which also gives it its dark color. There is a large variety of pies, pork pie being the most famous one. Most pies are filled with different kinds of ground meat or vegetables, or fruit if they are served as dessert. Bubble and squeak is a mixture of fried cabbage and mashed potatoes. Scotland is famous for its Angus cattle and lean beef, but traditional Scottish consumers are also proud of haggis, a kind of meat loaf made with sheep innards. Beef or mutton, carrots, potatoes, and onions are the main ingredients of Irish stew, which is probably more popular abroad nowadays than in its home country, Ireland. Kippers (smoked fish) are another traditional snack, and since the eighteenth century there have been sandwiches, named for the fourth Earl of Sandwich, who, according to legend, had his cook prepare slices of bread with meet and vegetables, which he and his guests could eat without having to leave their game of cards to sit down at the dinner table. The sandwich has come a long way since then, but layers of thinly sliced wheat bread cut in triangles with equally thin slices of cucumber in between are occasionally still served in British families.

With the conquest of India, tea rooms started to push coffee houses, which had been very successful in the eighteenth century, out of business, and ever since, tea has been taken seriously in the United Kingdom. Nevertheless, modern coffee bars offering espresso and *caffe latte* are on the rise again. The traditional afternoon tea may be served with shortcakes, fruit pies, trifles, crumpets drenched in butter, or sweet buns with clotted cream. After a long day at work, many people on the British Isles like to stop at their local pub for a pint of ale, which is brewed with top-fermenting yeasts and usually has a sweeter taste than lager beers. Most beer drinkers still prefer their beer less cold than American consumers do, as does the traditional Scottish whisky connoisseur, who likes his whisky pure and without ice. Scottish whisky and Irish whiskey have been distilled for centuries. Another famous liquor, with an alcohol content ranging from 37.5 to 47 percent, is gin, flavored with juniper berries and a variety of other herbs.

RESOURCE GUIDE

BOOKS

Anderson, Jean. *Food of Portugal*. New York: Hearst Books, 1994.

Bosrock, Mary Murray. *Put Your Best Foot Forward: Russia*. St. Paul, MN: International Education System, 1995.

Boxer, Lady Arabella. *Seven Centuries of English Cooking*. London: Weidenfeld & Nicholson, 1973.

Brook, Stephen. *The Wines of Germany*. London: Mitchell Beazly, 2003.

Casas, Penelope. *Tapas: The Little Dishes of Spain*. New York: Knopf, 1985.

Child, Julia and Alex Prud'homme. *My Life in France*. New York: Random House, 2006.

Dabars, Zita. *The Russian Way*. New York: McGraw-Hill, 2002.

Day-Lewis, Tamasin. *West of Ireland Summers, a Cookbook: Recipes and Memories From an Irish Childhood*. Boulder, CO: Roberts Rinehart Publishers, 1998.

Der Fischer Weltalmanach. Frankfurt am Main: Fischer, 2006.

Forristal, Linda J. *Mother Linda's Bulgarian Rhapsody: The Best of Balkan Cuisine*. Blandensburg, MD: Sunrise Pine Press, 1998.

Garten, Ina. *Barefoot in Paris: Easy French Food You Can Make at Home*. New York: Clarkson Potter Publishers, 2004.

Gergely, Aniko. *Culinaria Hungary*. Cologne: Konemann, 1999.

Goldstein, Darya. *A Taste of Russia*. Montpelier: Russian Life Books, 1999.

Gould-Marks, Beryl. *Eating The Russian Way*. New York: Gramercy, 1963.

Helou, Anissa. *Mediterranean Street Food*. New York: Harper Collins, 2002.

Jackson, Michael. *Scotland and Its Whiskies*. New York: Harcourt, 2001.

Klein, Donna. *The Mediterranean Vegan Kitchen*. New York: HP Books, 2001.

Kremezi, Aglaia. *The Foods of Greece*. New York: Workman Publishers, 1993.

Maher, Joanne, ed. *The Europa World Year Book*. 2 vols. London: Routledge, 2006.

Mayes, Frances. *Under the Tuscan Sun: At Home in Italy*. San Francisco: Chronicle Books, 1996.

Mayson, Richard. *The Wines and Vineyards of Portugal*. London: Mitchell Beazly, 2003.

Oliver, Jamie. *The Naked Chef*. New York: Hyperion, 2000.

Roalson, Louise, et al. *Norwegian Touches: History, Recipes, Folk Arts*. Iowa City, IA: Penfield Books, 2003.

Schwind, Martin, ed. *Die Staaten und Länder der Erde*. Hanover: Schroedel Verlag, 1959.

Strybel, Robert. *Polish Holiday Cookery*. London: Reaktion, 2004.

Trnka, Peter. *The Best of Czech Cooking*. New York: Hippocrene Books, 2001.

MAGAZINES

Alt om Mad. Copenhagen: Bonniers Specialmagasiner A/S.

BBC Good Food. London: BBC Worldwide Ltd.

Comer y Beber. Barcelona: Hymsa Grupo Editorial Edipresse.
La Cucina Italiana. Milan: Editrice Quadratum SpA.
Cuisine et Vins de France. Issy les Moulineax: Marie Claire Album.
Cuisine Gourmande. Paris: Prisma Presse.
Essen und Trinken. Hamburg: Gruner & Jahr.
Food and Travel. Sudbury Hill: Fox Publishing Ltd.
Gestgjafinn. Reykjavik: Frodi Ltd.
Koch und Backjournal. Vienna: Publicity Werbegesellschaft.
Kuchnia. Warsaw: Prózyski i S-ka.
Saisonküche. Spreitenbach: Limmatdruck AG.
The Vegan. St. Leonards-on-Sea: The Vegan Society.
Tip Culinair. Haarlem: Uitgeverij Spaarnestad, bv.

WEBSITES

BBC Food. Regularly updated information on food and new recipes. Accessed August 7, 2006. http://www.bbc.co.uk/food.

British Nutrition Foundation. Promotes the well being of society through nutrional knowledge. Accessed August 7, 2006. http://www.uk250.co.uk/frame/11003/british-nutrition-foundation.html.

La Cocinca Espanola. Regularly updated information on Spanish food and recipes. Accessed August 7, 2006. http://www.perso.wanadoo.es/recetasdecocina.

Cook Italian Today. Regularly updated information on Italian food and recipes. Accessed August 7, 2006. http://www.italy1.com/cuisine/english.

France Escapade. Regularly updated information on tourism and gastronomy in France. Accessed August 7, 2006. http://www.france-escapade.com/recettes/cuisine/recherche_cuisin_fr.php.

The International Restaurant Guide and Directory. Regularly updated information on European restaurants. Accessed August 7, 2006. http://www.restaurant-e-guide.com.

Michelin Guide. Regularly updated information on European restaurants. 7 August 2006. http://www.viamichelin.com/viamichelin/gbr/dyn/controller/Restaurants.

VIDEOS/FILMS

Babettes Gaestebud [Babette's Feast] (Denmark, 1986/7). Directed by Gabriel Axel, starring Stéphane Audran. Features elegant French cuisine.

Bella Martha (Germany, 2001). Directed by Sandra Nettelbeck, starring Martina Gedeck. A perfectionist's view on modern cooking.

Big Night (United States, 1996). Directed by Campbell Scott, starring Tony Shalhoub. A portrait a life and food in an Italian restaurant.

Chocolat (UK/United States, 2000.). Directed by Lasse Hallström, starring Juliette Binoche. Features delicious chocolate creations.

Cuisine Americaine (France/United States, 1998). Directed by Jean-Yves Pitoun, starring Jason Lee. Features the recipes of a French chef.

Dinner Rush (United States, 2000). Directed by Bob Giraldi, starring Danny Aiello. Portrays dinner at an Italian restaurant.

Die Gewürzstraße (Germany, 1999). Directed by John Lawton. A documentary that deals with the historic importance of spices.

La grande bouffe (France/Italy, 1973). Directed by Marco Ferreri, starring Marcello Mastroianni. Food is portrayed here as hedonistic excess.

My Big Fat Greek Wedding (United States/Canada, 2002). Directed by Joel Zwick. Features a variety of traditional Greek dishes.

The Naked Chef (UK, 1999). Directed by Patricia Llewellyn. A TV series giving Chef Jamie Oliver's view on the bare essentials of cooking.

Vatel (France, 2000). Directed by Roland Joffé, starring Gérard Depardieu. A portrait of three festive days at the court of Louis XVI.

ORGANIZATIONS AND MUSEUMS

Deutsches Kochbuchmuseum, Dortmund, Germany, Tel. +49 (231) 5025741. http://www.kochbuchmuseum. dortmund.de. Display of old cook books, tools, and historic kitchens.

European Aquaculture Society, http://www.easonline.org/home/en/default.asp. Promotes the interests of the European fishing business.

International Dairy Federation. http://www.fil-idf.org. Promotes the interests of the European dairy business.

International Hotel and Restaurant Association. http://www.ih-ra.com. Represents the European hotel and restaurant business.

Hotelli- ja Ravintolamuseo. Helsinki, Finland. Tel. +358 (9) 68593700. http://www.hotellijaravintola museo.fi/menus.htm. Explains the Finnish hotel and restaurant history.

The Irish Whiskey Corner Museum. Dublin, Ireland. Tel. +353 (1) 8725566. http://www. irish-whiskey-trail.com. Exhibits on the history and manufacture of Irish whiskey.

Musée de la Geuze, Brussels, Belgium, Tel. +32 (2) 5202891. http://www.brussels.org/mus.htm. Display on the history of beer brewing.

Musée de la Vigne et du Vin. Saint Lambert de Lattay, France. Tel. +33 241784275. http://www.mvvanjou.com. Displays a collection of machinery used by wine growers.

Museo del Cioccolato, Caslano, Switzerland, Tel. +41 (91) 6118888. http://www.alprose.ch. Exhibits on chocolate and its production.

Museo dell'Olivo, Imperia, Italy, Tel. +39 (183) 295762, http://www.museodellolivo.com/eng/vieni.htm. Explains the history of the olive industry.

Radbrook Culinary Museum, Shrewsbury, United Kingdom, Tel. +44 (1743) 232686. http://www.musee-online.org. Exhibits on food, nutrition, housecraft, and education.

NOTES

I would like to thank Astrid Bohner and Tatiana Zilotina for their helpful input.

1. Schwind 1959 (in Resource Guide), p. 568.
2. *Der Fischer Weltalmanach* (in Resource Guide), p. 344.
3. Ibid., p. 53.
4. Maher (in Resource Guide), Vol. I, p. 480.
5. *Der Fischer Weltalmanach* (in Resource Guide), pp. 299, 291, 173.
6. Ibid., p. 77.
7. Ibid., p. 301.
8. Maher (in Resource Guide), Vol. I, p. 779.
9. *InBev*. Accessed November 9, 2006. http://www.inbev.com.
10. *Der Fischer Weltalmanach* (in Resource Guide), p. 94.
11. Maher (in Resource Guide), Vol. I, p. 951.
12. *Der Fischer Weltalmanach* (in Resource Guide), pp. 421, 455.
13. Maher (in Resource Guide), Vol. I, p. 1458.
14. Ibid., Vol. II, p. 3903.
15. *Der Fischer Weltalmanach* (in Resource Guide), p. 642.
16. *Czechvar*. Accessed November 9, 2006. http://www.beersince1933.com/czechvar.htm.
17. *Der Fischer Weltalmanach* (in Resource Guide), p. 178.
18. Ibid., p. 625.
19. Ibid., pp. 642–643.
20. Ibid., p. 117.

21. Maher (in Resource Guide), Vol. I, p. 1898.
22. *Der Fischer Weltalmanach* (in Resource Guide), p. 193.
23. Maher (in Resource Guide), Vol. I, p. 1962.
24. Ibid., Vol. I, p. 2093.
25. *Der Fischer Weltalmanach* (in Resource Guide), p. 469.
26. Ibid., p. 625.
27. Maher (in Resource Guide), Vol. II, p. 4013.
28. *Der Fischer Weltalmanach* (in Resource Guide), p. 426.
29. Maher (in Resource Guide), Vol. II, p. 4013.
30. *Der Fischer Weltalmanach* (in Resource Guide), p. 426.
31. Ibid., p. 370.
32. Ibid., p. 625.
33. Ibid.
34. Ibid., p. 245.
35. Maher (in Resource Guide), Vol. I, p. 2360.
36. *Der Fischer Weltalmanach* (in Resource Guide), p. 334.
37. Maher (in Resource Guide), Vol. II, p. 3178.
38. *Der Fischer Weltalmanach* (in Resource Guide), p. 334.
39. Ibid., p. 623.
40. Heineken International. *Welcome.* http://www.heinekeninternational.com.
41. Grolsch Lager & Beer. http://www.grolsch.co.uk.
42. *Der Fischer Weltalmanach* (in Resource Guide), p. 367.
43. Maher (in Resource Guide), Vol. II, p. 3568.
44. *Der Fischer Weltalmanach* (in Resource Guide), p. 320.
45. Maher (in Resource Guide), Vol. II, p. 3012.
46. *Der Fischer Weltalmanach* (in Resource Guide), p. 374.
47. Maher (in Resource Guide), Vol. II, p. 3632.
48. Ibid., p. 3668.
49. *Der Fischer Weltalmanach* (in Resource Guide), pp. 376, 466, 493.
50. Ibid., pp. 114, 394, 341.
51. Ibid., p. 176.
52. Ibid., pp. 235–236.
53. Maher (in Resource Guide), Vol. II, p. 4140.
54. Ibid., Vol. I, p. 1476.
55. Ibid., p. 1474.
56. *Der Fischer Weltalmanach* (in Resource Guide), p. 396.
57. Maher (in Resource Guide), Vol. II, p. 4166.
58. *Der Fischer Weltalmanach* (in Resource Guide), p. 459.
59. Maher (in Resource Guide), Vol. II, p. 4378.
60. *Der Fischer Weltalmanach* (in Resource Guide), p. 459.
61. Maher (in Resource Guide), Vol. I, p. 1434.
62. *Der Fischer Weltalmanach* (in Resource Guide), p. 495.
63. Maher (in Resource Guide), Vol. II, p. 4512.
64. *Der Fischer Weltalmanach* (in Resource Guide), pp. 195, 234.

GAMES, TOYS, AND PASTIMES

MAJA MIKULA

Games, hobbies, and toys encompass a diverse range of practices and objects of material culture that often have very little in common, other than their association with recreation, leisure, and play. Play is a vital aspect of human culture, and games, hobbies, and toys make it happen. It is no wonder then that this area of human activity can reveal a great deal about the social and cultural context in which it occurs. It always involves rituals that can be read at a "deep" level to throw light on the values and myths prevalent in the society in which it unfolds.

Games can be categorized in many different ways. French anthropologist Roger Caillois divided them into four main categories: competition, chance, simulation, and disorientation. Competitive games involve training, skill, and discipline; games of chance largely depend on probability; simulation games require that the players escape from reality and become fantasy characters; and, finally, games of disorientation are based on a physical feeling of dizziness. If there is money or material gain involved, we are talking about gambling, which can contain traces of all four of these categories.[1] Hobbies, like games, are voluntary, uncertain, isolated in space and time, and bound by rules. Unlike games, however, hobbies such as handicrafts and collecting can be—and usually are—materially productive.

In *Centuries of Childhood*, French sociologist and historian Philippe Ariès argued that childhood, as we know it today, did not exist before the Victorian era. Children—especially those of the poorer classes—were not given toys or encouraged to play. Preserved texts and artifacts suggest, however, that toys and games have a long tradition in European societies, although they may not have always been considered the children's domain. Many European playthings were originally associated with fairs and festivals and were used by children and adults alike. The longer average life span and the generally higher standard of living associated with modernity have meant that people now assume adult responsibilities at an older age and devote more time and energy to recreational activities. Games and hobbies are widely practiced, in different ways, by both children and adults regardless of gender, class, affluence, or cultural belonging. Also, an object can be used as a toy in some societies or in certain historical periods while performing a more practical function in others. An example of this is the eighteenth-century fashion doll, which originally had the function of advertising women's clothing.

TOYS IN THE MEDIEVAL ERA

Our knowledge about play in the Middle Ages and the Renaissance is based on portraits and manuscript illustrations, the texts of laws, statutes, wills, and letters, and the actual playthings surviving from that period. Many medieval toys served both as playthings and as talismans protecting their owners from evil spirits. Rattles were made of horn, shell, dried gourds, and precious metals. War toys, such as swords, shields, hobbyhorses, and miniature soldiers, prepared young boys from aristocratic families for the exigencies of a military career. Dolls performed a similar function for medieval girls, training them for the role of wife and mother. Rag dolls (Latin *simulacra de pannis*) are mentioned in medieval manuscripts. Wooden dolls were manufactured in Germany and Holland (Middle German *Tocke* a "little block of wood"). There are records of professional dollmakers (Middle German *Tockenmacher*) in the Nuremberg area in Germany dating from the fifteenth century. In a category of their own, edible gingerbread dolls, sometimes with an inside compartment containing a small gift, were sold at German fairs. Other materials used to make toys were clay, wax, and *papier mâché* or composition, which is a mixture of wood pulp, paste, gum, and sand, or sawdust. Balls were popular in many European societies and were usually made either of animal skins or of the inflated bladders of sheep and goats. Spinning tops, drums, whistles, marbles, kites, and windmills are also mentioned or depicted in medieval manuscripts.

Ancient vases, reliefs, and coins show that the Greeks and the Romans had many different kinds of toys, such as dolls, miniature soldiers, balls, hoops, carts, and rattles. Dolls were usually made of wood, cloth, or painted clay, and were sometimes jointed, with the limbs separately attached to the torso by cord. Miniature replicas of soldiers, weapons, and war vessels were made of metal or clay. Although miniature furniture and other household items dating from the Roman period have been preserved, it is not certain whether these objects were used for play purposes.

Mechanical toys were powered by water and steam. Greek balls were made of wool, stuffed into a cover made of animal skin. Clay rattles often took animal forms and were used both in play and in the religious rituals related to the cult of Dionysus. Games of chance, such as dice and knucklebones, were widespread among adults, especially the upper classes. In Greek mythology the future of the human race was sometimes decided in a game of dice. Loaded dice used by professional gamblers in ancient Rome are preserved in a number of European museums.

Distinctive customs and artifacts developed in conjunction with religious and semi-religious festivals. Life-sized nativity scenes, which were on display at Christmastime in churches and city squares, gradually found their way into people's homes. Today the toy industry receives a regular yearly boost during the Christmas season, and Christmas paraphernalia is an industry of its own.

In the sixteenth century, specialized centers manufacturing wooden animals and dolls emerged in the German towns of Seiffen, Berchtesgaden, and Sonneberg, as well as in Oberammergau. Nuremberg was known for tin soldiers and the "Nuremberg kitchen," a forerunner of the dollhouse. The first elaborately furnished Dutch and German dollhouses, or "cabinets," also date from the sixteenth century.

The pastimes of sixteenth-century Flemish youngsters are richly documented in paintings by Martin Van Cleef (1507–37) and, most notably, Pieter Brueghel the Elder (1525–69), which show children playing with hoops, tops, stilts, kites, dolls, and musical instruments, and engaging in games such as leapfrog, tag, and blindman's buff.

Around the same time, an organized toy trade began to flourish in principal European cities. At first, peddlers carried mostly German and Dutch toys as part of larger shipments of other goods and sold them either at fairs or door to door. Later Nuremberg merchants gained control over the budding toy trade and encouraged artisans to standardize their products and to specialize in particular designs. "Flanders babies"—simple wooden dolls manufactured in the Low Countries, which were very popular in England at the time—are an example of toy mobility in that period. Noah's Arks can be traced back to the village of Oberammergau in the Bavarian Alps, known for producing intricate religious scenes in carved wood. In the sixteenth and seventeenth centuries, the peep-box theater (*Guckkastenbild* in German), presented by traveling entertainers, was popular in France, Holland, Germany, and Italy. Italian philosopher, poet, painter, and architect Leon Battista Alberti (1404–72) is credited with the creation of the first peep-box theater for his study of perspective.

Puppet theaters thrived along Europe's trade routes, taking the legends and folklore of cultures across the continent. Performed by itinerant puppeteers, these shows crossed borders and affected, and were affected by, the local traditions they encountered on their way, enriching them with elements of puppet design, performing techniques, stories, and principal characters.

Subsequent to the industrialization of parts of Europe in the late eighteenth century and the emergence of a wealthy middle class, handcrafted playthings slowly began to give way to mass-produced toys. At the same time, wood was increasingly replaced by metal and paper as the principal materials in toy production, and mechanical and optical toys became more common. The French *pantin*, a cardboard Dancing Jack puppet with articulated arms and legs manipulated by strings, became a fashionable toy among adults, used to make fun of nobility. Other cultures have had paper cut-out art traditions, including the well-known Polish *wycinanki* and the German and Swiss *Scherenschnitte*. Other toys—dollhouses, furniture, ships—were also often made of paper. Dolls with porcelain or bisque (unglazed porcelain) heads became more common at the end of the nineteenth century. Inexpensive mass-produced tin soldiers made by Andreas Hilpert of Nuremberg were particularly popular in Germany.

The advent of industrialization went hand in hand with a widespread fascination with mechanical toys. Life-size dolls, animals, and landscape and seafaring scenes that could produce a range of sounds or perform complex and precise movements were taken on tours and exhibited at fairs or given as precious presents to foreign dignitaries. The walking doll, precursor of today's toy robots, was popular in France in the 1830s.

In other parts of Europe, not yet affected by industrialization, handcrafted folk toys made of materials that were most commonly at hand—such as wood, cloth, or animal bones and skins—continued to proliferate. Folk toys preserved in museums throughout the former Eastern Europe testify to the rich toy-making traditions in certain areas.

A negative turning point in the history of the European toy industry, which also had an enormous impact on the international market of toys and games, was World War I. The toy industry in war-torn Europe came to a halt, and the United States and Japan emerged as the new leaders on the global toy scene. The United States in particular set a new trend by introducing licensed figures of Disney cartoon characters that were not merely miniature copies of the adult universe, but truly belonged to a new international world of children's popular culture. Europe kept its traditional attitudes toward childhood and play and was slow to adopt the American-style integration of playthings with children's media industries. It was also resistant to television advertising to children, with some countries banning it altogether in defiance of the impending Americanization of children's culture. Even today countries of the European Union have different measures that ensure that children are not excessively exposed to advertising. Sweden, for example, prohibits advertising aimed at children below the age of twelve; Germany and Denmark proscribe advertising for specific types of toys, and Greece restricts children's advertising between 7:00 AM and 10:00 PM In the period between the two World Wars, the American toy industry began to dominate the world market, and the strongest European toy-making countries, such as Germany and Great Britain, were unable to reestablish their former primacy.

In the second half of the twentieth century, two main strands of toy making continued the European tradition with considerable success. On the one hand, toys representing the adult world, such as Hornby electric trains and Matchbox cars by Lesney, enjoyed popularity in the 1950s and 1960s. On the other hand, products such as LEGO construction toys from Denmark, Playmobil sets from Germany, and wooden blocks by the Swedish company Brio developed a reputation as quality playthings that encourage children's creativity. LEGO stands out among European manufacturers of toys and games as one of the first companies to develop a global marketing scheme that included theme parks, displays in shopping malls, and, more recently, toy "systems" based on characters and storylines from children's popular and media culture.

By the 1980s, the manufacture of toys and games in Europe had yielded to the pressure of a global play industry. Most toys on the European market are currently designed and marketed through American and Japanese companies and manufactured in China, Hong Kong, and other parts of Asia. China currently produces from 70 to 80 percent of the world's toys. Most of China's toys are produced in the southern province of Guangdong, which has more than 4,500 toy factories.[2]

The latest shift away from traditional toys and games toward electronic or video games began in the 1980s and is now taking hold even in the poorest European societies. Video gaming is popular not only among teenagers, but also among adults of all ages. In less affluent countries, where dedicated desktop and handheld consoles are still considered a luxury, personal computers are more commonly used as a gaming platform. Online gaming is also popular among gamers with high-speed Internet access.

Currently, the strongest national toys and games markets in Europe are the United Kingdom, Germany, and France. Each country specializes in a certain product line: the United Kingdom in metal and plastic miniatures, as well as table and board games; Germany in model trains and plastic and paper toys; and France in die-cast, mechanical, and stuffed toys, as well as board games.

NORDIC COUNTRIES: NORWAY, SWEDEN, FINLAND, ICELAND, AND DENMARK

All countries in the Nordic group are characterized by relatively small households and higher-than-average employment rates for both women and men. All of these countries also boast high spending power, a relatively strong state support for families, and generally high living standards. It is therefore not surprising that their share of expenditure on recreational pursuits is higher than in most other European countries.

In the forest-covered areas of northern Europe, wood-carved toys and games have a long tradition. One such area is the Dalarna province in central Sweden, which is known for high-quality handcrafted toys. The best known is the *dalahäst* (the dala horse). This toy, carved from a single piece of wood and painted with traditional floral designs, has become Sweden's national symbol.

Do-it-yourself activities are among the most popular hobbies, with many Nordic people enjoying hands-on activities related to the construction and maintenance of their homes or summerhouses. Genealogy, collecting memorabilia, and traditional folk arts such as rug weaving, knitting, ceramics, and jewelry making are also widespread.

Popular outdoor games are versions of tag and hopscotch. Hopscotch markers made of heavy glass and engraved with designs from Hans Christian Andersen's fairy tales are part of

Denmark's cultural heritage. Among adult indoor games, bridge and chess are particularly popular in Denmark and Iceland. Iceland has more chess grand masters in proportion to the size of its population than any other country in the world, and many Icelanders have won youth division world championships in recent years. Board games such as Trivial Pursuit, Monopoly, Pictionary, and Jeopardy provide Nordic adults with an opportunity for socializing during long and cold winters. All Nordic countries are big on gambling, and Norway, Denmark, and Sweden are among the five countries with the highest per capita spending on gambling in the world.

People in the Nordic countries place a strong emphasis on the educational value of toys and their capacity to boost children's creativity. Throughout the region, there is a preference for locally produced toys, such as Danish LEGOs and the Swedish Brio. Globally produced toys thought to promote intolerance or gender bias—such as war-related toys or sexualized dolls—have met considerable resistance from parents in this area of the world. Activity and construction sets, dolls, and plush toys associated with television and film brands such as Sesame Street or Lord of the Rings are among the most popular children's toys in the region. The trendy Bratz dolls appeal to Nordic children more than the Barbie brand. Barbie dolls have been at the center of a heated public debate in Sweden for over three decades; many consider Barbie a negative role model for girls.

Levels of mobile or cell phone and Internet usage are high, and e-shopping is widespread. Broadband connections have boosted the popularity of personal computer and console video games. Growing numbers of children in the younger age groups—especially the "tweenagers," aged between ten and thirteen—are abandoning their traditional toys in favor of online and console gaming. The most popular games played online are Counter Strike, War Craft, and Battlefield 1942.

The local flavor of the toys and games industry in Sweden has been facilitated historically by the fact that no advertising of toys is allowed, according to Swedish law. However, this situation has been somewhat undermined in the last two decades with the penetration of e-commerce and global media, which are saturated with toy advertisements. The Swedish company Brio is among the strongest toy brands in the world. In addition to its famous wooden construction toys and model railways, the company also manufactures a range of indoor games under the brand Alga.

Denmark's leading toy manufacturer, LEGO, generally maintains a high profile in the global toys and games industry. The name comes from *leg godt* (Danish for "play well"). The company, founded in the 1930s, today employs more than 7,000 people and has operations in over thirty countries worldwide. LEGO's core products are construction kits consisting of little plastic bricks that can be snapped together to construct complex predesigned or invented models of mainly buildings, vehicles, and landscapes. Some LEGO sets include electronic motors, and some are computer controlled. One of LEGO's most popular product lines in recent years has been the Bionicles, a series of snap-together robots figuring in adventure stories set in the imaginary Mata Nui world. The company is known for its creative marketing efforts, which include four Legoland theme parks worldwide: Billund (Denmark), Günzburg (Germany), Windsor (the United Kingdom) and Carlsbad, California (the United States), and a series of promotional events, such as building competitions. However, like many other traditional toy manufacturers, LEGO has recently suffered from the increased popularity of interactive video games.

FRANCE AND THE BENELUX

The importance of toys and games in this group of European countries is evident from the fact that some of the most influential modern theories addressing the subject from different disciplinary perspectives come from the Netherlands and France. Johan Huizinga, a Dutch historian, was fascinated by the continuing popularity of game playing during the medieval period. His explanation of this phenomenon, which he developed in the study entitled *Homo Ludens*, was that play endured because it was the very basis of more "serious" cultural pursuits, such as law, education, and warfare. Huizinga's analysis was the starting point for the theory of play developed by French sociologist Roger Caillois. In his essay collection *Mythologies*, literary critic and semiologist Roland Barthes included toys among the "contemporary myths" underpinning bourgeois ideology. The French adult, says Barthes, sees the child as a smaller self. Therefore, construction sets that encourage the child's imagination are not as popular as those that purely represent a microcosm of the entirely socialized adult world, such as miniature soldiers, medical instruments, hairdressing equipment, transport vehicles, and the like.

Because France and the countries of the Benelux generally enjoy a high standard of living, spending powers are considerable throughout the region. Parents have a strong influence on the spending habits of their children, much longer than in some other European countries. This influence is due to a lower percentage of teenagers earning money from casual work, although the situation has been changing since the mid-1990s. The family unit is highly valued in the whole region, and many games are enjoyed together by parents and children in the family home. The annual peak time for giving and receiving toys in Holland and Belgium is not Christmas, but Saint Nicholas's (Dutch *Sinterklaas*) Day, in early December. Celebrations are shared by adults and children alike, and there are gifts for everyone.

Traditional crafts such as pottery, glasswork, and silverwork are practiced in some parts of the region. The province of Burgundy in France is known for woodcraft, the town of Delft in the Netherlands is known for its fine pottery, and Brussels, the capital of Belgium, is known for lace making. Belgium also has a wide variety of traditional folk games that still enjoy considerable popularity. These games include different bowl games and throwing games, as well as archery, crossbow shooting, and fencing. Traditionally the province of male players, some of these games increasingly attract female participants.

Domestic activities, such as cooking, gardening, and home improvement, are popular leisure-time pursuits in the entire region. Other popular hobbies include stamp collecting and model trains. The people of Luxembourg enjoy playing chess socially in their country's many restaurants, pastry shops, and cafés.

France and the countries of the Benelux are all characterized by rich traditions in toy making. As early as the Middle Ages, French locksmiths, jewelers, and basket makers produced trinkets for sale. By 1600, Paris was established as the center of fashion trade. Because printed catalogues did not exist then, costume dolls called "Pandoras" were sent from Paris to other European cities to advertise the latest lines of clothes and accessories. The most celebrated nineteenth-century doll manufacturer was the Parisian firm Jumeau.

In the nineteenth century, France was also known as a producer of sophisticated musical, optical, and mechanical toys. In particular, several optical inventions that originated in France are often considered predecessors of the cinema. In the praxinoscope, invented by the artist Émile Reynaud, strips of pictures with figures in various stages of movement were seen as animated when they were revolved in a drum, reflected from the facets of a looking-glass core. Another optical toy with a similar mechanism, the phenakistiscope, was developed by the Belgian inventor Joseph Plateau. The magic lantern, invented by the French tinsmith Auguste Lapierre, consisted of a tin box, a candleholder, a concave mirror, a lens, and a channel for slides. Images were projected onto a plain white wall or a special linen screen. Lapierre's lanterns were sold in Parisian toyshops, complete with sets of slides representing captivating stories from history, geography, and fiction.

As a result of the country's high birth rates and strong economy, France currently has the fastest-growing toys and games market in Europe. Despite the growing popularity of video games, traditional playthings still dominate the French market. Traditional board games, such as Trivial Pursuit, Monopoly, and Scrabble, are particularly well liked, because the whole family can play them together.

Belgium follows the trend, evident in most of Europe, of a rapid expansion of the video-games hardware and software market. PlayStation 2 is the most popular video game console. Among software titles, race, sports, and adventure games are the most widespread. Belgian teenagers and pre-teenagers are especially attracted to toys related to dance and music. Bands for children and television programs, such as Idol, in which contestants compete to become pop stars, are linked with highly popular toy ranges. Dance-related games from Konami, accompanied by dance mats and headgear, are also becoming fashionable because they appeal to Belgium's penchant for performance dance.

Educational games, often with a language-learning aspect, are a popular parents' choice for young children. This choice is not surprising in a country with three official languages: Dutch, French, and German. Brand consciousness and loyalty also play an important role in the rather traditional Belgian society; LEGO, Playmobil, Fisher-Price, and Barbie are the most popular brands.

Board games, quizzes, fashion dolls, and construction and activity toys enjoy a continuing popularity in Holland. A recent trend is the extreme popularity of toys and games based on television and film characters, such as SpongeBob SquarePants and Yu-Gi-Oh. Video games are now outperforming traditional toys and games in sales. Console games such as Nintendo's GameCube are extremely popular, and online gaming has become a recent trend among teenagers.

The only major toy manufacturer in the Netherlands is Jumbo. The company was founded in 1853 and now sells its board games and puzzles to other countries around Europe. Jumbo products are praised for their educational and developmental value. The rest of the Dutch industry either imports toys, mainly from China and Thailand, or has production facilities there.

THE UNITED KINGDOM AND IRELAND

For a long time, the living standards in the United Kingdom were on average much higher than those in Ireland, its closest neighboring country. Since the late 1990s, however, this disparity has been less pronounced. Although the Irish people are still relatively young by EU standards, the United Kingdom has a much higher proportion of people in the older age brackets. In both countries, spending on toys, games, and recreation in general has been considerable. The legalization of divorce in Ireland in 1997 is believed to have boosted toy sales in the country as guilt-ridden parents tend to lavish their children with toys. The growing numbers of women in the workforce throughout the region are said to have had the same effect: that is, working mothers compensate for their absence from home by providing their children with toys, especially with those toys that have educational value. Many high school and tertiary students in the United Kingdom are in the labor market, which means that they have more spending power at a younger age and that their consumption patterns are less influenced by their parents.

Traditional crafts, such as weaving, knitting, pottery, glassblowing, and woodcarving, have been making a comeback in recent years. Gardening is popular throughout the region, particularly in England. There even people living in apartment buildings sometimes rent a

THE BRITISH TOY INDUSTRY

One of the most prominent nineteenth-century toy manufacturers was William Britain in Hornsey Rise, north London. Initially a manufacturer of mechanical toys, Britain later specialized in making hollow-cast lead toy soldiers. Cheaper to make and to transport, Britain's glossy toy soldiers were treasured as collectable items throughout most of the twentieth century. Concerned with children's safety, the company switched from toxic lead to harmless pewter as its main raw material. Britain shifted its production work to China in the 1990s, and the industry was bought by a U.S. toy manufacturer in 1998. Other high-quality British toys in the nineteenth century included wax dolls, toy boats, and steam engines. One of the world's best-loved construction toy systems, Meccano, was invented in 1901 by Liverpudlian Frank Hornby. Hornby's versatile construction kits soon became so popular that Hornby had to open an office in Berlin to handle the export of Meccano toys to Russia, Germany, Austria–Hungary, and eastern Europe. Another Hornby classic, the model train, was introduced in the 1920s. Harbutt's Plasticine—the predecessor of Play-Doh—was patented in 1899, and commercial production began at a factory in Bathampton in 1901. Thriving in the first half of the twentieth century, the British toy industry suffered a sharp decline in the 1970s. This decline has been attributed to the overall inertia of British toy makers, who were used to dominating the colonial markets of the British Empire and became increasingly unable to compete with their counterparts in the United States, Japan, and Hong Kong after these favorable circumstances ceased to exist.

plot of land so they can indulge their passion for green, growing things. Pub culture contributes to the continuing popularity of traditional indoor games, such as darts, pool, billiards, chess, bingo, and bridge. Betting and gambling also retain their popularity. Traditionally associated with elderly women, bingo has attracted younger players in recent years, particularly in northern England.

The historical record of toys and games in the United Kingdom dates back to the Middle Ages. A spinning top made of maple wood, dating back to the eleventh century, has been excavated at Winchester in southern England. In medieval times, toys and games were often made by children themselves. The earliest marble games, for example, were played with cherry stones and cobnuts. Cloth dolls are mentioned in a fifteenth-century religious manuscript. Until the early nineteenth century, most commercial toys in Britain were imported from Switzerland, France, or Germany. Although a luxury toy market for dolls and mechanical toys had existed for several centuries, most children from the poorer social strata and from rural areas had no access to commercially produced toys before the mid-1800s. Before that time, toy making still depended largely on small artisan workshops, such as the one described in Charles Dickens's novel *The Cricket on the Hearth* (1845). Larger-scale industrial production of toys did not begin until the mid-1800s, when Birmingham became known for its glassmakers who specialized in glass eyes for dolls and stuffed animals.

Until recently, the seven-floor Hamleys toys and games store on Regent Street in London was the largest toy shop in the world. With its world-famous imaginative displays and interactive demonstrations, a visit to Hamleys easily outshines purchasing toys online by providing the ultimate shopping experience for children.

The high exposure of children to a wide range of media influences has contributed to the popularity of brand-name dolls and figures. Mattel's Barbie dolls are still well liked in the whole region, but the trendier Bratz dolls, made by Bandai, and Mattel's Flavas are steadily carving their own niche in the fashion doll market by appealing to the values and interests prevalent in teen culture. Craft sets, such as Bandai's Badge-it, a badge-making kit, or

Scoubidou, which features colorful hollow plastic tubes used for weaving key chains and friendship bands, are also very popular.

The United Kingdom is the largest market for video games in Europe and the third largest in the world, after the United States and Japan. The country's software houses, such as Eidos, Codemasters, and SCI, are famous worldwide for their creativity and excellence. An example of British innovation in this area is MUD (Multi User Dungeon), which was developed in 1979 by Roy Trubshaw and Richard Bartle at the University of Essex, England. MUD, which originally combined interactive fiction, role-playing, programming, and dial-up modem access to a shared computer, has since inspired hundreds of popular online games, which have been hosted on Internet servers since the mid-1990s. The most popular gaming console is Sony's PlayStation 2.

GERMANY, AUSTRIA, AND SWITZERLAND

This group of countries, like many others in the developed world, has been affected by declining birthrates. Here, too, children are abandoning traditional toys and games in favor of video games at an earlier age, but traditional toys and games are still holding strong as a parental choice. The economy of the region is not evenly balanced. Germany is still recovering from worldwide recession, exacerbated by the expenses of reunification in 1990, whereas Switzerland enjoys one of the highest per capita incomes in the world. This

TOYS IN GERMANY

Germany was the undisputed toy-making capital of the world until the beginning of World War I in 1914 when much of Germany's industry was converted to wartime purposes and German imports were banned in many countries. Germany has the longest and richest toy-making tradition of all European countries. The oldest preserved toys are dolls made of baked clay, which date from the thirteenth and fourteenth centuries. By the late seventeenth century, the city of Nuremberg had firmly established itself as a center of the emerging European toy trade. Located at the intersection of the ancient German salt-trading route and another route coming north over the Alps from Venice, Nuremberg traded in a wide variety of goods, including toys, which were then known as *Nürnberger Tand* (Nuremberg trinkets).

Nuremberg's annual *Internationale Spielwarenmesse* (International Toy Fair), which takes place in February, is the world's largest and most significant toy fair, bringing together thousands of exhibitors from around the world. Permanent showrooms are reserved for international industry leaders, such as Mattel, Playmobil, and LEGO. Germany also abounds with toy museums. The *Spielzeugmuseum* (Toy Museum) in Nuremberg, founded in 1971, is based on the collection of Lydia and Paul Bayer. Sonneberg has one of Germany's oldest toy museums, which was founded in 1901 and today houses close to 100,000 objects.

imbalance is to some extent reflected in consumers' buying patterns of toys and games because toy discounters seem to be more popular in Germany than elsewhere in the region.

Traditional crafts, which enjoy considerable popularity throughout the region, include woodcarving, ceramics, jewelry making, and embroidery. The Swiss still enjoy traditional games, such as *Hornussen*, also called "farmer's tennis," *Steinstossen*, or stone-putting, and *Schwingen*, or Swiss wrestling. Throughout the region, outdoor games and do-it-yourself hobbies are increasingly popular.

The Erzgebirge, or Ore Mountains, on both sides of the German–Czech border, supplied Nuremberg merchants with wooden toys such as Noah's Arks and toy farms. A thriving cottage industry still exists there, producing wooden toys, ornaments, and Christmas wares such as nutcrackers, wooden angels, and nativity scenes.

Another toy-making center was the Thuringian town of Sonneberg. The Sonneberg toy makers worked mainly in wood and *papier mâché* or "composition." This latter material, made by mixing paper or wood pulp with gum and sometimes sand or sawdust, had the advantage of being cheap, easy to mold, and resilient. The relatively cheap mass-produced *papier mâché* dolls were highly popular throughout Europe in the first half of the nineteenth century. In the Gröden valley in south Tyrol, the town of Oberammergau specialized in wooden tabletop lottery games, such as Tivoli or Bagatelle, which are similar to today's ubiquitous pinball machines.

In the sixteenth century, Nuremberg itself specialized in the manufacture of miniature tin animals. The same material was later used for the manufacture of toy armies, inspired by the military success of Frederick the Great. The leading manufacturers were the Hilpert family. Their armies were cast from pairs of slate molds, on which the front and the back of the figure had been engraved in low relief. The Hilperts also used this technique to manufacture rococo gardens, coaches, animals, and market scenes. Following the opening of the first German railway line between Nuremberg and Fürth in 1835, toy trains emerged as another specialty of local toy makers. By 1900, Nuremberg and the neighboring town of Fürth had as many as 300 toy factories, mostly engaged in work with metal.

Märklin, the most prominent German manufacturer of model railways today, was founded in 1859 by wife and husband Caroline and Theodor Märklin. Through skilful marketing and continuing innovation and expansion, this family-owned company based in the town of Göppingen soon became a major supplier of transport-themed toys to the world market.

Steiff, a German manufacturer of soft toys from Giengen, dates back to the late nineteenth century, when the founder of the company, Margarete Steiff, began to sew felt animals to give them away as Christmas presents. The original Steiff teddy bear was born in 1902 and was based on sketches of real-life animals from Stuttgart Zoo.

The famous Berlin doll maker Käthe Kruse made her dolls from impregnated fabric, molded realistically into the features of babies and toddlers. These lifelike dolls enjoyed considerable popularity internationally between the two wars. Interestingly, the model for Mattel's classic Barbie doll was a German doll named Lilli, launched in 1955 as a spin-off to a popular comic strip published in *Die Bild-Zeitung*. Today, Germany's largest doll manufacturer is Zapf, based in the Bavarian town of Rödental.

Ravensburger is a publisher and manufacturer of jigsaw puzzles, board games, and arts and crafts kits. The original bookshop was established in 1845 by bookseller, journalist, and publisher Carl Maier. The first Ravensburger jigsaw puzzles, originally made out of thin wood and later out of cardboard, were launched in 1964. The company's products are exported today to more than 50 countries around the world. Another German toy brand with a strong reputation worldwide is Playmobil, which makes sturdy plastic figurine sets based on pirate, police, and farm-life themes.

The German market for toys and games is Europe's largest after the United Kingdom. As it is elsewhere in Europe, toys and games associated with children's films, cartoons, television programs, and music bands are among the most popular products in the entire region. Younger children in Germany are encouraged to spend their out-of-school time outdoors so they are not as exposed to the video-game culture as children in some other European countries. Wooden toys, which have a long tradition in the region's many forested areas, are considered the safest choice for toddlers as synthetic materials may contain noxious chemicals. Most video games that top the charts were developed in the United States and manufactured by their German subsidiaries. Sony PlayStation 2 and Nintendo Game Boy Advance are the most popular consoles.

POLAND, CZECH REPUBLIC, SLOVAKIA, SLOVENIA, AND HUNGARY

In addition to their geographical proximity, the countries in this group have at least two other key characteristics in common: all five are still affected by their recent transition to liberal democracy and a free-market economy, and—along with five other countries—they all joined the European Union in the most recent stage of enlargement, which occurred on May 1, 2004. For the Czech Republic, Slovakia, and Slovenia, this transition also involved a newly gained political independence following the breakup of Czechoslovakia and Yugoslavia, the multinational states they were once part of. For all of them, the transition meant an opportunity to revitalize their historical links with their western neighbors and reestablish themselves as part of the European mainstream. This sweeping political and social change has been accompanied by a similarly far-reaching cultural transformation, in terms of lifestyles, consuming habits, and attitudes about leisure. Held back during Communist rule, consumerism—including the consumption of toys and games—is now boosted by the improvement of the economy and living standards in most of these countries.

Folk crafts in the region include pottery, woodcarving, wickerwork, lacework, knitting, and embroidery. Many of the folk crafts were neglected during the post-World War II period but gained a renewed popularity in the 1990s as part of an overall effort to recover the elements of the national cultural heritages that had been suppressed under Communist rule.

Paintings on glass are characteristic of the town of Zakopane at the foot of the Tatra Mountains in Poland. The traditional toy-making centers in Poland are the towns of Żywiec, Myślenice, Kielce, Rzeszów, and Cracow. This last city, an important historic center on the Vistula River, is primarily known for its dolls in regional folk costumes and animal-shaped whistles made of glazed clay. Other traditional Polish playthings include wooden toy horses, birds and butterflies with movable wings, cradles, and rag dolls.

Bohemia in the Czech Republic is known worldwide for its crystal glass. Wooden toys and Christmas crafts are a tradition of the Ore Mountains (Czech Krušné hory and German Erzgebirge) on both sides of the political border between Germany and the Czech Republic. The Slovak town of Modra, near Bratislava, specializes in handmade pottery painted with decorative flower ornamentation. Dolls made of corn husks are among the most characteristic traditional toys in Slovakia. The towns of Ribnica and Kočevje in Slovenia specialize in the manufacture of wooden objects, mainly kitchen utensils such as spoons, spatulas, and sieves. Ribnica is also known for its pottery, including clay toys and animal-shaped whistles.

Traditionally people in this region have enjoyed much of their leisure time outdoors. Many city dwellers spend their weekends in the countryside, where they enjoy walking, picking berries or mushrooms, and simply relaxing. Do-it-yourself home-improvement projects and gardening are also popular pastimes. Collecting is not as popular now as it was during most of the twentieth century, when commemorative badges, coins, and stamps were the most popular collectable items.

Card games and chess are popular throughout the region, especially in Hungary, where chess masters such as Judit Polgár are national celebrities. The so-called Hungarian deck of cards, first manufactured in 1835, features the characters from the story about the Swiss national hero Wilhelm Tell, immortalized by German poet Friedrich von Schiller. Board games such as Monopoly and Risk are also well liked.

The toys and games market in this group of countries is dominated by the international giants, such as Hasbro, Mattel, LEGO, and Brio. Overall, these countries' accession to the European Union in 2004 has improved the quality of toys and games on the market, as all products now have to comply with European standards. Hungary's strongest local players are Gulliver and Régió. In terms of innovative products, logic puzzles are Hungary's trademark. The most famous worldwide is Rubik's Cube, invented in the 1970s by Erno Rubik, lecturer at the Academy of Applied Arts and Crafts in Budapest. Other ingenious sliding and rotary puzzles, made most commonly of plastic or wood, have been developed in Hungary, but none of them has ever achieved international success comparable to that of Rubik's Cube.

A major Polish producer of toys and games is Cobi SA, which is best known for its military-themed building blocks similar to LEGO, called *Mala Armia* (Little Army). The company has also launched multimedia and video-game products to accompany its traditional toy range. Poland also has a number of innovative small manufacturers, such as the multi-award winning BAJO. Founded in 1993 by sculptor and architect Wojciech Bajor, the company specializes in high-quality wooden toys.

All countries in this group are experiencing a shift away from traditional playthings toward video games, albeit at a slower pace than those European countries with traditionally stronger economies. Because the expensive original software is out of reach for a majority of gamers, piracy has been widespread in this part of the world. Since 2004, the stricter controls that are in place within the EU market have put illegal producers under considerable pressure. Sony PlayStation dominates the console market, and Nintendo's Game Boy is the most popular handheld console. As more people gain access to the Internet, online gaming is also becoming increasingly popular.

ESTONIA, LITHUANIA, AND LATVIA

The three Baltic countries of Estonia, Lithuania, and Latvia gained independence from the Soviet Union in 1991 and joined the European Union in May 2004. Although they now boast relatively high living standards compared to other parts of the former Soviet Union, many effects of the recent transition to a market economy are still present. During the decades of Soviet occupation, the range of play products available for purchase was limited, and the quality was often substandard. Toys and games were often made or improvised by children themselves, depending on their imagination and the materials at hand. Although the poorer segments of the population still have hardly any funds for expenditure on recreation and leisure, the number of people with sufficient means to afford expensive toys and games by leading international manufacturers is steadily growing.

Before the accession of the Baltic countries to the European Union, piracy was widespread in almost any kind of consumer goods, including toys and games. The quality of counterfeit products was generally low, and there was little regard for safety. In recent years, the obligation to comply with strict EU regulations has contributed to a growing awareness of the importance of toy safety, and significant efforts have been made to curb piracy in the toy sector.

All Baltic countries have a rich tradition of folk crafts, including weaving, knitting, embroidery, silver jewelry making, leatherwork, ceramics, and woodcarving. Handmade wool sweaters, cardigans, mittens, and socks are preferred to factory-made ones and can be bought from specialized shops or market stalls. Toys and kitchen utensils made of aromatic juniper wood from the Estonian islands are among the most popular Baltic handicrafts, appealing to tourists and residents alike.

Many people in the Baltic countries enjoy gardening. Collecting is also widespread, with stamps, coins and postcards being the most popular collectables. Traveling abroad is another form of recreation that was completely out of reach for the average person during the decades of Soviet domination, but it is now becoming increasingly popular.

Estonia's largest toy retailer is the Tallinn-based Jukat Eesti Ltd. Lithuania's leading toy retail chain is Zaislu Planeta (Toy Planet). Its parent company, Voira, is an authorized dealer of over thirty different toy manufacturers, including top international brands such as LEGO, Hasbro, and Zapf Creation. The company operates successfully in all three Baltic countries. In Latvia, the award-winning wooden toys produced by Varis Toys and Stradu Indranes are considered to be among the most innovative local toy products. Recent trends in toys include playthings that promote children's development, and the opening of educational toy retailer BeBe offers evidence of this trend.

RUSSIA, BELARUS, MOLDOVA, AND UKRAINE

The countries in this region are currently facing many of the same social problems that were present during the Soviet era, as well as a new series of difficulties brought about by the momentous social change in the post-Soviet period. The supply of toys and games during the Soviet era was extremely limited. When the borders opened in the early 1990s, shops and open-air markets became inundated with cheap imports. Uneven wealth distribution has had a negative impact on local toys and games manufacturers, whose products are more expensive than those imported from Asia. At the same time, local products are often not as appealing to wealthier consumers as some well-known international brands. This situation is slowly changing as the economy in the region improves and the strongest local producers regain ground.

Traditional crafts include weaving, embroidery, knitting, tapestry, ceramics, and wood-carving. Knitting and embroidery are still popular among women of all ages. Painting and lacquerwork are used to decorate kitchen utensils, jewelry, and toys.

The region's toy-making tradition can be traced back to the medieval period. Clay rattles, dolls, and animal-shaped rattles dating back to the tenth century have been found in the excavations in the old Russian towns of Kiev, Novgorod, Moscow, Tver, Radonezh, and Dmitrov. Wooden rattles, balls, boats, and animal figures dating back to the twelfth century have been unearthed in the towns of Staraya Ladoga and Novgorod and in the excavations along the Oyat River. Wooden toys have a long tradition in the Volga region, especially in the villages of Lyskovo, Gorodets, and Fedoseevo. Russia's most sought-after artifact, the matryoshka nested doll, is a relatively recent addition to the region's folk craft. A symbolic decorative object rather than a plaything, the matryoshka represents the continuity of the Russian people. The concept of nested objects, however, is not originally Russian, but came to Russia from China and Japan, where it has a millennial tradition. The first Russian matryoshka was shaped by wood turner Vassily Zvezdochkin and painted by book illustrator and folk-art expert Sergei Maliutin in the second half of the nineteenth century.

Although some Western toys, such as Barbie dolls and action figures, are often criticized as models that encourage socially unacceptable behavior and instill objectionable values, their popularity among children is unwavering. Russia's response to Barbie's extraordinary success is a doll called Veronika, manufactured by the Moscow toy factory Krugozor. Taller than Barbie and significantly cheaper, Veronika has been Krugozor's most popular toy in the last decade.

Soft toys and baby dolls with real-life capabilities, such as singing, speaking, or crying, are popular among preschool girls. Locally produced dolls are not in favor, partly because they only come with a limited range of accessories. Boys like playing with action figures, cars, and weapons. Construction kits, embroidery sets, weapons, and musical instruments have been among the most widely used toys since the Soviet period. Danish LEGO, Canadian Mega

TOYS IN RUSSIA: TRINITY TOYS AND MATRYOSHKA DOLLS

Russia's most prominent toy-making center is Sergiyev Posad (called Zagorsk during the Soviet period), a picturesque historical town northeast of Moscow. The townspeople and the monks of the town's Trinity Monastery specialized in icon painting, wood turning, and carving. Their artifacts, including wooden toys, were sold to pilgrims in the open-air market in front of the monastery. Wooden horses and wooden dolls dressed in folk costumes are the most typical "Trinity toys." In the late nineteenth century, the artists of Sergiyev Posad developed a characteristic style of painting matryoshka dolls; it was realistic and based on the Byzantine tradition of icon painting. Two other distinct styles of matryoshka painting—both more symbolic and ornamental than the Sergiyev Posad style— were developed in the towns of Semyonov and Polkhovsky Maidan. During the Soviet era, folk crafts associated with religious painting had all but fallen into neglect, but the 1990s have seen a growing interest in their revival. Today's matryoshkas reflect the contemporary life and popular culture of the Russian people and can represent anything from contemporary Russian and foreign politicians to heroes and heroines of the Russian folk legend and the international, mostly American, pop cultural lore.

Bloks, and Poland's Cobi are currently among the most popular construction brands. Since the opening of the market in the early 1990s, the range of popular products has expanded, with educational and scientific toys and role-playing paraphernalia enjoying particular success. Board games produced by local manufacturers enjoy considerable popularity. Chess playing has been popular since the Soviet era when it was encouraged by the government, both as a social activity for adults and an extracurricular activity among schoolchildren. The range of outdoor games on the market is limited in comparison with the countries of the European West, and most children are happy with balls, skipping ropes, chalk, and improvised swings and slides. Sledges and ice skates are popular in winter.

Computer gaming is becoming increasingly popular in the region. Since licensed products are too expensive for most users, piracy in video-game software and hardware has been widespread. Moreover, affordable "jewel" versions of licensed software—without costly covers, packaging, and booklets—are popular among gamers. Russia's most successful video-game publishers are 1C and Buka, which also have in-house development teams. Furthermore, it is not uncommon for Western publishers to outsource part of a game's development, most commonly art-related work, to studios in Russia and Ukraine.

PlayStation 2 is the most popular of the latest consoles, mainly due to the fact that it can also function as a DVD player. However, since PlayStation 2, Microsoft Xbox, and Nintendo GameCube are often out of reach for the average consumer, inexpensive alternatives by Russian and Chinese companies (for example, Star Trek and Dendy) enjoy a considerable popularity. Computers are generally seen as a less expensive option than consoles because their functionality is far greater. Online video games are also widespread.

BULGARIA, ROMANIA, AND ALBANIA

Geographically close but ethnically and culturally diverse, the countries in this group are in the process of building democracy and developing free-market economies after decades of Communism. Living standards are among the lowest in Europe, and spending on toys and games is considerably lower than in the rest of the continent. Although the economic situation in Bulgaria and Romania is improving with their impending accession to the European Union, Albania has held the unenviable record of being Europe's poorest country for centuries. The common negative effects of transition to a market economy, such as unemployment and uneven wealth distribution, are evident throughout the region, but are nowhere as pronounced as in Albania. Many adult Albanian males are leaving the country to look for work abroad, while their families remain in Albania, struggling to make ends meet.

Knitting, weaving, embroidery, pottery, and copper engraving are some of the traditional handicrafts in the region. Children enjoy outdoor games, such as tag and hide-and-seek. Playing cards, chess, and other board games offers an opportunity to socialize with family and friends. In Albania, elderly men gather in bars to play dominoes and chess, whereas younger generations prefer pool and billiards.

The local toy production that existed in the region under Communism largely collapsed in the early 1990s, unable to survive the competition of cheap imports. Since then, new establishments have emerged, mainly producing eco-friendly toys made of wood, cardboard, and fabrics. Although these products do not seem to be popular among domestic consumers, they are in high demand on the European market. Romania is the strongest toy exporter in the region with exports mainly going to the EU market. Bulgaria's strongest toy retailer is Hippoland with stores in several major cities.

The use of video games is becoming increasingly widespread among teenagers and young adults. The international video-game publisher Ubisoft has had a development branch in Romania's capital, Bucharest, since 1992. There are also some local development teams in the region, working mainly on international collaborative projects.

CROATIA, BOSNIA–HERZEGOVINA, THE FORMER YUGOSLAV REPUBLICS OF MACEDONIA, AND SERBIA AND MONTENEGRO

To varying degrees, the countries in this part of Europe are still feeling the effects of the violent disintegration of the former socialist Yugoslavia, the country they were all part of in the second half of the twentieth century. Serbia and Montenegro and Macedonia were also affected by the Kosovo crisis of the late 1990s. Moreover, the process of transition to a market economy in this region has been plagued by problems such as uneven wealth distribution and high unemployment. The dismantlement of an all-Yugoslav market has deeply affected all branches of industry, including the production of toys and games.

The traditional handicrafts in the region include tapestry, weaving, embroidery, pottery, and woodcarving. In Croatia wickerwork and painted wooden toys, mostly carts, vehicles, wheeled animals, and miniature furniture, were made in the village of Vidovec in Hrvatsko Zagorje near Zagreb and in Zelovo in the Dalmatian hinterland. These items were usually manufactured in small workshops and sold at country fairs or religious festivals. The villages of Stubički and Bistrički Laz in Hrvatsko Zagorje are known for their decorative painted butterflies with flapping wings, animal-shaped whistles, and other musical instruments.

Although a modest toy industry emerged in the region in the late nineteenth century, commercially produced toys were often out of reach for the poorer segments of the population. A majority of children made their own toys, such as marbles made of hardened mud and rag dolls and balls made out of old socks. Popular games were hide-and-seek, leapfrog, and hopscotch.

A large-scale production of toys and games did not begin until after World War II, with manufacturers mostly concentrated in the Republic of Croatia. The openness of borders in the former Yugoslavia also meant that parents could buy toys for their children from abroad, mostly from Italy, Austria, and Germany. The conspicuous consumption of playthings in the post-World War II period was celebrated in a song well liked in the entire former Yugoslavia. The song was called "Moja Mala Djevojčica" ("My Little Girl," 1958) and was sung by the Croatian singer Zdenka Vučković.

There is currently no major manufacturer of toys and games in the region. The market is flooded by imported products, coming mostly from other European countries and Asia. In Croatia, the retail chain Turbo Limać stocks a wide range of toys for all ages, including Mattel's Barbie dolls, infant toys by Chicco, construction kits by LEGO, and toy cars by Burago and Majorette.

Both children and adults are increasingly interested in video games. Personal computers remain the most popular platform with online gaming increasing in popularity in recent years. The most successful game development company is Croteam, founded in 1993 in the Croatian capital, Zagreb. The company's best-known game is the first-person shooter Serious Sam, in which the hero Sam Stone fights against alien forces to save humankind.

ITALY, SPAIN, AND PORTUGAL

These three countries are characterized by the centrality of family ties in the lives of the vast majority of their inhabitants. This explains the popularity of toys that prepare children for their future household responsibilities, such as toy washing machines, vacuum cleaners, cooking equipment, and tool sets. Not surprisingly, these toys generally perpetuate the traditional gender divisions within the family unit. Another dominant social and cultural trait in this region is the strong influence of the Catholic church. Although Christmas is the peak time for toy sales in most of Europe, in Italy, Spain, and Portugal, Christmas accounts for up to 75 percent of the annual sales of play-related products. In Spain, children are also traditionally given toys on the sixth day of January, Día de los Reyes Magos (Epiphany).

The traditional crafts in Italy are lacework, pottery, marble carving, and gold and silver filigree work. Murano, an archipelago of islands in the Venetian lagoon, is famous worldwide for its glassmaking. In Spain, leatherwork is primarily a specialty of Cordoba, lace and carpets of Granada, pearls of the Balearic Islands, and jewelry, swords, and knives of Toledo. Spain is also known for its handmade guitars and other musical instruments. In Portugal, rug making is associated with Arraiolas, fine embroidery with Guimares, black pottery with Vila Real, and basket weaving with the Algarve. Folk art is increasingly recognized as a valuable part of a country's cultural heritage, boosting the tourist appeal of the three countries.

Gardening, do-it-yourself home-improvement projects, and collecting of rare artifacts, books, old music records, and comic strips are among the region's most popular hobbies.

The early Venetian and Genoese travelers are credited with introducing playing cards to medieval Europe. There are records of the existence of tarot cards, used for divination, in late medieval Italy and France. A subset of the tarot deck, called the Minor Arcana and divided into four suits, provides the basis for today's standard playing-card decks. Today the most popular Italian card games include Scopa and Scopone, Briscola, Tressette, and Terziglio. A form of lotto was widespread in sixteenth-century Genoa, derived from an earlier gambling tradition and related to the annual draw of senators-elect.

Another brand that contributed to Italy's reputation of excellence in toy making in the early 1900s is the famous car manufacturer Bugatti. Bugatti's exclusive range of electricity-powered cars for children, which were built in the 1920s alongside the company's real-life racing cars, are considered by experts the finest toy cars of all time.

Giochi Preziosi is currently the strongest toy and game manufacturer, retailer, and distributor on the Italian market. Other popular brands are Trudi for soft toys, Clementoni and Editrice Giochi for indoor and educational games, Grand Soleil for outdoor games, and Artsana for infant and preschool products.

Spain's toy industry is concentrated in the towns of Ibi and Onil in Alicante province. The country's leading toy manufacturer is Famosa SA, specializing in dolls and action figures. The company also has a strong presence in the Portuguese market.

As they do elsewhere in Europe, children in this region increasingly abandon traditional toys and games in favor of video games at an early age, usually in their preteens. Video games are also a popular pastime among young adults. Soccer-related video games, such as Pro Evolution Soccer, are well liked throughout the region, in which soccer fans are particularly passionate and widespread. PlayStation 2 and Game Boy Advance are the most popular consoles, but new-generation consoles such as Xbox and GameCube have been gaining popularity in recent years. Nokia's N-Gage—a video-games console that is also a mobile phone, an MP3 player, and a radio— is still considered too expensive by the majority of gamers in the region. Online gaming is also becoming increasingly popular, boosted by the relatively recent consolidation of broadband services. Local companies have not been able to compete with international leaders in video-game publishing, and some pioneering efforts in this field have not yielded significant results.

GEPPETTO AND GORNINI: PIONEERS OF ITALIAN TOY MAKING

Italy is also home to the world's most popular wooden marionette, the mischievous hero of Carlo Collodi's nineteenth-century novel for children, *The Adventures of Pinocchio* (Italian *Le Avventure di Pinocchio*). The story of Pinocchio, his loving father Geppetto, and the Blue Fairy, who breathes life into the wooden body of the puppet and eventually turns him into a real boy, is known and loved by children across cultures and continents.

In the Renaissance and early modern periods, Italy's toy making was the domain of artisans such as Collodi's Geppetto. One of the pioneers of industrial toy making was the Mantuan aristocrat Luigi Furga Gornini. In 1872, he began to manufacture *papier mâché* carnival masks in his summer villa in Canneto sull'Oglio near Mantua. Later he expanded his product range to include dolls, the product which was soon to gain him international fame. An undisputed leader in the Italian toy industry for more than a century, Furga was taken over by Grand Soleil in the early 1990s.

GREECE, TURKEY, AND CYPRUS

The traditionally strained relations between Greece and Turkey improved considerably after several earthquakes hit both countries in 1999, giving ordinary people of both nationalities an occasion to show compassion toward each other. Greece and Cyprus have been among the main advocates of Turkey's bid to join the European Union. However, this attitude of support is extremely volatile, and recent incidents involving Turkey's violations of Greek airspace have already upset the equilibrium.

Despite political animosities, the two cultures have elements in common, developed mostly during the Ottoman period (Greece was under Ottoman rule from the fifteenth to the early nineteenth century). Traditional crafts in the region include weaving, knitting, embroidery, carving, metalwork, and pottery. Some villages have developed a cottage industry manufacturing traditional toys. The best known is the village of Soganli in the Cappadocia region in central Turkey, known for its handmade dolls dressed in traditional costumes.

Coffee shops are popular gathering places where village men congregate to talk, drink coffee or tea, and often play backgammon, dominoes, checkers, or cards.

Greece's major chain retailers of toys and games are Jumbo, Moustakas, and Zaharias. Jumbo has recently expanded beyond the borders of Greece, mainly targeting other countries in the region, such as Cyprus, Bulgaria, and Romania. Cheap imitations of brand-name products, imported mainly from China and Hong Kong, are sold at bazaars and flea markets. In Greece, the most popular toys in recent years have been those related to the latest film productions, such as *Finding Nemo*, *Harry Potter*, *Matrix Revolution*, and *The Lord of the Rings*. Fashion dolls, such as Mattel's Barbie and My Scene, Hasbro's Cindy, and the Bratz line of hip-hop–inspired dolls by MGA Entertainment have been popular among pre-teenage girls. An additional attraction of these dolls for fashion-conscious pre-teenagers is that they come with a whole range of accessories, such as make-up, nail polish, and jewelry. New lines of construction toys targeted specifically at girls, such as LEGO's Belville range, which encourage creativity and role-playing, are gaining popularity on the Greek market. Monopoly, Trivial Pursuit, and the stacking game Jenga are the most popular indoor games, usually played at parties and family get-togethers.

In Turkey, where people rarely go shopping specifically for toys, most play products are sold in supermarkets and hypermarkets. The market leader in infants' toys and games is the Italian brand Chicco. Most soft toys are nonbranded imports from Asia. Licensed action figures, such as Spiderman and Action Man, and construction toys, such as LEGO's Robotics range, are well liked among Turkish boys. Model cars and other vehicles are increasingly seen as collector's items rather than children's toys. The leading brands are Maisto and Burago. Board games are increasingly popular among young adults, who play them at different social occasions. Outdoor games have always been a widespread form of entertainment in Turkey, where children often play outside after school.

Video gaming is increasingly taking hold in this region with the passion spreading primarily among teenagers and young adults. This latter group is mostly interested in football, racing, and war games. Sony's PlayStation 2, with its ability to read CDs and DVDs and allow for interactive gaming through the Internet, is the most popular console. Video-game piracy is a problem in Turkey where prices of the original software are higher than in most European countries.

RESOURCE GUIDE

PRINTED SOURCES

Ariès, Philippe. *Centuries of Childhood*. Translated by Robert Baldick. London: Jonathan Cape, 1962.

Barthes, Roland. *Mythologies*. Translated by Annette Lavers. New York: Hill and Wang, 1972.

Beaumont, Lesley. "Child's Play in Classical Athens." *History Today* 44:8 (1994). 30–35.

Biškupić, Iris. *Croatian Traditional Children's Toys*. Zagreb: Museum and Gallery Center Klovićevi Dvori, 1999.

Brewer, John. "Childhood Revisited: The Genesis of the Modern Toy." *History Today* 30:12 (1980). 32–39.

Brown, Kenneth. *The British Toy Business: A History Since 1700*. Rio Grande, OH: Hambledon Press, 1996.

Caillois Roger. *Man, Play and Games*. Translated by Meyer Barash. New York: The Free Press, 1961

Collodi, Carlo. *The Adventures of Pinocchio*. Translated by Ann Lawson Lucas. Oxford: Oxford University Press, 1883/1996.

Corredor-Matheos, José. *El juguete en España*. Barcelona: Espasa-Calpe, 1989.

Cross, Gary, and Gregory Smits. "Japan, the U.S. and the Globalization of Children's Consumer Culture." *Journal of Social History* 38:4 (2005). 873–90.

Culff, Robert. *The World of Toys*. London: Hamlyn, 1969.

Dickens, Charles. *The Cricket on the Hearth*. Kila, MT: Kessinger Publishing. 1845/2004.

Ehrmann Jacques, ed. *Game, Play, Literature*. Boston: Beacon Press, 1968.

Fleming, Dan. *Powerplay: Toys as Popular Culture*. Manchester, UK: Manchester University Press, 1996.

Fraser, Antonia. *A History of Toys*. New York: Spring Books, 1972.

Fritzsch, Karl Ewald. *An Illustrated History of Toys*. Leipzig, Germany: Edition Leipzig, 1968.

Geertz, Clifford. "Deep Play: Notes on the Balinese Cockfight." *Daedalus* 101 (Winter 1972). 1–37.

Giocattolo d'epoca e sua cultura: Il giocattolo nella storia. Florence: Alinari, 1995.

Hamlin, David. "The Structures of Toy Consumption: Bourgeois Domesticity and Demand for Toys in Nineteenth-Century Germany." *Journal of Social History* 36:4 (2003). 857–71.

Huizinga Johan. *Homo Ludens: A Study of the Play Element in Culture*. London: Routledge and Kegan Paul, 1949.

Joannis, Claudette. "Canons et soldats de plomb: jouets de princes, objets de musee." *La Revue du Louvre et des Musees de France* 51:5 (2001). 68–71.

Orme, Nicholas. "Child's Play in Medieval England." *History Today* 51:10 (2001). 49–55.

Petényi, Sándor. *Games and Toys in Medieval and Early Modern Hungary*. Translated by Alice Choyke and László Bartosievicz. Krems, Austria: Medium Aevum Quotidianum, 1994.

Remise, Jac, and Jean Fondin. *The Golden Age of Toys*. Lausanne: Edita, 1967.

Schramm, Manuel. "The Invention and Uses of Folk Art in Germany: Wooden Toys from the Erzgebirge Mountains." *Folklore* 115 (2004). 64–76.

Sutton-Smith, Brian. *Toys as Culture*. New York: Gardner Press, 1986.

PERIODICALS

Play and Culture. Champaign, IL, 1988–.

Das Spielzeug. Bamberg, Germany, 1909–.

Toys International. London, 1962–.

The Toy Trader and Exporter. London, 1908–.

Toy Trader Year Book. Watford, England, 1969–.

WEBSITES

Datamonitor. Accessed June 6, 2006. http://www.datamonitor.com/. Industry profiles, with extensive reports on the toys and games industry in Belgium, France, Germany, Greece, Hungary, Ireland, Italy, the Netherlands, Poland, Portugal, Russia, Spain, Sweden, Turkey, and the United Kingdom.

Economist Intelligence Unit. Updated August 16, 2006. Economist Group. Accessed June 5, 2006. http://www.eiu.com. Regularly updated consumer statistics and forecasts.

Toy Industries of Europe (TIE). Toy Industries of Europe. Accessed June 6, 2006. http://www.tietoy.org. An action group that interacts with the EU institutions and other European stakeholders on behalf of the toy industry.

Toy Traders of Europe (TTE). Toy Traders of Europe. Accessed June 6, 2006. http://www.toy-tte.org. An association representing the toy trade on issues related to the harmonization of standards at the European level.

Videos/Films

Bionicle and the Mask of Light. (U.S., 2003). Directed by David Molina and Terry Shakespeare. An animated feature film based on LEGO's Bionicle robots.

Bionicle 2: Legends of Metru-Nui. (U.S., 2004). Directed by David Molina and Terry Shakespeare. Another animated feature in the Bionicle series.

Bionicle 3: Web of Shadows. (U.S., 2005). Directed by David Molina and Terry Shakespeare. Another animated feature in the Bionicle series.

A Grand Day Out with Wallace & Gromit. (UK, 1989). Directed by Nick Park. The characters of this animated film are made of the well-known British modeling toy Plasticine.

The History of Toys and Games. (U.S., 2006). A feature-length History Channel documentary on the history of toys and games, presented by actor John Ritter.

Monty Python and the Holy Grail in Lego. (UK/U.S., 2001). Directed by Tim Drage and Tony Mines. A short LEGO-based animation that replicates the scenes from the homonymous Monty Python movie.

Wallace & Gromit in The Curse of the Were-Rabbit. (UK, 2005). Directed by Steve Box and Nick Park. The characters in this animated film are made of Plasticine.

Wallace & Gromit in A Close Shave. (UK, 1995). Directed by Nick Park.

Wallace & Gromit in The Wrong Trousers. (UK, 1993). Directed by Nick Park.

TOY FAIRS

Feria Internacional del Juguete y de los Juegos (International Fair of Toys and Games), Valencia, Spain. http://www.feriavalencia.com/fejuy.or.

Igrushki i igry (International Toys and Games Exhibition), Moscow, Russia. http://toys.mvdv.ru/exhibition/243/ex.htm.

Salone Internazionale del Giocattolo de Milano (International Toy Salon), Milan, Italy. http://www.salonedelgiocattolo.it.

Spielwarenmesse International Toy Fair, Nuremberg, Germany. http://www.spielwarenmesse.de.

Świat Dziecka (Child's World Trade Fair of Goods for Children), Poznań, Poland. http://www.swiatdziecka.mtp.pl.

The Toy Fair, London, United Kingdom. http://www.britishtoyfair.co.uk/files.

Univers d'enfants (*Kids' Universe*), Paris, France. http://www.univers-enfants.com/main.cfm.

MUSEUMS AND THEME PARKS

Badener Puppen- und Spielzeugmuseum (Baden Doll and Toy Museum), Villa Attems, Erzherzog Rainer-Ring 23, Baden, Austria. http://www.museum.com/jb/museum?id=808. A collection of nineteenth- and twentieth-century dolls and toys.

The Bear Museum, 38 Dragon St., Petersfield, UK. http://www.bearmuseum.co.uk. Founded in 1984 by antiquarian Judy Sparrow, the museum houses a large collection of antique and contemporary teddy bears.

Benaki Museum, 1 Koumbari St., Athens, Greece. http://www.benaki.gr/index-en.htm. The museum features a collection of 15,000 toys, games, and objects related to childhood, including Greek toys from the fifth century BC, as well as toys from the ancient Roman and Byzantine periods. More recent European, Asian, African, and American toys are also on display.

Bethnal Green Museum of Childhood, Cambridge Heath Rd., London, UK. http://www.vam.ac.uk/moc/index.html. The Museum of Childhood, a branch of the Victoria and Albert Museum, houses the United Kingdom's national collection of childhood-related objects dating back to the sixteenth century.

Brighton Toy and Model Museum, 52–55 Trafalgar St., Brighton, UK. http://www.brightontoymuseum.co.uk. A collection of over 10,000 exhibits, including rare model trains, arcade games, construction toys, puppets, and toy theaters.

Coburger Puppenmuseum (Coburg Doll Museum), Rückerstrasse 2–3, Coburg, Germany. http://www.coburger-puppenmuseum.de. Situated in Coburg, the center of German doll production, the museum houses more than 900 mostly German and French dolls as well as miniature furniture.

Deutsches Spielzeugmuseum (German Toy Museum), Beethovenstrasse 10, Sonneberg, Germany. http://www.spielzeugmuseum-sonneberg.de. One of Germany's oldest toy museums, founded in 1901, with a collection of close to 100,000 toys, including teddy bears, dolls, and tin soldiers.

Edinburgh Museum of Childhood, 42 High St., Edinburgh, UK. http://www.cac.org.uk/venues/museum_childhood.htm. The museum has five galleries across three floors of a restored eighteenth-century building. The exhibits include puppets, train sets, dolls, and dollhouses, spinning tops, arcade games, and children's costumes.

Erzgebirgisches Spielzeugmuseum (The Toy Museum of the Ore Mountains), Hauptstrasse 73, Seiffen, Germany. http://www.spielzeugmuseum-seiffen.de. A collection of more than 3,000 wooden folk art objects, including toys, Christmas ornaments, nutcrackers, chandeliers, and miniatures.

The House on the Hill Toy Museum, Stansted Mountfitchet, Essex, UK. http://www.stanstedtoymuseum.com. A collection of over 80,000 playthings, ranging from the late Victorian era to the 1990s. The collection includes dolls and dollhouses, puppets, tin and lead toys, model trains, toy soldiers, teddy bears, arcade games, die-cast toys, and rock-and-roll memorabilia.

Khudozhestvenno-pyedagogicheskiy muzei igrushki (Toy Museum of Art and Education), Pr Krasnoj Armii 123, Sergiyev Posad, Russian Federation. http://www.zagorsk.ru/history/mtoys. The museum displays toys found in archeological excavations, traditional Russian toys made of wood, clay, and *papier mâché*, toys from the Soviet period, and nesting dolls.

İstanbul Oyuncak Müzesi (Istanbul Toy Museum), Ömerpasha Caddesi Dr. Zeki Zeren Sok. 17, Göztepe, Istanbul, Turkey. http://www.istanbuloyuncakmuzesi.com/genel.asp. This museum, which opened in 2005, houses approximately two thousand toys from the collection of Turkish poet Sunay Akin.

Legoland, Nordmarksvej 9, Billund, Denmark; Legoland Allee, Günzburg, Germany; Winkfield Road, Windsor, Berkshire, UK. http://www.lego.com/legoland/portal. Theme parks in Denmark, Germany, and England, dedicated to LEGO toys. A fourth *Legoland* can be found in Carlsbad, California.

The Lilliput Antique Doll & Toy Museum, High St., Brading, Isle of Wight, UK. http://www.lilliputshop.com/museum.html. Originally based on a private doll collection started by the Munday family in 1960, the museum houses over 2,000 exhibits, including dolls, dollhouses, rocking horses, tin plate toys, trains, bears, and soft toys.

Mänguasjamuuseum (*Toy Museum*), Lutsu 8, Tartu, Estonia. http://www.mm.ee. The museum's collection consists of more than 6000 dolls and toys, including traditional Estonian handcrafted rag dolls, wooden horses, spinning tops, and reed ducks.

Miejskie Muzeum Zabawek ze Zbiorów Henryka Tomaszewskiego (The Municipal Museum of Toys from Henryk Tomaszewski's Collection), Ul. Karkonoska 5, Karpacz, Poland. http://www.muzeum zabawek.pti.pl. Among the museum's two thousand exhibits are tin, wind-up, wooden, porcelain, paper, wax, cloth, and terra-cotta dolls.

Muumimaailma (Moominworld), Naantali, Finland. http://www.muumimaailma.fi/englanti/index.html. A theme park based on a very popular series of books for children by Finnish writer Tove Jansson.

Musée de la Poupée (Doll Museum), Impasse Berthaud, Paris, France. http://www.museede lapoupeeparis.com. The collection of about 500 nineteenth- and twentieth-century dolls originates from the private collection of Guido and Samy Odin.

Musée du Jouet (Toy Museum), 5, Rue du Murgin, Moirans-en-Montagne, France. http://www.museedu-jouet.fr. Situated in Moirans-en-Montagne, the toy capital of France, the museum focuses on the history of European toy making since the early nineteenth century.

Museo del Giocattolo e del Bambino (The Toy and Child Museum), Via Pitteri 56, Milan, Italy. http://www.museodelgiocattolo.it. This museum houses a large collection of toys dating from 1700 to1960. The collection includes tin toys, model trains, toy soldiers, and puppet theaters.

Museu del joguet de Catalunya (Toy Museum of Catalonia), Hotel Paris/c. Sant Pere, 1 , 17600 Figueres, Catalonia, Spain. http://www.mjc.cat. Founded in 1982, the museum houses over 8000 toys, including puppet theaters, model trains, dolls and dollhouses, Meccano, and toys for the blind.

Museu do Brinquedo (Toy Museum), Rua Visconde de Monserrate, Sintra, Portugal. http://www.museu-do-brinquedo.pt. A collection of more than 20,000 toys from the private collection of João Arbués Moreira.

Museu Valencià Del Joguet (Valencian Toy Museum), C/ Aurora Pérez Caballero, 4, Ibi, Spain. http://www.museojuguete.com/noframes_e.html. The museum houses over 4,000 toys from around the world.

Museum hraček (Toy Museum), Jiřská 6, Prague, Czech Republic. http://www.muzeumhracek.cz. Part of the Steiger family collection of classic European and American toys.

Múzeum bábkarských kultúr a hračiek (Museum of Puppet Culture and Toys), Zámockáčíslo 1, Modrý Kameň, Slovakia. http://www.snm.sk. This museum, situated in a Baroque manor, is dedicated to the history of puppet theater and toys.

Österreichisches Spielemuseum Leopoldsdorf (Austrian Museum of Games), Raasdorferstrasse 28, Leopoldsdorf, Austria. http://www.spielemuseum.at. The museum houses a documentation center and a collection of contemporary games.

Pomskizillious Museum of Toys, 10 Gnien Xibla St., Xaghra Gozo, Malta. http://www.gozo.gov.mt. A private collection of mostly European toys from the nineteenth and twentieth century, the museum is housed within two rooms of an eighteenth-century converted farmhouse.

Speelgoedmuseum (Toy Museum), Nekkerspoel 21, Mechelen, Belgium. http://www.speelgoed museum.be. A permanent collection of toys from around the world. Highlights include an interactive Pieter Brueghel–style painting and a model of the Battle of Waterloo made with 8007 toy soldiers.

Spielzeugmuseum Nürnberg (Nuremberg Toy Museum), Karlstrasse 13–15, Nürnberg, Germany. http://www.spielzeugmuseum-nuernberg.de. The collection, originating from a donation by Lydia and Paul Bayer, includes dolls, dollhouses, wooden figurines, and tin toys. A major attraction is a 30-square-meter working model train set.

Spielzeugmuseum (Toy Museum), Bürgerspitalgasse 2, Salzburg, Austria. http://www.smca.at/spielzeugmuseum.html. A collection of toys from the fifteenth century onward.

Szórakaténusz Toy Museum, Gáspár András utca 11, Kecskemét, Hungary. http://www.szorakatenusz.hu. A collection of more than 15,000 toys, including folk toys and musical instruments from the Carpathian Mountains.

NOTES

1. In this book, sporting games and gambling on sports are separate topics, covered in the chapter "Sports and Recreation."
2. Cross and Smits 2005 (in Resource Guide), p. 885.

LITERATURE

LUCA PRONO

To address the problem of a "European popular literature" means to confront two terms, "European" and "popular," that are constantly shifting in their meanings. If the notion of "popular" is murky, then to impose homogeneity on diverse literary works under the rubric of "European" is problematic, too. Conceiving a unified "European literature" implies an ideological operation, a foundational myth of the common identity of diverse peoples. European literary unity, as well as the region's social and political unity, is constantly being negotiated as the European Union opens its borders eastward. How exactly to define one great culture shared from Reykjavik to Palermo remains problematic. In the past, critics have argued for the essential unity of European literatures whose common literary heritage originated in ancient Greece and Rome. This common past was preserved, transformed, and spread by Christianity both within Europe and, through colonization, throughout the regions settled by Europeans. More recently, the rise of postcolonial studies has challenged these assumptions.

Applying the term "popular" to literature raises problems as well. Since its beginning, the trade in printed books has been conceived of as a capitalist industry, whose main aim was to sell books for profit. Publishers, readers, and writers are thus linked by commodity relations: publishers buy manuscripts from writers in order to sell them to readers. The history of publishing has been characterized by a search for ways to increase the numbers of books published and the speed of their publication. The establishment of a mass market in the printing industry was facilitated by the invention of the cylinder press in the nineteenth century, which led to the quick printing of large quantities of books. The expansion of the printing industry is a typically bourgeois phenomenon, and it was induced by new formats of middle-class reading. These formats started to flourish in the eighteenth century and were developed fully in the nineteenth and twentieth centuries: the newspaper, the periodical, and the novel. The growth of popular literature corresponded with the spread of literacy. With the Industrial Revolution, literary works, which were previously produced for the consumption of small and well-educated elites, became accessible to large sections of European society.

Just how large these sections are, though, is still a disputed topic, and statistics are not always of help. For example, the *Publishing Market Watch Final Report*, presented to the

CAPITALISM AND THE EUROPEAN BOOK MARKET

In Western European countries the book market has not been completely shaped by the principles of laissez-faire capitalism. For decades, European legislators have debated whether book prices should be fixed or free. Fixed prices, also referred to as Retail Price Maintenance (RPM), imply that the publisher sets the sales price of a book. Free prices mean bookshops and other retailers may sell the book at whatever price they choose. States where fixed pricing for books applies include Austria, Denmark, France, Germany, Greece, Italy, the Netherlands, Portugal, Spain, and Hungary. The other European states have either never had a fixed price system or abolished it several years ago. Belgium has opted for a compromise between the two systems: the level of discount is restricted for six months, after which there are no restrictions.

In general, the European Union encourages free competition, and its member states usually aim at encouraging free prices on all goods. Yet in many countries, mainly based on cultural arguments, the book trade has been granted an exemption from this principle of free competition. Thus, as Marc Baruch and Jean Richard have argued, "culture is not a mere commodity which can be reduced to economic exchanges, nor is it to be treated as an 'exception' to market rules: it is part and parcel of the fabric and dynamic development of societies. Books and cultural products are therefore the object of specific cultural policies that can only be effective if they take into account the specific economic constraints under which cultural industries operate."[1] Baruch and Richard distinguish between an Anglo-Scandinavian and a Southern European model. The former "rejects any retail price mechanisms regulating demand on the ground of economic inter-liberalism" and because libraries constitute vast networks disseminated throughout the countries, "arrangements have long existed for compensating authors and publishers for the loss of earnings resulting from the lending by a library of the same work to different people who might otherwise have purchased it."[2] The extension of this system, which in English is called the "public lending right," has become one of the cultural policies of the European Union. In the Southern European model in contrast, libraries are not as central to the dissemination of books or have been only recently developed. Most experts on the book trade emphasize that books have a dual role as cultural and economic products.

European Commission in January 2005 by Rightscom, a specialist consultancy based in London, and by the Turku School of Economics and Business, contains statistics on book markets in EU member states. Yet the analysts themselves have had to admit that there are some serious gaps in the data from the countries included in the study. An additional problem is represented by the sources used to gain the data: the national branch associations of book publishers. Because these publishers only collect data from members, they usually underestimate the size of national markets. The data from booksellers would be more reliable, but these are only available for few countries. The total reported sales in European book markets amounted to €26.6 billion in 2000. But, as the *Final Report* admits, the data are hardly precise. The Federation of European Publishers has estimated the value of book sales at €29 billion.[3] With such conflicting data, all discussion has to proceed with caution.

The end of Nazi/fascist dictatorships in Central and Southern Europe as well as the later fall of Communist regimes in Eastern Europe were major events in the twentieth century that shaped book markets both ideologically and economically. The collapse of totalitarian regimes represented a loosening of censorship, which allowed literature to be produced more freely. The transition from rigidly planned economies to a free market system has fundamentally changed the conditions of the book market. In former Communist countries, this process has caused an enormous increase in publishing companies since the 1990s. This growth has, in turn, caused a significant growth in titles published. However, this phenomenon has not always meant a rise in book sales, given the adverse economic conditions that Easter European countries had to face in the aftermath of Communism's demise. The growing number of titles published and the decline of book sales led to a decrease in print runs. The Hungarian market exemplifies these apparently contrasting trends. The number of published titles steadily rose from 7,599 in 1989 to 10,626 in 1998 and decreased only slightly to 9,990 in 2002. Yet the average print run constantly declined from 14,300 in 1989 to only 3,690 in 2002. The amount of business done, or turnover, from books grew from 24.4 billion forint in 1997 to 53.6 billion forint in 2002. The sharp decrease in print runs threatens the existence of smaller, independent publishers, who cannot exploit their bestselling titles to compensate for those they publish at a loss.

Central and Eastern European governments tried to limit foreign acquisition of their publishers by supporting them in the transition to a market economy after 1989. Several foundations were established to encourage both the production of domestic literature and the translation of domestic literature into foreign languages. These efforts were also supported by Western European public and private institutions such as the Soros Foundation, the Council of Europe, the Frankfurt Book Fair, and the Fund for Central and East European Book Projects.

The end of the Cold War in the 1990s also meant a sharp decrease in the number of translations from Russian published in formerly Communist countries: translations from Russian as the source declined from 6,450 in 1980 to 1,193 in 1994. The same phenomenon, although in more limited proportions, occurred for translations from all Eastern bloc languages. The flow of translations is now dominated by a few influential languages: English, German, and French. Translation rights of popular Eastern European authors often pass through German or British agents, thus making it impossible for small local publishers to hold on to the writers they initially discover.

The following pages will survey the book markets and the contributions to popular literatures of the different European areas and countries. The phrase "popular literature" usually refers to those writings that are designed for the masses and those that reach large audiences. Their primary aims are practical: to entertain, to educate, and to enhance readers' knowledge in a particular area. In the past, this has led critics to draw a line between popular and artistic or "high" literature. Popular literature, in contrast to high literature, does not seek a formal complexity and is more ephemeral in its themes and contents. However, the boundary between artistic and popular literature is rather unstable.

The most important fictional genres in popular literature are the romance, describing the obstacles encountered by two people in their (possibly forbidden) love; fantasy or science fiction; detective fiction; and children's literature. According to the 2002 Eurostat report on "Europeans' Participation in Cultural Activities," the majority of readers in the original fifteen members of the European Union read books for reasons other than work or study (44.8 percent), while 42.1 percent indicated they had not read any books at all. Of those who had read for reasons other than work or study, 33.3 percent had read between 1 and 3 books, 25.3 percent had read between 4 and 7 books, 15.9 percent had read between 8 and 12 books, while 19.6 percent had read 13 books or more. According to a 2003 Eurostat survey on new member and candidate countries, the percentage of those who had not read any books increased to 47 percent, while the percentage of those who had read for reasons other than school or work decreased to 38 percent.

The biggest European market by sales value was Germany, totaling around €9.4 billion in 2000 and 2001, but decreasing slightly in 2002. This represented one-third of the total market within the fifteen original European Union member states. The second biggest market was the United Kingdom, with sales around €5.5 billion in 2002. France, Spain, and Italy also had large book markets. If the amount of money spent on books per capita was considered, Germany and Britain still led, but countries such as Austria, Belgium, Denmark, Finland, and Sweden moved higher in the comparison.

AUSTRIA

Between 1998 and 2002, book sales in Austria fell by 8.7 percent in terms of volume, but grew 7.8 percent in terms of value. These contrasting trends were largely the result of strong increases in book prices, while changes in leisure habits away from reading accounted for the lower volume sales. In 2002, 38 percent of Austrians said they had not read any books in the previous year, 12 percent had read books for work, 14 percent had read compulsory texts for their education, 21 percent had read noncompulsory texts for their education, while 43 percent said they had read books for reasons other than work or study. Book sales per capita were estimated at €80 in the year 2000.

As far as formats are concerned, paperback sales represented 51.6 percent of the market in 2002, compared with 45.5 percent for hardbacks and 2.8 percent for electronic formats. The latter, however, was the fastest-growing sector, experiencing a phenomenal increase of 83.5 percent in volume terms and 72.4 percent in value between 1998 and 2002. Nonfiction titles accounted for 64.1 percent of the market in 2002, although their share declined slightly between 1998 and 2002, reflecting a fall in volume sales of hardbacks, which is the main format for nonfiction.

The total number of printing and publishing companies decreased between 1996 and 2000, and two publishers now dominate the Austrian market: Österreichischer Bundesverlag (ÖBV), now owned by German company Klett Gruppe, and Ueberreuter. Contrary to what happened in most European countries, independent booksellers remained by far the most important outlet for institutional distribution, accounting for 82.5 percent of sales in 2002. Local schools and state-funded bodies such as libraries are encouraged to spend most of their budgets within their own community.

An important segment of Austrian nonfiction books has centered on the popular icon of Elisabeth of Bavaria, better known as Sisi or Sissi from the films based on her life, whose myth flourished particularly in the second half of the twentieth century. Her free spirit and her dislike for official protocol inspired many biographers such as Brigitte Hamann (*The Reluctant Empress: A Biography of Empress Elisabeth of Austria*), Ludwig Merkles (*Sissi: The Tragic Empress*), Egon C. C. Corti (*Elisabeth*), and Renate Stephan (*Kaiserin Elisabeth von Österreich 1837–1898*). She has also inspired the cookbook *Menues à la Kaiserin Elisabeth* by Tino Gleichenstein.

Although generally neglected by Anglo-American critics, detective fiction has a long tradition in Austria. In the earlier part of the twentieth century, Baldwin Groller created Detective Dagobert (*Detektiv Dagobert: Taten und Abenteuer* [Deeds and Adventures]). Adolph Weissl also acquired an extensive reputation as a writer of detective stories (*Schwarze Perlen*

[Black Pearls] and *Das grüne Auto* [The Green Car]). Heimito von Doderer contributed some excellent mysteries, including *Every Man a Murderer* and *The Waterfalls of Slunj*. The postmodern writer Peter Handke used mystery conventions in his *Der Hausierer* [The Peddler], and Marianne Gruberhas published several successful mysteries such as *Windstille* [Calm] and *Tod des Regenpfeifers: Zwei Erzählungen* [Death of a Plover and Trace of the Buckskin].

Two of the most important contemporary Austrian writers of children's literature are Reinhardt Jung, author of *Bambert's Book of Missing Stories* and *Dreaming in Black and White*, and Christine Nöstlinger (*Fly Away Home, Conrad the Factory-Made Boy*, and *A Dog's Life*). The Hungarian-born Felix Salten lived in Vienna for the most productive part of his life when he wrote the children's classic *Bambi* as well as the popular *Florian, the Emperor's Stallion*.

Internationally renowned for its Sacher torte, the chocolate glazed cake lined with jam, Austrian cuisine is described in several important cookbooks such as *To Set before the King: Katharina Schratt's Festive Recipes*, edited by Gertrud Graubart Champe; *Austrian Cooking and Baking* by Gretel Beer; *Tyrolean Cook-Book* by Maria Drewes; and *Die Gute Küche: Das Oesterreichische Jahrhundert Kochbuch* [The Good Cuisine: The Austrian Century Cookbook] by Plachutta and Wagner.

Among contemporary Austrian writers whose works have won international attention are Ilse Aichinger, Ingeborg Bachmann, and Peter Handke.

THE BALKANS: SLOVENIA, CROATIA, SERBIA AND MONTENEGRO, BOSNIA-HERZEGOVINA, MACEDONIA, AND ALBANIA

The breakup of the former socialist Yugoslavian Republic and the ensuing wars of the 1990s, characterized by ethnic cleansing and massacres, have had a disastrous impact on the lives of people in the region. Cultural symbols such as the Bosnian National Library were prime targets. The conflicts, which resulted in armed interventions of NATO forces, touched all the countries in the area with the exception of Slovenia, leaving their economies and their societies in ruins. Macedonia and Montenegro were only marginally involved, while Croatia, Bosnia, and Kosovo (an Albanian enclave in Serbia) were the lands where major battles were fought. As citizens of these countries have had to struggle for basic goods, it is no surprise that the book market there cannot be compared to that of other regions in Western Europe.

In spite of the totalitarian Communist regime led by General Tito from the 1940s to the 1980s, Yugoslavia had a rich cultural life. Belgrade and Zagreb had big universities, each with more than 50,000 students, while smaller universities could be found in Sarajevo and Ljubljana. Cities such as Pristina, Rijeka, Zada, Dubrovnik, and Novi Sad offered institutes of further education with corresponding libraries. The annual book fair in Belgrade was an international event for intellectual encounters and debates. Publishing was well developed and of a high standard in the six republics, and the most successful international titles of the 1970s and 1980s were translated. International co-production projects for atlases, cookery books, art books, or books for children often included Yugoslavian publishers. Nevertheless, censorship hit authors such as Milovan Djilas, Vlado Gotovac, and the future President of Bosnia-Herzegovina, Alija Izetbegovic, who were all charged with nationalistic thinking.

The dissolution of the Socialist Federal Republic of Yugoslavia, beginning in the 1990s, caused the disintegration of a unified cultural community as well as material damage to cultural infrastructures such as schools, academies, libraries, publishing companies, and sales and distribution facilities. Censorship was strongly enforced in Serbia, Croatia, and Kosovo, as well as in the Croatian- and Serbian-dominated parts of Bosnia during the 1990s. To a certain extent, this situation continued into the new millennium. However, Macedonia,

CHILDREN'S LITERATURE IN THE BALKANS

Modern trends in children's literature of the region alternate between the traditional genres of the folkloric tradition and a more complex realism in novels and science fiction. The founding father of twentieth-century Serbian children's literature was Alexandar Vuco. Grigor Vitez, Dusan Radovic, Dragan Lukic, Miroslav Antic, Milovan Danojlic, and Ljubivoje Rsumovic further developed this literary sector after World War II. More contemporary writers include Vladimir Stojsin, Vladimir Stojiljkovic, Mirjana Stefanovic, Zoran Stanojevic, Vladimir Andric, and Zoran Popovic. In Bosnia children's literature reflects the tragedy of war with titles such as Advan Hozić's stories *Na kraju placa* [In the End of Marketplace]; *Diary* by Zlata Filipović, a child's diary written during the war; and Alija Duboćanin's *Pas pismonoša* [The Post Dog], a photo-realistic picture book of the war horrors in Sarajevo as experienced by a young girl and her dog. Ferida Duraković is also a well-known writer of children's literature whose books include *Amilina abeceda* [Amilia's Alphabet], *Jos jedna bajka o ruzi* [Another Fairy Tale about a Rose], *Mikijeva abeceda* [Mickey's Alphabet], and *Najnovije vijesti iz Sarajeva* [The Latest News from Sarajevo].

In Albania, the modernization of children's literature is linked to the process of democratization after 1991. Fantasy began as a major mode of narration for Sokol Jakova's fairy-tale novels such as *The Adventure of Brave Mirosh* and Mira Meksi's *Planetthi i ngrirë* [The Little Icy Planet]. Jorgji Kodra writes collections of fairy tales and short stories such as *The Boy Who Ignored the Time* and *Vocabulary within One Week*. Thanas Pilafa has written ten novels for children such as *Great Dreams* and *How I Became a Robinson*. Gaqo Bushaka, Dalan Shapllo, Ferit Lamaj, and Stavari Pon all write within the fairy-tale tradition.

Viktor Canosinaj's *They Were Looking for Happiness* and *Meriyll*, Ramadan Pasmaciu's *Childhood Paths*, Chmiter Xhuvani's *Street Children*, and Bedri Dedja's *Revolution in a Flat in Tirana* and *A Dangerous Trip* all use a realistic mode to portray children's problems in the modern family, at school, and against the background of a changing society.

Slovenia, Bosnia, and, increasingly, Montenegro are emerging as democracies virtually free from censorship. The geographic extremes of the region are also at opposite poles as far as economic standards are concerned: Slovenia is close to European counties in terms of individual income and employment, while Kosovo is still dependent on international aid.

Data on the book market in the Balkans are still scarce and refer to the year 2000. Based on those data, about 4,000 new titles are published annually in Slovenia; 2,500 in Croatia; 5,000 in Serbia and Montenegro, and 1,000 each in Bosnia-Herzegovina and Kosovo. Every year about 3,000 new books are published in Albania. There are no figures for the total amount of book sales in Croatia and in Serbia, while in Bosnia they totaled $2.2 million, in Macedonia $1.2 million, and $5.6 million in Albania. Publishing firms were destroyed during the war, and, in the case of Serbia, the book market hardly thrived under the totalitarian state economy imposed by President Milošević until 2000. The Croatian market, while not run within a socialist economy since the country's secession, still suffered from the authoritarian regime of Franjo Tudjman until 1999. The Croatian cultural scene is characterized by high book prices, with an average of 129 kunas (€17) for both hardback and paperback; very few libraries and bookshops (a total of 80 bookshops was reported in 2003); and low print runs. To develop their markets more fully, Serbia and Croatia will have to learn to cooperate, given that they speak the same language and thus share a readership. Contrary to their counterparts in Bosnia, Croatia, Kosovo, and to a certain extent, Serbia, Slovenian publishers were not ruined by the war and continue to operate successfully in the international market.

The popular culture of the region is directly linked to the re-creation of the different identities after the conflicts. A new translation of the Koran into Bosnian appeared in 1995 by theologian and writer Enes Karic. Ivan Lovrenovic contributed to the establishment of a national heritage with his *Bosnia: A Cultural History*. In *Sarajevo Blues*, Semezdin Mehmedinovic described the eruption of war in Bosnia through poems and stories, while the poems in *The Ninth Alexandria* focus on the author's journey through the United States after 9/11. The siege of Sarajevo has also been the subject of Dzevad Karahasan's *Diary of Resettlement*, which has been translated into ten languages, and of his novels *Schahrijars Ring* and *Sara and Serafina*. Slavenka Drakulic chronicled atrocities against Bosnian women (*S: A Novel about the Balkans*) as well as the Serbian war-crimes trial in the Hague (*They Would Never Hurt a Fly*). Svetlana Broz, a granddaughter of Tito and thus a Serb living in Bosnia, reconstructed acts of mutual help and resistance in *Good People in Times of Evil*. Other Bosnian authors who have reached an international readership include Marko Vesovic, Irfan Horozovic, Miljenko Jergovic, and Aleksandar Hemon, who immigrated to the United States at the beginning of the war and now writes in English (*Nowhere Man* and *The Question of Bruno*). Many successful Serbian writers decided to live in exile rather than under the Miloševic regime, including Vidosav Stevanovic (*Milosevic: The People's Tyrant*), the Croat-born Bora Cosic (*My Family's Role in the World Revolution*), David Albahari, Mirko Kovac, and Dragan Velikic. Slovenian writers such as Tomaz Salamun, Ales Debeljak, Drago Jancar, Andrej Blatnik, and Peri Lainseck have succeeded in reaching a wide international audience.

Popular comics in the region also echo the tragedy of war. A comic book featuring Superman was distributed to thousands of Albanian children refugees in and near Kosovo to teach them to spot and avoid land mines. A similar Superman comic was distributed in Bosnia after the war.

BELGIUM

Belgian literary production is divided into works written in Flemish and in French, a division that reflects the separation of the country into two linguistic areas. The 2002 Eurostat report on "Europeans' Participation in Cultural Activities" singled out Belgium as an exception among Northern European countries. While in most of these countries there is a higher tendency to read than in other regions, 58 percent of Belgians admitted not having read any book in 2002, 4 percent had read books for work, 8 percent had read compulsory texts for their education, 18 percent had read noncompulsory texts for their education, while 23 percent said they had read books for reasons other than work or study. Between 1998 and 2002, total book sales in Belgium remained more or less stable at 63 million books. However, in value terms, the market increased from €1 billion in 1998 to €1.1 billion in 2002. The average household expenditure for books reached €120 in 2002, and Belgians regularly visit one of their 867 libraries. Because Belgium does not follow the fixed price system for books, there is a high degree of competition among booksellers.

The most famous Belgian popular author is the prolific Georges Simenon, the creator of Inspector Maigret and perhaps the most widely published author of the twentieth century. His total literary production consisted of about 425 books that were translated into fifty languages and sold more than 600 million copies worldwide. In addition to the Maigret novels, Simenon wrote autobiographical volumes as well as psychological novels that, like the Maigret novels, are characterized by their accurate observation of people and captivating rendering of the atmosphere. Contrary to those detectives who rely on their deductive powers to solve their cases, Maigret solves his by psychological insight into the minds of the murderers. In another genre, Pieter Aspe is considered the best contemporary Belgian short story writer.

Together with fellow novelists Thomas Owen (Gérald Bertot) and Stanislas-André Steeman, Jean Raymond Marie De Kremer, who wrote under the pseudonyms John Flanders and Jean Ray, was the author of popular detective and horror stories. Ray's stories were written both in Flemish and French and are among the most important fantasy writing in Belgium.

In comic strips, Belgium can claim the world-famous Tintin, Blake and Mortimer, Suske and Wiske, and Spirou. In particular, the Tintin strip by Hergé (Georges Rémi) proved internationally popular because of its realistic and relatively didactic content, centering on a kind of Boy Scout hero. Created in 1929, Tintin appeared in book form from 1948 onward. The books have been translated into about forty-five languages and dialects. Total sales are believed to exceed 160 million copies.

Belgian cuisine is celebrated in the cookbooks *Comme Chez Soi: Les Recettes Originales de Pierre Wynants* [Like at Home: The Original Recipes of Pierre Wynants], *Belgo Cookbook* by Denis Blais and André Plisnier, and *Everybody Eats Well in Belgium* by Ruth Van Waerebeek.

BULGARIA AND ROMANIA

Bulgaria and Romania are still struggling to come to terms with the disastrous economic and social legacies of their totalitarian Communist regimes, with an unemployment rate close to 20 percent and a high rate of inflation. Data on the book market are extremely scarce. In Bulgaria, total sales for the year 2000 amounted to roughly €6 million. In 2002, there were 7,976 titles produced at the average price of €7 for hardcover and €3 to €4 for paperbacks. Over 3,000 publishing houses were registered with ISBN prefixes in 2003; however, only 150 were actually productive, and most of the books were produced by 30 to 40 publishing firms. Bulgaria has about 400 bookshops.

In Romania 6,393 titles were produced in 2002, a 2 percent growth in comparison to the previous year. The number of new titles was also on the rise at 4,528, a 2.5 percent increase. Romania has a fixed price policy, and the average cost for a paperback is €2.7. There are no statistics available on the number of bookshops. Many of the former state-owned bookshops have been privatized, although some have closed down.

As far as popular genres are concerned, since the fall of Communism, Bulgarian children's literature has displayed thematic diversity and original authorial styles. Lilia Ratcheva, Tsvetan Peshev, Chavdar Shinov, and Anastas Stoyanov employ the fairy-tale structure to talk about contemporary problems. Kina Kadreva's *Prikazka za palavoto skakalche* [The Story of the Little Grasshopper Who Could Not Hop] and Yordan Radichkov's *Malki Zhabeshki Istorii* [Small Frog Stories] use animal tales as allegories of contemporary society. Kina Kadreva, Mile Markovski, Roumen Shomov, and Petya Aleksandrova all make use of nonsense in their writings. Mystery and fantasy are present in Ivan Tsanev's *Vesela misterija* [Funny Mystery] and in Krasimir Mircev's *Vampiri—Gunduraci—Zmej* [Vampires—Centaurs—Dragons].

A similar loosening of censorship has allowed for more creativity in Romanian children's literature with the development of realistic stories such as Monica Savulescu-Voudouris's *Un alt glob, va rog!* [A Different Globe, Please], as well as the more traditional folktales of Eugenia Doina Gemala's *Legende din tinuturi dobrogene* [Legends from Dobrudja].

Cookbooks for the region include Atanas Slavov's *Traditional Bulgarian Cookbook* and Nicolae Klepper's *Taste of Romania*.

THE CZECH REPUBLIC AND SLOVAKIA

The transition of the former socialist state of Czechoslovakia to the European Union has produced many internal tensions as well as the peaceful separation of the country into two states, the Czech Republic and Slovakia, which took place on January 1, 2003. With the standard of living in the region higher than in most of the formerly Communist countries, the Czech book market is the second largest of the ten new EU member states in terms of book published. In 2003 more than 16,000 titles were published for a turnover of about €140 million. In spite of the large number of books published, the Czech market is hampered by poor distribution. There are about 600 bookstores in the country, a number which increases to 2,000 if sales outlets such as supermarkets are included. Czech publishers complain about the lack of capital of wholesalers and bookstores. An important sector of the market is covered by the book club Euromedia—Knizhní Klub (the Czech branch of the German publisher Bertelsmann), which reaches about 230,000 readers. The average price for a hardback is about €6.25, and prices have undergone a substantial increase since 1989. The number of publishers increased enormously from around 100 before the fall of the Communist regime to 3,492 in 2004, with a traditionally large sector devoted almost entirely to children's literature. This large number of children's publishers is the result of the censorship imposed by the regime until 1989: books for children were thought to be less controversial than adult literature; therefore, many authors wrote children's books. Because of the uncertainties that are still plaguing the market, Czech publishers are keener to translate international bestsellers rather than risk publishing local authors.

Science fiction writing had one of its founding fathers in the former Czechoslovakia with the writer Karel Čapek, who first employed the word "robot" in its modern meaning in his *R.U.R.* [Rossum's Universal Robots] in 1920. Čapek also wrote detective stories. More contemporary authors who have written thrillers include Pavel Kohout (*The Widow Killer*) and the exiled Josef Škvorecký (*The Mournful Demeanor of Ltn. Boruvka* and *The Return of Ltn. Boruvka*).

The most successful Czech author internationally is Milan Kundera, whose books combine erotic tales with political criticism. Because Kundera took part in the brief revolution of 1967–68 against Stalinism, he later immigrated to France, where he worked as a university lecturer. His most successful works, such as *The Book of Laughter and Forgetting* and *The Unbearable Lightness of Being*, were published there. Because of their sarcastic view of the Communist regime, Kundera's books were banned in Czechoslovakia until 1989 in spite of being bestsellers in Western European countries.

Peter Sis is the best known Czech children's author and illustrator. He has been living in the United States since the mid-1980s. In *The Three Golden Keys*, Sis re-creates his childhood in Prague, celebrating the rebirth of the city after the years of the Communist regime. Several Czech children's books are devoted to the fate of the many Jewish children who were imprisoned and executed in the Terezin concentration camp when Czechoslovakia was occupied by Nazi Germany.

The Museum Guild of the National Czech & Slovak Museum & Library has produced two popular cookbooks: *Quality Dumplings Recipes* and *Czech & Slovak Kolache Recipes & Sweet Treats*. Joza Brizova is the author of the bestselling *Varime Zdrave Chutne a Hospodarne*, which has been translated in English as *The Czechoslovak Cookbook*.

ESTONIA, LATVIA, AND LITHUANIA

Commonly referred to as Baltic states, Estonia, Latvia, and Lithuania came under direct Soviet rule after the end of World War II and were thus subject to the restrictions imposed by the USSR. All publishers were owned by the state, and books were censored to conform to the ideology of the regime and to suppress national cultures. Independent by 1991, the Baltic states have undergone important economic and political changes affecting all sectors of society, including the book market. Neither state-owned publishing houses nor the former monopolistic distribution system characterize the book market any longer. The sector is now privatized, with the exception of some book stores that are still owned by town councils. Although the Baltic states have a strong cultural tradition as far as reading and writing are concerned, book markets in Estonia, Latvia, and Lithuania are still limited in size.

As in other Central and Eastern European countries, the transition to a free market economy has produced contrasting data. The high level of literacy did not stop the significant decline of reading activities during the 1990s. In the case of Latvia, readership surveys show that approximately 20 percent of the Latvian population does not read books at all (not a single book during the past five years). This is also reflected in a falling number of publications per capita. Latvia is in third place with only 2.9 books per capita, Estonia takes the first place with 4.9 books, and Lithuania is second with 3.5 books published per capita. The transition to a free market economy has multiplied the number of publishers and books published per year. In Latvia the number of titles produced doubled between 1991 and 1999. In Lithuania the number of publishers grew from 6 during the Soviet era to 500 in the year 2000, although only 4 produced more than 100 titles. Yet, at the same time, the number of titles sold has dramatically decreased. In Lithuania, this is particularly apparent: 35 million copies were sold in 1991 and only 13.4 million were sold in 1998. The result is increasing consumer prices and reduced purchasing power, implying that people in general buy fewer books and visit bookshops less.

The end of Soviet censorship provoked a renewed interest in books dealing with national cultures, spirituality, and esoteric topics. Books that had been forbidden because of these kinds of subjects, such as Saulius Tomas Kondrotas's *A Glance of the Serpent*, could be published after independence. Another important trend in Baltic book markets is the increase in the number of translated works. This reflects the demand for Western foreign literatures after independence. In Lithuania, for example, translations constitute almost a third of all published titles; in Estonia books have been translated from as many as fifty languages. By contrast, translations of Russian books have decreased and are limited in almost all cases to classics. Since the end of the Soviet domination, the crimes committed by the Communist regime and the dreary life under foreign rule have been the subject of many popular books, such as *Indigo* by Peeter Sauter, *The Conspiracy and Other Stories* by acclaimed Estonian writer Jaan Kross, *Three Moments of Sky* by Sigitas Parulskis, *The Poker in Vilnius* by Ricardas Gavelis, *Bille Trilogy* by Vizma

Belševica, and *Soviet Latvian Woman* and *Cheka, Bombs and Rock 'n Roll* by Pauls Bankovskis.

FRANCE

Between 1998 and 2002, the French book and publishing sector obtained strong results, which marked a considerable improvement from the early 1990s. Although book sales per capita remained low at a little more than €40 in 2000, total sales reached €2.5 billion in 2001, and the market enjoyed steady growth. Comics witnessed a disproportionate growth in comparison to the other sectors of the French book market. Although sales for the French book trade increased by an average of 3 percent in 2004, the figure was 4.5 percent for comics, and 2,618 new comics titles or new editions of comics were published in 2004. This was 37 percent more than the previous year, twice as many as in 2000, and four times as many as in 1995. In 2002, 40 percent of French people said they had not read any books in the previous year, 9 percent had read books for work, 11 percent had read compulsory texts for their education, 18 percent had read noncompulsory texts for their education, and 40 percent said they had read books for reasons other than work or study. Hardback is the most popular format, representing 70 percent of total books sales in 2001, while paperbacks accounted for 27 percent and electronic formats accounted for 4 percent of total volume sales. The average price for a hardback was €15, while it was €5 for a paperback.

In the years immediately following World War I, Paris became an international cultural center, attracting writers from Europe and the United States. The capital of France also became the capital of modernism and surrealism. Two poets who were originally part of the avant-garde, Jacques Prévert and Robert Desnos, later broke away from the movement and adopted more traditional forms; both also contributed screenplays for popular French films.

The two French women writers who worked most successfully in the romance genre are undoubtedly the prolific Colette (Sidonie-Gabrielle Colette) and Françoise Sagan (Françoise Quoirez). Their novels feature people involved in painful and, especially in Sagan's case, unconventional relationships.

Sometimes exploited by the writers of the Nouveau Roman, detective fiction was used in its more traditional and popular mode by writers such as Maurice Leblanc, Albert-Charles Simonin, and Léo Malet. Leblanc was a journalist who became famous as the creator of Arsène Lupin, the thief turned inspector. In his most famous works, *Touchez pas au grisbi!* [Don't Touch the Grisbi] and its sequel *Le cave se rebiffe* [The Angry Cave], Simonin used Parisian slang to more realistically represent the underworld of gangsters. The genre also received impetus from the establishment in 1945 of the *Série Noir* collection by the highly respected publisher Gallimard, which gathered the best French and international noir authors.

French children's literature in the first half of the twentieth century was marked by the publication of *Le Petit Prince* [The Little Prince] by the famous aviator-author Antoine de Saint-Exupéry. The book, which has become a children's classic, records the conversation between a little prince and an aviator who is trying to repair his plane in the Sahara. After 1945, important authors writing in the genre were Maurice Druon, who wrote *Tistou of the Green Fingers*, a moral tale reminiscent of *Candide*, and Henri Bosco, who focused on the adventure of Pascalet in an eerie world. In addition to books, the Astérix strip, created by René Goscinny and Albert Uderzo in the late 1950s, became a children's favorite even beyond France.

One of the most popular contemporary French writers, Daniel Pennac, has worked both in the genre of detective fiction and in children's literature, although his popularity is largely the result of the Belleville cycle, which includes the novels *La Fée carabine* [The Fairy Gunmother], and *Monsieur Malaussène*. Set in a rundown multiracial Parisian area, the series mixes the conventions of detective fiction with a surrealist tone and has proved highly entertaining to readers. The most controversial and successful French writer is certainly Michel Houellebecq, whose books, set in a darker future, have been branded as racist, homophobic, and pornographic as well as poetic and moving.

French cooking, whether the rich classical style or the Nouvelle Cuisine that became popular in the 1970s as a reaction to the former, is illustrated in famous cookbooks such as *Le Guide Culinaire* [The Complete Guide to the Art of Modern Cooking] by Auguste Escoffier and *La cuisine du marché* [The Cuisine of the Market] by Paul Bocuse.

GERMANY

The German book market is the largest in Europe and second in the world only to that of the United States, although it has been declining for several years. Important international publishing groups such as Bertelsmann (owner of Random House) and the Holtzbrinck group have their corporate headquarters in Germany. According to the European Bookseller Federation, Germany has 7,400 bookshops, which amounts to one bookshop per 11,000 inhabitants. There are quality bookshops in every town. In spite of this, 41 percent of Germans said in a 2002 survey that they had not read a book within the previous year, while 15 percent had read books for their work, 16 percent had read compulsory books for educational purposes, 21 percent had read noncompulsory books for educational purposes, and 40 percent had read books for reasons other than work or study.

In 2003 the industry's sales turnover dropped by 1.7 percent to €9.1 billion. This decline had been more evident in 2002, when sales fell by 2 percent. In fact, the classic retail book trade registered a drop in sales of 2.5 percent in 2003. Department stores (-2.6 percent) and book clubs (-1.3 percent) also noted decreased sales. The only sector gaining ground was the mail-order book trade, which increased its sales by 1.5 percent. This increase was largely the result of online book sales, which grew by 10 percent to between €350 million and €400 million. Sales turnover for German book publishing companies declined by 1.1 percent in 2003, an improvement after the 2.8 percent drop the previous year. Since the German book market has been affected by the weak overall economy, there has been little or no growth for more than a decade. Nevertheless, the number of books produced actually increased in 2003 by 2.6 percent to a total of 80,971. Since 2002, Germany has fixed book prices by law: the average price is €26.31 for hardbacks and €11.98 for paperbacks. The four top German publishing houses are Bertelsmann, the Holtzbrinck group, Bonnier/Piper, and Verlagsgruppe Luebbe. Taken together, they control 73.9 percent of the German book market.

In Germany there is a long popular tradition of detective fiction. The most successful German detective series is *Jerry Cotton*, which centers on the FBI agent Jerry Cotton. It has been published in more than fifty countries, has sold over 750 million copies worldwide, and is still in print today. The series, which started in the 1950s, was created by Delfried Kaufmann and has been continued by more than sixty writers, all of whom have remained anonymous. A popular writer in the genre and one of the best known outside Germany is Jakob Arjouni, who has created a Turkish-German detective named Kemal Kayankaya (*Happy Birthday Turk* and *One Man, One Murder*). Referred to as "the Queen of German Crime," Pieke Biermann is a prolific author of hard-boiled mysteries featuring inspector

Karin Lietze (*Violetta*). Other successful German women writers in the detective genre include Ingrid Noll (*Hell Hath No Fury* and *The Pharmacist*) and Doris Gercke, whose *How Many Miles to Babylon* features the policewoman Bella Block.

The German tradition of children's stories can count on illustrious names such as those of the Brothers Grimm, who are still very popular today. Michael Ende was one of the most celebrated children's authors, contributing to the genre such masterpieces as *Momo* and *The Neverending Story.* Contemporary bestselling authors in the fantasy realm include Cornelia Funke (*Inkspell, Inkheart,* and *The Thief Lord*), Hans Magnus Enzensberger (*Where Were You, Robert?*) and Kai Meyer (*The Flowing Queen*). There are also numerous authors of German children's books dealing with the Holocaust. For example, Mirjam Pressler, who also edited *The Diary of Anne Frank* with Otto Frank, wrote the compelling novella *Malka,* based on the true story of a Jewish girl who tried to escape the Nazis with her family. Monika Feth's bestselling *The Strawberry Picker* was written instead in the tradition of the German detective story.

While his books do not belong to the realm of popular literature, Nobel Prize winner Günther Grass continues to write successful and controversial novels that deal with Germany's repressed past. Heinz Konsalik was one of Germany's most prolific authors; his books have sold more than 80 million copies worldwide.

GREECE

Among the fifteen original members of the European Union, Greece has the third highest percentage of people (58 percent) who, in 2002, admitted they had not read any book during the previous year. Only 36 percent of Greeks said they read for reasons other than work or study, while 5 percent said they had read for their work, 11 percent had read compulsory books for their education, and 9 percent had read noncompulsory texts for their education. In spite of these unfavourable reading habits, the Greek book market has grown since the fall of the military regime in 1974. The number of books published doubled between 1990 and 2002, from about 3,000 to almost 7,000 per year, a number that stabilized between 1998 and 2002. The Retail Price Maintenance Law for books, enacted in 1997, has protected the profit margins of small publishing houses against large booksellers that were offering competitive discounts to readers. The Greek publishing industry, however, is changing fast, with a few big companies aspiring to become absolute market leaders.

Only 141 Greek companies publish more than ten book titles per year. Approximately 21 percent of Greek books are produced by the five biggest publishers, and the percentage increases to 37 percent if the largest fifteen firms are taken into account. Greek books are distributed through 2,000 bookstores, although fewer than 300 of them sell books exclusively. There are also 1,500 sale outlets, including press agencies, supermarkets, and kiosks. These data show a low degree of concentration in the retail sales channel: branches of the two largest chains, *Papasotiriou* and *Eleftheroudakis*, do not number more than twenty locations.

Popular Greek children's authors include Penelope Delta, Eugene Trivizas, Manos Kontoleon, Voula Mastori, and the prolific Loty Petrovits Androutsopoulou. Successful contemporary fiction authors include Andreas Staikos (*Les Liasons Culinaires*); Pavlos Matesis (*The Daughter*); Alexis Stamatis (*The Seventh Elephant* and *Bar Flaubert*); Petros Markaris, the creator of the successful mystery series featuring Inspector Costas Haritos; Rhea Galanaki (*Eleni, or Nobody*); and Ioanna Karystiani (*Jasmine Isle*).

HUNGARY

Hungary had an established book-buying and reading tradition before 1989 and the fall of the Communist regime. This phenomenon can be explained by the state subsidizing book prices and the comparative absence of leisure activities. More books were available to Hungarians during the Communist period than to citizens in other Eastern European countries because of the increasingly liberal cultural policy of the 1980s. Since the 1990s, the yearly number of titles and the average prices have grown steadily, while print runs have decreased. Between 1998 and 2002, titles published stabilized around 10,000 copies per year. The sales volume increased from €146 million to €232 million in 2003. The most popular volumes include business books, international bestsellers, illustrated lifestyle books, and children's books. The average price for a hardcover is €12, while a paperback costs an average of €8. There are around 400 publishing companies and 700 bookshops. Bookshops belonging to a chain account for 65 percent of total sales, while book clubs cover 15 percent of the market.

The increase in the number of publishing houses has been particularly beneficial to children's literature. Before 1989 only one publishing house (Móra) produced books for children; now more than twenty publishing houses list books for children in their catalogues, and five of them (Móra, Ciceró, Egmont, Passage, and Minerva Nova) publish children's books exclusively. Many Hungarian children's authors, such as Katalin Szegedi and Krisztina Rényi, have received national and international awards, while others (Dániel Varró and Gyula Böszörményi) are on the country's bestseller list. Ferenc Molnár has contributed the children's classic *Pál Street Boys* to world's literature. Other popular children's authors include Ágnes Nemes Nagy, Sándor Weöres, István Kormos, Éva Janikovszky, Ervin Lázár, István Csukás, Pál Békés, and Ferenc Szijj.

Contemporary Hungarian authors are trying to come to terms with the totalitarian regimes that ruled the country before and after World War II. Nobel Prize winner Imre Kertesz has dealt extensively in his novels with the memory of the Holocaust and the condition of Hungary after the fall of Communism. The controversial legacies of the Communist regime are often felt directly or indirectly in Hungarian fiction. In his international bestseller *Harmonia Caelestis*, Péter Esterházy chronicled his family's resistance to Communism only to discover, while consulting the country's secret archives, that his father had actually worked as a Communist spy, which necessitated a revised edition. Lajos Grendel, Laszlo Krasznahorkai, Aliz Mosonyi, and Dezsu Tandori all use more absurd tones to deliver their social and political satires on Hungarian society.

ITALY

Although the Italian economy is one of the most badly hit by the slow economic growth in Europe in the new millennium, every year the country's publishing industry produces between 53,000 and 55,000 titles. This considerable number reflects the increasingly complex and wide-ranging habits of Italian readers. Yet, with 0.95 titles per thousand inhabitants, Italy lags behind most Western European countries, surpassing only Greece and Portugal. The growth in the number of books published was also the result of an increase in the number of new publishing houses, which, between 1998 and 2003 increased at an average of 8.7 percent, reaching the figure of 5,281. Since the mid-1990s, the average print run per work has shown a constant decline and now stands in the range of 1900 to 2000 copies per title for a large number of Italian publishers. The weighted average price per book is €18.52. In 2003 the number of people between fourteen and eighty years old who were estimated to have bought at least one book was 17.6 million. The average number of books bought per purchaser was 5.3.

Book reading in Italy continues to remain low. In 2002, 50 percent of Italians said they had not read any books in the previous year; of those who had read books, 5 percent had read books for work, 6 percent had read compulsory texts for their education, 4 percent had read noncompulsory texts for their education, and 43 percent said they had read books for reasons other than work or study. This is a particularly discouraging figure since 2002 witnessed the launch of book sales attached to newspapers. According to the trade journal *Giornale della Libreria*, 2004 saw a total of more than 100 series and media projects; 1700 titles came onto the market, having a total print run of 80 million copies. There is a strong geographical imbalance in reading habits: while one northern Italian in two has read a book in the past year, only one southerner in three has.

During the Fascist regime, censorship encompassed all sectors of culture, including popular literature. But even during the twenty years' dictatorship, not all voices could be silenced. The last years of the dictatorship saw the formation of a neorealist group of writers who would become the most important authors of the postwar period: Alberto Moravia, Ignazio Silone, Cesare Pavese, Elio Vittorini, Carlo Levi, Vasco Pratolini, Carlo Cassola, Elsa Morante, Beppe Fenoglio, and Pier Paolo Pasolini. In spite of obvious differences, these writers shared a common left-wing inspiration and commitment that led them to document the social and political realities of postwar Italy. Their themes ranged from the chronic problems of southern Italy to the northern resistance against Nazi-Fascism, from the portrayal of urban working classes to the devastation of war.

Genre literature also influenced one of the most outspoken critics of the Sicilian mafia, Leonardo Sciascia, who often gives his books the structure of political thrillers as in *Il giorno della civetta* [The Day of the Owl] and *A ciascuno il suo* [A Man's Blessing]. The fellow Sicilian writer Andrea Camilleri also uses the detective story to investigate the criminal phenomena of Sicilian society. One of the most praised Italian crime writers was Giorgio Scerbanenco. Carlo Fruttero and Franco Lucentini were central to Italian popular literature both for their editorship of *Urania*, the most famous Italian science fiction series, and for the successful thrillers they wrote from the early 1970s to the late 1990s. Carlo Lucarelli has written successful adult thrillers, such as *Almost Blue*, and children's literature. The thriller conventions have also been used by poststructuralist critic Umberto Eco for his bestselling gothic novel set in the Middle Ages, *Il nome della rosa* [The Name of the Rose]. The comedian-turned-writer Giorgio Faletti has written two thrillers, *Io Uccido* and *Niente di vero tranne gli occhi*, which have been among the bestselling Italian books in recent years.

Italy's great culinary tradition is represented in popular culture by books authored by world-famous chefs such as Gianfranco Vissani (*La leggenda di un grande cuoco* [The Legend of a Great Cook]), Igles Corelli (*In cucina con Igles Corelli* [In the Kitchen with Igles Corelli]), Claudio Sadler (*Menu per quattro stagioni* [Menu for Four Seasons]) and Gualtiero Marchesi (*Il grande ricettario* [The Big Cookbook]).

Given the country's strong links with Catholicism, the market for spiritual and religious tends to be monopolized by the Roman Catholic Church. Both Pope John Paul II and Pope Benedict XVI authored books whose sales have rivaled those of the *Harry Potter* series. Other authors of religious bestsellers include Vittorio Messori (*Ipotesi su Gesù* [Hypothesis on Jesus]), Igor Sibaldi (*I maestri invisibili* [The Invisible Masters]) and Mario Pincherle (*Il quinto vangelo* [The Fifth Gospel]).

The 1980s and the 1990s also witnessed the commercial and critical success of women writers such as the feminist Dacia Maraini; Margaret Mazzantini; Melissa P., with her graphic erotic novel *Cento Colpi di Spazzola*; Luciana Littizzetto, with her humorous books;

and Susanna Tamaro, who is active both in children's literature and romance writing. Gay writers such as Pier Vittorio Tondelli and Aldo Busi have also achieved unprecedented visibility on the popular literary scene.

THE NETHERLANDS

According to data gathered in 2002, 53 percent of the Dutch population had read books for reasons other than work or study, 10 percent had read for their work, 14 percent had read compulsory texts for their education, 9 percent had read noncompulsory texts for their education, and only 37 percent said they had not read a book in the previous year. This high percentage of readers for pleasure accounts for the healthy book market, with 79 million books sold in 2001 (compared to 73 million in 1998) for a total value of €1.14 billion. In 2002 the number of publishing companies decreased to 488, with a total output of almost 20,000 volumes. Leading Dutch publishers are Wolters Kluwers, PCM, Malmberg, Veen, Bosch, Keuning Uitgeverij, and WPG Uitgeverij. Flemish publishers are also targeting the Netherlands in an attempt to expand their readership. The Netherlands has a mixed system in which the retail price of books is fixed for Dutch language books, while the price for books in foreign languages can be decided by individual booksellers. This means that books written in foreign languages often cost less than their translations. The fixed book price for a sector of the market has allowed independent booksellers to counter the increasing competition from bookshop chains. The Dutch have so far preferred the familiar and personal atmosphere of independent sellers rather than the global outlook of big chains.

Detective fiction is popular in the Netherlands, and several Dutch writers are the authors of best-sellers. Unfortunately, the inclusion in the plots of elements that closely echo Dutch politics and society has limited their marketability abroad. The prolific A. C. Baantjer (né Albert Cornelis), a former Dutch policeman, has written more than fifty bestselling novels; each book's first print run usually amounts to more than 100,000 copies. Chris Rippen is also a leading Dutch crime writer, whose books include *Sporen* [Tracks], *Playback*, and *Baltische Connecties*. Charles den Tex sets his mysteries among the middle class and uses his experience as a corporate consultant as the backdrop for his novels (*Dump*, *Claim*, and *Stegger*). Saskia Noort is the latest bestselling author in Dutch crime fiction. Her first novel, *Terug naar de kust* [To the Coast], sold more than 35,000 copies, which is a remarkable number in a country like the Netherlands with a comparatively small population of 16 million inhabitants. Her second novel, *De eetclub* [The Dining Club], was also a major success.

Annie M. G. Schmidt was one of most popular and productive Dutch children's writers of the twentieth century. Godfried Boman's children's classic *Eric in the Land of Insects* has proved very successful with different generations of young Dutch readers. Bette Westera is a more recent author; her poems about animals and short stories for children have already obtained prestigious awards.

Bestselling Dutch fiction writers include Cees Noteboom, Hugo Claus, Marcel Möring, Harry Mulisch, Marga Minco, and Tessa de Loo.

POLAND

Similar to other former Communist countries in Eastern Europe, Poland faced important economic challenges after 1989. State subsidizing of book prices ended, the state-owned distribution system dissolved, the bookselling sector was privatized, and the numbers of publishers increased considerably. Poland has a strong book-reading culture, especially in urban areas, and the book market is first in number of published titles within the new member states of the European Union with 22,430 published volumes in 2003. Increasing book prices have led many Poles to buy fewer books, and the total sales volume went down from €477 million in 2001 to €475 million in 2003. Between 1999 and 2002, general adult fiction and nonfiction sales fell from 23 percent to 18 percent of the market. By contrast, educational reforms stimulated the expansion of the textbook market from 21 percent to 25 percent. To try to increase sales and margins of profit, publishers have progressively opted for direct selling either via mail or the Internet. Book clubs and mail orders accounted for 30 percent of the market in 2003, while door-to-door sales represented 12 percent of the total. In spite of the decrease in sales, the Polish book market seems to be reaching Western European levels, fueled by the ongoing consolidation of the largest five publishing companies (now controlling approximately 40 percent of the market), a mixture of domestic and international investments in the top companies, the increasing use of information technology, copyright legislation, and a national biography prepared according to international standards.

Polish science fiction and fantasy can count a large number of bestselling writers who have won numerous awards and whose works have been translated into many different languages. Stanisław Lem, the founding father of Polish science fiction, has sold over 27 million copies of his works all over the world, and his books have been adapted for film by important directors such as Andrzej Vajda, Andrei Tarkovsky, and Steven Soderbergh. Jacek Dukaj is considered the most talented young Polish science fiction author, and his works have proven to be very popular with Polish as well as international readers. A short animated movie based on his short story *The Cathedral* was nominated for an Academy Award in 2003. Marek Huberath uses science fiction and fantasy settings to explore philosophical themes such as human resistance or surrender to evil. Tomasz Pacyński was the chief editor of *Fahrenheit*, Poland's first Internet science fiction fanzine, and the author of a popular fantasy trilogy based on the character of Robin Hood. Andrzej Sapkowski first obtained critical and commercial success with his short story *The Hexer* (translated as *The Witcher*) in 1986. Since then, he has created a cycle of stories based on the same character, Geralt, a mutant who has been trained to chase and kill monsters. Janusz Andrzej Zajdel employed science fiction conventions to explore totalitarian societies and has been an inspirational figure for many Polish sci-fi authors interested in dystopian novels, such as Edmund Wnuk-Lipiński, Antonina Liedtke, and Rafał Aleksander Ziemkiewicz. Other important Polish science fiction and fantasy writers include Marek Baraniecki, Ewa Białoęcka, Feliks Wiktor Kres, and Andrzej Pilipiuk.

With her novel *White and Red* (also titled *Snow White and Russian Red*), Dorota Masłowska became a cult author for Polish youth, and her book sold more than 100,000 copies. Małgorzata Musierowicz has written fiction for children and teenagers that has proven to be popular with adults, too. She is particularly renowned for her saga about the Borejko family from Poznan, which describes Poland at dramatic moments in recent history beginning in the late 1970s. Jan Brzechwa and Julian Tuwim have made important contributions to children's literature. Ryszard Kapuściński was probably the best-known Polish reporter and the author of successful books about international politics and travel.

RUSSIA, UKRAINE, AND BELARUS

Book markets in Russia, Ukraine, and Belarus were faced with important economic and political changes during the late 1980s that were at the same time beneficial and threatening. The collapse of the Soviet Union meant the emancipation of the book market from censorship and strict governmental control. However, the introduction of a free economy also implied the end of the centralized distribution system. The three countries have reacted to these changes with different strategies and strengths, and they have met with diverse results.

Russian publishers, which were mainly based in Moscow and St. Petersburg, could not reach the furthest regions of the country. By the mid-1990s, in spite of the freedom granted to writers and publishers, book production had plummeted to the lowest point since the early years of the twentieth century. The high level of inflation prevented people from spending money on less-essential items such as books. Yet, by 2001, also thanks to the abolition of taxes on books in 1996, the market started to improve, with the number of books published reaching the highest point at 70,332 titles. This number grew to 89,066 titles in 2004 with total sales of €1.17 billion, a 2.7 percent increase over the previous year. Publishing houses have also increased by sixty times in comparison with the Communist era and now number 5388. There are about 6,000 bookshops in Russia, and the average book price is approximately €2. As in other Eastern European countries, book prices have risen significantly since the introduction of a free market economy. The top five publishing houses are AST, Eksmo Press, Drofa, Prosveshchenie, and Olma Press. Only one, a publisher of textbooks (Prosveshchenie), is now state owned. Overall, the state share of the book market has been reduced to 12.6 percent. Political changes have also affected the subject matter of publications. While technology and the natural sciences were the major topics during the Communist regime, today there are more books devoted to the humanities and the social sciences, with a sharp increase in the number of titles on philosophy, economics, law, sociology, and religion.

The Ukrainian book market is still in transition. After its independence in 1991, Ukraine faced a severe economic crisis. The book trade and the publishing industry are still trying to create reliable channels of information. The Ukrainian book market is limited by marketing problems, bookshops without computer support, low consumer spending power, and the dominance of the Russian book market. The number of books published almost doubled from 7,749 titles in 2000 to 13,805 in 2003; however, the number of printed books per capita has remained low (0.8 in 2003). The average book price is €4 for hardcover and €2 for paperbacks. There are 2,100 officially registered publishing houses; of those, however, only about 600 are fully active. There are 390 bookshops in the country, a number that goes up to almost 600 if street stalls and kiosks are included. Bookshops cover 30 percent of the market, while supermarkets and kiosks account for almost half of Ukrainian book sales.

Data about the Belarus book market are scarce. The region has a high literacy rate, but books in Belarus are still few in number. Most books published in Belarus are in Russian. Bookstores, concentrated in urban areas, are largely state run and often have second-hand sections. This is an important part of the market since print runs of books are limited. In addition to bookstores, kiosks and stands also have a limited selection of books, with particular focus on popular novels, astrology, and children's books. The quality of printed volumes is still far behind European standards.

Since the region is becoming a free market economy after being the leading area of the Socialist bloc, several bestselling and popular books are self-help volumes for businesspeople that address how to develop companies and how to deal with corruption and crime. These include *Business Is Psychology* by Marina Meliya and *Hunting for Werewolves* by Aleksandr Khinshtein, which documents the spread of corruption among law enforcement officers. In addition, the region is rewriting its history by revising the myths of the Soviet past and creating new ones linked to the glorious past of the czars. Viktor Suvorov's books have proven to be extremely popular with their bitter satire of the supposed superpower status of the

USSR and its role of liberator in World War II. *The Liberators* gathers several stories that document the author's experience in the Ukrainian army, and *Icebreaker* controversially claims that Stalin was only a few weeks from launching a full-scale invasion of Europe when Hitler anticipated him by invading Russia. Aleksandr Bushkov has contributed to the renewed interest in the age of the czars with his patriotic biography of Catherine the Great, titled *The Diamond Cinderella*.

Since the opening of the region to Western literature, European and American crime writers have enjoyed a wide readership. This success has encouraged Russian authors to develop this genre. The most popular Russian crime writer is Daria Dontsova, who has produced over forty novels in just a few years. Her books often feature a strong female protagonist. In the domain of fantasy and children's books, the popular success of the *Harry Potter* series (which has sold about 1.2 million copies in Russia) has prompted several bestselling parodies, such as Dmitry Yemets's *Tanya Grotter and the Magical Double Bass* and Andrey Zhvalevsky's *Porry Gatter and the Stone Philosopher*.

SCANDINAVIA

The Scandinavian countries—Denmark, Norway, Sweden, Iceland, and Finland—have a strong book-reading tradition. According to the data quoted in the Eurostat survey "Europeans' Participation in Cultural Activities," 72 percent of Swedes have read books for reasons other than work, the highest percentage in Europe. This percentage remains high in the other two Scandinavian states that are part of the European Union: 66 percent in Finland and 55 percent in Denmark. Only 19 percent of Swedes had not read a book in the previous year. Such percentages increased only slightly for Finland (24 percent) and Denmark (33 percent), remaining well below the European average.

In 2001 the Swedish book sector generated total sales of around €280 million. There was strong interest in literary books (45 percent) and nonfiction books (35 percent), followed by children's books (16 percent), reference books (3 percent), and electronic media (1 percent). The Swedish book market had a dramatic 20 percent growth in 2002, when taxes on books were lowered from 25 percent to 6 percent. In 2003 the market kept this high level, with only sales in department stores declining slightly. The part of the Swedish book market that grew most decisively over the last decade was the paperback market.

In 2001, 14,319 titles were published in Denmark, producing a sales volume of about €300 million. Bookstores accounted for 75 percent of the sales, while supermarkets and newsagents took 8 percent of the market. Finally, 15 percent of books were sold through book clubs, and only 2 percent were sold on the Internet. Together with Finland, Denmark has one of the highest levels of book sales per capita among European Union member states. In 2001 there were 434 bookstores in the country and approximately 1,500 publishing houses.

The total number of books published in Finland grew by 8.5 percent between 2003 and 2004, increasing from 7,370 to 7,994 titles. The turnover from sales also grew by 4 percent. Finland abolished the fixed price system in the early 1970s, and since then the number of bookstores has declined. Yet, considering the size of the Finnish population, the bookstore network is still one of the most extensive in the world, although most of the stores are small. Sales through bookstores account for 40 percent of the market. The ten biggest publishers represent 80 percent of total book production. Although book sales per capita are the highest in the European Union, the Finnish book market is facing important problems. Public expenditure on books, including library acquisition, has dropped dramatically from the

1990s. While the number of published titles has increased, print runs have declined, and book prices are high.

Norway has one of the strongest book-reading cultures in the world. In 2003, 88 percent of Norwegians lived in communities with at least one bookshop, which 69 percent of them visited at least once during a month. With 600 bookshops, Norway had the highest number of bookshops per number of inhabitants in the region. In 2003, 92 percent of the population reported having read at least one book in the previous year. The turnover generated from book sales in the country totaled €625 million, with a per capita spending of €125, one of the highest in Europe. About 70 percent of the Norwegian population bought at least one book in the previous year. Bookstores represent 57 percent of the market, while 24 percent of the sales take place through book clubs, a sector which is expanding rapidly. Approximately 27 percent of the population has a book club membership, while 24 percent are members of more than one book club. There is no tax on books, and book prices are fixed for the first seventeen months after publication. However, booksellers may apply a 12.5 percent discount on the book price, a privilege that, until May 2005, was limited to book clubs only.

The most successful genre in Norwegian popular literature is the serial romantic novel. It is estimated that half a million Norwegians out of a total population of 4.5 million read serial novels. Mostly sold through kiosks, these novels often make it to bestseller lists thanks to their historical settings and melodramatic overtones, which appeal to many readers. Best-selling authors in the genre include Anne-Lise Boge, Kjellaug Steinslett, Eva Stensrud, Trine Angelsen, Frid Ingulstad, and Synnøve Eriksen.

Peter Høeg is a popular Danish author whose books (*Smilla's Sense of Snow*, *The Woman and the Ape*, *Borderliners*, and *The History of Danish Dreams*) have enjoyed a wide international audience. Other widely read Scandinavian authors include Jostein Gaarder (Norway); Karen Blixen (Denmark); Marianne Fredriksson and Bo Giertz (Sweden)—the latter writes spiritual novels and religious books; and the Nobel Prize–winning Halldor Laxness (Iceland).

SPAIN AND PORTUGAL

Neither Portugal and Spain has strong reading habits. Only 15 percent of the Portuguese population in 2002 read at least a book a year for reasons other than study or work, the lowest percentage of the original fifteen members of the European Union. Portugal also had the highest percentage of people who reported not having read a single book in a year (67 percent). In Spain, 39 percent of the population read for reasons other than study or work, and more than half reported not having read any books during the previous year. Because of this low reading level, the Spanish book market decreased by 5 percent in volume terms in 2002, reaching a low point of 235 million books sold for a total turnout of €2,630 million. In the same year, approximately 70,000 titles were published. Sales to consumers represented 90 percent of the Spanish market in terms of both volume and value. This reflects the poor quality of the Spanish library system. Hardback sales accounted for a striking 89 percent of the market, although paperback sales rose considerably because of improved quality and competition. The sales of fiction books experienced a dramatic growth of 49 percent from 1998 to 2002. The average book price in 2002 was €11.95. Few data are available about the Portuguese book market, which remains small. In 2002, 11,331 titles were published in Portugal, and book sales per capita had grown to over €60.

In spite of these statistics, both countries can count on a number of authors whose books sell well not only in their home countries but also abroad. The difficult situation of the Basque country and the impact of Basque terrorism on the national life and psyche are explored in Bernardo Atxaga's novels, particularly in *The Lone Man* and *The Lone Woman*. The Spanish Civil War and the ensuing fascist dictatorship of Francisco Franco have been dramatized in *Manolo, recuerdas?* [Manolo, Do You Remember?] by Manuel Altes. The impact of the dictatorship was also clear in the works by Gonzalo Torrente Ballester, who joined Franco's Falangist Party but soon fell victim to the regime's censorship. Carmen Martìn Gaite first wrote novels in a social-realist mode but progressively increased the psychological depth of her characters as well as introduced elements from Spanish folklore. In addition to several novels, poems, and short stories, she has written children's books. The more postmodern work of Agustìn Diaz Pacheco is frequently linked to those of internationally renowned writers Paul Auster and Salman Rushdie. Mystery and fantasy conventions have been successfully used by anthropologist-turned-novelist Albert Sachez Piñol as well as by Arturo Perez-Reverte and Manuel Vasquez Montalban. Almudena Grandes obtained overnight success with the erotic novel *The Ages of Lulu*, which was adapted for the screen by Bigas Luna. Her later bestselling works include *Atlas de Geografia Humana* [Atlas of Human Geography] and *Los Aires Dificiles* [The Difficult Airs].

Like Spain, Portugal experienced a long fascist dictatorship, which lasted from the 1930s to the mid-1970s. Popular novels such as *Sinais de Fogo* by Jorge De Sena, *Ballad of Dogs' Beach: Dossier of a Crime* by J. Cardoso Pires, *Seascape with Woman* by Teolinda Gersao, and *A loba e o rouxinol* by A. M. Pires Cabral testify to the enduring impact of the dictatorship on the Portuguese literary mind. Cardoso Pires is also the author of a book of impressions of Lisbon. David Mourão Ferreira wrote novels such as *Um Amore Feliz* [A Happy Love] that obtained considerable success. José Saramago was the first Portuguese author to win the Nobel Prize, and since the publication of *Baltasar and Blimunda*, his books have been international bestsellers whose style alternates allegorical narration with realistic descriptions. Also allegorical in style, Helder Macedo's *Pedro e Paula* [Pedro and Paula] depicts the country's conflicts throughout the past fifty years. Maria Velho Da Costa is one of the most popular Portuguese women writers, along with Maria Isabel Barreno and Maria Teresa Horta. Both Spain and Portugal held colonies in Latin America. Novels written by Latin American authors in Spanish and Portuguese have proved extremely popular in Europe. Works by Latin American authors such as Isabel Allende, Jorge Amado, and Gabriel García Márquez have been grouped under the style of Magic Realism.

SWITZERLAND

The Swiss book market reflects the country's division into three major linguistic areas: German, French, and Italian. The largest submarket is the German-speaking region, which represents 75 percent of the total market value, followed at 22 percent for the French-speaking region and 3 percent for the Italian-speaking region. Rhaeto-Romansh, the fourth official language, is spoken by comparatively few people and thus is of marginal importance in the book market. The total Swiss book market value in 2002 was €650 million; growth had slowed down between 2000 and 2002, but the market seemed to start growing again in 2004. The neighboring countries with the same languages are of vital importance for the Swiss market since they, together with English-speaking countries, represent the main export markets. Germany accounts for the largest portion (60 percent in 2002). The major export markets are also the major sources for imports, with Germany still in a leading position by the same percentage.

Internal diversity characterizes each linguistic submarket because of the large numbers of smaller publishing companies and the low level of concentration in publishing and retailing.

High education levels, the standard of living, and purchasing power make Switzerland an attractive market for foreign publishers. Per capita spending on books remained stable from 1998 to 2002.

There are about 500 publishers in Switzerland. Few of them are large ones, and the micro-enterprises represent 90 percent of the total. Most companies are limited to domestic activities because they lack marketing and distribution power. Trade associations and public foundations seek to remedy this through promotional activities at international book fairs and the provision of grants. German publishing multinationals targeted medium-sized Swiss publishers for acquisition in the 1990s, but this phenomenon was short lived. In spite of the limited international presence, the medium-sized Swiss publishing scene is enlivened by the constant emergence of new companies. The textbook market is the focus of renewed international interest as schoolbook publishers that were formerly owned by cantons are being privatized. As a result, German publishers have not lost the chance of entering the Swiss market.

The book retailing sector also has a low concentration. In 2001, only 2 booksellers out of 500 belonged to chains with ten or more outlets. Bookshop density, on the contrary, is high, with one outlet for each 11,000 inhabitants. Foreign acquisition is still low although German chains made some inroads in 2001. Between 1998 and 2003, Internet sales increased considerably, representing 6 percent of the total market value in 2002. Yet, paradoxically, this increase only reflected the Swiss preference for small outlets: customers chose to buy from the Websites of local bookshops rather than from virtual international suppliers. Accordingly, the Internet is not regarded as a threat to traditional booksellers, but rather as an additional sales channel.

Max Frisch and Friedrich Dürenmatt, whose works explored feelings of alienation and identity in modern society, were two of the most representative Swiss writers in the post–World War II years. Given the importance of business in Swiss life, it is not surprising that one of the most successful books in recent years was *Fünfunddreissig* [Thirty-five] by former manager Rolf Dobelli. The author mixes fiction and business, investigating the position of the workplace in everyday life. Business is also central to the writing of Martin Suter, whose fame is linked to the weekly column *Business Class*. He is also the author of four novels. Mariella Mehr is a controversial radical writer of Roma origins; she champions minority rights in her works, which have been translated into several languages.

TURKEY

Turkish book market operators have been somewhat disappointed that European Union requests for the modernization of the country before it can join the union have left out any discussion of the book trade. Access to books is limited to the big cities of Istanbul, Ankara, Izmir, Bursa, and Antalya, while reading levels in the countryside remain low. This is in part the result of the strong oral storytelling tradition of Turkey, and also in part because of the less-than-encouraging attitude of the government toward the book trade. Although the process of democratization has advanced in recent years, some writers still experience tensions in their relationship with political power. The government does not provide funds to libraries and bookshops. The Turkish state is itself a major publisher: several publishing companies are directly linked to ministries and public institutions. In total, there are approximately 1400 private publishing houses, half of which are active. Publishers mainly fall into three categories according to the subjects they select: companies primarily concerned with religious books, those that publish legal works, and those categorized as liberal and progressive publishers. Only twenty publishing houses employ more than five people.

The total number of volumes published every year reaches 20,000. New titles produced per year number about 6,000, with a print run of 2,000 copies per title. Total annual sales come to about €300 million. The average price for a paperback is approximately €8.50, while a hardback costs €17.20. These are quite expensive prices given standard salaries. Although there are about 1,300 localities where books are sold, only 100 of these are proper bookshops with large selections of volumes. Libraries are concentrated in big cities.

Popular literature of the country has drawn extensively on the contrasts implied in Turkey's ambiguous geographic and cultural position: a Muslim nation that enjoys a privileged relationship with the Western world rather than with Arab countries. Yaşar Kemal is one of the most prolific Turkish writers and one whose literary production covers the second half of the twentieth century. Kemal's series of novels on the Chukurova plain has been compared to the fictional worlds of William Faulkner and Gabriel García Márquez. Kemal's books portray the conflict between poor farmers and rural landowners. As a result of the political content of his books and his leftist views, Kemal was imprisoned in the 1970s. Orhan Pamuk, who received the Nobel Prize in literature in 2006, is a leading postmodernist author; he explores the conflicts between Muslim traditions and the Westernized customs of most Turkish citizens. Pamuk has also tried the murder mystery genre with his successful *My Name Is Red*, which sold 85,000 copies in three weeks. The novelist Ahmet Altan has addressed past events in Turkey's history: *Like a Sword's Wound* sold 150,000 copies and *Dangerous Stories* 250,000 copies. In spite of the historical subjects of his novels, Altan has always been a vocal critic of Turkish governments, their policies toward freedom of speech, and their administration of the legal system. Aziz Nesin was an extremely prolific writer, whose over 100 books satirized Turkish bureaucracy and denounced social inequalities in the country. For his criticism, Nesin was repeatedly jailed. Other important contemporary Turkish authors include Bekir Yildiz, Sevgi Soysal, Adalet Agaoglu, Furuzan, Tezer Ozlu, Tomris Uyar, Nazli Eray, Latife Tekin, Murathan Mungan, and Bilge Karasu.

UNITED KINGDOM AND IRELAND

After Finland and Sweden, the United Kingdom, in 2002, had the highest percentage of people who reported having read at least one book in the previous year for reasons other than work or study (63 percent). Only 25 percent of the population had not read a book in the previous year. In Ireland, on the contrary, the percentage of the population that had not read any books during the previous year was greater than the percentage of those who had read for pleasure (44 percent and 40 percent respectively).

The situation of the UK book market is consistent with the above statistics, showing volume and value gains of more than 10 percent from 1998 to 2002, reaching a value of almost £2.5 billion in that year. With 125,390 titles published each year, the UK market is second only to that of Germany. The consumer market was the main factor in the growth, accounting for 80.4 percent of sales in 2002. Publishers and retailers were eager to promote both bestsellers and new titles by lesser-known authors. The institutional market did not match the growth of the consumer one, and sales to libraries even decreased. Paperbacks have been the dominant format in the British book market, with sales growing by 18.4 percent between 1998 and 2002. Fiction was the fastest growing category, with a 13.8 percent increase in volume sales. Popular genres such as thrillers, science fiction, and children's novels were the main market drivers. Nonfiction titles also experienced a significant growth thanks to a renewed interest in history, biographies, and TV-inspired titles.

Independent booksellers are finding it increasingly difficult to face the competition of big chains. In 2002, for example, large chains accounted for 43 percent of the market, other bookshops took a 13 percent share, and sales through book clubs and the Internet reached 21 percent and 6 percent respectively. Institutional providers, particularly those dealing with libraries, have seen their profits reduced since the collapse of the Net Book Agreement in 1995.

Data on the Irish book market are scarce and not up to date. In spite of the high number of those who do not read books, the Irish book market in 2003 experienced an overall 8 percent increase. The educational market led this trend with a substantial growth of 16 percent, while the general literary market dropped by 8 percent. The nonfiction market experienced a 1.8 percent growth, with a corresponding decrease in the fiction and children's literature sections. Compared with previous data, the number of books printed dropped by 1 percent to a total of 8,253 volumes.

Some of the most popular contemporary fiction authors of the United Kingdom have demonstrated the multiculturalism of British society and have encouraged the country to come to terms with its imperial past. Writers such as Salman Rushdie, Vikram Seth, Kazuo Ishiguro, Hanif Kureishi, Timothy Mo, Buchi Emecheta, V. S. Naipaul, and Ben Okri have all explored the burden and the problematic legacy of the empire on local populations and immigrant communities in Britain. The tensions between Protestants and Roman Catholics in Northern Ireland have been powerfully documented in the fiction of William Trevor and Bernard MacLaverty. The importance of Scotland and its authors within British popular fiction is testified to by the success of writers such as Irvine Welsh, James Kelman, and Alan Warner.

Fantasy and science fiction have been used by feminist writers such as Angela Carter, Jeannette Winterson, and Doris Lessing to critique the predominance of male rationality in fiction. Male writers have contributed to the fantasy and science fiction genres, too. Arthur C. Clarke rose to international fame for his cooperation with director Stanley Kubrick on the screenplay for *2001: A Space Odyssey*. Stephen Baxter has written stories set in a distant future (the *Xeelee Sequence*) and in the present day, imaging an extensive exploration of space. Baxter also writes stories for children. J. Ballard's novels are set in dystopic societies where people are subjected to mechanization. Bob Shaw and Ian McDonald are popular science fiction authors from Northern Ireland. And thanks to the screen adaptations of his *Lord of the Rings* trilogy, J. R. R. Tolkien continues to be one of the most extensively read British fantasy authors.

The ultimate success in British children's literature is the *Harry Potter* series by J. K. Rowling, which takes advantage of recent trends in children's literature. Thanks to appealing marketing techniques, the development of bookshops and libraries for children, and the growth of the paperback market, the field of children's books has consistently expanded since the late 1950s. Fact books such as simplified biographies, manuals, history books, and junior encyclopedia represent an important tradition in British literature for children. Popular authors in children's literature include Roald Dahl; Beatrix Potter, of the *Peter Rabbit* series; Wilbert Vere Awdry, the creator of Thomas the Tank Engine; fantasy author Brian Jacques; and the more realistic Melvin Burgess, Michael Coleman, and Judy Blume.

The crime writings of Agatha Christie have enjoyed lasting popularity with a vast readership. More recent British authors whose books became bestsellers in this genre include P. D. James, Ruth Rendell, John Mortimer, Reginald Hill, Peter Robinson, Ian Rankin, and Val McDermid. Ian Fleming was the creator of the successful James Bond (007) spy stories. In Ireland the genre was first practiced by Sheila Pim and by Eilis Dillon, who was also a successful children's author.

Throughout the twentieth century, popular Irish literature addressed the problem of the national question, developing family sagas that mirrored the establishment of an independent country, such as Frank Delaney's *Ireland: A Novel*. Popular fiction also reflected the social changes that have taken place in the nation as an increasing number of novels have urban rather than rural settings. Widely read authors include Edna O'Brien, Maeve Binchy, Seamus Deane, Roddy Doyle, Dermot Bolger, Colm Tóibin, and Jennifer Johnston.

RESOURCE GUIDE

PRINT SOURCES

Barron, Neil, ed. *Anatomy of Wonder 4: A Critical Guide to Science Fiction*. New Providence, NJ: Bowker, 1995.

Caidi, Nadia. "Cooperation in Context: Library Developments in Central and Eastern Europe." *Libri* 53 (2003): 103–117.

Chernaik, Warren. *The Art of Detective Fiction*. New York: St. Martin's Press, 2000.

Clute, John, and Peter Nicholls, eds. *The Encyclopedia of Science Fiction*. New York: St. Martin's Press, 1993.

Davidson, Hilda Ellis, and Anna Chaudhri. *A Companion to the Fairy Tale*. Cambridge: D. S. Brewer, 2003.

Fritzsche, Sonja Rae. "Reconceptualizing East German Popular Literature via the Science Fiction Niche." *German Quarterly* 77.4 (2004): 443–461

———. *Science Fiction Literature in East Germany*. Bern: Lang, 2006.

Godsland, Shelley, and Nickianne Moody, eds. *Reading the Popular in Contemporary Spanish Fiction*. Newark: University of Delaware Press, 2004.

Goldthwaite, John. *The Natural History of Make-Believe: Tracing the Literature of Imagination for Children*. New York: Oxford University Press, 1996.

Gorrara, Claire. *The Roman Noir in Post-War French Culture: Dark Fictions*. Oxford: Oxford University Press, 2003.

Haines, Brigid, and Margaret Littler. *Contemporary Women's Writing in German: Changing the Subject*. Oxford: Oxford University Press, 2004.

Hunt, Peter. *An Introduction to Children's Literature*. Oxford: Oxford University Press, 1996.

———. *Understanding Children's Literature: Key Essays from the International Companion Encyclopedia of Children's Literature*. London: Routledge, 2000.

Hunt, Peter, and Sheila Ray, eds. *International Companion Encyclopedia of Children's Literature*. London: Routledge, 1996.

Klobucka, Anna, ed. *On Saramago*. Monographic issue of *Portuguese Literary and Cultural Studies* (2001, Spring).

Konstantinova, Bozhanka. "Bulgarian Children's Literature." *Bookbird: A Journal of International Children's Literature* 40.1 (2002, January).

Labon, Joanna. *Balkan Blues: Writing Out of Yugoslavia*. Evanston: Northwestern University Press, 1995.

Lumley, Robert. *Culture and Conflict in Post-war Italy: Essays on Mass and Popular Culture*. London: MacMillan, 1990.

Marjanovic, Voja. "Literature for Children and Young People in Serbia in the Past and Today" *Bookbird: A Journal of International Children's Literature* 42:1 (February 2004) 46–49.

Meek, Margaret. *Children's Literature and National Identity*. Stoke on Tent: Trentham Books, 2001.

Metcalf, Eve Maria, ed. *Children's Literature of the Nordic Countries*. Special issue of *Bookbird: A Journal of International Children's Literature* 37: 4 (1999).

Mullen, Anna, and Emer O'Beirne, eds. *Crime Scenes. Detective Narratives in European Culture since 1945*. Amsterdam: Rodopi, 2000.

Naess, Harald S., ed. *A History of Norwegian Literature*. Lincoln: University of Nebraska Press, in cooperation with the American-Scandinavian Foundation, 1993.

Pells, Richard. *Not Like Us: How Europeans Have Loved, Hated and Transformed American Popular Culture Since World War II*. New York: Basic Books, 1998.

Priestman, Martin. *The Cambridge Companion to Crime Fiction.* Cambridge: Cambridge University Press, 2003.

Rossel, Sven H., ed. *A History of Danish Literature.* Lincoln: University of Nebraska Press, in cooperation with the American-Scandinavian Foundation, 1992.

Rottensteiner, Franz, ed. *View from Another Shore: European Science Fiction.* Liverpool: Liverpool University Press, 1999.

Shavit, Zohar. *A Past without Shadow: Constructing the Past in German Books for Children.* London: Routledge, 2005.

Stableford, Brian. *Historical Dictionary of Science Fiction.* Lanham: Scarecrow Press, 2004.

———. *Historical Dictionary of Fantasy Literature.* Lanham: Scarecrow Press, 2005.

Tevis, Yvonne P., and R. Reginald, eds. *East of the Sun: Russian and Eastern European Science Fiction.* New York: Sagapress, 1987.

Vázquez de Parga, Salvador. *La Novela policiaca en España.* Barcelona: Ronsel, 1993.

Wachtel, Andrew. *Making a Nation, Breaking a Nation: Literature and Cultural History in Yugoslavia.* Palo Alto: Stanford University Press, 1998.

Warme, Lars G., ed. *A History of Swedish Literature.* Lincoln: University of Nebraska Press, 1996.

Whittingham, Charlotte. *Swedish Crime Writers.* Supplement to the *Swedish Book Review*, 2001.

Youssef, Magdi. "Il mito della letteratura europea." Pp. 67–105 in Franca Sinopoli (ed.), *La Letteratura Europea Vista dagli Altri.* Rome: Meltemi Editore, 2003.

Zuck, Virpi, ed. *A Dictionary of Scandinavian Literature.* Westport, CT: Greenwood Press, 1990.

Publishers Weekly has an international focus and is not limited to the United States.

Bookbird is a periodical on children's literature published by IBBY: International Board on Books for Young People.

Media History published by Taylor and Francis

WEBSITES

Association of Learned and Professional Society Publishers. http://www.alpsp.org.uk. *Learned Publishing* published by the Association of Learned and Professional Society Publishers.

Associazione Italiana Editori. *The Italian Book Market. Report 2004.* http://www.aie.it/Allegati/Stranieri/The%20Italian%20Book%20Market%20-%20Report%202004.pdf.

Baruch, Marc, and Jean Richard. "The Book Sector and the State: Relationships in Change." 1994; revised 2000. *Council of Europe.* http://www.coe.int/T/E/Cultural_Co-operation/culture/Completed_projects/Books/ecubook_A6.asp#TopOfPage

BIEF—Bureau International de l'Edition Française. http://www.bief.org.

Bookseller. http://www.thebookseller.com.

Booktrusted. http://www.booktrusted.com. International Website of children's literature.

Council of Europe. "Recommendations for the Reform of Library Legislation in Central Europe (1994–95)." http://www.coe.int/T/E/Cultural_Co-operation/culture/Completed_projects/Books/ecubook_A2.asp#P113_19464.

European Booksellers Federation. http://www.ibf-booksellers.org/ebf/studies.html.

Eurostat. "Europeans' Participation in Cultural Activities." 2002. http://epp.eurostat.cec.eu.int/portal/page?_pageid=1090,30070682,1090_33076576&_dad=portal&_schema=PORTAL.

Eurostat. "New Europeans and Culture." 2003. http://epp.eurostat.cec.eu.int/portal/page?_pageid=1090,30070682,1090_33076576&_dad=portal&_schema=PORTAL.

Frankfurt Book Fair. http://www.buchmesse.de/en/index.php?content=/en/brancheninformationen/tlp.html. Book markets worldwide.

IBBY—International Board on Books for Young People. http://www.ibby.org/.

Kabouropoulos, Socrates. *The Indisputable Gain of Confidence of the Publishing Market in Greece.* http://www.readingeurope.org/observatory.nsf?open.

Litrix–German Literature online. http://www.litrix.de.

Øverland, Janneken. *Trends in contemporary Norwegian literature.* http://odin.dep.no/odin/engelsk/ norway/history/032005–990479/index-dok000-b-n-a.html.

Reading Europe—Information Resource Centre on Books and Reading. http://www.readingeurope.org/ observatory.nsf?open.

Turku School of Economics and Rightscom. *Publishing Market Watch Final Report.* 2005. http:// www.publishing-watch.org/.

NOTES

1. Baruch and Richard (1994; revised 2000) (in Resource Guide, Websites).
2. Ibid.
3. The sources used for statistics on single European markets are the *Publishing Market Watch Final Report* and the Websites of the Frankfurt Book Fair, the European Booksellers Federation, and the Reading Europe—Information Resource Centre on Books and Reading (all in Resource Guide).

LOVE, SEX, AND MARRIAGE

ANNETTE OLSEN-FAZI

Since the beginning of the twentieth century, Europe has been the scene of great change on multiple fronts, especially those involving lifestyles and relationships. Evolving from a primarily agrarian system at the turn of the century to an increasingly industrial and technological model, Europe is in the vanguard of what might be a new social order. When Europeans fall in love, have sex, get married (and divorced), and recognize the rights of children, women, and persons with alternate lifestyles, their trajectory might herald the future of the industrialized world.

Across the board, European nations are experiencing decreased or negative population growths, aging of the population, low marriage rates, increased divorce statistics, and an age for first coitus seemingly in free fall. Romantic love is still the ideal state for sexual relations for most, although many accept casual relationships and even one-night stands. Contraception is gaining acceptance, while abortion is declining. Women are increasingly vocal, and children's rights are recognized as never before in the history of the world.

The number of sexual partners is increasing, as are sexually transmitted diseases. HIV rates are alarming in several nations, including Russia and the Ukraine. Sex education seems satisfactory only in the more pragmatic nations such as Germany and France. Others, such as Italy, Poland, and Portugal, have much room for improvement. Trafficking in women and children has reached pandemic rates. In fact, violence against females appears widespread, touching not only the former Soviet bloc but also progressive countries such as Belgium or the United Kingdom. Pedophilia is a great problem that might simply not have been recognized earlier.

As Europeans work fewer hours, enjoy more leisure, and greater material comforts than ever before, they have more time to devote to flirtation, relationships, love, and sex. The following provides detailed portraits of individual nations all across Europe at the dawn of the twenty-first century.

AUSTRIA

Austria is a 32,378-square-mile country with a population of over 8 million. The population growth rate is 0.25 percent, and life expectancy is 74.5 years for males and 81.0 years for

MARRIAGE AND DIVORCE IN AUSTRIA

Only civil marriages are legal in Austria, although many couples opt for an additional church wedding. Wearing the finished bridal gown before the wedding can bring bad luck; some brides leave a stitch undone until the last moment. Over 30 percent of Austrian unions end in divorce. Reasons given for divorce are extramarital sex, selfishness, and inflexibility.

females. The largest ethnic group is German (98 percent), with Hungarian, Slovakian, Czech, and Roma (Gypsy) minorities (2 percent). The major religion is Roman Catholicism (78 percent). Protestants, Muslims, and others account for 22 percent. The official language is German.[1]

During the first part of the twentieth century, the state as well as the Catholic Church prescribed abstinence for single persons. During Austrian Fascism (1934–38) women were legally inferior to men and urged to bear racially "pure" children while, like the Virgin Mary, eschewing indulgence in sexuality for their own pleasure.

Today, Austrians experience love and sexuality like most Europeans. Austrians fall in love around age thirteen. Heterosexual petting starts at fifteen on average, followed by intercourse some six months later. Some 3 percent of girls and 4 percent of boys experience intercourse before age 13.[2]

In addition to school sex education, Austrians get information from the Internet and the advice columns in publications such as *Bravo*, a German magazine for teenagers, and the Viennese newspaper *Kronen Zeitung*. The Austrian Society for Planned Parenthood has counseling centers all over the country.

In 1996 the Austrian Parliament repealed anti-homosexual articles, and homosexual acts between males are legal if both parties are between 14 and 18 years old or if both parties are over 18. If one partner is over 19 and the other under 18, the older partner is liable to prosecution. As recently as 1974 the mentally handicapped were sterilized by the state.[3]

Romantic love is considered the ideal basis for sexual relationships. Sexuality and procreation are recognized as separate, and there is little stigma to sexual activity for pleasure. In spite of a desire for companionship, more and more Austrians (18–22 percent) live alone. Five percent of Austrians describe themselves as "swingers"; paradoxically, 42 percent seek a stable relationship.[4]

Extramarital births have been rising since the early 1960s, today accounting for 33 percent of births. Since contraception is available (42–45 percent of Austrian women ages 15–44 take the pill) and abortion legal through 12 weeks, the birth of a first child before marriage is usually a welcome event.[5]

Since 1975, abortion does not result in imprisonment if performed in the first trimester in the case of normal pregnancies, during the first four months for medical or ethical reasons, or if the female is a minor. There has been debate about the so-called morning-after pill as well as the right of minors to an abortion without written permission from a parent or guardian.

THE BALKAN STATES: SLOVENIA, CROATIA, SERBIA, MONTENEGRO, BOSNIA-HERZEGOVINA, MACEDONIA, AND ALBANIA

The Balkan Peninsula is an area of some 200,000 square miles. Nationalities are Serbs (8.5 million), Albanians (6 million), Croats (4.5 million), Bosniaks (2.4 million), Slovenians (2 million), Macedonians (1.4 million), and Montenegrins (0.265 million). Religions are

Christianity (Eastern Orthodox and Catholic) and Islam. Eastern Orthodox Serbia and Montenegro have their own national churches. Roman Catholicism is the principal religion in Croatia and Slovenia, while Islam is practiced by a majority in Albania. The median birthrate in the Balkans is 9.85 per 1,000 population. The life expectancy is 71.8 years for males and 78.1 years for females.

Albania is one of the least developed states in Europe. It has the highest birth rate and one of the youngest populations. Arranged marriages were customary into the twentieth century. It became illegal to betroth infants in 1946. Now, especially in rural areas, a bride is often under the legal age of 16. In northern Albania an unmarried daughter can be a source of shame. Should she lose her virginity, the family is sometimes shunned. The ancient Code of Lek, allowing a man to beat his wife and bind her in chains if she defies his orders, disappeared only well into the twentieth century. Church weddings, banned by the Communists in 1967, are again common. The man is no longer head of the household, and a woman can request divorce. Although abortion was legalized in 1992, rates peaked around 1997. Today contraceptives are available, a partial explanation for the current decrease in abortions. A sad fact is that 57 per 1,000 Albanian women die during pregnancy or childbirth.[6]

Muslims in Bosnia-Herzegovina call a young, unmarried woman a *cura*, literally a "big girl," physically mature, but still a virgin. A girl becomes a *cura* with the onset of menstruation; before that, she is a *curica,* or "little girl." Usually a girl can dance and socialize after her fourteenth year, the beginning of courtship age. Since 1977 abortion has been available during the first 10 weeks to preserve the mother's life or health, for socioeconomic reasons, in case of fetal impairment, or if the pregnancy is the result of sexual violence. A minor must obtain written permission from a parent or legal guardian unless she is over 16 and earns her living. There is a sizable but subdued homosexual community in Sarajevo. Sexual contact between men was illegal until 1998; today the community has a Website called *Queer Bosnia,* and activists who campaign for equal rights. There is little acknowledgment of lesbians.

In Serbia and Montenegro, people postpone marriage until they can earn a living. The age of marriage is 28.2 years for men and 24.7 for women. In 2001, only 60 percent of cohabitant couples were legally wed; 20 percent of children were born out of wedlock.[7] Anti-gay laws were extant in Serbia until the 1990s. In the mid-1990s, homosexual movements emerged such as Labris, a lesbian political group. Soon after, the first gay and lesbian center, Deve, opened in Belgrade. These groups organized the first Belgrade Gay Pride demonstration in June 2001.

In Slovenia, the median age for first intercourse is 18.5 years. Reasons stated for initiating sexual activity are love (45 percent), an "accident" (22 percent), and simple curiosity (15 percent). The marriage rate is dropping while cohabitation is increasing. In 2002, 7201 couples legalized their unions, nearly 7 percent fewer than in 1999. The age of marriage is rising. In 2000, the average man married at 29.6, and the average woman at 26.7 years. Slovenia's divorce rate increased from 0.14 in 1995 to 3.0 in 2002. Premarital cohabitation often includes the birth of children; births outside marriage are rising: in 2000, 37.1 percent births were to unmarried mothers.[8] Homosexuality was decriminalized in 1976. A gay student group, Magnus, organized in the mid-1980s. In spite of visible gay and lesbian groups, the Slovenian community has been slow to acknowledge the equality of homosexuals.[9]

BALKAN WEDDING TRADITIONS

A hundred years ago, many Balkan brides wore black. In traditional ceremonies, the couple remains seated and bridesmaids hold a red or a white canopy above their heads. A feast with food, dancing, and toasting of the couple follows.

COMING OF AGE IN LITHUANIA

Until the beginning of the twentieth century, a Lithuanian girl's first menstrual period was celebrated with a slap from her mother, who would wish her to "bloom like a rose and be beautiful."

Croatia has long been receptive to Western influence. Urban youth enjoys one of the most liberal lifestyles of the Balkan states, accepting premarital sexuality as a right. Older generations are more conservative, subscribing to gender roles and rejecting homosexuality. Fifty percent of women and 40 percent of men believe love forms the ideal basis for sexuality. 87 percent of Croatians disagree that marriage is an outdated institution. Surveys indicate 24.5 percent of girls and 46.3 percent of boys aged 15–17 have experienced coitus. Most persons adopt serial monogamy. Few people (2 percent) cohabit. Couples marry rapidly, and only 7 percent of children are born out of wedlock.[10] Except for large cities, where approximately 30 percent of marriages end in divorce, the divorce rate is low and most children grow up in two-parent homes. Abortion during the first 10 weeks was legalized in 1978, yet many facilities turn away women requesting abortions. The Women's Ad Hoc Coalition is fighting to maintain free, safe abortion and contraceptives.

During the beginning of the AIDS epidemic in the 1980s, the Ministry of Health classified homosexuals with prostitutes and drug users. Today 75 percent of Zagreb University students say sexual orientation is unimportant. Croatian gays and lesbians are increasingly active, often standing up to attack. The first homosexual organizations were established in the 2000s.[11]

One alarming post-Communist development is the enslavement of children and young women, many forced into prostitution in Western Europe. Victims are beaten, tortured, even murdered.[12]

THE BALTIC STATES: ESTONIA, LATVIA, LITHUANIA

Estonia is a 17,462-square-mile country with a population of 1,332,893 and a growth of –0.65 percent. Life expectancy is 66.3 years for men and 77.6 years for women. Estonians are the major ethnic group (67.9 percent), followed by Russians (25.6 percent), Ukrainians (2.1 percent), Belarusians (1.3 percent), Finns (0.9 percent), and others (2.2 percent). Religions are Evangelical Lutheran (13.6 percent), Orthodox (12.8 percent), other Christian (1.4 percent), unaffiliated and unspecified (3.2 percent), and none (6.1 percent).[13]

Latvia has a population of 2,290,237 and a population growth of –6.9 percent. Life expectancy is 65.8 years for men and 76.6 years for women. Ethnic groups are Latvian (57.7 percent), Russian (29.6 percent), Belarusian (4.1 percent), Ukrainian (2.7 percent), Polish (2.5 percent), and Lithuanian (1.4 percent). Major religions are Lutheran, Roman Catholic, and Russian Orthodox. Languages are Latvian (official; 58.2 percent), Russian (37.5 percent), Lithuanian and other (4.3 percent).[14]

Lithuania is a 65,200-square-kilometer country with a population of 3,596,617 and a growth rate of –0.3 percent. Life expectancy is 66 years for men and 78 years for women. Ethnically, its people are Lithuanians (83.4 percent), Poles (6.7 percent), Russians (6.3 percent), and others (3.6 percent). Religions include Roman Catholicism (79 percent), Russian Orthodoxy (4.1 percent), and various Protestant groups (1.9 percent). Lithuanian is the official language (82 percent), followed by Russian (8 percent), Polish (5.6 percent), and others (4.4 percent).[15]

Today youth in the Baltic region experience adolescence like most Europeans. Although there is sex education in schools, most get their information from peers, parents, the Internet, and pornography.

Dating and courtship is on the European model, with teens socializing in groups until couples are formed. Basketball games are popular, as is dancing or eating out. The Baltic states are more traditional than their Scandinavian neighbors, and gender differences more marked. Chivalry is appreciated, and men are expected to open doors for women.

HIV rates are high, and statistics indicate that fewer than 50 percent of people aged 16–20 practice safe sex. In Latvia, Genders, classified as an NGO (nongovernmental organization) in 1996, provides information about HIV and safe sex, strives to improve women's condition, and distributes condoms. In Estonia, Living for Tomorrow, an AIDS prevention organization, is aimed at young people.[16]

WEDDING TRADITIONS IN THE BALTIC STATES

Only civil marriage is recognized in the Baltic, although many also opt for a religious ceremony. City couples commonly choose Western-style weddings, yet there is a gradual return to traditional nuptials. Engagements last about six months; in some areas, the exchange of rings is a contract. A Latvian bride wears her veil until midnight, when it is passed to a younger female. At a traditional Lithuanian wedding, the flower girl and ring-bearer wear replicas of the bridal couple's outfits.

In spite of the declining population, many (approximately 50 percent) marry outside their ethnic and national groups. Divorce rates could soon overtake marriage rates in Estonia. Most people in Latvia and Estonia marry between the ages of 26 and 29.8, and more than half of all children are born outside wedlock. Abortion statistics continue to be high. In Latvia, more than 40 percent of children are born outside wedlock, and the country counts 110 abortions per 100 live births. In Lithuania, the age of first marriage is 22 years, and the abortion rate is lower: approximately 60 per 100 live births.[17]

Divorce is obtained through the courts or the Vital Statistics Office. There is no legal separation in Estonia. In 2002, 46.7 per 100 Estonian marriages ended in divorce; in Lithuania, the rate was 38.9 per 100; in Latvia, 34.4 per 100.[18]

In 1990, Tallinn hosted a congress on homosexuality. Laws against sodomy were repealed in 1992. In 1998, the Estonian Association for Lesbian and Bisexual Women was registered. Because of Lithuania's Catholic tradition, there is greater bias against homosexuality than in the other Baltic states, although homosexuality was decriminalized in 1993. Latvia has a thriving homosexual scene, but the Latvian Evangelical Lutheran Church excommunicated all active gays in 1995.[19]

BELGIUM

Belgium, a Western European country, won its independence from the Netherlands in 1830. Dutch (known in Belgium as Flemish) is spoken by the greatest number of inhabitants (60 percent), followed by French (39 percent), and German (less than 1 percent). Roman Catholicism is the major religion (60 to 75 percent). Others are Islam (6 percent and growing), Protestant faiths (1.2 percent), and Judaism (less than 1 percent). The birth rate is 10.48/1000 population, and life expectancy is 75.4 years for males and 81.9 years for females.[20]

Belgium is tolerant of homosexuality. In 2003, Belgium legalized same-sex marriage. In 2005, the government announced a total of 2,442 same-sex unions. Asylum can be requested by homosexuals claiming discrimination in their home countries.[21]

CEREMONIAL WEDDING CUSTOMS IN BULGARIA

Most Bulgarian couples opt for Western weddings; however, some choose traditional nuptials. One involves the bride's tossing a bowl of wheat (health), coins (prosperity), and raw eggs (fertility) over her head. If the bowl breaks, the union will endure. In some rural communities, a professional matchmaker finds partners for young women. The groom goes from home to home, toasting his upcoming wedding with *Palinca* (plum brandy). People who have not found a spouse can attend the annual "Maidens' Fair" in Transylvania.

There is controversy concerning abortion; the current law as of 2006 allows termination of pregnancy until the end of the twelfth week. Afterwards, abortion is allowed if there is risk to the health or life of the mother or if the fetus suffers from an incurable condition. Contraception is used by 78.5 percent of married or cohabiting females.[22]

While Belgians proclaim romantic love the best basis for sexual relationships, they do not equate sex with marriage. Cohabitation elicits no reaction, even among older generations. Children are often born out of wedlock. In 2002, Belgium had one of the lowest marriage rates in Western Europe (3.9 per 1,000). Those who marry are older (30.6 years for men, 28.4 years for women) than many other Europeans. In 2001, divorces exceeded marriages.[23]

Violence against women is a serious problem; others are prostitution and pedophilia. A 1998 study found that nearly 17 percent of women had been victims of domestic physical or sexual abuse. Many of the women and children taken from the Balkan states and sold into sexual slavery in Western Europe end up in Belgium. Close to half a million prostitutes work in Belgium, 50 percent of whom are imported by Eastern European traffickers. Brothel keepers earn 25 million euros a year.[24]

BULGARIA AND ROMANIA

The population of Bulgaria is 7.9 million with a birth rate of 9.66 per 1000. Life expectancy is 68.4 years for males and 75.9 for females. Ethnic groups are Bulgarians (83.9 percent), Turks (9.4 percent), Roma (4.7 percent), Armenian (0.1 percent), Vlach (0.1 percent), Macedonian (0.05 percent), and other (5.5 percent). Religions are Bulgarian Orthodox Christianity (82.6 percent), Islam (12.2 percent), Roman Catholic (0.6 percent), Protestant (0.5 percent), and undeclared (4.1 percent). The major language is Bulgarian.[25]

Romania has a population of 23 million and a growth rate of −0.21 percent. Life expectancy is 66.1 years for males and 74.0 years for females. The population is Romanian (89.5 percent), Hungarian (6.6 percent), Roma (2.5 percent), German (0.3 percent), and Ukrainian (0.3 percent). In terms of religion, Romanians are Romanian Orthodox (86.7 percent), followed by Roman Catholics (4.7 percent), Protestants (3.7 percent), Pentecostals (1.5 percent), Eastern-rite Catholics (0.9 percent), and atheists (9271 individuals).[26]

Family has always been important in Bulgaria and Romania. Into the late 1970s, Bulgarian women said a female's fulfillment comes through husband and children. Bulgarians typically marry young (18–25 for women; 20–25 for men). Matrimony is between man and woman; the legal age is 18. Only civil ceremonies are binding. Sexual activity involving persons 14 or younger is called "lechery"; yet among the Roma, very young marriages are common.

In 2000, however, 60 percent of Bulgarians stated marriage is not preferable to cohabitation. A considerable number cohabit, yet only marriage is recognized. Marriage is in slow decline. Today 25 percent of all marriages in Romania end in divorce.[27]

Until the mid-1950s, divorce carried stigma in Bulgaria. Rates started rising in the 1970s, and today 30 percent of marriages are dissolved. The state issued restrictions on divorce in the 1985 Family Code, making divorce extremely expensive. Divorce by mutual consent can be obtained after three years of marriage. Family law in Communist Romania was modeled on Soviet law. Divorce can be obtained by joint statement at the registry office. Divorce rates have been rising since the mid-1970s; today 25 percent of marriages end in divorce, most within seven years. Causes are violence, infidelity, and alcoholism.[28]

There is a historical reluctance to disseminate birth control, although abortion has long been available. In 1976, only 6 percent of females aged 15–44 used modern contraceptive methods; 94 percent did not use any birth control. However, by the late 1990s, 47 percent aged 15–44 used the pill, condoms, or an IUD. Nevertheless, Bulgaria has one of the highest teen pregnancy rates in the world, 83.3 per 1000. Furthermore, in 1970 the number of pregnancies ending in abortion was 50.4 percent; by 1996 the number had climbed to 57.7 percent. Bulgaria recognized the right to abortion early (1957), and the procedure is easily accessible and free for women under 18 and over 35.[29]

Romania started experiencing declining birth rates in 1960s and was the only European Communist nation to ban abortion and contraception. Abortion was possible for women over 40, those who already had five or more children, or if the mother's life was in danger. In December 1989, after the overthrow of Ceausescu, abortion was legalized. By the mid-1980s, Romania had the highest maternal death rate (abortion caused 80 percent of those deaths), and the highest infant mortality rate in Europe. Today the average woman wants two children. Between 1993 and 2001 there was a 40 percent decline in abortions, but Romania still has the highest abortion and infant mortality rate in Europe.[30]

The median age for first coitus in Bulgaria and Romania is 17.1 years. Bulgarians pride themselves on their sex lives. The average citizen reports 151 sexual encounters per year (world average is 103). Role-playing, watching pornography, and dressing up are favored stimulants; 21 percent say they enjoy a good spanking. More somberly, 44 percent have had unprotected sex without knowing the partner's sexual history.[31] Homosexuality was legalized in 1968, and discrimination against gays and lesbians made illegal in 2003. There are no sodomy laws, but "scandalous homosexuality," presumably public displays, is prohibited. Bulgarian society is generally negative about homosexuality.

In spite of the 2000 repeal of Article 200 making public displays of homosexuality punishable in Romania, homosexuals are routinely denied rights guaranteed by international law. Since homosexuality is viewed as contributing to a declining population, there is widespread belief that homosexuality can, and should, be eradicated.[32]

THE CZECH REPUBLIC AND SLOVAKIA

In 1993 the Czech and Slovak Federal Republic became separate nations. The Czech Republic has a population of 10,224,000. Life expectancy is 71.5 years for males and 78.7 years for females. Ethnically, inhabitants are mostly Czech (95 percent); other groups include Germans (0.4 percent), Roma (0.1 percent), Poles (0.5 percent), and Slovaks (2 percent). Most Czechs claim to be atheists (59 percent); otherwise the major religion is Roman Catholicism (27 percent), and there is a small Jewish community. In Slovakia the population is 5,431,363, and life expectancy is 70.5 years for men and 78.7 years for women. The population growth is 10.62 per 1000. Ethnic groups are Slovak (85.5 percent), Hungarian (9.7 percent), Roma (1.9 percent), and Ukrainian (1 percent). Roman Catholicism is the leading religion (68.9 percent), followed by Protestantism and Eastern-rite Catholicism (14.9 percent).[33]

FERTILITY IN THE CZECH REPUBLIC

Many Czechs and Slovacs opt for a Western-style wedding, but traditional customs endure. A baby is sometimes laid in a Czech wedding bed to ensure fertility.

Schools provide information about anatomy; safe sex education was introduced in the 2000s. However, most teens learn about sex from their peers (45 percent boys; 35 percent girls), followed by books, parents, the media, and the Internet. In the Czech Republic the median age of first sexual experience is 15.8 years; in Slovakia the median age is 17–18. Premarital sex is the norm, and most do not use contraceptives the first time (57 percent men; 64 percent women). Men report an average of 8.1 partners; women, 6.6 partners.[34]

Until 1990, most women used withdrawal or the rhythm method for birth control. The condom was used by 22–25 percent, and the pill by only 8–10 percent. Sterilization was chosen by 2 percent. In the late 1990s, pregnancy among girls under 15 was low (0.03 percent), with 70 percent ending in abortion. There is a growing anti-abortion stance in both countries. Slovakia has signed an agreement with the Vatican, allowing the Church control over school sex education.[35]

High employment and poor health care contributed to a population decline starting in the 1960s. Since 1987, abortion through the twelfth week has been available on demand. In 2004, the number of abortions fell for the first time since 1958; in 2004, 27,574 pregnancies were terminated, and 97,664 live births recorded. Today 40–50 percent of Slovak and Czech women take the pill, and these republics have the lowest abortion rates in the former Eastern bloc.[36]

Czechs and Slovaks have no courtship rituals such as the Maidens' Fair in Romania. Couples marry around age 20 to 21; spouses tend to be the same age. Serial monogamy is common. In the first quarter of 2005, 8,000 Czechs divorced; in 2002 the Slovakian rate was 11,000.[37]

Attitudes toward homosexuality are ambivalent. Consensual homosexuality was decriminalized in the early 1960s. Large cities have gay/lesbian clubs and organizations; Lambda, a gay campaigning organization, was registered in the Czech Republic in 1990. Yet, mores are slow to catch up. In 1995, 33 percent of men and 41 percent of women considered homosexuality a disease.[38]

FRANCE

France is a 547,030-square-kilometer country with a population of 60,000 and a growth of 0.37 percent. Life expectancy is 75 years for males and 83 for females. The population is French, with Teutonic, Slavic, North and West African, Indochinese, West Indian, and Basque minorities. The major language is French. Most French describe themselves as Roman Catholic (90 percent), followed by various denominations of Protestant (2 percent), Jewish (1 percent), Muslim (3 percent), and unaffiliated (4 percent).[39] Young people are informed about sexual matters, and premarital sex is common. A survey among 4,255 students aged 11–19 showed 31 percent had experienced intercourse. Although sexuality is considered a healthy part of life, parents rarely discuss sex with their children. Children receive sex education in school, including information about safe sex, contraception, and relationships.[40]

Although romance is the desired basis for sexual relationships, Adolescents (called *ados*) go to clubs, to the café, or out to eat with groups of friends that frequently form in primary school and last a lifetime. When pairing occurs, it leads to a monogamous sexual relationship. There is no stigma attached to an experienced girl; both genders express affection through sexuality. Birth control is freely available, and prophylactic vending machines are found in school and university rest rooms, clubs, and youth hostels.

In 1998 the PACS (*pacte civil de solidarité*) was given recognition in law. The PACS is a contract between two persons having many of the implications of marriage, such as common property, joint tax matters, social protection, inheritance, and synchronized vacation time. Common law marriage (known as *concubinage*) is common, and spouses have many of the rights and responsibilities of marriage and the PACS.[41]

Divorce became legal in 1792, was abolished in 1816, and reestablished in 1884. The latest law (2005) makes divorce practical and nonpunitive. Divorce by mutual consent is encouraged.

France has no sodomy laws. Although at variance with traditional values, homosexuality is accepted. André Labarre, member of the French Senate, and Bertrand Delanoe, Mayor of Paris, are gay. The French Family Court recognized a lesbian couple as parents in 2004, using the word "family" to describe the couple and their three daughters.[42]

THE ORIGINS OF "BRIDAL WHITE" AND OTHER FRENCH WEDDING CUSTOMS

Most French dream of a romantic wedding followed by a lifelong relationship. Only civil marriages are legal, but many also opt for a religious ceremony. Bridal white originated in France, as did the hope chest. French couples prefer to marry between May and July; nobody weds on August 15, the day celebrating *la sainte Vièrge* (the Virgin Mary). In rural areas, friends gather under the bridal pair's window, banging on pots and pans, singing and joking loudly.

GERMANY

Germany is a 137,838-square-mile country with a population of 82.5 million and a growth rate of 0.1 percent. Life expectancy is 74.3 years for men and 80.6 years for women. Ethnic groups are German (91.5 percent), Turkish (2.4 percent), Serbo-Croatian, Italian, Russian, Greek, Polish, Spanish, and others (6.1 percent). The population is divided between Protestants, mainly Lutherans (38 percent), Roman Catholics (34 percent), and Muslims and unaffiliated make up 28 percent.[43]

Prior to World War II, Germany pioneered the study of sexuality. Hitler's Third Reich (1933–45) squelched such research, promoting a return to traditional roles. Women were encouraged to adhere to *Küche, Kirche, Kinder* (kitchen, church, children), reinforced by the concept of *Lebensborn*, the "ideal" of producing pure "Aryan" children. The Cross of Honor of the German Mother was bestowed on women bearing four or more children.

Today, Germany is again in the vanguard of sexual liberty. After puberty, both males and females enjoy sexual autonomy. It is not unusual for minors (under 18) to leave the parental home to live with a partner or friends. Sex education starts in elementary school; however, most youngsters get their primary information from peers, books, magazines, and the Internet.

Young people have social "appointments," with each expecting to pay his or her own way. They go to movies and museums, engaging one another in discussions about politics, art, and philosophy. While there is a tendency to postpone marriage or cohabitation, nearly everyone expresses a desire for a solid, loving relationship. Most people answer "love" when explaining why they choose to share their lives with another. Teens, asked what they value highest in relationships, list trust, understanding, compatibility, and respect for individuality.

GERMAN MARRIAGE CUSTOMS

Germans are attached to customs concerning love and marriage. One is the wedding booklet, created by family and friends, with pictures and anecdotes about the couple. The booklet is "sold" during the reception, raising money for a honeymoon. Only civil marriage is legal, but many also opt for a religious ceremony. Sometimes guests bring old dishes they can break to the *Polterabend* (rehearsal dinner).

Romantic attachment is followed by sexual contact, intercourse occurring among 50 percent of couples within three months. There is no value attached to virginity, and couples are roughly the same age. Adolescents idealize first intercourse as something to look forward to. The average age for coitus is 17, although 30 percent experience intercourse before 16. Young Germans often have the partner sleep over at their parents' home. Most teens experience serial monogamy before settling down.[44]

Contraception is freely available. More than 80 percent of women use contraception for their first act of intercourse, and 90 percent of those who want to avoid pregnancy practice regular birth control. Conscious of the dangers of HIV, a majority of young males avoid intercourse without a condom. The most popular contraceptive is the pill, and 94 percent women aged 30–45 have taken it.[45]

Yet, differences separate population groups. With the influx over the past 40 years of guest workers (notably from Islamic Turkey), there is growing tension between the immigrant patriarchal model of gender differentiation and female chastity, and the German ideal of gender equality and tolerance for difference.

Germany records fewer marriages, more divorces, and smaller families yearly. In 2004, only 395,992 persons said *Ja* to matrimony, while 213,691 couples divorced. After decades of declining birth rates, Germany is witnessing a renewed population increase, mostly as a result of immigrant populations.[46] The first abortion laws were passed in the nineteenth century. In 1992 the *Bundestag* (Parliament) allowed first-trimester abortion on demand. Although a considerable percentage of teen pregnancies are terminated by abortion, the rate is still only about one-fifth of that in the United States.[47]

Antigay legislature was repealed in 1994, four years after the unification of Germany. The greatest growth of homosexual groups occurred during the 1980s, when many lesbians were involved with the feminist movement. In 1985 a public ceremony was held to commemorate homosexuals murdered under the Nazi regime.

Now Berlin's annual Christopher Street Day Parade, a gay pride event, draws over 400,000, and the same city boasts the Schwules Museum, housing the world's largest collection of gay and lesbian artifacts. In June 2001, openly gay Klaus Wowereit was elected mayor of Berlin.[48]

GREECE

Formerly the Hellenic Republic, Greece is a 51,000-square-mile country with a population of 11 million and a growth rate of 0.21 percent. Life expectancy is 75.9 years for males and 81.2 years for females. Most citizens are Greek (98 percent), although there has been considerable Turkish and Albanian influx into the population. Other groups include Jews and Roma. The Greek Orthodox Church (98 percent) is followed by Islam (1.3 percent), and other (0.7 percent) in religious affiliation. The official language is Greek (spoken by 99 percent).[49]

Greece is a traditional patriarchy. Women in ancient Greece were little more than chattel, ruled over by males of the family. Today the primary role of women is still that of mother and homemaker, and females are underrepresented in the electorate.

Since there is no formal school sex education, young Greeks get knowledge from their parents, their peers, the media, and the Internet. Contraceptive dissemination is limited. The government has established over 50 Family Planning Centers showing limited effectiveness. Abortion on demand through the twelfth week was legalized in 1986; however, abortion has long been accepted. Although precise rates are elusive, the World Health Organization estimates more than 150,000 yearly abortions are performed, one of the highest rates in Europe. A 2004 survey showed the most common contraceptive method to be the condom (33.9 percent), followed by coitus interruptus (28.8 percent), the pill (4.8 percent), and the IUD (3.6 percent); no birth control was used by 23.8 percent.[50]

GREEK WEDDING CEREMONIES

After the rings are blessed outside the church, a Greek couple is led inside to stand on a platform. The bridal pair holds lighted candles, symbolizing happiness. The Greek Orthodox Church allows three marriages, and 90 percent of divorced Greeks optimistically marry again.

Love is taken seriously, and many believe sex should imply the possibility of children. Adolescents are romantic, placing greater emphasis on the emotional than the physical aspect of relationships. The median age of first coitus is 15 to 17. Cohabitation is frowned upon, yet, as more young Greeks acquire cars, they have greater autonomy. Courtship tends to be long (4 to 6 years). Rural areas remain conservative, and premarital sex the exception. In some villages matchmaking (*proksenio*) still exists, and women may go into marriage with a dowry (*prika*).[51]

Marriage is the desirable state for all adults, with emphasis on becoming a good husband or dutiful wife. Yet, with a gradually increasing single population, cities constitute a paradigm shift. Greeks can choose between a religious and a civil wedding; before 1982, only religious marriage was valid. Most choose the Greek Orthodox Church, and Greek weddings are among the most festive in the world. Divorce is increasingly common, although rates remain lower than in most industrialized nations. Children are the glue holding marriage together; divorcing couples typically have only one child or none.

Greece is often associated with a reputation for homosexuality because of relationships between older men and pubescent boys in ancient Greece. The Greek Homosexual Liberation Movement (AKOE) was founded in 1978, publishing *Amphi*, the first gay Greek magazine. The April 2000 Gay Pride march in Athens attracted homosexuals from everywhere. There remains tolerance for male homosexuality, and occasional same-sex encounters are not considered indicative of homosexuality. Lesbians have difficulty gaining acceptance because of the idea that woman's fulfillment lies in marriage and children.[52]

HUNGARY

The Republic of Hungary has a population of 10,198,315 with a growth rate of –0.33 percent. Life expectancy is 67 years for men and 76 years for females. Ethnic groups are Hungarian (93 percent), Roma (2 percent), German (1.2 percent), Romanian (0.8 percent), Slovakian (0.4 percent), Croatian (0.2 percent), Serbian (0.2 percent), and Ukrainian (0.1 percent). A majority of Hungarians are Roman Catholic (68 percent), followed by Protestant (Calvinists, 21 percent; Lutherans, 6 percent). There are small groups of Greek Catholic and Orthodox congregations, and approximately 80,000 Jews.[53]

Mores were traditionally conservative in Hungary. In the early 1980s, young women often discovered the facts of life on their wedding night. Masturbation was thought to drain a

WEDDING TRADITIONS IN HUNGARY

In times past, a Hungarian groom fetched his bride on horseback. After exchanging vows, the couple now heads a procession of guests. In rural areas the procession can circle through the town, people leaving their homes to congratulate the couple.

boy's spinal fluid. Girls were expected to have no sexual feelings, and chastity was highly prized. Hungary now has school sex education, although quality varies from district to district. Most teens learn about sex from parents, peers, the media, the Internet, and pornographic materials, now often locally produced.[54]

Hungary is moving into the European model, and young adults increasingly emancipated. Teenagers have started American-style dating, especially in Budapest and other large cities. Favored activities are going to dance clubs, eating at restaurants, and watching foreign movies. Teenagers become sexually active at a median age of 16.8 years. However, substance abuse among the young is rampant, and as many as 300,000 teens live on the streets. Rates of sexually transmitted diseases, including HIV, are rising.[55]

Hungarians are romantic, laying emphasis on chivalry and courtship. Men give flowers to women, and expect to pay on a date. Women seek a monogamous, loving relationship, and casual sex is not the norm, even in cities.

Contraceptives were difficult to obtain under Communism, and abortion was used as birth control. The abortion rate is approximately 50,000 per annum, a rate of 74 per 100 live births. As a result of declining population growth and ethical and patriotic concerns, abortion is under fire. In 1993, the state medical agency stopped subsidizing contraceptives. Nevertheless, statistics indicate that 73 percent of women in a steady relationship use birth control. Hungary was a pioneer in emergency contraception.[56]

Today more than 40 percent of marriages end in divorce. Dissolution of marriage can be granted if one or both spouses declare the marriage irretrievably broken down.

Although homosexuality was decriminalized in 1961, homophobia still exists, and most gays and lesbians live discreetly. Today Hungary celebrates Gay Pride Day, and organizations, clubs, restaurants, and other venues cater to gays and lesbians.[57]

ITALY

Italy is a 116,334-square-mile country with a population of 58,057,477 (2004). Life expectancy is 76.6 years for men and 82.7 years for women. The population growth is 0.09 percent. Inhabitants are Italian, with small groups of Germans, French, Slovenians, Albanians, and Greeks. The language is Italian, although clusters of German, Slovene, and French speaking populations exist. The religion is Roman Catholicism (97.20 percent). Because of Albanian and North African immigration, there is a Muslim minority.[58]

At the beginning of the twentieth century, as a result of the growing presence of women in the work force, traditional gender roles came under discussion. The Fascist era (1922–43) witnessed a reversal of the egalitarian trend. Starting in the 1960s, female education has increased dramatically. Although gender inequalities exist in rural areas, women in large cities enjoy more freedom than before, and premarital sex is accepted among students and young professionals.

In the early 2000s, the Ministry of Education funded sex education in public schools. Today Italians get their information from parents, peers, the media, and the Internet. Magazines and television offer articles and programs about sexual matters. Italians, especially those from towns, are relatively well informed about sexuality.

In cities the median age of first coitus is 17 to 19. About 50 percent use modern contraceptives. Some prejudice still persists; in 1997 condom dispensers in high schools caused a public outcry.[59]

Abortion was a common form of birth control under Fascism. After lobbying by feminist groups, first-trimester abortion on demand was legalized in 1978. Abortion remains controversial and harshly condemned by the Catholic church. Statistics show abortion is declining among women of Italian ethnicity (in 2000, 140,000 were performed), a reflection of improved access to contraceptives.[60]

ELABORATE ITALIAN WEDDINGS

When Italians wed, they choose a Roman Catholic or a civil ceremony. Italian weddings are among the most impressive and expensive in the world. The celebration might start with a religious ceremony in the morning, followed by a multicourse meal lasting 4–6 hours, and end with dancing.

One-on-one dating is uncommon in Italy. Young people prefer group activities, going to cafés, movies, or restaurants with friends. Strolling through the streets eating a *gelato* (ice cream) and picnics or soccer matches in the countryside are popular. Men take the lead in romance, and chivalry is practiced by even the young and educated. Men open doors for women, light their cigarettes (nearly 25 percent of Italian women smoke), and might request a kiss at the end of an evening. Text messaging has become a popular method of flirtation, and clever *repartée* an important part of courtship.

A majority of Italians (80 percent) say love is a requirement for a satisfying sexual relationship; yet both genders admit sexual feelings for persons other than their partners. Faithfulness is deemed primordial for a successful union; yet 35 percent of men and 15 percent of women report relations with other persons. Today the average age of marriage is 30.0 years for men and 27.1 years for women. As a result of the high cost of living, increased unemployment, and strong family traditions, many young, single professionals in their 30s or older remain in, or move back into, the childhood home.[61]

In 2004, there were 50,828 divorces, below the European average. Although legalized in 1970, divorce is not the norm because of religious custom and the importance placed on family. Three years must pass between legal separation and a petition for divorce.[62]

Legislation does not permit same-sex marriage, and no law protects homosexuals. Gay men are exempt from military service. Mostly thanks to Arcigay, a homosexual lobbying association, convictions based on discrimination are increasing. As in all areas, there is a schism between northern Italy and the southern areas. Whereas the north is increasingly tolerant, homosexuality is still derided in the south, where many consider it a disease or perversion.[63]

THE NETHERLANDS

The Netherlands is a 15,770-square-mile northwestern monarchy with a population of 16,407,491. Life expectancy is 76.3 years for males and 81.5 years for females. Persons of Dutch ethnicity are the majority (83 percent), followed by other Europeans (8 percent), and Turks, Moroccans, Antilleans, Surinamese, and Indonesians (9 percent). Dutch is the official language, and religions are Roman Catholic (31 percent), Dutch Reformed (13 percent), Calvinist (7 percent), Muslim (5.5 percent), other (2.5 percent), and no religious affiliation (41 percent).[64]

THE ORIGIN OF BRIDAL SHOWERS

Wedding showers originated in the Netherlands. If a girl's father disapproved of her husband, he could refuse her a dowry. Her girlfriends and female relatives would then shower her with household items so she would not go empty-handed into marriage.

A historically liberal society, Holland is undergoing a process, sometimes termed "Americanization," involving increased conservatism. Many matters accepted by ethnic Dutch are offensive to immigrant families, often Muslims. Dutch parents practice tolerance coupled with vigilance, acknowledging their children's sexuality while counseling self-protection. Children learn about sex at school or from their parents and peers, the media, and the Internet.

The Dutch subscribe to the idea of romantic love, but recreational sex is not condemned. There is sympathy for persons alone, and visiting a prostitute is regarded as a healthy outlet. Contraception is available, even to minors. Sex education is compulsory, although slightly different programs respect variations in ethnic and religious backgrounds.

Since 1971 modern contraceptives have been available upon request. By 2006, 96 percent of women of childbearing age were using contraception. The Netherlands has one of the lowest teen pregnancy rates of all industrialized nations. Abortion was tolerated already in 1972; in 1984, it became available upon demand. The abortion rate for women 15 to 19 is 4.2 per 1,000, 10 times lower than in the United States.[65]

One-on-one dating is uncommon. Going out with groups of friends is preferred, and only established couples spend evenings alone together. Women open their own doors and drive themselves or bicycle to their destinations. There is no value attached to virginity, except in Muslim communities.[66]

In the first half of 2005, the marriage age had risen to 30.7 years for men and 28.3 years for women. Some elect not to marry, opting for one of three other legal unions: a Registered Partnership, Cohabitation with Registration, or Cohabitation without Registration. In 1992, 93,638 weddings were celebrated; in 2004, only 75,056 heterosexual partners married. However, 2004 also saw 949 Registered Partnerships and 69 same-sex unions (36 male; 33 female). Only civil marriage is recognized. In 2001 the Dutch parliament legalized same-sex marriage. Since then 1,075 marriages between women and 1,339 unions between men have been performed.[67]

Divorce rates are rising, and the system is geared toward making divorce easy. Couples can choose a "blitz divorce" (*Flitsscheiding*) where marriage is downgraded to Registered Partnership and processed through City Hall.

The General Equal Treatment Act was enacted in 1994. It prohibits discriminatory acts based on gender, sexual orientation, religion, political affiliation, race, or civil status. Since 1998, homosexual partners can share custody with same-sex partners.[68]

POLAND

The Republic of Poland has a population of 38,536,869 (July 2006 census). Life expectancy is 70.4 years for men and 78.5 years for women. The population growth rate is 0.02 percent. Ethnic groups are Polish (96.7 percent), German (0.4 percent), Belarusian (0.1 percent), Ukrainian (0.1 percent), and other (2.7 percent). The dominant religion is Roman Catholic (95 percent), followed by Eastern Orthodox, Protestant, and other (5 percent). A majority (80 percent) describe themselves as deeply religious. The official language is Polish (97.8 percent).[69]

Poland is a traditionally conservative society, strongly influenced by the Roman Catholic faith. People with rural backgrounds feel strong ties to the church and its doctrines, whereas educated Poles are more progressive, eager to embrace the pragmatic attitudes of their European neighbors. Issues related to love, sex, and relationships divide Poles. One is sex education with its emphasis on safe sex and contraception; others are abortion and homosexuality.

POLISH CUSTOMS

Poles prefer to marry on Saturdays so that the festivities can last into the night. In a custom still practiced in rural areas, the bride's mother pins the veil to her daughter's hair right before she enters the church, then removes it at the wedding party, symbolizing the bride's passage from childhood to adulthood.

Surveys reveal that peers are the main source of sexual information, followed by magazines and the Internet. Approximately 20 percent have intercourse before 16; by age 19, 55 percent boys and 44 percent of girls have had coitus. Women place importance on emotional connection (75 percent), and men cite affection/love (41 percent), followed by curiosity (35 percent), and desire to be a man (16 percent). More than 75 percent have sexual relations before marriage. Cohabitation is rare (1.2 percent). Married couples often live with parents, even after the birth of the first child.[70]

Under Communism abortion was common. The Anti-Abortion Act of 1993 made it illegal except if the pregnancy endangers the woman's life or health, the embryo is seriously damaged, or the pregnancy is a result of sexual crime. Even women with HIV have been refused abortion because fetuses are not automatically infected. Some 80,000 to 250,000 illegal abortions are performed yearly, most through the "abortion underground" (illegal operations performed by licensed physicians), causing hundreds of deaths. The United Nations Human Rights Committee demanded in 2004 that Poland reform abortion laws, make contraceptives widely available, and address sex education. Teen pregnancy rates are rising; surveys from the late 1990s indicate only 10 percent of sexually active girls 11–19 years old were familiar with contraception or believed sex causes pregnancy.[71]

Poland is a chivalrous society. A man might kiss a woman on the hand, although this is typically reserved for older ladies. Poles are not accustomed to casual sex; both genders expect relationships to endure. Females appreciate the emotional support of a steady relationship, and spurn the advances of males they suspect of being flighty. A 1991 survey indicated that 50 percent of women and 25 percent of men had experienced a single sexual partner. Among married couples, 85 percent of wives and 56 percent of husbands claim to never cheat.[72] The average Pole marries at 24 to 34 years. There were 319,200 marriages in 1948; in 2003 only 195,000 couples tied the knot. Informal relationships are gaining ground because emphasis is on finishing an education and establishing a career before marriage.[73]

In 2002, 41,000 marriages ended. Women filed nearly 80 percent of the petitions. The Catholic Church does not recognize divorce, and people cohabiting with a new partner cannot receive Holy Communion.[74]

Despite liberal laws, equality for homosexuals has not been reached. In 2005, the mayor of Warsaw banned Gay Pride celebrations for the second time, and in 2000 Catholic former president Lech Walesa reportedly stated that homosexuals need medical treatment.[75]

RUSSIA, UKRAINE, BELARUS

Russia is the world's largest country with 6.5 million square miles. The population is 143.4 million (2005 estimate), and population growth is –0.37 percent. Life expectancy is

VALENTINE'S DAY

Under Communism, women were given flowers on International Women's Day (March 8). Although the Soviet holiday is still observed, Valentine's Day is becoming the day when women are celebrated. In 2003, television featured programs on how to show affection on Valentine's Day, and police presented women who committed traffic offenses with flowers instead of tickets. In Ukraine, Valentine's Day has become enormously popular, and the custom is to send not only roses but also champagne or a bottle or two of vodka.

60.6 years for men and 74.0 years for women. The ethnic makeup is Russian (78.8 percent), Tartar (3.8 percent), Ukrainian (2 percent), Bashkir (1.2 percent), Chuvash (1.1 percent), and other (12.1 percent). Religions are Russian Orthodox and Muslim. The official language is Russian.[76]

Ukraine, a 603.700-square-kilometer country, has a population of 47.4 million (2005 estimate), with a population growth of –0.63 percent. Life expectancy is 61.6 years for males and 72.38 years for females. Ethnic groups include Ukrainians (77.8 percent), Russians (17.3 percent), Belarus (0.6 percent), and small groups of Romanians, Poles, and Hungarians. The dominant religion is Ukranian Orthodox, with a minority of Ukrainian-rite Catholics and pockets of Protestants and Jews. Ukranian is the official language; other groups speak Romanian, Polish, and Hungarian.[77]

Belarus is a 207,600-square-kilometer country with a population of 10,300,483. The population growth is –0.09 percent and life expectancy is 63.0 years for men and 74.7 years for women. Belarusians are most numerous (81.2 percent), followed by Russians (11.4 percent), Poles (3.9 percent), Ukrainians (2.4 percent), and others (1.1 percent). Religions are Eastern Orthodox (80 percent), with Roman Catholic, Protestant, Jewish, and Muslim making up the remaining 20 percent.[78]

Since sexuality among the young was denied under socialism, Soviet children received virtually no sexual information. The fall of Communism created availability of sexual material and outlets. Concurrently, prostitution, sexually transmitted diseases, and trafficking in women and children exploded. Today HIV rates are climbing and the birth rate plummeting. A systematic program of Russian sex education in schools is still lacking, although more than 80 percent of the population is in favor. Youngsters learn about sex from peers, the media, and the Internet. Pornography is another source of "information." In Ukraine, educators and health specialists have created programs to inform the young about intimacy, reproduction, pregnancy, contraception, abortion, and STDs.[79]

Divorce was prevalent under Soviet rule, yet that rate is now higher, with 45 for every 100 Russian marriages ending yearly. In the Ukraine, 65 percent of marriages end in divorce; in Belarus, the figure is 68 percent. Single-parent families are increasing as a result of divorce, increased childbirth outside marriage, and economic problems.[80]

Courtship in Russia, Ukraine, and Belarus is taken seriously, and love considered a foundation for a good sexual relationship. Pragmatic attitudes sometimes carry the day. Women, especially, state their willingness to forego love if a relationship carries financial security.

Today the dating style in Russia, Belarus, and Ukraine is closely tied to the economic situation. Conversation over a drink or a cup of coffee is common, as is going to parties and clubs. Teens are sexually active, many starting as young as 15. Serial monogamy is the norm, with young adults experiencing successive relationships.

Most females undergo at least one abortion. According to the *United Nations Demographic Yearbook*, Russia is a country where abortions outnumber live births (2:1). In Ukraine, nearly 50 percent of people under 17 have had at least three partners, and more than 50 percent of sexually active teens become pregnant at least once. Russia accounts for

70 percent of HIV cases in Eastern Europe and Central Asia. In 2003, 860,000 Russians were infected. In Ukraine in 2004, more than 68,000 persons were living with HIV. For Belarus, the number is about 43,000.[81]

A recent phenomenon involves "mail-order brides" for Western husbands. Business is booming, with hundreds of agencies competing for clients. Most of the women are under 35 and attractive; many head single-parent households. Reasons for wanting a Western husband are the desire for financial security, the need for a "strong" man, and the hope of finding a new life elsewhere. Men who seek Russian, Ukrainian, and Belarusian wives often hope they will be less modern than American or Western European females.

Couples wanting to wed submit a request to the local registrar. Only civil marriage is legal; however, many couples also choose a church ceremony. Rings are plain gold bands worn on the right hand. A band on the left signals a widow or widower. At the wedding supper following the *Zags* (the signing of the registry), many toasts are drunk to the couple's happiness.

In 1933 homosexuality became a criminal offense. After the breakup of the Soviet Union, many republics revised anti-homosexual laws. Today Russia has registered gay magazines and associations devoted to ending discrimination against homosexuals. Homosexuality was decriminalized in the mid-1990s. However, homosexuals remain among the most reviled minorities in Russia, Belarus, and Ukraine.[82]

SCANDINAVIA

Scandinavia refers to the Kingdoms of Denmark, Norway, and Sweden; sometimes Finland is included.

Swedes are the majority inhabitants of Sweden, followed by a sizable population of Sweden-Finns along the Swedish-Finnish border, and a small population of Saamis (Laplanders) to the north. Swedish is the dominant language, and the Church of Sweden the official religion (87 percent). A small immigrant Muslim population exists. The population is 9 million; the birthrate is 10 per 1000. Life expectancy is 77.1 years for males and 82.5 years for females.[83]

Denmark has a population of 5,432,335 with a birthrate of 12.2 per 1000. The language is Danish, although minorities speak Faroese and Greenlandic. Danes are the largest ethnic group (93.8 percent) with Asian, Turkish, African, English, German, Swedish, Inuit, and Faroese minorities (6.2 percent). The state religion is Lutheran (84.3 percent). Others are non-Lutheran Protestant and Roman Catholic (2 percent) and Muslim (3 percent). Danish is the official language (98 percent).[84]

Norway is a 324,220-square-kilometer country with a population of 4,574,560. The population growth is 0.41 percent, and life expectancy is 76.6 years for males and 82.0 years for females. Norwegians are the dominant ethnic group (92.7 percent). The official language is Norwegian. Religions are Lutheranism (86 percent), other Protestant denominations (3.5 percent), Roman Catholicism (1 percent), and Islam (2 percent).[85]

Finland, with a population of 5.2 million, is Europe's largest archipelago. Finnish is the official language (91.3 percent), followed by Swedish (5.4 percent) and Saami (a few thousand). The major religion is Lutheran (85.6 percent).[86]

The Scandinavian countries are liberated and egalitarian. The advent of the birth control pill in the 1960s resulted in great sexual pragmatics. Scandinavians, including Finns, enjoy freedom to experiment with different partners and lifestyles without censure. Gender equality is genuine: all countries report women in high positions, and Finland counts a female president of the republic.

SCANDINAVIAN WEDDING CUSTOMS

Danish weddings often involve a Gate of Honor through which the couple walks in a symbolic passage to married life. A traditional Norwegian groom wears his *bunda* (the costume from his village or region), consisting of a white silk shirt, a vest, coat, short trousers, and knee-stockings. At some Swedish weddings, the tradition of a gold coin (given by the mother) in one shoe, and a silver coin (given by the father) in the other is still observed.

School sex education starts at 12–14 years, covering anatomy and puberty, later including information about contraceptives, sexually transmitted diseases, cohabitation, and same-sex relationships. When Finns turn sixteen, they receive a pamphlet on relationships, sexuality, and family planning. It includes sample condoms. Scandinavians also get information from parents, peers, the media, the Internet, and pornography. Only child pornography is illegal in Scandinavia. Sexuality is found in movies, on television, on billboards, in the arts, in research. It should be noted that Danish feminist groups are agitating for a return of privacy to sexuality.

Adolescents experience intercourse at ages 14 to 17 on average. Premarital sex is the norm, and the old Nordic custom of children before marriage commonplace (more than 50 percent of Scandinavian children are born outside marriage). Although marriage now enjoys renewed popularity, many still never wed (marriage rates dropped some 50 percent between 1960 and the early 1970s). In spite of sex education and availability of contraception, abortion rates are higher in Scandinavia than in such countries as the Netherlands.[87]

Females commonly take the initiative in courtship, and excessive chivalry is viewed with suspicion. Men often wait for women to demonstrate willingness before showing interest. Once the ice is broken, sex can happen rapidly. The one-night stand is frequent and can lead to a long-term relationship. Over 50 percent of Finns of both genders exchanged their first kiss before age 13; approximately 5 percent of the same age group also experienced intercourse. Love forms the basis for sex, and most 15-year-olds have, or hope to have, loving intimacy with a steady partner. Forty percent of single males and 28 percent of single females enjoy regular sex with different partners. Finnish women often lead the dance, taking the sexual initiative in 15 percent of encounters. Men and women aged 18–54 now report at least ten sexual partners over a lifetime. Finns believe the elderly and the physically or mentally infirm are entitled to love and sex, and want residential facilities to provide private rooms for such purposes.[88]

Scandinavians form romantic attachments at work, at school, in public places, or in private homes. Going out for coffee or a beer and enjoying a lively discussion are favored activities. Other pastimes are bicycling or walking in the countryside. In Finland, the cell phone is an important part of flirtation, used to approach a potential partner. Among Finns, 67 percent of women and 59 percent of men report being in love. Engagement rings are plain gold bands. Most engaged couples are already cohabiting, and engagement does not necessarily herald marriage in the near future. The average age at marriage is 33–36 years for men and 30–33 years for women.[89]

When Scandinavians marry, they choose a civil or religious ceremony. Same-sex couples can enter a Registered Partnership, followed by an ecclesiastical blessing. By 2002, more than 2000 Danish partnerships had been registered. Heterosexual marriage and same-sex unions carry the same rights and responsibilities.

When marriage in Scandinavia is terminated, it starts with separation, regulated by civil authority, followed by divorce. However, divorce without prior separation is possible when one spouse has remarried, there has been domestic violence, one spouse has committed adultery, or a couple has lived apart over 2 years.

Homosexuality was decriminalized in Denmark in 1933; in 1941 the first explicit lesbian novel was published. Following World War II, homosexuals were persecuted and "masturbation patrols" entrapped gays. Sex with male minors was punished by aversion therapy and even castration.[90] In 1954, *Pan*, the first homosexual publication in the world, was founded. The Lutheran Church began blessing homosexual partnerships in 1997. The Norwegian Association for Lesbian and Gay Liberation (LLH) lobbies to improve the life of gays, lesbians, and transexuals. Sweden passed an amendment to the Constitution in 2002 making it a crime to target homosexuals with "unfavorable speech." Today homosexuals see themselves as citizens first, homosexuals only incidentally.[91]

TRADITIONAL WEDDINGS IN SPAIN

Spanish couples can choose a civil or religious wedding. In a traditional wedding, the groom gives his wife 13 coins (*arras*), symbolizing future support. Sometimes bride and groom exchange coins. Spanish weddings usually involve dancing, singing, and many delicious dishes, including squid served in a sauce cooked with its own ink.

THE IBERIAN PENINSULA: SPAIN AND PORTUGAL

Spain and Portugal lie in the Iberian Peninsula. Spain is a 194,896-square-mile country with a population of 43.2 million (2005 estimate) and a growth rate of 2.1 percent. Life expectancy is 75.3 years for men and 82.5 for women. The major religion is Roman Catholicism (99 percent); others are mostly Muslim (1 percent). Spanish is the official language (74 percent), but minorities speak Catalan (17 percent), Galician (7 percent), and Basque (2 percent). Portugal is a 35,550-square-mile country with a population of 10.6 million (2005 estimate), and a growth rate of 0.18 percent. Life expectancy is 72.2 years for men, and 79.5 years for women. In addition to ethnic Portuguese, the country has a 100,000 population of black African descent. Roman Catholicism is the dominant religion (94 percent), followed by Protestant and Muslim minorities. Portuguese is the official language.[92]

Spanish women earned the right to vote and divorce in 1931, but under the rule of Francisco Franco (1939–1975) women returned to the role of homemakers, and sex to procreation within marriage. After Franco's death in 1975, freedoms were reclaimed. Couples began to cohabit, school sex education was suggested, and divorce was again possible. The 1980s and 1990s witnessed legalization of abortion and the rise of feminist and gay movements.[93]

The church no longer dominates mores; most Spaniards disregard its teachings about relationships. Society is increasingly tolerant about sexual matters. Sixty-seven percent of women aged 15–49 use modern birth control. In 2002, 9.82 percent of female visits to Barcelona emergency rooms on summer weekends were for emergency contraception.[94]

Portugal also experienced fascist rule (1932–1974), with ramifications on sex and marriage. Portugal has a tradition of *Marianismo*, the cult of the Virgin Mary, holding maternity without sex as the feminine ideal. In 1999, a Ministry of Equality was created. Today only about 20 percent of elected officials are women; however, they constitute 80 percent of the university population. Teenagers are more likely to accept sex without strings than any previous generation. The average 17-year-old in Lisbon regards premarital sex as normal, although criticism is attached to one-night stands. Women no longer place value on virginity, a sentiment not

MARRIAGE IN PORTUGAL

In Portugal, both civil and religious marriage is legal, as is marriage between first cousins. Same-sex marriage is illegal. Wedding feasts are memorable for their seafood and copious servings of local wines.

always shared by males. Love is the ideal basis for a sexual relationship, with older generations more likely to believe sex should happen within a committed relationship. Although contraceptives are available and free, Portugal has one of the highest teenage pregnancy rates in Europe: 25 per 1,000 for females aged 14–19.[95]

There is sex education in Spanish schools; youngsters also get information from peers, the media, and the Internet. In cities boys engage in coitus at a median age 15.4 years, and girls at 16.1 years. Sex play without penetration is common (14 percent girls; 33 percent boys). Nearly half of Spaniards and Portuguese have had intercourse before age 15 (52 percent males; 37 percent females). It is increasingly common for urban Portuguese to have sex as early as 12.[96]

Portugal enacted legislation in 1984 making sex education mandatory. However, such education is sporadic, and many Portuguese learn about sex from parents, friends, and the Internet. A TV program, *A. B. Sexo*, debuted in September 2005. The first episode involved how to put on a condom, causing a minor revolution among the older, Catholic population.[97]

A scandal shook Portugal in the early 2000s when a state-run orphanage, Casa Pia, was revealed to be a decades-old center for pedophilia. Children were not only abused by staff but reportedly also rented out to prominent citizens.[98]

Abortion remains a controversial subject in Spain and can be obtained only if the woman's life is in danger, the fetus irrevocably damaged, or the pregnancy the result of sexual crime. Although consistent data is hard to obtain, 300,000 has been quoted as the number of annual abortions,[99] although some data from 1987 (abortion was legalized in 1985) indicate 16,766 legal abortions were performed that year and 5,900 more took place abroad.[100]

Portugal has one of the harshest laws in Europe, with abortion allowed only if the woman's health is in danger, the fetus irrevocably damaged, or the pregnancy a result of sexual crime. In 2001, seventeen females were tried for having undergone illegal abortions. The Ministry of Health estimates over 20,000 illegal abortions every year, and unreported numbers of "abortion tourists" go to Spain. Over the past 20 years, more than 100 women have died from abortion.[101]

Young Spaniards like group outings, where bonding can take place among friends. Though 80 percent of women in a monogamous relationship report sexual activity, cohabitation is rare. In 2004, the average age of marriage was 28.6 years for women, and 30.6 years for men. Today Spain has the second-lowest marriage rate in the European Union (only Swedes marry less). Motherhood comes late, with the first child born to women averaging 29.2 years. However, with only 5 percent of children born out of wedlock, Spain has one of the lowest rates in Europe.[102]

Divorce has been legal in Spain since 1981. In 2003, 347 divorces per day were pronounced, twice as many as a decade earlier. Separation precedes divorce, but separation can be requested only after one year of marriage. Currently, divorce takes about 2 years from beginning to end.

In Portugal, divorce can be obtained by mutual consent or through the petition of one spouse. Grounds for divorce are physical separation, violation of conjugal duty of respect, infidelity, deserting the marital home, failing to participate in family life, and failing to provide financially to the family unit.

Spain and Portugal have known harsh repression of homosexuals. For many years gay Portuguese could be locked in *Mitras,* institutions for undesirables. Under Franco, homosexuals were classified a public danger; in 1977, a gay pride demonstration brought homosexuality out of the closet. In 1978, homosexuality was decriminalized in Spain, and support groups grew up all over the country. In June 2005, Spanish parliament legalized same-sex marriage, also granting gay couples the right to adopt children and inherit from one another. The Catholic Church has condemned the law, predicting the collapse of Spanish society. Portugal recognizes same-sex partnerships, and grants them the rights and responsibilities accorded heterosexual marriages. Homosexuals are excluded from military service.[103]

> ## WEDDING CUSTOMS IN SWITZERLAND
>
> Weddings are traditionally held between June and September and consist of an early afternoon church ceremony followed by a reception. In times past, kidnapping the bride was a tradition, and the groom would pay ransom for her release.

SWITZERLAND

Switzerland has a population of 7.1 million (2005 estimate). Life expectancy is 76 years for men and 82 years for women. The growth rate is 0.49 percent, and ethnic groups are German (65 percent), French (18 percent), Italian (10 percent), Romansch (0.6 percent), and other (8.9 percent). The official languages are German (63.7 percent), French (19.2 percent), and Italian (7.6 percent), followed by Romansch (0.6 percent), and other (8.9 percent). Major religions are Roman Catholicism (46.1 percent), Protestant faiths (40 percent), other (5 percent), and none (8.9 percent).[104]

Switzerland is a developed, prosperous nation. In times past it was believed stuttering was a result of masturbation; today Swiss children evolve in a climate of tolerance and freedom.[105] Swiss learn about sexuality primarily from state-funded school programs. Debate over the quality of the programs has arisen, and people question whether minority groups receive needed information. Swiss also learn about sex from peers, the media, and the Internet. Magazines for teens contain relationship advice.[106]

Age of first coitus is 15 to 17. Switzerland has the lowest adolescent fertility rate in Western Europe, with 4.6 births per 1,000 women aged 15–19. Reasons include sex education, availability of contraceptives, emergency contraception, and abortion. Statistics for 1978 show 15,562 legal abortions. By 2002, the number had decreased to 11,792. Mothers under 20 tend to be married or in a monogamous relationship.[107] Condoms are first choice for casual relationships; the pill is preferred in stable unions. When queried about reasons for intercourse, tenderness and emotion are cited (97 percent girls; 91 percent boys), followed by pleasure (76.9 percent girls; 82.7 percent boys).[108]

Dating is not quite on the American model. People often go out with friends to restaurants, cafes, and clubs, hoping to meet members of the opposite sex. If a young Swiss meets someone interesting, he or she requests a *rendez-vous* (i.e., a date). The idea that males should pay for females is rapidly disappearing, and the more solvent member of a couple typically foots the bill.

Switzerland has higher marriage and divorce rates than most of Europe. Although having a child before marriage was looked at askance a few years ago, today most Swiss see it as acceptable. The Swiss marry late (30.8 years, men; 28.2 years, women). Only civil marriage is legal; the couple is issued a certificate and a Family Book to record births, deaths, and eventual remarriages.[109] In case of marital breakdown, a petition for divorce is filed with a judge. No explanation for the divorce is necessary, and fault is not assigned.

Same-sex marriage is not legal in Switzerland, but same-sex unions are common. In 1992, homosexual behavior was subjected to the same rights and responsibilities as heterosexual relations. In April 1999, a new Constitution included homosexuals as a group against which it is illegal to discriminate. Homosexual acts between two consenting members of the armed forces are legal. In 2005, 58 percent of Swiss voted for legal recognition of same-sex partnership rights.[110]

TURKEY

Turkey is a 300,948-square-mile country with a population of 73.3 million and a growth rate of 1.09 percent. Major ethnic groups are Turkish (80 percent) and Kurdish (20 percent). Religions are Islam (99.8 percent), other (0.2 percent). Life expectancy is 69.9 years for men and 74.9 years for women. Languages are Turkish, Kurdish, Arabic, Armenian, and Greek.[111]

Turkey is in the throes of modernization. The traditional extended clan coexists with the nuclear family, and professional women live next door to veiled wives. In spite of motions towards gender equality, Turkey remains a patriarchy where the husband is head of the family. Boys are prized over girls, and a Turkish mother is closer to her sons than to her daughters. In many homes the oldest son is responsible for all females, including his mother, in the absence of the father.

Although Turkey granted suffrage to women before many progressive countries, marriage and motherhood are still considered the ideal state for females. Turkish society tends to keep women in the home and reserve public life for males. The suicide rate for women trapped in hopeless, loveless marriages is unusually high.[112] However, the number of women in the professions and on university campuses is growing, and Turkey has had a female prime minister.

Because of scarcity of contraceptives, abortion, legal through the tenth week, was long a means of birth control. With better access to modern methods, rates are now declining. Preferred methods of contraception include the IUD and tubal ligation.[113]

Turks meet future partners through family and friends. Marriage is based on practical considerations, and a contract between families is typically signed. Bride price is practiced, and it can be so high that the entire clan must contribute. First and second cousin marriage is common. Virginity is prized, and brides can wear a red ribbon belt to proclaim their purity. A bloodstained sheet is later displayed to prove the bride was a virgin.[114] Although illegal, society accepts a man's murder of a wife suspected of sexual impropriety.

Only civil marriage is recognized, although many (50 percent) also take vows before an imam.[115] Average age of marriage for girls is 18; the husband might be considerably older. Divorce is uncommon although legal; 6 out of 100 marriages end in divorce. Divorce takes 1 to 3 years to be pronounced, and females cannot remarry for 300 days.[116]

Physical contact between persons of the same gender is common. Men kiss and hold hands with other men; women walk down the street with linked arms. Public contact between men and women, even married couples, is unacceptable. Men who take the penetrative role in homosexual acts are not considered gay; when homosexual acts between enlisted men are reported, only the receptive partner is discharged. Although many celebrities are known homosexuals, Turkish society rejects a proclaimed homosexual lifestyle, and gays risk losing their jobs.[117]

THE UNITED KINGDOM AND IRELAND

The United Kingdom is a 94,226-square-mile monarchy composed of England, Wales, Scotland, and Northern Ireland. In 1922, Southern Ireland became a republic; six counties in Ulster in northeastern Ireland chose to remain with the United Kingdom. The population is

60,441,457, and life expectancy is 75.9 years for males and 81.0 years for females. The population growth is 0.28 percent, and religions are Anglican (Church of England) and Roman Catholic. There is also a sizable Muslim population. Inhabitants are English (81.5 percent), Scottish (9.6 percent), Irish (2.4 percent), Welsh (1.9 percent), and Ulstermen (1.8 percent). The remaining 2 percent are West Indians, Indians, Pakistanis, and West Africans.[118]

THE GROOM'S CAKE

The groom's cake originated in England during the Tudor period. Although both bride's and groom's cakes were originally fruitcake, today the groom's is likely to be chocolate.

The Republic of Ireland is a 32,544-square-mile independent state covering five-sixths of the island of Ireland. The population is 4,016,000, and life expectancy is 75 years for men and 80 years for women. The population growth is 1.87 percent, and religions are Roman Catholicism (92 percent), the Church of Ireland (Anglican), Methodist, Presbyterian, Muslim, and Jewish. English and Gaelic are the official languages.[119]

Although World War II brought women into the UK labor force, the post-war years saw a return to more traditional gender roles. In the 1980s, the United Kingdom resolved to abolish gender differences, and women have made strides in the workplace and at home. Domestic violence is a problem, and in similar crimes of passion, females tend to get heavier prison sentences than males.[120]

Age of first coitus has steadily declined since the 1960s. Today, although the average age for both genders is 16 years, nearly 25 percent have intercourse at 15 or younger, most without contraception. Only 40 percent of women aged 16–17 use modern contraceptives. Dispensing contraceptives to females under 16 is still an issue because UK laws question the capacity of young girls to make informed choices about reproductive health. School sex education is also controversial, as some believe it encourages experimentation.[121]

Britons learn about sex principally from the media and the Internet. Television programs that explore sexuality are common, and magazines carry question and answer columns. Abortion is legal through the twenty-fourth week to save the life of the mother, to preserve her health, in case of fetal damage, and for socioeconomic reasons. In Northern Ireland, abortion is illegal, and health practitioners are reluctant to release data. The United Kingdom has the highest teen pregnancy and abortion rate in Western Europe. It is estimated that in 2003 over 25,000 minors underwent abortions.[122]

People begin to date early, 13–17 years. Those who learn about sex in a positive manner are more likely to use contraceptives and enjoy positive, long-term relationships. Sexual experimentation is common. Britons typically have multiple sexual partners; approximately 60 percent of young men report 10 partners or more.[123]

Marriage rates are declining, and only 22 percent of young people consider marriage the ideal state. Women, more than men, are happy with single life, and 41 percent of females prefer separate living arrangements even in a committed relationship. It is increasingly common for couples to have sexual encounters with persons other than the official partner.[124]

Couples must give a three-month notice of intent to marry and obtain a license from the local registrar. Civil and religious marriage are both recognized.

The United Kingdom and the Republic of Ireland have had historically strong anti–gay and lesbian attitudes. Male homosexuality was partially decriminalized in 1967. Large gay communities exist in London and other big cities. Groups offer telephone hotlines, counseling, and guidance. Homosexual magazines, film festivals, and radio programs flourish, and state-run television airs sympathetic broadcasts. In 2005, same-sex unions were legalized.[125]

The Republic of Ireland has one of the strongest Roman Catholic traditions in Europe. The church has promoted censorship, strict gender expectations, and bans on sexual congress outside of marriage and on birth prevention. The Irish wed late, often for economic reasons. In the late 1960s increasing urbanization heralded a new prosperity, reducing the hold of the church and the rural way of life. Until the past decade, however, Ireland produced more educated people than could be employed, and many left to seek their fortunes elsewhere.

One of the most controversial issues in Ireland has been the ban on abortion, a situation that captured the world's attention during the 1980s and 1990s when several very young girls were denied therapeutic abortions. Some of the girls were able to travel to the United Kingdom; others miscarried spontaneously. One died of exposure after giving birth in a grotto to the Virgin Mary.[126]

Although this is evolving, gender roles and expectations are pervasive. The female is subordinate to the male, and Ireland remains a patriarchy where woman's fulfillment should come from marriage and motherhood. Except in the new class of educated, technologically savvy young residents of Dublin and other cities, sex is considered a reproductive issue. Yet extramarital birth is on the rise (16.6 percent in 1991), as are single-parent households. More than 30 percent of extramarital births are to teenagers.[127]

Teens get most of their information about sex from peers, foreign media, books, and the Internet. Romantic love is idealized, and couples take great pride in the longevity of marriage. Children are the normal outcome of marriage, and women are expected to be sexually compliant to their mates.[128]

Divorce was illegal in Ireland until 1995. The court must be convinced there is no hope of reconciliation.[129] Although an annulment from the Church is popularly called "Catholic divorce" and allows people to remarry, the Church insists that it is actually a finding that no true marriage existed.

Homosexual rights have been long in coming since family is a cornerstone of Irish society. Into the 1970s, homosexuals could be dismissed from jobs, denied promotions, even deprived of their children. Today large cities have gay bars, saunas, and clubs. In 1993, Ireland repealed anti-homosexual laws, making it illegal to discriminate on sexual orientation.[130]

RESOURCE GUIDE

PRINTED SOURCES

Baban, A. "From Abortion to Contraception: A Resource to Public Policies and Reproductive Behavior in Central and Eastern Europe from 1917 to the Present." *Romania*. Edited by H. P. David. Westport, CT: Greenwood Press, 1999.

Boxer, Marily J., and Jean H. Quataert, eds. *Connecting Spheres: European Women in a Globalizing World, 1500 to the Present,* 2nd edition. New York: Oxford University Press, 2000.

Erskine, Angus, et al., ed. *Changing Europe: Some Aspects of Identity, Conflict and Social Justice.* Perspectives on Europe, Contemporary Interdisciplinary Research. Aldershot, UK: 1996.

European Union Annual Report on Human Rights. Brussels: Council of the European Union, 2003.

Flandrin, Jean-Louis. *Families in Former Times: Kinship, Household, and Sexuality*. Translated by Richard Southern. Cambridge, UK: 1979.

Hall, Peter, ed. *Europe 2000.* The European Cultural Foundation. New York: Columbia University Press, 1977.

Jowell, Roger, et al., ed. *British—and European—Social Attitudes,* 15th report. Aldershot, UK: Ashgate Publishing Limited, 1998.

Mazower, Mark. *Dark Continent: Europe's Twentieth Century*. New York: Knopf, 1999.

Ozment, Steven. *Ancestors: The Loving Family in Old Europe*. Cambridge, MA: Harvard University Press, 2001.

Stearns, Peter N., ed. *Encyclopedia of European Social History*. New York: Charles Scribner's Sons. The Gale Group, 2001.

Therborn, Göran. *European Modernity and Beyond: The Trajectory of European Societies, 1945–2000*. London: Sage Publications, 1995.

WEBSITES

Advocates for Youth. http://www.advocatesforyouth.org. Provides information on adolescent sexual behavior and reponsibility.

Alan Guttmacher Institute. 2006. http://www.agi-usa.org/. Provides a wealth of information on the sexual and reproductive health of young people.

Center for Reproductive Rights. *The World's Abortion Laws*. Copyright 2005. Accessed August 2005. http://www.crlp.org_fac_abortion_laws.html. Information on contraception and abortion.

CIA. *The World Factbook*. Accessed July 2005. http://www.cia.gov/pub/countries/factbook. (As of November 2006, moved to https://www.cia.gov/cia/publications/factbook/index.html.)

Divorcemagazine.com. Accessed August 2005. http://www.divorcemag.com/statistics/index.shtml.

Draghici, Daniela. "Psychology and Reproductive Choice." Pro-Choice Forum. Opinion, comment and reviews. http://www.prochoiceforum.org.uk/psy-ocr9.asp#top.

Expat Focus. http://www.expatfocus.com/. Provides news, information, financial, and practical advice about life in different countries.

FPA. *Teenagers: sexual health and behaviour.* . Family Planning Association. http://www.fpa.org.uk.

Francoeur, Robert T., ed. *The International Encyclopedia of Sexuality*. Online edition. Copyright 1997-2001 by Robert T. Francoeur. The Continuum Publishing Company. Accessed July 2005. http://www2.hu-berlin.de/sexology/IES/index.html.

Gay, Lesbian, Bisexual, Transgender, Queer Encyclopedia. Accessed September 2005. http://www.glbtz.com/. A comprehensive resource of arts and cultural information relating to alternative lifestyles.

Gay World. http://www.actwin.com/eatonohio/gay/world.html. A comprehensive gay, lesbian, transgender website.

Generation Expat. http://www.generationexpat.com/. A blog devoted to Budapest, Prague, and other Eastern European cities.

Hester, Carla. *The Holland Ring*. Accessed September 10, 2005. http://thehollandring.com/. Website with information regarding the Netherlands.

ILGA. *The International Lesbian and Gay Association*. Accessed August 2005. http://www.ilga.com.

Institute for the Study of Marriage, Law, and Culture. *International Perspectives*: Copyright 2003. Accessed December 2005. http://marriageinstitute.ca/internat.htm.

International Planned Parenthood Federation—European Network. http://ippfen.org/site.html.

Janssen, Diederik F. *Growing Up Sexually*. Updated August 2006. Accessed November 6, 2006. http://www2.hu-berlin.de/sexology/GESUND/ARCHIV/GUS/GUS_AFS.HTM. Anthropological study that examines childhood sexuality and the scripting of sexual development.

Library of Congress, Federal Research Division. *Country Studies*. Accessed July/August 2005. http://countrystudies.us.

Make Love Not Sex: SexDex in Romania. http://sexdex.ro. Guide for Romanian teenagers.

Population Reference Bureau. Updated December 9, 2005. Copyright 2005. http://prb.org/datafinder6.htm. Provides timely and objective information on U.S. and international population trends and their implications.

Wedding Traditions and Customs Around the World. Euroevents and Travel. Copyright 2002-2005. http://www.worldweddingtraditions.com/. Describes international wedding customs.

NOTES

1. CIA (in Resource Guide, Websites).
2. Francoeur (in Resource Guide, Websites).
3. ILGA (in Resource Guide, Websites).
4. Francoeur (in Resource Guide, Websites).
5. Center for Reproductive Rights (in Resource Guide, Websites).
6. Population Reference Bureau (in Resource Guide, Websites).
7. International Perspectives: Institute for the Study of Marriage, Law, and Culture (in Resource Guide, Websites).
8. Library of Congress, Federal Research Division (in Resource Guide, Websites).
9. ILGA (in Resource Guide, Websites).
10. Library of Congress, Federal Research Division (in Resource Guide, Websites).
11. ILGA (in Resource Guide, Websites).
12. Wikipedia. *Trafficking in Human Beings*. Accessed December 2005. http://en.wikipedia.org/wiki/Human_trafficking.
13. CIA (in Resource Guide, Websites).
14. Ibid.
15. Ibid.
16. Nordisk institut for Kvinne og Kjønsforskning. "NIKK—Living for Tomorrow—Best Practices Case Studies." http://www.NIKK.UIO.no/forskning/nikk/living/lft_unaids_e.html.
17. Center for Reproductive Rights (in Resource Guide, Websites).
18. Divorcemagazine.com (in Resource Guide, Websites).
19. ILGA (in Resource Guide, Websites).
20. Library of Congress, Federal Research Division (in Resource Guide, Websites).
21. ILGA (in Resource Guide, Websites).
22. International Planned Parenthood Federation Western Hemisphere Region. http://www.ippfwhr.org/.
23. Population Reference Bureau (in Resource Guide, Websites).
24. *Human Trafficking and Modern Day Slavery*. Accessed November 2005. http://gvnet.com-humantrafficking/maldova.htm.
25. Library of Congress, Federal Research Division (in Resource Guide, Websites).
26. Ibid.
27. Population Reference Bureau (in Resource Guide, Websites).
28. Ibid.
29. International Planned Parenthood Federation, European Network (in Resource Guide, Websites).
30. Ibid.
31. Sofia News Agency. "Bulgarians Are Champions in Lovemaking." November 9, 2005. http://www.novinite.com.
32. ILGA (in Resource Guide, Websites).
33. CIA (in Resource Guide, Websites).
34. Janssen (in Resource Guide, Websites) .
35. Center for Reproductive Rights (in Resource Guide, Websites).
36. Ibid.
37. Divorcemagazine.com (in Resource Guide, Websites).
38. Myers, Bill. *Homosexual Rights Around the World*. Gay Rights Information. Established 1998. September 2005. http://www.actwin.com.eatonohio/gay/world.htm.
39. *Country Studies*. Federal Research Division of the Library of Congress.
40. Alan Guttmacher Institute. *Teenagers' Sexuality and Reproductive Health*. Accessed August 2005. http://www.guttmacher.org/sections/adolescents.php.
41. Gais et Lesbiennes Branchés. *France QRD: PACS, contrats d'union et mariages*. Accessed November 2005. http://www.france.qrd.org/texts/partnership/index.html.

42. Gay, Lesbian, Bisexual, Transgender, Queer Encyclopedia (in Resource Guide, Websites).
43. CIA (in Resource Guide, Websites).
44. Francoeur (in Resource Guide, Websites).
45. Ibid.
46. Divorcemagazine.com (in Resource Guide, Websites).
47. Francoeur (in Resource Guide, Websites).
48. ILGA (in Resource Guide, Websites).
49. Library of Congress, Federal Research Division (in Resource Guide, Websites).
50. Francoeur (in Resource Guide, Websites).
51. Ibid.
52. ILGA (in Resource Guide, Websites).
53. CIA (in Resource Guide, Websites)
54. Janssen (in Resource Guide, Websites).
55. Patt, Martin. *Prevalence, Abuse, and Exploitation of Street Children—Republic of Hungary.* Accessed December 2005. http://gvnet.com/streetchildren/Hungary.htm.
56. Borthuiser, Zoltan, and Attila Kereszturi. *Reproductive Health in Hungary.* Accessed October 2005. http://www.gfmer.ch/International_activities.En/Reproductive_health_in_Hungary.htm.
57. ILGA (in Resource Guide, Websites).
58. CIA (in Resource Guide, Websites).
59. Francoeur (in Resource Guide, Websites).
60. Spinelli, Angela, and Michele Grandolfo. "Abortion in Italy." *Bollettino epidemiologico nazionale* 4.14 (2001, April). Accessed September 2005. http://www.ben.iss.it/precedenti/aprile/1apr_en.htm.
61. Francoeur (in Resource Guide, Websites).
62. Divorcemagazine.com (in Resource Guide, Websites).
63. ILGA (in Resource Guide, Websites).
64. CIA (in Resource Guide, Websites).
65. Netherlands Ministry of Foreign Affairs. *Q&A Abortion in the Netherlands.* 2003. http://pvnewyork.org/contents/pages/742/abort.pdf.
66. Hester, Carla. *The Holland Ring.* 10 September 2005. http://thehollandring.com/.
67. Netherlands Embassy, Washington, DC. *Marriage and Divorce.* http://www.theNetherlands-embassy.org/listing.asp?categoryvalue=dcmarriageanddivorce.
68. ILGA (in Resource Guide, Websites).
69. CIA (in Resource Guide, Websites).
70. Francoeur (in Resource Guide, Websites).
71. Ibid.
72. Ibid.
73. UNICEF. *At a Glance–Poland-Statistics.* http://www.unicef.org/infobycountry/poland.statistics.html.
74. Divorcemagazine.com (in Resource Guide, Websites).
75. ILGA (in Resource Guide, Websites).
76. CIA (in Resource Guide, Websites).
77. Ibid.
78. Ibid.
79. Francoeur (in Resource Guide, Websites).
80. Americans for Divorce Reform. *Non-US Divorce Rates.* Accessed November 2005. http://www.divorcereform.org/nonus.html.
81. Francoeur (in Resource Guide, Websites).
82. ILGA (in Resource Guide, Websites).
83. CIA (in Resource Guide, Websites).
84. Ibid.
85. Ibid.
86. Ibid.
87. Francoeur (in Resource Guide, Websites).

88. Ibid.
89. Ministry of Foreign Affairs of Denmark. *Family.* Accessed October 2005. http://denmark.dk/portal/page?_pageid=374,520402&_dad=portal&_schema=PORTAL.
90. Francoeur (in Resource Guide, Websites).
91. International Homosexual Web Organization. *First Parnership Page.* Accessed October 2005. http://users.cybercity.dk/~dko12530/.
92. CIA (in Resource Guide, Websites).
93. Francoeur (in Resource Guide, Websites).
94. Checa, M. A., J. Pascual, A. Robles, and R. Carreras. "Trends in the Use of Emergency Contraception: an Epidemiological Study in Barcelona, Spain (1994-2002)." *Contraception* 70.3 (2004, September): 199–201.
95. International Planned Parenthood Federation—European Network (in Resource Guide, Websites).
96. Francoeur (in Resource Guide, Websites).
97. *TVI, Televisao Independente.* http://www.tvi.iol.pt.programas/programa.php?id=2386.
98. Pedroso, Paulo. "Casa Pia and Portugal's Paedophile Panic." http://www.richardwebster.net/print/xportugueseconcora.html.
99. Singh, Susheela, and Jacqueline E. Darroch. "Adolescent Pregnancy and Childbearing Levels and Trends in Developed Countries." *Family Planning Perspectives* 32.1 (1999, January/February). http://www.guttmacher.org/pubs/journals/3201400.html.
100. Johnston, Wm. Robert. "Historical Abortion Statistics—Spain." *Johnston's Archive.* Updated May 2 2005. Accessed October 2005. .http://www.johnstonsarchive.net/policy/abortions/ab-spain.html.
101. Women on Waves. *Criminalisation of Abortion in Portugal.* http://www.womenonwaves.org/article-1020.52-en.html.
102. Library of Congress, Federal Research Division (in Resource Guide, Websites).
103. ILGA (in Resource Guide, Websites).
104. CIA (in Resource Guide, Websites).
105. Janssen (in Resource Guide, Websites)
106. Swiss Federal Office of Public Health. "Sex Education. National Coordination Needed." *Spectra: Prevention and Health Promotion* 36. December 2002. http://www.suchtundaids.bag.admin.ch/imperia/md/content.
107. Henshaw, Stanley K., Susheela Singh, and Taylor Haas. "The Incidence of Abortion Worldwide." *Family Planning Perspectives* 25 Supplement (1999, January). http://www.agi-usa.org/pubs/journals/25s3099.html.
108. Narring, Francoise, Pierre-Andre Michaud, and Vinit Sharma. "Demographic and Behavioral Factors Associated with Adolescent Pregnancy in Switzerland." *Family Planning Perspectives* 28.5 (1996, September-October). http://www.guttmacher.org/pubs/journals/2823296.html.
109. Micheloud & Cie. "Marrying a Swiss in Switzerland." *Switzerland.isyours.com.* Accessed November 2006. http://www.isyours.com/e/immigration/marriage/marrying_a_swiss_in_switzerland.html.
110. ILGA (in Resource Guide, Websites).
111. CIA (in Resource Guide, Websites).
112. Frantz, Douglas. "Turkish Women Who See Death as a Way Out." *The New York Times on the Web* (2000, November 3). The New York Times Company. Accessed November 2005. http://www.library.cornell.edu/colldev/mideast/batmnt.htm.
113. Genç, Metin, Gülsen Günes, Mustafa Sahin, Leyla Karaoglu, and Erkan Pehlivan. "Family Planning Knowledge and Practices of Reproductive Age (15–49) Married Women in Yesilyurt (Malatya)." *Turkish Journal of Population Studies* 17–18 (1995–96): 61–81. Abstract at Committee for International Cooperation in National Research in Demography. http://www.cicred.org/rdr/rdr_a/revues/revue89-90/02-89-90_a.html.
114. "Virginity Testing." *Women and Global Human Rights.* Accessed November 2005. http://www.webster.edu/~woolflm/virginitytest.html.
115. "Marriage." *Turkish Odessey/about Turkey/AnotolianCulture/People.* Accessed November 2005. http://www.turkishodyssey.com/turkey/culture/people.htm#MARRIAGE.

116. U.S. Department of State. *Divorce Regulations: Ankara, Turkey.* Accessed November 2005. Http://ankara.usembassy.gov/divorce_regulations.html.
117. Netherlands Ministry of Foreign Affairs. *Focus Countries—Turkey—specific groups and issues (sexual orientation).* European Country of Origin Information Network. http://www.ecoi.net/doc/en/TR/contents/5/2520-2548.
118. CIA (in Resource Guide, Websites).
119. Ibid.
120. Francoeur (in Resource Guide, Websites).
121. FPA (in Resource Guide, Websites).
122. Center for Reproductive Rights (in Resource Guide, Websites).
123. Francoeur (in Resource Guide, Websites).
124. "Women Happier on Their Own." *Mirror: the Best Newspaper on the Web.* Mirror.co.uk-news. All news archives. 22 December 2003. Accessed November 2005. http://www.mirror.co.uk/news/allnews/content_objectid=13748238_method=full_saiteid=50143_headline=WOMEN-HAPPIER-ON-OWN-name_page.html.
125. ILGA (in Resource Guide, Websites).
126. "Pro-Life, Even in Death." *Salon.com Life.* Accessed November 2005. http://www.salon.com/mwt/feature/2002/03/01/abortion/print.html.
127. Francoeur (in Resource Guide, Websites).
128. Ibid.
129. Irish Government. *Divorce Decrees in Ireland.* On-line Access to Services, Information and Support (OASIS). Accessed December 14, 2006. http://www.oasis.gov.ie/relationships/separation_divorce/divorce.html
130. ILGA (in Resource Guide, Websites).

GAMES, TOYS, AND PASTIMES

GAMES, TOYS, AND PASTIMES: The city of Windsor re-created at Legoland in London.
© Art Directors.co.uk / ArkReligion.com / Adina Tovy.

GAMES, TOYS, AND PASTIMES:
Traditional Russian nesting dolls.
Courtesy of Shutterstock.

LOVE, SEX, AND MARRIAGE

LOVE, SEX, AND MARRIAGE: Supporters of gay marriage embrace outside the Spanish parliament in Madrid, 2005. The parliament legalized gay marriage, defying conservatives and clergy who opposed making traditionally Roman Catholic Spain the third nation to allow same-sex unions. © AP Photo/Jasper Juinen.

LOVE, SEX, AND MARRIAGE: Macedonian bishop blesses the rings during a traditional wedding ceremony near Skopje, 2004. © AP Photo/Boris Grdanoski.

MUSIC

MUSIC: A drumming troupe take part in the Love Parade in Berlin. © Art Directors.co.uk / Ark Religion.com / Tibor Bognar.

MUSIC: A rave party in Belgium, 2001. Courtesy of Shutterstock.

PERIODICALS

PERIODICALS: Magazines in Berlin focus on a potential war in Iraq, 2003. © Kurt Vinion/Getty Images.

PERIODICALS: An information kiosk in Costa del Sol, Spain. © Juergen Henkelmann Photography / Alamy.

PERIODICALS: A Paris display with various comics about reporter Tintin by Belgian author Hergé (Georges Rémi), 2000. © Jean-Pierre Muller/AFP/Getty Images.

PERIODICALS: A businessman in Paris relaxes with his coffee and a newspaper. Courtesy of Shutterstock.

RADIO AND TELEVISION

RADIO AND TELEVISION: Winner of the Eurovision song contest Helena Paparizou of Greece, left, and winner of a previous contest Ruslana stand side by side after the finale in Kiev, 2005, with famous Ukrainian boxer Vitaliy Klitschko at right. © AP Photo/Mykola Lazarenko, Pool.

RADIO AND TELEVISION: A sattelite dish can be found in such remote places as on the roof of old Russian monastery near Solovetskiy. Courtesy of Shutterstock.

SPORTS AND RECREATION

SPORTS AND RECREATION: Zinedine Zidane celebrates with his teammates during the Group E Champions League soccer match between Hamburger SV and Juventus in Hamburg's Volkspark Stadium, 2000. © AP Photo/Christoph Stache.

SPORTS AND RECREATION: Estonia's Erika Salumae gestures after capturing a gold medal in the women's cycling sprint in the Summer Olympics in Barcelona, 1992. © AP Photo/Lionel Cironneau.

THEATER AND PERFORMANCE

THEATER AND PERFORMANCE: Exterior of the Abbey Theatre in Ireland as it stood in 1965. © Bettmann/Corbis.

THEATER AND PERFORMANCE: The world famous Moulin Rouge. Courtesy of Shutterstock.

THEATER AND PERFORMANCE: Exterior of the Burgtheater in Vienna. Courtesy of Dreamstime.

TRANSPORTATION AND TRAVEL

TRANSPORTATION AND TRAVEL: Seen from the Swedish side, some 35,000 Swedish and Danish bicyclists cross the Oresund Bridge that ties the Danish capital Copenhagen with Sweden's third largest city Malmö. AP Photo/Henrik Montgomery.

TRANSPORTATION AND TRAVEL: A train preparing to depart a London tube station. Courtesy of Shutterstock.

ANDREAS JACOB

Music has played a major role in the development of the European culture since its very beginnings. Analogous to the often divergent tendencies of both social and ethnic struggle that led to the cultural diversity of the continent, there is a wide range of traditional as well as contemporary styles of music. Therefore, the outline of the subject of European popular music requires some reflection on its methodological premises.

There are several difficulties to be met when discussing the types and genres of music that are popular throughout the different regions and states of Europe. First of all, it should be stated that in the course of this article the term *popular music* will not be used in order to express a concept of music that is defined by the opposition to its "arty rival," the so-called classical music. Common as that contrast may be, it might turn out to be misleading for many readers: Regarding these two postulated kinds of music, it can be shown in many cases that the ways of their propagation, as well as the receptive strategies of the audiences listening to them, do not always differ substantially—or at least not more than they may differ between certain genres of the so-called popular music (e.g., traditional folk music versus such forms of electronic dance music as techno). For this reason, this chapter confines itself to the description of the types of music that happen to be popular with the audience at certain places (countries or regions) and at the time given.

Second, the complex image arising from analysis of the listening habits of Europeans may be explained by a wide range of historical reasons that include language barriers and cultural particularities as well as the contingencies that struck the eastern part of the continent after the collapse of the Communist system or the different degrees of dissemination of new technologies and media of communication. Further difficulties come to the fore regarding the quality of the information accessible on the various countries. For example, an interpretation of musical predilections based on the retail values of music sales may be problematic for countries that show a very high level of physical piracy for products of the music industry, according to the estimates of the International Federation of the Phonographic Industry (IFPI). From a socio-economic point of view, it still is significant to note that these countries tend to be situated in Eastern Europe, where the gross domestic product (GDP) is considerably lower than in the Western states. The reliability of legal and economic institutions affects not only the dependability but sometimes even the sheer availability of information. For a country such as Belarus (often considered the last post-Soviet dictatorship in Europe), it is hard to deliver any valid data concerning the current musical life at all.

In spite of all the variety of vernacular styles and local traditions in Europe's popular music, it can be observed that a varying but usually very large amount of the music listened to consists of pop music of Anglo-American descent on the one hand, and locally produced music based on that global model (sometimes with "scents" of regional influences) on the other. Thus, European music makes no exception to the trend of industrial and cultural globalization, whereas idiosyncratic styles still persist in many variants—partly as niche products, partly as genres of national (and, rarely, of international) importance.

To give but two examples: In Finland—with no more than 5.2 million inhabitants, a remote geographical situation at the Northern edge of Europe, and the prevailing Finnish language offering similarities only to the few other Finno-Ugric languages—more than half (54 percent) of the music repertoire sold in 2004 was of domestic origin.[1] To a large extent, this repertoire will not be popular outside the boundaries of Finland, although not all of it belongs to specific vernacular styles such as *iskelmä*. Only a few Finnish bands, the ones that adapt international popular styles and use English texts (like HIM or The Rasmus), are successful in attracting a greater international audience. The United Kingdom, which still is the third largest music market of the world (after the United States and Japan), provides a counterexample: A good half of the repertoire sold in 2004 came from domestic artists (51 percent). But because of the international importance of the English language and a vibrant music scene, the United Kingdom may be said to be the only truly relevant "export nation" of music in Europe. For the most part, British pop music will rather be considered as an international phenomenon than a "vernacular" one. The borderline between local music traditions and international, Anglo-American pop sound is not always easy to draw, especially because there has been vivid interchange between the different styles (e.g., American country music, which is partly rooted in Scots/Irish balladry). So on the one hand, it may be possible to detect the specific Scottish influences in, say, the music of Wet Wet Wet or Franz Ferdinand (as well as the "Finnishness" of the aforementioned HIM); on the other hand, even remote local repertories limited to very small audiences may give room to an Anglo-American strain.

This diagnosis of manifold interdependencies also holds for many of the national and vernacular genres that often arose from the meeting and blending of styles of different origin. To stick with the example of Finland, specific appropriations of tango developed during the 1940s, which led to a unique tradition of that originally Argentinean dance and made Finland one of the international strongholds of tango dancing and playing. Another example of the mixed descent of apparently truly local styles is *rebetika* music, often identified by listeners as the prototypal national music of Greece: It is not, as might be supposed, a genuine country-bred folk music growing exclusively from Greek roots, but an urban popular music developed at the beginning of the twentieth century, with sources not only in older Greek folk music (*dimotika*) but also in Roma music and in Turkish and even Near Eastern styles.

As for the different genres of music and their market shares in Europe, it is noticeable that most of the internationally known music genres are represented within the spectrum of musical predilections as expressed by the data published by the phonographic industry. The strongest position usually is held by "middle-of-the-road" pop songs, whether of national or international provenience. Genres to follow usually are rock music and music based on traditional styles of folk music (mostly in a commercialized version). Styles such as hip hop (partly performed in the national languages), rhythm and blues, dance, and classical music may come next in liking, taking their positions according to particularities of the concerning country (in many cases with a market share between 2 and 10 percent, classical finding even more enthusiasts in Austria and Italy, hip hop doing especially well in Poland). As a general rule, jazz and blues range a little lower in popularity (2–5 percent), always taking account of possible exceptions such as Italy (9 percent) and Poland (8 percent). Genres of smaller importance include a vast amount of international productions and ethnic styles (such as the so-called world music).

All in all, the European music market is one of the largest worldwide, currently—with $12.3 billion retail value in 2004—surpassed only by the North American market (combining the United States and Canada, with $12.8 billion retail value). In fact, the described situation of the economic market is already a result of a remarkable recession that struck the European music industry in the early years of the twenty-first century. There were permanent losses in the retail value for music products during the early 2000s (e.g., a 5.4 percent loss for Europe from 2003 to 2004, in contrast to a modest gain of 2.2 percent for North America). This development, with double-digit market declines in such major countries as France or Spain, may be due to the growing influence of more or less illegal downloads from the Internet or CD burning, but it may also be an expression of the consumers' discontent with the actual structures of the music industry and its products. It is for that reason that some managers of the international music industry began thinking about strengthening the influence of domestically produced music during those years.

As democracy has spread over the largest parts of the continent after the fall of Communism in the early 1990s, censorship is hardly an issue in the European countries (with the possible exception of countries, such as Belarus, Russia, or some of the post-Yugoslav states, that have not installed as liberal a political system as their neighbors have).

THE BALKANS: ALBANIA, BOSNIA-HERZEGOVINA, CROATIA, MACEDONIA, SERBIA AND MONTENEGRO, AND SLOVENIA

The states of the former Yugoslavia and Albania cannot be discussed in one paragraph without problems, because the development of these states differed vastly from the 1990s on. On the one hand, Slovenia, for example, built up a democracy with functioning institutions and became a member of the European Union (not being its least successful economy, by far); on the other hand, Albania still suffers to a certain extent from anarchic political situations that came about after the fall of the rigid Communist system that the dictator Enver Hoxha had established after World War II. Furthermore, the musical cultures of the various countries feed on different roots but are mingled with each other to the utmost complexity, largely as a result of the multiethnic populations and their divergent religious backgrounds (Roman Catholic, Orthodox, and Islamic): The traditional music of Slovenia (an Alpine country bordering Austria and Italy) bears resemblances to Austrian or even German music, whereas its southern neighbors show some of the typical characteristics of the southeastern Slavic countries (in that respect rather to be compared with the music of Bulgaria); the influence of the 500-year Ottoman Turkish reign is strongly to be felt in Albanian and Macedonian music and sometimes also in that of Bosnia-Herzegovina; Greek strains can be heard in the southern countries (especially Macedonia). To make it even more complicated, the transnational ethnic group of the Roma (Gypsies) exerted strong musical impact within great parts of the region.

In this context, it must suffice to take the state of Croatia as an example. With a population of 4.5 million inhabitants in 2004, it is the fiftieth largest music market of the world: 2.8 million record units were sold in 2004, which equaled a retail value of $17.5 million. A good half (54 percent) of the sold recordings was of domestic origin. Although international (especially American) music is of immense popularity among the younger generation, the greatest part of the top-selling albums were by Croatian artists (such as Miroslav Škoro) and also produced by domestic record labels (such as Croatia Records).

That domestic music—whether in a genuine vernacular style (such as the *zabavna muzika* in former Yugoslavia) or in adaptation of some international style (such as rock or dance music)—often uses idiomatic elements of the regional traditional music. This can be heard, for example, from Albanian artists of different genres, such as Sinan Hoxha or Adelina Ismajli. It is only rarely that musicians from these countries achieve any international acclaim, one of the few examples of which being the Slovenian rock band Laibach.

Traditional instruments of the region include different types of zithers and accordions as well as flutes and bagpipes; also popular are lutelike instruments such as the one-stringed *gusle* (in Serbia and other countries), the *saz* (a long-necked lute of Turkish origin, common in urban Muslim settings, such as in Bosnia-Herzegovina), or the similar *çifteli* of Albania. Particular musical productions of the region worth emphasizing are, for example, the rural brass bands of some Serbian regions or the tradition of bell ringing (*pritrkavanje z zvonovi*) in Slovenia.

BALTIC STATES: ESTONIA, LATVIA, AND LITHUANIA

The three Baltic states are situated on the eastern shore of the Baltic Sea, adjacent to Poland, Belarus, Russia, and (divided by a narrow gulf) Finland. It is not only for this geographical position that these countries (now belonging to the European Union) take a transitional function between the cultural spheres of Russia, Scandinavia, and Central Europe.

The annual sales numbers as well as the retail values for recordings in these three countries are subject to quite heavy fluctuations for several reasons: For one, the reliability of the statistics is flawed by institutional shortcomings and by a level of piracy that is estimated well beyond 50 percent of the overall value (with Lithuania taking a pivotal role in illegal trade of the pirated products). Furthermore, the economy of these states is boosting, but still not stabilized—sudden changes in economic or financial conditions may affect these markets as strongly as unpredictable alterations in consumer behavior.

Nonetheless, it is possible to draw some conclusions from a comparison of two of the states that offer accessible data at the moment: Estonia (with a population of 1.3 million) is the fifty-third largest music market of the world. With a total of 0.9 million record units sold in 2004, a retail value of $11.5 million was achieved. The most important music medium was the CD (about 90 percent of the sold units), whereas cassette tapes lost their importance. About a third of the sold repertoire was of domestic origin. The situation in Latvia shows characteristic differences: Though having a higher population (2.3 million inhabitants), Latvia is not such an important music market (only sixtieth worldwide position), with a total of 0.6 million units sold in 2004 that had a retail value of only $4.4 million. With great certainty, that finding can be traced back to the country's weaker economic position. This might also be the reason for the larger share of cassettes within the total of record units sold (about a third of the overall revenue). The portion of the domestic repertoire is a little higher than in Estonia (usually about 40–45 percent) but rocketed to 65 percent in 2004. Both Estonia and Latvia were successful in drawing some international attention to their music life during the last years by each winning the Eurovision Song Contest (a show format televised all over Europe) in 2001 and 2002, respectively. For the most popular genres, the sales data from Latvia of 2004 seem to be significant: As in most European countries, "middle of the road" pop music holds the first position in listeners' approval (35 percent of the records sold may be said to belong to that style). In second place (22 percent of the sales), there follows music with strong reference to traditional Baltic music, a fact that may have to do with the importance of music for the coining of a national identity. Rock music (including metal and alternative variants) comes third in popularity (18 percent of the sales), other genres took portions of 5 percent or less in the music market of 2004.

Baltic independent record labels (such as Latvian Microphone Records or Platforma Records) placed many of their artists (such as re:public or Fomins & Kleins) among the top-selling albums of their countries, without arousing much wider notice. Such international impact is achieved only sporadically, when Baltic pop groups singing in English and adapting international stylistic characteristics make contact with record labels from abroad (as in the example of the Estonian girl band Vanilla Ninja).

Furthermore, there are strongly felt vestiges of the attempt of the Soviet dictatorship to break the indigenous Baltic identity by settling large Russian-speaking populations in these countries while deporting the Baltic ones to Siberia. So, for example, about one third of the people living in Estonia actually are ethnic Russians (partly not speaking the national language and rather cultivating their own cultural roots).

Thus, the traditions of choral singing and of folk ensembles (music and dance), which were first shown as great public events in the late nineteenth century, not only played a

NATIONALISM IN THE MUSIC OF THE BALTIC STATES

In order to understand the crucial role of music with traditional background in the Baltic states, it is important to remember the complex history of these countries, because much of the music played and listened to still has the function of reassuring the Baltic peoples of their national identity. These countries have shared a common history for many ages, with frequent occupation by foreign powers (during the twentieth century Russia, Germany, and the Soviet Union); they declared their independence during 1991–92 following a political movement relying not on the use of violence but largely on the display of symbols of their national cultures during folklore song-festivals—the so-called Singing Revolution. Significant differences among the states, which have left traces in their musical cultures, lie in their national languages (Estonian is not a Baltic language as Latvian and Lithuanian are, but a Finno-Ugric one) and their religious preference (Protestant Lutheranism is the religion with the largest membership in Estonia and Latvia, whilst Lithuania has a majority of Roman Catholics).

major role during the struggle for independence from the Soviet empire but continue to be used as means for propagating national culture and identity. For that cause, the folk revival is often encouraged for political reasons as much as it is supported by scientific research (which may be seen from such a group as the Vilnius University Ensemble). Traditional instruments include plucked zithers in different related forms (called *kanklės* in Lithuania, *kokles* in Latvia, *kannel* in Estonia) as well as flutes and reed instruments (such as bagpipes) of various constructions.

BENELUX STATES: BELGIUM, THE NETHERLANDS, AND LUXEMBOURG

The Netherlands and Belgium are, relative to their population sizes, rather important music markets, whereas the small Grand Duchy of Luxembourg (with a population of less than half a million) is of minor significance. The Netherlands (with 16.3 million inhabitants) ranks tenth in the global list of the music industry, Belgium (with 10.3 million inhabitants) holds the fifteenth position. Selling 29.9 million record units in the Netherlands and 18.5 million in Belgium, the industry's total yield was $507.7 million for the Dutch and $275.1 million for the Belgian market in 2004.

Situated in western Europe and bordered by the larger states of France and Germany, the people of the so-called Benelux states show strong inclinations toward the international music taste and favor pop music of Anglo-American descent. In 2004, only about 20 percent of the music products sold in the Netherlands and Belgium were of domestic origin. In Belgium, the language divide (between Dutch-speaking Flemish people in the north, French-speaking Walloons in the south, and even a small German-speaking ethnicity in the southeast) to some extent corresponds to different music tastes: Artists from the Netherlands (such as Marco Borsato and Andre Hazes) are popular with the Flemings, Francophone singers with the Walloons. This cultural interchange works either way, so Belgian-Flemish music often finds its audiences in the Netherlands as well as in its own country.

An analysis of the music sales by genre shows a vast lead of the popularity of "middle of the road" pop (45 percent in Belgium, 49 percent in the Netherlands), followed by rock music (28 percent and 16 percent, respectively). Jazz and Blues hold a slightly over-average percentage in the market (5 percent in the Netherlands as well as in Belgium), as does rhythm and blues/urban music (9 percent in Belgium, 4 percent in the Netherlands). Classical music gained a market share of 6 percent in the Netherlands in 2004, whereas in Belgium only 1 percent of the sold records belonged to that genre. Traditional folk music and country styles are hardly of any importance with regard to the music sales of either of the two states.

Most of the popular music (whether of domestic or international origin) is distributed by international labels. If aiming at wider success, Flemish and Dutch groups or singers usually employ English for their song texts (as did, for example, Vaya con Dios from Belgium during the 1980s and 1990s, or Golden Earring from the Netherlands a decade or so earlier), whereas French is often regarded as being sufficiently international in the French-speaking regions. Artists from the Walloon region made considerable contributions to French popular culture (to name only *chansonniers* such as Jacques Brel or Adamo on the one side, rock singers such as Plastic Bertrand on the other). During the last decade of the twentieth century, the Flemish music scene of Belgium left a more lively impression than the Wallonian one (an observation that well connects to the economic growth of the two regions in the recent past). Particularly in the Netherlands, there is a strong liking for British music and a certain cultural orientation toward the United Kingdom. A particularity of the Dutch music market is the strong share of music DVDs: 22 percent of the overall turnover was produced by that format (a percentage to be found nowhere else in Europe). With 5.3 million music DVDs sold in 2004, the Netherlands were the sixth most important market worldwide. That remarkable fact is even more astonishing when looking at the provenience of the Top 10 Music Videos, as more than half of them featured Dutch artists such as Marco Borsato.

BULGARIA, ROMANIA, AND MOLDOVA

The Southeastern European countries are facing a period of radical change in the first decade of the twenty-first century, which also affects the music industry. Valid statistical data was submitted from Bulgaria only in 2004, but much of the information seems to hold as well for its larger neighbor Romania (that has a population of estimated 22 million inhabitants, in this respect about three times as large as Bulgaria). The former Soviet republic of Moldova shares much of its cultural heritage with Romania, but (in spite of having over 4 million inhabitants) is not yet a sizable music market because of very poor economic conditions.

For a European country of its size, Bulgaria does not constitute a large music market: 7.5 million inhabitants bought 0.9 million record units with a retail value of $5.2 million in 2004, which made Bulgaria the fifty-seventh in the worldwide list of the music industry. There were steep declines in sales during the later years (in 2001, there were still 2 million record units sold), a finding that might be due to the very high estimated level of piracy (more than 50 percent). Furthermore, the portions of repertoire of domestic origin fell dramatically during three years (from 73 percent in 2001 to 35 percent in 2004), the reason for which might be sought in the predilection of young people for pop, rock, and dance music from the United States. The decline in sales from 2003 to 2004 was particularly steep for LPs (54.5 percent) and cassette tapes (35.6 percent), whilst singles and DVDs boosted (with gains of 72.4 percent and 133.8 percent, respectively). This fact expresses the change in music propagation brought about by a strongly growing economy, because the consumers of those EU candidate states could afford to buy new entertainment technology.

The traditional music of the Balkan states is still influential for popular music, especially in Bulgaria. Because of the complex history of the region, generalizations of the styles and instruments of the countries can hardly be satisfying. Regional music traditions absorbed different influences including Slavic and Turkish culture (in particular in Bulgaria and Southern Romania), Roma and Jewish music, as well as Austro-Hungarian traces in Transylvania (western Romania). Some features of the local styles, attracting the interest of foreigners, are the changing or asymmetrical meters (such as 5/16 or 7/16) and the two-part singing in some Bulgarian regions on the one hand, and on the other the use of alpenhorns in the Carpathian Mountains or of mouth harps (*drîmba*) and panpipes (*nai*) in Romania.

A major portion of music heard in Bulgaria and Romania is of nondomestic origin, but there is still quite a number of local artists who make their way into the national Top 10 (such as Anna Lesko of Romania or Mariana Popova of Bulgaria). It appears that dance music of national production is particularly popular and, in the (rare) case of the Moldovan band O-Zone, sometimes even gathering international acclaim.

The Czech Republic, Slovakia, and Hungary

The three Central European states have shared a common history in many respects: After having been part of the Hapsburg Empire for centuries, they enjoyed short independence between the two World Wars and came under Communist rule thereafter, with insurgencies suppressed by the Soviet empire. After the fall of Communism, the standard of living rose quickly, and the states eventually became members of the European Union. These commonalities are partly mirrored in the musical life of the states, which have developed a vibrant musical culture. The Czech Republic and Hungary have similar-sized populations (10.2 million and 10 million inhabitants, respectively, whereas Slovakia has 5.4 million inhabitants) and a similar gross domestic product per capita, but the amount of money spent on music products by the Hungarians is considerably higher: In 2004, the retail value for records in Hungary amounted to $59.1 million (7.6 million record units having been sold), whilst in the Czech Republic only a yield of $39.6 million was achieved (with 4 million records sold). This finding is extraordinary, as the estimated penetration of technical equipment for playing music products is higher within the Czech than within the Hungarian population. A possible explanation for the smaller Czech return for music products might be the higher level of physical piracy in the Czech Republic (estimated more than 50 percent). Also, a remarkably high share of music of domestic production was sold in the Czech Republic: 61 percent of the total turnover originated from the country itself, whereas in Hungary only 38 percent came from Hungarian production (although there is a solid portion of Hungarian pop music within the country's Top 10, too). From a look at the Slovakian charts, it can be seen that local artists (such as the rock group Peha) are very popular in that country as well. Most of the music of domestic artists was produced by big international labels.

A broad variety of musical styles is appreciated within the three states, with rather high values for the shares of dance music (9 percent of the total turnover in the Czech Republic, 6 percent in Hungary). Classical music has a long-standing tradition in Central Europe, which is reflected by the solid percentages of the retail value attained by it in the Czech Republic and Hungary (6 percent and 4 percent, respectively). Traditional folk music is not a major issue within the sales rates, but constitutes a vital source for some of the more popular genres. To name some of the particularities, up to 80 percent of the folk music in regions within the Czech Republic and Slovakia (which offer many similarities for the foreign listener) are intended for dance. Roma music had major impact on the musical culture, especially in Hungary, where professional Gypsy bands were much in favor in urban and aristocratic settings of the nineteenth century and many people identified "Hungarian style" with their music (not without stirring reactions from conservative or racist circles in the twentieth century that claimed amateur peasant music to be "real Hungarian"). A remnant of the Hapsburg times is the widespread style of *verbunk* (Czech) or *verbunkós* (Hungarian), a fiery type of music formerly used when recruiting soldiers. Instruments frequently used in traditional folk music include clarinets as well as violins and cymbaloms (a type of hammered dulcimer). Yet, it should be remembered that the large number of ethnographic districts prevents generalization about folk styles (so, for example, the music of the region of Bohemia often reminds one of German influences more than that of Moravia and Slovakia does; also, the instrumental music of professional Gypsy musicians and the vocal-based peasant music in Hungary are widely divergent).

Well-known festivals for popular music include "Rock for People" held annually in Český Brod in the Czech Republic, the Pohoda Festival of Slovakia (at the Airport of Trencin), or the large Sziget Festival taking place right in the center of Budapest (Hungary).

FRANCE

With about 60 million inhabitants, France is one of the largest European nations. As a music market, it holds the fifth position worldwide—in 2004, 126.6 million record units were sold, having a retail value of $1,979.3 million. Furthermore, the concept of a distinct French cultural identity is held up strongly in a state that unites many different nationalities (the Basque and Catalan people near the Spanish border, the Corsicans and Provençals in the south, the Celtic Bretons in the north, the German-related Alsatians in the east, and, not to be forgotten, the large number of immigrants from former colonies in Africa, the Caribbean, and elsewhere). The rather high share of domestic-produced music within the total turnover for records (63 percent in 2004) is an expression of the importance that is bestowed on French national culture. In addition, the predominance of French songs among the genres of popular music as mirrored by the sales numbers (French music was responsible for 35 percent of the record sales in 2004 as compared to a share of 25 percent for international songs) may partly be explained by governmental affirmative action: So, for example, broadcast stations are advised to go on the air with a considerable quota of domestic music. (Similar directions concern the movie industry or the cultivation of the French language.)

The French audience is rather diversified, but for all relevant styles of popular music, there is a long row of successful artists performing in French. The spectrum includes rock music (with such a veteran of the 1960s as Johnny Hallyday still being one of the stars of the French show scene) as well as rap (as an example for that style, the current top act Sinik could be named).

Typical for multinational music with an immigrant background is the adaptation of styles of foreign descent, as for example the northern African (*maghreb*) popular music *raï* that is present in France with artists such as Cheb Khaled. The mixing of musical influences of different national origins and popular styles is represented by musicians such as Manu Chao or the band Les Negresses Vertes.

THE *CHANSON*

It may be because music often serves as a means of national self-assurance that genres of originally rather limited scope, such as the *chanson*, have become symbols of French culture and find larger audiences well beyond their initial target group. The *chanson* (literally "song") is a type of music that grew in urban settings on the basis of older light music (*vaudeville*, or *voix de ville*). It absorbed literary artistic tendencies, with singers such as Edith Piaf or the Belgian Jacques Brel becoming icons of that musical genre in the 1950s and 1960s. Even in the twenty-first century, the *chanson* has lost little of its creative vitality, and artists such as Michel Sardou or Patrick Bruel may be found not only to reach the Top 10 in the national charts but also to find interested listeners in other European countries.

Classical music holds 5 percent of the French music market, and within that genre it may be observed that classical music of French descent is considered as one of the pillars of national cultural identity.

As French culture derives in large part from the influence of the courtly sphere, it is hardly a surprise that traditional folk music does not play as large a role in the definition of cultural identity as it does in other European countries. Nonetheless, there is a rich and regionally very specific scene within that genre (with vast stylistic differences between, say, the music of the Celtic Bretons and the Mediterranean Corsicans). Traditional instruments include all common types; as examples for rather more unusual popular instruments it may suffice to mention the hurdy-gurdy (*vielle*) or the bagpipe (the *cornemuse*, with a specific type of dance, the *musette*, relying on the particularities of that instrument).

Some of the most interesting festivals of popular music in France are held in Brittany, such as the open-air Festival de Vielles Charrues at Carhaix, La Route de Rock at Saint-Malo, or the Festival Art Rock at Saint-Brieuc (to name but a few).

GERMANY AND AUSTRIA

The two German-speaking countries not only have strong common cultural traditions but are also interlinked in economic respects. Germany, being the larger of the two by far (with about 82 million inhabitants, almost exactly ten times the population of Austria), is the fourth most important music market of the world: In 2004, 181.3 million record units were sold, achieving a retail value of $2149 million. Furthermore, Germany was the second largest market worldwide for single track downloads from the Internet in 2004 (numbers still showing a vast gap to the world leader for that medium, the United States). Compared

SCHLAGER: A HYBRID OF STYLES

A peculiarity of German and Austrian music is the phenomenon of *Schlager*, a term that identifies light popular music sung in German that may touch on several genres such as pop, sometimes even rock or rap (the different variants exemplified by artists such as Wolfgang Petry, Herbert Grönemeyer, or the group Die Fantastischen Vier). Quite often, it blends into hybrid styles that use elements of traditional folk music (*Volksmusik*), in particular the forms of folk originating in the Alpine regions; the so-called *volkstümliche Musik*, for example, is a commercialized version of traditional folk that is popular especially in Austria (with a market share of 9 percent in 2004) and southern Germany (particularly in the region of Bavaria). The tendency of much of the traditional music toward a kind of chamber style (*Stubnmusi*), applying instruments such as zithers or acoustic guitars and complex part-singing, often is replaced there by the use of electronically amplified instruments, drum set, and an easily graspable vocal line (as in the case of the combo Zillertaler Schürzenjäger). Wind bands are common in both the traditional and the commercialized variant of folk. Singing in regional dialects is not limited to folk-based styles but also spreads to music with an orientation toward pop or rock. "Austropop" (with artists such as Wolfgang Ambros or the group Erste Allgemeine Verunsicherung) may serve as an example for that, as well as the Cologne rock group BAP.

to that, Austria ranks fourteenth in the list of international music markets, with 11 million record units sold in 2004, which amounted to a value of $288.6 million. In both markets, a decline in sales can be observed during the first years of the twenty-first century, which affected all media formats with the exception of music DVDs. A decisive difference lies in the share of domestic-produced music within the total market of the countries: Whereas music of domestic origin made constant gains during the last years, reaching up to 49 percent in Germany in 2004, that portion is considerably lower in Austria and came up only to 7 percent in that country in the same year. The reason for that is the strong influence in Austria of music produced in Germany, snapping away much of the potential audience of German-singing Austrian artists.

Classical music is relatively popular in both countries, compared with the European average, attaining 8 percent of the overall turnover in Germany and a remarkable 12 percent in Austria in 2004. So, the classical genre came out as the second most popular one in Austria (after pop, but before rock) and as the third most popular one in Germany (after pop and rock). That phenomenon of rather widespread liking of classical music corresponds to a high number per capita of opera and concert houses as well as communal or state-run symphony orchestras and other ensembles. Particularly in the case of Austria, a sociopsychological approach may be taken by identifying the predilection for classical music as a means of defining national culture, postulating Austria to be an "art music nation."

Dance and electronic body music goes strong in Germany (getting up to 6 percent of the overall turnover in 2004), where techno raves like the Berlin Love Parade attracted hundreds of thousands each year during the first decade of the twenty-first century. DJs such as WestBam gained international acceptance in the 1990s, and there is still a vibrant scene in Germany and Austria (e.g., with the Austrian drum and bass duo Kruder and Dorfmeister).

At times, proponents of German rock music have become known beyond national borders. This applies to phenomena of the past such as the West German "Krautrock" of the 1970s (featuring such bands as Kraftwerk and Can) as well as to more recent metal acts such as Rammstein, originating from East Germany, which are popular especially in the Eastern European countries and find fans even in the United States.

Of the numerous popular music festivals taking place in Germany, Rock am Ring should be mentioned, a large open-air event taking place at the Formula 1 racing track around the castle of Nürburg in the mountain area of the Eifel.

GREECE AND CYPRUS

The Greek music scene strongly relies on the rich musical tradition of the country that once constituted the cradle of Occidental culture. More than half of the repertoire sold in Greece comes from domestic production (57 percent in 2004). With about 11 million inhabitants, Greece is the thirty-second most important music market of the world: In 2004, 7.6 million record units were sold for a total retail value of $89.3 million. It is typical of Greek musicians that different streams of pop, folk, and local classical music can mingle within their oeuvre. Two of the most prominent classical composers of the late twentieth century, Mikis Theodorakis (born 1925) and Thanos Mikroutsikos (born in 1947), wrote pieces belonging to such genres as symphony, opera, and—in the case of Theodorakis—film music (as for *Zorba the Greek*) that took up influences of traditional music, but they also

GREEK MUSICAL GENRES

The Greek musical genres to come to international reputation can be subdivided according to their origin (urban or rural) and to their historical genesis. Thus, the genre of *rebetika* (also transliterated *rembetika*, briefly described in the introductory section of this article) may be said to be the Greek variant of urban blues, blending several musical traditions into one expressive style during the first half of the twentieth century. The more popular genre to develop from the fundamentals of *rebetika* in the cities, especially during the second half of the twentieth century, was named *laika*, sharing with its ancestor some instrumental commonalities (such as the use of the bouzouki). For the traditional folk music, the term *paradosiaka* is used, whereas the folk music still vivid in rural settings is often referred to as *dimotika*. Different types of lutes (*tambouras*) form the most conspicuous group of instruments used within these styles: Related to the Turkish *saz*, a variety of forms were developed, including the aforementioned long-necked bouzouki as well as the so-called *lauto*.

composed popular songs and collaborated with musicians of the nonclassical genre. That multivalent artistic approach was certainly stimulated by a political incentive, because the musicians belonged to the democratic anti-dictatorship movement that fought the Greek military junta between 1967 and 1974; the political orientation is clearly expressed by Mikroutsikos's function as a Minister of Culture for a leftist government from 1994 to 1996. But in the same way it may be seen as part of a genuine Greek conception of music not to erect rigid barriers between traditional and contemporary music, nor between the genres of folk, pop, and classical. For that reason, educational goals for elementary schools may be expressed as allowing an understanding for the tradition of Byzantine chant as well as for folksongs.

From these older and newer musical styles, a large number of popular music phenomena take their starting point. This may be seen from the rejuvenating tendencies of *New Rebetika* (with artists including Babis Tsertos) or from a musician such as George Daralas (also transliterated Giorgos Ntalaras) recombining different stylistic influences ranging from the "classical" contemporary composer Theodorakis to the "classical" popular genre of rebetika and not seldom dealing with social issues. In a similar manner, a rock musician of the older generation, the still-popular Vasilis Papakonstantinou (born 1950), collaborated with Theodorakis and Mikroutsikos within the antifascist movement and performed their songs, showing that political matters were of utmost importance to the popular music scene that lay the foundations for present musical life.

Apart from the domestically produced music, it is the usual array of international main-stream pop music that finds its way into the Greek top-selling charts. In the early 2000s, rock (and explicitly hard rock) music is a major factor within the Greek music market for international as for domestic productions.

The most important cultural festival in Greece probably is The Hellenic Festival, taking place from June to September in Athens' Herodes Atticus theater, which shows a wide spectrum of events ranging from theater to music (both classical and popular) to ballet and dance.

Most of the findings described for Greece also are valid for Cyprus, as far as the Greek-speaking majority of the island, with currently about 770,000 inhabitants, is concerned (the Republic of Northern Cyprus, where a population of about 200,000 Turkish-speaking people lives, was established after a military intervention of Turkish troops in 1974 and is diplomatically acknowledged only by Turkey). Due to the common language and similar cultural roots (presenting a blend of *laika* music and pop), artists from Cyprus such as the singers Anna Vissi and Michalis Chatzigiannis will find large parts of their audiences in Greece. Another, strongly diverging example for the Cypriot music scene is given by the hard rock band The Unleaded, at the moment living in the United Kingdom. As for the Northern Cypriot music, a corresponding orientation toward Turkish music may be stated, although many peculiarities of that area can be found on a closer look; a folklore group engaged in that regional music is Yeksad.

ITALY

Renowned as one of the most important European "music nations" and, with about 58 million inhabitants, being one of the largest European economies, Italy harbors a most vital music scene that is perceived well beyond its geographical and linguistic borders. In 2004, 37.8 million record units were sold in Italy, amounting to a retail value of $652.5 million, thus making the country the world's eighth largest music market. Almost half of the sold repertoire comes from domestic production, a fact that relates to the position of Italian pop as the customers' most appreciated genre (followed by international pop). Further music styles of economic impact are (in order of their market shares): rock music, classical music, alternative, and jazz/blues (the latter reaching a respectable portion of 9 percent). As in many other European countries, the number of records sold has declined considerably going into the twenty-first century. In the case of Italy, this finding corresponds to a level of physical piracy that (with an estimated 25–50 percent of the total turnover) is remarkably high for a Western European nation.

A general predilection for light pop music can be observed in Italy; that mainstream style may absorb other genres such as rock as well as jazz or more literary forms of songwriting. The Italian tradition of song (*canzone*) is held up by song contests and music festivals, the most famous one being the festival held in Sanremo, which is not strictly limited to songwriting and therefore is remarked by large parts of the public as an indicator for the development of Italian popular music in general.

Pop musicians singing in Italian, such as Eros Ramazotti or Tiziano Ferro, are well known throughout Europe, many listeners cherishing the Mediterranean flair transported by that type of music. Rock music has also found a specifically Italian formulation that exerts impact to European audiences. To name but a few examples: Adriano Celentano, a rock and roll musician of the older generation (born in 1938), is still valued by many Italians as a singer as well as a figure of public (and even political) life. Rock singer Gianna Nannini had celebrated stage appearances all over Europe. Perhaps the most successful, already having been active in the music business for a long time, is the rock guitarist and singer Zucchero (by surname Fornaciari), who has worked with such different international artists as B. B. King, Eric Clapton, Miles Davis, and Paul Young. Of less international reputation but of equal popularity among young Italians is Vasco Rossi, a rock singer who (like Zucchero) was born in the 1950s in Northern Italy. There exist different variants of rock music in Italy that take up influences of regional traditional music, perhaps best known being the Neapolitan style (with bands such as Spaccanapoli).

Italian songwriting may be said to be influenced by French *chanson* to some extent (as can be seen from the music and lyrics of artists such as Fabrizio De André or Paolo Conte) and by traditional regional music or world music as well (an example being the Sicilian singer-songwriter Pippo Pollina).

Among the music styles to be mentioned as reaching great popularity, dance music and hip hop/rap from Italy should not be forgotten: Musicians such as Gigi D'Agostino and Jovanotti have found wide acclaim throughout Europe. Also, classical music takes a large share within the Italian music market (11 percent of the retail value of the music industry of 2004 belonged to that genre). There is still a widespread liking for such classical Italian genres as the opera of the nineteenth century, and it is not seldom that an opera singer (for example, Andrea Bocelli) should turn to lighter, commercialized music in records and concerts, attaining great success by doing so.

A circumstance to be remembered not only when speaking of traditional folk music is the regional diversity of Italy, a country that became a nation only in the nineteenth century, rather late by European standards. The most obvious divide, which also concerns the economic welfare of the country, is the contrast of northern and southern Italy: While northern Italian traditional music in many cases relates to the products of the neighboring countries (such as the Piemonte region bordering the Savoie in France, or the Trentino with its Alpine, Austro-Tyrolian influences), the music from the southern parts (especially Sicily) is often said to be already participating in the Arab cultural sphere. Accordingly, the instruments used differ widely, ranging from the Alpine *alpenhorn* to accordions (*organetto, fisarmonica*), mandolins, guitars, pipes (*pifferi*), and flutes (*fiati*) to different percussion instruments (such as the *tammorra*, a kind of tambourine). Often the cultivation of traditional folk music and dance (such as the *saltarello* in central Italy or the *tarantella* in Southern Italy) is used to define regional rather than national identity.

POLAND

With about 39 million inhabitants, the largest of the new European democracies to become a member of the Western political alliances (both the European Community and the NATO), Poland hosts a highly original and innovative music scene. The country is the thirty-first largest music market worldwide: In 2004, a total of 12.3 million record units was sold, which attained a retail value of $92 million. A solid portion (40 percent) of the repertoire listened to in Poland is of domestic production. Some characteristics of the preferences of the Polish audience immediately strike the eye when one compares the country's music market to those of other European nations: An extraordinarily high percentage (17 percent) within the sales rates is owed to the genres of hip hop and rap (often performed in Polish), making that style the second most popular one (after pop, but ahead of rock). For both dance music and jazz/blues, a rather high market share of 8 percent was counted in 2004. The strong liking for jazz, which has a long-standing and vital tradition in Poland, can be regarded as symptomatic for the structure of the Polish audience with a considerable fraction being followers of more complex music. On that background, it is hardly a surprise that classical music achieves a high market share (of 9 percent) as well.

In a remarkable way, much of the Polish music scene is influenced by some classical tradition, and many artists of popular music experienced a classical education. That finding is true not only for some jazz musicians or political songwriters but also for such a hip hop performer as O. S. T. R., who attended courses as a classical violinist at a music college. On the other hand, much of the classical music even of contemporary composers can be found to be popular with the audience: Composer Krzysztof Penderecki (who began his career as an avant-garde musician) is often considered to be one of the protagonists of public life, perhaps because of the role he played in the pro-democratic movement struggling for political freedom during the reign of Communism. Henryk Mikołaj Górecki, another living composer, had a remarkable public success with his Third Symphony ("Sorrowful Songs"), which held a position within the English Top 10 in 1992.

In a similar way, some musicians, taking their starting point from classical music, reach great popularity by cultivating a style between the rigid genre frontiers (a good example for that is the violoncellist and composer Piotr Rubik, who currently is very successful within the Polish charts).

For jazz musicians such as the 1971-born pianist Leszek Mozdzer (who also received a classical instrumentalist education), the confrontation of jazz and classical music turned out to be fruitful, as documented in Mozdzer's albums from 1994 and 1999, which presented improvisations on themes by Chopin. In general, Polish jazz showed autonomous qualities during the 1990s and 2000s, with musicians such as trumpet-player Tomasz Stanko reaching international reputation.

The actual spectrum of music popular in Poland is quite wide; it ranges from, say, Krzysztof Krawczyk (a vocalist with roots in political songwriting and mainstream rock) to hip hop acts such as Verba to heavy metal (two prominent groups being the death metal combos Vader and Decapitated). Judging from that width of musical scope, it may be more than a coincidence that album compilations of various artists persistently take great shares of the turnover for records; in 2004, 32.8 percent of the record units sold within the Polish music market (with a value of 24.4 percent of it) were compilation albums.

As for the traditional folk music, much of it is dance music. Ensembles often consist of such instruments as fiddle, clarinet, accordion (sometimes as pedal accordion), and frame drum (*grajcary*). Also, the bagpipe (*kocioł*) is met frequently, with bagpipe ensembles constituting a typical ingredient of Polish traditional folk music.

One of the great festivals of popular music in Poland is the National Festival of Polish Song held in Opole since 1963, one of the biggest European open-air rock festivals, Przystanek Woodstock (The Woodstock Stop), takes place annually in changing cities. There are also important festivals for traditional folk music, such as the annual Festival for Rural Bands and Singers in Kazimierz Dolny or the International Festival of Mountain Folklore held each year in Zakopane.

RUSSIA, UKRAINE, AND BELARUS

The three large Slavic-dominated states that came out of the Soviet empire still own a problematic character as far as the development of state institutions (e.g., an autonomous legal system) is concerned, a condition that also affects their cultural life in some respects. Russia, being the largest country of the world in area and counting more inhabitants than any European nation (with a population of about 144 million people), certainly is the most important music market of the three: In 2004, a total of 118.9 million record units were sold, amounting to a retail value of $490.8 million, making Russia the eleventh largest music market worldwide. As in the neighboring Ukraine, the level of physical piracy for music products is very high (more than 50 percent of the overall revenue). Another similarity of the two countries is the comparatively high share of cassette tapes within the propagated music media (16.8 percent in Russia, 22.4 percent in Ukraine in 2004), with the consequence of Russia being the third largest market of the world for that format. A decrease of the share of cassettes can be observed (especially in Russia), which may be interpreted as a sign of the dynamic economic growth that these countries undergo, raising the penetration of CD players within the music audience. Ukraine has no comparable impact on the international music market: 15.4 million record units with a retail value of no more than $41.7 million were sold to a population of about 48 million people in 2004 (thus making Ukraine the fortieth largest music market of the world). That finding corresponds to the fact that the gross domestic product per capita in Ukraine was only about a third of that of Russia in that year. As there is no functioning music industry in Belarus, exact numbers are not available for that country, which is run by a government often considered to be the last dictatorship in Europe.

Quite a high portion (more than 60 percent) of the music sold in the post-Soviet states is of domestic or regional origin. Especially in Russia, with its immense extent and multi-ethnic population (not only of Slavic descent, but including Siberian, Turkic, Caucasian, and Ugric ethnicities), it is hard to give a concise description of the musical tastes of the audience. But in general, pop and rock have taken the role as the most popular genres after the fall of Communism, musical styles that had been suppressed by the former totalitarian regime for a long time as being suspected of transporting Western values. With the reforms of *perestroika* in the 1980s, a vivid scene of popular music other than folklore or workers' movement songs was growing (especially important within the genre of rock music, with bands such as DDT or Aquarium). After the breakup of the Soviet empire, a large variety of popular music styles was established, ranging from pop and rock to hip hop, techno, trance, and punk.

In Russia, artists such as the dance pop duo t. A. T. u. have reached international acclaim. Artists known beyond the national borders often come from the genre of rock: Some bands, such as Zveri or Leningrad, are influenced by punk (the latter also by ska); others (such as Zemfira) play melodic mainstream rock/pop. The Eurovision Song Contest had its share in making some Russian or Ukrainian music acts popular in other European countries, such as the alternative rock group Mumiy Troll (having a significant following in Scandinavia), the rhythm and blues singer Alsou, and the pop singer Dima Bilan, all from Russia, and artists such as Ruslana (combining ethnic music of the people of the Huzuls with dance music) or the pop singer (and former beauty queen) Tina Karol from Ukraine.

In Ukraine and Belarus, singing in the vernacular language (rather than in the closely related Russian) is often regarded as a means of strengthening the national identity. For that reason, the use of the native language is still subject to censorship as far as the state-run broadcast stations are concerned in Belarus, because the current regime urges an intense orientation toward Russia. Popular music sung in the national language (as, for example, by the alternative rock band N. R. M.) is propagated by the organization Belaruskaya Muzychnaya Alternatyva (Belarus Musical Alternative) and thereby becomes a political act as much as a genuinely musical one. Even in Ukraine (which held free elections after the so-called Orange Revolution), a music festival such as Kiev's Rock Sich still is defined by the stress laid on national culture and language.

Traditional instruments include button accordions (such as the Russian *livenka*) in all three of the states. Balalaika ensembles are frequently found in Russia; the perhaps most typical folk instrument in Ukraine is the *bandura* (a kind of zither), other popular instruments being the violin, the hammered dulcimer (*tsymbaly*), or specific kinds of drums (*baraban*); tambourines also playing a major role within the traditional music of Belarus.

SCANDINAVIA: FINLAND, DENMARK, ICELAND, NORWAY, SWEDEN

The Northern European states are, by European standards, wealthy nations, a fact that is also reflected in their relative importance (compared to their size) as markets for popular music. Thus, Norway (a state of about 4.5 million inhabitants only, but with one of the highest GDPs per capita in Europe) is the sixteenth most important music market worldwide: 13.1 million record units were sold in 2004, amounting to a retail value of $273.8 million. Norway holds a special position as far as popular music in the Nordic nations is concerned, because the adaptation of international music taste seems to be more advanced there: Only 30 percent of the value of records sold in 2004 was owing to domestic production, although some national artists singing in Norwegian (such as Bjørn Eidsvåg) were successful in placing their albums within the Top 10. It is not rare for Nordic pop musicians to sing in English, which may be due at least in part to the international cultural orientation of the Scandinavian people. Some Norwegian pop music acts (like the band a-ha) have attained international importance, but the most vital scene for popular music within the Nordic countries appears to be situated in the largest of the nations in question, Sweden. According to self-estimates, Sweden is the third largest "export nation" of popular music (after the United States and the United Kingdom). Starting with the 1970s band ABBA, quite a bit of pop music of Swedish origin—such bands as Ace of Base, Roxette, or The Cardigans, to name but a few—has been brought forward to the international audiences. Also, the share of domestically produced music within the national music market is higher than in Norway (39 percent of the retail value). With 9 million inhabitants, Sweden is the seventeenth largest music market of the world: in 2004, 18.1 million record units were sold that added up to a retail value of $267.9.

Of smaller international impact is the popular music of Denmark, a nation that has well over 5 million inhabitants and constitutes the twenty-first largest music market worldwide (with 9.6 million record units sold in 2004, amounting to a retail value of $187.4 million). Forty-one percent of the turnover was due to music of national origin (e.g., TV-2), but only few of the musicians won audiences abroad. The case is different with Finland, which hosts a scene of popular music that (at least at the moment) is able to stir international interest, the current top act as of 2005 probably being the band Nightwish. Of all the Nordic music markets, Finland has the highest share of domestic produced music (54 percent). With about 5 million inhabitants, it is the twenty-seventh largest music market of the world: In 2004, 9.6 million records were sold for a retail value of $133.6 million. Even in such a small country as Iceland (only about 290,000 inhabitants), there is a lively artistic scene, and sometimes local popular musicians (e.g., the singer Björk) succeed in finding international acclaim.

Jazz music has developed strongly in Scandinavia, in some cases—as in the music of the saxophonist Jan Garbarek or the guitarist Terje Rypdahl from Norway—showing affinities to local traditional folk music (in this case the rural *bygde* music). There is a long custom of singing in private as well as public gatherings. Some of the older genres—epic poems and historical ballads—still persist in such places as Iceland or the Faroe Islands. The different ethnicities cultivate specific traditions of popular music as part of their national identities, as may be seen from the sung genre of *joiks* within the Saami (Lapp) people, living as an ethnic minority in the arctic, circumpolar zone of Norway, Sweden, and Finland. Traditional instruments include different types of violins and fiddles—perhaps most famous the ornamented *hardingfele*, or Hardanger fiddle, from Norway or the Swedish keyed fiddle (*nyckelharpa*)—as well as plucked zithers (the Norwegian *langeleik* or the Finnish *kantele*). Some form of folk music revival has taken place in all of the Nordic countries, but easy-listening pop music (whether of international orientation or in a vernacular style such as the Finnish *iskelmä*) constitutes by far the most widespread type of music.

The largest festival of popular music in Northern Europe is the Roskilde Festival, an open-air event held in Denmark every summer by a nonprofit organization that hands the revenue of the festival over to humanitarian and cultural purposes.

SPAIN AND PORTUGAL

Situated on the Iberian peninsula in the southwest of Europe, Spain and Portugal both have developed distinct musical cultures not easily compared. Spain—with a population of about 41 million inhabitants, by far being the larger of the two—is the ninth most important music market of the world: In 2004, a total of 38.4 million record units were sold (a dramatic decline in contrast to the figures of 2001, when a total of 80.4 million record units was reached). The retail value of these sales amounted to $572.8 million. For comparison, 11.7 million record units with a retail value of $121.8 million were sold in Portugal in 2004, making the country of about 10.5 million inhabitants the twenty-ninth largest music market worldwide.

A further difference is to be noticed regarding the origin of the sold repertoire: whereas almost half of it in Spain (46 percent) came from domestic production, Portuguese-produced music reached a market share of only 29 percent in that country.

That statistical finding repeats itself in the top-selling music charts: In Spain, most of the Top 10 albums regularly come from Spanish artists, which does not apply in an analogous way in neighboring Portugal. A further dissimilarity lies in the grade of homogeneity of the two countries' native population (here not taking account of the numerous descendants and immigrants from the former colonies): Within the Spanish state, the regional differences between various nationalities (with distinct languages, such as the Basques, Catalans, and Galicians) are much stronger than in Portugal.

Accordingly, a considerable number of popular Spanish musicians can be described as cultivating some regional style or other, which has its function within the definition of the national identity of the concerning region. For that purpose, a phenomenon such as the *Nova Cançó Catalana* (New Catalan Song), personified by singer Joan Manuel Serrat, is as much part of a typical "Catalan music" as the traditional dance of the *Sardana* (a complex group dance accompanied by a unique ensemble of eleven musicians). The intricate Catalan rhythms appear in different stylistic contexts, similar findings apply to the complicated metrical models in Basque music. Traditional music and instruments sometimes blend into new stylistic developments. To give but two examples, the group Berrogüetto uses Galician traditional instruments in a fusion of folk and rock music, whereas another exponent of the new folk movement, the group L'Ham de Foc from Valencia, employs instruments of all epochs and cultures. Thus, popular styles with more traditional background (like flamenco music and dance, performed by such prominent musicians as the guitarist Paco de Lucia) are only part of a multifaceted image. On that background, it is no surprise that the music of a transnational ethnic minority, the Roma, should play a considerable role within the development of Spanish popular music in changing contexts.

In some historical respect, Portuguese popular music shares the lot of its Spanish counterpart: An authoritarian regime (in this case that of the dictator Salazar) oppressed wide

SPANISH ROCK AND POP ROOTS

Pop and Rock Music often takes its starting points from traditional musical patterns. The style of one of the current top acts of popular music, Ojos de Brujo, may be described as *Rumba Flamenca.* Spanish pop music for a long time suffered from a repressive cultural climate during the times of the fascist Franco regime. Once democracy was established in the 1970s, a new and innovative sound (and, also, more liberal thematic contents of pop songs) spread within Spain's popular music. In that respect, the *Movida madrileña* (Madrilene movement), with pop bands such as Mecano, was a characteristic phenomenon of the post-Franco era. Such a singer as Julio Iglesias had the opportunity to become one of the true international top acts of pop during the 1980s. Meanwhile, Spanish pop music appearing within the national Top 10 (e.g., David Bisbal or the girl band Las Ketchup) often retains some characteristic folklore-related elements but, generally speaking, obeys the laws of the international music market. The international acceptance of Spanish popular music is partly due to the fact that Spain is a major destination for tourists from many European nations.

parts of cultural life up to the 1970s, and a number of productions of popular music was suspected to foster "non-Portuguese" tendencies. So one of the most famous music styles of Portugal, the *fado*, was not in official esteem for a long time. Perhaps for good reasons, that urban genre was associated with influences from black African culture and a fatalistic approach to life. The heritage of *fado* (exemplified by the singer Misia) meanwhile has perpetuated to a new generation of musicians (such as the singer Amália Rodrigues) and has become a symbol of Portuguese national identity by transporting the melancholic feeling of *saudade*. In contemporary Portuguese popular music, a variety of styles can be met. A political songwriter active for decades who takes up traditional musical structures is Zeca (José) Alfonso. Jazz and blues are represented by such musicians as Maria Joao and Rui Veloso. Immigrants from the former colonies make their contribution to Portuguese musical life, as can be seen from the reggae band Kussundulola with musicians from Angola. One of the rare cases of a Portuguese pop music act to find international acclaim is Madredeus. Folk music is cultivated by formations using traditional (sometimes even medieval) instruments from Portuguese and Galician music history. Such a traditional instrument, encountered both in Portugal and in Spain, is the bagpipe (*gaita*), and ensembles like Gaiteiros de Lisboa (Bagpipers of Lisbon) or Sétima Legião show the unbroken vitality of its use. One of the largest festivals of popular music held in Europe is the spin-off of the Rock in Rio music event that is held in Lisbon.

SWITZERLAND

Although situated within a country of comparatively minor extension and population, the Swiss music scene shows a number of characteristics worth mentioning under a separate heading. Compared to its population numbers (about 7.5 million inhabitants), Switzerland holds a high position within the world's music economies: In 2004, 20.4 million record units were sold, amounting to a retail value of $258.8 million and making Switzerland the eighteenth largest music market worldwide. The culture of this small but by European standards wealthy state is defined by the regional diversity of the speakers of the four official languages: German (or rather, the Alemannic dialect of Schwyzerdütsch), French, Italian, and Rhaeto-Romansch. The last is spoken only in some valleys of Switzerland, the other three are shared with very much larger neighboring countries. In many respects, Swiss culture can be seen as a combination of regional identities and of national as well as transnational predilections. It may be for that reason that the share of music produced outside Switzerland is very high within the Swiss music market (usually around 80 percent of the total turnover).

The stress laid on the different regional cultures can be seen from performers of popular music—and not only of traditional folk music, but of more contemporary styles—who use the local language variants. There is a veritable movement of dialect pop and rock music, especially in the German-speaking parts of Switzerland (exemplified by the group Plüsch of Interlaken). Stephan Eicher, an influential rock chanson singer-songwriter, became famous by singing songs in all different Swiss languages. Also, the regional or local heritage of folk music is held in high esteem, especially in the Swiss-German speaking areas of Switzerland, with such Alpine musical traditions as yodeling, the blowing of alpenhorns, and whip-cracking (*chlepfe*) still well cultivated by special organizations and clubs. Other traditional instruments (rather appealing to chamber styles) include hammered dulcimers (*Hackbretter*) and accordions (e.g., the diatonic *Schwyzerörgeli* or *fisarmonica a nümar*). Traditional dance music is performed by ensembles such as the *bandella* of the Italian-speaking Ticino area, which consists of a clarinet and usually four brass instruments.

In contemporary Swiss popular music, all of the familiar genres are present. Artists as different as the pop singer Patrick Nuo, the dance music singer-producer DJ Bobo, the electronic dance music duo Yello (whose music is often used for dance samples or film music), and the hard rock combo Krokus have achieved international success. Such acclaim often coincides with the choice of the English language for the texts of the concerning artists. Although the Swiss charts usually are dominated by international Anglo-American pop music, music performed in French or German as well as in dialect will also reach good sales numbers regularly. The largest music festival is held annually in Lucerne; furthermore, the jazz festival in Montreux has grown to international importance.

TURKEY

Positioned right at the border between Europe and Asia (the Middle East), and being Europe's largest Islamic country with about 70 million inhabitants, Turkey plays a significant role within the cultural spectrum of the continent. Furthermore, the country gained decisive importance for the music of southeastern Europe, as the former Ottoman empire covered the whole Balkan region and stretched as far as southern Hungary, thereby exerting vital influence on the cultural life of the countries concerned.

Today, Turkey is the twenty-second largest music market of the world, with 43.5 million record units sold in 2004 totaling $166.2 million retail value (which does not include the figures for pirated products, with an estimated level of physical piracy of more than 50 percent). A cultural particularity may be seen in the very high portion of cassette tapes within the total of music products: More than half of the record units sold in 2004 were cassettes, thus making Turkey the world's most important market for that format. A closer look at the other top ten markets for cassettes—including India, Russia, Indonesia, China, and even Saudi Arabia—confirms the hypothesis that the dominance of cassettes is closely linked to the ways of propagation of recorded music in these countries on the one hand and to the level of penetration of newer technical audio devices on the other. Also, it may be more than mere coincidence that within a country where recorded music circulates mainly on cassettes (making it easy to record and copy music), there should be a predilection for local and

ROCK, RAP, AND CLUB MUSIC IN TURKEY

Anatolian (*Anadolu*) rock is a musical phenomenon that came about in the 1960s, when the music of American and British bands was transformed and combined with Turkish folk music by artists such as the band Mogollar (whose former mastermind, Murat Ses, later went on to form a new style of fusion music called Electric Levantine). Rock music with less regional influences is represented by musicians such as Erkin Koray or Demir Demirkan. There even exists a club music scene of international impact, which may be seen from the band project Baba Zula. A genre first developed by a migrant community outside the motherland (especially in quarters of West Berlin) is Turkish hip hop, which at the same time also gained a following in Turkey.

regional popular music rather than for international production. Accordingly, the Turkish music market is characterized by a high share of domestic music (with a staggering 94 percent of the total revenue in 2004).

The most popular music style in Turkey belongs to the genre of mainstream pop with Western orientation, but even here the cultural heritage of the region can hardly be overheard. Artists such as the singers Tarkan and Mustafa Sandal have reached international success, at least partly because of the wide dissemination of Turkish-rooted migrants all over Europe. Other important pop musicians are such female singers as Sezen Aksu or Sertab Erener (winner of the 2003 Eurovision Song Contest). Genres of popular music that show a deliberate synthesis of Western styles with regional music (whether of folk or of classical descent) are Arabesque and Anatolian rock. Arabesque arose from the waves of migration within Turkey, when the rural population from the southeastern areas moved to the big cities (especially Istanbul), where the older taverna music (*fasil*) was often superseded by these Arabic influences. A musician amalgamating Arabesque with Anglo-American rock and roll is Orhan Gencebay.

The folk music of Turkey is very diversified, breeding on the local particularities of regions between the Caucasus, the Middle East, and the Balkans. Also, classical Turkish music fed on different sources, including Arabic, Persian, and Byzantine music. Characteristic instruments for classical music are the *oud* (a lute-type instrument used especially for solo improvisation within the form of *taksim*) and the *ney*, a flute of great antiquity. The drum *darabuka* (or *darbuka*) finds use both in classical and in folk music. Within the traditional folk music, the long-necked lute *saz* (or, more specifically, *baglama*) may perhaps be said to be the most common instrument all over Turkey.

Several great music festivals are held in the big cities; worth mentioning are the International Istanbul Music Festival and the International Istanbul Jazz Festival, taking place from June to July.

UNITED KINGDOM AND IRELAND

The two English-speaking states, and in particular the United Kingdom, surely have had the greatest European impact on the international scene of popular music. An explanation for that prominent role should not be contended with pointing out the function of English as the modern *lingua franca* but will also draw attention to the vibrant music scene of such cities as London, Manchester, or Dublin.

The United Kingdom (with about 60 million inhabitants, larger by far than Ireland with its population of 4 million people) takes a central position within the world's music industry: With a total of 194.1 million record units sold in 2004, amounting to a retail value of

$3.5 billion, the United Kingdom is the world's third largest market for music products, only giving way to the United States and Japan. The numbers for the smaller state, Ireland, accordingly were lower: In 2004, a retail value of $145.8 million was earned by the sale of 8.6 million record units of music products, thus making Ireland the twenty-fourth largest recorded music market worldwide. Partly because of its vicinity to the strong British music industry, the share of domestically produced recorded music within the sold repertoire is considerably lower in Ireland: Only 25 percent of the music products sold in Ireland in 2004 originated there, whilst in the United Kingdom about half of the records were produced in the country itself.

Taking a closer look at the music genres present within the records sold in the United Kingdom, very typical findings come to the fore: Pop music and mainstream ("middle of the road") combine to the strongest portion, followed by rock. Rhythm and blues, dance music, and hip hop take a market share between 5 and 10 percent, while jazz, classical music, and country together sell less than 5 percent of the total of records.

The paramount importance of British popular music for the worldwide music scene dates back at least to the 1960s, when bands such as the Beatles, the Rolling Stones, the Who, and Cream (featuring guitarist Eric Clapton) rocked the audiences of the world. Innovative approaches were taken during the 1970s in diverse areas of popular music; genres ranged from experimental, rather composed music (by such bands as Pink Floyd, Genesis, and Queen), to straightforward heavy metal (e.g., Led Zeppelin, Deep Purple, Black Sabbath, Iron Maiden, and Judas Priest) to punk rock (exemplified by the Sex Pistols or the Clash).

As of the first decade of the twenty-first century, virtually all styles of popular music have prominent exponents in the United Kingdom, be it in the genre of pop music (e.g., Dido, Sugababes, Robbie Williams), soul (Simply Red), or dance music (The Prodigy, Massive Attack). Innovative fusion of genres is often to be found in Britain, a recent example being the blend of hip hop, dub, and electronic music introduced by the band Gorillaz.

With all its international appeal, it may sometimes be hard to define the typical British element within the country's popular music. An example for a "vernacular" style in British music is the phenomenon called Britpop (with bands such as Oasis or Blur), which arose in Britain in the 1990s. Also, younger rock bands (e.g., Franz Ferdinand or Arctic Monkeys) show a clear orientation toward a genuinely "British" style.

Music of the immigrants (especially from the former British colonies) transformed the British popular music scene in several cases. The Caribbean genre of ska developed into an English style in the 1970s (the so-called two-tone-ska, represented by bands such as Madness). A more recent example is the adaptation of the Punjabi dance music *bhangra* into a fusion style of popular music, which took place since the 1990s, propagated by artists such as Panjabi MC.

The musical scene in Ireland brings forth internationally acknowledged top acts every once in a while. For rock music, U2 was the highest-selling Irish band from the 1980s into the 2000s; Sinéad O'Connor and Ronan Keating (former member of the boy group Boyzone) are examples of pop music from Ireland. Some of the current top acts of pop, such as the female singer Enya or the band The Corrs, show affinity to different strains of Celtic music and traditional folk music. Folk music generally plays a great role within the popular music of Ireland and is kept alive by several successful ensembles such as the Chieftains, the Dubliners, or Planxty. Fusion styles that adapt folk influences even include punk rock (as to be seen from the band The Pogues).

The traditional folk music of Ireland commonly uses the fiddle, the flute, the tin whistle, the bellows-blown *uilleann* bagpipes, the harp, accordions (especially the button accordion), the concertina, and the frame drum *(bodhrán)*. Some of these instruments also exist in different forms in Britain—the bellows-blown bagpipe in Northumbria being as familiar as the harp in Wales or the fiddle and concertina in England. A traditional instrument known worldwide is the mouth-blown bagpipe of the Scottish type (called "warpipes" in Ireland).

Some important festivals of popular music are the Glastonbury Festival, the Godiva Festival (held in Coventry), the revitalized Isle of Wight Festival, and the pop concerts taking place in different British cities under the name of Party in the Park. In Ireland, the Sligo Live Festival unites popular Irish musicians of different styles every summer.

RESOURCE GUIDE

PRINTED SOURCES

Smith, C., ed. *The Greenwood Encyclopedia of Rock History*. Westport, CT: Greenwood, 2006.

Frith, S., ed. *The Cambridge Companion to Pop and Rock*. Cambridge, UK: Cambridge University Press, 2001.

Frith, S., ed. *Popular Music*. 4 vols. London: Routledge, 2004.

IFPI. *The Recording Industry in Numbers*. London: International Federation of the Phonographic Industry, 2005a.

IFPI. *The Recording Industry: World Sales*. London: International Federation of the Phonographic Industry, 2005b.

Mitchell, T. *Popular Music and Local Identity: Rock, Pop, and Rap in Europe and Oceania*. London: Leicester University Press, 1996.

Rice, T., et al., eds. *Europe. The Garland Encyclopedia of World Music, Vol. 8*. New York: Garland Publishing, 2000.

FILMS

Carmen (Spain, 1983). Directed by Carlos Saura, starring Laura del Sol and Paco de Lucia. The second of Saura's five films dealing with the flamenco, based on the the famous opera of that title by Georges Bizet and its inspiration, the French nineteenth-century novel by Prosper Mérimée.

The Commitments (Ireland/UK/United States, 1991). Directed by Alan Parker. An Irish take on the scene of young working-class musicians.

Crossing the Bridge: The Sound of Istanbul (Germany/Turkey, 2005). Directed by Fatih Akin, starring Alexander Hacke and Baba Zula. Both a musical documentary on the diversified music scene of Istanbul and a commentary on the vast social and cultural contrasts within the European-Asian capital.

Leningrad Cowboys Go America (Finland/Sweden, 1989). Directed by Ari Kaurismäki. Road movie featuring the bizarre folk-punk combo Leningrad Cowboys—a very Finnish kind of musical.

Yellow Submarine (UK/United States, 1968). Directed by George Dunning. Rather psychedelic animation movie starring (as cartoons) the Beatles at the height of their fame.

RECORDINGS/VIDEOS (LISTED BY REGIONS):

The Balkans: Albania, Bosnia-Herzegovina, Croatia, Macedonia, Serbia and Montenegro, and Slovenia

Laibach. *A Film from Slovenia—Occupied*. Mute 0724382452294. DVD, 2004.

Miroslav Škoro. *Milo moje*. Croatia Records/Campus 5545194. CD (also as DVD), 2003.

Belgium, the Netherlands, and Luxembourg

Marco Borsato. *Zien*. Universal Music 0602498661635. DVD, 2004.
Vaya con Dios. *The Best of Vaya con Dios*. Ariola 0743214098622. CD, 1996.

Bulgaria, Romania, and Moldava

Marcel Cellier. *Le mystère des voix bulgares*. Nonesuch 79165, 79201. 2 CDs, 1987, 1988.
O-Zone. *Disco-Zone*. Universal Music 060249870095. CD, 2004.

Czech Republic, Slovakia, and Hungary

Andras Farkas and Ensemble. *Famous Hungarian Gypsy Tunes*. ARC Music 5019596164729. CD, 2001.
Peha. *Experiment*. Epic 5099751132028. CD, 2003.

Estonia, Latvia, and Lithuania

Lithuanie, le pays des chansons. Ocora C 600005. CD, 1997.

Finland and the Scandinavian states: Denmark, Iceland, Norway, Sweden

The Cardigans. *Life*. Stockholm Records LC 5865. CD, 1995.
Him. *Dark Light*. Reprise B000ATT2QO. CD, 2005.
Jan Garbarek Group. *Twelve Moons*. ECM 519500-2. 2 CDs, 1993.
Tango Orkesteri Unto. *Finnish Tango*. ARC Music 5019396183025. CD, 2003.

France

Manu Chao. *Clandestino*. Virgin Fra 0724384578329. CD, 1998.
Cheb Khaled. *Aiysha*. Movieplay 8712177033676. CD, 2001.
Michel Sardou. *Du Plaisir*. Universal Music 0602498191811. CD, 2005.

Germany and Austria

Die Fantastischen Vier. *Viel*. SMD COL 5099752444427. CD, 2004.
Herbert Grönemeyer. *Mensch live*. Groenland 0724349097797. DVD, 2003.
Zillertaler Schürzenjäger. *Am Morgen, wenn die Sonne lacht*. MCP 9002986526056. CD, 2004.

Greece and Cyprus

George Dalaras. *A Tribute to Markos Vamvakaris*. Tropical 0764916884023. 2 CDs, 2004.
Thanos Mikroutsikos and Vasilis Papakonstantinou. *Thalasssa sti skala*. Minos-EMI 724352439126. CD, 1999.
Yeksad. *Music of Northern Cyprus*. ARC Music 5019396198326. CD, 2006.

Italy

Zucchero Fornaciari. *Blue's*. Polygram LC 0309. CD, 1987.
Jovanotti. *Buon Sangue—Live*. Universal Music 0602498574577. DVD, 2006.
Eros Ramazotti. *Dove c'è musica*. BMG 74321354402. CD, 1996.

Poland

Perruche/Sinfonia Vasovia/Alti. *Henryk Mikołaj Górecki: Sinfonie 3.* Naive 0822186050293. SACD Hybrid, 2005.
Sources of Polish Folk Music. Polish Radio PRCD 150–155. 6 CDs in series (more in process), 1996–.

Russia, Ukraine, and Belarus

Leningrad. *Hleb.* Eastblok 4015698692723. CD, 2006.
Ruslana. *Wild dances.* EMI 0724386445322. CD, 2005.
t. A. T. u. *Dangerous and Moving.* Interscope 0602498851036. CD, 2005.

Spain and Portugal

Julio Iglesias. *Divorcio.* SMI COL 5099750632499. CD, 2003.
Paco de Lucia. *Gold.* Universal Music 0602498325964. CD, 2005.
Misia. *Drama Box.* Tropical 0764916885020. CD, 2005.

Switzerland

Schweizer Volksmusik: Traditional Swiss Music: Tag der Schweizer Volksmusik IMF Luzern. DRS: Zytglogge 4532. 2 CDs, n.d.
Yello. *Flag.* Vertigo 0602498307571. CD, 2005.

Turkey

Orhan Gencebay. *Klasikleri.* Kervan Plakç_l_k 4039664203423. 2 CDs, 1998.
Mogollar. *Mogollar + 8.* World Psychedelica 9990601087603. CD, 1990.
Mustafa Sandal. *Seven (reloaded).* Universal Music 0602498717264. CD, enhanced (with videos), 2005.

United Kingdom, Ireland

Dido. *No Angel.* BMG/Arista LC03484. CD, 2000.
Franz Ferdinand. *Franz Ferdinand.* Domino Recording WIGCD 136. CD, 2004.
Gorillaz. *Phase One: Celebrity Take Down.* Parlophone 0724349013308. DVD, 2002.
Planxty. *The Planxty Collection.* Shanachie 0016351791221. CD, 1989.
U2. *War.* Island 0042281114823. CD, 1985.

Festivals or Events

The following are only a selection; for a more comprehensive overview see http://www.yourope.org or http://www.2camels.com/festivals/):

Festival de Vielles Charrues: Open-air event in a natural amphitheater at Carhaix (Brittany/France), end of July. http://www.viellescharrues.asso.fr/en/festival/.
Glastonbury Festival of the Contemporary Performing Arts: UK's biggest open-air festival, held in a valley in Somerset/England, usually on the last full weekend in June. http://www.glastonbury festivals.co.uk/.
Love Parade: Huge, free open-air techno rave held in the center of Berlin one weekend in July. http://www.loveparade.net/.

Montreux Jazz Festival: One of the most influential jazz festivals of Europe, held all over the town of Montreux (Switzerland) during two weeks in summer (end of June to middle of July). http://www.montreuxjazz.com/index_en.aspx.

Przystanek Woodstock (The Woodstock Stop): Open-air rock festival taking place in a different city in Poland each year, in July. http://www.wosp.org.pl/en/przystanek/2005/.

Rock in Rio-Lisboa: European spin-off of the world's biggest music event (originally held in Rio de Janeiro), taking place in Lisbon (Portugal) every few years. http://rockinrio-lisboa.sapo.pt/?lang=en.

Roskilde Festival: The largest festival of popular music in Northern Europe, an open-air event held in Denmark every summer (end of June). http://www.roskilde-festival.dk.

Sziget Festival: Big open-air rock festival taking place on the Danube island Óbudai, right in the center of Budapest (Hungary), in August. http://www.sziget.hu/festival_english/.

ORGANIZATIONS, MUSEUMS AND SPECIAL COLLECTIONS

International Federation of the Phonographic Industry (IFPI), IFPI Secretariat, 54 Regent Street, London, W1B 5RE, United Kingdom. http://www.ifpi.org. Principal organization of the music industry, with branches in many European countries as well as all worldwide.

Institute of Popular Music (IPM), School of Music, University of Liverpool, Roxby Building, Chatham Street, Liverpool, L69 7ZT, United Kingdom. http://www.liv.ac.uk/ipm/index.htm. University institute teaching popular music and providing scientific resources on that subject.

International Association for the Study of Popular Music (IASPM), http://www.iaspm.net/iaspm/. International organization with central seat at the Institute of Popular Music (IPM). Promoting research on popular music; European branches in the Benelux states (Belgium, The Netherlands, Luxembourg), Bulgaria, German-speaking countries, Scandinavia, Spain, and UK/Ireland.

Klaus-Kuhnke-Archiv of Popular Music, Dechanatstr. 13–15, D-28195 Bremen, Germany. http://www.kkarchiv.de/. Collection of about 90,000 recordings and 8000 books on popular music.

Musée de la Musique, 221, Avenue Jean Jaurès, F-75019 Paris, France, http://www.cite-musique.fr/anglais/musee/index.html, Showing a large permanent collection of musical instruments as well as temporary expositions often focusing on contemporary musical life.

Musées de musiques populaires, BP 3249, F-03106 Montluçon cedex, France, http://www.musees-montlucon.com/, Collection of instruments and recordings of traditional and contemporary popular music.

Museum of Popular Music, Kaštan, Bělohorská 201/150, 16900 Prague 6, Břevnov, Czech Republic. http://www.popmuseum.cz/. Centre of information on Czech and Slovak popular music, also including a collection of musical instruments.

Museum of Popular Instruments—Research Centre for Ethnomusicology (MELMOKE), 1.3 Diogenous Str., Aeridon Square, 10559 Plaka, Athens, Greece. http://www.culture.gr/4/42/421/42109/e4210901.html. Collection of about 1200 instruments of traditional popular music.

Musical Instrument Museum, Rue montagne de la cour 2, B-1000 Brussels, Belgium. http://www.mim.fgov.be/. Large collection of musical instruments.

rock'n'popmuseum, Udo-Lindenberg-Platz 1, D-48599 Gronau, Germany. http://www.rock-popmuseum.de/. Features cultural history of popular music of the twentieth century.

Society for Traditional Music in Switzerland, http://www.gvs-smps.ch/. Promoting traditional Swiss folklore music.

NOTES

1. All given statistical information is taken from the publications of the International Federation of the Phonogaphic Industry, IFPI 2005a,b in the Resource Guide.

PERIODICALS

CHRISTINA SVENDSEN

Periodicals are a typically modern form of communication. Three qualities are necessary for a text to be considered a periodical: it must appear at intervals, even if the intervals are somewhat irregular; it must inform readers on current events or developments in some area of life or knowledge; and it must be affordable. Legends about the invention of the first periodical usually center around the figure of the Parisian doctor Théophraste Renaudot, who founded an early newspaper called *La Gazette* on May 30, 1631. However, while Renaudot's history provides a clear and straightforward narrative for the origin of the newspaper, periodicals had been founded and sold in France and elsewhere before that date.

It is difficult to trace the origin of the periodical, because these ephemeral documents were often not preserved in libraries since it was presumed they were no longer interesting once their contents were out of date. It is nonetheless clear that the earliest ancestor of the periodical was the *occasionnel*, a manuscript often composed of several letters that had been copied together and circulated among bankers, sovereigns, or other influential figures to pass on news of political events in distant places. These *gazettes de la main* (gazettes of the hand) were soon printed and circulated regularly whenever a newsworthy event occurred; the earliest printed example of this genre is a Hungarian *occasionnel* printed in 1480 containing news about the war against the Ottomans. The earliest *occasionnels* had titles like *News of the Court* or much shorter descriptive titles like *Courant* or *Tydnighen* [Tidings]. The origin of news about events in Italy might have been marked "from Madrid," because the news would have come from a letter from Madrid, and the same piece of news might be recounted several times as emanating from different cities. Only later would an editorial voice be used, where the journalist might intervene to state the origin of a news item or present an independent analysis. These more-edited accounts of the news were called *extraordinaires* and appeared less frequently.

If *occasionnels* are the ancestor of newspapers, then the low-cost books published serially with some continuity in content are most likely the ancestors of the magazine. These books often contained a hodgepodge of topical political, literary, and cultural issues and could be similar to almanacs. The earliest is the *Mercure francais*, begun under the title *Chronologie novenaire de Palma Cayet* and published by the brothers Jean and Etienne Richer in 1589; it became the *Mercure* in 1611. Even now, European magazines tend to be issued by publishing houses that also print books, whereas newspapers have their own presses. France and Holland had the earliest and liveliest publishing scenes; periodicals from their capitals, published in French, English, and Dutch, traveled across Europe and set the standard for the newly invented periodical industry. Only later did London enter the fray: the world's first copyright law was enacted in the United Kingdom in 1710. The heyday of periodicals publishing was probably in the nineteenth century, when several editions of a newspaper might come out in a single day, and readers subscribed to and shared a large range of newspapers, magazines, and serials.

Today, periodicals are still popular. Newspapers, for example, are read by over 180 million people across Europe. Within publishing, newspapers are the most important subsector, with 36.8 percent of production value in 2001, followed by journals and magazines (32 percent), and then by books (24.6 percent). But periodical advertising revenue is falling, core readership for periodicals is over forty-five years of age, and younger readers appear to prefer other media. Digital technologies are quickly changing the ways in which content is created, combined, distributed, and consumed. Currently, periodicals face competition from new media such as television and the Internet—forcing an ever-quicker news cycle time and reaction time. Nonetheless, the theory that new media replace old media is an oversimplification that is generally not true: despite the advent of radio, TV, and Internet technologies, print is still a dominant medium and continues to grow alongside the new media, differentiating itself and serving different needs from those served by newer media.

AUSTRIA

Austria has a small periodicals market that flourishes in the shadow of its larger neighbor, Germany. Austria's two largest daily newspapers, *Die Neue Kronenzeitung* and *Kurier*, together reach more than half the population. Better-educated Austrians, especially in the larger cities, read either the conservative *Die Presse* or the liberal *Der Standard*, quality newspapers published in Vienna with circulations of less than 100,000. The weekly news magazine *News* has one of Europe's highest rates of household penetration; it competes with other weeklies such as *Profil* and the business weekly *Wirtschaftswoche*. The magazine *Der Falter* publishes an influential weekly guide of events as well as restaurant, music, and museum reviews for Vienna.

Several waves of press concentration have hit Austria since World War II; by early 1997, this trend left the country with a small but stable number of papers. Austria has, however, strong regional newspapers that dominate up to 90 percent of the regional markets, the most important being the *Salzburger Nachrichten*, the conservative *Tiroler Tageszeitung*, and the liberal Catholic *Kleine Zeitung* based in Linz. With a few exceptions, each Austrian province is supplied by just one regional publisher; the remaining small, secondary papers do not sell more than 10,000 copies each. Many Austrians read German periodicals such as *Der Spiegel*, but local magazines are also popular, including *Wiener Journal* [Viennese Journal] (culture and politics), *Ladylife*, *Wienerin*, *AUF* (fashion), *Feine Küche* and *Kochen und Küche* (cuisine), *Bier Akademie*, and *Alles Auto*. Austria has a relatively high rate of Internet penetration. Traditional media still dominate online, but a wide variety of local, German, and international sites are accessed.

THE BALKANS: SLOVENIA, CROATIA, SERBIA AND MONTENEGRO, BOSNIA-HERZEGOVINA, MACEDONIA, AND ALBANIA

There has been great disruption in the periodical market in the Balkans because of the war that split apart the former Yugoslavia into the post-socialist nations of Slovenia, Croatia, Serbia and Montenegro, Bosnia-Herzegovina, and Macedonia. A few Serbian presses still publish magazines from Belgrade that are distributed in Serbia, Montenegro, Macedonia, and parts of Bosnia, such as the tabloid *Svet* (270,000) and the magazine *Lepota i Zdravlje* (270,000), which focuses on health and beauty. Magazines targeted specifically toward women—*Lea* (70,000)—or men—the new *CKM* (40,000)—also sell well.

Slovenia

Despite almost no foreign investment after Slovenia's bloodless secession from the Yugoslav federation in 1991, six newspapers flourish in the small Slovenian market for daily periodicals, selling a total of 380,000 copies to a population of 2 million. The two dailies with the highest circulation are *Delo* (93,000) and the tabloid *Slovenske Novice*, both owned by the same holding company. Although *Delo* is a quality newspaper and *Slovenske Novice* a tabloid, on Sunday they jointly publish the popular *Nedelo* (70,000). Two regional dailies originally founded in the 1970s are still popular: *Dnevnik* (65,000) circulates in the capital, Ljubljana, while *Vecer* (67,000) is read in the northeast region. The newest specialized dailies are the sports paper *Ekipa* (30,000) and a business daily titled *Finance* (5,000). The two biggest political weeklies are *Mladina* and *Mag*, although smaller political magazines from across the political spectrum are also published (*Demokracija*, *Panorama*). The Catholic Church issues a number of important magazines that exert political influence, including *Druzina*. Foreign investors have lately entered the market with *Finance* and through licensing Slovenian versions of *Playboy*, *Cosmopolitan*, and *Men's Health*. Although men's magazines outsell women's, *Naša Žena* (fashion) and *Dober Tek* (food) are popular, as are a plethora of car and computer magazines.

Croatia

In Croatia as well, official figures are hard to come by, but the post-socialist period has been harsh for the press: five years of war and five more of international isolation have taken their toll. Independent or accurate reporting is rare. In this country of over 4 million inhabitants, two political weekly magazines compete with the large audience interest in tabloids and women's magazines. The only quality daily newspaper is the state-owned *Vjesnik*, which has a circulation in the low thousands. The largest private newspapers, *Vezernji list* [Evening Paper] and *Jutarnji list* [Morning Paper], compete to be the more up-to-date and sensational. The third national newspaper, *Slobodna Dalmacija*, is printed in Split for the population of the Dalmatian region. Regional papers such as the Rijeka daily *Novi list*, have formed a news pool, giving readers a better selection of news from across the country. In an attempt to boost their 2004 sales, daily newspapers sometimes offered novels or cookbooks as a bonus for buying a newspaper.

The leading weekly political magazines are the rivals *Globus* and *Nacional* and the lesser-known *Feral Tribune*. They are, however, far outclassed in total sales by the women's magazine *Gloria*, which is Croatia's best-selling magazine and reaches 15 percent of the market. *Story*, another women's magazine, and the periodical *Auto Klub* reach 10 percent of the market each, while the political *Globus* reaches a mere 8.5 percent, according to research by Puls.

281

Reading periodicals on the Internet is increasingly popular. More than half of Croatian homes have computers. The top ten Croatian Websites have a low ratio of news to entertainment, however; the daily newspapers *Vecernji list* and *Slobodna Dalmacija* are the only two among the top ten Croatian sites that feature news and politics. Prominent among the top-ten Croatian Websites are the lonely hearts site *Iskrica* and two job search sites.

Bosnia-Herzegovina

Newspaper readership has always been limited in Bosnia-Herzegovina and has been sinking recently as a result of the devastated economy of the region and the lack of quality in available periodicals. Newspapers and magazines often cater to ethnic identities, thereby limiting their potential audiences. Six daily newspapers are published in Bosnia, four of them in the Federation of Bosnia-Herzegovina: *Dnevni Avaz, Oslobodjenje*, and *Jutarnje Novine* in Sarajevo, and *Dnevni List* in Mostar. The nationalist Serb *Nezavisne Novine* and *Glas Srpski* are published in Banja Luka in the Republic of Srpska. *Glas Srpski* is the only daily owned by the government; the others are more or less independent, depending on the political situation.

There are no reliable data on the circulation of most of the papers published in Bosnia-Herzegovina. According to some assessments for 2001, *Dnevni Avaz* had the highest circulation—approximately 40,000 copies—followed by *Oslobodjenje* with 15,700 copies, and *Jutarnje Novine* with a circulation of around 10,000 copies. *Nezavisne Novine* and *Glas Srpski* circulated 7,500 and 7,200 copies respectively. Several weekly magazines also circulate: *Slobodna Bosna* (28,000), *Dani* (25,500), *Nedeljne Nezavisne Novine* (18,000), and *Reporter* (10,000).

Albania

Until the end of the Communist regime in 1990, Albania was a highly controlled society; by far the most important daily newspaper was *Zeri i Popullit* [Voice of the People], published by the Communist Party's central committee. As a result of the changed political situation, *Zeri i Popullit* lost its substantial circulation to the new, independent papers that started to emerge. By 1991 several opposition papers were being published, including the popular and outspoken *Rilindja Demokratike*. In response to the changing public mood, *Zeri i Popullit* dropped the hammer and sickle insignia from its masthead, along with the Marxist slogan "Proletarians of the World Unite." It then joined with opposition newspapers in the campaign to expose and denounce the corruption and privileges of the ruling elite. Now, *Zeri i Popullit* is stable and is published as the newspaper of the Socialist Party. Its contemporary competitors include *Rilindja Demokratike* (the Democratic Party organ); *Panorama* and *Shekulli* (centrist); *Ballkan, Metropol, Korrieri, Gazeta Shquiptare, Gazeta Tema*, and *Koha Jonë* (all independent); and the English-language entries, the *Albanian Daily News* and the weekly *Tirana Times*. Two business periodicals have a reasonable circulation: *Biznesi* and *Ekonomia*. Despite the illiteracy and poverty still prevalent in Albania, the biweekly cultural magazine *Spektër* has also become popular.

BELGIUM

The contemporary trend of ownership concentration of newspapers began in Belgium in the 1960s. This has resulted in a shrinking number of newspapers and, in particular, a decrease in the number of independent newspapers. Of today's twenty-six Belgian newspapers, only ten are autonomous; the remaining sixteen papers are parallel editions of the main papers and differ only slightly from them.

Initially, the six major newspaper companies in Belgium were family enterprises, but gradually all have come to be controlled by Belgian or French conglomerates. Some of the major papers are *De Financieel Economische Tijd* (a financial paper), *De Morgen* (independent), *De Standaard* (Catholic oriented), *Gazet van Antwerpen* (regional), *Het Belang van Limburg* (regional), *Het Laatse Nieuws* (sports), *Het Volk*, *La Libre Belgique* (Catholic oriented), *Le Soir* (centrist), *L'Echo* (financial), *La nouvelle Gazette* (regional), *La Meuse* (regional), and *La Wallonie* (progressive), as well as weeklies such as *Le Peuple* (socialist) *Spectator*, *Le Vif/L'Expres*, and *New Europe*. In the German-speaking part of Belgium, *Grenz Echo* (11,000) is published. Many newspapers also run weeklies, freely distributed advertising papers, and Websites.

In 1995 the overall circulation of the Belgian press amounted to 1.54 million, the Flemish press accounting for 64.3 percent of sales and the French-language press 35.6 percent. Currently, only 36 percent of Belgians subscribe to any newspaper, and circulation figures declined slightly between 2000 and 2005. Some Belgians read the international press, particularly newspapers and magazines published in the Netherlands or France. Popular Belgian magazines include *Menzo* (for men), *Flair* (fashion for women), *In Vino Veritas* (wine), *Jet Magazine* (youth), *Loving You*, *Freeze* (snowboarding and surfing), *Le Soir* (current events), *Auto Magazine*, and *Sport and Vie*.

GRAPHIC NOVELS AND COMICS IN BELGIUM

Another medium that competes with newspapers for the attention of both young and old is the extremely popular Franco-Belgian serialized *bandes dessinées*, a genre that includes comic books and graphic novels. In the early twentieth century, comics were only published within newspapers as episodes or gags. One of the earliest Belgian comic books was Hergé's *Tintin in the Land of the Soviets*, published in *Le Petit Vingtième* in 1930. When France and Belgium were invaded during World War II, the Nazis banned imports of American comic books—giving a boost to local artists who would retain their popularity when the war was over. The main publishers of comics include Editions Dargaud and Dupuis, which promoted the famous Belgian "clean line style." Besides *Tintin*, the *Smurfs*, *Spirou*, *Charlie Hebdo*, and *Vaillante* are other famous Belgian cartoons. In the 1960s, erotic "adult" comics became popular, and in the 1980s, Japanese manga began to exert an influence. The Belgian Center of Comic Strip Art, located in an art nouveau glass warehouse in Brussels, provides a good guide to what Belgians call the "ninth art," as does the annual Angoulême International Comics Festival in France.

BULGARIA AND ROMANIA

Bulgaria

The Bulgarian periodical market underwent sudden changes after the fall of Communism in 1989: new publications were founded overnight, while others abruptly disappeared. There is little press regulation in Bulgaria, making it nearly impossible to gather accurate statistics. However, it is fair to say that the market is dominated by tabloids, both dailies and weeklies. The eleven existing dailies are hybrids between news and entertainment publications. The old political party papers that dominated Bulgaria's market in the 1990s have disappeared, with the exception of *Duma*, the mouthpiece of the Socialist Party, which has a very low circulation. The daily of the Union of Democratic Forces, *Demokratsiya*, disappeared in 2002.

The German media giant WAZ owns the two dailies with the biggest circulation in Bulgaria: *Trud* [Labor], the only newspaper title to survive the political changes, and *24 Chassa* [24 Hours], the first privately owned paper in Bulgaria. Other Bulgarian dailies include *Standart News*, *Sega*, *Monitor*, *Telegraph*, *Zemya*, and the evening tabloid *Noshten Trud*. Despite the popularization of tabloid weeklies and sensational journalism in recent years, readership continues to drop. The statistics available suggest that the total current circulation of daily papers is 400,000 or less in a country of 8 million people. In 2006, four weekly papers were in print: *Capital* and *Banker* (business), *168 Chassa* and *Politika* (current events), and the new *Tema* (political and social commentary for more educated readers).

In Bulgaria the Internet is probably the most independent media platform available. The information it offers is unregulated, but it has been establishing itself ever more firmly as a news source, particularly at the site www.Mediapool.bg. As far as magazines are concerned, *Maximum* (gossip), *Bakchus* (food), *Egoist*, the *Bulgarian Medical Journal*, car magazines, and *Computer World Bulgaria* are top sellers.

Romania

Romania's press followed a pattern similar to Bulgaria's after the revolution that ended the Communist regime: proliferation and the rise of tabloids. However, Romania's press market is larger and more active. At its peak in 1996, there were 106 dailies and 1781 other periodicals, as compared to 36 dailies and 459 other periodicals in 1989. The number of periodicals in print tends to fluctuate in relation to the political cycle, producing an upswing around electoral periods (for example, 1996, 2000, and 2004) when political and economic groups finance new or expanded papers.

In this country of 22 million inhabitants, over twenty dailies are published in the capital Bucharest, most with a national circulation. In Constanta, Timisoara, and Iasi, up to six dailies compete for an audience. The best-selling national daily is *Libertatea* (200,000), a tabloid owned by the Swiss media group Ringier. *Jurnalul National*, owned by the Voiculescu family, has managed to make its daily print run skyrocket from below 20,000 to a peak of 350,000 copies by publishing a series of commentaries on recent history. *Evenimentul Zilei*, which started in 1992 as a tabloid but is now considered among the most serious dailies in Romania, sells roughly 100,000 copies a day. It was recently bought by Ringier, which also owns the sports daily *ProSport* (100,000), a rival of the Voiculescu family's sport daily *Gazeta Sporturilor* (also 100,000). *Adevarul*, formerly known as the Communist-era national daily *Scinteia*, has built a new reputation for quality and remains among the best-selling dailies (100,000 to 120,000). The most important finance and business newspapers are *Ziarul Financiar* (circulation of approximately 15,000) and *Bursa*.

The number of national weeklies has decreased since the early 1990s. Weeklies featuring political debate have disappeared or have turned into entertainment magazines. Among the few that remain are the satirical *Academia Catavencu* (50,000 to 70,000); the business weekly *Capital* (50,000 to 60,000); and *Formula As* (250,000 to 300,000 in 2002), a magazine focusing on health, cooking, politics, and art. TV guides are also among the best sellers: *ProTV Magazin* has a circulation of 130,000 copies a week and *TV Mania* sells 160,000. Monthly magazines are a mixture of local and translated international magazines: women's fashion magazines are popular (*Unica*, *Cosmopolitan*, *Elle*, *Avantaje*, *Burda*, *Lumea Femeilor*), as are soft pornography magazines (*FHM*, *Playboy*, *Penthouse*, *Hustler*), youth magazines (*Bravo*,

Popcorn), auto magazines (*AutoMotor & Sport*, *Auto Show*, *Auto Mondial*), and information technology magazines. All have print runs ranging from 20,000 to over 100,000 copies per month. *Flacara* and *Lumea Magazin* are among the few general-interest Romanian monthlies.

The Internet is gradually becoming accessible in Romania. The government estimates Internet penetration at about 24 percent, although independent experts argue this figure is too high.

THE CZECH REPUBLIC

After the Velvet Revolution of 1989, the Czech Republic (at the time still united with Slovakia as Czechoslovakia) saw a dramatic shift from political party–owned newspapers to a press independent of party supervision. After the press was privatized, a significant number of papers were forced to close because of financial problems and shrinking readership. New papers appeared quickly but often did not survive the competition, except for the former dissident paper *Lidove Noviny* and the tabloid paper *Blesk*.

The Czech Republic currently has eight national newspapers: *Mlada Fronta DNES*, *Lidove Noviny*, *Hospodarske Noviny*, *Pravo*, *Slovo*, *ZN Zemske Noviny*, *Sport*, and *Blesk*. *Mlada Fronta DNES* is the best-selling newspaper in the country, with a 22.3 percent market share. It reaches over 1.3 million readers every day. The runners-up are the tabloid *Blesk*, with 16.3 percent of the market, and *Pravo*, with 13 percent. All the national weekly papers are published in the capital, Prague. The national papers have regional supplements distributed in locations outside the capital city, but they nonetheless face stiff competition from the regional papers, which make up over 26 percent of the market. The free *Metro* magazine, distributed at subway and bus stations in Prague, is another source of competition for advertisers and readers.

The Czech market is dominated by German publishing chains. International monthlies are popular here, especially *Esquire*, *Playboy*, and *Cosmopolitan*; local magazines such as *Leo*, *Privni kuryr*, *Prajhski Ogni*, *Silva Bohemica*, and *Rock and Pop* also sell well.

LATVIA, LITHUANIA, AND ESTONIA

Latvia

The Latvian press underwent a sea change in 1991 when this Baltic nation, like its neighbors, became independent from the Soviet state. During the Soviet era, censorship was

THE FALL OF COMMUNIST PRESSES

The media landscapes of most Eastern European countries were powerfully affected by the rise and fall of Communism. During the Communist period, presses were owned by the national government, and therefore were nominally owned by the people. Private presses were often illegal, and official censorship bodies controlled what information could or could not be disseminated. Illegal underground presses were sometimes able to circumvent these constraints, most famously in the case of the samizdat presses in the Soviet Union. After the end of the Iron Curtain in 1989, periodicals were privatized, and official censorship ended. This gave rise to financing crises, foreign buyouts, and a wild proliferation of new print and online periodicals in the immediate wake of the political changes. After a period of culling, most periodical markets reached a certain stability by the beginning of the twenty-first century. In these markets, sales of tabloids and entertainment periodicals currently dominate sales of more serious publications, reflecting the unrestrained capitalism that replaced the Communist structures.

frequent, and little news of interest was published in official papers. During the tense period when Latvia was gaining its independence, readership soared and has remained relatively high ever since, despite being dampened by recent economic hardships.

Latvia's population of 2 million supports roughly 140 newspapers, 24 of which are dailies, while 117 appear less frequently and have lower circulation rates. Fourteen of the dailies are national and are issued in Riga, the capital, where one-third of the population is concentrated. The average circulation per issue for all dailies combined is 284,000 copies. The biggest national daily morning newspaper is *Diena* (publishing 64,300 copies in Latvian and 10,000 copies in Russian); it is followed by *Panorama Latvii* (31,200 copies in Russian), *Neatkariga RA* (23,800 copies in Latvian), and *Cas* (20,000 copies in Russian). These papers represent about 60 percent of the total daily newspaper circulation. Three national evening newspapers also circulate: *Rigas Balss* (35,000 copies in Latvian and Russian), *Vakara Zinas* (13,000 copies in Latvian), and *Spogulis* (12,000 copies in Latvian). Regional papers are published at least three times a week, if not daily. Major Latvian magazines include *Kapital Latalii*, *Kapitals*, *Likums un Tiesibas*, *Lyublu!*, and *Studija*.

The years 1988 through 1994 saw rapid and unsustainable growth in periodicals. The total number of titles tripled; however, because of economic difficulties, the number of titles and circulation dropped sharply.

Lithuania

In Lithuania, three national daily papers are published: *Lietuvos rytas* (bought by 60 percent of newspaper readers), *Respublika* (22 percent) and *Lietuvos aidas* (9 percent), as well as the regional paper *Kauno Diena*, which is struggling to go national. Lithuanians also read one local tabloid newspaper, *Lietuvos Zinios*, and an increasingly popular business newspaper, *Verslo Zinios*, owned by the Bonnier media group from Sweden.

After Lithuania gained independence from the Soviet regime, newspaper publishing houses were privatized, and some, like *Lietuvos rytas* and *Respublika*, created their own distribution operations in the bigger cities. In addition to their main section, all these daily newspapers have added various regional supplements and special sections on topics such as culture, fashion, or lifestyle to increase readership. A satirical newspaper, *Sluota*, is also reasonably popular.

The Lithuanian magazine sector has been growing considerably since 1994. The market is dominated by *TV Antena* and *Stilius*, weekly magazines published by the parent company *Lietuvos Rytas*. The quality weekly *Veidas* circulates close to 10,000 copies each week. Foreign titles such as *Cosmopolitan* and *Harpers Bazaar* entered the market starting in 1998. The number of magazine titles on the Lithuanian market increased by about 50 percent between 1989 and 1999. The Internet is also a popular way of gaining access to periodicals in Lithuania.

Estonia

The Estonian media is vibrant after the isolation of the Soviet days. Seven daily papers cater to the Estonian readers (close to a world record of dailies per thousand of population) as well as a range of weekly papers and magazines for a population of just 1.4 million.

Before the restoration of independence in 1991, the Estonian press was controlled by the Communist Party, and censorship was routine. Despite these strict controls, Estonians were avid readers even during the Soviet period, largely because of the low price of Soviet newspapers and the long tradition of readership. The first regular Estonian newspaper dates only to 1857, when Perno Postimees started a newspaper venture, but Estonians often had read Swedish, Russian, French, and Yiddish periodicals before that. In 1990, during the political crisis in the country, Estonia was among the countries with the highest number of newspapers sold per thousand people (523 copies). By 1995, after the dramatic political changes in Estonia were over, the figure had dropped to 171.

The first new privately owned newspapers, set up at the end of the 1980s, introduced a new, bolder style of reporting. The *Postimees* daily was the first to be privatized, and it is still the nation's top-selling title, with a daily circulation close to 60,000. At the beginning of 1999, the country supported seven national dailies (five in Estonian, two in Russian), eighteen weeklies (eleven in Estonian, seven in Russian), and twenty-two regional papers (eighteen in Estonian, four in Russian). Estonia has seen an increasing tendency toward a concentration of ownership of the press.

FRANCE

In a country of nearly 60 million people, French daily newspapers have a total diffusion of around 8.7 million. One out of every four in the French population reads a national newspaper on a regular basis, and two out of three read a regional or a local newspaper.

The three newspapers of record, in order from the least to the most conservative, are *Libération*, *Le Monde*, and *Le Figaro*. The French newspaper market is surprisingly regional, given the long-standing centralist tradition in other fields of French society; the national newspapers, all of which are based in Paris, make up just 25 percent of the daily newspaper market. In 2004, for example, *Le Monde*, with a circulation of 360,000, reached 35 percent of French readers; *Le Figaro* reached 26 percent (347,000); *Libération*, 15 percent (216,000); *La Croix*, 9.1 percent (96,000); *France Soir Plus*, 5 percent (61,000); and *L'Humanité*, 4 percent (50,000). Specialized papers are also popular, particularly the two financial newspapers *Les Echos* (166,000) and *La Tribune* (92,000), and the sports papers *Paris Turf* (96,000) and *L'Equipe* (350,000). On Sundays *Le Journal du Dimanche* (291,000) comes out. Apart from this, special editions of *Le Parisien* and *L'Equipe* appear regularly. Two free newspapers, *Metro* and *20 Minutes*, are distributed at railway and metro stations in Paris and Marseille five times a week.

The regional daily newspapers have always had a more stable readership than their national counterparts, which saw their numbers fall from 4 million in the early 1970s to just above 2 million at the beginning of the new millennium. *Ouest France*, based in Rennes, is the largest daily newspaper in the country, with a diffusion of 785,000. Other important regional newspapers include *Sud Ouest* (Bordeaux, 329,000), *Le Voix du Nord* (Lille, 317,000), *Le Progrès* (Lyon, 263,000) and *Le Dauphiné libéré* (Grenoble, 260,000).

If the French read relatively few daily newspapers, they are among the biggest readers of magazines and periodicals in the world. The magazine market in France flourishes with 590 weeklies and biweeklies, 1350 monthlies and bimonthlies, and 1570 quarterlies. Leading weekly magazines of general interest are the center-right, heavily illustrated *Paris Match* (707,000); the patriotic *Marianne* (118,000); and the trio of *Le Nouvel Observateur* (544,000), *L'Express* (554,000) and *Le Point* (358,000), all of which are situated at the center-left end of the political spectrum. Also popular is the *Courrier International* (180,000), a weekly survey in French of the international press. In addition, there are about 170 local weekly newspapers, mostly with small circulations.

A large range of niche magazines is popular, such as the highly respected *Jeune Afrique* (ground-breaking reporting of news from African countries), *Europ* (an EU-oriented quarterly), and *Maghreb Hebdo* and *Ad-Dawliya*, (both written for a French-North African readership). For the extreme right, news kiosks stock *L'Action française* (30,000) and *Royaliste* (10,000); for the extreme left, they sell *La Nouvelle Vie Ouvrière* (120,000) and *Informations Ouvrières* (20,000). Catholics may purchase *Pélerin Magazine* (302,000), *La Vie* (176,000), *Témoignage chrétien* (20,000), and *France Catholique* (18,000); Protestants support *La Voix protestante* (6,000); and the Jewish community publishes *L'Arche* (20,000) and *Actualité Juive* (17,500).

France has a strong tradition of intellectual and literary periodicals. Addressing the general public are *Le Monde Diplomatique* (240,000), *Etudes* (140,000) and *Passages* (35,000). *Le Monde Diplomatique* is owned by the Monde group, but it has an autonomous, radical-left editorial staff. French intellectuals also read *Esprit* (10,000), *Commentaire* (5,500), *Les Temps Modernes* (5,000) and *Le Débat* (5,000). *Magazine Littéraire* and *Lire* focus more on literary matters, while the notorious satirical and investigative weekly *Le Canard Enchaîné* (430,000) concentrates on scandals in the governmental, juridical, and business circles of France. *Le Canard* is known for its independence; it does not publish any advertisements, and its owners are not tied to any political or economic group. *Paris Vogue* has an artistic edge missing from incarnations of the fashion magazine in other parts of the world; it also enjoys great popularity in France. Finally, the French tabloid press exists but is relatively mild. Weeklies such as *France Dimanche* (575,000), *Voici* (575,000), *Ici Paris* (442,000), *Gala* (304,000), and *Entrevue* (308,000) cover celebrities and scandal. People in France tend to have very good Internet access, and all major periodicals have their own Websites.

Serial comic books are extremely popular in France among adults as well as children. *Asterix et Obelix* and *Tintin* continue to be popular, although they are supplemented with superhero fare, political graphic novels, and comics influenced by Japanese manga.

GERMANY

Since the early 1990s, the number and circulation of newspapers in Germany have shown signs of decline, although roughly 355 daily newspapers continue to circulate, and the penetration of these dailies hovers around 77 percent. Circulation figures show that the local and regional press is very important in Germany, reflecting the impact of Germany's late transition from many principalities into a single nation in 1871. The German market for daily newspapers is nonetheless dominated by a small number of publishers, the largest being the Axel Springer Group with around 24 percent of the market (*Bild, Welt, Hamburger Abendblatt, Berliner Morgenpost*). Its rivals are the WAZ Group (Westdeutsche Allgemeine Zeitung) and Gruner + Jahr.

Germany has only a few national papers: the excellent liberal *Süddeutsche Zeitung*; the conservative *Frankfurter Allgemeine Zeitung*; the conservative *Welt*; the popular right-wing tabloid *Bild*; the liberal *Frankfurter Rundschau*; and the small left-wing *Tageszeitung*, which was begun in 1979 and is still owned cooperatively among several thousand owners. These papers strive to be objective but generally have leanings easily located on the political spectrum.

The format of the weekly newspaper became popular in Germany after 1945. It presents less actual news and more analysis and background information. One of the most successful and important weeklies is *Die Zeit* (500,000), a liberal and independent paper. Its main competitor on the market is *Die Woche*. The Protestant Church edits the *Deutsches Allgemeines Sonntagsblatt* (50,000) and the Catholic Church publishes the *Rheinischer Merkur* (111,000). Free newspapers distributed in subway and train stations are a recent European-wide trend, appearing within Germany in Berlin, Hamburg, and Cologne.

The German magazine sector supports 780 general magazines (total circulation of roughly 126.98 million copies) and nearly 3,400 specialized periodicals (17.27 million). The most famous and respected German news magazine is *Der Spiegel*, with a weekly circulation of roughly 1.04 million and considerable political influence thanks to its strong investigative journalism. It competes directly with the magazine *Der Stern* and the flashier, conservative magazine *Focus* (780,000). Germany's best-selling magazines are the erotic *Girlsgate*, *Beate Uhse*, and *Piep!* Other popular periodicals include *auto motor und sport*, *Auto Bild*, and *Autonews* (cars); *Mädchen* and *Brigitte* (fashion); *Kicker* (the leading soccer magazine); *Bravo* and *Teens mag* (youth); *Die Welt der Mode* and other sewing, knitting, and dress pattern magazines put out by the Burda publishing house; literary magazines; and the widely distributed pop cultural Berlin weekly *Zitty*.

GREECE

In Greece today, a total of eighty-eight newspapers circulate among a population of 10.6 million people: nine morning, fifteen evening, twenty-two Sunday, and seventeen weekly newspapers. The Greek market also supports six financial papers and nineteen sport newspapers. Sunday papers sell best, making up 51.2 percent of sales in 2004, followed by evening newspapers (17.5 percent), sports (15.7 percent), weekly (9.1 percent), morning (6.3 percent) and financial papers (0.1 percent). Among morning dailies, the market leaders are the liberal *To Vima* (57,100) and the conservative *Kathimerini* (51,400). The major evening papers are the liberal *Eleftherotypia* (83,400), the centrist *Ethnos* (50,800), and the liberal *Ta Nea* (86,100). Their Sunday editions also dominate the Sunday market. Smaller papers include *Niki* (socialist), *Apogevmatini* (conservative), *Ena* (independent), and *Pontiki*, a satirical weekly paper. Total newspaper sales figures show a continual decline from the late 1980s to the beginning of the 1990s, thanks to the introduction of private television channels in 1989 and competition from Internet-based news sources. From 1989 to 1992, national newspapers lost approximately 28 percent of their circulation, forcing many to close down.

Unlike in other countries, many Greek newspaper houses also own and publish magazines. One major player, the Lambrakis publishing group, owns *Hi Tech*, *ROM*, *RAM*, and the monthlies *To Paidi Mou Ki Ego*, *Diakopes*, and *Gamos*, as well as the Greek versions of *Marie Claire*, *Cosmopolitan*, and *National Geographic*. Its competitor, the Tegopoulos Publishing Group, owns *Cinema*, *Idaniko Spiti*, and *Menu ke Alla*. It also publishes Greek versions of *Elle*, *MAX*, and *Car and Driver*, as well as Greek magazines *Armonia*, *Astra ke Oroma*, and *Lipon* in cooperation with Hachette Rizzoli. *Auto Motor & Sport* is also popular. Greece shares the European trend toward a concentration of press ownership. In addition, glossy publications now have to compete with free supplements provided in newspapers; however, in 2004, astrology and cooking magazines took the lead in sales and advertising (26 percent), followed by TV magazines (22 percent), women's magazines (13 percent) and recreation and leisure magazines (9 percent).

Because of the large and far-flung diasporic Greek community, media companies in Greece have been involved in ongoing negotiations for an expansion of Greek media abroad, particularly in the Balkans and Eastern Europe. The Internet is slowly gaining ground in Greece.

HUNGARY

Hungary boasts ten national newspapers and twenty-four local dailies, all privately owned, that serve a population of 10 million. The vast majority of Hungarian papers are owned by Western investors, because Hungarian entrepreneurs did not have enough capital to acquire them in the wake of the Communist collapse.

The Hungarian periodicals market is remarkably stable. The old Communist Party newspaper, *Népszabadság*, has managed to preserve its position as market leader among quality dailies with a circulation of just under 200,000. The second largest quality daily, *Magyar Nemzet*, has a circulation of around 100,000. The smaller newspapers *Magyar Hírlap* and *Népszava* have circulations of 49,000 and 31,000 respectively. All of these titles existed before 1989; no new quality political daily has been successfully launched in the period after the fall of Communism. Apart from tabloids, newspaper circulation numbers dropped throughout the 1990s. However, some new weekly newspapers have been successful, particularly periodicals for business people such as *Budapester Zeitung*, *Budapest Business Journal*, and the independent political weekly *168 Ora*.

Local dailies enjoy virtual monopolies in the counties where they are published. Although there were several attempts to launch rival local newspapers, these mostly failed because of the inflexibility of local markets, where subscribing to the family county daily is a tradition going back decades.

Tabloids were not permitted during the Communist era, but they flourish now and provide the greatest degree of competition in the Hungarian periodical market. Two foreign-owned magazines, *Blikk* (204,000) and *Mai Nap* (67,000), compete for readers' attention with upstarts like *Esti Hirlap* and the satirical magazine *Ludas Matyi*. Hungarians can also browse in cultural magazines (*2000*, *Kritika*), women's magazines (*Nok Lapja*), and an English-language daily newspaper (*Budapest Sun*). The old Communist-era sports daily survived under the name *Nemzeti Sport* and is now the only newspaper dedicated exclusively to sports, with a circulation of 93,000. Newspaper kiosks also offer many international magazines in Hungarian editions, such as *Cosmopolitan*, *Elle*, *Playboy*, and *Story*. Other important magazines include *Nok Lapja*, *Kiskegyed*, and *Hölgyvilág*.

The percentage of Hungarians with access to the Internet is currently around 20 percent but is growing steadily. Most Hungarian periodicals have online editions.

ITALY

There are 177 daily newspapers in Italy, most of them owned or controlled by a small number of publishing trusts. The paper of record is the centrist *Il Corriere della Sera*, based in Milan and owned by RCS Mediagroup, which also owns Italy's other best-selling daily newspaper, the sports-oriented *Gazzetta dello Sport*. The *Corriere della Sera* was first published in 1876, and it now boasts well over 667,000 copies in daily circulation and a readership of approximately 2.97 million. As a cultural institution, it also administers a foundation that organizes literary and political events as well as the exchange of ideas.

The mildly leftist *La Repubblica* is Italy's second national daily paper. The other dailies can usually be purchased in different parts of Italy but have strong regional flavors: these include *La Stampa* (Turin), *Il Gazzettino* (Venice), *Il Giorno* (Milan), *Il Mattino* (Naples), *Il Messaggero* (Rome), *Il Tempo* (Rome's more conservative daily), *Il Resto del Carlino* (Bologna), *L'Unione Sarda* (Sardinia), *La Nazione* (Florence), *La Gazzetta del Mezzogiorno* (Bari and southern Italy), *Giornale di Sicilia* (Sicily), *Corriere delle Alpi* (originally founded by Resistance fighters in 1945 and now the leading paper of northernmost Italy), and *L'Osservatore Romano* (the renowned Vatican newspaper). The newspaper of the formerly separatist Northern League (*Ligua Nord*) is titled *La Padania*. Current Italian president Silvio Berlusconi's brother, Paolo, owns a center-right daily called *Il Giornale*. Italy supports two financial dailies, *Il Sole 24 Ore* and *Italia Oggi*. Italy's historic Communist paper, *L'Unità*, has been bought out and is run now by non-Communist leftists in rivalry with the new Communist paper, *Liberazione*. The Italian market supports several well-known Catholic dailies besides *L'Osservatore Romano*, including *L'Avvenire* and *L'Eco di Bergamo*. A crisis in 1990 precipitated the closing, merging, or changing hands of many Italian newspapers. Total national newspaper circulation has risen since then and is back to roughly 6 million total copies sold per day for a country of 58 million inhabitants.

Italy does not have tabloid daily newspapers. This is mainly because of the existence of a successful weekly press of genuine popular character, particularly the beloved sporting papers, chief among them *La Gazzetta dello Sport*. Italy also supports a multitude of magazines focused on tourism as well as monthlies for men (*Boss*, *Max*, *Maxim*) and women (*Donna Moderna*, *Cosmopolitan*), for brides (*Vogue Sposa*), for readers interested in general topics (*Panorama*, *Kiss Me!*), and for those interested in food (*La Cucina Italiana*, *Cucina Bella e Buona*); in addition, there are Catholic magazines, children's magazines, and comics.

THE NETHERLANDS

The Netherlands has an old and lively tradition of periodicals publishing. Dutch national newspapers take up about 45 percent of the market, with a total of 2.08 million copies sold daily. There are eight national newspapers, all broadsheets, not counting specialized dailies such as the *Financieel Dagblad* (a business newspaper) and the *Agrarisch Dagblad* (agriculture newspaper). Of these eight, two are small Protestant papers (58,000 and 31,000 copies sold daily) that depend almost totally on subscriptions. The other six together have a circulation of 2.02 million: the populist *De Telegraaf* (850,000) and *Algemeen Dagblad* (395,000), and the more respected *de Volkskrant* (350,000), *NRC Handelsblad* (270,000), *Trouw* (112,000), and *Het Parool* (90,000). Between 77 percent and 94 percent of sales occur through subscription. Sunday newspapers were never successful in the Netherlands, and neither were sensationalist tabloids.

Until the late 1960s, the national newspapers were entangled in a Dutch social structure known as "pillarization": the deeply rooted division of society along lines of religious or political convictions. Newspapers were officially or unofficially attached to one of these four pillars (Catholic, Protestant, socialist, or liberal). Starting in the late 1960s, these ties between the national newspapers and political parties or the church were loosened or severed as newspapers developed editorial statutes declaring their autonomy.

The twenty-nine regional newspapers together sell roughly 2.6 million copies per day. The largest regional papers are *Dagblad de Limburger* and *De Gelderlander* (both 90,000); the smallest is *Goudsche Courant* at 16,000 copies. A third category consists of the small local papers published one to three times a week, often free and delivered door-to-door, which function mainly as advertising opportunities for local businesses. In 1999 these local publications were joined by two free tabloid newspapers for urban areas, distributed to commuters at public transport stations. The free *Metro* is the sister publication of a Swedish paper by the same title, while *Spits* is an initiative of *De Telegraaf*.

There are over 200 magazines in The Netherlands. The major opinion magazines are *Elsevier* (133,000), *Vrij Nederland* (67,000), *HP/De Tijd* (41,000), *De Groene Amsterdammer* (17,500) and *Hervormd Nederland* (14,000), all on the center-left of the political spectrum by Dutch standards. The only—and mild—form of tabloid journalism is found in international celebrity magazines such as *Story*. Other popular magazines include *Libelle*, *Margriet*, *Cosmopolitan*, *Knip Mode* (fashion), *Culinaire Saisonnier* (food), *Lover*, *Break Out!*, and *Gay News*, as well as art, cinema, and design magazines.

POLAND

Although newspaper readership is now in decline, Poland has a strong tradition of written press. In a country of 38.6 million people, the sixteen national dailies sell about 4 million copies. *Gazeta Wyborcza* (600,000) is one of the most widely read daily newspapers in Poland, reaching about 17 percent of the market. It was founded by leaders of the Solidarity movement in 1989, although it is now also owned in part by U.S. investors. It also publishes local inserts in major Polish towns. The other top dailies are *Rzeczpospolita* (260,000), which reaches 7 percent of daily newspaper readers, and the tabloid *Super Express* (500,000), which reaches 14 percent, as well as the smaller sports daily *Dziennik Sportowy*, the Catholic newspaper *Nasz Dziennik*, and the leftist newspaper *Trybuna*.

Poland has seventy-eight regional dailies and a strong, steadily growing magazine sector. Several privatized Communist papers continue to be published (*Gazeta Poznanska, Dzis, Gazeta Krakowa*) alongside capitalist business papers (*Gazeta Prawna*, the weekly *Gazeta Bankowa, Prawo i Gospodarka*) and digests of foreign papers such as *Forum* and *Angora*. The collapse of the old political system and the rise to power of local regional political formations has resulted in a rapid growth of regional press. Most are weekly; have circulations of 1000 to 3000; are published by local governments (40 percent), church parishes (10 percent), or private corporations (24 percent); or are owned by a school. The rapid growth of local periodicals has been a spontaneous process with three distinct phases: the heroic phase, based on broad public support for the Solidarity movement; the political phase, which followed a split within the anti-Communist forces when different factions sought their own media outlets; and the more current market-oriented phase, where the emphasis is on profit.

The prestigious weekly news magazines *Polityka* and *Wprost* have a circulation of about 300,000 each; they compete with the new Polish edition of *Newsweek*. Men's magazines such as *CKM, He*, and *Moda Meska* are very popular, as are women's magazines such as *Claudia, Pani*, and *Twój Styl* as well as the Polish editions of *Reader's Digest, Playboy*, and *National Geographic*. The government subsidizes periodicals for the ethnic minorities. There are also a number of English language papers, such as the weekly *Warsaw Business Journal* and *Warsaw Voice*. Most sales occur at kiosks, and subscriptions represent less than 4 percent of sales. The Internet is becoming an important source as well, and many Polish periodicals are available online.

The major Polish daily available abroad is *Nowy Dziennik*, published in New York. Thanks to the large Polish emigrant population, Polish language periodicals are also produced in the United Kingdom, Australia, South Africa, Germany, France, Canada, Lithuania, and Ukraine.

RUSSIA AND UKRAINE

Russia

During the Soviet era, Russia had a well-established tradition of newspaper readership. Nearly every Russian household subscribed to several papers between 1970 and 1990, including one or two national newspapers (*Pravda, Izvestiya, Trud*, or *Sovetskaya Rossiya*), at least one local newspaper, and several niche magazines (targeted toward members of the Communist Party, members of a particular profession, farmers, women, workers, or children). Soviet media reached a height of activity during perestroika, when state control and censorship were present but waning, and economic and financial pressures had not begun to affect periodicals.

In the early 1990s, when President Yeltsin helped to lead Russia into a new democratic, capitalist regime, countless new periodicals were founded but went bankrupt soon after. The situation started changing in the mid-1990s, when a new class of Russian business people emerged and began to finance glossy entertainment and fashion magazines. The presidential elections of 1996 turned the attention of the new Russian business leaders to the political role of the media. By the second half of the 1990s, the majority of the print media had new owners who expected loyalty and extensive personal coverage in exchange for financial support. The so-called Russian media wars reached their peak in 1999, featuring biased reporting and harsh critiques of political opponents.

Although the periodicals market has continued to grow since 2000, it is less chaotic. According to Ministry of Press data, there are over 37,000 officially registered print media outlets in Russia, including 22,200 newspapers and 12,700 magazines. Despite the impressive numbers, many of these have very low circulations. The increase in newspapers' prices since the end of the Soviet era has inevitably brought a serious decline in readership. In general Russians buy only one newspaper a week, mostly for financial reasons. In order to adjust to the new preferences of their readers, many newspapers have moved from daily editions to a weekly format or have introduced a special weekly edition—a previously unheard-of format that now enjoys great popularity.

Some leading Soviet-era newspapers such as *Pravda*, *Izvestiya* (263,700), *Trud* (1.7 million), and *Moskovskie Novosti* continue to be published and read in the new Russia. However, the perestroika-era newspapers *Argumenty i Fakty* (2.88 million), *Komsomolskaya Pravda* (27 million), and *Moskovsky Komsomolets* remain the best sellers. Yeltsin-era newspapers from the early 1990s that are still successful include *Nezavisimaya Gazeta* (50,000), *Kommersant* (117,300), and *Novaya Gazeta* (670,000). *The Moscow Times* is the most popular English-language daily in Russia. Literary magazines, such as *Lituraturnaya Rossiya* and *Glas*, continue to be widely read, and a satirical weekly known as *Krokodil* also enjoys success.

The Internet has developed rapidly since the 1990s, although Russia still lags behind—it had 18 million Internet users in 2001, or just 12.42 percent of the population, concentrated in urban areas such as Moscow and St. Petersburg. Nonetheless, the evolution of online media is progressing rapidly. Serious attention is paid to online-only news organizations, which often have a much more independent editorial line than do print periodicals: they are more difficult to censor and do not require capital investments from business people to finance their production and distribution. The large numbers of young people with technical and journalistic education but few job prospects have also favored the rise of online papers, such as the first Internet daily, Gazeta.ru; the first round-the-clock news service, Lenta.ru; the international hit *Naked News*, where announcers removed their clothing while reading news reports on streaming video; and the *Russky Zhurnal* online papers Utro.ru and Vesti.ru. There was a new wave of popularity for online media in the spring of 2001, when President Putin expanded Russian state control over privately owned news media during the conflict in Chechnya

Putin has since centralized media control, forcing two leading media magnates of the Yeltsin era—Gusinsky and Berezovsky—to give up much of their media empires and flee the country. Major shareholder Gazprom and Russian state officials attempted to present the conflict as entirely financial. However, it became clear they were shutting down the independent and critical coverage of current events—particularly when Gazprom fired the staff at two other periodicals, the daily paper *Segodnya* and a weekly magazine, *Itogi*. Arrests and physical threats against journalists continue in the country.

Ukraine

Although reliable statistics are hard to come by, 355 national, 464 regional, and 1,732 local newspapers are officially published in Ukraine for a population of 47 million. The tabloid *Fakty i Komentarii* is the national favorite, selling 1.02 million copies per day; this tabloid is followed by *Silski visti* (476,000), whose target audience is rural villagers, and the daily political paper *Golos Ukrainy* (180,000). The national weekly, *Zerkalo nedeli*, which is considered to have the highest quality reporting, has a circulation of 48,000, or 8,000 more copies per issue than its rival, the Russian national daily *Den*. *Molod Ukraiiny*, a youth newspaper, is also popular. Regional newspapers sell better than the national papers because they are perceived to be more in touch with the concerns of average people.

Beginning in the Soviet glasnost era, Ukraine experienced an explosion in the number of periodicals but a drop in circulations. The country still has some of the lowest readership numbers in Europe today. The daily circulation of the Russian-language press in the country is about 25 million copies per day, while the circulation of the Ukrainian one is nearer to 16 million copies per day. This is true even though 37.6 percent of periodicals are published in Ukrainian, 21.8 percent in Russian, and 20 percent are bilingual. Some periodicals, such as the daily broadsheet *Den*, also print a digest version in English. The *Kiev Post* publishes entirely in English, as do smaller free publications.

Ukrainian periodicals have been largely privatized; only 8.9 percent are published by government institutions, and fully 55 percent are owned by Ukrainians. However, many are owned by politicians or political parties, or are under political and economic pressure from them. Unofficial censorship is not unknown in Ukraine, despite being forbidden by national laws. Independent media can also be targeted for tax inspections, another, which is another form political pressure can take.

Ukraine's periodical market must also compete with a vast array of foreign print media, mostly Russian and Polish, smuggled across the border at a rate of 1 million copies a day. Popular contraband publications include *Spid-Info*, *Cosmopolitan*, *Playboy*, and *Ogonek*. They coexist with the roughly 100 legal magazines published in Ukraine, usually niche publications such as the auto magazine *Za kermom*. Women's monthlies are the largest and most stable category of Ukrainian magazine publication; profitable titles include *Natalie*, *Academia*, *Eva*, *Lisa*, and *Otdohni*.

Ukrainians also publish local imitations of *Newsweek*, such as *PIK* and *Korrespondent*, but they are expensive and sell less well in Ukraine than do the American periodicals. Internet use is growing in Ukraine, and many Ukrainian papers can now be found online.

SCANDINAVIA: FINLAND, DENMARK, NORWAY, SWEDEN, ICELAND

Finland

Like other Nordic countries, Finland has a lively press. Newspaper readership rates are the third highest in the world, with 455 copies sold per each 1,000 inhabitants in 1998. Since Finland is officially a bilingual country with a Swedish-speaking minority of 310,000 people (6 percent of the national population), it possesses a range of Swedish-language periodicals. The newspaper market is stable since there is not much room for growth in a saturated market that caters to a population of 5.2 million. The biggest changes in recent years have been related to the growth of the Internet in this highly technologically advanced society.

Finland supports roughly 226 newspaper titles with a total circulation of 3.4 million copies. Of these, 56 are dailies, appearing four to seven times a week. Major titles include the centrist *Helsingen Sanomat*, the independent *Turun Sanomat*, the Social Democratic *Suomen Sosialidemokraatti*, the independent *Ilta-Sanomat*, and the Swedish-language *Hufvudstadsbladet*. Some 170 newspapers are issued one to three times a week, with a combined circulation of 1.1 million copies. In addition there are 100 free newspapers on the market, with a total print run of 3.3 million copies. Ownership structures tend to be concentrated, thanks to a rash of mergers; of the 56 dailies in Finland, only 11 have independent ownership.

Magazines have always been popular in Finland and have been increasing their sales since the 1990s. Most Finnish magazines are trade, professional, and business magazines (41 percent); consumer magazines, including general interest, women's, men's and children's magazines (40 percent); periodicals published and paid for by large businesses, banks, and trade organizations (15 percent); and opinion journals dealing with current affairs, society, politics, and culture (3 percent). While magazine ownership is split between local and foreign ownership, Finnish companies also own controlling shares in the periodicals of other countries, particularly Sweden and other countries of the Baltic region. *Reader's Digest* (297,000), the Scandinavian magazine *7 Days* (217,000), a news and culture magazine called *Suomen Kuvalehti* (95,000), and foreign news magazines are top sellers in Finland, as are the magazines *Birka*, *Eeva*, *Demi*, *Me Naiset*, and *Kauneus*.

Denmark

Denmark has experienced a steady decline in the number of newspapers since World War II, as much because of the trends of consolidation and concentration as because of a decline in readership. With an average decrease in titles of more than 25 percent each decade, only thirty-five newspapers remain today; twenty-nine of these are independent, while the rest are linked to political parties or platforms. Denmark possesses three large nationally distributed newspapers. The independent *Morgenavisen Jyllands-Posten* (publisher of the notorious cartoons of the Prophet Mohammed in 2005) is the market leader, with a growing circulation of over 175,000. The moderate *Politiken*, the left-wing *Information*, the liberal *Dagen*, the *Bornholms Tidende*, the *Århus Stiftstidende*, and the Lutheran daily *Kristeligt Dagblad* are also popular. Denmark supports a financial daily, *Børsen*, as well as an English-language newspaper, the *Copenhagen Post*. It also supports two rival tabloids, although they have lost 40 percent of their combined readership in the last fifteen years; *Ekstra Bladet* is the one most likely to survive.

Competition has been decreasing in regional markets because of increasing sales of the national Danish newspapers. Regional papers have begun to cooperate with each other in response, pooling stories and forming alliances. The Copenhagen-based media group *Berlingske Officin* is the most important as far as direct and indirect control over circulation are concerned. However, all newspapers must cope with a general decline in readership, a trend that shows signs of continuing, caused in part by competition with electronic media and foreign newspapers in English.

Free newspapers are a growing phenomenon: 137 free district papers, distributed weekly based on inhabitants' shopping patterns, have a combined circulation of almost 5.04 million per week. By international standards, this puts Denmark in a league of its own. The district press has increasingly come to assume the role previously played by local newspapers. Surveys have found that as much as 28 percent of the local adult population names the district papers as the primary source of local information. Danish magazines also sell widely, particularly *Meals* (food), *Alt for Damerne*, *Climax* (cinema), *Smag & Behag*, *Euroman*, *Eurowoman*, children's magazines, and adult magazines for men and women.

Norway

Norway has the highest daily newspaper readership in the world: 600 copies per every 1000 inhabitants. It possesses two popular national newspapers, *Verdens Gang* (365,000) and the liberal *Dagbladet* (206,000). In addition, there are six medium-to-small-sized national political or ideological papers, and a plethora of regional papers. Norwegians from all geographic and economic classes tend to read a combination of quality and popular papers. In 1998, 218 newspapers were supported by a country with a population of less than 5 million, even though most papers had circulation runs of fewer than 10,000 copies. Regional papers make up more than 75 percent of daily papers sold in Norway, and five regional newspapers—the *Aftenposten* (288,000), the *Bergens Tidende* (94,000), the *Adresseavisen* (89,000), the *Stavanger Aftenblad* (73,000), and the *Faedrelandsvennen* (47,000)—account for 20 percent of total newspaper sales. Sunday newspapers were banned from 1919 until 1990, and even now readership is much lower on Sundays than on other days of the week.

Weekly family magazines used to be best sellers, but they are now being overtaken by music, fashion, and special interest magazines. Norwegian top-sellers include *Henne, Tique, Trendmagasinet, Kvinneforskning, Det Nye, Hjemme PC, Apéritif, Scream* (heavy metal), *Computerworld*, and *Spirit* (rock).

Sweden

The Swedish newspaper market has traditionally been lively. Currently, more than 80 percent of the adult population read a newspaper on an average day. Most newspapers are local or regional rather than national; in fact, only two tabloid newspapers and one business paper can be regarded as having a national readership. Nearly 100 percent of the morning newspapers are sold by subscription, with early morning home delivery. Home delivery is highly valued by readers and very reliable, even in remote areas of Sweden.

Sweden has one of the earliest to develop and most strongly protected independent press systems. The Swedish Freedom of the Press Act is a constitutional law that dates back to 1766. Nearly all social groups read newspapers—the only exception is in Stockholm, where a small segment of the working class does not. The Swedish press still has traditional links to political parties. There are about 160 papers on the market in Sweden. Of these, about 50 are published only once or twice a week and have a very low circulation. The total circulation of newspapers on any given day is about 4.2 million copies, in a country of just over 9 million people. This places Sweden close to the top in per capita newspaper consumption in the world, after Norway and Finland.

Roughly 25 percent of the Swedish newspaper market consists of metropolitan morning papers, dailies published in Sweden's three biggest cities: the *Dagens Nyheter* (361,000 copies) of Stockholm, the *Göteborgs-Posten* (262,000) of Göteborg, and *Sydsvenska Dagbladet* (128,000) of Malmö. Another large market segment is made up of urban tabloids (20 percent), the main ones being *Aftonbladet* (412,000) and *Expressen* (327,000). A third important segment consists of regional and local papers (45 percent), which are usually issued at least three times a week. Weekly or biweekly papers tend to have a small circulation and represent less than 10 percent of total newspaper circulation. Specialized papers such as the business dailies *Dagens Industri* (110, 000) and *Finanstidningen* (12,000) have significant circulation figures, as does the Christian daily *Dagen* (17,000). Finally, free papers have existed for a long time in Sweden but began to play a bigger role in the market in 1995, when *Metro* was introduced into subway stations in Gothenburg and Malmö—before spreading to the capitals of other countries. Free newspapers rely on advertisers for funding, and their content is usually based on material from wire reports, press releases, and publicity offices. Swedish newspapers have been active in creating online publications, and most Swedes have good Internet access.

The general magazine press in Sweden has seen a long-term decline in circulation, mainly affecting family and women's magazines, although some, such as *Vår Bostad* [Our Home], published by the Association for Tenants, still enjoys great popularity and a circulation of roughly 1 million copies. Papers published by trade unions for their members are popular, as are lifestyle magazines such as *Henne, Amelia, bang, Silikon* (computers), *Allt om Mat* (food), *Habit, Bröllopsmagasinet* (brides), *Vecko Revyn*, and *Hemmets Journal*.

Iceland

Although Iceland is large geographically, its population numbers a mere 290,000 people living in just over 100,000 households. Iceland is one of the most urbanized countries in Europe, with 60 percent of its people live in the capital, Reykjavík. Icelanders are devoted newspaper readers. In 2002 newspaper readership was among the highest in Europe: roughly 390 copies purchased for every 1,000 inhabitants. In a recent Gallup poll, 80 percent of the adult population claimed to read a newspaper daily and 96 percent claimed to read a newspaper every week.

There are three national daily newspapers: *Dagblaðið Visir* (DV), *Fréttablaðið*, and *Morgunblaðið*. All are published in the morning in Reykjavík. *Morgunblaðið* is generally considered a more serious newspaper than *Fréttablaðið*. Iceland had no tabloids until 2003, when DV evolved toward that status after a change in ownership. Two papers of special interest are published weekly: *Fiskifréttir*, which reports on the fishing industry, and *Viðskiptablaðið*, a business newspaper. They have a combined weekly circulation of about 6,000. In addition, twenty-three local and regional papers are published weekly; nine of them are sold, while fourteen are free of charge. Their combined average weekly circulation is 49,000.

The newspaper market has gone through significant restructuring in recent years, in contrast to the incremental change typical during the previous century, when there were several national newspapers, usually five or six, all of which had formal or informal ties to political parties. Many were partly funded by political parties, and their readership was to a large extent based on political affiliation. Those ties have gradually faltered, forcing the papers to find new bases for their sales.

Icelanders have warmly embraced the Internet, and in 2002 more than 80 percent had access. The largest Website, whether in terms of visitors or page impressions, is www.mbl.is, run by Árvakur, publisher of *Morgunblaðið*.

SPAIN AND PORTUGAL

Spain

Until 1966, the mass media in Spain was tightly controlled under guidelines imposed by Generalissimo Francisco Franco's regime after his victory in the Spanish Civil War in 1939; censorship was routine. During the transition period to democracy, which began around the time of the dictator's death in 1975, control on the media was liberalized. All Spanish newspapers and periodicals are now privately owned, and Spain has seen a concentration of press ownership paralleling that in other European countries.

Most Spanish magazines have a national distribution; newspapers tend to be regional, except for the market leader, *El Pais*, which sells about 450,000 copies daily and 1 million on Sundays in a country of 40.3 million. The ever-popular sports press also reaches a national audience, including the daily *Marca* (417,000), *AS* (140,000), and the regional Catalan sport dailies, *Sport* and *El Mundo Deportivo*, which sell slightly over 100,000 copies per issue. Two new regional daily sports newspapers, *Estadio Deportivo* and *Super Deporte*, sell about 10,000 copies per issue. The three major economic daily newspapers are published in Madrid and Barcelona. In 1999, *Expansión* (59,000) was the best seller, rivaled by *Cinco Días* (28,000) and the growing *La Gaceta de los Negocios* (13,000).

The newspapers *ABC* (450,000) and *El Mundo* (302,000) struggle for a national audience but are often outsold within a given province by regional papers. Spain contains a number of politically autonomous provinces, and newspapers focusing on local news sell briskly. In Catalonia, *La Vanguardia* (212,000) and *El Periódico* (208,000) are popular, while the Basques read *El Correo* (133,000); in Galicia, *La Voz de Galicia* sells 135,000 copies.

Most newspapers are published in Spanish. Six are published in Catalan, one in Basque, and a few more are bilingual. The circulation rate of all bilingual newspapers except *El Periódico* is generally low. Readership also varies greatly between regions. The total circulation rate of newspapers in the province of Navarra is about 188 copies per 1,000 inhabitants, while in Castilla La Mancha, it is a mere 52 copies per 1,000 inhabitants. In 1999 roughly 38 percent of the population read a newspaper. Low rates are in part related to the fact that Spain has a weak periodicals tradition and no popular daily newspapers.

Spain supports approximately 350 periodicals. Most of them have small circulations, with only a few exceeding 500,000 copies. Among these are *Pronto* (877,000) and *Hola* (597,000), representing the so-called *prensa del corazón* or "press of the heart." Other popular Spanish periodicals include *Fusion, Mujer 21, Epoca, Sobremesa, Crecer feliz,* and *Casa Viva,* as well as computer, cinema, fashion, and car magazines.

Portugal

Portugal registered the biggest increase in newspaper circulation in the European Union in 1999 (12.5 percent), although it still holds last place in readership numbers: only 73.5 people out of 1000 buy a paper on any given day. Portugal's population is 10.5 million, and over 10 percent of the population is still illiterate. Portugal has had a free press since the "Revolution of the Carnations" in 1974, when censorship laws that had lasted for the previous half century were lifted.

The daily news press that covers current issues is dominated by the popular papers *Jornal de Notícias* (101,400) and *Correio da Manhã* (89,000), followed by the more serious papers *Diário de Notícias* (65,500) and *Público* (53,200). Of the three afternoon papers published at the beginning of the 1990s, only one, *A Capital* (10,000), is still in print. The weekly market is clearly dominated by *Expresso* (136,800), followed by the news magazine *Visão* (100,900). However, the largest number of printed copies in the Portuguese press belongs to the TV, soap opera, and fashion magazines. Portugal's bestselling magazine is *Maria* (314,400), while others with circulations over 100,000 include *Telenovelas, Nova Gente, Caras,* and *TV Guide.* Specialized magazines are the most dynamic sector, with dozens of titles on economic topics, automobiles, computer technologies, and travel. The sports press, almost exclusively dedicated to soccer, shows a particular vitality. Of the three sports dailies, two have circulations over 100,000: *A Bola* and *Record.*

Regional and local presses also number in the hundreds and include daily, weekly, and fortnightly papers. The Catholic Church is a major owner of these periodicals, publishing over 600 small newspapers and magazines. Press ownership is concentrated in the hands of four Portuguese media conglomerates; the Catholic Church; and foreign groups such as Hachette Filipacchi, the Brazilian groups Abril and Globo, and Bertelsmann, which runs the *Círculo de Leitores,* the largest book club in the country.

SWITZERLAND

Switzerland has long upheld freedom of the press and nourished a flourishing periodicals culture. Switzerland's media conglomerates own media empires within Switzerland and across Europe. The largest company, Ringier, owns leading tabloid newspapers *Blick* (309,300) and *Sonntagsblick*, and additionally publishes the weekly magazine *Schweizer Illustrierte*. Tamedia AG publishes *Tages-Anzeiger* (268,200) and *SonntagsZeitung*, a Sunday paper with a circulation of 218,500 copies, as well as the news magazine *Facts* (104,500). However, Switzerland's newspaper of record, the culturally influential *Neue Zürcher Zeitung* (169,600), is independently owned and published. Other than the *Neue Zürcher Zeitung*, Swiss newspapers tend to be highly regional in character. Other major dailies include *Die Südostschweiz* (138,900), *Berner Zeitung* (136,600), *Neue Luzerner Zeitung* (133,600), *Aargauer Zeitung* (118,100), *Basler Zeitung* (114,500), *St. Galler Tagblatt* (109,600), *24-heures* (88,500), *Neue Mittelland Zeitung* (81,200), *Tribune de Genève* (77,400), *Der Bund* (68,500), *Le Matin* (65,120), and *Le Temps* (53,500). The leading daily newspapers in the Italian-speaking part are *Corriere del Ticino* (39,100), *La Regione Ticino* (32,300), and *Giornale del Popolo* (27,400).

The forces of ownership concentration have been putting small- and medium-sized papers out of business: between 1990 and 2000, the number of fully staffed newspapers fell from sixty-seven to forty-three. In addition, two free newspapers, *20 Minuten* and *Metropol*, have been launched by Swedish publishers for commuters in Zurich and other major Swiss cities, thus creating more competition for regular newspapers.

The weekly and monthly Swiss press has enormous diversity, including the political papers *Die Weltwoche* (92,300), *L'Objectif*, and *24 Heures*, as well as more culturally oriented magazines like the *Beobachter* (333,200) that are devoted to consumer interests and practical advice. Mountain-climbing magazines such as *Alpin,* gastronomical magazines such as *Saison Küche*, car magazines such as *Auto Bild*, fashion magazines such as *Freundin* and *Brigitte*, and children's magazines such as *KinderMAX*, *Blättli*, and *Troubadour* reach large audiences. The *Swiss Review* has one of the largest circulations of all Swiss magazines—over 360,000—because it is sent by the Swiss Embassy to registered Swiss citizens living abroad and doing business around the world.

TURKEY

Turkey has twenty-nine national newspapers, of which the best selling is *Hürriyet* [Freedom], with a circulation of more than 495,000 in 2004. *Hürriyet* is widely read by the Turkish diaspora population living in Germany and other European countries; it also produces regional supplements for readers in different regions in Turkey. There are three other major daily papers, with daily circulations ranging from 200,000 to 300,000: *Günaydin* [Good Morning], *Tercuman* [Interpreter], and *Milliyet* [Nationality]. One much smaller paper, *Cümhüriyet* [Republic], is considered influential because it is read widely by the country's economic and political elite. Regional papers are popular in Turkey: more than a dozen dailies are published in Istanbul, nine are published in Ankara, three in Izmir, and at least one daily is published in each of the other major cities, including Adana, Bursa, Diyarbakir, Gaziantep, Konya, and Mersin. Weekly and biweekly newspapers also sell well. Turkey has at least 199 regional newspapers.

Periodicals are privately owned in Turkey, but they are subject to certain government controls. Censorship is enforced on any periodicals that encourage "separatism" (usually understood as advocating Kurdish rights) or publish material considered obscene or likely to offend public morals. Top-selling Turkish magazines often focus on cars, travel, fashion, comics, or computers; these include *Eva, Matangi Tonga, Arabadergisi, Fanatik, Atlas, Aktuel,* and *PC Life.*

UNITED KINGDOM AND IRELAND

United Kingdom

The newspaper and magazine market in the United Kingdom is healthy: total sales of national daily newspapers are nearly 14 million in a country of 60 million, and sales of national Sunday papers total nearly 15 million. Roughly 60 percent of people in the United Kingdom read a national daily paper, and 70 percent read a national Sunday paper. Readership has been in decline since the peaks of the 1950s, but the national market still supports fourteen major daily and fifteen Sunday titles.

Despite concentration in press ownership, British newspapers face lively competition with each other. The *Daily Express,* once the most popular daily in the United Kingdom, now sells fewer than 1 million copies. Currently, the tabloid paper the *Sun* (3.5 million) and its Sunday edition, *News of the World* (4 million), lead the pack; the *Daily Mail* and *Mail on Sunday* now have the second largest daily and Sunday circulations (2.4 and 2.3 million), having overtaken the *Mirror,* the *Sunday Mirror,* and *Sunday People. The Guardian* and the *Observer,* both quality papers, have circulations of 401,000 and 440,000 respectively. The *Times* of London, with a daily circulation of over 700,000, has recently surpassed its rival middlebrow heavyweights, the *Daily Telegraph* and the *Evening Standard,* in popularity.

The lowest-selling titles of the fourteen national papers, the *Racing Post* and *The Scotsman* (among dailies) and *Sunday Business, Sport First,* and the *Non-League Paper* (on Sunday) sell between 44,500 and 88,000. "Middle-market" papers continue to be squeezed out by quality and tabloid newspapers, which attract the middle-market readership. The United Kingdom is famous for having some of the most aggressive tabloid reporters and photographers in Europe.

The United Kingdom also has a buoyant regional and local newspaper market. There are about ninety regional morning and evening titles, and six Sunday papers. There are distinctive "national" markets for newspapers in Scotland, Wales, and Northern Ireland. Sales of regional newspapers vary considerably. The best-selling regional newspaper is the Wolverhampton, England, *Express & Star* (just under 180,000 copies). Weeklies that charge prices tend to have very small circulations; the largest, the *West Briton,* sells just under 50,000 copies a week. By contrast, at least twenty-five free local weeklies have circulations of over 100,000. About 80 percent of people in the United Kingdom read a local paper.

The magazine sector in the United Kingdom is large and has been growing consistently over the past decade. The highest circulating magazine in the United Kingdom in 2005 was *Sky the magazine* (6.78 million), a free guide to cable and satellite television offerings, followed by the low-cost *What's on TV* (1.67 million) and *Radio Times* (1.2 million). Another of the highest circulating magazines in the United Kingdom is the *National Trust Magazine* (1.66 million), about the British countryside and its heritage sites, followed closely by *Saga* (1.25 million), a magazine for retired people; the cooking weekly *Take a Break* (1.2 million); the BBC pre-school magazines (929,500); and *Reader's Digest* (776,900). Popular fashion magazines include *Glamour, Chat, Marie Claire, Eve,* and *New Woman.* The American *Times* magazine (551,100) just barely beats out its more serious and substantive British competitor, the *Economist* (503,100) in sales. Tabloids also rank high (*OK! Magazine, Daily Star*), as do parenting magazines, buyers' exchanges such as the *Exchange & Mart, Nuts* (for men), *Dazed and Confused* (youth), *Auto Express,* and *Car.*

All the major media in the United Kingdom have established online presences, a trend that started in 1994, and more than half of all adults regularly use the Internet.

Ireland

Ireland supports four national dailies, two national evening newspapers, five national Sunday newspapers, approximately fifty regional and twelve local newspapers, and thirty-two free newspapers. The national daily *Irish Times* is the newspaper of record. Roughly 600,000 national newspapers are sold in the Republic each day, as well as 650,000 regional newspapers each week, and sales have been increasing ever year since 1999 because of Ireland's booming economy. Most Irish newspapers are politically conservative and have a middle-class orientation. The only tabloids are *Ireland on Sunday*, *Sunday World*, and the *Star*. This small number is probably linked to the wide availability of British tabloids, which can be bought all over Ireland and are cheaper in Ireland than are Irish newspapers. Approximately 25 percent of daily and 33 percent of Sunday newspapers sold in Ireland are British.

Ireland has a small but lively magazine sector distinct from the British press, although many British magazines also circulate there. The most successful magazine is *RTE Guide* (145,900), a weekly guide to Irish radio and television channels. *CIRCA* is Ireland's highest-circulating magazine on the visual arts and contemporary culture, while *Image* is the leading women's magazine; other popular titles include *Ireland's Eye*, *Oxygen*, *Phoenix*, *Business & Finance*, *Reality* (a Catholic lifestyle magazine), *Irish Computer*, *Red & Black Revolution*, *Motoring Life*, *Irish Garden*, *Ireland Afloat* (boating), and *Country Sports and Country Life*. *Cuisle* covers current affairs, the environment, and Gaeltacht culture in Gaelic. Dublin's *New Riot Magazine* is a free alternative-culture magazine for young people. In addition, the *Irish Echo* (based in New York), the *Irish Post* (based in London), and the *Irish Emigrant* all provide news to members of the Irish diaspora living in other countries.

Internet access is becoming commonplace in Ireland; e-zines, blogs, and the Websites of traditional print media are popular.

RESOURCE GUIDE

PRINT SOURCES

Asante, Clement. *Press Freedom and Development*. Westport, CT: Greenwood Press, 1997.

Barker, Hannah. *Newspapers, Politics, and English Society*. Essex, UK: Pearson Education Limited, 2000.

Black, Jay, Jennings Bryant, and Susan Thompson. *Introduction to Media Communication*. New York: McGraw, 1997.

Boehm, Eric. *Historical Periodicals Directory: Europe, the West, North, Central, and South*. Santa Barbara, CA: ABC-CLIO, 1992.

Christin, Anne-Marie. *Histoire de l'Ecriture*. Paris: Flammarion, 2001.

Durham, Meenakshi, and Douglas Kellner. *Media and Cultural Studies: Keyworks*. Malden, MA: Blackwell, 2001.

Ezell, Margaret. *Social Authorship*. Baltimore: John Hopkins Press, 1999.

Fritzsche, Peter. *Reading Berlin 1900*. Cambridge, MA: Harvard University Press, 1998.

Internationales Handbuch Medien 2004/2005. Frankfurt: Nomos, 2004.

Japp, Phyllis, Mark Meister, and Deborah Japp. *Communication Ethics, Media, and Popular Culture*. New York: Peter Lang, 2005.

Kuhn, Raymond. *The Media in France*. London: Routledge, 1995.

Rossel, André. *Le Faux Grand Siecle*. Paris: A L'Enseigne de l'Arbre Verdoyant, 1982.

Stokes, Jane, and Anna Reading. *The Media in Britain: Current Debates and Developments*. New York: St. Martin's Press, 1999.

Studies in Newspaper and Periodical History. Westport, CT: Greenwood, since.

WEBSITES

All newspapers and magazines mentioned in this article have Websites; some are listed below.

AllYouCanRead.com. Accessed March 30, 2006. http://www.allyoucanread.com. A site listing bestselling periodicals in Europe.

The Audit Bureau of Circulations, UK. Accessed March 30, 2006. http://www.abc.org.uk.

BBC. Accessed March 30, 2006. www.bbc.co.uk.

The British Library's Newspaper History Website and Reading Room. Accessed April 16, 2006. http://www.bl.uk/collections/histnews.html.

CIA Country Guides. *CIA—The World Factbook*. Accessed April 14, 2006. https://www.cia.gov/cia/publications/factbook/index.html.

Corriere della Sera. Accessed March 30, 2006. http://www.corriere.it.

DIEPER: Digitised European Periodicals. Accessed September 10, 2006. http://gdz.sub.uni-goettingen.de/dieper. A centralized access point that makes retroactively digitized periodicals from ten European countries available to readers.

Economist Intelligence Unit. Accessed March 30, 2006. http://www.eiu.com/.

El Pais. Accessed March 30, 2006. http://www.elpais.es.

The European Journalism Centre. Accessed March 30, 2006. http://www.ejc.nl. *Frankfurter Allgemeine Zeitung*. Accessed March 30, 2006. http://www.faz.net.

The Guardian. Accessed March 30, 2006. http://www.guardian.co.uk.

Hürriyet. Accessed March 30, 2006. http://www.hurriyetkurumsal.com/eng.

Institute of Press Development. Accessed March 30, 2006. http://www.pdi.ru.

The Joint Industry Committee for Regional Press Research. Accessed March 30, 2006. http://www.jicreg.co.uk/.

Le Monde. Accessed March 30, 2006. http://www.lemonde.fr.

MATESZ. Accessed April 14, 2006. http://www.matesz.hu. Hungarian statistics.

The Nations Encyclopedia. Accessed April 14, 2006. http://www.country-data.com/. Provides specific information about periodicals from most countries.

Online project focused on Russia media. Accessed March 30, 2006. http://www.smi.ru.

Press Display. Accessed April 14, 2006. http://www.pressdisplay.com. Digital images of periodicals from across Europe.

Press Research Centre at Jagiellonian University in Krakow. Accessed April 14, 2006. http://www.onet.pl/.

Project Rastko. Accessed April 14, 2006.

http://www.rastko.org.yu/isk/mbjelica-journalism.html. An online encyclopedia of Serbian culture.

PubList. Accessed April 14, 2006. http://www.publist.com. An online database containing bibliographic information on periodicals from around the world.

Reporters without Borders. Accessed March 30, 2006. http://www.rsf.org.

Süddeutsche Zeitung. Accessed March 30, 2006. http://www.sueddeutsche.de.

World Press. Accessed March 30, 2006. http://www.worldpress.org.

MUSEUMS

International Newspaper Museum of the City of Aachen. Pontstraße 13 • D-52062 Aachen. http://www.zeitungsmuseum-aachen.de/. Founded in 1886, the museum contains one of the world's largest collections of newspapers in nearly all of the world's languages, as well as scholarly books about the history of newspapers.

Newspaper Museum Fjell-Lom. Stigersveien 1, N-7374 Røros, Norway. A museum covering the history of newspapers and printing technology in Norway.

RADIO AND TELEVISION

HOLGER BRIEL

In its 1976 *Recommendation Concerning the International Standardization of Statistics on Radio and Television*, UNESCO gave a poignant definition of radio and television (TV). Radio was defined as "broadcasting of sound signals only" and TV as "broadcasting of transient images of fixed or moving objects, with or without sound." In the same document, UNESCO announced that, because of the everincreasing importance of both broadcasting media, it was launching an international program to monitor such broadcasts on a global basis.

In the twenty-first century, this recommendation seems as timely as ever. It is fair to say that TV has supplanted the book as the primary means of global storytelling. Although the United States is still the market leader in production and consumption of broadcasting material, other areas of the world have been following its example and have become important players in their own right. This is certainly true for Europe.

Europe is a heterogeneous entity with very divergent cultures. To attempt to write about a European mediascape is to be either rather naïve about its diversity or very optimistic about the growing together of a European cultural sphere. Furthermore, throughout the last two centuries there have been numerous and competing ways of defining Europe, such as: the European Union (EU) with twenty-five member states; the Organization for Security and Co-operation in Europe (OSCE) with fifty-five states from Europe, Central Asia. and North America; the Council of Europe (CoE, forty-six member states with 800 million people); the "Schengen States" (fifteen members); the European Free Trade Association (EFTA) with four non-EU European countries as members; and also the European Broadcasting Union (EBU) with fifty-two member states.

It is this last organization's lead which will structure the following discussions. In 2004 the EBU's Legal Director Werner Rumphorst stated that "Europe covers *all* the countries situated in the European Broadcasting Area."[1] For the sake of brevity and to make clear that the status of Armenia, Azerbaijan, Georgia, but also Moldova, Belarus, and Ukraine are far from clear at this point, those countries have been excluded from this chapter.

THE HISTORY OF ELECTRONIC MEDIA IN EUROPE

From their inception, starting with books and continuing with newspapers, the media's means of mass information have exerted a compelling influence over people's lives. With the rise of audiovisual technology, this influence reached an astonishing scale. Already before the turn of the twentieth century, telephony had begun to inspire the European and American elites. But it was its wireless variety which would have an even greater impact. Largely as a result of World War I (1914–1918), countries realized that wireless communication was an important factor in conducting and winning the information war and, a bit later on, the economic war. Add to that the rising star of cinema, with Hollywood and Paris as major centers, and it was only a question of time before attempts would be made to broadcast wireless sound and pictures.

In the early 1920s all major European countries experimented with television. The first public demonstrations were held in 1923 in Leipzig and in 1925 at the department store Selfridges in London. The new technology received a further boost with the 1936 Berlin Olympics, much of which was broadcast to large screens in Berlin and Hamburg. In 1937 the coronation of George VI in London was broadcast from Hyde Park Corner, and French National Television started shortly afterwards. While the U.S. market continued to flourish, European television was all but erased in the run-up to World War II as many European nations concentrated their research on war technology. All major European powers also tried to get their propaganda sent on radio waves across demarcation lines. The Axis powers, especially, feared these broadcasts.

After the end of World War II in 1945, Western Europe quickly restructured its media landscape. Despite reservations during the 1950s, the European TV market grew at a rapid pace and set up the platforms for much of the later enlargement of the 1970s. Most countries followed the "BBC model" of public broadcasting corporations: more or less independent agencies governed by laws of the individual states. These stations were meant to "inform, educate, and entertain the public" (in that order) and thereby differed greatly in their mission from American commercial broadcasters, whose aim was strictly entertainment. Meanwhile, in Eastern Europe, tightly run state broadcasters ensured that no independent opinions threatened the Communist hegemony of the airwaves.

Things changed again in the 1980s as a result of developments that had already started in the 1950s, when "pirate" (i.e., unlicensed) radio stations began broadcasting into many European countries. Soon, Western European governments were put under pressure to license private radio and TV stations fashioned after the North American mediascape. Britain had already experienced commercial broadcasting since 1955, when ITV was licensed. This new public–private "dual broadcasting system" was installed in most Western European countries during the first half of the 1980s. Satellite and cable television quickly established themselves, and pay TV soon followed.

The demise of the Soviet Empire also changed the media landscape. With the fall of the Berlin Wall in 1989, Eastern European states began emancipating themselves from Soviet dominance. As their markets opened up during a time when satellite and cable programming had already become the norm, bandwidth scarcity did not preclude multiple channels (as had been the case earlier in Western Europe). At that time, with a weakened state government unable to assert media sovereignty, private audiovisual providers were quick to jump into the market. This led to a situation in which public broadcasters had and continue to have an exceedingly difficult time to establish themselves in these new markets.

THE EUROPEAN MEDIA SITUATION TODAY

The European media situation must be considered both in terms of the types of media consumed and the quantities of media consumption.

Hardware

Over the last few decades there has been an explosion of media outlets in Europe. It is now home to over 3000 TV and about 15,000 radio stations. On the consumer side, virtually every European household has at least one TV. When it comes to individualized programming abilities, hardware such as the video recorder or DVD player has become ubiquitous. In 2004, their figures for the major European media markets were as shown in Table 1.[2] Although VHS video tape recorders were still in the majority, figures indicate that they were on their way out and that the future belonged to DVD players and recorders.

Country	DVD %	VHS %
UK	61.3	60.2
Germany	58.0	60.7
France	61.0	61.7
Spain	49.5	48.0
Italy	31.1	31.5
Western Europe	50.5	52.2

TABLE 1 Video Hardware Penetration in the Largest European Markets

When it comes to the modes of broadcast reception, almost all national public radio and TV broadcasters reach close to 100 percent of their intended national audiences via terrestrial (that is, broadcast from ground-based antennas) analog TV. Shortly after the millennium, some European countries launched Digital Video Broadcasting terrestrially (DVB-T), mostly in metropolitan areas. This relatively new mode of broadcasting has the potential to become quite important in the future as analog broadcasting will cease by 2010.

Satellite TV naturally aims for a larger, international audience. In 2005, more than 102 million European homes owned satellite dishes capable of receiving over 1400 TV and radio channels from 12 Astra and 26 Eutelsat satellites.[3] These satellites provide coverage from northernmost Scandinavia to Kazakhstan in the east, Sudan in the south, and the Canary Islands in the southwest. Satellite uptake is still on the rise: in 2004, Denmark had the highest number of satellite dishes (42 percent), followed by Austria, Germany, and Norway.

Cable is also available in most European countries, albeit at a smaller scale. While cable offers many advantages over satellite, such as the larger amount of transmittable data and other interactive services, initial startup costs for cable are substantial, and therefore cable penetration reaches high penetration (90 percent and more) only in densely populated and affluent countries such as Germany, Belgium, and the Netherlands. Southern and most

Eastern European countries have a very low cable uptake. Greece, to name only one such country, at present does not have any cable transmissions at all.

Media Consumption

In general one can say that in Europe media consumption has been on the rise. Judging by the demographics of leisure activities alone, it is fair to say that today TV has firmly supplanted the book as the primary means of global storytelling. Much of this increase in electronic media consumption has to do with the multiplication of radio and TV channels during the 1980s and 1990s. The countries with the highest viewing levels (about 4 hours daily) tend to be in Eastern and Southern Europe (e.g., Estonia, Hungary, and Greece), and the ones with the lowest viewing rate (about 2.5 hours daily) in Northern and Central Europe (e.g., Austria, Sweden, and Denmark). In Britain, viewers also spent more than 4 hours per day in front of the "telly." According to Eurodata TV Worldwide, in 2004 Western European television viewers also spent on average 4 more minutes per day in front of their televisions than in 2003, a trend that has gone on uninterrupted for the last decades.

THE DUAL SYSTEM

Media in European countries is provided by both a national, public broadcasting system and commercial broadcasters. The relationship between the two varies from country to country.

Public Broadcasters

The European public broadcasting system goes back to the 1920s. Just as with newspapers, the states then insisted on having a say in this new medium. Radio stations were also entwined with other state institutions, such as postal, telephone, and telegraph agencies. Until the end of World War II, radio and early TV were seen by the state as its mouthpiece. At least for Western Europe, this would change with the more liberal commercial broadcasting input provided by the United States. Broadcasting was taken away from the influence of the state and overseen by more neutral supervisory bodies. Much of Eastern Europe would have to wait until the early 1990s to enter into a more liberalized broadcasting sphere.

By the 1970s, Western governments started to allow commercial offers as well. The first country to attempt this was Britain in 1955. In 1975, Italy followed suit, and by the mid-1980s almost all Western European countries had such programs with almost instant success. Concerns persisted of a "dumbing-down" of the populace through TV; of crass, U.S.-style consumerism holding sway; and of the loss of cultural diversity. Most nations therefore added passages to their broadcasting laws to ensure that at least public broadcasters would send a minimum of informational, educational, and highbrow entertainment content. Another passage would usually also deal with the right of minorities to receive pertinent programming.

Lastly, the European countries also differ in their levels of funding allocated through the license fees or government grants. In general, most national public broadcasters receive over 50 percent of their funding through license fees. In some countries, revenues rely more on commercial activities than on government funding. This model seems to be the trend of the future, as public funding continues to dwindle by several percentage points each year.

Governments and public broadcasters had feared that commercial TV would do away with tested recipes for a TV programming mix and only cater to the baser instincts of people. However, new advances in technologies, the force of "pirate" (illegal) broadcasters and "border blaster" stations (legal, but with their target audiences located in countries other than where the transmissions originate from), and the general wishes of citizens, led governments to allow commercial players. Initially, they did broadcast many of the programs it was feared they would, sometimes quite violent and sexual in nature. But frequently the amount of sexually oriented material diminishes once a new technology is established; this was also the case with commercial TV. As regards to violence, strict laws were passed to hold it at bay or to allow such broadcasts only late in the evening. But governments are not only upset with these commercial stations. In secret many of them welcomed then, as now the public broadcasters had to justify their oftentimes overly expensive programming structures, thus making them more financially accountable.

Commercial broadcasters finance themselves mostly through advertising. Most public broadcasters, however, are allowed to transmit commercials only during small and tightly regulated program slots. Their main source of revenues would come from license fees and government subsidies or grants. Table 2 shows the spread of revenues for the most important European public broadcasters.[4]

In general, public broadcasters have been losing audience share as a result of the introduction of commercial radio and TV. They have also been losing profits, with the exception of the Italian RAI and the British BBC. The BBC remains the only large public broadcaster that does not transmit any commercials on its flagship TV stations, although it allows its newer stations to gather revenues from advertisements. The much smaller public broadcaster of Estonia has recently also removed advertising. Conversely, most other public broadcasters have been forced to increase the amount of advertising in order to stay afloat financially.

The percentage of their audience losses, however, differs from country to country. Overall, Northern European public broadcasters enjoy a higher audience share than their eastern and southern neighbors. Austria and Denmark have public TV services that capture more than 50 percent of the audience share. In France, Italy, and the UK, public TV has more than a 40 percent share of the national audience, as shown in Figure 1.[5] At the other end of the scale are Southeastern European countries such as Greece and Turkey and some of the new eastern EU members such as Lithuania, where the public broadcasters' audience share is in the single digits.

These negative audience trends, however, pertain mostly to TV. Public broadcasting radio channels have remained largely stable in audience share, some even gaining. One reason, of course, is cost; one hour of radio costs merely 5–10 percent as much as of one hour of television. Even in Eastern Europe, the future of public-service radio looks quite good.

License Fees

License fees had originally been levied to pay for broadcasts. They were introduced with the beginning of organized European radio broadcasts in 1922 in England and in 1923 in Germany. Most European countries levy them; exceptions include Bulgaria, Cyprus, Estonia, Hungary, Latvia, Lithuania, the ex-Yugoslavian countries, Luxembourg, Flemish Belgium, Spain, and Portugal (since 1999). In Greece and Hungary, there are no license fees as such, but a percentage of the electricity bill goes toward funding the Public Broadcasting Companies. The absence of these fees has dire consequences for the public broadcasters, because their loss of autonomy impairs their ability to perform their services to the public.

Country	Aids/ Grants	License Fee	Other Public Income	Advertising	Sponsorship	Sales of Programs	Merchandising	Pay TV	Other Commercial Revenues	Others	Total
Switzerland	1,9	98,2	—	44,3	—	5.1	—	—	7	—	156.5
Iceland	—	80.7	0	36.3	3	3	0.9	—	—	—	121
Austria	1.3	45.5	0	45	4.6	4.4	0	—	4.3	11.6	116.7
Denmark	—	78.7	—	27.5	0.,	1..,	1.1	—	6.6	—	115.2
Great Britain	6.7	60.7	0.2	18.1	0	5.6	8	0.6	2.7	1	103.7
Germany	3.9	73.6	—	8.1	0.3	0.4	—	—	10.1	0.8	97.2
Norway	0	79.2	6.1	—	0	0	0	—	0	0.6	85.9
Sweden	—	70.6	—	—	0.4	1.8	—	—	0.6	6.4	79.9
Ireland	—	22.3	—	36.2	—	—	—	—	11.3	—	69.8
Finland	0.2	53.8	9.3	0	0	0.8	0.2	0	2.7	0	67
Belgium	0.5	34.9	—	12.3	2.2	0.2	0.2	—	3.1	2.8	56.3
France	2.3	34.4	—	11.9	0.2	0.7	—	0.3	4.2	1.8	55.8
Slovenia	0.8	36.5	—	6.4	4.2	0.2	0.3	—	3.7	3.1	55.2
Italy	0.1	22.7	1.2	19.2	1.4	2.6	—	0.7	0.5	0.8	49.2

Netherlands	25.6	0	0	14.9	0.1	—	0	—	—	4.4	45
Spain (estimated)	7.3	—	0.1	20.5	—	2.7	0	0.5	2.1	0.7	33.9
Portugal (estimated)	7.4	6	0	6.8	0.2	0.2	0.1	0	0.5	4.1	24.8
Greece (estimated)	0.7	—	18.3	2	—	—	—	—	—	—	20.9
Poland	0	4.4	—	6.5	0.4	0.1	—	—	—	1.1	12.4
Estonia	7.2	—	—	2.2	0.3	0	—	—	0.9	0.2	10.8
Slovakia	2	5.6	—	0.9	0.2	0.2	0.1	—	0	0.2	9.2
Macedonia	0,1	5	—	2	0	—	0,1	—	0,1	1	8,3
Turkey	0	—	4	0,4	0,2	0	0	—	—	1,4	6

TABLE 2 Average Revenue Per Capita of the Public Broadcasting Systems, 2000 (Euros per Inhabitant)

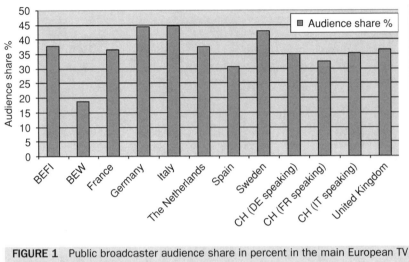

FIGURE 1 Public broadcaster audience share in percent in the main European TV markets, 2004.

Annual European public broadcasting license fees and other public broadcaster revenues amounted to over €30 billion in 2004. Fees vary greatly amongst European nations and can be viewed as an indication of how affluent a country is and how much it cherishes its public broadcasting units. The license fee figures for 2005 are as shown in Table 3.[6]

Two public broadcasters are the heavyweights in Europe: the UK-based BBC, with over €5 million revenues and about 27,000 employees, and the German ARD, with over €6 million revenues and almost 24,000 employees. The BBC broadcasts 25 channels by cable and satellite. Besides its prime channel, the ARD also controls all German third channels (discussed in the later section on Germany) and several other national and international channels.

Programming strategies vary between the large European public broadcasting services. The BBC achieves audience loyalty mainly through its news programs, generally a public broadcasting domain. The French and German public broadcasting services entrusted their futures to a mix of home-produced fiction and information programs, while the Spanish services bet on a mix of fiction and entertainment. Lastly, Italy's public broadcasting service leads the way with home-produced miniseries.

Commercial TV

Most commercial TV in Europe is of the free to air (FTA) variety; that is, it relies on advertising revenues for its financing. Generally speaking, commercial television broadcasters do not have the same programming obligations as public broadcasters do. A minimum service, such as news programs, is required of them in only a handful of countries. They do, however, garner a large number of viewers. In France, TF1; in the United Kingdom, ITV; in Germany, RTL; in Italy, Canale 5; and in Spain, Tele 5 and Antena 3—they all give their national public broadcasters a run for their money. They have at least as high an audience share as individual public stations and often completely dominate the annual ratings. In the United Kingdom for instance, ITV regularly garners eight to nine out of the annual top ten programs.

Other kinds of commercial TV and radio providers are pay radio and pay TV. These systems rely on subscription charges to finance themselves. For radio, this is usually done via

Country	Euro
Iceland	389.26
Switzerland	291.60
Denmark	274.30
Norway	239.70
Austria	238.18
Sweden	213.91
Germany	204.36
Finland	193.95
Britain	178.86
Ireland	155.00
Belgium	145.49
France	116.00
Italy	99.60
Greece	39–45
Turkey	6.00

TABLE 3   2005 Television License Fees in Europe

the Internet, but pay TV is still dependent on set-top boxes. In the early 2000s, pay TV became the biggest audience winner, with the United Kingdom and Germany achieving audience increases between 13 and 17 percent, and Spain and Italy around 7 percent. It is expected that the United Kingdom will remain the largest pay TV market in Europe, with France, Germany, Scandinavia, and Spain following shortly behind. There are small, but powerful numbers of pay TV providers in Europe, as Table 4 indicates.[7]

Other major players, such as the American firms Home Box Office (HBO) and Time-Warner, as well as several Scandinavian and French companies, have become active in Eastern Europe, generally with high audience gains. As is clear from the monthly charges levied, this is a money-intensive industry with potentially high profit margins, and therefore it is attracting a large number of investors.

The Special Case of Eastern Europe and the Newer EU Members

Most Western European countries can look back upon a relatively stable 60-year history of mostly public broadcasting. But the state of affairs was different in Eastern Europe. Up until 1989, broadcasters were directly answerable to totalitarian regimes, which exerted complete control over the airwaves. While in Western Europe there had been the slow process of the formation of a public broadcasting sphere that only later on opened itself up to a competitive system, things happened rather more speedily (and chaotically) in the southeast of Europe.

Market	Pay TV Provider	Main Stockholder	Launch	Subscribers	Minimum Subscription (Euro/Month)
Germany	Premiere	Permira Fund (pan-European)	1991	3,300,000	5.00
Greece	Nova	Multichoice Hellas (Greece)	1999	223,000	12.30
France	ABSat	ABGroup (France)	1995	25,200,000	N/A
	Canal +	Canal+ (France)	1984	4,900,000	28.80
	Canal Satellite	Canal+ (France)	1992	2,700,000	11.00
	TPS	TF1 (France)	1996	1,200,000	11.00
Italy	SKY Italia	News Corp (USA)	2003	2,400,000	22.00
Portugal	TV Cabo	PT Multimedia (Portugal)	1994	1,400,000	13.49
Scandinavia	Canal Digital	Telenor (Norway)	1997	710,000	20.50
	Viasat	MTG (Sweden)	1991	600,000	13.29
Spain	Canal +	Sogecanal (Spain)	1990	1,930,000	24.97
	Digital+	Sogecanal (Spain)	2003	18,000,000	22.00
UK	(Sky USA)	News Corp (USA)	1989	72,000,000	20.20

TABLE 4   Major European Pay TV Providers (2004/5)

The new political and economic developments after independence facilitated the development of a legislative vacuum in the broadcasting sector. When those countries were still ruled by Communist governments, a regulation process for the media simply did not exist. Conversely, complete freedom from censorship would not come until 1989. From then on, commercial broadcasters simply transferred their business know-how with little changes to the eastern markets. The newly created public broadcasters, however, faced a host of difficulties. These included: the mindsets of their own workforces, untrained for the new liberal environment; the mindset of their audiences, often unwilling to be informed by what they still considered to be state agencies; the lack of government funding; and the very competitive business milieu.

In the East European countries, TV is by far the strongest medium in the broadcasting industry. It represents between 92 percent (in Romania) and around 60 percent (in the Baltic states) of the entire broadcasting economy. In the larger states, the industry is almost completely driven by advertising revenues, favoring private networks. Only in smaller and less developed markets do public broadcasters hold their own. There is hardly any broadcasting production money available, which impoverishes the broadcasts and drives audiences to the privates.

In broadcasting issues, size does matter; many of the new markets are small and do not offer the profit margins public and commercial providers are looking for. Only Poland, with a 2004 audiovisual sector turnover of close to €3 billion, offers sufficient incentive. Thus, it has become the most fought-over eastern market. Hungary, the Czech Republic, and Turkey follow at a distance, the latter (73 million people) offering a vast growth potential. Pay TV is relatively well developed, as the strong rates of cable subscriptions testify. However, these private broadcasters are almost exclusively Western media conglomerates.

Public radio, on the other hand, is in a much better state than its TV counterpart. It is cheaper to produce and therefore better financed and technically well equipped. It covers the whole of the national territories and is able to offer diverse programming. Largely thanks to its generalist formats, for the most part it remains a (if not the) market leader.

PROGRAMMING

Despite a rapprochement between public and commercial broadcasters in funding and programming structures, important differences remain. The most important one is arguably the number of American productions shown. American programs have always had a dominant position in the international markets, and Europe is no exception. It is mostly the commercial providers that broadcast American materials: soap operas, sitcoms, Hollywood feature films.

In 2003, the major Hollywood studios earned $1.35 billion from licensing films to pay TV channels in Europe's top five media markets. Overall, the United States generates over $9 billion annually from program sales in Europe, whereas its own imports from Europe, even if strong British productions are taken into account, are negligible at less than 10 percent of its export figures. Western European channels annually buy over 300,000 hours of American programming, and although the volume of American imports is shrinking in Western Europe, Eastern Europe has become a major growth market. However, as a result of the recent and continuing expansion of the European broadcasting market, European broadcasting net revenues are nearing their American counterparts; both are roughly worth an annual $80 billion. Speculation as to why there is such an American dominance of the market is rife; many commentators cite the model function of American culture or the American way of life. But perhaps the reasons are more of a pedestrian nature; the average cost of an American production is usually five to ten times higher than that of its European counterpart and is therefore likely to achieve superior production quality.

One decidedly American adherent in Western Europe is the UK, which imports over 90 percent of its feature films from the United States. The total volume of fiction and film programming imported and broadcast by Western European television channels in 2001 reached 320,239 hours, a 3 percent increase on the 2000 level. Though the volume of American imports fell back for the third year in succession, American-initiated programming continued to dominate program imports, due to the growth in the number of U.S. co-productions imported.

Figure 2 illustrates the relationship between U.S. imports and non-U.S. imports in the five largest European markets.[8]

Apart from this dominance of American imports in the categories of feature films, sitcoms, and drama series, fiction continues to be the largest and most influential prime time program category in Europe. The category "fiction" generally refers to films made for TV, series, miniseries, soap operas, *telenovelas*, and similar. The European Union is well aware of this trend and for some time has been spending considerable energies in trying to rectify this imbalance (see the section "The Role of the EU").

313

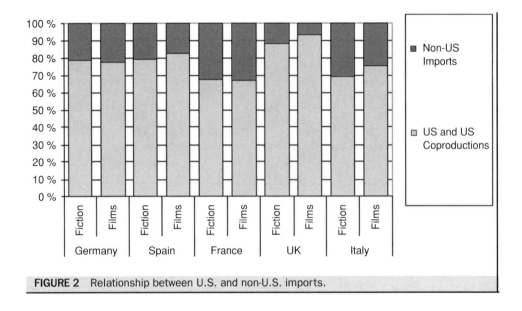

FIGURE 2   Relationship between U.S. and non-U.S. imports.

But national differences exist. Since 2000, drama series were the most important category in the United Kingdom and in Spain, whereas Italy depended more on its home-produced miniseries. In France and Germany, the locally produced made-for-TV-film category dominated. The larger European broadcasting markets generally produce a fair share of their own programming. In the United Kingdom and Germany over 50 percent of prime time fiction is now of domestic origin. France's figure remains the highest, with over 75 percent home-produced programming.

Relatively new program categories are reality shows and revamped game shows. Although these shows have garnered much interest and sometimes even cult followings (at least for their first runs), overall they have had little impact on European programming, which still seems to prefer fiction over "reality." The most successful reality show in the first few years of the new millennium was *Big Brother*. Conceived by Dutchman John de Mol's Endemol production company, it went on to become a global TV phenomenon. In terms of game shows, the biggest pan-European draw was *Who Wants To Be a Millionaire?*, which has so far run in some ninety countries and met with huge audience successes everywhere. Since the 1980s, audience fragmentation has increased as a result of channel proliferation. Audience members now often drift away from general broadcasting into niche narrowcasting. It seems that apart from soccer, which still ranks highest in European audience attraction, the big national media events have now become a phenomenon of the past.

THE ROLE OF THE EU

For the longest time, the EU and its predecessors have expressed an interest in the coalescence of a pan-European broadcasting market. However, major obstacles had to be removed. From its very beginning, the EU has always insisted that cultural matters were the sole domains of its member states. Therefore, broadcasting has always been left in the hands of the individual countries. Even within those countries, different regulations applied. This is still the case in Germany, where the individual *Länder* (states) have broadcasting sovereignty, or in Belgium and Switzerland, where different linguistic areas have their own broadcasting laws. The EU doctrine finally changed in the 1980s, when it became clear that—because emergent commercial broadcasters were not bound by country borders—a new framework was needed. The EU therefore turned to a somewhat forgotten institution from the early days of European broadcasting: the European Broadcasting Union (EBU). The EBU had been collaborating with national TV stations since 1954. An important step on the road to an integrated European broadcasting market was the Treaty "European Agreement Concerning Programme Exchanges by Means of Television Films" (ETS No. 027), signed by the members of the Council of Europe in 1958 and effected in 1961.

Eurovision, Europe's television exchange, had already been conceived in 1950. Its first official broadcast was the coronation of Britain's Queen Elizabeth II on June 2, 1953. Regular programming began in 1954. The Eurovision broadcast jingle has become an audio icon in Europe; it can be heard before the broadcast of every European song contest, every European Champion's League football game, and every other large trans-European broadcast.

The first European television season, in 1954, was deemed a major success. Demand was on the increase, especially as the market already comprised 3.5 million viewers in eight countries (Belgium, Denmark, France, West Germany, Italy, the Netherlands, Switzerland, and the United Kingdom). The popular Eurovision Song Contest first aired in 1956 to ten countries. The game show *Jeux Sans Frontières* (Games without Borders), in which various European national teams competed against each other, would bring Europe together—at least on television. Later on, agreements with American and Asian networks were added, allowing for such record one-offs as the 1969 broadcast of Neil Armstrong's moon walk.

To counterbalance this successful internationalizing Western trend, the Eastern bloc founded its own international broadcasting organization, OIRT (Organization for International Radio and Television), which created the Eastern bloc program exchange, Intervision. After 1989, broadcasting reforms led to the 1993 absorption of OIRT into the EBU.

The EU also continues to encourage diversity in broadcasting and program production. In 1989 it presented its controversial directive, "Television Without Frontiers" (TVWF). It stipulated the free flow of media programs within the EU, forbade advertising of tobacco products on European TV, and insisted on strict rules for advertising quotas. It also extended the Right of Reply (i.e., the legal right to respond to statements about oneself and have one's response printed) from print media to electronic media. It furthermore included the protection of minors. Finally, the directive stated that the European audience must be allowed general and free access to major events considered of major importance to society (mostly applicable to big sporting events).

The most contentious article of the Directive was perhaps Article 4, which mandated that at least 50 percent of broadcasts would have to consist of European productions. This passage was introduced to protect the European broadcasting market from a complete dominance of American productions. Although the EU produces more films than the United States, 75 percent of EU cinema revenues stem from American productions. Article 5 sets quotas for material created within the EU (e.g., 10 percent of the broadcast time should be used for recent—not older than 5 years—independent EU productions). After a lengthy process, the World Trade Organization sanctioned this act of protectionism through a clause called "cultural exception."

The European Union and the Council of Europe also encourage transborder broadcasting projects. Many individual states have begun TV broadcasts (largely via satellite) in their local language to audiences abroad. Examples for this are Deutsche Welle (Germany), BBC World (UK), TV 5 (France), TVE International (Spain), and RAI International (Italy). Another inter-European initiate is the German-French co-production ARTE, aired simultaneously in

ANDORRAN MEDIA ON THE WEB

http://www.rtvasa.ad/ is the Website of Radio Nacional d'Andorra, which operates Radio Andorra and music station Andorra Musica. The commercial radio station Andorra1 is on the Web at http://www.andorra1.ad.

French and German. One last trans-European initiative to be mentioned here is the Médaille Charlemagne pour des Médias Européens, which is awarded annually to a respected member of the European media environment.

These European political and cultural activities just described all bear witness to the fact that the media have been gaining an ever greater influence over European societies. After all, society today is referred to as "media society" or "information society." As the EU Lisbon strategy called for Europe to become the most advanced knowledge based economy in the world, it also acknowledged that this knowledge nowadays is mostly gained via electronic mass media outlets. To achieve this goal, the EU policy holds that a well-organized media marketplace is the best guarantor for achieving this goal. In many ways, the EU has therefore taken over the functions of national broadcasting regulators.

In the following sections, a few representative European broadcasting markets are displayed. Generally speaking, the larger national find mention here because of their financial weight and broader reach. Some others, however, were chosen because they might offer a few surprises of their own.

ANDORRA

Andorra is largely dominated by the airwaves from its two neighbors. As the national language is Catalan, the broadcasts from Catalonia are especially well received.

Already in the 1950s the commercial Andorran radio station Sud Radio broadcast a mix of music and peppy commentary into France, thereby undermining strict French broadcasting laws. For the longest time, the French government tried in vain to suppress it. Nowadays commercial radio stations are Radio Valira, Flaix FM, Andorra1, and others. There also exists one church radio station, Ràdio Principat.

The national public broadcaster is Ràdio i Televisió d'Andorra, and it operates a TV channel (TVA) and radio stations.

In total there exist one TV channel and approximately 15 radio channels.

BOSNIA AND HERZEGOVINA

Bosnia and Herzegovina is a very new country, and therefore the broadcasting market is still in formation. Furthermore, there exist several ethnic groups within the country who need to be catered for by individual broadcasting outlets. Not surprising then that there are 183 licensed commercial broadcasters (42 TV, 141 radio), plus three additional statewide public broadcasters that form the public broadcasting system for the country: The Public Broadcasting Service of BiH (Bosnia and Herzegovina) (PBS BiH) for all of the country, Radio and Television of the Federation Bosnia and Herzegovina (RTV FBiH, two TV channels and two radio channels), and Radio and Television of the Republic of Srpska (RTRS, one TV channel, one radio channel). Sixteen public and twenty-six private TV stations compare with sixty-two public and seventy-nine private radio stations. Cable exists only in rudimentary form. The statewide public broadcaster transmits one radio channel, BH Radio (since 2001), and one TV channel, BHTV 1 (since 2003).

In contrast to other former Eastern bloc countries, the Law on Public Broadcasting System was quickly ratified in 2002 and allows the public broadcasters to gain funding from subscription fees, advertising, sponsorship, and direct state funding.

Commercial radio and TV stations are forming at a rapid pace. The most popular commercial TV stations across Bosnia and Herzegovina are Mreza Plus and the Open Broadcast Network. There are also local stations such as Studio 99 and TV Hayat from Sarajevo, TV Tuzla, TV Mostar, and TV Zetel Zenica. Commercial radio competes mostly with local stations. Several radio networks have also developed, the biggest one being Bosanka Radio Mreza (BORAM).

DENMARK

The first radio station in Denmark was the Statsradiofonien (later Danmarks Radio), which began transmitting in 1920. In 1926 it was given the monopoly to broadcast one channel, P1. On a national level, the monopoly lasted until 1995. In 1951 a second radio channel (P2) was added for regional use.

Pirate radio stations began targeting Denmark very early on. The first one was Radio Mercur (1958–1962), transmitting from a ship anchored in international waters. Recording its programs was prohibited by Danish law. In order to counter the pirate youth appeal, in 1963 the Danish public broadcaster added a third radio channel, P3, whose broadcasting consisted mostly in contemporary music. In 1986, private stations were allowed to broadcast. Today there exist about 300 local commercial radio stations.

TV broadcasting began in 1953 with TV1; a second channel, TV2, was added in 1987. Unlike its older brother, TV2 received mixed funding from the beginning. Both public channels affect a 98 to 100 percent coverage countrywide. In 1983 commercial radio and TV channels were allowed to broadcast on a local basis and without advertising. As with radio before, pirate TV stations caused the state to act. From 1988 onward these stations were also allowed to broadcast advertising. Today there exist more than 300 local radio and over 50 local TV stations. Furthermore, almost all households are able to receive foreign TV stations. Local pay TV channels exist as well, mostly of Swedish and UK origin.

Recently, popular Danish productions such as the police/clairvoyance series *Sensing*

BOSNIA-HERZEGOVINA MEDIA ON THE WEB

The Public Broadcasting System of Bosnia-Herzegovina (PBSBiH) is on the Web at http://www.pbsbih.ba, while the Federation Bosnia and Herzegovina TV (FTV1 and 2) can be found at http://www.rtvbih.ba/Program/index.html. The Radio-Television of the Republic of Srpska (RTRS) is at http://www.rtrs-bl.com.

Among commercial TV providers, Mreza Plus, which has several TV and radio stations and started operating in 1992, is at http://www.mrezaplus.com commercial. The Open Broadcast Network (OBN) is on line at http://www.obn.ba, and Alternative TV Banja Luka is at http://www.atvbl.com.

Commercial radio is represented on the Web by commercial Bosanska Radio Mreza (BORAM) at http://www.boram.ba, Radio Stari Grad at http://www.rsg.ba, and Radio M at http://www.radiom.ba.

DANISH MEDIA ON THE WEB

The Danish Broadcasting Corporation is on line at http://www.dr.dr. The Greenland public broadcaster is at http://knr.gl, and Faroese public broadcasting is at http://www.svf.fo/.

Murder have left their mark on the European TVscape. Much of its success, though, can be attributed to the worldwide triumph of the American *CSI* (Crime Scene Investigators) format. Other popular TV series in Denmark are *Robinson Ekspeditionen* (the local version of *Survivor*) and the screenings of the classic children's series *Olsen Banden* [The Olsen Gang], which had also enjoyed immense popularity already in the German Democratic Republic.

Greenland

Greenland is an autonomous Danish dependent territory with limited self-governance and a population of approximately 56,000. It does have its own radio and television stations. Greenland Broadcasting Company (KNR, Kalaallit Nunaata Radioa) is an independent public radio and TV broadcaster financed by the national treasury, advertising, and sponsorships. It broadcasts in both native Greenlandic and Danish. KNR TV also transmits TV news from the Danish PBS, while radio broadcasts from Danmarks Radio are broadcast on a separate radio channel. Three other AM and ten FM stations are also on the air. Lastly, there also exists one local TV station, NUUK TV. In August 2005 it launched terrestrial digital TV services in the capital, with seventeen digital TV channels.

Faeroe Islands

Another autonomous self-governing Danish overseas territory are the Faeroe Islands, with a population of about 50,000. The Faeroes have one AM, thirteen FM, and three TV broadcasting stations. In 1957, the Faroese Public Radio Station was established; the Faroese Television Company followed in 1984. It is the only station on the islands broadcasting in Faroese. It produces almost 20 percent of its content and translates into Faroese about the same percentage of foreign programs. Its costs are met by license fees, advertising, and bingo. It garners a high audience rating, up to 80 percent in peak times.

FRANCE

France was one of the first countries to conduct trial broadcasts. In 1897 the first of them went out from the Eiffel Tower. In 1922, Radiola (later renamed Radio Paris) began its regular broadcasts. In 1932, Radio Luxembourg was set up (largely with French financing but situated in Luxembourg in order to circumvent strict French broadcasting laws). In the late 1930s, there already existed fourteen commercial and twelve public sector radio stations.

In the 1950s, five large radio networks commenced broadcast in France. Four foreign commercial radio stations proved especially to be forces to be reckoned with: These so-called *périphériques* were RTL (Luxembourg), Europe No. 1 (near Saarbrücken, Germany), RMC (Radio Monte Carlo in Monaco), and the small Sud-Radio (Andorra). 1965 therefore saw a major revamping of the public radio broadcasters with the renaming of France I, II, and III to France Inter, France Musique, and France Culture.

As with most other European nations, it was the pirate radio stations that also spurred on the process towards the liberalization of the French airwaves. From 1981 on, local commercial radio stations were licensed; from 1986 they were allowed to go national. Commercialization forced the state radio broadcasters once again to revamp their programs and introduce new ones, oftentimes local stations. Today there exist seven national radio channels.

The new independent broadcasting sector very quickly began to dominate the public broadcasting sector. Today the commercial radio sector is mainly concentrated in three groups: the popular NRJ group and the two *périphériques*, Europe 1 and RTL. All in all, there are over 1,500 radio stations broadcasting in France today, with a daily audience of about 85 percent of the population.

TV broadcasting in France started relatively late; the first experimental broadcasts began in the mid-1930s. In 1945 the French state formed a national broadcasting company, today called France Télévisions. A second channel was added in 1964, and a third channel in 1973. Today, there exist the following public TV channels in France: France2, France3, France4, TV5, and Réseau France Outre Mer (RFO, the overseas French TV). Another publicly funded TV channel is ARTE, a German-French co-production with its headquarters in Strasbourg. Advertising was allowed on public broadcasting station from 1968 onward. Films may not be interrupted by advertising on the public channels, and only up to 12 minutes per broadcasting hour may be occupied by advertisements. Today FR2 receives over

FRENCH MEDIA ON THE WEB

The national public TV stations are on line at http://www.france2.fr, http://www.france3.fr, and http://www.france5.fr. Commercial TV stations are at http://www.tf1.fr, and http://www.m6.fr.The pay TV channel Canal+ is at http://www.canalplus.fr.

The national and regional public radio channels are on line at http://www.radiofrance.fr, while http://www.europe1.fr and http://www.rtl.fr are commercial radio stations. A large, internationally operating commercial radio network is on line at http://www.nrj.fr.

The island of Corsica, also belonging to France, has a public TV broadcaster on line at http://www.corsefrance3.fr, while http://www.alta-frequenza.com is the site of a commercial radio station.

half of its revenues from advertising, FR3 20 percent, whereas ARTE and the radio stations continue to receive almost 99 percent of their revenues from the license fees and state/EU subsidies.

In 1982 the general state monopoly on broadcasting ended, with commercial channels being licensed. The first and prime public French channel, TF1, was sold off in 1987, and right away took over the ratings. Today it dominates almost all of the popular program sections, consisting mostly of football, movies, series, and the annual Miss France contest. Privatization was a hotly discussed issue and connected to the fear of the Americanization of French culture and, here especially, the French language. In France, as in other large European countries, most foreign language programs are dubbed into French. Daily television usage in France has been increasing steadily, in 2004–05 clocking in at over 3 hours a day. In August 2005, TF1 held a 34.5 percent audience share, followed by the public stations F2 (18.8 percent) and F3 (14.7 percent).

France is also home to the arguably most successful European pay TV company, Canal+. It was launched in 1984 and has interests in France, Belgium, Spain, Scandinavia, and a host of co-owner business interests in media companies all over Europe. In France, Canal+ has more than 5.9 million subscribers, a 66 percent market share. It has also become an important production company in its own right. In second place is satellite TPS (Télévision Par Satellite), a joint venture between France Télévision, M6, TF1, France Telecom, and Lyonnaise Communication. Last but not least is the satellite company ABsat.

Programming is comparable to that in other European countries. Emphasis lies on the screening of local and Hollywood films, TV talk shows (many with a strong culture element), and, more recently, reality shows. One particularity can be observed in children's programming: in 2005, all top ten children's programs were animated ones. The top four were *Dora L'Exploratrice*, *Boule et Bill*, *Arthur*, and *Alien Bazar*. This is fitting when one remembers that together with Japan and Belgium, France has a very strong affinity not only for children's but also for adult animation.

GERMANY

With a population of over 80 million and a highly developed infrastructure, Germany is the second most important broadcasting market in the world after the United States.

Broadcast experiments were already taking place in Berlin in 1897. Beginning in the late stages of World War I, when Hans Bredow, generally considered the father of German broadcasting, experimented with music and lectures on the German western front, radio was used for relaying information. After the war it was used for postal and business purposes. This postal usage also explains the fact that, as in most other European nations, the post office had, at least for some time, authority over the airwaves. In 1920, a radio station near Berlin broadcast the first concert in Germany. Regular broadcasts began in 1923 in Berlin, with nine further regional broadcasting companies set up within the next year, among them the Westdeutsche Funkstunde AG (WEFAG). This would be the beginning of what today is the WDR, Germany's largest regional public broadcaster. Financing for these stations mostly came from business people and political parties, although the post office had a 51 percent share in all of them. Even then these stations carried commercials and relied on a license fee of two Reichsmarks. In 1926, Deutsche Welle GmbH was launched, which broadcast on a national level. From 1929 on, shortwave programs were sent out internationally, and an exchange with the American station NBC began.

Experimental television also had its beginnings in the late 1920s. Experimental broadcasts began in 1928, when still pictures were transmitted by wire to viewing booths in post offices. In 1930 motion pictures were transmitted on radio frequencies when radio was off the air.

When the Nazis came to power in 1933, all broadcasting was subsumed under government control. Josef Goebbels quickly understood how to utilize the power of broadcasting and launched a major offensive to equip all Germans with their own radio set, the *Volksempfänger* [People's Receiver]. The newly created national radio channel exercised strong censorship on news and even music. Weekly news programs were produced for cinemas and nascent television heavily promoted, for instance during the 1936 Olympics in Berlin, when large screens were set up in venues in the capital to broadcast the games.

In 1945 a defeated Germany was split up into the American, French, British, and Soviet zones. Every zone endeavored to emulate broadcasting structures from the home countries of the occupying forces. Thus, in the American zone, efforts were made to set up commercial TV, in the British zone the BBC model of public broadcasting was preferred, and in the French zone a centralized broadcasting system was envisaged. In the end, the three Western zones accepted a somewhat modified British system.

In the Soviet zone, a centralized broadcasting corporation (DFF) was run by the state. Radio broadcasts started in 1946. The first television program was aired in December 1952 on Stalin's birthday. However, most people in the German Democratic Republic (GDR) were eventually able to receive the more popular West German television. When the West German public broadcasting service began concerted broadcasting into the GDR in 1966, its uptake rate was immediately up to 60 percent.

In West Germany, radio broadcasts began in the late 1940s. As regards to TV, the first test picture was broadcast by the NWDR (North-West German Broadcasting Corporation) in 1950. In the first year the broadcasts lasted for two hours per day in the evening, but soon afternoon and early evening programming was added. The programming structure closely followed cinema programs (weekly news review, followed by a cultural segment and then the main film of the evening) and radio broadcasts (variety shows, advice columns, cultural shows). In 1954 the *Arbeitsgemeinschaft der öffentlich-rechtlichen Rundfunkanstalten der Bundesrepublik Deutschland* [Association of Public Broadcasting Corporations in West Germany] (ARD) was founded. It cocoordinated all regional television stations, allowing for exchanges of programs between the regional stations. Just as with print media, the freedom and independence of the ARD was guaranteed by Article 5 of the German Basic Law. However, the ARD had to adhere to the cultural norms of the state from which programs originated. Although the actual broadcast was regulated by federal broadcasting law, the actual programming content was decided by a body composed of representatives from significant groups of citizens, including educators, church administrators, local business people, and, last but not least, politicians. Its programming mainstay was the continuously popular news show *Tagesschau*. In 1963 the *Zweites deutsches Fernsehen* [Second German Television] (ZDF) began its broadcast, with the intention of providing a conservative counterbalance to the more liberal ARD. However, the public's hunger for more in television was not sated, and beginning in 1964 the German regional stations introduced their "third" channels.

After unification in 1989, the West German and East German broadcasting corporations were joined, and most of the GDR's broadcasting structure was subsumed under West German law. German federal states broadcast about three to five radio stations and also have at least one TV channel each. In 1992, ARTE was created, a French-German co-production. Another quasi-public station is 3SAT, a channel run by the ARD and ZDF, together with their counterparts from Switzerland (SRG) and Austria (ORF). Another public channel, Phoenix, broadcasts mostly documentaries, political discussions, and live coverage of sessions of the *Bundestag* (legislature). While there is one national public radio (Deutschlandfunk) and one international public radio and TV (Deutsche Welle), there are no national commercial radio stations in Germany.

As elsewhere in Europe, the German broadcasting market was liberalized in the 1980s. State-run television and radio, which had catered to the information and entertainment needs of the populace, had lost their monopoly. What had already been hinted at with the popularity of transnational radio, such as Radio Luxembourg and American Forces Network in the radio sector, had now become reality in the even more powerful medium of television.

Because commercial TV had irrevocably begun, the German government saw fit to incorporate several new laws into the broadcasting legislation. Following American, Scandinavian, and Dutch examples, cable companies had to reserve one or more channels for community broadcasting. Public access channels (PACs), or open channels, were defined as a forum for all kinds of audiovisual material, initiated and produced by people living within the broadcast range of its signals. A 1987 act further specified the running of PACs, providing funding from the existing licensing fees. Today, there exist over eighty different PACs in Germany.

Commercial radio has been a great success. Today there are more than 800 German commercial radio stations on the air. Viewer demographics suggest that their success is region-specific, however; commercial radio is strongest in Berlin (with over 70 percent of the audience tuning in) and generally in Northern Germany.

Commercial TV in Germany is largely in the hands of two media conglomerates: Springer (which owns Sat1 and PRO7 among others, and which is also Germany's largest press conglomerate), and Bertelsmann (RTL, RTL2, and others). The commercial stations RTL and Sat1 each reach about the same audience figures as the public ARD and ZDF (around 14 percent each).

GERMAN MEDIA ON THE WEB

The two public broadcasters ARD and ZDF are on line at http://www.ard.de (with newscasts from Hamburg) and http://www.zdf.de (from Mainz), respectively. The most popular commercial TV broadcaster is at http://www.rtl.de, followed by http://www.sat1.de. The largest regional TV broadcaster, from Cologne, is at http://www.wdr.de, while http:// www.rok-tv.de/home is the Website of a community TV channel from Rostock. Another regional station is http://www.tvnah.de. There is a commercial radio station at http://www.planetradio.de.

As a result of the proliferation of stations and the introduction of new program schedules, Germans today watch more TV than ever. In 2004 the average viewing time was about 203 minutes TV a day. In terms of leisure activities, TV is clearly the leader, with 89.1 percent watching it at least once a week. It is followed by radio (81.3 percent) and newspapers (78.5 percent). There are over eighty German channels available free to air (FTA) via satellite and cable. In 2004, 55.8 percent of German households were cabled, while satellite had an acceptance of 38.7 percent. Almost all broadcasts of foreign films are dubbed into German. On cable, however, dual channel transmissions allow one to choose whether to listen to the soundtrack in the original language or in German.

Popular entertainment programs in Germany are largely produced by commercial TV companies. Examples are *Die Ultimative Chart Show* [The Ultimate Chart Show], *Verstehen Sie Spass?* (similar to *Candid Camera*) and *Wer wird Millionär?* (similar to *Who Wants to Be a Millionaire*). However, when it comes to more serious programing—and here especially, made-for-TV films requiring large budgets—public TV continues to have the upper hand. Next to soccer and the screening of Hollywood blockbusters, these made-for-TV shows regularly receive the highest ratings.

Germany is also home to one pay TV company, Premiere. After a troubled past, it now has new owners, and in September 2005 it began the first German HDTV broadcasts. In the same year it also successfully bid for the transmission rights to the German soccer league. As in Britain, Italy, France, and other large European media markets, football is viewed as the prime lead-in to pay TV subscriptions.

Digitalization has also made a large impact on Germany. The government announced that by 2010 all analog signals would cease and only digital ones would remain on the air. In addition, digitalization has allowed the newest broadcasting trend, digital terrestrial broadcasting, to become a commercial fact.

Although all these new formats might have a dizzying effect on the German consumer, the biggest threat to TV at the moment has to be the Internet. In 2004 69 percent of Germans in the more prosperous southwest of the country made use of the Internet, up from only 14 percent in 1998.

HUNGARY

Broadcasting has a long history in Hungary. Already in 1893 a contraption was in use for which the rest of the world would have to wait quite a bit longer: the *Telefon Hirmondó*. In order to understand its revolutionary impact, one has to remember that the invention of the telephone was actually the beginning of broadcasting. Telefon Hirmondó established a service in Budapest that would enable its subscribers to listen to the latest news or an opera from the local concert hall in their own living rooms. Its inventor, Tivadar Puskás, had created a dissemination device that was available on a continuous basis for over 12 hours a day.

Several "news readers" would take turns reading the news, stock market reports would be broadcast three times a day, and sessions from the Hungarian parliament analyzed. Authors would read from their works, and other entertainment items would be sent out to a subscriber base of an amazing 6,200 people (in 1901) across Budapest. While there had been similar transmissions from the opera in 1890 in Paris, Hirmondó was the first station inventing the transmission formats that would later be used by almost all radio stations worldwide. The service continued until 1926, when it was beaten out by radio.

Radio services were introduced in Hungary in 1925. The first station was owned by the Hungarian Telephone-Journal and Radio Company. It continued its broadcasts even during World War II. Shortly after the war, a second channel was added.

HUNGARIAN MEDIA ON THE WEB

The public broadcaster MTV is on line at http://www.mtv.hu, and two commercial stations are at http://www.tv2.hu and http://www.online.rtlklub.hu.

Hungarian public radio broadcasts from four national stations (Kossuth, Petofi, Bartók, and the external service Radio Budapest) and several regional ones can be heard at http://www.english.radio.hu. Commercial stations can be found at http://www.danubius.hu and http://www.slagerradio.hu, the latter of which is owned by the Emmis group.

During the 1956 revolution the first skirmishes took place in front of the Hungarian radio building, on the front of which was displayed "Free Radio Kossuth"—the name of one of the radio channels. Unfortunately, it would not be able to live up to this name. Television was launched in Hungary in 1957, broadcasting a variety of theatrical programs, folk dancing, and musical shows. A second state TV channel was launched in 1968, and color TV became available in 1976.

Since the early 1970s, there existed three national radio channels and two TV channels. Television and radio were later on split into two separate state entities. The new Magyar Televízió [Hungarian Television] (MTV) enjoyed a monopoly until the late 1980s. During the second half of the 1980s, two commercial radio channels were introduced. After the collapse of the Soviet bloc, public broadcasting was turned into a stock company, but it remained wholly state-owned. As of 2006, MTV is financed by a license fee, but it also carries advertising. The first satellite TV channel was launched in 1996, followed by national commercial TV in 1997. Broadcasts such as RTL Klub's *Heti Hetes* [Weekly Seven], in which seven public personalities discussed weekly political events in rather irreverent tones, were a welcome phenomenon for Hungarian viewers. Recently, as everywhere else, *Big Brother* proved to be a big local success, eclipsed only by the national ratings topper, RTL Klub's soap *Barátok közt* [Between Friends], which regularly draws up to 65 percent of the 18-to 49-year-old audience group. Unlike in other former Eastern bloc countries, the new broadcasting regulatory body, ORTT, does flex its muscles and gives out fines for offenses. The now defunct commercial station TV3 was forced to stay off the air for a whole day at one occasion for violations of the broadcasting laws.

Today, there exist three terrestrial television networks: MTV, the public broadcasting channel, with two channels; commercial TV2; and RTL Klub. Cable penetration is around 45 percent, and there are numerous commercial channels available via cable or satellite. In 1992, a third public channel was launched, Duna TV. It addresses itself mostly to Hungarians living abroad and can be received via satellite. Audience preferences, however, lie with the commercial stations. In 2003 the audience numbers were as follows: The three public channels (M1, M2, and Duna) received only 17 percent of audience share, compared to commercial TV2's 31.2 percent and commercial RTL Klub's market-leading 31.5 percent.

Radio has also greatly profited from deregulation. The three public radio stations now have to compete with two large, successful, and foreign-owned national commercial stations, while a host of commercial local and regional stations are also seeking a share in the market.

ITALY

Italian broadcasting began in 1924, when the government-controlled URI was formed. After being renamed EIAR in 1927, its name was changed once again to Rai in 1944. Rai would remain the only legal broadcaster until 1976.

In 1950 Rai broadcast three national radio channels. Television transmissions began in 1954. At first the programs would be watched mostly in bars until TV sets became slightly more affordable. TV quickly established itself as a national medium, surpassing newspaper uptake with ease. This trend continues even today, with advertising revenues twice as high for TV as for the print media.

The second national channel, Rai2, began broadcasts in 1961, and a third, region-based network was inaugurated in 1979. In 1975, the Italian government paved the way for commercial television. From a European perspective, this was very early. What the government had not expected, however, was the explosion that happened next. Within a few years, over 600 television stations and more than 2,500 radio stations went on the air. Since then, the situation has become less frantic. Today, there are over 800 local commercial TV stations and more than 1300 radio stations in Italy. In order for commercial TV stations to keep their broadcasting licenses, they have to send at least a small amount of news programs.

In the early 1980s powerful businessmen established four national commercial broadcast networks. Silvio Berlusconi, who would become Italian Premier in 1994, was one of them. After some transactions throughout the 1980s, the 1990 Broadcasting Act unified the by then three commercial networks into Berlusconi's Fininvest company, but it also granted Rai continuous possession of its three national channels and the right to go on collecting license fees, which still form about 60 percent of its financial base. Both networks were allowed to air advertisements, whose length would take up no more than 15 percent of the daily transmission time and no more than 18 percent of the hourly transmission time, a rather generous amount. According to an EU directive, 50 percent of the programs aired were to be European-made, and of these, again 50 percent of local origin. This last provision proved to be a boon for Italian production companies. Italian series and miniseries became some of the favorite transmissions. Public TV has been successful in maintaining Italian heritage through Italian music, dance, and high- and lowbrow Italian TV series. Italy also has its very own kind of miniseries, usually in four to eight parts, often based on novels or conceived as a televisual continuation of printed photo stories. Commercial TV broadcasts those as well, together with large doses of sports (soccer) and American fiction. Ever since the days of Italian emigration to the United States, America has had a special place deeply rooted in Italian fantastic imaginary. Therefore audience figures are very high for such American media products, especially when linked to

"Italian" themes. In terms of factual and more highbrow entertainment, the public Rai stations continue to enjoy viewer support. Shows such as the daily current events program *Batti e Ribatti* [Strike and Counterstrike] continue to keep Rai's ratings and reputation intact.

Satellite penetration is very high in Italy, but cable still remains a negligible quantity. Pay TV does exist and is broadcast either via satellite or terrestrially. Unlike the practice in smaller countries and much of Northern Europe, foreign language programs are dubbed in Italian.

LUXEMBOURG MEDIA ON THE WEB

RTL Lëtzebuerg, RTL's domestic network, is on line at http://rtl.lu. A commercial radio station, Den Neien Radio, can be found at www.dnr.lu, and public cultural radio at www.100komma7.lu.

Staying with its reputation as one of the forerunners in all things TV, Italy was the first European country to introduce digital television. Since November 1995 direct-to-home (DTH) digital satellite broadcasts were aired from the three existing pay TV channels. In 2003, Telepiù and the other smaller pay TV provider Stream fused to form Sky Italia.

The average viewing time in Italy is around 4 hours a day, very much on the high side when compared to other European countries. In terms of audience share, the three public channels are at the low 40 percent mark, followed by the commercial Canale 5 in the mid-twenties, the commercial Italia 1 in the lower teens, and the pay TV Rete 4 with 10 percent.

LUXEMBOURG

Although Luxembourg is one of the smallest countries in Europe, with less than half a million inhabitants, it has had a tremendous influence on European broadcasting. The reasons for this are twofold: CLT and SES.

Broadcasting began at the end of the 1920s with French capital. After World War II, the Compagnie Luxembourgeoise de Télédiffusion (CLT, Luxembourg Broadcasting Company) broadcast into France, as Luxembourg broadcasting laws were much more liberal than French laws were. The station was funded by French and Belgian publisher money, but German media group Bertelsmann has since become the major stakeholder. From the onset, CLT's radio programs were broadcast in various languages into Germany, Switzerland, England, France and a host of surrounding countries. Due to the fact that it was not government-regulated, it was able to offer all the good aspects of a commercial service that a deeply regulated European audience craved.

However, the people in Luxembourg themselves did not profit much from this arrangement. It took until the end of the 1970s for RTL, as the broadcasting arm of CLT was called, to air a few hours in Letzeburgesch. And it took even longer for RTL Lëtzebuerg to be established as a local-language TV station.

CLT itself feared for its market when in 1984 the Luxembourg government wanted to sponsor TV programs via satellite, mostly funded by American money. There was a sharp outcry from RTL as well as from other European governments. Eventually, an indigenous company was formed, the Société Européenne des Satellites (SES, European Satellite Company). It launched its first satellite in 1988. Today, it owns twelve satellites, had a €1.1 billion turnover in 2004, and, together with Paris based Eutelsat (2003–04 turnover: €760 million, over twenty satellites), constitutes the duopoly of satellite broadcasters in Europe.

In 1990, CLT's monopoly was abolished, paving the way for legalizing at least some of the pirate radio stations to which many people listened. In order to fight the pirates, some of them were given licenses, and thus another twelve legal local radio stations were established. However, in a country as small as Luxembourg, sustained economic development for these stations might be hard to achieve.

THE NETHERLANDS

Broadcasting started in the 1920s in the Netherlands, when the electric goods company Philips started taking an interest in broadcasting amateurs. From 1930 onwards the government regulated who was allowed to broadcast. A very unique Dutch system of broadcasting began. The ones chosen were those considered to be "pillars" (*zuil*) of Dutch society: the Socialists, the liberal bourgeoisie, the Catholics, and the Protestants. This system continued on after World War II and was then also extended to TV broadcasting, which began in 1955. Today, the system is equally liberal: with a certain number of signatures, one can start one's own licensed TV channel. The organization allowing for such broadcasts is Omroep. It is member-run and nonprofit. Thus, there are a large number of broadcasting organizations catering to minority audiences, such as a Buddhist broadcaster, an environmentalist one, a secular humanist one, a Dutch-Jewish broadcaster, an Islamic broadcaster, a channel for the 50+ generation, a Frisian one (the second official language in the Netherlands), and many more.

Starting with the 1969 Broadcasting Act, some advertising was allowed for the first time on the public broadcasting channels. A more neutral regulating body was also set up, the Dutch Broadcasting Foundation (NOS), which later on allowed stations such as the ex-pirate radio broadcaster Veronica to broadcast. The first broadcast company not bound to one of the "pillars" was TROS; it commenced broadcasts in 1969.

The 1988 Media Act specified that public channels had to adhere to the following programming percentages: 25 percent information, 20 percent culture, 25 percent entertainment, and 5 percent education. The formula was slightly changed on a number of occasions, but the main ingredients remain the same. This kind of quality programming was intended to set the public broadcasters apart from the proliferating commercial channels. It was also used to justify the levied license fees. In 1988–89 the commercial RTL Veronique (later renamed RTL4) began broadcasting from Luxembourg, followed in 1993 by RTL5.

Today there are three national public channels, with the pillars providing the programming via a complex timing formula. The license fee provides the majority of funding. There also exist eight national commercial channels and about 120 local channels, including community channels. In radio there exist five national channels, nine nationwide commercial channels, and about 470 local stations. The cable system in the Netherlands is very developed. The high population density lent itself to profitable cabling, which had started already in the 1970s, reaching a market penetration of about 90 percent today.

As everywhere else in Europe, the time the Dutch spend watching TV is increasing. In 1988 the average Dutch viewer spent 124 minutes per day in front of the TV set; in 2004 the time had increased to 192 minutes. RTL4 is the most popular station (24 percent market share), followed by the three national public channels (a combined 36 percent).

Since about 1995, Dutch programming has been able to set trends rather than follow them. To a large part this is due to the worldwide domination of Endemol, John de Mol's production company, which gave the world hits such as the reality show *Big Brother* and other "leisure entertainment" shows such as *Changing Rooms* and *Ready, Steady, Cook*. The TV soap *Goede Tijden, Slechte Tijden* [Good Times, Bad Times], Europe's first daily soap, has been a ratings hit since its inception in 1990, easily beating the screening of Hollywood films on a regular basis. As many other Dutch formats, *Goede Tijden, Slechte Tijden* was sold to German TV and has had a very successful run there as well.

NORWEGIAN MEDIA ON THE WEB

The Norwegian national public broadcasting service can be found on line at http://www.nrk.no/. The commercial national terrestrial TV service is at http://pub.tv2.no, and the commercial satellite TV channel TV3 is at http://www.tv3.no. A commercial national radio station is at http://www.kanal24.no.

Radio is also very popular in The Netherlands. Just as in TV, the public broadcasters, which used to have a 70 percent market share, now only garner 44 percent of the market and slightly lag behind the commercial stations (49 percent).

NORWAY

Radio broadcasting began in the early 1930s in Norway on a public-broadcasting basis. After World War II, television was introduced on an experimental basis, but a full-fledged program did not go on the air until 1960, a very late start indeed. Intense discussions on the value of TV and the possibility of television undermining national ethics and culture preceded the launch. Although such discussions were also held in most other European countries, Norwegian public opinion against TV was particularly strong and mostly based on fears that TV would lead to an American-style consumerism. Eventually, the public-broadcasting status of the envisaged TV broadcaster was confirmed by law, and Norsk Riksringkasting (NRK, Nordic Imperial Broadcasting) commenced transmissions. A second TV channel was started in 1996. Today, NRK operates three radio channels and two TV channels, mostly funded by a license fee.

In 1980 the public broadcaster lost its monopoly and new stations appeared. In 1988 commercial radio stations were for the first time allowed to broadcast advertising. In the same year, a Norwegian consortium began broadcasting the channel TVN, and Swedish commercial broadcaster Kinnevik broadcast a Norwegian-language channel, TV3, via satellite. Transmissions of the latter station originated from London, as British broadcasting law was and remains more liberal than its Norwegian counterpart. In 1992 the first national terrestrial commercial channel began its broadcasts. In terms of market share, the public broadcasting service still has the advantage with a rating of just under 50 percent. Local radio stations also thrived with deregulation. Currently, there exist several hundred of them.

Every year at the *Gullruten* (the Norwegian version of the Emmy Awards), the best TV shows are crowned. In 2005 the winning entertainment program was *Idol 2005* (Norway's version of *Pop Idol*), the best reality show was *71 grader Nord* [71 Degrees North], the best docusoap *Canada på tvers* [Across Canada], and the best humor programm *Nytt på Nytt*. The latter is the Norwegian version of the British comedy/current events show *Have I Got News for You*. It has been on the air since 1999 and has advanced to become one of the most popular Norwegian TV programs ever.

SPANISH MEDIA ON THE WEB

Radiotelevisión Española (RTVE), Spain's public radio and television broadcasting corporation, including numerous TV and radio channels, can be found on the Web at http://www.rtve.es/. Tele 5, the largest national commercial TV station, is at http://www.telecinco.es, while pay TV channels and cable are at http://www.sogecable.com. A Catalan TV station from Barcelona is at http://www.tvcatalunya.com.

Commercial radio stations are at http://www.ondacero.es and http://www.radioatlantico.com, the latter being on Gran Canaria, Canary Islands.

SPAIN

Radio broadcasts began in 1923, when Radio Ibérica began transmitting from Madrid. Soon other stations followed in Barcelona, Seville, and the Canary Islands. From 1939 to 1975, the year of Franco's death, Spain was a dictatorship. This had important repercussions for its national mediascapes. Although conditions got better towards the end of the 1960s, censorship was the rule, freedom of speech practically nonexistent. After the end of the dictatorship it was therefore important that newscasts quickly became politically independent. This happened in 1977, when the government ended its requirement for all stations to read the government news on their channels.

Television broadcasts started in 1956 as a state monopoly and closely regulated by the government. A second government channel was launched in 1965. Television in Spain, just as in other Mediterranean countries, is the main source of entertainment, but also of information. Spain has the second highest European per diem TV viewing rate (after Britain) at over 4 hours a day.

The state monopoly of Televisión Española (TVE) completely ended in 1988, with the passing of the Private Television Law. By 1989, three commercial stations were on the air. As Spain consists of politically autonomous and linguistically differentiated regions such as the Basque country, Catalonia, and the Balearic and Canary Islands, the public broadcaster had to provide separate channels for them as well. As there are no license fees, Radiotelevisión Española (RTVE) and its radio counterpart (RNE) must finance themselves wholly by advertising; a small state subsidy to make up for low advertising revenues does not account for much. Another national radio broadcasting network already in existence under Franco is the Catholic Church–governed COPE network with more than eighty stations.

By the end of 1998, thirty-eight licenses had been awarded for digital cable telecommunication services. The two main players have been Telecom Italia and Cableuropa. In 2003, Vía Digital and Canal Satélite Digital became Digital +. A further change happened in 2005 when the leading pay TV provider in Spain combined its channels into one pay TV network and opened a new FTA, Cuatro. Digital terrestrial TV had a rough start in Spain, with pay TV operator Quiero forced to close down in 2002.

Another important Spanish media group is PRISA. It owns the most important local TV network in Spain, Localia. In radio, it is the owner of the leading commercial radio network, Cadena SER, which operates six radio channels with a combined daily audience of about 10 million listeners. It also has interests in Spanish speaking areas and countries in the Americas.

Since the 1990s at the latest, Spain has adopted many globally successful programs such as *Trato Hecho* [Let's Make a Deal] and *El Precio Justo* [The Price is Right]. Other popular formats proved to be dating shows such as *Uno para todas* [Man O Man], and *Ay mi Madre* [Mother Knows Best]. More recently, the Latin American soap opera format called the *telenovela* (basically a soap opera with a finishing date) has gripped the world. Naturally, because of its linguistic proximity, Spain has been a testing ground for *telenovelas* for the rest of Europe. In 2005 the adaptation of the successful Colombian *telenovela El Autentico Rodrigo*

Leal [Finding Rodrigo] and the Spanish version of the German police series *Niedrig und Kuhnt*, titled *Suarez y Mariscal: Caso cerrado*, proved to be ratings winners. Likewise, as with many other countries in Europe, cooking shows such as the 2004 Spanish production *Karlos Arguiñano en tu cocina* [Karlos Arguiñano in Your Kitchen] have lately proven to be very popular as well.

A peculiarity of Spanish TV is the so called "contra-programming": a station simply does not release any information on what it is going to broadcast during a certain time slot. While this is quite a fanciful and popular idea, advertisers are for the most part not amused.

Today there exists a deep funding crisis in Spanish public broadcasting, as government funding is drying up. However, the audience is not completely defecting to commercial TV. Rather, it is evenly split between commercial and public broadcasters. In 2003, the first and second public broadcasters achieved an audience share of 30.6 percent, whereas the two biggest commercial stations, Tele 5 and Antena 3, achieved a combined 30.9 percent. Overall, there exist two national public TV channels, three national commercial ones, and a host of cable, satellite, regional, and local channels. There are also over 800 commercial radio stations available.

UNITED KINGDOM

The United Kingdom is the second largest media market in Europe after Germany. In terms of media production and media concentration, London is the biggest player in all of Europe.

The history of broadcasting in the United Kingdom is also the history of what is arguably the best known broadcaster in the world—the British Broadcasting Corporation (BBC). Broadcasting began around the turn of the twentieth century, when Guglielmo Marconi experimented with radio broadcasting, first connecting the United Kingdom and France (1899), and then Europe with the American continent (1901). The BBC was founded in 1922 and right away levied a broadcasting receiver fee on its listeners. From 1924 onward it used the Big Ben daily time signal in its broadcasts. In 1926 it became a staple in the British media diet during the general strike, when it went on the air five times a day. In 1929 it made its first experimental TV transmission. While experimental transmissions were continued throughout the 1930s, from 1939 on they were abandoned because of World War II and resumed only in 1946. Regular TV broadcasts did not start until 1955. In the same year, Europe's first commercial TV station, ITV, went on the air in England. BBC 2 started in 1964.

The 1960s also saw the rise of "pirate" radio stations, broadcasting from offshore into Britain. The most famous of these was Radio Caroline. It ceased broadcasts from 1967 to 1972, but then returned. Today, it has become a legal satellite and Internet broadcaster.

Legal commercial radio broadcasting commenced in 1973 with London's LBC and Capital Radio. Channel 4, the second commercial TV station, began in 1982. In the late 1980s, two satellite networks also entered the market, Sky Television and British Satellite Broadcasting. Sky was more successful and soon took over its rival. Radio Luxembourg also tried to enter the British satellite market, but it did not succeed and consequently closed its satellite broadcasts in 1991. Finally, commercial national terrestrial Channel 5 began broadcasts in 1997.

Today, media continue to thrive in the UK. The BBC continues to broadcast several channels, adding more as it avails itself of digital technology and also embraces the Internet. ITV has launched a digital service, and Sky TV is one of the global leaders in satellite TV. The British audience watches the most TV in all of Europe, for over 4 hours a day, and long-running soaps such as *Eastenders* (BBC1) and *Coronation Street* (airing uninterrupted

UK MEDIA ON THE WEB

BBC, the UK's national public broadcaster, with multiple TV and radio channels, can be found online at http://www.bbc.co.uk. Radio's BBC World Service is arguably the best-known (English-language) radio news channel in the world. BBC World is the BBC's commercially funded 24-hour TV news channel on its way to matching the radio service's fame.

The national commercial broadcaster ITV is at http://www.itv.com; its station on the isle of Jersey is at http://www.channeltv.co.uk.

Sky TV, the pay TV digital satellite network, is at http://www.sky.com.

One of the most popular radio stations, started by entrepreneur Richard Branson, is at http://www.virginradio.co.uk. A national commercial radio station transmitting classical music is at http://www.classicfm.co.uk. The most famous of the former pirate stations is at http://www.radiocaroline.co.uk.

On the Channel Islands, Guernsey radio is at http://www.islandfm.com, and Jersey radio is at http://www.channel103.com. A commercial radio broadcaster on the Isle of Man is at http://www.manxradio.com.

The Gibraltar Broadcasting Corporation, public radio and TV broadcaster in Gibraltar, is at http://www.gbc.gi, and the British Forces Broadcasting Service (BFBS) for Gibraltar can be found at http://www.ssvc.com/bfbs/radio/gibraltar/.

on commercial ITV since the mid-1950s) have achieved broadcasting fame. In terms of the most watched shows, ITV is clearly the leader, continuing to sweep the ratings, except for the BBC's *Eastenders*. The Australian soap *Neighbours* has also been popular for a long time. Besides the Hollywood block-busters, other popular shows are *Who Wants to Be a Millionaire?*, any and all soccer matches, home improvement shows, gardening *(Ground Force)* and cooking shows *(Ready, Steady, Cook)*. One particularly strong feature of British television are its comedies. On TV, they go back to the 1950s and 1960s, but are still going strong today. Recent hits include *Father Ted*, *The Kumars at Number 42*, *Absolutely Fabulous*, *The Royle Family*, and many others. One particularly successful show is the BBC-produced *Have I Got News for You*, a review of weekly political/cultural events in the form of a comical quiz show with invited and regular guests matching wits and slightly reminiscent of the Weekend Update on the American *Saturday Night Live* show.

Largely thanks to the BBC, radio is an important part of British media landscape. BBC Radio 4 is home to the longest running radio soap opera, *The Archers*. It started as a pilot in the Midlands during Easter 1950. Today it is available countrywide, airing six times a week.

Despite the overwhelming presence of the BBC, commercial radio is also doing well, with over 600 legal stations and a host of illegal ones on the air.

OTHER BRITISH EUROPEAN TERRITORIES

The Channel Islands (Alderney, Guernsey, Herm, Jersey, Sark and others)

The Channel Islands hold a special legal status because they are generally thought to be part of the British Isles but not of the Europe Union. There is one commercial TV station on the islands, Channel TV, which is part of the ITV network and broadcasts mainly from Jersey. A commercial radio station, Channel 103FM, is also located in Jersey. Finally, the BBC maintains a studio in Jersey, whereas a commercial radio station, Island FM, operates from Guernsey.

Isle of Man

There are currently four analog television stations broadcasting on the Isle of Man over the terrestrial network. They are BBC North West, BBC2, ITV Borders, and Channel 4. Currently, there are three local radio stations: Manx Radio, Energy FM, and 3FM.

Gibraltar

PAN-EUROPEAN BROADCASTERS ON THE WEB

The European Union's Europe by Satellite can be found on line at http://ebs.net, whereas the EU's TV News channel can be found at http://www.euronews.net and the sports channel at http://www.eurosport.net.

Arte, a German–French channel, has its home page at http://www.arte-tv.com/fr/70.html, whereas http://www.3Sat.de represents a co-production of German, Austrian. and Swiss public broadcasters.

Radio Free Europe/ Radio Liberty lives on at http://www.rferl.org.

Gibraltar is another special case. It is considered to be part of the European Territories of the United Kingdom and is served by the two radio channels of the British Forces Broadcasting Service (BFBS) and by one public broadcaster, the Gibraltar Broadcasting Corporation (GBC), which offers radio and TV services. Its format is similar to commercial local radio stations in the United Kingdom.

PAN-EUROPEAN STATIONS

Besides national European broadcasters, there also exist a number of stations whose broadcasts transcend borders. These pan-European stations address audiences in various parts of Europe or even the whole of Europe. Already from the 1950s onwards, pirate stations and "border blasters" targeted audiences across national borders, legally or illegally. A genuine pan-European approach has only been in effect since satellite broadcasts began in the 1980s.

One organization targeting such transborder audiences in Europe is the EU itself. It operates a Europe by Satellite (EbS) service, broadcasting live from EU sessions in Strasbourg and disseminating other informational programs. Two other very successful EU initiatives are the Eurosport and Euronews channels.

There are also various Armed Forces Services. Arguably the most famous one is AFN, American Forces Network. It began broadcasting from a London basement in 1943, and its European base is nowadays found in Frankfurt, Germany. AFN has influenced the musical tastes of several generations of Europeans.

One more American channel, with a long and somewhat controversial history, is Radio Free Europe/Radio Liberty. It was established in 1949 as a nonprofit, private corporation to broadcast Western ideals to the Eastern bloc. Radio Liberty, established in 1951, had the same remit but was directed toward the Soviet Union. Until 1971 both stations were funded by the American Congress via the CIA and through private donations. They were fused in 1975.

Lastly, there are religious broadcasters. Especially since the fall of the Berlin Wall, several evangelical organizations have begun targeting mainly Eastern European audiences. While their zeal is boundless, in broadcasting terms their impact remains negligible.

NEW MEDIA AND THE OUTLOOK FOR THE FUTURE

Broadcasting media are a booming market throughout Europe. Pay TV is especially set to make major inroads, with 100 million pay TV homes expected in Western Europe by 2010. Already worth more than €20 billion in Western Europe, it will more than double this figure by 2008. Digital TV will be the technology of choice, with 99 million homes equipped to receive digital signals by 2010.

In both dissemination standards and programming, pay TV is the industry's avant-garde. Regular HDTV programming was introduced by the German pay TV channel Premiere in September 2005. First-run films and major sports events are almost exclusively found on pay TV, unless these events are deemed of "national importance." An example for such a case is the All England Lawn Tennis Championships at Wimbledon, which have received this label in the United Kingdom and is carried by the BBC.

Industry analysts expect video on demand (VOD) to be the largest growth segment in the near future, thereby switching the emphasis from individual channels to individual programs. Similar claims can be made by the personalized video recorder (PVR), which is in the process of gaining the upper hand over both VHS and DVD players. Its advantage is the ease with which it can be operated and its ability to cut out advertising during the recording process.

Radio seems set to continue prospering in both its public and commercial guises. There is a wide consensus that the basic structure of radio is likely to continue unchanged. Radio did make it onto the satellite platform, with over 600 channels available free to air. Furthermore, technological advances continue to improve its quality. Digital audio broadcasting (DAB) has been available in Europe since the mid-1990s, and Digital Radio Mondiale (DRM) is set to revolutionize the almost forgotten short-wave and medium-wave bands. Another innovation likely to expand in the future is Radio Data Service (RDS). It is a way of adding information in digital form to FM transmissions. The advantage over conventional radio is that it tunes to a program identification signal rather than to a frequency. It can also transmit song titles at the same time as the songs themselves and can stream news or traffic information.

Radio is furthermore able to take on the aura of a very local provider. Nowadays many European stations are located in the centers of towns and cities, with passers-by able to quickly cast a glance through "their" station window. This feeling of immediacy cannot be matched by TV, mainly due to its need for a much larger technological apparatus.

A crucial point for the future concerns the convergence of digital media. This trend will perhaps have the strongest consequences for the European mediascape. With the advent of computers and the Internet in the 1990s, all kinds of data can now be equally rendered in a single environment. On the consumer front, new software that allows the computer to be used as the centerpiece for home entertainment units only further exemplifies this trend of convergence between the classical broadcast media and the Internet.

If at one time electronic media were discussed on a national level, this soon gave way to a discussion of media in a European context; nowadays the discussion decidedly veers towards a global broadcasting perspective. And yet specificities abound. Because of the abundance of media, a trend toward what has been called "glocalization" can be observed: while individuals consume a distinct menu of differing media outlets and media contents, they may originate from very far away and very near at the same time. A hungry person in Paris may search for a recipe on an Australian Web page and at the same time browse the menu of a café around the corner.

National and linguistic borders, for the longest time guarantors of mechanisms of mass medial exclusion and inclusion, have been broken up and do not any more play the very important role in broadcasting they used to. Again, the Internet has arguably had the strongest impact, since it allows for cheaper broadcasting than radio and TV. Indeed, according to recent research, heavy Internet users tend to watch up to one-third less TV than non-Internet users. However, the cable operators have begun to claw back customers by offering their medium through high-speed access. They view digital TV as a way to attract customers to a triplet of services that includes TV, telephony, and high-speed Internet.

The Internet also serves as an extension of what has been called the "prosumer" trend, the convergence of the producer with the consumer. It is wholly and instantaneously interactive. While national broadcasters allowed for experimental attempts by individuals to broadcast their own materials through Open Channels or Public Access Channels, consumers have now firmly taken the production and dissemination of their own material into their own hands. Perhaps this also explains why so many people flock to such new services and why the older, less mobile broadcasting companies encounter difficulties in keeping up.

But while extolling the virtues of new media, one has to be careful not to overlook the social differences still in existence. Even in fairly homogeneous Europe, these continue to inform media access and usage. In most EU countries, less than half of households had home access to the Internet in 2002. The highest household Internet access was reported by Denmark (56 percent) and the United Kingdom (50 percent), whereas in Spain 17 percent, in Portugal 16 percent, and in Greece less than 10 percent of households had home Internet access. Households with dependent children reported much higher Internet access rates than those with no dependent children. Broadly speaking then, the more affluent north of the continent is on the forefront of Internet use, whereas Eastern and Southern Europe are lagging behind. Generally, the newer media are also the domain of the younger generation. In 2003, for the first time, more German 14-year-olds were Internet users than were not.

Lastly, the Internet bills itself as a decentralized and nonhierarchical space and it therefore lends itself much better than traditional broadcasting media to a mode of resistance to the existing political, economic, and cultural status quo. For better or worse, this "repurposing" of technology has advanced discussions about copyrights and media access more than any other technology of recent times has been able to accomplish. And it continues to invent ways in which to challenge the traditional media; for instance through blogging, which is challenging the print media, and through podcasting, which may pose a threat to radio.

CONCLUSIONS

As this survey of European broadcasting media has shown, it is virtually impossible to draw together a unifying interpretative strand when confronted with the present-day plethora of rapidly changing media phenomena. However, this might already be an important insight in itself.

The abundance of different media (print, private and public radio and television, the Internet, etc.) already points to the fact that the producers as well as the audiences are on the one hand becoming more and more heterogeneous, while on the other the difference between producer and consumer becomes less pronounced. This development had already begun early on with the photographic camera, continued then with video cameras, then computer printers, and is now best symbolized by podcasting and blogging. As historical and present-day experience with all media reveals, the "hype" surrounding new media needs to be moderated. Every new technology requires sacrifices from older technologies: with the invention of the printing press the public scribes became fewer, with the invention of photography the portrait painters fell on hard times, radio had newspapers worried, the cinema threatened the stage, TV in turn threatened cinemas, and the Internet nowadays worries all of the above. But new media tend to get superseded by the next technological advance and die a slow death on the ever increasing scrap heap of old media technology.

By the same token, the fact that the world is rapidly moving towards a globalized media market once again raises the question of who controls the media. Especially in TV there exist few but large major players, and media concentration continues to increase. In a global market dominated by only a handful of players, programs will increasingly look and sound alike, constituting a uniform stream of information. Strong national public broadcasters and careful policymaking by the EU can help to ensure that local content can still be seen and heard. In general, the dual system of commercial and public broadcasting has worked quite well for Europe. Most governments' (and now the EU's) insistence on leveling a license fee to support public broadcasting has allowed for quality programs to be created and aired on a large scale. And while the fees can be quite hefty, in comparison to other leisure activities they are still rather good value for the money. Private enterprises have led the market with innovations and continue to do so, thereby fulfilling their audiences' entertainment needs.

NOTE ON THE STATISTICS IN THIS CHAPTER

As the broadcasting markets deal in perishable goods (i.e., mostly news and *Zeitgeist*), they are also very volatile markets. Data permitting, this chapter endeavors to present a picture of the European broadcasting landscape in 2005. Likewise, numbers for radio and TV channels in the individual markets are bound to change quickly. It is hoped, however, that in particular the Web resources provided in the sidebars and the Resource Guide will help the reader to receive more up-to-date information than this chapter might be able to provide.

GLOSSARY/ABBREVIATIONS

AM	Amplitude modulation, a technique for imposing an audio signal on a radio wave by varying the power output of a transmitter
DAB	Digital audio broadcasting, digital radio FM broadcasting standard
DRM	Digital Radio Mondiale, short-wave and medium-wave digital broadcasting standard
DTH	Direct-to-home satellite TV
DVB-T	Digital video broadcasting, terrestrial, a newer mode of broadcasting digital signals on a local level via land-based antennas; also known as digital terrestrial television (DTT)
FM	Frequency modulation, A technique for imposing an audio signal on a radio wave by varying the frequency of the wave
FTA	Free to air, satellite channels broadcast free of charge
Fiction	Made-for-TV films and feature films
HDTV	High-definition television, new digital TV broadcasting standard
NTSC, PAL, SECAM	Older color TV broadcasting standards. North America in general uses NTSC, and the rest of the world PAL and SECAM.

Pay TV	A TV channel or a package of channels (usually satellite or cable) for which a charge is levied.
PVR	Personalized video recorder
RDS	Radio Data System, a way to impose digital text on emitted radio signals carrying audio; in use since the 1990s.
VOD	Video-on-demand

RESOURCE GUIDE

PRINTED SOURCES

Allen, Robert C., and Annette Hill, eds. *The Television Studies Reader*. London: Routledge, 2003.

Bondeberg, Ib, and Francisco Bono, eds. *Television in Scandinavia*. Luton: University of Luton Press, 1996.

Briel, Holger. "The Media of Mass Communication: the Press, Radio and Television." Pp. 322–338 in Eva Kolinsky and Wilfried van der Will (eds.), *The Cambridge Companion to Modern German Culture*. Cambridge, UK: Cambridge University Press, 1998.

Chapman, Robin. *Selling the Sixties: Pirates and Pop Music Radio*. London: Routledge, 1992.

Crisell, Andrew. *An Introductory History of British Broadcasting*. London: Routledge, 2002.

Faulstich, Werner. *Grundwissen Medien*. Stuttgart: UTB, 2004. One of the main texts on German Media, in German.

Hoffmann-Riem, Wolfgang. *Regulating Media: the Licensing and Supervision of Broadcasting in Six Countries*. Guildford, UK: Guilford Press, 1996.

Humphreys, Peter J. *Media and Media Policy in Germany*. Oxford: Berg, 1994. An excellent overview of the changes in the mediascape, looking at the legal and political wrangling over privatization in the 1980s and the effects German unification had on it.

Jarren, Otfried, Rolf H. Weber, Patrick Donges, Bianka Dörr, Matthias Künzler, and Manuel Puppis. *Rundfunkregulierung: Leitbilder, Modelle und Erfahrungen im internationalen Vergleich*. Zürich: Seismo, 2002.

Kelly, Mary, Gianpietro Mazzoleni, and Denis McQuail. *The Media in Europe: The Euromedia Handbook*. London: Sage, 2003.

Padovani, Cinzia. *A Fatal Attraction: Public Television and Politics in Italy*. Lanham, MD: Rowman and Littlefield, 2004.

Papathanassopoulos, Stylianos. *European Television in the Digital Age*. London: Polity, 2002.

Robillard, Serge. *Television in Europe: Regulatory Bodies; Status, Functions and Powers in 35 European Countries*. Strasbourg: The European Institute for the Media, Media Monograph No.19, 1995.

Tornos Mas, Joaquín. *Las autoridades de regulación de lo audiovisual*. Madrid/Barcelona: Consell de l'Audiovisual de Catalunya, Marcial Pons, 1999.

Wieten, Jan, Graham Murdock, and Peter Dahlgren, (eds). *Television Across Europe: A Comparative Study*. London: Sage, 2000.

WEBSITES

ARD. Accessed November 16, 2006. http://www.ard.de. Union of German Public Broadcasters.

Astra. Accessed November 17, 2006. http://www.ses-astra.com/. Homepage of the Astra satellite company.

BBC. http://www.bbc.co.uk. British Broadcasting Corporation.

Bakker, Piet. *Dutch Media*. March 2005. Accessed November 16, 2006. http://users.fmg.uva.nl/pbakker/werk/dutchmedia.pdf. A description of the state of the media in the Netherlands.

Council of Europe. *European Convention on Transfrontier Television*. Accessed November 17, 2006. http://conventions.coe.int/treaty/en/Treaties/Html/132.htm.

EPRA. Accessed November 17, 2006. http://www.epra.org/. European Platform of Regulatory Authorities in Düsseldorf, Germany; much information, including addresses of all European national regulatory bodies for television and radio.

European Association of Regional Television. *Circom.* Accessed November 17, 2006. http://www.circom-regional.org.

European Audiovisual Observatory. Accessed November 16, 2006. http://www.obs.coe.int/. The media arm of the Council of Europe. An excellent site with much information on European media.

European Broadcasting Union. http://www.ebu.ch. European body for the common transmission of television programs, such as Eurovision. Established in 1954.

European Commission. *Audiovisual and Media Policies.* Accessed November 17, 2006. http://ec.europa.eu/comm/avpolicy/index_en.htm. The framework of the European Union Audiovisual Policy, including the Television Without Frontiers directive.

European Journalism Centre. Accessed November 16, 2006. http://www.ejc.nl. Much information on all European media.

European Union. *Europe by Satellite.* Accessed November 17, 2006. http://europa.eu/comm/ebs/index_en.html.The European Union's TV news agency.

Eutelsat Communications. Accessed November 17, 2006. http://www.eutelsat.org. The Website of the European Satellite Corporation.

International Press Institute. http://www.freemedia.at. Based in Vienna.

Kiefl, Barry. *International TV Programming and Audience Trends 1996–2001.* 2003. http://www.crtc.gc.ca/eng/publications/reports/drama/drama3.htm.

Machet, Emmanuelle, Eleftheria Peretzinidou, and David Ward. *A Comparative Analysis of Television Programming Regulation in Seven European Countries: A Benchmark Study.* 2002. http://www.eim.org/Events/Downloads/Davidstudy1.pdf.

Médiamétrie. Accessed November 17, 2006. http://www.mediametrie.fr/. French/international broadcasting statistics bureau, In French and English.

Mediendaten Südwest. Accessed November 16, 2006. http://www.mediendaten.de. Information on all areas of German media, in German.

Museum of Broadcast Communications. Accessed November 17, 2006. http://www.museum.tv/. Very well-researched information about all things televisual.

Rumphorst, Werner. *Public Service Broadcasting in an Enlarging Europe: Contributing to European Policy Objectives.* 2004. http://www.ebu.ch/CMSimages/en/leg_p_psb_wr_300804_tcm6-15161.pdf.

Statistisches Bundesamt Deutschland. Accessed November 17, 2006. http://www.destatis.de/. German Federal Statistics bureau.

NOTES

1. Rumphorst 2004 (in Resource Guide, Websites).
2. Graph adapted from *Screen Digest*, 2004.
3. http://www.spacenewsfeed.co.uk/2005/1May2005_10.html.
4. European Audiovisual Observatory (in Resource Guide, Websites).
5. Ibid.
6. Information compiled from EU Audiovisual Observatory fact sheets.
7. Data adapted from http://www.mm.uni-koeln.de/mitarbeiter-loebbecke-publications-proceedings/Conf-085-2005-Business%20Opportunities%20and%20Risks%20from%20Pay-TV%20Piracy-The%20Case%20of%20Europe.pdf.
8. European Audiovisual Observatory (in Resource Guide, Websites).

SPORTS AND RECREATION

STEPHAN WASSONG AND THOMAS ZAWADZKI

The sports scene in Europe has developed with an astonishing dynamism and continuity since the 1960s, reaching large parts of the European population. Approximately 60 percent of Europeans are engaged in sports in some way or other. Research shows that between 60 and 80 million people in the present member states of the European Union are organized in about 694,000 sports clubs.

Without a doubt, people engage in sports for various reasons. Motives differ; aspiring to achieve and winning are no longer the prevailing reasons for participation. People now take up sports as a leisure activity for adventure as well as for social, educational, fitness, and health reasons, making sports activities attractive to a wide range of the population. For at least the past two decades, the power of sports to support social integration has been highly valued. Programs have been developed that aim at better integration of so-called social fringe groups, including elderly people, persons with disabilities, drug addicts, juvenile delinquents, and immigrants. The popular slogan "sport for all" and, above all, the political endeavors of local and national organizations such as the various National Olympic Committees in Europe are clear signs of the educational and sociopolitical promotion of sports. Initiatives to support sports for all often focus on children and young people as there is a growing concern about improving the fitness of children and adolescents. Experts agree that some 30 percent of children and young people do not participate in enough sports or daily exercises. Many reasons can be given for this lack of activity, including the ever-increasing popularity of computers, computer games, and television. These less strenuous pursuits have replaced outdoor games.

ENGLAND—HOME COUNTRY OF SPORTS AS POPULAR CULTURE

The growth of modern industry from the late eighteenth century onward has had a big impact on the rise of sports as a mass phenomenon. The main reasons for this increased interest in sports were the technological developments that contributed to the Industrial Revolution and mass urbanization as a consequence of industrialization. In Europe industrial cities developed into metropolises as economic opportunities brought huge numbers of migrants from rural communities to the cities. Industrialization and urbanization occurred and developed first in England. Therefore it is no accident that England can also be regarded as the cradle of modern sports.

Technological Progress

The following section illustrates how technological progress provided a basis for the expansion of sports in England. Reference will be made to the development of the railroad network, the progress in information technology, the invention of the light bulb in 1879, and the rise of mass production resulting from new manufacturing techniques in factories.

The increase of both the popularity of spectator sports and participation in sporting activities benefited from the expansion of the railroad network. Between 1835 and 1845, the railroad network grew from 471 to 3,277 miles in England and Ireland. Athletes and spectators as well as sporting equipment, such as horses, rowboats, or sailboats could be transported faster and easier. The development of horse racing, which was already a well-established sport in the eighteenth century, is a good example of the railroad network helping to popularize sports. In 1837 the "Racing Calendar" listed the names of 1,214 horses; the number increased to 2,534 in 1869.

Innovations in communications technology also contributed much to stir popular general interest in sports. Without television, people interested in sports depended on daily newspapers for their sporting news. With the invention of telegraphy in 1844, news on business, politics, and sports could be transmitted more quickly. Receivers were often installed in bars or in front of main stations. Improved printing technologies resulted not only in the mass production of newspapers but also led to lower costs for consumers. As a consequence, the sale of sporting papers rose enormously. From the 1880s onwards, the English sporting magazines *Sportsman*, *Sporting Life*, and *Sporting Chronicle* sold over 300,000 copies a day.

Another signifcant factor in the expansion of sports was the light bulb, invented in 1879 by Thomas A. Edison. Electric lighting was commonplace at leading indoor sports venues and gymnasiums by 1890. Prior to 1879 indoor sporting facilities were often poorly lit by dangerous gas lamps, which often prevented people from taking part in indoor sports or gymnastic activities. The invention of electric light not only contributed to increased participation in healthful indoor sporting activities, but also to an increase in spectator sports.

Perhaps one of industrialization's main impacts on sports was the mass manufacturing of sporting goods. With the help of new production techniques, sports articles such as rubber balls, tennis rackets, cricket bats, golf sets, and so on swamped the market. The English safety bicycle of the late 1880s, with equal-sized pneumatic tires and efficient coaster brakes, became one of the most important new sporting goods.

Urbanization played a more indirect role in the development of sports than the technical innovations just mentioned; but the rise of cities contributed much to the increase of spectator sports. Because trade unions had become more and more successful in their demand for a free Saturday afternoon since around 1850, the masses of urban workers had more time to spend on sports venues. Soccer was the sport with the highest number of spectators. In the soccer season of 1888–89, matches were watched by over 600,000 spectators. In the season of 1895–96, this number grew to 1,900,000. The Cup Final, the highlight of every soccer season, developed into a real magnet for spectators. From 1885 to 1894, the average number of spectators was 23,400. Between 1895 and 1904, this average number increased to 668,000. Fewer spectators attended cricket games and horse races, but the organizers of these sports events could still sell 10,000 tickets on average. On public holidays, 50,000 visitors could show up at the turfs or the cricket grounds.

Educational and Social Effects of Sports

Urbanization also led to an increasing interest in utilizing sports as an educational remedy for solving social problems that had their source in the modern metropolis. On the sunny side of urbanization, there were, among many other things, the rise of new business areas, a large entertainment scene, beautiful neighborhoods in the suburbs, and an improved inner-city transport system. On the darker side, there was the emergence of social districts with high population density caused by huge numbers of migrants from rural communities. The social hot spots were a breeding ground for high rates of illnesses, delinquency, and homicides. In general urbanization required new patterns of behavior in order to master the personal, political, economical, and social demands of city life. Education was expected to help citizens as they faced modern challenges. But what was the role of sports in this educational hope?

A belief in the educational power of sports was first and foremost based on the ideology of "muscular Christianity." The philosophy behind muscular Christianity can be connected with Charles Kingsley, who used this phrase in his novel *Two Years Ago* (1857). The basic argument of muscular Christianity was that participation in sports contributed to the development of Christian morality, physical fitness, and manly character. According to this view, sports were no longer regarded as a waste of time and as incongruous with the strict Puritan work ethic. Prejudices against sports, which were mainly put forward by the middle classes, decreased, and it was expected that sports would support the education of the Christian gentleman. In fact, Kingsley produced a kind of moral defense for sports. He argued:

> Through sport boys acquire virtues which no books can give them; not merely daring and endurance, but, better still, temper, self-restraint, fairness, honour, unenvious approbation of another's success, and all that "give and take" of life which stand a man in good stead when he goes forth into the world, and without which, indeed, his success is always maimed and partial.[1]

This view gained popularity at English public schools and universities. Teachers, headmasters, and the presidents of Cambridge and Oxford tolerated the sporting activities of their pupils and students. Moderate athletic activities were said to help to improve standards of health and contribute to the development of highly moral and social character traits. Character traits such as fair play, team spirit, self-confidence, and goal-oriented behavior were believed to be not only of great use within athletic settings but also applicable to the daily life of the students. It was further expected that the acquisition of said character traits could help students to become future leaders in politics, business, and administration. At many schools and universities, athletic activities were organized as extracurricular activities, run by the students themselves. Through self-government, students were supposed to learn to take responsibility for their actions, develop efficient leadership skills, and become sensitive to dynamic group processes.

It is noteworthy that the pupils of Rugby School were the first, in 1845, to fix the rules of their beloved football game, thenceforth called rugby. The rules aimed at taking away the brutality of the game. For example, hacking with the heel or above the knee was no longer allowed in the "Laws of Football as Played at Rugby School." Eton Public School preferred to play a variant of football that did not allow the students to play the ball with the hand. The rules of Rugby and Eton were the beginning of the separation between rugby and what

KEEPING LOWER CLASSES OUT OF COMPETITIVE SPORTS

The impact of muscular Christianity could also be felt beyond the school and university walls. Particularly, members of the middle classes were convinced that, in moderation, sports were not harmful and could help to educate useful citizens. The result was a growing interest in sports and the widespread founding of sports clubs. Unfortunately these clubs were often not open to laborers. Either they could not afford the high club membership fee, or they were excluded by amateur regulations in which workmen were classified as professionals by rule, as this quote from the English Amateur Rowing Association (ARA), founded in 1882, shows:

An amateur is any person who has never competed in an open competition, or for public money, or for admission money, and who has never at any period of his life taught or assisted in the pursuit of athletic exercises as a means of livelihood or is a mechanic artisan or labourer.[2]

This class amateur rule was clearly designed to control social exclusiveness in sports. It was argued that workingmen trained their bodies by their daily work and therefore had an advantage in athletic competition. Of course, this thought of preserving fair play was no more than a pretense. Moral arguments were utilized to prevent social mingling in sports. The socially exclusive amateur rule was followed most strictly by the famous Henley Royal Regatta. Shortly before the Olympic Games in Antwerp in 1920, the U.S.-American rower John Kelly was excluded from the regatta because of his former job as a bricklayer. At the Games in Antwerp, Kelly finished first in the single and double sculls. Ironically Kelly's work as a bricklayer did not prevent Prince Rainier III of Monaco from marrying Kelly's daughter, Grace Kelly, a famous actress who thus became Princess of Monaco.

became known as "association football," or "soccer" for short.

The attempt to regulate social exclusiveness in sports through banning amateurs from the lower classes did not remain unchallenged. Many advocates of muscular Christianity severely criticized this class-conscious attitude and demanded a more democratic amateur rule that allowed almost all people to take part in sports on amateur level. The Amateur Athletic Club, founded by Oxford and Cambridge men in 1866, set up amateur rules excluding only those who had competed in athletic events for money. Manual workers were allowed to participate. Dr. Furnivall from Cambridge was very clear when he dismissed the social exclusivity of the ARA:

We feel that for a university to send its earnest and intellectual men into an East End or other settlement to live with and help working men in their studies and sports, while it sends its rowing men into the ARA to say to those working men, "You're labourers; your work renders you unfit to associate and row with us" is a facing-both-ways, an inconsistency and contradiction which loyal sons of the University ought to avoid.[3]

The message of this quotation is unmistakable: sports must be accessible to all. In particular, educators, progressive politicians, and above all social reformers claimed that the educational value of sports must take its effects also where it was most needed: in the social hot spots of the cities. The population of these city districts was often composed of both employed and unemployed working men and their families. Particularly during the third quarter of the nineteenth century, concerns about the way the lower classes enjoyed themselves were often voiced. Organized sporting activities were regarded as a remedy for both an increasing decay of morality and an increasing rate of illnesses. Apart from the foundation of many sport clubs for working men in which boxing—a more or less questionable sport because of its brutality and negative side effects such as betting—became very popular, attempts were made to establish inner-city playing fields. Sports on these playing fields or play centers provided opportunities for team games and track and field disciplines. Above all, young people could participate in sports legally and away from the overcrowded streets. In general, football, stickball, or catch-and-run games in the streets were forbidden. The ban was controlled by policemen who took their jobs seriously.

DIFFUSION OF SPORTS IN EUROPE

Of course, the impact of industrialization and urbanization was not only felt in England but also in other parts of Europe and in the United States. In the late nineteenth century, a more or less strongly developed sports scene began to be seen in many European countries. The sporting scene in England became the model to adopt. The best example of this is the work of the French nobleman Pierre de Coubertin. Since the 1880s, he had traveled extensively in England to study the sporting scene. His impressions, completed by his insights into U.S. sports culture, drove him to establish a strong athletic scene in France.

At least two more major forces supported the rise of sports to a phenomenon of popular culture beyond England in the late nineteenth and early twentieth century. The first force was the tradition of World's Fairs or universal exhibitions, which had influenced the spread of sports from the time such events began in 1851. At the 1851 World's Fair in London, an international sailing regatta took place at Cowes. The prize was the so-called 100 Guinea Cup. On August 22, in a race open to all nations, the cup was won by the sailors of the New York schooner *America*. After the victory, the cup was offered by the New York Yacht Club as a permanent prize for a sailing competition—the well-known America's Cup, which still enjoys great popularity today. At the exposition organized in Paris in 1867, sports became part of the program again. Teams from Germany, England, Belgium, France, and the Netherlands started in the regattas, held from July 8 to 12. At the 1889 World's Fair in Paris, de Coubertin organized the International Congress on Physical Education. In his preparations for the congress, de Coubertin initiated a worldwide survey on the role of physical education. In it he was able to reveal an impressive worldwide interest in the topic of sports and education.[4] The 1900 World's Fair in Paris and the 1904 event in St. Louis integrated the modern Olympic Games into the universal expositions, stressing the strong link between sports and industry.

The modern Olympic Games were indeed the second major force alongside the World's Fairs that supported the development of sports internationally. Again de Coubertin, whose belief in the educational power of sports and whose organizing abilities led to the successful reinstitution of the Olympic Games, was a key figure. In June 1894 the congress *Pour Le Rétablissement des Jeux Olympiques* (for the reestablishment of the Olympic Games) took place at the Sorbonne in Paris. The group decided to organize the first modern Olympic Games in Athens in 1896 and set down amateur rules for the eligibility of athletes. The International Olympic Committee (IOC) was founded, and the Greek academic Dimitrios Vikélas became its first president.

WOMEN AND SPORT

Without a doubt, the Olympic Games have contributed much to stimulate the growth of sports in Europe and beyond. But is this also true of the participation of women in sports? In the 1920s, women's sports were on the rise, although it was slow going. But there still existed the traditional prejudice that women's engagement in sports would be damaging to their health. It was, for example, often said that sports impaired women's fertility. Although the ladies of the English upper class participated mainly in golf, tennis, and hockey for social reasons, sports remained a male domain at the close of the nineteenth century in spite of the founding of the Ladies' Golf Union in 1893 and the All English Women's Hockey Association in 1895. At the public schools for girls, athletic activities were almost completely neglected. Instead, the female pupils often had to do therapeutic gymnastics, which was said to strengthen the women's health and grace. Since the first decades of the twentieth century, however, female participation in sports improved slowly. The emancipation of women's competitive sports, which mainly emanated from the United States, is connected with the female track and field athlete Mildred "Babe" Didrikson and the tennis players Helen Wils and Suzanne Lenglen, who became very prominent in Europe. The Frenchwoman Lenglen fascinated the audience not only with her athletic skills but also with her appearance. At the young age of fifteen, she won the hard-court championship, which was followed by many triumphs in Wimbledon and Paris in the 1920s.

After the Olympic Games in Paris in 1900, women took part in various sports, including croquet, golf, tennis, archery, swimming, and ice skating. But their full acceptance as Olympic athletes was above all impeded by de Coubertin's dislike of women's sports. After long discussions, women were allowed to start in gymnastics and track and field events at the Games of the Ninth Olympiad in Amsterdam in 1928. They started in the high jump, discus throwing, the 100-meter run, the 800-meter run, and the 4 × 100-meter relay. After the 800-meter run, which was won by the German Lina Radke-Batschauer, the participation of women in running competitions was again the object of heated discussions because many female runners gave up or broke down, totally exhausted, on the track. It was only at the Olympic Games in Rome in 1960 that women were allowed to compete in running competitions longer than 200 meters again.

It was mainly because of the foundation of the Fédération Sportive Féminine Internationale (FSFI) in 1921 that women were allowed to participate at the Olympics in track and field events. Under the pressure of the FSFI, chaired by the Frenchwoman Alice Milliat, the International Olympic Committee (IOC) decided to organize the five mentioned track and field events for women at the Games in Amsterdam. But this was not enough for the FSFI, as it demanded track and field competitions for women in ten events. As a protest, they organized the women's world games, which were hosted by Paris in 1922, by Gothenburg in 1926, by Prague in 1930, and by London in 1934. Actually the first of these events in 1922 was named the Women's Olympic Games. After a protest by the IOC and the IAAF in 1926, the FSFI was forced to rename its games the World Games of Women. In 1936 the FSFI was dissolved under the pressure of the IOC. But the participation of women at the Olympic Games was no longer the problem that it once was. Today's participation of women at the Olympic Games shows that the former "weaker sex" succeeded greatly in its struggle for emancipation.

As for Europe, a strong sporting scene has developed in almost all countries since the beginning of the twentieth century at the latest. People engage in sports for different reasons. The major stimuli are commercial, educational, health, social, and competitive interests, which drive people to participate in sports as a profession or in their leisure time. As a consequence, a diverse sport scene has developed, whose organizational and institutional structure has become more and more complex.

THE DARK SIDE OF MODERN SPORTS

But, of course, the world of sports is not without blemish. Doping scandals often overshadow popular sports events. The history of doping at the Tour de France can serve as an example. In 1967 the legendary Briton Tom Simpson died at this famous cycling race.

During the ascent to Mont Ventoux, he collapsed and fell off his bike. After some seconds of recovery, he continued the race until he collapsed a second time. He could not be revived, and he died. An autopsy revealed that Simpson had been doped by an amphetamine cocktail. Today a tomb has been placed where Simpson collapsed, but the message of this tomb has often been ignored. At the Tour de France in 1998, forbidden preparations were found in the possession of the Festina Team to which the French star Richard Virenque belonged. In a raid at the team hotel, the police detected mainly erythropoietin (EPO), a preparation that facilitates the transport of oxygen. Although none of the professionals from Festina could be tested positively for lack of methods, the team was banned from the Tour. The Spanish teams withdrew from the tour to protest against the rude raid and legal procedure of the French administration, and the tour was in danger of being canceled. Finally the race was won by the Italian Marco Pantani, who himself was excluded from the Giro d'Italia one year later because of his high hematocrit value, indicating the consumption of forbidden substances. Virenque, who had been the favorite to win the tour in 1998, admitted in a trial in 2001 that he had been doped in 1998. He was excluded from all cycling competitions for six months. Ironically he won the mountain stage at the Mont Ventoux at the Tour de France in 2001. A major doping scandal also overshadowed the Tour de France in 2006. One day before the prologue, officials published a list with fifty-eight doping suspects, which led to the exclusion of top athletes, including Jan Ullrich, Ivan Basso, Francisco Mancebo, and many other top-class cyclists. But things escalated at the end of the tour as the winner, Floyd Landis, tested positive on doping. For the first time in the history of the tour, the winner was disallowed the title belatedly. The new winner of 2006 became Oscar Pereiro Sio, who had finished second.

Another danger of sports, and a very current one, is betting, which can no longer be confined to such sports as horse racing and boxing. The betting business in these two sports has a long tradition dating back to the end of the eighteenth century. Today soccer betting dominates. It is very popular to make bets on the matches of the European top-level leagues, the European Cups, and international matches. In Germany, the host country of the soccer world championship—the Fédération International de Football Association (FIFA) World Cup—in 2006, a scandal was uncovered in 2005. A few referees of the German Football Association had manipulated matches in the first and second league as well as in the German Cup competition in order to reach unexpected scores through which high amounts of money could be made. The referees themselves had been paid for their bias by the Croatian bet mafia. It is said that one referee had been paid money amounting up to €6000. The few referees involved in the scandal were suspended and taken to court.

But even before the betting scandal, the Committee for Development of Sport of the Council of Europe had become active in securing the individual, social, and moral values of sports. In 1996 a round-table discussion was organized with the authorities of the Netherlands to discuss fair play and ethics in sports. Other conferences on this topic soon followed, resulting in the nomination of ambassadors of fair play in many countries of the European Union. It is the task of the ambassadors to promote fair play and mutual respect in sports. In addition to this, the project Eurofit, a test to measure schoolchildren's mobility, endurance, strength, and speediness, was launched in 1988. Since 1995 a Eurofit test has been developed for adults, too. In 1985 the European Convention reported on the brutality and misbehavior of spectators at sports events, particularly soccer matches. A permanent commission of the convention gives practical advice for the prevention of violence at sporting events and has published a safety manual whose key lines have to be checked before a big event. Last but not least, the program Sprint (Sports Reform Innovation and Training) was developed to help establish—mainly among new member states—a comprehensive reform program, which concentrates on sports laws, financing in sports, management in sports, and support of honorary service in sports.

BJARNE RIIS

Although Bjarne Riis was born (April 3, 1964, in Herning) in a country not known for its cycling tradition, he became a world-class professional cyclist. He achieved this stature with his triumph in 1996, when he won the Tour de France with his Team Telekom. In the following year, he supported Jan Ullrich, and after the end of his career as an athlete, he became the athletic director of the Danish team, which boasted top cyclists such as Laurent Jalabert and Tyler Hamilton.

All in all, it can be said that sports are widely accepted in Europe as a useful means of contributing to individual and social well-being. In the end, it is the duty of athletes, coaches, managers, companies, and politicians to help avoid abuses in sports.

SCANDINAVIA

Denmark

Danish sport is mainly organized by two national organizations: Denmark's Sport Confederation (Danmarks Idræts-Forbund, or DIF) and the Danish Gymnastics and Sports Association (Danske Gymnastik- og Idrætsforeninger, or DGI). The DIF represents approximately 1.5 million members and has its roots in Olympic and English amateur sports. As an umbrella organization for fifty-six specialized national federations, the DIF covers the field of elite sports in Denmark and also represents the National Olympic Committee. Swedish gymnastics and rifle shooting were the original interests of the DGI, a national governing body that represents approximately 1.5 million members as well. The DGI holds regional competitions only and includes twenty-five regional associations. A third national organization in Danish sports is the Danish Companies' Sports Federation (Dansk Firmaidrætsforbund, or DFIF), which comprises about 200,000 members and covers sporting activities done by the workers in the companies. Besides these organizations, many special associations were founded during the second half of the twentieth century, for example, Danish School Sports, Danish Trim Committee, Association for the Promotion of Exercise and Sport during Daytime, Danish Heart Foundation, Team Denmark, and so on.

Most up-to-date research displays the very positive trend in sports participation in Denmark.[5] In all, 72 percent (seventy-three male, seventy-one female) of the interviewees answered "yes" when asked whether they "normally practice sports or exercise." The participation in sports among youngsters (sixteen to nineteen years of age) was especially high at 80 percent. Even 58 percent of the seventy- to seventy-four-year-olds participate in sporting activities. The Danish ardor for participating in sports was also displayed by the amount of time Danish citizens spent on the whole in physical activities: here the range differed from more than seven hours among the youngsters, to four hours and twenty minutes among thirty- to thirty-nine-year-olds, and more than seven hours among the sixty- to sixty-nine-year-olds.

The sports association with most members younger than eighteen years is the football union, followed closely by federations representing swimming, handball, gymnastics, and horse riding. Danish citizens more than twenty-five years old prefer—according to the number of sports association members—golf, football, badminton, gymnastics, and sailing. Nonorganized sports that are highly accepted in Denmark are jogging, walking, gymnastics, cycling, soccer, and badminton.

In the late 1990s, the state provided about €325 million in funding to these clubs—€650 per member.[6]

Finland

The Finnish Sports Federation (Suomen Liihunta ja Urheilu, or SLU) is the umbrella organization for seventy-four national sports federations, fifteen regional organizations, the Finnish Workers' Sports Federation, eight Swedish-language sports organizations, four student and school organizations, two fitness sports organizations, eight sports organizations for special groups, the Finnish Olympic Committee, Young Finland, and another twelve supporting members.

Some 7,800 local sports clubs offer sports services to the Finns. Around 400,000 young Finns—every third Finn under nineteen—participate in physical activities provided by sports clubs. Another 400,000 adults are active members.

The Finns are very active in sports: they are the sportiest nation in Europe. Some 92 percent of the Finns participate in physical activities at least once a week, and only four out of a hundred stated that they did not participate in sports at all. More than a third of the Finns participate in sports very intensively: within the age groups of twenty to twenty-four and sixty to sixty-four, 46 percent state that they participate in sports more than 120 times per year. Forty-four percent of Finns between thirty-five and forty-nine years old participate in sports regularly (12–120 times per year), and only 20 percent participate in sports occasionally or are reluctant to do physical activities.

The most common sports in 2001 were walking, cycling, cross-country skiing, and jogging. For children and youngsters, the most popular sports were soccer and cycling. Swimming, cross-country skiing, and floorball/bandy followed, ranking third to fifth, whereas track and field athletics only ranked tenth. Walking enjoyed the greatest popularity with adults. Other highly ranked activities were cycling, cross-country skiing, swimming, and weight exercises. Jogging was preferred to Nordic walking, gymnastics, aerobics, and floorball.

Finnish sports are funded by an annual budget of more than €80 million from the Ministry of Education; approximately €380 million more come from local authorities for financing, constructing, and maintaining sports facilities.

Norway

The umbrella organization for all sports in Norway is the Norwegian Sports Confederation and Olympic Committee (Norges Idrettsforbund og Olympiske Komité, or NIF). Fifty-five national federations, nineteen regional confederations, three hundred sixty sports councils, and over twelve thousand clubs are registered as members of NIF.

Nearly 60 percent of Norwegians aged sixteen to twenty-four participate in physical activities two or more times per week. In older age groups, the figures are somewhat lower but remain at a very high level. Only the sixty-seven- to seventy-nine-year-olds are reluctant to participate in sports: 25 percent do not participate in physical activities anymore, but the remaining 64 percent take part in sports activities regularly, once a week or even more often.

The most popular sports for children aged between six and twelve are soccer, skiing, handball, gymnastics, and swimming with a total of 300,000 registered members in the national federations. In the next age group, the thirteen- to nineteen-year-olds, swimming and gymnastics are replaced by golf and volleyball, with the number of youth participating in all five sports at 200,000.

In 2003, Norwegian sports received a total of over €130 million (over 1 billion kroner) from national lottery funds for sports.[7]

BJØRN DÆHLIE

Bjørn Dæhlie (born June 19, 1967, in Elverum) was the dominant cross-country skier of the 1990s with eight Olympic titles, which is a record for an athlete at the Winter Olympics. He also won four silver medals. Daehlie won the medals at the Olympic Winter Games in Albertville, Lillehammer, and Nagano. In addition, he was very successful at the world championships (seventeen medals; nine of them gold), especially in 1997, when he won medals in all five events.

BJÖRN BORG

Without a doubt, Björn Borg (born June 6, 1956, near Stockholm) must be listed among the greatest tennis players of all times. Besides five consecutive Wimbledon victories, he gathered many more titles. He won six times in Roland Garros, twice at the Masters, and once at the World Team Cup (WTC) tennis championship. He led the Swedes to the Davis Cup in 1975. His accomplishments brought the Swedish "Sportsman of the Century" into the media spotlight. Unfortunately, nothing remains of his fame and his prizes, as a consequence of private and business-related flops.

PETER FORSBERG

On ice, Peter Forsberg (born June 20, 1973, in Örskjöldsvik) may be described as a hockey player with "technical skills perfectly combined to physical utilizability." His offensive work and his qualities as a goal getter brought him two Stanley Cups, the Art Ross Trophy, the Hart Trophy, the Calder Trophy, world championships in 1992 and 1998, and two Olympic gold medals in 1994 and 2006. The National Hockey League professional is one of the best all-around players in the league.

Sweden

Sweden is divided into twenty-one regions. In every region a district sports federation acts as the extension of the Swedish Sports Confederation (Riksidrotts Förbundet, or RF). The RF represents sixty-seven special sports federations, which include around 22,000 clubs and another 7000 company sports clubs. The Swedish Olympic Committee represents the Olympic sports and the high-performance sports.

Almost half of the Swedish population aged between seven and seventy are members of a sports club. Over three quarters (76 percent) of Swedish children between seven and fourteen years of age belong to a sports club. In the older age groups, the total number of sports club memberships decreases to between 40 and 46 percent but remains relatively constant. It is only among sixty- to seventy-year-olds that sports club membership declines to 28 percent of the Swedish population. In all, 30 percent of Swedes are reluctant to participate in sports. On average, 11 percent of Swedes are active irregularly, 25 percent are active intensively, and 12 percent are active in a competitive and organized way.

The most common sport in Sweden is soccer for both women and men, followed by gymnastics, equestrian sports, golf, and track and field athletics for women, and golf, skiing, ice hockey, and floorball for men.

Swedish sports receive financial support from the state: approximately €50 million from the Ministry of the Interior, €350 million from local authorities, and €120 million from the national bingo lottery.

IRELAND AND THE UNITED KINGDOM

Republic of Ireland

Irish sports are mainly organized by the Irish Sports Council, an umbrella organization for sixty-seven recognized national governing bodies in Ireland. The council is responsible for educating future coaches as well as for providing strategic support in the organization and administration of most Irish sports. The Olympic Council of Ireland and the Paralympic Council of Ireland act as "embassies" for Irish sports in international contexts.

Of the Irish, 28 percent never practiced or played sports in 2004, whereas at least 53 percent did physical exercises once a week. In order of preference, women engaged in swimming, aerobics, cycling, golf, tennis, and jogging; men participated in golf, soccer, swimming, Gaelic football, pool (billiards and snooker), and cycling. Another leisure practice is walking, which makes an enormous difference when the proportion of the Irish population who participated in physical exercise during the past twelve months is considered. When walking is included, 78 percent of the Irish participated in sports; when walking is excluded, only 43 percent did so.

Very popular sports in Ireland are Gaelic football and hurling, both played by teams only at a national level for lack of other nations playing this amateur sport. Almost every city in Ireland has its own club.

In 2002 the Department of Tourism, Sport, and Recreation provided over €75 million in capital grants to voluntary and recreational organizations throughout Ireland. Further subsidies were given by the government to sport facility financing programs; for example, the swimming pool program received a total of €58.6 million in 2000–02.

DAVID BECKHAM

Since the end of the 1990s, David Beckham (born May 2, 1975, Leytonstone) has been one of the world's best soccer players and one of the most chatoyant figures on the turf. With his transfer from Manchester United to Real Madrid, he may be regarded as a mega-star or pop star. With his colorful lifestyle, he crossed the line between sports and show business, especially through his marriage with Victoria Adams, one of the Spice Girls. His victories in soccer are nearly countless: several times English Champion, World Cup participant in 1998 and 2002, and Champions League winner in 1999. In 2003, he was made an Officer of the British Empire. Although he has received all these honors, Beckham's performance at the 2006 World Cup in Germany was described as disappointing, and his future in the national team seems uncertain.

United Kingdom

The Central Council for Physical Recreation and the British Olympic Association operate at a national level. Besides these two groups, the specialized national federations can be considered as umbrella bodies for the different sports in the different home countries. For example, the United Kingdom is represented by the soccer teams in England, Scotland, Wales, and Northern Ireland.

Only 45 percent of the British participate in sports at least once a week, an average that ranks the United Kingdom sixth in comparison with other member states of the European Union. Thirty-one percent never participate in sports. Among sixteen- to nineteen-year-olds, 53 percent participate in sports more than 120 times per year. This number decreases in the following age groups until only every fourth Briton aged forty to forty-four participates in sports, and only ten out of a hundred aged sixty-five or over do so. The number involved in sports between twelve and 120 times per year is more stable. Although only 25 percent of fifteen- to twenty-year-olds answered that they participated in sports this frequently, the number actually increases among thirty-five- to thirty-nine-year-olds and then begins to decrease steadily.

Britain's favorite sport is walking, with a total of nearly 20 million British participants aged sixteen and older. Swimming, general fitness activities, and all kinds of billiards follow. Among the British top ten sports, one also finds cycling, weight training, running, soccer, and golf, as well as tenpin bowling. The membership figures of 2002 show another very interesting situation. Although walking is the number one sport in general, soccer is the number one sport as far as the number of members who belong to organizations is concerned. Two and a half million Britons are members of a soccer club, over 880,000 are organized in golf clubs, and 830,000 are members of gymnastics associations.

SOUTHERN EUROPE

Portugal

On a national level three nongovernmental sports organizations, the National Sports Confederation, the National Olympic Committee, and the Sports Foundation, act as bodies for promoting sports. Besides these organizations, sports clubs, sports federations, the professional league of clubs, and sports-promoting organizations act to further physical activities.

The Portuguese population has the highest number of people not affiliated with sports in the European Union. Sixty-six percent stated they do not participate in any sports at all. Thus it is not surprising that only 22 percent of the Portuguese engage in physical activities at least once a week, with only one nation in the European Union yielding a lower percentage. Among the sixteen- to nineteen-year-olds, 26 percent participate in sports on average more than three times a week. This number decreases steadily to 2 percent among those aged 65 and older. Among those who participate in sports regularly (once a month and more), the highest number (24 percent) is also found with the youngsters; it decreases to 11 percent among persons aged forty to forty-four and continues to decline to only 1 percent among the seniors (age sixty-five and older). The number of Portuguese participating in sports occasionally, that is, less than once a month on average, is noteworthy: 50 percent of the youngsters are physically active occasionally, and the number increases to 97 percent for the seniors age group.

The number of members of soccer clubs (nearly 114,000) and the percentage of those who said they play soccer in their leisure time (30 percent) clearly reveal that soccer is the most popular sport in Portugal. Other top sports in Portugal are swimming, track and field, sports at fitness clubs, gymnastics, cycling, basketball, volleyball, and tennis, practiced by two to eleven percent of the Portuguese population. With reference to membership figures in sport-specific clubs, soccer is followed by handball and basketball, both with more than 20,000 members; athletics, judo, skating, and tennis, with less than 20,000 members; and, at last, volleyball, golf, and gymnastics, with less than 10,000 members.

Spain

National federations, the Spanish Olympic Committee, and the Paralympic Committee represent sporting activities on a national level. Besides these professional leagues, club associations and sports promotion entities act as national representative organizations.

Thirty-eight percent of the Spanish population practices sports or physical activities once or twice a week. Forty-nine percent participate in sports three times per week or more. Only 13 percent participate in sports less than once a week.

Swimming is the most popular sport in Spain, with 39 percent of the Spanish participating in it. Thirty-six out of one hundred play soccer, and twenty-two prefer cycling. Fitness, mountaineering, tennis, aerobics and dancing, basketball, running and jogging, and track and field athletics are the other top ten activities, according to the number of people involved. According to membership figures, soccer, with over 650,000 members, is by far the most popular club-related sport. Basketball and golf follow with approximately 290,000 and 240,000 members, respectively. Judo, tennis, handball, and mountaineering clubs have about 100,000 members each; karate, shooting, and underwater sports clubs have around 50,000 members each.

Italy

Forty-two Italian sports federations are assembled in the National Olympic Committee (Comitato Olimpico Nazionale Italiano, or CONI) together with nineteen other federations representing non-Olympic sports and fourteen associations for the promotion of sports. Altogether these federations represent 72,000 Italian sports clubs and 16,700,000 persons (if multiple affiliations are not considered).

Almost always men dominate in Italian sports; thus 16.5 percent of male children and teens participate in sporting activities 120 or more times per year whereas only 6.7 percent of female children do so. In Italy, 27.9 percent of the boys and 22.6 percent of the girls participate in sports between sixty and 120 times per year. This trend is reversed in the case of participation in physical activities not considered to be sports; in that case, 26.2 percent of the girls are involved, compared to 17.1 percent of the boys. No physical activities at all are performed by 22.4 percent of the girls and 15 percent of the boys. Analogous trends can be seen for Italians from sixteen to seventy-four years old: on the whole, 3.5 to 4.9 percent participate in sports in a regular or even intensive and competitive way. Other physical exercise is done by an average of 33.7 percent of the population, and thirty-seven of the interviewees said they do not take part in any sports or physical activities at all.

The popularity of soccer in Italy remains uncontested. Over the years the number of soccer clubs has steadily increased. In 1997 the Italian Soccer Federation registered 13,268 soccer clubs and issued 1,000,288 licenses to players. Twenty-six percent of Italians said that soccer was their favorite sport. The activities of gymnastics and sports at fitness clubs were each practiced by 21 percent of respondents, and aquatics and winter sports followed at 13 percent each. Racket sports, cycling, volleyball, and track and field were mentioned by 8 to 6 percent. Basketball (at 4 percent) and running (at 3 percent) completed the survey of the Italian population. According to the number of registered players, soccer is by far the most popular sport in Italy. Basketball and volleyball follow with approximately 280,000 and 240,000 licensees, respectively. Tennis, winter sports, track and field, and martial arts are represented by over 100,000 participants each, followed by bowls (boccia), motorcycling, and sailing.

The most relevant funding source in Italian sports is private funding. Approximately €29 billion was allocated to sports in 1996.

MIGUEL INDURÁIN LARRAYA

After twelve years of professional cycling, Miguel Induráin Larraya (born July 16, 1964, in Villava) ended his outstanding career in 1997. Spain's most popular athlete ruled the cycling world from 1991 until 1996. Five times he won the most exclusive cycling competition in the world, the Tour de France; twice he won the Giro d'Italia (in 1992 and 1993). Through his efforts, Don Miguel, as the Basque was called, made cycling popular. Although he was the world champion in 1993 and 1995 and the Olympic champion in 1996, he remained a modest and fair sportsman.

ALBERTO TOMBA

Between 1986 and 1998, Alberto Tomba (born December 19, 1966, in San Lazaro die Savenna) dominated the technical disciplines in alpine skiing. Among his outstanding successes are three Olympic gold medals, two World Championship titles, and one World Cup title. Not fitting into any pattern, the Italian ski legend enjoyed great popularity. For the Olympic Winter Games in Turin, Tomba was hailed as one of the goodwill ambassadors of the games.

Greece

Greek sports are organized predominantly autonomously although the General Sports Secretariat with its affiliation to the Hellenic Ministry of Culture belongs to governmental sports structures. Together with the Hellenic Olympic Committee, it is the umbrella organization for the forty-seven national federations and the Hellenic Paralympic Committee.

Although Greece is regarded as the home country of athletics, physical activity is not widespread. Only 26 percent of Greeks participate in physical exercise at least once a week, whereas 57 percent never take part in sports.

According to data collected by the Hellenic General Secretariat of Sports in 1997 and 1998, soccer once again plays a dominant role in sporting activities, with 2 million players organized in 5,773 clubs. Other very popular sports are volleyball with 108,470 participants, karate and tae kwon do with 48,419 licensees, handball with 18,425 players, basketball with 15,760 participants, and sailing with 13,260 licensees.

Cyprus

By Kathleen J. O'Shea

As in Greece, the sports history of Cyprus dates back many centuries. Inscriptions found in various archaeological sites both on the island and in Greece bear witness to Cypriots' love for sports. That love continues, and in recent decades, programming and financial support have allowed sports and recreation to again become more central to the people of Cyprus.

The most popular sports among all age groups in Cyprus are football and basketball; track and field, tennis, and skiing are also popular sports. In earlier years, football was popular only with men, but today many women and girls are actively participating in this sport as well.

Basketball is the second most popular sport in this country. The Cyprus Basketball Association was founded in 1966 and became a member of the International Basketball Federation, FIBA (Fédération Internationale de Basketball), in 1974. The first organized league played in 1967, with Digenis Morphou winning the first title. The sport is expanding to women and youth as well as men. Most of the teams also have basketball academies where young children go and learn the game.[8]

The history of basketball in Cyprus can be divided into three periods: from 1966 to 1974, from 1974 to 1988, and from 1988 to the present. Until 1974 the best teams on the island were Digenis Morphou and PAEEK Kerynia. But the Turkish invasion on July 20, 1974, turned the members of those two teams into refugees and destroyed the team economically.

In the second period, between 1974 and 1988, the teams had no foreign players so the level of play was lower. In the last period, from 1988 to the present, the Cyprus teams introduced foreigners, especially Americans, so their basketball teams became better and the first successes in international play followed predictably.

Until the early 1980s, the teams were forced to play in open courts with asphalt parquet, but later in the decade, the Cyprus Sports Authority (KOA) started building modern arenas. Stadiums like Eleftheria in Nicosia, Kition in Larnaca, the AEL arena in Larissa, and Apollon stadium in Limassol were built to modern standards. In the 2005–06 season, eight teams will compete in the first division.

The range of Cyprus's sporting activities in recent years has broadened. The World Shooting Cup and three international tournaments (basketball, track and field, and tennis) have been held in Cyprus. Many sporting opportunities are available, including cycling, tennis, golf, freshwater fishing, and diving. Skiing on Mount Olympus is enjoyed by many during the winter.

Cyprus was first recognized by the International Olympic Committee in 1978 but has yet to win a medal in the summer Olympics.

ERIKA SALUMÄE

Erika Salumäe (June 11, 1962, in Pärnu) won the gold medal for the former Soviet Union during the 1988 Summer Olympics. Four years later in Barcelona, she repeated this victory under different conditions. After the breakdown of the former Soviet Union, Salumäe was no longer supported by Soviet sports promotion. Without her own material—even her bike was borrowed from the Australian team—she competed successfully for the young Estonian nation and was the very first Estonian to win an Olympic gold medal.

Between 1982 and 1989, Salumäe won gold ten times, silver three times, and bronze three times at the World Championships and set fifteen world records. She was awarded the honor of Estonian athlete of the year nine times.

THE BALTICS

Estonia

The umbrella organization of Estonian sporting life is the Estonian Olympic Committee (Eesti Olümpiakomitee; or EOK); it unites all clubs and societies. Approximately 2000 sports clubs unite around 140,000 Estonians—according to figures in surveys provided by the European Union, 28 percent of sixteen- to twenty-four-year-old Estonians were members of a sports club.[9]

In Estonia, 7.6 percent of eighteen- to thirty-four-year-old men, 3.4 percent of thirty-five- to forty-nine-year-old men, and 2.7 percent of fifty-plus-year-old men participated in intensive and competitive sports. Fewer women were active in sports: 4.1, 1.9, and 0.4 percent, respectively. Thirty percent of women and 37 percent of men between eighteen and thirty-four years of age engaged in physical activity at least once a week. Between the ages of thirty-five and forty-nine, 19 percent of men and 26 percent of women participated in sports, and for women and men older than fifty, 9 percent of men and 22 percent of women remained active. On average, 79 percent of Estonian women and 70 percent of Estonian men never participate in sports.

On an international level, Estonian athletes were most successful in track and field, wrestling, and weight lifting before the breakdown of the former Soviet Union. Now the sports most popular among Estonians are track and field, basketball, sailing, and cycling.

Latvia

Since 1993, the Latvian Sports Administration (Latvijas Sporta Pärvalde; or LSP) has been the umbrella body for all sporting activities in Latvia.

ULJANA SEMJONOVA

Uljana Semjonova (born March 9, 1952, in Daugavpils), the famous 2.12-meter (6´11´´) basketball center for the former Soviet Union, earned many honors during her career, which began in 1968. She was a double Olympic champion (in both 1980 and 1984), a triple world champion, and ten-time European champion. She was nominated as the first non-U.S. player to the Basketball Hall of Fame in 1993.

Thirty percent of Latvian women and 33 percent of Latvian men between the ages of eighteen and thirty-four participated in physical activities at least once a week. Only 12 percent of females and 18 percent of males between the ages of thirty-five and forty-nine did so, and even fewer Latvians over the age of fifty, 15 percent of women and 20 percent of men, were active at least once a week. This means that on average 85 percent of Latvian women and 80 percent of Latvian men do not participate in physical activities. Nonetheless Eurobarometer reported in 2003 that 25 percent of Latvian sixteen- to twenty-four-year-olds are involved in club-related sports.

The most popular sports in Latvia are track and field athletics, basketball, and ice hockey.

Lithuania

Seventy-eight Olympic and non-Olympic sports federations in Lithuania cover ninety-six sports disciplines. The Lithuanian Union of Sports Federations was founded in 1993 and acts as an umbrella organization at a national level with over 800 sports clubs in the country.

Thirty-two percent of eighteen- to thirty-four-year-old women and 37 percent of men in that age group participate in sports once a week or more; 21 percent of women and men aged thirty-five to forty-nine take part in sports at least once each week; and 23 of women and 26 percent of men fifty or more years of age participate in sports once a week or more. On average 76 percent of Lithuanians (77 females, 75 males) say that they never participate in sports.

The most popular sports are basketball, soccer, bodybuilding, track and field athletics, sport dances, and tennis. More than 52,000 people of all ages attend sports clubs on a regular basis.

EASTERN EUROPE AND THE BALKAN STATES

Poland

In Poland, 4339 sports clubs and approximately 8000 school sport associations are represented by sixty-six national federations and the Polish Olympic Committee (Polski Komitet Olimpijski; or PKOl). Thus approximately 385,000 Poles participate in sports.

Between 1997 and 2003, Polish participation in sports rose from 26 percent to 41 percent; Nine percent of Polish citizens took part in sports regularly, 11 percent participated in sports rather often, and 21 percent said that they were seldom active in sports. A still higher number of Poles, 59 percent, did no physical exercise at all.

According to club membership figures in Poland, soccer is the number one sport with over 180,000 participants. Only one-tenth are involved with track and field (18,400) and volleyball (17,200), followed by basketball (14,300), karate (13,600), table tennis (11,800), and handball (10,000).[10]

Czech Republic

The Czech Sports Association (Český svaz tělesné výchovy; or ČSTV) involves thirty-eight Olympic sports federations, thirteen non-Olympic sports federations, eighteen associations with a special affiliation to sports, and 8763 sports clubs. The ČSTV has more than 1.3 million members. A second national body for sports is the Czech Olympic Committee.

Thirty-six percent of the Czech population never participate in sports activities, and 31 percent participate in sports at least once a week. In the nine- to fifteen-year-old age group, 70.5 percent of females and 66.9 percent of males take part in sports regularly. Among women aged sixteen to seventy-four, 48.1 percent take part in sports regularly, whereas only 57.9 percent of men in the same age do so. In the Czech Republic, 16.5 percent of females and 16.3 percent of males do not engage in any physical exercise.

The membership figures for organized sports once again display a strong preference for soccer: 478,205 Czechs are members of a soccer club. Only 61,013 persons are registered as members of tennis clubs, 58,439 persons are members of ice hockey clubs, and 53,047 persons are involved in volleyball. Basketball, track and field, skiing, floorball, equestrian sports, and cycling follow. Cycling enjoys the greatest popularity among non-club-related sports, with 11 percent of women and 10 percent of men saying that they do cycling and mountain biking. Women prefer aerobics, swimming, volleyball, jogging, and basketball, whereas men say that soccer is their number two sport, followed by swimming, volleyball, jogging, and bodybuilding.

ADAM MAŁYSZ

At the age of fifteen, Adam Małysz (born December 3, 1977, in Wisła) started his ski-jump career and soon became a national hero. In 2001 he won the Four Hills Tournament, the most sought-after title for ski jumpers, He was also a triple World Champion and a World Cup winner. Małysz is the most successful Polish winter athlete of all time, winning both a silver and a bronze Olympic medal in Salt Lake City in 2002.

Slovakia

The most important nationwide nongovernmental sports organizations are the 101 national sport federations, seven special sports organizations, and 20 confederation like organizations.

On regional and local levels, there are some 4000 sport clubs and associations that provide appropriate services for practicing organized and unorganized sports. Altogether the sport-specific federations had a total of approximately 687,000 members in 2003; 568,000 members took part in competitions.

According to the membership figures, soccer is by far the most popular sport in Slovakia with 458,000 members, dwarfing basketball, handball, tennis, ice hockey, bodybuilding and power lifting, and table tennis with from 10,000 to 20,000 members, and karate, volleyball, and mountain running with fewer than 10,000 members.

MARTINA NAVRÁTILOVÁ

Martina Navrátilová (October 18, 1956, near Prague) started her tennis career in Czechoslovakia, and in 1973 she began to represent her country at international lawn tennis tournaments. The serve-and-volley specialist and left-hander Navrátilová emigrated to the United States in 1976 and with her doubles partner Chris Evert took first place at Wimbledon. Her many titles and records, including 18 Grand Slam victories and a series of 74 undefeated games, guaranteed her entrance to the Tennis Hall of fame.

ZINEDINE ZIDANE

Young Zinedine Zidane (June 23, 1972, in Marseille) learned soccer techniques in the streets of Marseille. His talent was discovered by the residential school of the A.S. Cannes and at 17 he played in the first division of French soccer. In 1994 he was a first-time member of the "Equipe Tricolore," the French national team, and in 1998 he played with them when they won the World Cup final. Further honors followed. He also played for some of the most successful European soccer clubs: Juventus Turin and Real Madrid. In the 2006 World Cup final between France and Italy, his last game for France, Zidane was red-carded for headbutting an Italian player who had provoked him.

Hungary

About eighty national sports federations represent the different disciplines in Hungary. In 2004, 7000 sports clubs had a total of 840,000 members, and over 200,000 of them participated in official competitions. Additionally over 3000 school sports clubs promoted physical activity in Hungary.

Bicycling is the most popular sport in Hungary, with 19 percent of women and 16 percent of men deciding in its favor. After cycling, women listed dancing, swimming, and jogging at 9 percent each, aerobics at 8 percent, and badminton and billiards at 7 percent, followed by darts, skating, basketball, and handball. Men, on the other hand, ranked soccer second at 12 percent, followed by billiards at 10 percent, swimming at 8 percent, jogging at 7 percent, darts and chess, each at 6 percent, badminton, dancing, and table tennis, each at 4 percent, and basketball at 3 percent.

Sports financing in Hungary is secured by the government, with 0.25 percent of the national budget and additional subsidies of €73.5 million by municipal authorities allocated to sports in 2000.

Slovenia

The national governing body in Slovenian sports is the Olympic Committee of Slovenia and Association of Sports Federations (Olimpijski Komite Slovenije—Združenje Športnih Zvez; or OKS-ZSZ). This group acts as an umbrella organization for thirty-one federations for Olympic sports, seventeen federations of IOC-recognized sports, twelve federations for non-Olympic sports, twelve municipal sports federations, ten federations of general or expert nature, and three associations of bordering regions. All of these groups represent approximately 3,500 sports clubs with 300,000 to 400,000 members.

Forty-six percent of the Slovenian population over eighteen are engaged in physical activity once a week or more, and only 20 percent participate in physical activities three times per month or less. Thirty-four percent of Slovenian citizens state that they do not participate in sports at all.

State support for Slovenian sports amounted to approximately €50 million in 2000. In addition, lotteries provided sports with approximately €4 million in 2001.

RUUD GULLIT

Ruud Gullit (born September 1, 1962, in Amsterdam) was one of the most outstanding European soccer players of the late 1980s and early 1990s. Because of his all-around abilities, he was regarded as the prototype of the future soccer player. Nonetheless, he won his only international title in 1988 at the European Championship. Afterward he won national titles with A. C. Milan in the Italian A-Series and later changed to FC Chelsea, where he stayed as a coach. In 2004 he went back to his native club, Feyenoord Rotterdam.

CENTRAL EUROPE

France

The Comité National Olympique et Sportif Français (CNOSF) acts as the umbrella body for twenty-nine Olympic sport federations, forty-six national sports federations, fourteen multisport and related sports federations, and five school and university sports federations. It represents over 170,000 sports associations and clubs and nearly 14 million members.

In 2000 72 percent of the French population engaged in physical activity at least once a year, with 60 percent participating at least once a week and 12 percent even participating in a competitive context. Two years later 35 percent stated they did not participate in sports at all, whereas 43 percent said they participated in sports at least once a week.

In 2002 non-club-related leisure activities such as walking (21 percent), swimming (15 percent), and bicycling (13 percent) were very popular sports among fifteen- to seventy-five-year-olds. Twelve- to seventeen-year-old youngsters preferred swimming (39 percent), cycling (38 percent), and soccer (32 percent). Soccer is also a very popular sport, according to 2004 club membership figures that claim 2,140,100 members; it is followed by tennis (1,064,800), judo/ jujitsu (564,800), equestrian sports (432,500), basketball (426,900), pétanque (23,200), golf (301,900), handball (300,500), rugby (256,000), and sailing (224,500).

Netherlands

The National Olympic Committee Netherlands Sport Federation (Nationaal Olympisch Comité*Nederlandse Sport Federatie, or NOC*NSF) is the umbrella organization for more than ninety sports federations and 30,000 clubs and associations. Thus the number of athletes organized in clubs amounts to over 1.5 million.

In 1999 41 percent of the Dutch said they did engage in some physical activity, whereas 41 percent were involved in irregular and occasional physical exercise. Eighteen percent of the Dutch population participated in sports frequently. In 1999–2000, 86 percent of twelve- to nineteen-year-olds spent 2.6 hours participating in sports, 74 percent of twenty- to thirty-four-year-olds spent 1.3 hours in

ANTON GEESINK

Anton Geesink (born April 16, 1934) may be regarded as the person who changed the world of judo. He was the first European to become World Champion in Paris in 1961, leaving the Japanese in second place. He repeated this victory at the 1964 Olympic Games in Tokyo and put an end to the idea that the Japanese were unbeatable. The International Judo Federation made him the first European to receive the tenth *dan* (or rank). He was elected one of the fifty most successful athletes of the century by UNESCO in 2000.

PIETER CORNELIS MARTIJN VAN DEN HOOGENBAND

Pieter van den Hoogenband (born March 14, 1978, in Maastricht) started his swimming career with the PSV Eindhoven, and at the age of eighteen, he surprised the world by finishing fourth in both the 100- and 200-meter freestyle events at the 1996 Summer Olympics. With six gold medals at the European Championships in 1999, he was one of the favorites for the 2000 Sydney Olympics. In an exciting final in the 200-meter freestyle, van den Hoogenband equaled Australian Ian Thorpe's new world-record time from the semifinals to win the gold medal. Other world records and titles followed, including three Olympic gold medals, two Olympic silver medals, and two Olympic bronze medals.

FRANZISKA VAN ALMSICK

The career of Franziska van Almsick (born April 5, 1978, in Berlin) had many turning points: "World class," "world record," "brat," "tragic heroine," and "athletic loser" were some ways that headlines in several German newspapers described her. Her career started in 1991, and she proceeded to garner records and titles until the Olympic Games in Atlanta. Due to her rapid rise, she was one of the media's favorite athletes—until she lost strength, and enthusiasm turned into malice. The inglorious climax of her career was reached during the Sydney Olympic Games in 2000: "Leaden duck," the media proclaimed. Nevertheless van Almsick started a comeback, which she managed to sustain in 2002 but which did not last long enough for the 2004 Olympic Games in Athens.

sports, 63 percent of thirty-five- to forty-nine-year-olds spent 1.1 hour in sports, and 48 percent of fifty- to sixty-four-year-olds and 35 percent of sixty-five- to seventy-nine-year-olds spent 0.9 hours each in sports.

In club-related contexts, soccer ranks first as the most popular sport. Tennis, gymnastics, golf, ice skating, field hockey, swimming, equestrian sports, skiing, and volleyball follow. Among sports that are not organized, swimming predominates, followed by fitness, walking, cycling, soccer, tennis, gymnastics, running and jogging, and aerobics.

The Ministry of Health, Welfare and Sport subsidizes provincial sports organizations with around €60 million each year. In addition, the state lottery provides approximately €37 million. Other sources of revenue are sponsors (€270 million), television broadcast rights (€450 million), and membership fees (€635 million).

Belgium

The Comité Olympique et Interfédéral Belge (COIB) has the task of representing both the Olympic movement and non-Olympic sports federations in Belgium. Furthermore the COIB must combine the regional federations in the Flemish-, French-, and German-speaking areas. The COIB incorporates thirty-four Olympic, thirty non-Olympic, eleven affine federations, and three multisport and sport-promoting federations. Its approximately 17,000 sports clubs comprise around 1.35 million members.

In 2000 the most popular sport in Belgium was cycling, practiced by 31 percent of the Belgian population. Cycling was followed by swimming with 23 percent, walking with 20 percent, sport in fitness clubs with 15 percent, soccer with 13 percent, jogging with 12 percent, and tennis, gymnastics, basketball, and badminton with less than 10 percent.

FRANZ BECKENBAUER

The soccer player Franz Beckenbauer (born September 11, 1945, in Munich) is one of the most popular Germans and one of the world's best players ever. In 1990 the former captain of the 1974 World Champion team led the German team into the World Cup final and won. But his biggest coup was making Germany the site of the World Cup in 2006. During months of travel as the president of the bid committee, "Kaiser" (or "Emperor") Beckenbauer, as he is called due to his fame, persuaded the officials of the FIFA to vote for Germany.

Luxembourg

The umbrella organization for sports in Luxembourg is the Comité Olympique et Sportif Luxembourgeois (COSL). In 2002 120,000 athletes were organized in 1534 clubs and sixty-one national federations.

The membership figures for 2000 make soccer the most popular sport in Luxembourg with 26,318 members. Tennis, which has become more and more popular during the last decades, is played by over 16,000 Luxembourg citizens. Gymnastics claims 7,747 participants, basketball is preferred by 5,754 citizens, and table tennis is in fifth place with 4,262 players.

Germany

In 2006 the German Sports Confederation and the National Olympic Committee merged into the German Olympic Sports Confederation (Deutscher Olympischer Sportbund, or DOSB). Fifty-five national federations, eleven federations with special tasks, six associations for education and science, and two supporting associations are organized within the DOSB. Furthermore sixteen regional confederations are represented. Thus 27 million Germans are members of 90,000 sports clubs and associations.

In 2001 37 percent of German females and 49 percent of German males aged sixteen to twenty-five participated weekly in sports. Nearly 28 percent of Germans aged twenty-five to fifty-five engaged in physical activity. In the over-sixty-five age group, 13 percent of females and 14 percent of males participated in sports.

Thus 31 percent of Germans engaged in sports or physical exercise once a week or more. Fourteen percent engaged in sports one to three times per month, and 55 percent took part in sports or exercise less than once per week or never.

In 2004 running was the most popular activity, followed by swimming, cycling, gymnastics, sports in fitness clubs, walking, and soccer. According to sports association membership figures for 2003, 5.5 million German men were organized in soccer clubs, 1.5 million were members of gymnastics associations, 1.2 million did shooting, and 1.1 million played tennis. Women preferred gymnastics, with 3.5 million enrolled as members of gymnastics clubs. Other activities favored by women were soccer with 850,000 women, tennis with 748,000, horseback riding with 539,000, and track and field athletics with 421,700.

German sports are supported by the federal government with around €185 million and by the federal states and communes with approximately €3.5 billion.

Austria

The Federal Austrian Sport Organization (Österreichische Bundes-Sportorganisation; or BSO) is the umbrella body for Austrian

DIRK NOWITZKI

As early as the 1990s, people predicted that Dirk Nowitzki (born June 19, 1978, in Würzburg) would become a leading basketball personality. And he did: in 1998 Nowitzki joined the NBA and soon found his place in the world's top basketball league. The "German Wunderkind," as U.S. fans called him, soon became a star with the Dallas Mavericks and set new records. Nowitzki had been the leading figure on the German national team, which achieved fourth place in the European Championship in 2001, and third place in the World Cup one year later.

HERMANN MAIER

Hermann Maier (born December 7, 1972, in Flachau) appeared on the alpine skiing scene in 1997 and quickly began to place among the best in international competitions. His spectacular purler at the Olympic games in Nagano in 1998, which he overcame without any injuries, and his Super-G Olympic gold medal two days later made him the world's top alpine skier. In 1999 he became double World Champion and had further success in the World Cup. Even a motorcycle accident in 2001 did not stop the "Herminator's" career: he made a comeback in 2003.

sports. It comprises three national governing bodies, fifty-seven national federations, and the Paralympic and Olympic committees as ordinary members, and one representative of the Austrian state, nine regional representatives, and twenty-one all-Austrian associations of high rank as extraordinary members. It represents approximately 12,300 clubs throughout Austria.

Forty-eight percent of Austrians aged 14 and older are regularly involved in physical activity—from once or twice a month to over three times a week. Nineteen percent state that they rarely engage in physical activity, and 33 percent said they never paraticipate in sports.

According to sports club membership figures, Austrians prefer mountaineering with 455,312 members registered in 2003. Second is soccer with 427,600 members, followed by tennis, skiing, gymnastics, curling, golf, swimming, equestrian sports, and cycling. The predominant non-club-related activities are cycling with 53 percent of the total population naming this sport, swimming with 45 percent, hiking with 34 percent, skiing with 28 percent, walking with 26 percent, tennis with 16 percent, inline skating and gymnastics with 12 percent each, and mountain biking and soccer with 8 percent each.

Austrian sports are supported by the government and its provinces and municipalities. Thus the state subsidized sports with €48 million in 2000; in addition the provinces spent approximately €80 million to support physical activities and sports.

RESOURCE GUIDE

PRINT SOURCES

Borgers, Walter. "From the Temple of Industry to Olympic Arena—The Exhibition Tradition of the Olympic Games." *Journal of Olympic History* 10 (September 2002): 7–20.

Bottenburg, Maarten van, Bas Rijnen, and Jacco van Sterkenburg. *Sports Participation in the European Union. Trends and Differences.* Nieuwegein/Netherlands: Arko Sports Media, 2005.

Breedveld K., and Maarten van Bottenburg. Sports in the Netherlands: Policy, research, participation, harmonization. Paper presented at third Compass workshop, Rome, Italy, May 23–25, 2002. Accessed March 15, 2006. http://www..uniroma1. it/compass/ workshop.htm.

Central Statistical Office of Poland, ed. *Concise Statistical Yearbook of Poland 2004.* Warsaw: Zaklad Wydawnictw Statystycznych, 2005.

Christensen, Kristina, Allen Guttmann, and Gertrud Pfister, eds. *International Encyclopedia of Women and Sport.* 3 vols. New York: Gale Group, 2001.

Cox, Richard, Grant Jarvie, and Wray Vamplew, eds. *Encyclopedia of British Sport.* Oxford: ABC Clio, 2000.

Directorate General Education and Culture. *The Citizens of the European Union and Sport.* Special Eurobarometer 213/Wave 62.0—TNS Opinion & Social. Brussels: European Commission, 2004.

Eisenberg, Christiane. *English Sports und Deutsche Bürger. Eine Gesellschaftsgeschichte des Sports 1800–1939.* Paderborn: Schöningh, 1999.

Glader, E. *Amateurism and Athletics.* West Point, NY: Leisure Press, 1978.

Guttmann, Allen. *From Ritual to Record. The Nature of Modern Sport.* New York: Columbia University Press, 2004.

Hartmann-Tews, Ilse. *Sport für Alle!?* Schorndorf: Hofmann, 1996.

Herlihy, D. V. *Bicycle. The History.* New Haven: Yale University Press, 2004.

Holt, R. *Sport and the British. A Modern History.* Oxford: Alden Press, 1989.

Holt, R., ed. *Sport and the Working Class in Modern Britain.* Manchester: Manchester University Press, 1990.

Jones, S. G. *Sport, Politics and the Working Class. Organised Labour and Sport in Inter-war Britain.* Manchester: Manchester University Press, 1988.

Kluge, Volker *Olympische Sommerspiele. Die Chronik I. Athen 1896—Berlin 1936.* Berlin: Sportverlag Berlin, 1997.

Ladd, T., and J. Mathisen. *Muscular Christianity. Evangelical Protestants and the Development of American Sport.* Grand Rapids, MI: Baker, 1999.

Liponski, Wojciech, ed. *Encyklopedia Sportów Swiata*. Poznan: Atena, 2001.

Magee, S. *Ascot. The History*. London: Methuen, 2002.

Mangan, J. *Athleticism in the Victorian and Edwardian Public School. The Emergence and Consolidation of an Educational Ideology*. London: Frank Cass, 2000.

McIntosh, P. C. *Sport in Society*. London: West London Press, 1987.

Müller, Norbert. *Pierre de Coubertin (1863–1937). Olympism. Selected Writings*. Lausanne: International Olympic Committee, 2000.

Norges Idrettsforbund og Olympiske Komité. *Sport and Physical Activity in Norway*. Oslo: Akilles, 2004.

Roberts, G. "The Strenuous Life. The Cult of Manliness in the Era of Theodore Roosevelt." Ph.D. dissertation, Brandeis University, 1970.

Steinbach, Dirk. "Das Sportverhalten in Europa: Tendenz beachtlich." *DSB Jahresmagazin 2005/2006. Eine Publikation des Deutschen Sportbundes*, 100–02.

Tokarski, Walter, and Dirk Steinbach, eds. *Spuren. Sportpolitik und Sportstrukturen in der Europäischen Union*. Aachen: Meyer & Meyer, 2001.

Tokarski, Walter, Dirk Steinbach, Karen Petry, and Barbara Jesse. *Two Players, One Goal? Sport in the European Union*. Aachen: Meyer & Meyer, 2004.

Vamplew, Wray. *Play Up and Play the Game. Professional Sport in Britain 1875–1914*. Cambridge: Cambridge Press, 1988

Wassong, Stephan. *Pierre de Coubertin's American Studies and Their Importance for the Analysis of His Early Educational Campaign*. Web-Publishing: Amateur Athletic Foundation of Los Angeles. Accessed December 28, 2006. http://www.aafla.org.

———. "The Playing Fields Sub-Commission of the International Olympic Committee (1926–1930)." *Stadion: International Journal of the History of Sport* 24: 167–83.

———. *Internationale Einflüsse auf die Wiedereinführung der Olympischen Spiele durch Pierre de Coubertin*. Kassel: Agon, 2005.

SELECTED PERIODICALS AND DAILY NEWSPAPERS

Corriere dello Sport, Italy

Diario Sport, Barcelona, Spain, 1975–

Gazzetta dello Sport, Milan, Italy, 1896–

Kicker Sportmagazin, Nurenberg, Germany, 1920–

Lancilotto e Nausica. Critica e Storia dello Sport, Rome, Italy, 1984–

L'Equipe. Le Quotidien du Sport et de l'Automobile, Paris, France, 1946–

Sovetskiy Sport, Moscow, Russia, 1924–

Sport Bild, Hamburg, Germany, 1988–

Sport in History, Oxford, United Kingdom, 1983–

Sport in Society. Culture, Commerce, Media, Politics (formerly: Culture, Sport, Society), Oxford, United Kingdom, 1997–

Sportwissenschaft, Schorndorf, Germany, 1970–

Stadion. International Journal for the History of Sport, St. Augustin, Germany, 1975–

Tuttosport, Turin, Italy, 1946–

VIDEOS/FILMS

Billy Elliott: I Will Dance (United Kingdom, 2000). Directed by Stephen Daldry. A film about a boy who does not want to do boxing but ballet and starts dancing against his father's will.

Das Wunder von Bern (Germany, 2004). Directed by Sönke Wortmann. A reconstruction of the World Cup final in soccer played in Bern, Switzerland, seen from a nine-year-old boy's viewpoint.

En forarsdag in Helvede (Denmark, 1977). Directed by Jorgen Leth. A documentation of the Paris-Roupaix spectacle in 1976.

Fimpen (Sweden, 1973). Directed by Bo Widerberg. Comedy about the discovery of a young talent who finds out the disadvantages of professional soccer.

Höllentour. Der Film (Germany, 2004). Directed by Pepe Danquart. A movie on the Tour de France on its 100th anniversary in 2003.

Kick It Like Beckham (original title Bend It Like Beckham) (United Kingdom/United States/Germany, 2002). Directed by Gurindher Chadha. A problem-oriented movie about an Indian girl who wishes to play soccer against her family's wishes and her religion. Also examines other aspects of an immigrant's life in Britain.

Olympia. Fest der Völker and Olympia. Fest der Schönheit (Germany, 1938). Directed by Leni Riefenstahl. The first movie that dealt solely with the Olympic Games of 1936.

People and Leisure (United Kingdom). Directed by John Taylor. A film that deals with sports development in the United Kingdom and depicts the problems associated with it.

2. Paralympics Revival 1995 (Germany, 1995). Directed by Otto Bock. This documentary deals with the preparation of athletes with disabilities in Duderstadt, Germany, in 1995 for the Atlanta Paralympic Games, which took place a year later.

WEBSITES

European Commission. Accessed December 28, 2006. http://ec.europa.eu/sport/index_en.html. Home page on sports in the European Union, legislation, actions, and further information.

European Committee for Sport History (CESH). Accessed December 28, 2006 http://www.cesh.eu. Home page on the history of sports in Europe.

Giro d'Italia. Accessed December 28, 2006. http://www.giroditalia.it. Home page of the second largest cycling event in the world after the Tour de France.

International Association for Sports and Leisure Facilities (IAKS). Accessed December 28, 2006. http://www.iaks.org. Home page for architects and engineers of sports facilities. The organization has its seat at the German Sport University in Cologne.

International Olympic Committee (IOC). Accessed December 28, 2006. http://www.olympic.org. Official home page of the Olympic movement headquartered in Lausanne, Switzerland, with other links to sports organizations worldwide.

International Paralympic Committee (IPC). Accessed December 28, 2006. http://www.paralympic.org. Official home page of Paralympic sports headquartered in Bonn, Germany, with links to other organizations for sports for the disabled.

Rychtecky, Antonin. *Participation in Sports and Physical Activities in the Czech Republic.* Updated March 15, 2005. http://www.uniroma1.it/compass/czech.htm.

Slovakia and Its Sports. Accessed March 15, 2006. http://www.sportslovakia.sk.

Tour de France. Accessed July 10, 2006. http://www.letour.fr. Official home page of the Tour de France.

Union of European Football Associations (UEFA) Champions League. Accessed December 28, 2006. http://www.uefa.com/Competitions/UCL/index.html. Home page of the crown of European soccer run by the European soccer federation UEFA.

World Equestrian Festival CHIO Aix-en-Provence. Accessed December 28, 2006. http://www.chioaachen.de/. Home page of the world's most popular equestrian event outside of the Olympic Games.

MUSEUMS

Sport Museum of Finland, Olympic Stadium, FI-00250, Helsinki, Finland. www.urheilumuseo.fi. The Sports Museum of Finland is a national institution devoted to the history of sports and physical activity in Finland. It is located at the Olympic Stadium of Helsinki, the venue of the Olympic Games of 1952.

Norwegian Olympic Museum, Håkon Hall, 2618 Lillehammer, Norway. www.ol.museum.no. The Norwegian Olympic Museum is situated in Lillehammer, the host city of the 1994 Olympic Winter Games. The museum displays the history of the Olympic Games and sports from their ancient Greek origins up to the present day by audiovisual means, photographs, and texts. It also has a unique collection of artifacts.

Latvian Sports Museum, Alksnaja iela 9, Riga, LV-1050, Latvia. www.sportamuzejs.lv. The museum houses a rich collection of materials about Latvian sporting activities abroad as well as in Latvia. In January 2000 the museum began the implementation of its long-term project "The Hall of Honour," which currently displays an exhibition dedicated to Latvian Olympic champions.

Vilnius Sportsmen's House, 8 Asmenos St, LT-01135, Vilnius, Lithuania. http://www.muziejai.lt/ Vilnius/sporto_muziejus.en.htm. The museum keeps exhibits representing achievements of sportsmen from Vilnius, activities of sports organizations, and participation of the Lithuanians in the Olympic Games, as well as the World Lithuanian Games. The museum depicts the establishment of the first Lithuanian athletic organizations. Its expositions include material about the First National Games in Lithuania in 1938 and focus on the participation of some Lithuanian athletes in the Olympic movement. The permanent exposition documents the history of the All-Lithuanian Games and contains collections of prizes won by well-known Vilnius athletes.

Muzeum Sportu i Turystyki (Sports and Tourism Museum), Wybrzeże Gdyńskie 4, 01–531 Warszawa, Poland. http://www.muzeumsportu.waw.pl/english.htm. The Sports and Tourism Museum houses 44,000 exhibits connected mostly with Polish sports, including medals, badges, plaques, cups, sports and tourist clothes, art work on sports, and postage stamps. The museum's collection also includes 55,000 photographs, 16,000 books, 2700 volumes of journals and archival documents, as well as video and audio documentation. Some of the oldest exhibits are connected with the activities of the Gymnastic Society "Sokół," the Warsaw Rowing Association, the Warsaw Cycling Association, and the Warsaw Skating Association.

Musée National du Sport, 24, rue du Commandant Guilbaud 75016 Paris, France. http://www. museedusport.jeunesse-sports.gouv.fr/. The National Sports Museum of France houses over 100,000 exhibits and displays a wide range of objects relating to the history of sports and physical education. The objects are medals and coins, diplomas, paintings, engravings and lithographs, sculptures, books and periodicals, photographs and films, stamps and posters, and several other pieces of art.

Sportimonium—Sports Museum Flanders and the Flemish Folk Games Central, Bloso-domain Hofstade, Trianondreef, 1981 Hofstade, Belgium. http://www.sportimonium.be. Sportimonium allows the visitor to trace the interesting story of sports and games by means of surprising objects; wonderful posters, remarkable pictures, and clips from television and radio. Other exhibits are trophies and personal belongings of great sports heroes.

Deutsches Sport und Olympia Museum, Rheinauhafen 1, 50678 Köln, Germany. http://www.sport museum.info. On 2000 square meters the German Sports and Olympic Museum displays over 3000 exhibits, including media and film projections from over 2500 years of athletic history. Different aspects of German, international, and Olympic sports are shown in permanent and temporary exhibitions. In all, 100,000 objects are in the possession of the museum.

NOTES

1. Holt 1989 (in Resource Guide), p. 93.
2. Glader 1978 (in Resource Guide), p. 88.
3. Holt 1989, p. 108.
4. Pierre de Coubertin, "Les Exercises Physiques dans les Ecoles d'Angleterre, d'Amerique, d' Australie et dans les Colonies Anglaises," in *Exposition Universelle de 1889. Congres des Exercises Physiques. Compte Rendu des Seances et Concours.* Paris: Publications des Annales Economiques, 1889, pp. 1–7.
5. Most of the information used in this article is taken from van Bottenburg et al. 2005 (see Resource Guide).
6. Bjarne Ibsen and Per Jørgensen, "Sports Structures in Denmark", in Tokarski et al. 2004 (in Resource Guide), pp. 137–146.
7. Norges Idrettsforbund og Olympiske Komite 2004 (see Resource Guide).

8. Erodotos Miltiadous, http://www.eurobasket.com/cyp/intra.asp.
9. The Gallup Organisation. 2003. "Public Opinion in the Candidate Countries. Youth in New Europe," in *Eurobarometer* 2003.1: http://ec.europa.eu/public_opinion/archives/cceb/2003/2003.1_youth_analytical_report_en.pdf, p. 13. Survey requested by the European Commission Directorate General Education and Culture.
10. Central Statistical Office of Poland 2005 (in Resource Guide).

THEATER AND PERFORMANCE

KEVIN BROWN

Popular theater and performance in Europe developed from a wide variety of influences. Some folk traditions date back to the early medieval period or earlier. Distinct traditions appear around various regions, including those identified with the Viking, Celtic, Ottoman, and Germanic cultures. There was a prevalent influence of the Catholic Church throughout the Middle Ages, as well as a steady tradition of Jesuit school drama. In some places Islamic influences existed, such as in Albania, Bulgaria, Greece, and Turkey, all once part of the Ottoman Empire. Jewish theater occasionally arose, such as at the Bucharest Jewish State Theatre in Romania and the Zydowski Theatre in Poland. During the Renaissance, there was a resurgence of classical influences as Europeans gained inspiration from looking back to ancient Greek and Roman drama.

During the eighteenth and nineteenth centuries, theater began to play a larger role, especially in relation to the formation of various national cultures. In many countries, theater has been used as a revolutionary force, sometimes leading to declarations of independence. Theater has also been used as a conservative force, with many state theaters cropping up across Europe toward the end of the nineteenth century.

Theater as popular entertainment has always been strong, from the music halls of England to the boulevard theaters of France. The twentieth century saw several companies dedicated to a "people's theater" movement, including the Théâtre National Populaire in France, the Theatre Workshop in England, and the Work Theatre in the Netherlands. Folk traditions continued to play a role and were often assimilated into regional mainstream theater styles, such as in the *dainas* of Latvia and the *orta oyunu* of Turkey. Popular theater and performance in Europe at the turn of the twentieth century was very lively. A rich variety of theater and cabaret traditions still continues in many European countries, especially at venues such as the Wintergarten Varieté in Germany and the Folies Bergère in France.

The twentieth century saw major disruptions accompanying World War I and World War II. The breakup of the Ottoman Empire in 1923 and the fall of Nazi Germany in 1945 both resulted in the splintering of nation states. There was a suspension of most theatrical activities in those areas hardest hit by the wars. During the period from the end of World War II

THE BURGTHEATER COMPANY

Vienna, the capital of Austria, was the center of the popular theater in the eighteenth and nineteenth century, when dialect comedies and spectacular dramas were featured on the stage. Vienna is the home of the Burgtheater (National Theatre), founded in the eighteenth century, and became the center of Austrian theater under the long-ruling Habsburg dynasty. The Burgtheater is the home of one of Europe's foremost repertory companies, mostly performing modern and classical plays in German, the official language of Austria. Leading actors of the Burgtheater company currently include Raoul Aslan, Ewald Balser, and Paula Wessely. Vienna is also the home of the Wiener Volkstheater and the Akademietheater.

until the late 1980s, the Soviet Union gained influence in most of Eastern Europe, and censorship became prevalent in many of the countries behind the Iron Curtain.

Occasionally during the post–World War II period, underground theaters sprang up, including the "cellar theaters" in Czechoslovakia, "basement theaters" in Ireland, and "free groups" in Switzerland. In 1989, the fall of the Soviet Union and the collapse of Communism in Eastern Europe sent reverberations across Europe. The immediate effect in Eastern Europe was the easing of many restrictive censorship laws, as State subsidies for the theatre dwindled. More recently, the formation of the European Union has changed the theatrical landscape as well: in most cases, theater has flourished as new models of subsidization have taken hold and have created a space for experimentation in the arts.

The turn of the twenty-first century has seen a revival of folk traditions as people of contemporary Europe remember their traditional pasts; examples of this trend include revivals at the Vlaamse Volkstoneel in the Netherlands, the Folklór Centrum in Hungary, and the Dora Stratou Folk Dance Theatre in Greece. Various arts festivals are now prevalent in Europe, often including the traditional arts of drama, music, opera, and ballet, and sometimes offering a blend of new forms of performance such as cinema, multimedia installations, and performance art. Some of the most popular festivals are the Salzburg Festival in Austria, the Avignon Festival in France, and the Edinburgh Festival in Scotland.

ALBANIA

Over twenty professional theater groups are active in Albania. Located in a politically contentious area between the Balkans and Greece, and with a population of 3.13 million,[1] Albania has experienced many influences on the growth of its drama. Traditions of folk theater have long been prevalent in Albania and give a distinctive style to the country's drama.

Because it was part of the Ottoman Empire from the fifteenth century until 1912, Islamic restrictions on theater have slowed the development of drama in Albania. The first play written in Albania was *The Wedding of Lunxheria* (1874), by Koto Hoxhi. After the formation of the Albanian Republic, some European touring companies visited there, including Italian companies that played there during the occupation of the country during World War II. After the war, Albania fell under Communist influence, and during the 1960s and 1970s, the government began funding theater. The first state theater in Albania was founded in 1945 in the capital city Tirana; it was renamed the National Theatre in 1989.

AUSTRIA

Although Austria, with a population of 8.19 million, is most famous for its music, all the performing arts have flourished there. For most of the eighteenth, nineteenth, and twentieth centuries, state-sponsored theater has been at the center of the Austrian stage, and popular folk theater has been either censored or pushed to the outskirts of the cities. Opera has been and is the most popular performance form in Austria. Mozart's operas continue to be featured at the Wiener Staatsoper (State Opera) in Vienna, considered one of the best opera houses in the world. Salzburg boasts the Festspielhaus and Landestheater, both of which offer a mixture of drama, opera, and music.

Many Austrian-born artists were at the center of German-speaking drama in the nineteenth and twentieth centuries. The famous actor and director Max Reinhardt, sometimes considered the "father" of modernism, was born in Austria in 1873 and came to influence the theatrical world through his eclectic productions in Berlin. Hugo von Hofmannsthal wrote symbolist drama in the early twentieth century, notably *Der Tor und der Tod* [Death and the Fool] (1893), as well as adaptations of classical plays. Other notable Austrian playwrights include Fritz Hochwälder, Franz Werfel, and Ferdinand Bruckner. One of the more successful Austrian playwrights of the later twentieth century was Peter Handke, whose experimental plays like *Offending the Audience* became popular internationally in the late 1960s.

There are also many summer festivals in Austria, including the Salzburger Festspiele (Salzburg Festival), founded in 1918 by Reinhardt, Hofmannsthal, and Richard Strauss. Each summer, the Salzburg Festival produces plays, operas, and concerts. Austria boasts a network of popular cabarets and beer gardens, which sometimes offer floor shows, dancing, and music. Other popular performance traditions include performances by the dancing Lipizzaner stallions at the Spanish Riding School, the Vienna Boys' Choir, and the Glockenspiel (carillon) of Salzburg.

BALKANS: SERBIA, MONTENEGRO, CROATIA, BOSNIA-HERZEGOVINA, MACEDONIA, SLOVENIA

The Balkan states have always been culturally diverse. This diversity is reflected in the post–Cold War separation of the former Yugoslavia into the present states: Serbia and Montenegro with a population of 10.5 million, Croatia with 4.55 million, Bosnia-Herzegovina with 3.9 million, Macedonia with 2.03 million, and Slovenia with 1.97 million.

Croatia and Slovenia were once part of Austria, and therefore the German-language theater has been dominant there. Players from Germany were known to visit this region in the early 1800s, and by mid-century, native companies roamed the countryside. A National Theatre of Croatia was formed in Zagreb in 1860. A group of actors, led by Mladen Skiljan, founded the Zagreb National Theatre in 1953. The Comedy Theatre in Zagreb continues to feature musicals and puppet theater.

The Serbian theater was more influenced by France and Russia. The Serbian National Theatre began in Belgrade in 1869 and later housed the Yugoslav Dramatic Theatre. Their repertoire included plays by European dramatists such as Henrik Ibsen, as well as many by Serbian playwrights. In the early twentieth century, Branislav Nusic was an influential theater manager who also wrote popular social comedies. He was an influence on Ivan Cankar, who was a central figure of the modernist movement. The Belgrade Dramatic Theatre was formed as an offshoot of the Serbian National Theatre in 1952.

Under Communist control of the Yugoslavian state, between the end of World War I and the early 1990s, theater was subsidized. Although Yugoslavia was ruled by Marshal Tito from 1945 to 1980, Tito rejected Soviet Communism; one result was that theater flourished in the absence of the strict dictates governing the arts that were felt in most Eastern European countries. While there were only twelve theaters in Yugoslavia in 1939, by 1949 there were sixty-six spread throughout the country, many in remote regions. Six of these were in Macedonia, offering plays produced by Dimitar Kjostarov, who was trained in Stanislavski's naturalistic methods. Theater in Slovenia during this period was centered around the city of Ljubljana. A cultural center was established in Trbovlje in 1957, featuring touring companies as well as local productions. The Ljubljana Opera continued to be active during this period. The Dubrovnik Festival of the Arts was established in Bosnia in 1950. The Belgrade International Theater Festival started in 1968.

Since the breakup of Yugoslavia in the 1990s, theater has struggled, although with some successes. The shake-ups of the late 1990s provided themes for many contemporary plays, such as Croatian playwright Slobodan Snajder's *Snake Skin* (1998) and Macedonian playwright Goran Stefanovski's *Euroalien* (1998).

BALTIC STATES: LITHUANIA, LATVIA, ESTONIA

In Lithuania, with its population of 3.43 million, theater has been influenced by folk traditions, and plays are often written in rhyming verse. The Lithuanian State Theatre in Kaunas had its heyday between the country's declaration of independence from Russia in 1920 and its incorporation into the Soviet Union in 1940. The leading playwright of this era was Balys Sruoga, whose plays, such as *Kazimieras Sapiega* (1942), commented on the common people and the fight for independence. During the Soviet era, playwright Justin Marcinkevicius was popular, and director Eimuntas Nekrosius rose to international acclaim shortly after Lithuania' declaration of independence from the Soviet Union in 1991. Even in contemporary times, Jesuit school drama is performed in the street.

At the turn of the twentieth century in Latvia, the best-known playwright was Janis Rainis, who became renowned for incorporating Latvian history and folk heroes into his plays. In 1918 Latvia's independence from Russia was announced on the stage of the Latvian National Theatre in Riga. Like Lithuania, the country lost its independence a second time in 1940, and theater atrophied under Soviet domination. Since the second independence was declared in 1991, Latvian drama has looked to folk traditions for inspiration, particularly to *dainas*, Latvian folk music. Because of the German influence in Latvia, opera is popular, particularly as performed at the Latvian National Opera. Today, Latvia's population numbers approximately 2.3 million.

During the 1800s, Estonian folk traditions experienced a revival but were once again suppressed when the Soviet Union took over the country in 1939. In the postwar period, the most famous Estonian dramatist was Artur Alliksaar. His play *The Nameless Island* (1966) attacked Stalinism; as a result, it was censored for a long time. In 1991 Estonia became independent again, and the country's theater experienced a revival at venues like the Estonia Theatre in Tallinn. Estonia's population is approximately 1.33 million.

BENELUX: BELGIUM, NETHERLANDS, LUXEMBOURG

Belgium, with a population of 10.41 million, is a bilingual country (French and Flemish), split between its French-speaking side (Wallonia), where theater is based on French forms, and the Dutch-speaking side (Flanders), where drama resembles the theater in the Netherlands. One of the best-known playwrights from Belgium was the symbolist Maurice Maeterlinck, whose plays first became famous in Paris. Comédiens Routiers was a popular theater company, directed by Jacques Huisman, which toured Belgium at the turn of the twentieth century. Huisman would later become the director of the touring National Theatre, formed in 1945 after World War II. Today, the tendency toward decentralization in theater is kept alive through a government subsidy program that favors small local groups over large groups in the big cities. In the first few years of the twenty-first century, there has been much experimentation in the arts, with many crossover performance artists, such as Jan Fabre, whose work challenges the boundaries between theater, dance, and sculpture. The Cirque Royal, originally a circus, hosts opera, ballet, and concerts. Also notable is the Théâtre Royal de Toone, a puppet theater that features classical plays.

In the Netherlands, with a population of 16.3 million, drama is also split between two language traditions; French tragedies and Dutch comedies were traditionally the most popular dramatic forms. The first major theater was the De Koninklijke Vereeniging Het Nederlands Tooneel (Royal Society of Netherlands Theatre), producing mainly French plays and the works of Shakespeare. One of the first managers was Louis Henri Crispin, who was influenced by the naturalism of the French Théâtre Libre.

The early twentieth century saw Flemish revivals and the creation of the Vlaamse Volkstoneel (Flemish Folk Theatre), based in Flanders and touring throughout Belgium, the Netherlands, and Luxembourg. The Netherlands was the home of two of the most significant Flemish playwrights of the twentieth century: Joost van den Vondel, who wrote constructivist plays based on classical stories and the Bible, and Hugo Claus, who was a practitioner of poetic realism. Subsidies became available to theater troupes in the 1950s. In the 1960s, 1970s, and 1980s, underground groups, particularly in the progressive city of Amsterdam, called for the end of domination by elite foreign influences and attempted to establish a people's theatre. One example was the Work Theatre, which created plays collaboratively and performed them in schools or in the streets. Amsterdam continues to boast lively experimental theaters and cabarets, with groups like Felix Meritis offering experimental theater and dance in cabaret settings and Boom Chicago offering improvisational comedy. The Netherlands has a lively festival season, including the Lowlands Festival, the Oerol Festival, Dance Valley, and the Parade. Also popular in the summer is the Vondelpark Openluchttheater (Open Air Theatre).

Luxembourg, with a population of 0.46 million, is also very multicultural, with three official languages. Plays in French and German have long been popular, but a greater number of plays are being produced in the local language, Letzeburgesch. The Théâtre Ouvert Luxembourg (Open Air Theatre of Luxembourg) and the Théâtre du Centaure (Centaur Theatre) both opened in the 1970s, and 1985 saw the formation of Théâtre des Capucins de la Ville de Luxembourg.

BULGARIA

Bulgaria, with a population of 7.73 million, has over forty professional theaters. The arts in Bulgaria show the diverse influence of its Ottoman past, as well as the influence of the Greek upper class. The first Bulgarian acting company was formed in 1881 by Stephen Popov. The National Theatre was begun in the capital, Sofia, in 1904; it was fully operational by 1907 and was based on Russian models. The playwright Ivan Vazov was a dominating figure in turn-of-the-century Bulgarian literature, and his plays captured the nationalist spirit of

VÁCLAV HAVEL, CZECH PLAYWRIGHT

Václav Havel's absurdist plays, *Zahradni Slavnost* [The Garden Party] (1963) and *Vyrozumení* [The Memorandum] (1965), satirized the Communist Party and contributed to the liberal ideas that led to the Prague Spring in 1968. His plays were banned, and he was put in prison for five years. Samuel Beckett's play *The Catastrophe* (1982) was dedicated to Havel during the latter's imprisonment. Later, Havel participated in the "Velvet Revolution" of 1989. He was the last president of Czechoslovakia, resigning in 1993 when the country agreed to be split into two parts; later, he was elected the first president of the Czech Republic.

those times. Another playwright, Petko Todorov, was known for creating plays based on Bulgarian folktales and traditional songs, such as *Zidari* [The Builders] (1899). The 1920s and 1930s saw the rise of psychological realism with plays by Stefan Kostov and Iordan Iovkov. Following World War II, the country came under Communist rule, and theaters came under state control. During this period, theater was largely a tool for propaganda, with plays like *The Promise* (1949) by Andrei Gulyashki. Censorship in the theater was common until 1956 when it loosened slightly after the death of Stalin, and plays critical of Communism were able to be written, such as *Fear* (1956) by Todor Genov.

Since the fall of the Soviet Union, Bulgarian performance has become largely experimental and sometimes mixes genres, often incorporating folk dancing, folk singing, mime, and ballet. Numerous popular attractions feature folk music, folk dancing, sound-and-light shows, and even performances of Black Sea coast fire walking. Many new theaters have sprung up across Bulgaria, such as the open-air theater at Primorska Gradina (Seaside Park) and the baroque Dramatichen Teatur (Drama Theatre) in Varna. Pantomime is a very popular form in Bulgaria, with schools like Studio Pantomime, operated by Velyo Goranov. Opera is also well represented, with the Sofia National Opera House among the best in the world.

CZECH REPUBLIC, SLOVAKIA

Drama in what are now the Czech Republic (2004 population 10.22 million) and Slovakia (population 5.4 million) had its origins in the rituals of Slavic tribes of the fifth century, which remain an influence. The modern age of Czech theater was ushered in with the founding of the Národní Divadlo (National Theatre) in Prague in 1883. This gave rise to a period of naturalistic comedies and folk tragedies, which often featured farmers as stock characters; there also existed some symbolist drama. Around the turn of the nineteenth century, popular playwrights included Alois Jirásek and Frána Srámek.

Karel Hugo Hilar was an important theater manager who directed the Czech Municipal Theatre and the National Theatre; he also encouraged the development of new artists such as Karel Čapek. In the play *R.U.R.* [Rossum's Universal Robots] (1921), Čapek coined the term "robot," derived from a Czech word meaning "to toil in servitude." World War II brought an end to a golden age of Czech drama, with the German and Soviet influences producing an end to experimental theater and a shift toward Socialist Realism.

Experimental theater saw a resurgence in the 1950s with artists like designer Josef Svoboda, who found new ways to combine theater, cabaret, and film. The Theatre on the Balustrade was formed, featuring a mime company led by Ladislav Fialka, and plays directed by Jan Grossman. Plays by Josef Topol were performed at the Divadlo ze Branou (Theatre before the Gate), founded by director Otomar Krejca. The 1970s saw more experimentation and the formation of "cellar theaters," covert performances at private homes. Experimental theater is found at the Archa Theatre and the Laterna Magika in Prague. One of the most popular summer festivals in the Czech Republic is the Prague Spring Music Festival.

The Slovenské Národné Divadlo (Slovak National Theatre) in Bratislava was formed in 1920, featuring director Jan Borodac. Slovakian playwrights of the twentieth century include Jozef Gregor-Taijovsky, Ivan Stodola, Leopold Lahola, and Peter Karvas. Ferko Urbánek is credited with nearly forty plays, often performed by amateur theater groups in Slovak villages.

FRANCE

In France (whose 2004 population was 60.5 million), theater first emerged in the Middle Ages with traveling folk performers. The French national theater, the Comédie Française, was established in 1680. The neoclassical drama of the late Renaissance soon gave way to a theater of the people, *drame bourgeois*, at the end of the eighteenth century, when the philosopher and dramatist Denis Diderot called for plays that depicted middle-class heroes living everyday lives. Theater continued to be reformed throughout the 1800s by such writers as the romanticist Victor Hugo, who wanted to replace the old restrictive forms, exclaiming in his *Preface to Cromwell* (1827) "Let us take a hammer to their theories and systems and treatises."

The end of the nineteenth century saw the establishment of one of the most important modern theaters in Europe, the Théâtre Libre, created by the director André Antoine in 1887 as a reaction against the commercial boulevard theaters that had sprung up earlier in the century. Antoine became known for a naturalistic style, influenced by the philosophy of Emile Zola. Soon after came the introduction of alternative theaters, such as the Théâtre de L'Œuvre, directed by Lugné-Poë, and the Théâtre d'Art, directed by Paul Fort. The early twentieth century saw the formation of the Théâtre du Vieux-Colombrier by Jacques Copeau. Notable theater artists who emerged in the early twentieth century included actor, director, and producer Jean-Louis Barrault; playwright and poet Guillaume Apollinaire, who coined the term *realism*; and Antonin Artaud, who proposed the "theater of cruelty." Surrealist Jean Cocteau collaborated on a ballet with Pablo Picasso in 1917.

During the German occupation of France in World War II, Jean Anouilh adapted Sophocles' *Antigone* with an anti-Nazi message. In the middle of the twentieth century, Jean-Paul Sartre, Albert Camus, Jean Genet, and Fernando Arrabal all wrote influential plays. Mime was and is very popular in France, evolving from artists such as Etienne Decroux and Marcel Marceau. Ariane Mnouchkine's Théâtre du Soleil (Theatre of the Sun) produces unique works combining classical texts with Asian and African performance styles. France has a long tradition of street theaters and circuses, including Cirque d'Hiver (Circus of the Winter) and Luc Zalay's Cirque de la Mer, a company that tours the many summer festivals. Paris has had a lively cabaret scene since the founding of the Folies Bergère in 1886, and shortly thereafter at the Moulin Rouge, both still in operation.

JEAN VILAR, PROMOTER OF PEOPLE'S THEATER

A very important populist French actor, director, and manager was Jean Vilar. He first became known as a classical actor at the Théâtre de l'Atelier. He created a touring ensemble of actors in 1941 that took over the Théâtre de Poche in 1943. He started the Avignon Festival in 1947, which became an internationally recognized event centered on classical repertory theater. Vilar founded the Théâtre National Populaire, where he created a people's theater at the Palais de Chaillot. He promoted theater in the remote parts of France, especially to young people who could not afford the price of seats at Parisian theaters, and offered classical works to thousands of people who had never been to the theater before.

BERTOLT BRECHT

Bertolt Brecht was one of the most influential directors and playwrights of the late twentieth century. He moved to Berlin in 1924 and worked as a dramaturge for the great Austrian director Max Reinhardt. Influenced by Marxist ideals, Brecht invented Epic Theatre, an attempt to implement a Marxist philosophy of dramaturgy primarily through distancing techniques designed to expose the theatrical means of production. One very successful technique was the *Verfremdungseffekt* (alienation effect) through which Brecht sought to neutralize empathy, which he considered a tool of authority. His first successful production was *Die Dreigroschenoper* [The Threepenny Opera] (1928), an adaptation of John Gay's *The Beggar's Opera*. Brecht fled Germany during World War II and lived in exile in the Soviet Union, Denmark, and the United States. After the war, he moved to East Berlin and founded the Berliner Ensemble with his wife, Helene Weigel. His plays include *Mutter Courage und ihre Kinder* [Mother Courage and Her Children] (1941), *Der gute Mensch von Sezuan* [The Good Person of Szechuan] (1943), and *Der kaukasische Kreidekreis* [The Caucasian Chalk Circle] (1945).

GERMANY

There are over 180 public theaters in Germany, a country with a population of 82.69 million where the arts are heavily subsidized. One early form of drama was *Fastnachtspiel*, a kind of folk comedy that developed from a mix of Germanic pagan rituals and religious drama. In the late nineteenth century, a directors' theater movement began in Germany that eventually spread throughout Europe. It began with the formation of the company of George I, the Duke of Saxe-Meiningen, in 1874. A performance by the company at the Freie Bühne (Free Theatre) in Berlin, and its touring of other countries, inspired other directors and quickly led to a trend toward naturalism in theaters across Europe. Theater has been subsidized in Germany since the 1920s. One of the leading modernist movements to come out of Germany was expressionism, in which playwrights like Georg Kaiser commented on the dehumanization resulting from industrialization. Other important German playwrights include Georg Büchner, Frank Wedekind, and Gerhart Hauptmann.

After World War II, Germany was divided into the Communist East Germany and the democratic West Germany. Theater in East Germany became devoted to propagandizing Socialist Realism, but occasionally it was used as a way to stage protests. An important director to emerge around the middle of the century in Germany was Erwin Piscator. The early 1990s saw the fall of the Berlin Wall and the reunification of Germany, creating a new era of collaboration between artists from the East and the West.

Opera is hugely popular in Germany, especially as performed at the Deutsche Staatsoper and the Deutsche Oper in Berlin, the Nationaltheater in Munich, the Hamburgische Staatsoper in Hamburg, and the Alte Oper in Frankfurt. Beer gardens offer traditional German folk dancing and music. Variety theaters and cabarets have been popular in Germany since the late 1800s. The most famous is the Wintergarten Varieté in Berlin, where American vaudeville was introduced to Germany. Reconstructed in 1992, the Wintergarten Varieté offers everything from chorus girls to Russian acrobats. Another popular variety theater is the Schmidt Theater in Hamburg, offering live music, vaudeville, chansons, and cabaret.

GREECE

Greece, with a 2004 population of 11.12 million, has a rich theatrical tradition stretching back to the Athenian theater of the sixth through the third centuries BC; however, after centuries of Roman, Byzantine, and Ottoman rule, Greece did not have a single theater as of the early 1800s. During this time, the *karagöz* shadow puppet theater of Turkey was imported and adapted by the Greeks as *karagiozis*.

In the early twentieth century, Greek theater was dominated by visiting companies from Italy and France. In 1888 a municipal theater was founded in Athens, featuring a Greek opera company, and the Ethnikon (National Theatre) was founded in 1930. After World War II, revivals of classical plays became very popular. Opera is common in Greece, staged by the Greek National Opera at the Olympia Theatre. Traditional Greek folk dancing in authentic costumes can be found at the Dora Stratou Folk Dance Theatre on Philopappos Hill. The new Technopolis is a former foundry that has been converted into an arts complex, featuring galleries and performing arts. Sound and light shows are also popular; they light up the ancient ruins from the Pnyx, the hill across from the Acropolis.

Festivals have been popular in Greece since the days of the Panathenaic Festival and the Olympic games, starting in the sixth century BC. Every summer the Hellenic Festival features live performances that showcase the history of ancient Greece. The Theatre of Epidauros was built in fourth century BC by Polykleitos; it seats over 14,000 people and was one of the few buildings not pillaged during the many wars. The Epidauros Festival of Ancient Drama features productions of classical Greek theater at the well-preserved ancient amphitheatre in the Peloponnese. The Athens Festival features plays, folk dancing, folk music, operas, and ballets, all of which are staged June though September at the Odeion of Herodes Atticus, a second-century theater at the foot of the Acropolis. Also popular is the Lycabettus Festival, which stages theater and popular music on the slopes of Mount Lycabettus. The Festival of Delphi each June features ancient works and new plays inspired by the classics.

HUNGARY

Hungary, with a population of 10.1 million, is the home of numerous professional theater companies and thousands of amateur groups. The first Hungarian National Theatre was started in 1837. One of the most popular playwrights was Karoly Kisfaludy, who wrote plays such as *Csalodasok* (1824) and *Partutok* (1825), which featured lovable Hungarian peasant characters. This period saw the founding of the Peoples' Theatre in the 1860s, as well as a handful of private theaters where musicals were performed, including the Vigszinház (Comedy Theatre) in 1896, which featured a naturalistic acting style. Hungarian playwright Ferenc Molnár became known internationally for his comedies, most notably the play *Liliom* (1909), performed in the United States at the Theatre Guild and adapted into the musical *Carousel* by Rogers and Hammerstein in 1945. Hungary is known for its operettas, and the country houses some of the world's finest opera houses, including the Magyar Állami Operaház (Hungarian State Opera House) in Budapest.

A Communist regime was established in Hungary in 1949; the theaters were taken over by the state and forced to produce plays promoting Socialist Realism. Since the fall of Communism in 1989, theater has flourished again in Hungary, including folk revivals such as the *tánchaz* (dance house), which features dance lessons and live folk music. The Budapest Spring Festival showcases theater, opera, music, and dance, and the BudaFest opera and ballet festival takes place every summer. Puppet theater is also popular. Hungarian folk dancing can be seen at the Folklór Centrum (Folklore Center) in Budapest. Hungary is also known for its cabarets, many of which were shut down in the early years of the twenty-first century because of scandalous excesses.

COMMEDIA DELL'ARTE

Commedia dell'arte was a form of popular entertainment that originated in Renaissance Italy in the mid-sixteenth century. Eventually, the style spread throughout Europe and influenced mainstream drama, particularly in France, England, Germany, Russia, Spain, and Turkey. Commedia dell'arte means "play of professional artists" and probably evolved from the Greek and Roman mime of the classical age. Primarily physical comedy, this form was performed by small troupes of male and female actors, who would travel from town to town and play outdoors. These performances were improvised around a scenario (synopsis), of which about 1000 have survived. The plot usually involved two young lovers (the innamorati: Florindo and Isabella), frustrated in their romance by the older generation (Dottore, the doctor; Capitano, the braggart soldier; and Pantalone, the duped father) and helped along by the clever servants (the zanni: Arlecchino, Truffaldino, Pulcinella, Colombina, and Brighella). Although commedia dell'arte died out in the middle of the eighteenth century, it left a permanent mark on the theater world, influencing playwrights such as Molière, Marivaux, and Goldini, as well as comedians such as Charlie Chaplin, the Marx Brothers, and the Three Stooges.

IRELAND

In Ireland, a country with a 2004 population of 4.15 million, a nationalist movement in the arts was launched at the end of the nineteenth century, headed by the wealthy arts patron Lady Augusta Gregory, the poet and symbolist playwright William Butler Yeats, and Edward Martyn. Together, they founded the Irish Literary Theatre in Dublin in 1899. In the same spirit, the National Irish Theatre Society was begun by actors William and Frank Fay. These brothers would later build the Abbey Theatre in 1904, and the Abbey has been at the center of Irish theater ever since. Artists to emerge from the Abbey include playwrights John Millington Synge, Sean O'Casey, and Lennox Robinson. Actors that became known at the Abbey Theatre include Sarah Allgood, Marie O'Neill, Cyril Cusack, and Barry Fitzgerald.

Ireland's most famous postwar playwright was Samuel Beckett, known for his absurdist dramas that express the condition of human existence, such as *Waiting for Godot* (1953), *Endgame* (1957), and *Happy Days* (1961). Raised in a suburb of Dublin, Beckett eventually moved to Paris, where he wrote many of his plays in French. Playwright Brendan Behan spent fourteen years in prison for activities with the Irish Republican Army before he wrote *The Hostage* (1956) and *The Quare Fellow* (1954). Brian Friel is also known for political dramas such as *Translations* (1980) and *Dancing at Lughnasa* (1990). At experimental "basement theaters," such as the Pike Theatre in Dublin, amateur theater groups perform plays that have been rejected by the mainstream. The Dublin Theatre Festival began in 1957, featuring Irish writers and actors, and continues to be held every year.

ITALY

Ancient ruins from the Roman Empire abound in Italy (whose 2004 population was 58.1 million), and classical Rome has had a palpable effect on the theater of Italy. The Renaissance in Italy was known for several developments in theater, particularly technical developments in staging such as forced-perspective scenery, the proscenium arch, and the raked stage. The Teatro Olimpico in Vicenza, completed in 1584, is the oldest surviving theater of the Italian Renaissance.

Opera was the dominant form of theater in Italy from the seventeenth through nineteenth centuries. Opera was performed at the Teatro dell' Opera in Rome, the Teatro Comunale di Firenze in Florence, and the Teatro alla Scala in Milan. For a brief time in the early 1900s, futurists led by Filippo Tommaso Marinetti stirred up trouble with their short-lived movement devoted to the speed and frenetic energy of the future. The great Italian actress Eleonora Duse toured Europe and the United States around the turn of the twentieth century. Another important Italian theater artist of the twentieth century was Luigi Pirandello, known for his grotesque plays and for creating his own touring theater company in 1925. Other well-known Italian playwrights included Ugo Betti, Eduardo de Filippo, and Diego Fabbri. Later in the century, such directors as Franco Zeffirelli became known for stage productions as well as films.

Popular festivals abound in Italy, including the Maggio Musicale Fiorentino, a festival held during the summer in Florence that features opera, ballet, music, and films. Every two years, the Biennale dell'Arte is held in Venice, attracting a variety of contemporary artists, including a cross-discipline mix from theater, dance, music, visual art, and performance art.

POLAND

Poland, with a 2004 population of 38.53 million, has over 100 professional theaters, including 17 major theaters in Warsaw. The first national theater of Poland was built near Warsaw Castle in the eighteenth century; it was managed by Wojciech Boguslawski, considered to be the "father" of Polish theater. In the nineteenth century, the actress Helena Modrzejewska (also known as Helena Modjeska) gained an international reputation across Europe and the United States. A new National Theatre complex was built in 1833, including the Teatr Wielki for opera and ballet and the Teatr Rozmaitosci for drama.

One of the most intriguing Polish theater artists at the turn of the twentieth century was the actress and dramatist Gabriela Zapolska, who wrote over forty popular naturalist comedies addressing social issues; these included *Zabusia* (1896) and *Panna Maliczewska* [A Miss What's Her Name] (1912). One of the most famous actors of this period was Jerzy Leszczynski. Naturalism dominated, with room for the occasional symbolist dramatist such as Stanislaw Wyspianski, a painter, designer, and writer.

Following World War II, when the Soviet Union controlled the reestablishment of the Polish state, mainstream theaters saw nationalistic revivals of the romantics. Unlike in many Iron Curtain countries, where Soviet censorship had a stifling effect on the theater, the postwar period in Poland saw the emergence of several underground dramatists who were able to gain international recognition: Stanislaw Witkiewicz, who wrote over thirty grotesque dramas; the absurdist Witold Gombrowicz; surrealist Tadeusz Róziewicz; and Slawomir Mrozek, whose play *Tango* (1965) was produced widely in the United States and Europe. Director Jerzy Grotowski became known internationally for his actor-centered theater experiments, especially his production of Wyspianski's *Akropolis*. Other influential Polish directors include Andrzej Wajda and Tadeusz Kantor. The Zydowski Theatre, Warsaw's Jewish theater, featured performances in Yiddish. Poland's Solidarity movement eventually led to that country's independence in 1990, but recent economic hardships have led to cutbacks in government subsidies to the arts.

ROMANIA

Romania, with a population of 21.71 million, boasts over eighty professional theater companies, with at least half of them devoted to performing strictly drama, as well as thousands

CONSTANTIN STANISLAVSKI AND THE MOSCOW ART THEATRE

The Moscow Art Theatre (MAT) was founded in 1898 by Constantin Stanislavski and Vladimir Nemirovich-Danchenko. The studios of the MAT, where Stanislavski worked to perfect his naturalistic system of acting, have trained some of the greatest actors the world has ever seen. Vsevolod Meyerhold trained there; he later became a well-known director on his own and developed a system for acting based on the physical actions of the human body, which he called biomechanics. The first several seasons of the MAT featured plays by Anton Chekhov, with their distinctive naturalistic style. His plays, such as *Tri Sestry* [The Three Sisters] (1901) and *Vishnyovy Sad* [The Cherry Orchard] (1904), are touching tragicomedies that document the decline of czarist Russia.

of amateur acting groups. Theater in Romania has its roots in the religious pageants and festivals of folk culture. Romanian theater has also been influenced by the fact that the country was once part of the Ottoman Empire, as well as by its classical Greek and Roman past.

During the early nineteenth century, the Dramatic Society in Bucharest was formed. Actor Costache Caragiale managed the Teatrul des Mar (Big Theatre), built in 1852 and later renamed the Teatrul National (National Theatre) in 1854. Caragiale's nephew, Ion Luca Caragiale, was one of the first writers of Romanian comedy. Romania has a large Jewish population; in 1876 Avram Goldfaden founded the first Jewish theater in Romania, which would eventually inspire the opening of the Bucharest Jewish State Theatre after Word War II.

The most internationally famous Romanian playwright was Éugene Ionesco, who left Romania in 1938 and became known for his absurdist plays while he was living in Paris. One of the most influential directors of that time was Paul Eusty, who followed the naturalistic ideals of Constantin Stanislavski and André Antoine. In 1948, following World War II, theaters were nationalized and enforced the rules of Stalinist socialist realism. One star actress of this time was Lucia Sturdza Bulandra, who would eventually have a theater named after her.

Opera is very popular in Romania, with the Ion Dacian Operetta and Opera Româna in Bucharest staging operas, operettas, and ballets. Puppet theater is also very popular, and the Turkish *karagöz* shadow puppet theater has been performed in Romania since Ottoman times. One of the most famous groups is the Tandarica Puppet Theatre, founded in Bucharest in the 1950s. Censorship of the theater was lifted after the collapse of Communism in late 1989.

RUSSIA, UKRAINE, BELARUS, MOLDOVA

Early Russian drama consisted mainly of secular drama and presentations by foreign theater groups brought in by the czars, most notably Italian *commedia dell'arte* troupes. In the eighteenth century, a national repertory began at the Comedy House in Moscow. Later, the Bolshoi (big) theater was used for opera and ballet, and the Maly (small) theater hosted drama and musical comedy. Playwright Nikolai Gogol's *Revizor* [The Inspector General] (1836) is still perhaps the most widely performed play in Russian repertory. Notable Russian playwrights around the turn of the twentieth century included Anton Chekhov, Alexander Ostrovski, and Maxim Gorky. Gorky's *Na Dne* [The Lower Depths] (1902), a grotesque play about the pathetic tenants of a lodging house in Volga, became a rallying cry for Communist sentiments.

For a brief period after the Communist Revolution in 1917, theater was freed from the strictures of the czarist past, and a period of experimentation ensued. This short period saw the advent of the modernist movements of futurism and constructivism. Soon after Stalin took over from Lenin, however, censorship of the theater became prevalent. The culmination was Stalin's declaration that socialist realism was the official mode of production, and creativity in the theater came to a standstill. Plays were mostly propaganda pieces centered on a "positive hero" of the working class. Russia experienced a "thaw" under Khrushchev in the 1950s and 1960s, and the theater began to come alive again. A typical play of this period is *The Heart of a Dog* (1987) by Alexander Chervinski, adapted from a story by Mikhail Bulgakov, which uses the allegory of a human-to-canine heart transplant as a metaphor for Stalinism. In 1991 the Soviet Union collapsed—and so did state funding for the arts in Russia, whose population amounted to 143.2 million in 2004.

In Belarus, with a 2004 population of 9.8 million, the puppet theater Battaleika has been a tradition since the sixteenth century. The first professional theater in Belarus started in 1907. By the 1940s, there were over twenty professional theaters in the country. In Ukraine, whose 2004 population was 46.48 million, puppet shows featured the character Petrushka. The Golden Lion International Theatre Festival was founded in 1993 in Lviv. It features experimental theater and performance, attracting many young artists and students from throughout Europe. In Moldova (2004 population 4.2 million), puppetry is also popular and is performed at the Likuritch National Puppet Theatre, founded in 1945.

Throughout all the states that made up the former Soviet Union, there is a long tradition of popular performance, with groups of wandering minstrels called *maskharoboz* (maskers), who travel from village to village, singing and performing improvisational comedy.

SCANDINAVIA: SWEDEN, DENMARK, FINLAND, NORWAY, ICELAND

Theater in Scandinavia has its origins in religious festivals and folk traditions of the Middle Ages. Throughout Scandinavia, May Day celebrations have been popular for centuries and are still held in contemporary times. Celebrations of dancing and music last well into the evening, since the sun only sets for a couple of hours during the summer, and in some of the northernmost regions, the sun never sets at all for many days. For the same reason, outdoor summer drama performances are popular throughout Scandinavia.

Theater is subsidized and remains vibrant in Sweden (2004 population: 9.04 million). Stockholm alone hosts over twenty professional theatres. One of the oldest theaters in the world still in use is the Drottningholms Slottsteater (Drottningholm Court Theatre), built in 1766. The Royal Dramatic Theatre opened in 1788 and later became the National Theatre. August Strindberg, one of the first modern playwrights, is known for incorporating psychology into his naturalistic plays, such as *Fröken Julie* [Miss Julie] (1889). His later plays, such as *Ett Drömspel* [A Dream Play] (1901), border on expressionism and surrealism. Much of his work was performed abroad, as well as in Scandinavia at his own Intimate Theatre. A famous Swedish actor and director at the turn of the century was Gösta Ekman, who worked at the Våsa Teatern in Stockholm. Perhaps the most famous Swedish director was Ingmar Bergman, who managed the Royal Dramatic Theatre in Stockholm in the 1960s and directed films that have received international acclaim. Dance halls and cabarets continue to be popular in Sweden.

In Denmark (whose 2004 population was 5.43 million), theater originated with religious drama, especially Easter plays and plays about the lives of saints. Det Kongelige Teater (Royal Theatre) of Denmark was formed in 1748 and presented operas and ballets. One of the premier

JOHN LIND

John Lind (shortened from John Lindström) was a female impersonator, singer, and dancer of international acclaim in the early twentieth century. Lind got his start at the Alhambra Variety Theatre in Stockholm, with the help of director Hildur Carlsberg. He originally toured with a partner as *Fanny och John Lind*, performing in the United States, Europe, South America, and Africa. Lind, along with Paul Schneider-Duncker, founded the group *Les Petits Filous* in Hamburg. The show *?Lind?*—a variety show in which Lind played female historical figures and satirized contemporary dancers—was featured at the London Pavilion in 1904. Lind toured England, France, Russia, Finland, and Germany, but he only performed his act once in Sweden since female impersonators were not as well accepted at the time.

directors in Denmark was Sam Besekow, known for realistic productions at the Riddersalen Theatre in Copenhagen in the 1930s and 1940s. The actress Betty Nansen, who was well known for her roles in the plays of Strindberg and Ibsen, founded the Betty Nansen Theatre in Copenhagen in 1917. Another famous Danish actor was Poul Reumert, who lived in Denmark for six years during World War II; Reumert's acting style was said to have influenced Bertolt Brecht. After World War II, subsidized theaters flourished with the formation of many new repertory theaters. The 1960s and 1970s saw much experimental work, and Peter Langdal's eclectic adaptations of classical works continued the experimentation through the 1980s and 1990s.

In Finland, whose 2004 population was 5.25 million, a distinct theater did not develop until the late 1800s, during a time of struggle for a national culture after years of Swedish and Russian domination. The Finish poet Aleksis Kivi adapted *The Seven Brothers* into Finnish, inspiring the establishment of a national theater in 1873. It found a permanent home in 1902, and in the 1950s, director Arvi Kivimaa created a repertory company there. During the summer, the Helsinki Festival continues to present dance, music, and performances of poetry.

In Norway, whose 2004 population was 4.62 million, the Dramatic Society of Norway emerged at the turn of the nineteenth century, and in 1849 the Norwegian Theatre was founded in Bergen. This theater was where the most famous Norwegian playwright, Henrik Ibsen, got his start. Ibsen became internationally known for naturalistic dramas such as *Et Dukkehjem* [*A Doll's House*] (1879) and *Hedda Gabler* (1890). The Nationaltheatret (National Theatre) was established in 1899. The largest theater in Norway, the Folk Theatre, opened in Oslo in 1933. In the late twentieth century, theaters became subsidized, and many experimental groups emerged, including the Odin Teatret, started by Eugenio Barba in 1964. Norwegian folk dancing continues to be performed at the Oslo Konserthus (Oslo Concert House) and at the Norwegian Folk Museum.

In contrast to other Scandinavian countries, there is no evidence of early religious dramas in Iceland (2004 population 0.3 million). However, long-standing folk art traditions have flourished for centuries. In the nineteenth century, Sigurður Guðmundsson used theater as a tool in the struggle for national independence from Denmark. The Leikfelag Reykjavíkur (Reykjavík Theatre Company) was created in 1897, and a national theater was founded in 1950. Reykjavík currently hosts a two-week arts festival each summer.

SPAIN, PORTUGAL

In Spain, whose population amounted to 43.06 million in 2004, early theater was influenced by visiting players from Italy, who introduced Spain to *commedia dell'arte* during the

Renaissance. An early form of drama unique to Spain was the short, religious *autos sacramentale* (sacramental act), which began as court drama but soon spread to the *corrales* (courtyards) of inns and public houses. The works of playwrights like Pedro Calderón de la Barca and Lope de Vega (Lope Felix de Vega Carpio) led to a true people's theater. At the height of the golden age of drama in the mid-1600s, Spain had over 300 theater companies including over 2,000 actors.

Another form of theater native to Spain and Portugal was the *zarzuela*, an early form of musical theater based on folk traditions. Since the eighteenth century, opera has been popular in Madrid and Barcelona. During the early twentieth century, the careers of playwright Federico García Lorca and actress Margarita Xirgu were cut short by the onset of civil war in 1936. Censorship became common during the dictatorship of Francisco Franco from 1939 to 1975. Despite this censorship, a state-sponsored Experimental Theatre was established in 1965.

After Franco's death, Spain became a democratic constitutional monarchy and began to subsidize the theater. One important playwright of the late twentieth century was Alfonso Sastre, whose plays often comment on social issues. At the turn of the twenty-first century, theater in Spain is flourishing. Nightclubs are devoted to different types of traditional dance, including Salsa dancing, and *flamenco tablaos* (flamenco clubs) feature live dancing, singing and music. Cabarets such as Barcelona City Hall are also popular. Bullfighting is still performed, with bullfighting rings in the center of many Spanish cities, such as Las Ventas in Madrid. The San Isidro Festival features bullfighting for five weeks around May.

In Portugal, whose population in 2004 was 10.5 million, theater began with the formation of the *Teatro National Doña Maria II*, which began in Lisbon in 1834. This theater is still active, with the majority of its productions in Portuguese. For most of the 1900s, a repressive military regime ruled Portugal, and strict censorship laws slowed the progression of theater. Censorship slightly lessened in the 1940s, leading to the establishment of many theaters. Theater was used for propaganda purposes in a political movement that eventually led to a left-wing coup in 1974 that produced democratic reforms.

SWITZERLAND

The Swiss Confederation, with a 2004 population of 7.25 million, was founded in 1291 as a union of three separate cantons. Different parts of Switzerland speak German, French, Italian, and Rhaeto-Romansh. Switzerland has a rich tradition of popular theater, stretching back to the German-language peasant theater of medieval times. During the sixteenth and seventeenth centuries, theater was prevalent in Protestant and Catholic traditions, both of which used theater as a means to spread competing religious viewpoints. In modern times, there is a rich tradition of Nativity plays and bell ringing at Christmas time.

Because of Switzerland's political neutrality, Swiss theater gained momentum during more recent times. The Zurich Schauspielhaus became internationally known as the last refuge of the German-speaking theater, and it hosted actors from Germany and Austria. After World War II, the most popular writer was Fritz Hochwälder, who fled from Austria during the war to seek refuge in Switzerland. Another great playwright to emerge from Switzerland was Friedrich Dürrenmatt, whose grotesque plays show the influences of German expressionism. The most popular on the international stage was *Der Besuch der alten Dame* [The Visit, or The Visit of the Old Lady] (1956), in which a rich heiress returns to her hometown and talks the villagers into helping her murder a lover who had betrayed her. Similarly, Swiss writer Max Frisch's plays explore the cruelty and dehumanization of war, and the individual's struggle for control and happiness.

In the French-speaking part of Switzerland, there is a long tradition of theater outreach involving the public and the schools, typified by the Théâtre Populaire Romand. One of the most popular French-speaking theaters in Switzerland is the municipal theater in Lausanne, which featured the work of the internationally known designer Adolphe Appia. The Grand Théâtre in Geneva is famous for opera, ballet, and concerts. The 1970s saw the formation of small experimental theaters called *freie Gruppen* (free groups), such as Studio am Montag, created by performance artist Norbert Klassen. Mime is very popular in Switzerland. The mime group Mummenschanz, founded in 1972, is internationally acclaimed for a surrealist style that uses masks and props. Arts festivals are popular in Switzerland: during July and August at Theaterspektakel, for example, avant-garde theater and performance art are performed in circus tents by the lake in Zurich. The Lucerne Festival is a year-round music festival that includes opera and musical theater. Folk performers such as yodelers and dirndl-clad dancers perform in the Swiss Alps. At the end of every September, the alpine "Descent of the Cattle" is accompanied by folk music, folk dancing, parades, and alpenhorn blowing.

TURKEY

Turkey, with a 2004 population of 73.19 million, is home to over nine state-sponsored and numerous private theaters. The Ottoman Empire ruled Turkey from 1299 until the country became an independent, secular state in 1923; however, Islamic restrictions on the creation of images have made theater in Turkey a precarious enterprise. Nonetheless, many popular traditions have survived for hundreds of years, including village theater and folk theater. Village theater, which consists of folktales and fertility rituals performed by peasants to celebrate the change of seasons, predates Islam. Folk theater, on the other hand, was performed at Islamic sultans' festivals during Ramadan. Several forms of folk theater include the storytelling *meddah* (singer of praise); *karagöz*, a type of shadow theater imported from Asia; and *orta oyunu* (or "play in the middle"), similar to the Italian *commedia dell'arte*. A modern form of improvisational theater that developed in the early twentieth century and had its roots in *orta oyunu*, is the *tulûat tiyatrosu*.

Touring European theater companies brought European-style theater to Turkey in the mid-1800s. The first theater was built in Istanbul in 1868, but it was closed by an anti-European sultan in 1882. A drama school was founded at the Dar-ül-Bedayi (Place of Art) in 1914, led by French director André Antoine. In the early 1930s, this school developed into a state theatre, and was named the Sehir Tiyatrosu (municipal theatre) in 1934. The State Conservatory for Music and Drama was founded in Ankara, the capital of Turkey, in 1936.

Although censorship was prevalent in the nineteenth century, theater became subsidized by the Turkish government after World War II. In 1969, the "house of culture" opened in Istanbul, housing productions of drama and opera. Turkey's most well-know dramatist is Nazim Hikmet, who studied drama in the Soviet Union. He escaped to the Soviet Union in 1951 after years of imprisonment in Turkey for being a member of the Communist Party. His most famous work is *Byl li Ivan Ivanovich* [Did Ivan Ivanovich Exist?] (1956). In modern Turkish drama, about two-thirds of the plays produced are by foreign playwrights, and the remaining one-third are by playwrights from Turkey. Some other well-known Turkish playwrights are Cahit Atay, Refik Erduran, Orhan Asena, Haldun Taner, and Turgut Özakman.

The most popular arts festival in Turkey is the Istanbul International Festival, held in June and July in historic buildings throughout the city and featuring theater, opera, ballet, and music. Also, the Selçuk Ephesus Festival of Culture and Art is held in an ancient Ionian outdoor amphitheater. In Konya, the "whirling dervishes," who are Muslim mystics, perform ecstatic dances to flute music.

UNITED KINGDOM: ENGLAND, SCOTLAND, WALES, AND NORTHERN IRELAND

During the later part of the nineteenth century, nondramatic forms such as melodrama and pantomime dominated the English stage. The end of the nineteenth century brought a turn toward naturalism throughout Europe that was felt in the British Isles as well. One of the most prolific and longest-performing theater groups has been the Royal Shakespeare Company, started in 1879 at Stratford-upon-Avon. As a way around government restrictions, the private Independent Theatre Club opened in 1891 and began producing the social dramas of George Bernard Shaw and Henrik Ibsen. The Victoria Theatre, or Old Vic, was once a music hall for variety shows. It was closed temporarily in 1880, and then reopened as a temperance hall that offered lectures, concerts, and drama. In 1912 Lilian Baylis became the manager, and the Old Vic became well known for productions of classical plays.

MUSIC HALL PERFORMANCES

One of the most popular places of entertainment in England during the nineteenth century was the music hall, which featured a variety of popular entertainments for working class audiences. Some of the acts offered included comic songs, sketches, ballet, and even cinematic events. The music hall created its own brand of stars. They traveled throughout the country, performing at various music halls in England as well as abroad. Some of the most famous acts were the male impersonator Vesta Tilley, singer Marie Lloyd, comedian Dan Leno, and minstrel comic Little Tich. Charlie Chaplin emerged as a star from a group of comedians led by Fred Karno. Some well-known music halls in England include the Alhambra, the Canterbury, Collin's, the Empire, and the Metropole. Although the music hall tradition died out with the advent of cinema, its influence on the theater has been permanent, particularly through its impact on the development of vaudeville and musical theater in the United States.

In 1963, actor Laurence Olivier started a new national theater in England, which moved to the South Bank in 1976. From 1964 to 1973, former actor Sir Peter Daubeny directed the World Theatre Season at the Aldwych Theatre in London. Visiting companies from Russia, France, and Germany influenced the development of British theater in those years.

England is home to many arts festivals, from the mainstream to the fringe. The Chichester Festival, begun by Olivier in 1961, features plays from a wide range of artists, from Chekhov to Brecht. George Devine directed the experimental offshoot called the Young Vic; he also founded the English Stage Company in 1956, which took up residence at the Royal Court Theatre, producing plays like John Osborne's *Look Back in Anger* (1956), which challenged the assumptions of the upper class and started an "angry young man" movement that appealed to blue-collar workers. Director Joan Littlewood strove to create a "British people's theater" and founded the Theatre Workshop, which ran from the 1930s until the 1970s. Important contemporary artists include directors Peter Brook and Sir Peter Hall; actor Kenneth Branagh, who started the Renaissance Theatre Company in the 1980s; feminist playwright Caryl Churchill; the Czech-born playwright Tom Stoppard; Alan Bennett; and Andrew Lloyd Webber, whose musicals were some of the most widely popular works of the twentieth century and remain so today.

One internationally known Scottish playwright is Sir James Barrie, who wrote *Peter Pan* (1904), still performed as a popular children's play. John Brand, the founder of Scottish

Players Limited, is considered the "father" of Scottish drama. The Glasgow Repertory Theatre produced drama from 1909 until the outbreak of World War I in 1914. After the war, the Scottish National Players was formed, producing plays by native Scottish dramatists, and playwright James Bridie founded the Citizen's Theatre in Glasgow in 1943. The Edinburgh Festival was started in 1947 by Rudolph Bing, and for three weeks every summer it has featured productions by hundreds of international theatre, music, dance, and performance groups. In the 1950s, the Edinburgh Fringe Festival was added to the mix, featuring more experimental acts.

In Wales, a folk tradition of theater has existed since the days of the *eisteddfods*, festivals that featured ancient songs and plays. Welsh playwright Saunders Lewis was at the center of the Welsh-speaking theater movement of the early 1900s. Poet Dylan Thomas also wrote plays, including *Under Milk Wood* (1956), which lovingly tells the story of a day in the life of a Welsh fishing village. The famous stage and film actor Richard Burton was born in Wales, as was Anthony Hopkins, who also began his career on the stage. There are more than 130 theater companies currently operating in Wales. Northern Ireland is also considered part of the United Kingdom. Theaters to emerge in Northern Ireland include the Ulster Theatre in Belfast (opened in 1904) and the Belfast Arts Theatre (founded in 1947).

Theatrical activities throughout the United Kingdom are supported by a population that, in 2004, numbered 59.67 million.

RESOURCE GUIDE

PRINT SOURCES

Allain, Paul. *Polish Theatre in Transition*. Amsterdam: Harwood Academic Press, 1997.

Arnott, Peter D. *An Introduction to the French Theatre*. Totowa, NJ: Rowman and Littlefield, 1977.

Banham, Martin, ed. *The Cambridge Guide to World Theatre*. Cambridge/New York: Cambridge University Press, 1995.

Bushenhofen, Paul F. *Switzerland's Dramatists in the Shadow of Frisch and Dürrenmatt: The Quest for a Theatrical Tradition*. Berne/New York: P. Lang, 1984.

Constantinidis, Stratos E. *Modern Greek Theatre: A Quest for Hellenism*. Jefferson, NC: McFarland, 2001.

Csató, Edward. *The Polish Theatre*. Translated by Christina Cenkalska. Warsaw: Polonia Publishing, 1963.

Dobrowolsky, Ferdinand, trans. *Theatre in Yugoslavia*. Belgrade: Museum of Theatre Art, 1955.

Edwards, Gwynne. *Dramatists in Perspective: Spanish Theatre in the Twentieth Century*. New York: St. Martin's Press, 1985.

Esslin, Martin. *The Encyclopedia of World Theatre*. New York: Scribner, 1977.

Gassner, John. *The Reader's Encyclopedia of World Drama*. Edited by John Gassner and Edward Quinn. New York: Crowell, 1969.

Hartnoll, Phyllis, and Peter Found, eds. *The Concise Oxford Companion to the Theatre*, 2nd edition. Oxford/New York: Oxford University Press, 1992.

Innes, Christopher. *Modern British Drama: The Twentieth Century*. Cambridge/New York: Cambridge University Press, 2002.

Kennard, Joseph Spencer. *The Italian Theatre*. New York: B. Blom, 1964.

Klaniczay, Tibor, Jósef Szauder, and Miklós Szabolcsi. *History of Hungarian Literature*. Translated by József Hatvany and István Farkas. Budapest: Corvina Press, 1964.

Lamb, Ruth Stanton. *The World of Romanian Theatre*. Claremont, CA: Ocelot Press, 1976.

Leach, Robert, and Victor Borovsky, eds. *A History of Russian Theatre*. Cambridge: Cambridge University Press, 1999.

Lee, Vera. *Quest for a Public: French Popular Theatre Since 1945*. Cambridge, MA: Schenkman Publishing, 1970.

Lohner, Edgar, and Hunter G. Hannum, eds. *The Modern German Theatre*. Boston: Houghton Mifflin, 1966.

London, John, ed. *Theatre under the Nazis*. Manchester/New York: Manchester University Press, 2000.

Luciani, Vincent. *A Concise History of the Italian Theatre*. New York: S. F. Vanni, 1961.

Mályuszné Császár, Edith. *The Theatre and National Awakening*. Translated by Thomas Szendrey. Atlanta: Hungarian Cultural Foundation; Arlington, VA: Monograph Publishing, 1980.

Marker, Frederick J. *A History of Scandinavian Theatre*. Cambridge/New York: Cambridge University Press, 1996.

Martinovitch, Nicholas N. *The Turkish Theatre*. New York: B. Blom, 1968.

Morash, Chris. *A History of Irish Theatre: 1601–2000*. Cambridge/New York: Cambridge University Press, 2002.

Osnes, Beth. *Acting: An International Encyclopedia*. Santa Barbara, CA: ABC-CLIO, 2001.

Patterson, Michael. *German Theatre Today: Post-war Theatre in West and East Germany, Austria and Northern Switzerland*. London: Pitman, 1976.

Prévert, Jacques. *Popular French Theatre and Cinema*. Translated by Claire Blakeway. Rutherford, NJ: Fairleigh Dickenson University Press/London: Associated University Presses, 1990.

Rubin, Don. *The World Encyclopedia of Contemporary Theatre*, vol. 1. London/New York: Routledge, 1994–2000.

Shank, Theodore. *Contemporary British Theatre*. New York: St. Martin's Press, 1994.

Shoulov, Iosif. *The Bulgarian Theatre*. Translated by Elena Mladenova. Sofia: Foreign Language Press, 1964.

Slonim, Marc. *Russian Theatre: From Empire to the Soviets*. Cleveland: World Publishing, 1961.

Smeliansky, Anatoly. *The Russian Theatre after Stalin*. Translated by Patrick Miles. Cambridge/New York: Cambridge University Press, 1999.

Yates, W. E. *Theatre in Vienna: A Critical History*. Cambridge/New York: Cambridge University Press, 1996.

WEBSITES

European Theatre Convention. http://www.etc-centre.org/home.asp. Accessed June 20, 2006. Home page of an organization comprised of thirty-six theater companies from twenty-one European countries.

Finkelstein, Richard. *International Theatre Resources*. Updated June 12, 2005. Artslynx. Accessed June 20, 2006. http://www.artslynx.org/theatre/.

Magic Theatre Links Site. Updated May 27, 2006. Horse and Bamboo Theatre. Accessed June 20, 2006. http://www.horseandbamboo.org/magic.html. An international list of alternative theaters.

McCoy, Ken. *McCoy's Guide to Theatre and Performance Studies*. Updated August 2005. Stetson University. Accessed June 20, 2006. http://www.stetson.edu/csata/thr_guid.html.

Muratori, Fred. *Selected Resources in Theatre*. Updated February 3, 2006. Cornell University Library. Accessed June 20, 2006. http://www.library.cornell.edu/olinuris/ref/theaterbib.html.

Murphy, Donn B. *DBM's Theatre Netsearch*. Updated 1997. Georgetown University. Accessed June 20, 2006. http://www.georgetown.edu/faculty/murphyd/netsearch/europe.html. General links to theater resources on the Web.

Nellhaus, Tobin. *Theatre Studies Research Guide*. Updated January 11, 2006. Yale University. Accessed June 20, 2006. http://www.library.yale.edu/humanities/theater/history.html.

North European Amateur Theatre Alliance. International Amateur Theatre Association. Accessed June 20, 2006. http://www.neata.dk/. Association of amateur theaters from Denmark, Estonia, Finland, Iceland, Latvia, Lithuania, Norway, and Sweden.

Theatre. Updated 2006. Goethe-Institut. Accessed June 20, 2006. http://www.goethe.de/kue/the/enindex.htm. Links about German theater.

Theatre. SearchEurope.com, Inc. Accessed June 20, 2006. http://www.searcheurope.com/search/Arts_And_Entertainment/Theatre/index.shtml.

Theatre and Performance Studies. Updated January 11, 2006. University of California–Berkeley. Accessed June 20, 2006. http://www.lib.berkeley.edu/doemoff/theater/.

Theatre Archive Project. The British Library, University of Sheffield and AHRC. Accessed June 20, 2006. http://www.bl.uk/projects/theatrearchive/homepage.html. Links about British theater.

Theatrehistory.com. Accessed June 20, 2006. http://www.theatrehistory.com/. Commercial Website with general links to international theater history.

University of Michigan. *Internet Public Library: Drama and Performance.* Accessed June 20, 2006. http://www.ipl.org/div/subject/browse/hum20.40.00/. General theater resources.

Wolcott, Jack. *Theatre History on the Web.* Updated May 31, 2006. University of Washington. Accessed June 20, 2006. http://www.videoccasions-nw.com/history/theatrer.html.

PLAYS

Austria

Handke, Peter. *Kaspar and Other Plays.* Translated by Michael Roloff. New York: Farrar, Straus, and Giroux, 1969.

Czech Republic

Čapek, Karel. *Four Plays.* Translated by Peter Majer and Cathy Porter. London: Methuen, 1999.

Havel, Václav. *The Garden Party and Other Plays.* New York: Grove Press, 1993.

France

Anouilh, Jean. *Jean Anouilh: Five Plays.* New York: Hill and Wang, 1986.

Benedikt, Michael, and George E. Wellwarth, eds. and trans. *Modern French Theatre: The Avant-Garde, Dada, and Surrealism; an Anthology of Plays.* New York: Dutton, 1964.

Sartre, Jean Paul. *No Exit, and Three Other Plays.* New York: Vintage International, 1989.

Germany

Benedikt, Michael, and George E. Wellwarth, eds. and trans. *Postwar German Theatre: An Anthology of Plays.* New York: Dutton, 1967.

Brecht, Bertolt. *Collected Plays.* New York: Pantheon Books, 1971.

Fuchs, Elinor, ed. *Plays of the Holocaust: An International Anthology.* New York: Theatre Communications Group, 1987.

Hungary

Molnár, Ferenc. *All the Plays of Molnár.* Edited by David Belasco. Garden City, NY: Garden City Publishing, 1937.

Ireland

Beckett, Samuel. *Samuel Beckett: The Complete Dramatic Works.* London: Faber and Faber, 1986.

Harrington, John P., ed. *Modern Irish Drama.* New York/London: W. W. Norton, 1991.

Italy

Pirandello, Luigi. *Pirandello's Major Plays.* Translated by Eric Bentley. Evanston, IL: Northwestern University Press, 1991.

Poland

Mrozek, Slawomir. *Six Plays by Slawomir Mrozek*. Translated by Nicholas Bethell. New York: Grove Press, 1967.

Romania

Ionesco, Eugène. *Plays*. Translated by Donald Watson. London: J. Calder, 1985.

Russia

Chekhov, Anton. *The Plays of Anton Chekhov*. Translated by Paul Schmidt. New York: HarperCollins, 1997.
Glenny. Michael, ed. *Stars in the Morning Sky: New Soviet Plays*. London: Nick Hern Books, 1989.
Reeve, Franklin D., ed. and trans. *An Anthology of Russian Plays*. New York: Vintage Books, 1963.

Scandinavia

Ibsen, Henrik. *Ibsen's Selected Plays*. Edited by Brian Johnston. New York: Norton, 2004.
Strindberg, August. *The Plays*. Translated by Gregory Motton. London: Oberon, 2000.

Spain

Benedikt, Michael, and George E. Wellwarth, eds. *Modern Spanish Theatre: An Anthology of Plays*. New York: Dutton, 1968.
Dodgson, Elyse, and Mary Peate, eds. *Spanish Plays: New Spanish and Catalan Drama*. London: Nick Hern Books, 1999.
García Lorca, Federico. *Three Plays*. Translated by Michael Dewell and Carmen Zapata. New York: Farrar, Straus, and Giroux, 1993.

Switzerland

Dürrenmatt, Friedrich. *The Visit: A Tragi-Comedy by Friedrich Dürrenmatt*. Translated by Patrick Bowles. London: Cape, 1962.
Frisch, Max. *Four Plays*. Translated by Michael Bullock. London: Methuen, 1969.

United Kingdom

Churchill, Caryl. *Plays*. London: Methuen, 1985.
Coming on Strong: New Writing from the Royal Court Theatre. London: Faber, 1995.
Modern Drama: Plays of the '80s and '90s. London: Methuen, 2001.
Osborne, John. *Plays*. London: Faber and Faber, 1996.
Shaw, Bernard. *George Bernard Shaw's Plays*, 2nd edition. Edited by Sandie Byrne. New York: W. W. Norton, 2002.

NOTES

1. All population figures are from *World Population Prospects: The 2004 Revision*. United Nations: Department of Economic and Social Affairs, 2005.

TRANSPORTATION AND TRAVEL

MARTIN SACHS AND GERD BAYER

Europe has long been the meeting ground and crossroads for much of the world. The imperialistic past of European states dates back at least to the Roman Empire (third century BC to fifth century AD) and has also been shaped by such massive travel experiences as the fourth–to–sixth century AD mass migration of European peoples or the sea exploits of the Vikings between the eighth and eleventh centuries AD, which may have reached as far west as North America. The early modern and modern global empires of the Spanish and English monarchies relied on advanced weaponry and a combination of mercantile attitudes and missionary or pilgrim morality; they also owed their success to the colonizers' ability to move quickly and efficiently to remote places.

But Europe has not simply extended its forceful reach into the far corners of the globe; it has also developed the various means of transport necessary to do so. The ship, the train, the car: each vehicle has seen technological advancement in Europe, leading to a system of transportation in the twenty-first century that, in combination with the overall affluence and the very high population density, is marked by a very sophisticated network of railroads, highways, airports, channels, and even bicycle paths. To travel in Europe in many cases means to choose among numerous different means of transport. The general wealth of Europe, with the possible exception of some of the states formerly belonging to the Eastern bloc and some of those affected by the Balkan conflict of the 1990s, further contributes to a rather luxurious system of transportation that can turn travel from a drudgery into a pleasure.

Historically, the issue of transportation in Europe was shaped by two geographical aspects, both challenges that also stimulated transportation solutions: first, the great proximity of the sea, which lead to the building of military and mercantile navies that supported a system of global trade; and second, the mountain range of the Alps, which separated the North from the South, leading often to disjoint developments. While other places around the world might have longer or higher bridges and deeper tunnels, probably no region can compare with the Alps in terms of density of bridges and tunnels. During the Middle Ages, the importance of such cities as Venice, Nuremberg, and Amsterdam relied to a large extent on their location: they dominated land or sea routes that led into or through Europe, enabling them to gain wealth through trade and turning that wealth into political clout.

During the period in the eighteenth and nineteenth centuries known as the Industrial Revolution, the transportation of industrial raw materials and finished goods lead first to the increased building of canals and later to the development of railroads. The system of canals was already growing in England during the late eighteenth century; by the 1830s, there were over 4,000 miles in use, mostly for transporting industrial goods. In 1825 the first train company went into operation in England, powered by steam locomotives. The continent followed soon, with three countries opening railroad lines in the year 1835: the first train ran in May from Brussels to Mechelen in Belgium; in July France joined the railway age with the St. Etienne–Lyons line; the first German train ran from Nuremberg to Fürth in December. In the early twenty-first century, both rail and canal systems seem to have reached a stage of saturation, with smaller rail lines even being discontinued. One of the latest extensive water routes to have been completed is the Rhine–Main–Danube canal, opened in 1992. It provides a connection between the North Sea and the Black Sea that runs across Europe at a total length of 3,500 kilometers.

For the transportation of people in Europe, automobiles and airplanes have gained in importance. The history of flight in Europe goes back at least to the technical drawings of Leonardo da Vinci (1452–1519). In 1783, Jean-François Pilatre de Rozier und Marquis d'Arlandes succeeded in taking off in a hot-air balloon in Paris. In 1891, Otto Lilienthal invented a machine that enabled him to engage in artificial and controlled flight. By the end of the twentieth century, air travel had become a normal means of transportation for many Europeans, for travel both within the European Union and around the world. Long dominated by national airlines such as Air France, KLM, British Airways, and Lufthansa, the European airline market in the early twenty-first century has experienced new pressure from small bargain airlines such as Air Berlin and Ryanair, which offer inexpensive flights to select locations throughout Europe. Many European travelers also rely on charter airlines for their holiday travels: during the tourist season, many airports see a huge increase in flights to popular destinations around the Mediterranean Sea.

Due to the relatively high standard of living in most European states, private car ownership is overall high: in 2000, the average number for the fifteen countries of the European Union was 469 cars for every 1,000 people.[1] However, gas prices are also high, mostly as a result of hefty government taxes, which aim to deter people from using individual cars for commuting to work and to give incentives for the use of public transportation instead. In general, the public transportation systems are very elaborate, linking even smaller and rural communities to the larger cities. Every larger city in Europe has a train station with frequent service connecting it to the rest of the country. Major cities may have hourly express trains connecting them to other metropolises, making travel by plane unnecessary.

In post–World War II Europe, tourism saw huge increases. For instance, international tourists increased from 25 million in 1950 to 160 million in 1970, reaching 429 million in 1990.[2] At the same time, Europeans are very keen travelers. Estimates for the whole of the European Union state that 55 to 60 percent of the population take at least one holiday per year, with 65 percent of these trips being domestic, 22 percent to a fellow EU country, and 13 percent reaching beyond Europe.[3] Table 1 shows how diverse travel patterns across Europe are.

The use of different means of transportation also differentiates European states. Table 2 shows what kinds of vehicles travelers use for their holiday journeys.

Compared to the rest of the world, Europe receives high numbers of visitors. If one calculates the number of incoming visitors who stay overnight to the number of inhabitants, Europe clocks in at 0.64, compared to a global average of 0.13. Select other countries in Europe show even more impressive numbers, as summarized in Table 3.

	Domestic Travel	Travel Within EU	Travel Outside EU
Austria	31.8	36.8	31.4
Belgium	17.9	60.8	21.3
Denmark	30.9	47.1	22.0
Finland	71.4	17.4	11.2
France	83.2	7.8	9.0
Germany	34.0	43.7	22.3
Great Britain	49.6	29.8	20.6
Ireland	39.9	47.8	12.3
Italy	77.2	12.6	10.2
Netherlands	37.0	47.0	16.0
Portugal	82.0	13.4	4.6
Spain	89.7	6.1	4.2

Adapted from Mose and Jacobs 2004 (in Resource Guide, Print Sources), p. 50.

TABLE 1 Travel Patterns of Select European Countries, 2000

	Private Car	Airplane	Train	Bus	Ship or Boat
Austria	54.9	28.5	5.2	9.6	0.5
Belgium	57.9	28.9	5.5	7.0	0.6
Denmark	45.0	35.7	5.6	10.3	3.2
Finland	53.7	22.5	10.7	7.2	5.0
France	72.1	11.4	12.7	2.7	0.9
Germany	51.9	29.8	6.9	10.7	—
Great Britain	40.4	44.5	5.9	6.6	1.9
Greece	55.1	6.9	2.2	13.5	22.0
Italy	63.3	17.3	9.7	4.9	4.8
Netherlands	64.3	22.9	3.6	7.1	1.8
Portugal	70.5	14.3	3.3	10.0	1.8
Spain70.7	11.0	5.5	10.9	1.5
Sweden	61.1	22.2	7.6	6.5	2.4

Adapted from Mose and Jacobs 2004 (in Resource Guide, Print Sources), p. 49. The figures are for 2001, with the exception of Greece and Sweden (1997) and Denmark (2000).

TABLE 2 Transportation Methods Used by European Travelers

	Republic of Ireland	Spain	France	Sweden	Europe (average)	Norway	Finland	UK	The World
Visitors per Inhabitant	1.74	1.3	1.24	0.85	0.64	0.61	0.54	0.42	0.13

The numbers, for 2005, are adapted from Nutek, the Swedish Agency for Economic and Regional Growth, available at: http://www.nutek.se/content/1/c4/30/59/Tourism20060522.pdf.

TABLE 3 Visitors per Inhabitant for Various European Countries, Europe, and the World

The new member states of the European Union (such as Poland, Latvia, and Slovenia) also receive their share of tourist income. However, the amount of money spent by each visitor in the new states is still less than 50 percent of what visitors spend in the average EU country.[4] At the same time, the ten new member states are expected to produce 3 million jobs and generate close to €50 billion in the travel and tourism sector.[5]

During a time of growing fuel costs and concerns over airline security, the tourism industry in Europe finds itself in a state of transition. Still, many Southern European countries still see significant contributions to their gross national product coming from tourism. Many Eastern European countries hope to see continued economic growth from tourism. Overall, though, the forecasts are less optimistic. In 2005 the World Travel and Tourism Council warned of decreasing visitor spending and shrinking employment.[6] At the same time, however, the figures published by the European Travel Commission spoke a strong language. In Europe, tourism produces directly 5 percent of the gross domestic product, adding up to over €260 million in 2004. Over 415 million visitors arrived in Europe, giving the region a 54 percent share in the global number of tourism arrivals. Europe is also home to six of the world's top ten tourism destinations (France, Spain, Italy, United Kingdom, Germany, and Austria), with the guests arriving mostly from Europe (90 percent), followed by the Americas (5 percent), Asia-Pacific (3 percent), and Africa/Middle-East (1 percent).[7]

In the early twenty-first century, all aspects of mass transportation are affected by security concerns. The terrorist attacks on commuter trains in Spain in March 2004, on the London subway in July 2005, and the attempted attacks on planes from the United Kingdom to the United States as well as on trains in Germany in August 2006 all speak volumes about the importance of travel for everyday life. The way of life in Western Europe depends to a large degree on mobility, and the attempt to disrupt life in Europe is therefore aimed at transportation systems.

NORTHERN EUROPE

Baltic States: Estonia, Latvia, Lithuania

The three Baltic states are still in the process of recovering from the years of Soviet rule, which ended only in the early 1990s. The transportation networks in all three nations have yet to catch up with the rest of Europe. Despite the relatively small size of the states, the transportation network figures are still low: Estonia has less than 1,000 kilometers of railways and about 55,000 kilometers of roads; Latvia claims 2,300 kilometers of railways and almost 70,000 kilometers of roadways; Lithuania claims over 1,700 kilometers of railways and almost 80,000 kilometers of roadways.[8] Train routes are thus few, and many tracks have not yet been electrified. Diesel locomotives are a frequent sight. There are regular flights connecting the capital cities Tallinn,

Riga, and Vilnius. The road system is seeing steady improvements. Around Tallinn, four-lane highways are the norm. Further away from the capital cities, road surfaces may be riddled with potholes—a situation, however, that does not prevent the numerous buses from reaching the far corners of the countries. Cross-border buses connect cities such as Vilnius with Western metropolises such as Berlin, making bus travel a popular alternative compared to expensive flights. The train network across national borders, however, shows hardly any signs of improvement.

The amount of money spent on business travel in the Baltic states does not yet reach the EU average, which lies at just under 2 percent of the GDP. Only Estonia surpasses that figure, reaching about 2.4 percent; Latvia with about 1.25 and Lithuania with under 1 percent fall short. Consumer spending on travel and tourism in the states also falls short of the EU average by about 50 percent.[9] The numbers of cars owned per 1000 people were, as of 2000, also significantly lower in the Baltic states than the EU average of 469: with 353 (Estonia), 317 (Lithuania), and 235 (Latvia), the countries range at the bottom of the European list.[10]

However, recent economic development in the Baltic states favors the growth of tourism and in turn benefits from it. Visitors are attracted by the medieval architecture of cities such as Tallinn or the Art Nouveau beauty of Riga. In addition to architecture, tourists also enjoy the natural landscape; ecotourism to islands, seacoasts, and nature reserves is growing. The proximity to high-priced Scandinavia (Helsinki being only some 50 miles away from Tallinn) has brought numerous Finns and other visitors who benefit from the significantly lower prices in the Baltic states; cheaper alcohol has brought countless visitors to Tallinn and Riga. However, the tourist focus on the capital cities not only brings financial blessings; it also leads to an ever-growing disparity between the metropolitan and rural populations. Few visitors to Estonia make it to the university town of Tartu or the castles of Narva. Lithuania also has former capital cities Kaunas and Trakai as well as the stunning Aukštaitija National Park to offer. Many tourists to Latvia would also enjoy the castles along the Daugava river or the coastal resort Jurmala.

Many visitors still come from the neighboring countries: in Latvia, 36 percent of guests are from Lithuania, 23 percent from Estonia, 7 percent from Finland, 6 percent each from Germany and Poland, and 5 percent each from Russia and Sweden. The average length of stay is only 1.3 nights. About 78 percent arrived on the road, around 15 percent by plane, 5 percent by train, and less than 2 percent by sea. Latvians also predominantly visited the countries immediately around them. For 27 percent the purpose was to visit relatives or friends, 22 percent traveled for leisure, 17 percent for shopping, and 15 percent for business reasons.[11]

Benelux: Netherlands, Belgium, Luxembourg

Located on Europe's Atlantic coast, Belgium and the Netherlands have a long tradition of sea travel. Given the relatively uneventful geographic profile of the two countries, ships have also long been used for domestic transportation, leading to an elaborate system of canals. Still today, the canals are popular for ice skating in the winter. Both countries have major sea ports: Rotterdam still claims the title of being the world's largest seaport but has serious rivals in Asia. With over 30,000 sea-going vessels and over 10,000 barges, it still is the most important seaport in Europe.

Air transportation also plays a central role in the Benelux countries. Brussels airport serves 16 million passengers annually; with 44 million travelers per year, Amsterdam's Schiphol airport is the fourth largest airport in Europe.[12] In 2000, the over 1,300 travel agents and travel operators in Belgium had a total turnover of €4.5 million.[13]

In the Netherlands, bicycles are very popular. Not only most cities, but also cross country roads will have designated bike paths, even though the wind can be an obstacle to riders. The

THE LONDON TUBE

The London Tube is the world's oldest subway. The network's total length exceeds 250 miles, has around 300 stations, and serves about 15 million people each week. Started in 1863, the first electric trains ran in 1890. A recent major addition to the tube system, the Jubilee line extension, was completed in late 1999, linking Westminster with Waterloo and Stratford, providing direct subway access to some of the most deprived areas of London south of the river. During World War II, many of the underground tubes also served as air raid shelters during the German Blitz, when rockets launched from the continent frequently hit London. Not really part of the tube system, the Dockland Light Railway started service in 1987; it is a fully automated train running on an elevated track above the street level through the newly developed business district in the former dock areas in East London.

Dutch are also known throughout Europe as lovers of campers, traveling in them across the Alps to the sunny coasts along the Mediterranean.

One of the smallest countries in Europe, Luxembourg is less than 1,000 square miles in size (similar to Rhode Island) and has fewer than 500,000 inhabitants. It nevertheless has a very dense network of railways, totaling over 270 kilometers, and over 5,000 kilometers of roads,[14] connecting it very well to its neighboring countries. Given the affluence of Luxembourgers, private car traffic ranks high. Its thousand-year history, scenic landscape, and wine-growing traditions nevertheless make Luxembourg a popular destination for travelers.

British Isles: Great Britain and Ireland

London remains one of the global air travel hubs. Heathrow Airport has the most travelers per year (68 million); Gatwick (32 million), Stansted (22 million), and Luton (9 million) take this annual number well over 130 million. London City Airport allows only smaller planes to land but also offers direct flights to many European metropolises. In Ireland, Dublin Airport also has impressive numbers—18 million for the year 2005—and Shannon airport in the western part of the country serves over 3 million travelers per year.

Having pioneered railroad transportation in the nineteenth century, England continues to have a densely woven web of tracks. Given the relative wealth of most citizens, the high percentage of private car ownership has also led to an immense increase in road traffic. Especially in London, the most frequently seen car on the street is often a cab, followed by the famous double-decker buses. The long-distance buses operated by National Express reach about 1000 destinations in England, Wales, and Scotland; the company claims to transport 16 million passengers each year.

The traditional vacation takes the British family to a seaside resort such as Brighton or Whitby, complete with beaches, game parlors, and evening entertainment. Many Britons also fly to the sunny parts of the Mediterranean. Tourists to the United Kingdom visit predominantly London, famous for its historic sights, its museums, its theater, and its shopping. The Roman city of Bath, Stonehenge, the theater festival in Edinburgh, and the Lake District also attract both domestic and international travelers. Europe's second largest travel agent, Thomas Cook, is based in the United Kingdom. Britain's travel agents had a total annual turnover of €50 million in 2000, almost as much as the next four largest national turnovers (Germany, France, Spain, and Italy) combined.[15]

Visitors to Ireland predominantly aim for the historic and literary city of Dublin, but they often also take in the green hills and rural backcountry. The economic boom in Ireland during the 1990s provided the Irish with additional resources to spend in traveling internationally.

Ireland's national bus company, Bus Éireann, connects most places on the island. Except for the routes connecting such major cities as Dublin and Belfast, many roads are small and often lined by hedges and walls made from field stones.

Poland, Czech Republic, Slovakia, Ukraine, Belarus

Since the end of the Cold War, the numbers of both inbound and outbound visitors to Eastern Europe have significantly increased. Poland had fewer than 10 million outbound visitors in 1988, but in 1997 more than 50 million Poles traveled outside their home country; the corresponding numbers for Slovakia and the Czech Republic are almost identical.[16]

The Czech Republic is well connected to Western states. It has about a dozen border crossings each to Germany and Austria, making car, truck, and bus traffic across the former Iron Curtain simple. The connections by international buses and planes to most European cities are very good, for example through the national airline, CSA. Trains are very affordable, and the bus network is very dense. Car operators using the major highways need to purchase a toll pass known as a vignette.

Air travel to Prague arrives at Ruzyne Airport, which receives 10 million travelers annually, whereas Poland's Warsaw Airport welcomes 7 million guests per year.[17] Poland's national airline, LOT, competes domestically with the highly popular bus company PKS and the (struggling) train network PKP. As of the first decade of the twenty-first century, Poland is seeing huge increases in the percentage of car ownership, but road construction has not yet caught up with the increased traffic volume. The quality of the road surfaces is not always up to European standards.

Many travelers to the Czech Republic stay exclusively in Prague, making the city almost unaffordable to many Czech travelers. Other popular destinations are the traditional spa cities such as Karlsbad and Marienbad and the mountain ranges. Tourists come by train and bus, and also by plane. Public transportation in Prague is very efficient, with streetcars and subways alongside buses and private cars. As in most large cities, many locals do not own a private car. In general, car ownership in the eastern countries is lower than in the EU average (469/1000). In Poland, the number of cars owned per 1,000 people is 259, in the Czech Republic it is 335, and in Slovakia 236.[18]

Prostitution and sex tourism are serious concerns in many Eastern European states. Reports of human trafficking and forced prostitution indicate that the proximity of Western Europe wealth and Eastern European poverty lead to travel and work patterns that are anything but laudable. However, the short distances to Western neighbors also cause positive economic developments. For instance, between 1991 and 1997, the Slovak Republic added over 3,000 new beds to their tourist offerings, creating close to 5,000 new jobs in the tourist industry.[19]

Ukraine's major airport is located near Kiev and has frequent flights to all major cities in Western Europe and the neighboring countries. Trains in Ukraine have four classes, and railroads with a total length of over 22,000 kilometers connect most parts of the country very well. Travel times can be long, though, especially across the border. The trip from Kiev to Berlin, for example, takes 25 hours. Buses are very popular, departing from central cities and stopping frequently. The road system, just under 170,000 kilometers in length, leaves much to be desired.[20]

Belarus has over 5,000 kilometers of railways and almost 100,000 kilometers of roadways.[21] Given the population of just over 10 million and the size of the country (just over 200,000 square kilometers, making it smaller than Kansas), this still leaves many areas of the country badly connected, making traveling for the people of Belarus a more strenuous ordeal than for most fellow Europeans.

HIGH SPEED: THE GERMAN AUTOBAHN

The German Autobahn is world famous for not having speed limits. In reality, though, many areas, especially around cities, do have limits of 130 kilometers per hour or less. However, outside urban areas, drivers may encounter cars approaching from behind going faster than 200 kilometers per hour (about 125 miles per hour). The high speeds are made possible first of all by an intensive driver education program. The minimum age for driving a car is eighteen, and training involves frequent sessions of highway code, night driving, city driving, and, of course, Autobahn driving. Many students fail their first attempt at passing the exam, which means they have to take extra hours before retaking the test. To gain a license, the average student pays at least €1000. Apart from training the drivers, Germany also monitors all motor vehicles through mandatory safety checks on cars administered by a state-run office of technological surveillance called TÜV (*Technischer Überwachungsverein*). The final piece of the Autobahn speed puzzle is the money spent on building and maintaining road surfaces that will allow such high speed.

Germany

One of the economic leaders of Europe, Germany can boast an extensive transportation system. The German highway system is legendary, but there is also an extensive rail system, recently privatized. Although the Transrapid, a magnetic levitation train developed by German companies that reaches speeds of up to 500 kilometers per hour, has not found much support within Germany, it is in use in Shanghai, China. In addition to national train connections, larger German cities have extensive public transportation systems, including buses, streetcars, and subways.

With a train trip from Munich in the south to Hamburg in the North taking less than six hours on the fast ICE (Intercity Express) trains, which can reach speeds of up to 300 kilometers per hour (almost 190 mph), air transportation plays a minor role for domestic trips. However, Germans are known for spending their vacations in exotic places. It is no surprise, therefore, that Europe's largest travel agent, TUI, is based in Germany. In 2000, the combined annual gross income of German travel agents reached €20 million.[22] However, Germans also love to vacation at home, with Bavaria and the German Baltic and North Sea coasts being the top three destinations. In 2003, a survey found that almost 39 percent had vacationed in Germany, a significant increase from the 31 percent in the year 2000.[23]

Frankfurt Airport is Germany's largest international airport and, with 52 million travelers in 2005, nearly ties Paris's Charles de Gaulle Airport, with 53 million guests in 2005, for second place behind the United Kingdom's Heathrow. Most other larger cities in Germany have international airports that will reach many European metropolises. Berlin's Tegel Airport, with 11 million travelers per year, pales besides Frankfurt and is also surpassed by Munich's 29 million.[24] Work on Berlin-Brandenburg International Airport, which will replace its current two airports, is scheduled to open in 2011, with a capacity of 20 to 40 million passengers a year.

Scandinavia: Norway, Sweden, Finland, Iceland, Denmark

Given the distances across Scandinavia, air travel also is of major importance. In Denmark, Copenhagen's Roskilde Airport served 20 million travelers in 2005, Finland's Helsinki Vantaa Airport was used by over 10 million travelers, and Sweden's capital, Stockholm, saw 17 million travelers at its Arlanda Airport.[25] In Norway, Oslo's Gardermoen Airport served 15 million travelers in 2005, and Bergen's Flesland Airport still had close to 4 million.[26]

Given the length of Norway's coast and the distribution of the population alongside the ocean and its deep fjords, the sea has for a long time served as a transportation route. Still today, Hurtigrouten combines tourist travel with mail ship services and stops at all major cities on Norway's coast, calling at about thirty-four ports. The trip from Bergen to Kirkenes, near the North Cape, and back takes about 12 days. Started in 1893, the service is hugely popular both with Norwegian business and leisure travelers and with international tourists looking for a special way of experiencing Norway's spectacular coastlines. However, the numerous fjords, remnants of the past ice ages, not only add drama for the visitor; they also create obstacles to car travelers, creating the need for frequent ferry crossings. The train system in Norway is rather thinly developed and does not feature the most technologically advanced speed trains. The trip from Bergen to Oslo, for instance, takes close to 7 hours.

THE ØRESUND LINK

Since the completion of the land connection across the Øresund between the Danish capital, Copenhagen, and Malmö in Sweden, travel time by car and train from the continent to the northern Scandinavian countries has been significantly shortened. The Øresund link consists of a 4-kilometer tunnel, an artificial island 4 kilometers long, and a bridge spanning another 8 kilometers with an upper level for car traffic and a lower deck for trains. In 2005, almost 12,000 people per day crossed the bridge in private cars; the annual number for train travelers adds up to 6.6 million. The bridge is especially important for local travelers, with forecasts that see commuter traffic in the year 2015 making up a 42 percent share of all traffic across the link.[27]

In terms of incoming tourists, Sweden in the early years of the twenty-first century passed Denmark as the most important Scandinavian country. In 2005, Sweden had a 32 percent market share, followed by Denmark (30 percent), Norway (22 percent), and Finland (15 percent). Sweden, with almost 200,000 hotel beds, enjoys growing numbers of tourists. In 2005, guests in Sweden spent almost 45 million nights, only 10 million of which were for international guests. Swedes themselves took about 2 million business trips and over 10 million leisure trips abroad. In return, the country received almost 15 million international visitors. With over 3 million visitors, the Liseberg amusement park in Gothenburg attracted the most visitors, followed by the Sälen ski resort with over 2 million. The most popular museum in all of Scandinavia, the Vasa Museum in Stockholm, which teaches visitors about early modern sea travel with the help of the ship *Vasa*, built in 1628, still makes it into the top ten with over 800,000 visitors. When they travel, most Swedes do so by car. For leisure trips, the car is used by almost 75 percent, followed by the train (12 percent), buses (7 percent), and airplanes (almost 3 percent). International travel takes Swedes predominantly to Finland (14 percent) and Denmark (13 percent); the next most popular destinations are Spain (9 percent), Norway (8 percent), Germany (7 percent), and the United Kingdom (6 percent); other destinations are all below 5 percent. For international travel, Swedes travel predominantly by air (51 percent), followed by car (24 percent), ferry (12 percent), and bus (6 percent); trains are hardly of importance, at just over 2 percent.[28]

Finland is well connected by air, with frequent flights to major cities by SAS and Finnair. The national train system (VR) offers car-sleeper-trains that people use to travel efficiently across the far distances in the country. Also popular for long-distance traveling are the reliable cross-country buses. The many lakes in Finland have also occasioned a lively network of lake cruises.

Iceland is connected to many international cities through direct flights operated by Icelandair. Flying is also an affordable and thus popular option for moving across the island.

Many cities are connected through flights by Air Iceland. In addition, buses make up for a large segment of transportation. The circular road around Iceland has been completed, and only some segments of the 875 miles have not yet been paved. The total road length in Iceland is just over 6,000 miles, with many of the smaller roads unpaved. Given the proximity of most cities to the coast, the ocean serves an important function in transporting people both between parts of the country and to the rest of the world. There is even a weekly service by boat to Denmark.

Switzerland

Like Austria, Switzerland has to deal with its location in the middle of the Alps. In addition to finding ways of navigating their own country, the Swiss also have to deal with millions of cars and trucks crossing the Alps and passing through the scenic valleys of Switzerland. One of the solutions that should also appease those voicing environmental concerns is a massive train tunnel. The gigantic Gotthard-Base Tunnel is scheduled for completion in 2015. With the total length of all tunnels exceeding 90 miles, it will be the world's longest train tunnel, connecting Switzerland with Italy. At just over 20 miles in length, the Lötschberg Base tunnel, connecting regions within Switzerland, would still be an impressive technological achievement in many other areas of the world.

SOUTHERN EUROPE

Austria

Austria is a highly developed industrial nation. For that reason the number of passenger cars per 1,000 population is rather high at 495, even on a global scale.[29] Its means of transport are state-of-the-art, and public transportation in particular is heavily used by the Austrians. As of 2005 there are eighteen superhighways (about 2000 kilometers), and the total length of the road network is about 200,000 kilometers. The superhighways have a speed limit of 130 kilometers per hour, and everybody has to pay a toll in order to use them, most economically by purchasing a ten-day *Vignette* for €7.60. Trucks over 3.5 metric tons are required to be electronically tracked using a device known as a GO-Box. Austria has five international airports, the largest of which by far is Vienna International Airport,[30] which serves close to 16 million travelers annually.[31] Austria also has a modern railway network, with clean, comfortable, and reasonably frequent trains. This way of traveling can be considered the most environmentally responsible.

It is cheaper, but also somewhat slower and less comfortable, to use the bus services. However, sometimes buses are the only way to reach a remote destination, especially when doing a hiking tour in the Alps.

Bicycling is popular in Austria, as well. There are many cycling trails with different levels of difficulty. The most famous one runs along the river Danube from Germany to Vienna and beyond.

Except for the eastern part of the country including the capital Vienna, Austria is very mountainous and comprises the eastern part of the Alps. The climate is generally moderate but is more continental in the east with less rainfall and higher temperatures in the summer and colder winters. With the mountains reaching heights up to 3,798 meters on the Grossglockner, the climate varies dramatically with the respective altitude. In the mountains transportation is provided by cable cars of various types, cable chairs, and ski lifts.

Austria is an extremely popular holiday resort, not only for its own people but especially for people from other European countries. In 2004 it was ranked ninth among the most important holiday destinations in the world. Most people came from European countries, with the Germans being the absolute majority (57 percent of all nonresident guests). Dutch (10 percent), Swiss, British and Italians (4 percent each) are also important. The Austrians themselves like traveling, as well. Their favorite holiday destinations are the neighboring Italy, Hungary, and Slovenia.[32] The most interesting places in Austria are first and foremost the Alps, with their fascinating landscape and the contrast of areas seemingly untouched by civilization in the snow-covered regions of the highest mountains and the pulsating life in places such as Kitzbühel or Zell am See. Cultural life also plays a vital role. Vienna alone is worth a complete vacation, but places such as Salzburg (the Mozart town), Innsbruck, or Linz (the recent European Capital of Culture) are every bit as interesting as the capital.

THE HIGH ROAD THROUGH THE ALPS

Tunnels through the Alps can reach impressive dimensions. Numerous passes offer those travelers looking for scenic beauty the opportunity to climb from lush river valleys through increasingly desolate tundra areas to alpine heights featuring glaciers, rare plants and animals, and stunning views. One of the most impressive of its kind, the road over the Grossglockner pass in Austria, was commissioned in 1924, work began in 1930, and the road was opened to traffic in 1935. Climbing from about 1,500 meters above sea level to over 2,500 meters, the road goes by the Pasterze glacier and underneath the peak of the Grossglockner.

The Balkan States

The countries making up the former Yugoslavia—Bosnia-Herzegovina, Croatia, Macedonia, Montenegro, Serbia, and Slovenia—share the horrible memories of the Balkan conflict in the 1990s. Today, many of those countries still suffer from the destruction of their infrastructure and economy, as Albania, which was not part of Yugoslavia, does from its especially severe Communist past. The only exceptions are Slovenia, which is a rather prosperous country close to the Central European states with a booming tourism sector, and Croatia, whose tourism sector has also overcome many of the difficulties after the war and displays impressive growth rates.

Very often travel is still a demanding activity, with the streets being in a pitiable state in places, roads still being in bad condition and fuel stations being only sparsely distributed. Again the exceptions are Croatia and Slovenia, where the quality of the roads has reached a satisfactory level. These two countries also provide a rather comfortable public transportation system with modern buses and trains. In the other countries people usually go by bus because often it is the only appropriate means of transport available. Driving with a private car cannot really be recommended except in Croatia and Slovenia.

Tourism is a booming sector in Croatia and Slovenia, with rapid growth rates and a reasonable contribution to the GDP. Serbia and Montenegro also had rapidly increasing tourist arrivals in 2005, a consequence of an improved infrastructure and a concentration on higher-quality skiing and spa tourism. In the other countries tourist arrivals were quite low, all of them in the last fifth in Europe. Nevertheless, there is also hope for those countries, because they offer many natural beauties.[33] Tourists in Slovenia mainly come from Italy, Austria, and Germany, the same being true for Croatia. Slovenians tend to spend their holidays abroad. Most of them go by car and travel to neighboring countries such as Italy, Austria, and Germany.

In the capitals of the countries Western European influences are prevalent everywhere, and the younger generation tries to enjoy life as much as possible. Croatia especially offers many scenic beauties, including the beautiful Dalmatian coast. In Slovenia the short Adriatic coastline is also very interesting with many small, but lively, towns.

The climate in the Balkan states varies considerably. Slovenia in the north has a moderate, almost central European climate with rather cold, snowy winters and reasonably warm and dry summers. The coastal regions have a Mediterranean climate, whereas in the hinterland, except for the mountain regions, the climate is often continental, with cold winters and rather hot and dry summers.

Bulgaria and Romania

Bulgaria and Romania have been subject to dramatic changes since the 1990s. Within a few years the inhabitants had to face the collapse of the Eastern bloc, which provided new freedom and changes, and the struggle to meet the requirements for their accession to the EU scheduled for January 1, 2007. After the collapse of the Eastern bloc, many state-owned companies had to close or were privatized; many people became unemployed and now desperately try to make a living. The prospect of an EU membership gives hope to many, although there is still a long way to go. With this background, it is not surprising that the transportation systems in those two countries are not without problems.

Most flights to Romania arrive at Bucharest's Otopeni international airport, but there are also flights to the holiday resorts at the Black Sea. Traveling around in the country by plane is possible as well, because the most important cities are sufficiently linked. The road system in Romania is not very dense but is sufficient to reach the most popular places. Unfortunately, the road conditions are very poor, and there is just little more than 100 kilometers of super-highway. The speed limit on these roads is 90 kilometers per hour, and there is no toll. Because of the limited quality and quantity of roads, use of public transportation is widespread. There are various types of trains, and they vary in speed, comfort, and costs. Reservation is mandatory. Bus and train are probably the most accepted means of transport in Bulgaria, because the networks are extensive and rather cheap.

On average, people in Bulgaria and Romania are not very well-off as of the early twenty-first century. Thus, not many can afford to go on vacations abroad. Many stay at home during their holidays and visit the shores of the Black Sea. This is also true for most visitors from abroad, because the Black Sea region is known for being similar to such places as the Italian Adriatic coast but much cheaper. As a result, the Black Sea coast is an increasingly popular destination for young people and not-so-well-off families all across Europe. In 2004, 4.6 million people went on vacation to Bulgaria and 1.3 million to Romania. In 2004 Bulgaria had impressive growth rates as a result of visitors from the Netherlands, the United Kingdom, Italy, and France, but also from the United States and from Japan.[34]

Despite incoming tourist numbers being lower in Romania, this country has a lot to offer for both inhabitants and visitors. In addition to the Black Sea coast, the Carpathian Mountains offer a fantastic scenery and wildlife, with many attractive hiking trails.

The climate in Bulgaria and Romania is largely continental, with hot, rather dry summers, especially on the Black Sea coast, and cold winters, with temperatures often below 0°C. In the south of Bulgaria the winter is somewhat milder.

France

France, as one of the largest countries in Europe, is not easy to characterize on a general level. With its population of about 60 million, it is a massive economic power and has strongly influenced politics and culture in Europe for hundreds of years. Paris is the absolutely dominant center of the country in politics, economy, and culture, although some efforts toward decentralization have been made over the last decades.

France is highly motorized, and almost everyone has a car. People are generally not as pretentious about their cars as, for example, the Germans, so small ones dominate the scene, especially in highly congested urban areas. However, SUVs can be increasingly seen, as well. France has an excellent road and railway network. Both have the shape of a spider web, as almost all bigger roads and railway tracks start or end in Paris. There are about 11,000 kilometers of superhighways, most of which consist of privatized toll roads.[36] The speed limit outside the cities ranges between 80 and 100 kilometers per hour depending on the quality of the road. On the superhighways the speed limit is 130 kilometers per hour, with fines being very high and quickly reaching several hundred euros.

The railroad network has been improved and extended rapidly around the turn of the twenty-first century to become perhaps the best in Europe. Especially the French high-speed train TGV (*train de grande vitesse*), which reaches 320 kilometers per hour in commercial use, has largely replaced air travel between connected cities, as there are no long check-in queues and boarding formalities. In 1994 a railway link between France and England was established via the Channel Tunnel, with Eurostar trains frequently running between London, Brussels, and Paris.[37]

In Paris and the other larger cities, public transportation is excellent and absolutely necessary. Subway trains (the Metro) run frequently and help to ease the chaos above ground, especially in Paris, where traffic jams seem part of daily life. With the excellent railway network, air travel within the country has considerably decreased, but businessmen, especially, still make regular use of it. Although bicycles are not often used in the bigger towns and cities, there are many excellent bike paths across France, especially along the River Loire with its many castles and chateaux.

France is an excellent vacation destination, as can be seen by its status as first in the world in tourist arrivals, totaling 75 million in 2003. What makes France so special and inviting is probably its combination of scenic beauty, its fascinating capital, and the French way of life, especially its cuisine. Tourists primarily come from the United Kingdom, Germany, Italy and the United States. Together these four countries contribute to more than 50 percent of all guests.[38]

The French like traveling, as well, but they prefer to stay in their own country, with more than 80 percent doing so. When they travel abroad, they prefer Spain as their favorite vacation destination.[39]

THE CHANNEL TUNNEL

The Channel Tunnel links England with France, on the European continent. After the original plans were approved by Margaret Thatcher and François Mitterrand in 1986, building was completed in 1994. The tunnel runs about 60 yards below the bottom of the ocean, is about 24 feet high, and is over 30 miles long. There are two tubes for train traffic and a central service tube. In 2005, the 25 shuttle trains transported 1.3 million trucks, over 2 million passenger cars, 77,000 buses, and a total of almost 7.5 million travelers.[35] The "Chunnel" has not been a complete success: a fire broke out in the tunnel in 1996; there were frequent union disputes and strikes; and in 2006, the tunnel operators were still looking for a solution to their multibillion-dollar debt situation.

In the northern and central parts, the climate can generally be described as mild in the winter and rather warm in the summer, with the temperature range being wider in the eastern parts of the country. In the south the climate becomes Mediterranean with mild, humid winters and hot, dry summers. Especially in the coastal regions and along the Rhone Valley, winds can be heavy at times. In the Rhone Valley this wind is famous as the *Mistral.* In the Massif Central and, even more, the Alps, the climate varies with the altitude and can be very cold, windy and wet, even in summer.

France offers so many interesting and fantastic places and regions that it is impossible to name them comprehensively. With respect to natural beauty, the French are very proud of Normandy in the northwest, the Loire valley with its many famous castles, the Massif Central, and of course the Alps with their fascinating environment, sometimes bizarre and threatening but also beautiful and romantic in other places.

Greece

Greece, a country still renowned by many as the ancient birthplace of the Western world, actually has changed considerably over the last decades of the twentieth century. Although the Greeks care about their ancient roots, the country has been widely modernized. Tourism plays a vital role for the economy of the country, and agriculture is still relatively important in comparison with other western European countries.

Domestic travel in Greece is mainly done by bus, because there is an extensive network with relatively low prices. Trains provide a good alternative where available. There are flights between many islands and cities as well, but the prices are invariably higher compared to taking a ferry. Not too many Greeks do longer-distance travel by car, as there is only 470 kilometers of superhighway, and driving on the often mountainous side roads is quite stressful and tiresome.[40] The superhighways charge toll, and the speed limit is 120 kilometers per hour.

The climate in Greece is typically Mediterranean: mild, wet winters and hot, dry summers. In Greece these hot summer days often appear a bit cooler because of the northerly winds that often blow during that time. The northern part of Greece is somewhat more continental, with colder winters and less precipitation.

The combination of many (archaeological) sites of the antiquity and the country's beautiful scenery is an incentive for millions of tourists all over the world to visit Greece. With more than 13 million arrivals in 2004, it was ranked eleventh in Europe.[41] The majority of tourists come from Germany and the United Kingdom. These two countries alone make up almost 50 percent of all foreign guests in Greece, followed by France and Italy. Many tourists spend their entire holidays on one of the beautiful islands or on several of them: island hopping has become a very popular activity.

The Greek love their own country, and about 90 percent spend their vacations in their own country. Those who travel abroad prefer the other Mediterranean countries, especially Italy.[42]

Hungary

Like all Eastern European countries, Hungary has experienced tremendous changes since 1989. It has had to get used to a completely new economic system, the free-market economy. In 2004 it joined the European Union, along with nine other countries, and was planning to join the European Single Market. Generally put, the situation in Hungary has improved considerably in the early 2000s, but it still has a long way to go to reach the economic standards and level of development of its Western European neighbors.

The domestic transportation system in Hungary is cheap but efficient, especially the yellow buses that run between neighboring cities and towns or the yellow-and-red long-distance buses, which reach more distant, smaller communities. Going by train is comfortable, but the network is far less extensive, and thus far less used than the bus system. Travel by car is common. There are about 500 kilometers of superhighways, and the speed limit is 130 kilometers per hour.[43] All superhighways run toward the capital, Budapest. The road infrastructure is subject to constant improvement, and two new superhighways were under construction in 2005. All superhighways are toll roads. Local transport is well developed in the cities and towns, and Budapest also has a subway.

Hungary as a vacation destination is popular. It was ranked twelfth in Europe in 2004 on the basis of international tourist arrivals.[44] The climate is quite continental because the country is surrounded by mountains in almost all directions. The winters can be described as rather cold and dry, with temperatures well below 0°C, especially in the northern parts. The summers are hot and dry with maximum temperatures well above 30°C. Precipitation is highest in the west and lowest in the east.

When Europeans talk about spending their vacation in Hungary, they normally have two places in mind: either Budapest, with its ancient history and its status as the dominant city in the country, or the Balaton, which is Central Europe's largest lake. The lake is rarely deeper than a few meters, so in summer its water is very warm. However, health/wellness, river cruises, and cultural and sporting events have been quite successfully promoted recently. Other spots popular with tourists are the cities Eger and Pecs, the Baradla-caves in the National park Aggtelek, and the Dzalajka valley with the famous Lipizzaner horses grazing there.

One in three foreign tourists in Hungary comes from Germany, followed by Austrians, and Italians. The biggest growth rate in visitors to Hungary among the European countries, however, could be observed with the British. In 2003, 37 percent more arrivals were counted in Hungary than the year before. Hungary is also increasingly popular with people from the United States and Japan.

With an increasing standard of living, Hungarians like to travel as well. But about 70 percent still spend the best days of the year at home. When the Hungarians go abroad, they prefer Italy as a vacation destination.[45]

The Iberian Peninsula

Although Portugal and Spain are close neighbors and together form a peninsula in the southwest of Europe, the two countries display differences in many ways. The most striking difference is probably one of mentality. Whereas Spain, together with Italy, is seen as the typical Mediterranean country, the Portuguese lifestyle is often compared to and associated with the *fado*, the somewhat sad, melancholic type of song typical for the former seafarer nation. However, both countries are important industrial nations in the European Union (Spain more than Portugal) and offer a high-standard infrastructure and way of life.

The car is probably the most popular means of transport, especially in Spain. Both countries offer an extensive road network, with some limitations in Portugal (and to some extent also in Spain), as it is not possible to reach remoter areas by superhighway. Thus, travel by bus is popular in both countries because of low prices and an extensive network. Going by train is more expensive and, especially in Portugal, slower, but more comfortable. Flying is not really popular in Portugal because of the short distances, except for travel between the mainland and the Azores. Likewise, in Spain air travel is reasonable to the Balearic Islands or the Canary Islands. All those islands can be reached by ferries as well, which takes longer but is usually less expensive. In general, people think that the climate in Portugal and Spain is typically Mediterranean. This, however, is only true to some extent depending on season and location.

In Spain, most tourist destinations are situated along the Mediterranean coast, which has a climate of mild, wet winters and hot, dry summers. The same is true for the southernmost part of Portugal. The central parts of Spain and the eastern part of Portugal have a much more continental climate with less precipitation in winter, but also lower temperatures. The northern parts of both countries have a climate very unlike the expectations of most foreigners: although the winters are mild and wet, the summers still have lots of rainfall and moderate temperatures. The Atlantic coast of Portugal is generally much milder than the hotter regions along the Mediterranean coast.

Tourism is very important for both countries, especially for Portugal with its weaker economy, although the absolute numbers see Spain as second in the world in arrivals from abroad and Portugal in fourteenth place.[46] To both countries, the United Kingdom and Germany send the greatest numbers of tourists. In Spain those two countries provide about 60 percent of all tourists, in Portugal 50 percent. Other important source countries for visitors are France and Italy (for Spain) and Spain and the Netherlands (for Portugal).[47] In Spain Madrid, Barcelona, San Sebastian, Toledo, and Valencia are the most popular cities (for domestic and foreign tourists), with many architectural highlights. The same is true for Lisbon, Porto, and Coimbra in Portugal.

Both peoples share the love of their own country, so they predominantly stay at home during their vacations. Many Spanish like to spend some cooler days in the north, off the tourist tracks. When they decide to travel to another country, the Portuguese tend to travel to Spain and the Spanish to France.[48]

Italy

For Central and Northern Europeans Italy is the ideal of Mediterranean lifestyle and culture. Italian cuisine, culture, and fashion are famous all over the world, and many people dream of retiring in this country. But Italy is more than that. It is one of the most powerful members of the European Union and, despite some serious problems with organized crime and corruption, one of the dominant industrial nations in Europe.

Italy provides an extensive road network, with the superhighways being private, well-maintained, and subject to tolls. Fuel is expensive, and the speed limit on superhighways is 130 kilometers per hour. As a result, the stereotypical image of the hot-tempered Italian cannot often be verified on superhighways. In stark contrast to that, the stereotypical image of the Italian in a small car or on a Vespa motor scooter is still true to some extent in the cities. This always makes it a demanding but always interesting experience to dare driving in the chaos of noise, horns, shouting, and traffic jams, even for the locals.

Italians eager to spend their hours on the way in a more relaxed way make use of the excellent train services, which are rather cheap, usually on time, and quite comfortable. There is a good bus network as well, with even cheaper prices but less comfortable and slower than train travel.

Italy offers a wide array of interesting cities and scenic beauty for both Italians and tourists from abroad. The most popular are probably the Alps in the north and northwest, Tuscany in the north central part with its beautiful towns and landscape, Rome as one of the most beautiful cities in the world, Venice as a unique way of urban settlement in a lagoon, and the northern part of the Adriatic coast with its long, sandy beaches as ideal background for mass tourism.

Sicily in the south is very popular as well, especially with the more culturally and histori-cally interested visitor, and Naples as the "capital" of the south combines urban lifestyle with the hot-tempered mentality of southern Italy. Generally put, tourism is most prevalent in the northern and central parts of Italy, but all the more important for the economically much weaker south.

In 2004 Italy was ranked third in Europe and fourth in the world with respect to tourist arrivals from abroad.[49] Most people arrive in the summer, and since the typical vacation month is August in Italy as well, it is no surprise that the country is bursting with tourists from home and abroad during this time. One in three tourists in Italy comes from Germany, followed by the British, Americans, and French. Italians themselves like staying in their own country; about 75 percent do so. If they travel abroad, Italians prefer France, but also Spain and Germany.[50]

In general, Italy has a typical Mediterranean climate, with hot and dry summers and mild but wet winters. Temperatures increase from north to south and decrease with altitude. The skiing resorts in the Alps are very popular, because there is usually lots of sunshine in winter.

Turkey

Turkey is a country that has many faces and is not easy to describe in brief. A comparison of its per capita GNP with that of other (western) European countries implies that it is still an economically underdeveloped country.[51] While this really may be true for some of its eastern parts, the west and south, with Istanbul and the holiday resorts along the Mediter-ranean coast, offer a completely different impression. Istanbul, for example, is an interna-tional metropolis with a fascinating mixture of European and Islamic influences.

Only 66 out of 1000 people have a car, which is a very low number compared to 546 out of 1,000 people in Germany, for example.[52] In general, however, the transportation system is pretty good. There are numerous links from and to Europe and all over the world to the most important cities such as Istanbul, the capital Ankara, or Antalya, the biggest holiday resort in Turkey.

Traveling in the country is mainly done by plane or bus, because 1,859 km of superhigh-ways is not really much for a country that size.[53] Besides, Turkish car traffic, especially in the cities, is very chaotic and traffic jams are widespread, especially in Istanbul. Buses reach even the remotest areas of the country.

Turkey is very popular with tourists all over the world, but especially from Europe, and the tourism sector plays a very important role in the Turkish economy. In 2003 more than 13 million people visited Turkey from abroad. In 2004 this number increased by 20 per-cent.[54] Turkey has mainly been visited by tourists from Germany and the UK over the last years, but recently countries in Eastern Europe have discovered the good price/value ratio in this country, especially tourists from Russia. Additionally, the number of tourists from the United States visiting Turkey increased more than 90 percent from 2003 to 2004.[55]

The climate can be divided into four main zones. The southern part along the Mediter-ranean coast has mild, rainy winters, but hot, dry summers. Istanbul has a comparable cli-mate but it is a touch colder than in the south. The Black Sea region in the north is mild and rather rainy in summer, and chilly and even rainier in winter. The central part, with Ankara in the northwest, is hot and dry in summer and very cold in winter, with the mountainous regions in the east being pleasantly warm only in high summer. The southeast is dry and mild in winter and very hot in summer.

The Turks like to travel as well, but they mainly stay in their own country. During the sum-mer many avoid the hubbub of the Mediterranean coast and spend their free days on the

Black Sea coast, also to avoid the heat. If they travel outside the country, they prefer the main European tourist destinations, but also Germany, which is strongly linked to Turkey by millions of Turks who have moved to Germany as working migrants since the end of World War II.

For tourists, Istanbul is some kind of must-see, as it is the only city in the world that is situated on two continents. It is easy to see the different influences in many places, be it mosques or churches, markets, or architecture. Those seeking to relax in the sun spend their holidays on the beautiful beaches along the Mediterranean coast.

RESOURCE GUIDE

PRINT SOURCES

Ashworth, G. J., and J. E. Tunbridge. *The Tourist-Historic City: Retrospect and Prospect of Managing the Heritage City*. Amsterdam: Pergamon, 2000.

Bovagnet, François-Carlos. "Industry, Trade and Services/Population and Social Conditions/Science and Technology." *Eurostat Statistics in Focus* (2005, issue 13).

Briassoulis, Helen, and Jan van der Straaten, eds. *Tourism and the Environment: Regional, Economic, Cultural, and Policy Issues,* 2nd edition. Boston: Kluwer, 2000.

Bull, Adrian. *The Economics of Travel and Tourism*. New York: Wiley, 1991.

Burkart, A. J., and S. Medlik. *Historical Development of Tourism*. Aix-en-Provence: Centre des Hautes Studes Touristiques, 1990.

Elliot, J. *Tourism: Politics and Public Sector Management*. London: Routledge, 1997.

European Travel Commission. *European Tourism Insights 2005—Outlook for 2006*. Brussels: European Travel Commission, 2006.

Goeldner, Charles R., and J. R. Brent Ritchie. *Tourism: Principles, Practices, Philosophies,* 9th edition. Hoboken, NJ: John Wiley and Sons, 2003.

Höltgen, Daniel. *Terminals, Intermodal Logistics Centres and European Infrastructure Policy*. Nürnberg: GVB, 1996.

Ioannides, D., and K. G. Debbage, eds. *The Economic Geography of the Tourist Industry: A Supply-Side Analysis*. London: Routledge, 1998.

Leidner, Jürgen. *The European Tourism Industry*. Luxembourg: Office for Official Publications of the European Communities, 2004.

Mose, Ingo, and Anne-Katrin Jacobs. *Tourismus in Europa*. Vechta: Vechtaer Druck und Verlag, 2004.

Page, S. *Transport for Tourism*. London: Routledge, 1994.

Rae, W. Fraser. *The Business of Travel: A Fifty Years' Record of Progress*. London: Thomas Cook and Son, 1891.

Schmidt, Hans-Werner. "Industry, Trade and Services/Population and Social Conditions/Science and Technology." Eurostat. *Statistics in Focus* (2006, issue 5).

Webster, F. V. *Changing Patterns of Urban Travel*. Paris: OECD, 1985.

Williams, Allan M., and Vladimír Baláž. *Tourism in Transition: Economic Change in Central Europe*. London: Tauris, 2000.

WTO. *Sustainable Development in Tourism: A Compilation of Good Practices*. Madrid: World Tourism Organization, 2000.

WTO. *Tourism and Air Transport*. Madrid: World Tourism Organization, 2001.

WTO. *Tourism Economic Report*. Madrid: World Tourism Organization, 1998.

JOURNALS

Annals of Tourism Research. University of Wisconsin—Stout, since 1974.

Hospitality Research Journal. University of Surrey, UK, since 1990.

Journal of Sustainable Tourism. Sheffield Hallam University, UK, since 1993.
Journal of Tourism Studies. James Cook University, Australia, since 1990.
Journal of Travel Research. Virginia Polytechnic Institute and State University, since 1972.

WEBSITES

CIA. *The World Factbook.* U.S. Central Intelligence Agency. https://www.cia.gov/cia/publications/factbook.

Die Bahn. http://reiseauskunft.bahn.de/bin/query.exe/en. Probably the best Website in Europe for international railway links; despite being a German company, it also provides all-European information on timetables and links in English.

The European Eco-Label for Tourist Accommodation Service and Camp Sites. http://www.eco-label-tourism.com.

European Travel Commission. http://www.etc-corporate.org/. Detailed insight into tourism in Europe, with lots of facts, tables and figures.

European Union. http://europa.eu/abc/travel/index_en.htm. Accessed August 6, 2006. The EU's official website on traveling in the twenty-five member states. Provides helpful advice and practical tips for travelers on a wealth of subjects.

European Union. *Eurostat.* http://epp.eurostat.ec.europa.eu. The official statistics website of the European Union.

United Nations' World Tourism Organization. http://www.unwto.org.

World Travel and Tourism Council. Home page. http://www.wttc.org. Run by the travel industry, the site provides facts about the business side of tourism.

World Travel and Tourism Council. *EU Manifesto 2004.* http://www.wttc.org/publications/pdf/WTTC%20EU%20Manifesto.pdf.

World Travel and Tourism Council. *Viewpoint* (2005, 4th quarter). http://www.wttc.org/publications/pdf/VP%20WTM%202005%20(2).pdf.

Films

Alice in den Städten [Alice in the Cities] (Germany, 1974). Directed by Wim Wenders. A journalist takes young Alice throughout Germany to find her parents.

La ardilla roja [The Red Squirrel] (Spain, 1993). Directed by Julio Medem. About to commit suicide, a young man is rescued by a young woman and taken on a motorcycle ride across Spain.

Ariel (Finland, 1988). Directed by Aki Kaurismäki. An unemployed miner drives through Finland, increasingly turning criminal.

Baise-moi [Rape Me] (France, 2000). Directed by Virginie Despentes and Coralie. Two brutalized women go on a road trip of violence and sex across France.

Caro diario [Dear Diary] (Italy, 1994). Directed by Nanni Moretti. Moretti's very personal view toward Rome, Italian islands, and the medical system.

Drole de Felix [Adventures of Felix] (France, 2000). Directed by Olivier Ducastel and Jacques Martineau. About a gay man of Arab descent traveling through France, finding himself.

Im Juli [In July] (Germany, 2000). Directed by Fatih Akin. A love triangle takes the protagonists from Hamburg, Germany, to Istanbul, Turkey.

Im Lauf der Zeit [Kings of the Road] (Germany, 1976). Directed by Wim Wenders. Two men travel across Germany, fixing cinemas, trying to figure out life.

Reise der Hoffnung [Journey of Hope] (Switzerland, 1990). Directed by Xavier Koller. About a young Turkish family's desperate and fateful attempt to cross the Alps in order to live in wealthy Europe.

Sans toit ni loi [Vagabond] (France, 1985). Directed by Agnès Varda. Portrait of the life of a female drifter.

MUSEUMS

Deutsches Museum, Munich, Germany. http://www.deutsches-museum.de. Huge collection of all kinds of technologies, including space travel, ships, tunnels, and bridges.

London Transportation Museum, London, England. http://www.ltmuseum.co.uk/. London Tube and public transportation in one of Europe's greatest cities.

Museo Storico Navale di Venezia [Venice Museum of Naval History], Venice, Italy. http://www.marina.difesa.it/venezia/index.htm. Exhaustive collection, including room with gondolas.

Museum of Technology, Sinsheim and Speyer, Germany. http://www.technik-museum.de. Museum with two locations; includes the French high-speed passenger plane Concorde, a Boeing 747, a German submarine, Formula 1 cars, and numerous other vehicles.

Museum of Transport, Budapest, Hungary. http://www.fsz.bme.hu/hungary/budapest/bpmuz/bpmuz10.htm. Permanent exhibitions on the history of road and railway traffic and sailing and some original vehicles.

National Maritime Museum, Greenwich, England. http://www.nmm.ac.uk. Includes over two million objects related to seafaring, navigation, astronomy, and measuring time.

National Museum of Science and Technology Leonardo da Vinci, Milan, Italy. http://www.museoscienza.org/english/Default.asp. Based on Leonardo da Vinci's inventions and machines, the museum covers all kinds of transportation vehicles.

National Railway Museum, York, England, http://www.nrm.org.uk. The world's largest railway museum, covers three hundred years of global train history.

Scheepvaartmuseum, Amsterdam, Netherlands. Navy Museum http://www.scheepvaartmuseum.nl. History of Dutch maritime history from the sixteenth century onwards.

Vasa Museum, Stockholm, Sweden. http://www.vasamuseet.se/Vasamuseet/Om/Museet.aspx?lang=en. Seafaring museum centered on a seventeenth-century ship.

The Virtual Aviation Museum. http://www.luftfahrtmuseum.com. Virtual museum with extensive information about European aviation; includes links to numerous actual museum webpages.

Zeppelin Museum, Friedrichshafen, Germany. http://www.zeppelin-museum.de. Museum dedicated to zeppelins; includes replica of the *Hindenburg*.

NOTES

1. European Union, *Eurostat* (in Resource Guide, Websites).
2. Williams and Baláž 2000 (in Resource Guide, Print Sources), p. 7.
3. Ibid.
4. World Travel and Tourism Council 2004 (in Resource Guide, Websites).
5. Ibid.
6. World Travel and Tourism Council 2005 (in Resource Guide, Websites).
7. European Travel Commission. *Factsheet 2005*, p. 5. http://www.etc-corporate.org/resources/uploads/ETC_Fact%20Sheet_13%2010.pdf.
8. CIA, *The World Factbook* (in Resource Guide, Websites).
9. World Travel and Tourism Council 2004 (in Resource Guide, Websites).
10. European Union, *Eurostat* (in Resource Guide, Websites).
11. The numbers are for 2005, released by the Central Statistical Bureau of Latvia at http://www.csb.lv/ateksts.cfm?tem_kods=rob&datums=%7Bts%20%272006%2D08%2D17%2013%3A00%3A00%27%7D.
12. European Union, *Eurostat* (in Resource Guide, Websites).
13. Mose and Jacobs 2004 (in Resource Guide, Print Sources), p. 62.
14. CIA, *The World Factbook* (in Resource Guide, Websites).
15. Mose and Jacobs 2004 (in Resource Guide, Print Sources), p. 62.
16. Williams and Baláž 2000 (in Resource Guide, Print Sources), p. 61.
17. European Union, *Eurostat* (in Resource Guide, Websites).

18. Ibid.
19. Williams and Baláž 2000 (in Resource Guide, Print Sources), p. 43.
20. CIA, *The World Factbook* (in Resource Guide, Websites).
21. Ibid.
22. Mose and Jacobs 2004 (in Resource Guide, Print Sources), p. 62.
23. Ibid., p. 52.
24. European Union, *Eurostat* (in Resource Guide, Websites).
25. Ibid.
26. Ibid.
27. All data from the bridge's website: http://osb.oeresundsbron.dk.
28. Figures are from the 2005 report of Nutek, the Swedish Agency for Economic and Regional Growth, available at: http://www.nutek.se/content/1/c4/30/59/Tourism20060522.pdf.
29. Statistisches Bundesamt. 2005. *Länderprofil Österreich 2005.* http://www.destatis.de/download/d/veroe/laenderprofile/lp_oesterreich.pdf.
30. World News Network. *World Fact Book.* http://worldfactbook.com/country/Austria/2005/trans.
31. European Union, *Eurostat* (in Resource Guide, Websites).
32. Statistik Austria. *Tourismus in Österreich 2005.* Vienna: Verlag Österreich GmbH, 2006. pp. 61, 86.
33. European Travel Commission 2006 (in Resource Guide, Print Sources), p. 16.
34. European Travel Commission 2006 (in Resource Guide, Print Sources).
35. Data from http://www.eurotunnel.com.
36. World News Network. *World Fact Book.* http://worldfactbook.com/country/France/2005/trans.
37. http://www.raileurope.com/us/rail/eurostar/channel_tunnel.htm.
38. Bovagnet 2005 (in Resource Guide, Print Sources).
39. Schmidt 2006 (in Resource Guide, Print Sources).
40. World News Network. *World Fact Book.* http://worldfactbook.com/country/Greece/2005/trans.
41. Bovagnet 2005 (in Resource Guide, Print Sources).
42. Ibid., p. 10.
43. World News Network. *World Fact Book.* http://worldfactbook.com/country/Hungary/2005/trans.
44. European Travel Commission (in Resource Guide, Websites).
45. European Travel Commission (in Resource Guide, Websites); Bovagnet 2005 (in Resource Guide, Print Sources).
46. *Fischer Weltalmanach 2006* (CD-ROM).
47. Schmidt 2006 (in Resource Guide, Print Sources).
48. Bovagnet 2005 (in Resource Guide, Print Sources).
49. European Travel Commission (in Resource Guide, Websites), *Fischer Weltalmanach 2006* (CD-ROM).
50. Bovagnet 2005; Schmidt 2006 (in Resource Guide, Print Sources).
51. *Fischer Weltalmanach 2006* (CD-ROM).
52. http://www.destatis.de/download/d/veroe/laenderprofile/lp_tuerkei.pdf.
53. World News Network. *World Fact Book.* http://worldfactbook.com/country/Turkey/2005/trans.
54. European Travel Commission (in Resource Guide, Websites).
55. Ibid.

GENERAL BIBLIOGRAPHY

Adorno, Theodor W. *The Culture Industry: Selected Essays on Mass Culture*. Edited and introduced by Jay M. Bernstein. London: Routledge, 1991.

Anderson, Benedict. *Imagined Communities: Reflections on the Origin and Spread of Nationalism*. London: Verso, 1983.

Bayer, Gerd, ed. *Mediating Germany: Popular Culture between Tradition and Innovation*. Newcastle, UK: Cambridge Scholars Press, 2006.

Dean, John, and Jean-Paul Gabilliet, eds. *European Readings of American Popular Culture*. Westport, CT: Greenwood Press, 1996.

Denham, Scott, Irene Kacandes, and Jonathan Petropoulos, eds. *A User's Guide to German Cultural Studies*. Ann Arbor: University of Michigan Press, 1997.

Eagleton, Terry. *The Idea of Culture*. Oxford: Blackwell, 2000.

Ewen, Stuart. *All-Consuming Images: The Politics of Style in Contemporary Culture*. Revised edition. New York: Basic, 1999.

Fiske, John. *Reading the Popular*. Boston: Unwin Hyman, 1989.

Hall, Stuart. "Notes on Deconstructing 'The Popular.'" In *People's History and Socialist Theory*, edited by Raphael Samuel. London: Routledge, 1981. 227–240.

Harrington, C. Lee, and Denise D. Bielby, eds. *Popular Culture: Production and Consumption*. Malden, MA: Blackwell, 2001.

Hebdige, Dick. *Subculture: The Meaning of Style*. London: Routledge, 1995.

Highmore, Ben, ed. *The Everyday Life Reader*. London: Routledge, 2002.

Kaplan, Steven L., ed. *Understanding Popular Culture: Europe from the Middle Ages to the Nineteenth Century*. Berlin: Mouton, 1984.

Pells, Richard H. *Not Like Us: How Europeans Have Loved, Hated, and Transformed American Culture since World War II*. New York: Basic Books, 1997.

Ramet, Sabrina P., and Gordana P. Crnkovic, eds. *Kazaaam! Splat! Ploof!: The American Impact on European Popular Culture since 1945*. Lanham, MD: Rowman & Littlefield, 2003.

Richards, Greg, ed. *Cultural Tourism in Europe*. Wallingford, UK: CAB International, 1996.

Schildt, Axel, and Detlef Siegfried, eds. *Between Marx and Coca-Cola: Youth Cultures in Changing European Societies, 1960–1980*. New York: Berghahn, 2006.

Stephan, Alexander, ed. *The Americanization of Europe: Culture, Diplomacy, and Anti-Americanism after 1945*. New York: Berghahn, 2006.

Storey, John. *Inventing Popular Culture: From Folklore to Globalization*. Malden, MA: Blackwell, 2003.

ABOUT THE EDITORS AND CONTRIBUTORS

THE VOLUME EDITOR

GERD BAYER holds graduate degrees in English and geography. He currently teaches English literature and culture at the University of Erlangen, Germany. He previously taught at the University of Toronto, at Case Western Reserve University, and at the University of Wisconsin–Whitewater. He is the author of a book on John Fowles and nature (2004) and the editor of *Mediating Germany* (2006), and has published essays on twentieth-century British literature, postcolonial literature, popular culture, and cinema studies. He is currently working on an edited book on British Heavy Metal.

THE GENERAL EDITOR

GARY HOPPENSTAND is Professor of American Studies at Michigan State University and the author of numerous books and articles in the field of popular culture studies. He is the former president of the national Popular Culture Association and the current editor-in-chief of *The Journal of Popular Culture*.

THE CONTRIBUTORS

HOLGER BRIEL teaches Cultural and Media Studies at Aristotle University, Thessaloniki, Greece, and the University of New York in Skopje, Macedonia. His research interests include the philosophy of new media, public broadcasting, technoculture, and electronic literature. Apart from a large number of essays on media and culture, he has published *Adorno und Derrida oder wo liegen die Grenzen der Moderne?* (1993) and has edited *German Culture and Society* (2002) and *Field Studies: Language, Media and Culture* (2005).

MALIN LIDSTRÖM BROCK is a doctoral candidate of English Literature at Oxford University, United Kingdom. She is completing a dissertation on women's biography and feminist theory and teaches British and American literature. She has also written on the cultural history of reading and coedited a book on the Finnish author Tove Jansson.

KEVIN BROWN is an Instructor in the Department of Theatre at the University of Colorado at Boulder. He has recently published articles in the *International Journal of Performance Arts and Digital Media* and the *Journal of Religion and Theatre*. He is currently working on a theater ethnography about the performance of karaoke.

ROBERT VON DASSANOWSKY is Professor of German and Film Studies at the University of Colorado, Colorado Springs. He writes on Central European and American film and literature and works as an independent producer. The author of *Austrian Cinema: A History* (2005), he was named a Carnegie/CASE Professor of the Year in 2004.

HEIKE GRUNDMANN is a Postdoctoral Fellow at the University of Munich, Germany, where she teaches English and Comparative Literature. She has published a book on the hermeneutics of memory and articles on Romantic authors (Byron, Coleridge) and Shakespeare, with an emphasis on performance aspects. Her current research project deals with fools and the carnivalistic in Shakespeare's plays.

ANDREAS JACOB is Associate Professor of Musicology, Potsdam University, Germany. He has published on various subjects, including the music of Johann Sebastian Bach, the music theory of Arnold Schoenberg, and contemporary music. As an organist, he has played concerts throughout Europe and Japan. He has won several prizes for both his scientific and his artistic oeuvre.

ENNO LOHMEYER is lecturer in German at Case Western Reserve University in Cleveland, Ohio. His research concentrates on nineteenth- and early twentieth-century German and Austrian prose, with a special emphasis on social and gender studies. He is the author of *Marie von Ebner-Eschenbach als Sozialreformerin* (2002). In September 2006, his article, "Hedwig Courths-Mahler and the Everlasting Desire for Royal Romance," was published in *Mediating Germany*.

MAJA MIKULA is Senior Lecturer and Head of Italian Studies at the Institute for International Studies, University of Technology Sydney. Maja researches and publishes in the areas of popular culture, cultural studies, Italian culture, national identity, and gender. She is the author of *Key Concepts in Cultural Studies* (forthcoming 2007).

ANNETTE OLSEN-FAZI took her European Doctorate from the University of Montpellier (France). Having taught in the French University system and at Louisiana State University—Alexandria, she is currently an Associate Professor of English and French at Texas A&M International University. She has published articles about Southwestern literature, world poets and poetry, and various aspects of food culture. She received the Howard Endowed Professorship as well as the Provost's Award for Faculty Excellence at LSUA in 2004 and was recommended by CIES for a Fulbright award in Tunisia.

KATHLEEN J. O'SHEA is Professor of English at Monroe Community College in Rochester, New York. She is a recipient of the Chancellor's Award for Excellence in Teaching and the NISOD Award for Teaching Excellence.

LUCA PRONO holds a Ph.D. in American Studies from the University of Nottingham, UK. He is the volume editor of *The Encyclopedia of Gay and Lesbian Popular Culture,* forthcoming from Greenwood Press. He has also contributed chapters to the volumes *Modernism and Photography* and *New England: The Greenwood Encyclopedia of American Regional Cultures*, published by Greenwood Press. His research interests include American and Italian literature, popular culture, film history, and queer studies.

MARTIN SACHS took a graduate degree in Geography and English at Erlangen University, Germany. In his thesis, he researched tourism patterns related to karst caves in Franconia. The results were published in *Mitteilungen der Fränkischen Geographischen Gesellschaft* (1998). He currently teaches English and geography at the Willibald Gluck Gymnasium in Neumarkt, Germany.

JOY SPERLING is Associate Professor of Art at Denison University. She holds graduate degrees from Edinburgh University and the University of California—Santa Barbara. Her special interests are art history, modern art, and the history of photography. She has written on the nineteenth century as well as on modern and postmodern art.

CHRISTINA SVENDSEN is a Ph.D. candidate in the department of Comparative Literature at Harvard University. She has also studied at the Freie Universität Berlin while on a Fulbright fellowship and recently spent a year of research in Paris on a Sheldon grant and a fellowship from the Lurcy Foundation. Her dissertation will treat the rhetoric of architecture in nineteenth- and early twentieth-century European literature, particularly in the writings of Benjamin, Proust, Ruskin, and Hegel.

STEPHAN WASSONG is Senior Lecturer at the Liverpool Hope University. He researches historical, cultural, and educational aspects of the modern Olympic movement, Pierre de Coubertin, United States and European sports culture, and outdoor education. He is the president-elect of the European Committee for Sport History (CESH) as well as the editor of the *Journal of Olympic History*. He has published widely in his research fields.

ECKARD WOLF works as an architect in Potsdam, Germany, with a focus on environmentally friendly buildings: He was the German delegate to the COST project "European Outskirts," a scientific cooperation project about urban development. He is also the editor of the German architectural journal *Mensch + Architektur*.

THOMAS ZAWADZKI is a Ph.D. student at the German Sport University, Cologne. His special research interests are the Olympic Games, Olympic sport leaders and history, and the history of golf. He is the technical director of the *Journal of Olympic History* and the winner of the 2005 scholarship of the International Society of Olympic Historians.

INDEX